W9-BKH-297

## The Tyndale New Testament Commentaries

*General Editor:*
THE REV. CANON LEON MORRIS, M.Sc., M.Th., Ph.D.

# MATTHEW

DEDICATION

In grateful memory of

MY MOTHER

2.1.1909 – 19.6.1984

# THE GOSPEL ACCORDING TO MATTHEW

*AN INTRODUCTION AND COMMENTARY*

by

R. T. FRANCE, M.A., B.D., Ph.D.

*Vice-Principal and Senior Lecturer in New Testament Studies,*
*London Bible College*

**Inter-Varsity Press**
**Leicester, England**

**William B. Eerdmans Publishing Company**
**Grand Rapids, Michigan**

**Inter-Varsity Press**
*38 De Montfort Street, Leicester LE1 7GP, England*

**Wm. B. Eerdmans Publishing Company**
*255 Jefferson S.E., Grand Rapids, MI 49503*

© R. T. France 1985

*First published 1985*
All rights reserved. No part of this publication may be reproduced, stored in a retrieval system, or transmitted, in any form or by any means, electronic, mechanical, photocopying, recording or otherwise, without the prior permission of Inter-Varsity Press.

Unless otherwise stated, quotations from the Bible are from the Revised Standard Version, copyrighted 1946, 1952, © 1971, 1973 by the Division of Christian Education, National Council of the Churches of Christ in the USA, and used by permission.

Published and sold in the USA and Canada only by
Wm. B. Eerdmans Publishing Co.

**British Library Cataloguing in Publication Data**

France, R. T.
 The Gospel according to Matthew:an introduction
and commentary. — (The Tyndale New Testament
commentaries)
1. Bible. N.T. Matthew — Commentaries
I. Title    II. Bible. N.T. Matthew.    *English. 1985*
III. Series
226'.206    BS2575.3


IVP PAPERBACK EDITION 0-85111-870-4
EERDMANS EDITION 0-8028-0063-7

*Reprinted, September 1987*


Set in Palatino
Typeset in Great Britain by Parker Typesetting Service, Leicester
Printed and bound in USA by Eerdmans Printing Company, Grand Rapids, Michigan

*Inter-Varsity Press is the publishing division of the Universities and Colleges Christian Fellowship (formerly the Inter-Varsity Fellowship), a student movement linking Christian Unions in universities and colleges throughout the United Kingdom and the Republic of Ireland, and a member movement of the International Fellowship of Evangelical Students. For information about local and national activities write to UCCF, 38 De Montfort Street, Leicester LE1 7GP.*

# GENERAL PREFACE

The original *Tyndale Commentaries* aimed at providing help for the general reader of the Bible. They concentrated on the meaning of the text without going into scholarly technicalities. They sought to avoid 'the extremes of being unduly technical or unhelpfully brief'. Most who have used the books agree that there has been a fair measure of success in reaching that aim.

Times, however, change. A series that has served so well for so long is perhaps not quite as relevant as it was when it was first launched. New knowledge has come to light. The discussion of critical questions has moved on. Bible-reading habits have changed. When the original series was commenced it could be presumed that most readers used the Authorized Version and comments were made accordingly, but this situation no longer obtains.

The decision to revise and up-date the whole series was not reached lightly, but in the end it was thought that this is what is required in the present situation. There are new needs, and they will be better served by new books or by a thorough up-dating of the old books. The aims of the original series remain. The new commentaries are neither minuscule nor unduly long. They are exegetical rather than homiletic. They do not discuss all the critical questions, but none is written without an awareness of the problems that engage the attention of New Testament scholars. Where it is felt that formal consideration should be given to such questions, they are discussed in the Introduction and sometimes in Additional Notes.

But the main thrust of these commentaries in not critical. These books are written to help the non-technical reader understand his Bible better. They do not presume a knowledge of Greek, and all Greek words discussed are transliterated; but the authors have the Greek text before them and their comments are made on the basis of the originals. The authors are free to choose their own modern translation, but are asked to bear in mind the variety of translations in current use.

The new series of *Tyndale Commentaries* goes forth, as the former series did, in the hope that God will graciously use these books to help the general reader to understand as fully and clearly as possible the meaning of the New Testament.

LEON MORRIS

# CONTENTS

# ACKNOWLEDGMENTS

I would like to offer my thanks:

To my students and other friends, who for many years have badgered me to know when the commentary would be finished. I hope they will not be disappointed.

To the authorities of Ahmadu Bello University, Zaria, Nigeria, of Tyndale House, Cambridge, and of the London Bible College, in whose employment, successively, I have found the opportunity and the encouragement to complete what at times has seemed an endless task.

To Ann Bradshaw, Brenda Fireman and Mary Griffin, who turned my much-corrected manuscript into type.

Above all to Matthew, whom I have come to appreciate over the last ten years as both a skilful literary artist and also a disciple of rich theological insight. If those who use this commentary can share a little of the satisfying biblical perspective which he has given me, I shall be content.

DICK FRANCE

# ABBREVIATIONS

Standard abbreviations follow the scheme set out in the *New Bible Dictionary* (²1982), pp. x-xiii. The following abbreviations are used for books and periodicals which are referred to more than once.

*AB*         *The Anchor Bible*, vol. 26: *Matthew*, Introduction, Translation and Notes by W. F. Albright and C. S. Mann (New York: Doubleday, 1971).

BAGD         W. Bauer, *A Greek-English Lexicon of the New Testament and Other Early Christian Literature*, translated and adapted by W. F. Arndt and F. W. Gingrich; second edition revised and augmented by F. W. Gingrich and F. W. Danker (University of Chicago Press, 1979).

Banks        R. J. Banks, *Jesus and the Law in the Synoptic Tradition* (*SNTS Monograph* 28. Cambridge University Press, 1975).

Beare        F. W. Beare, *The Gospel according to Matthew: a Commentary* (Oxford: Blackwell, 1981).

*BJRL*        *Bulletin of the John Rylands Library.*

Black        M. Black, *An Aramaic Approach to the Gospels and Acts* (Oxford University Press, ³1967).

Blinzler     J. Blinzler, *The Trial of Jesus* (E.T. Cork: Mercier Press, 1959).

Bonnard      P. Bonnard, *L'Evangile selon Saint Matthieu* (Neuchâtel: Delachaux & Niestlé, ²1970).

Brown        R. E. Brown, *The Birth of the Messiah: a Com-*

|   |   |
|---|---|
|  | *mentary on the Infancy Narratives in Matthew and Luke* (London: Geoffrey Chapman, 1977). |
| Bruce | F. F. Bruce *New Testament History* (London: Pickering & Inglis, ⁵1982). |
| *BTB* | *Biblical Theology Bulletin.* |
| *CBQ* | *Catholic Biblical Quarterly.* |
| Daube | D. Daube, *The New Testament and Rabbinic Judaism* (London: Athlone Press, 1956). |
| Davies | W. D. Davies, *The Setting of the Sermon on the Mount* (Cambridge University Press, 1963). |
| Derrett | J. D. M. Derrett, *Law in the New Testament* (London: Darton, Longman & Todd, 1970). |
| Didier | M. Didier (ed.), *L'Evangile selon Matthieu: rédaction et théologie* (BETL 29. Gembloux: Duculot, 1972). |
| Dunn | J. D. G. Dunn, *Jesus and the Spirit* (London: SCM Press, 1975). |
| *EQ* | *Evangelical Quarterly.* |
| *ExpT* | *Expository Times.* |
| Finegan | J. Finegan, *Handbook of Biblical Chronology* (Princeton University Press, 1964). |
| Garland | D. E. Garland, *The Intention of Matthew 23* (SNT 52. Leiden: E. J. Brill, 1979). |
| *GP* | R. T. France and D. Wenham (eds.), *Gospel Perspectives: Studies of History and Tradition in the Four Gospels* (Sheffield: JSOT Press, vol. I, 1980; vol. II, 1981; vol. III, 1983; vol. IV, 1984). |
| Green | H. B. Green, *The Gospel according to Matthew* (*The New Clarendon Bible.* Oxford University Press, 1975). |
| Guelich | R. A. Guelich, *The Sermon on the Mount: a Foundation for Understanding* (Waco, Texas: Word Books, 1982). |
| Gundry | R. H. Gundry, *Matthew: A Commentary on his Literary and Theological Art* (Grand Rapids: Eerdmans, 1982). |
| Gundry, *UOT* | R. H. Gundry, *The Use of the Old Testament in St. Matthew's Gospel* (SNT 18. Leiden: E. J. Brill, 1967). |

Guthrie      D. Guthrie, *New Testament Introduction* (Leicester: IVP, ³1970).

Hare      D. R. A. Hare, *The Theme of Jewish Persecution of Christians in the Gospel according to St. Matthew* (SNTS Monograph 6. Cambridge University Press, 1967).

Hill      D. Hill, *The Gospel of Matthew* (*New Century Bible.* London: Marshall, Morgan & Scott, 1972).

*HTR*      *Harvard Theological Review.*

*ICC*      *The International Critical Commentary: The Gospel according to S. Matthew* by W. C. Allen (Edinburgh: T. & T. Clark, ³1912).

*ISBE*      G. W. Bromiley (ed.), *The International Standard Bible Encyclopedia,* revised edition (Grand Rapids: Eerdmans, 1979– ).

*JBL*      *Journal of Biblical Literature.*

Jeremias, *EWJ*      J. Jeremias, *The Eucharistic Words of Jesus* (E.T. London: SCM Press, 1966).

Jeremias, *NTT*      J. Jeremias, *New Testament Theology, Part One: The Proclamation of Jesus* (E.T. London: SCM Press, 1971).

Jeremias, *PJ*      J. Jeremias, *The Parables of Jesus* (E.T. London: SCM Press, ²1963).

*JETS*      *Journal of the Evangelical Theological Society.*

*JOT*      R. T. France, *Jesus and the Old Testament* (London: Tyndale Press, 1971; Grand Rapids: Baker, 1982).

*JSNT*      *Journal for the Study of the New Testament.*

*JTS*      *Journal of Theological Studies.*

Kingsbury      J. D. Kingsbury, *Matthew: Structure, Christology, Kingdom* (Philadelphia: Fortress Press, 1975).

Ladd      G. E. Ladd, *The Presence of the Future: the Eschatology of Biblical Realism* (Grand Rapids: Eerdmans, 1974).

Lindars      B. Lindars, *New Testament Apologetic: the Doctrinal Significance of the Old Testament Quotations* (London: SCM Press, 1961).

| | |
|---|---|
| McNeile | A. H. McNeile, *The Gospel according to St. Matthew* (London: Macmillan, 1915). |
| Meyer | B. F. Meyer, *The Aims of Jesus* (London: SCM Press, 1979). |
| MM | J. H. Moulton and G. Milligan, *The Vocabulary of the Greek Testament, illustrated from the Papyri and other Non-Literary Sources* (1930, reprinted Grand Rapids: Eerdmans, 1974). |
| *NBD* | J. D. Douglas and N. Hillyer (eds.), *New Bible Dictionary* (Leicester: IVP, ²1982). |
| *NIDNTT* | C. Brown (ed.), *The New International Dictionary of New Testament Theology* (Exeter: Paternoster Press, 1975–78). |
| *NovT* | *Novum Testamentum.* |
| *NTS* | *New Testament Studies.* |
| Robinson | J. A. T. Robinson, *Redating the New Testament* (London: SCM Press, 1976). |
| SB | H. L. Strack and P. Billerbeck, *Kommentar zum neuen Testament aus Talmud und Midrasch* (München: C. H. Beck, 1926–61). |
| Schweizer | E. Schweizer, *The Good News according to Matthew* (E.T. London: SPCK, 1976). |
| Senior | D. P. Senior, *The Passion Narrative according to Matthew: a Redactional Study* (*BETL* 39. Leuven University Press, 1975). |
| Sherwin-White | A. N. Sherwin-White, *Roman Society and Roman Law in the New Testament* (Oxford University Press, 1963). |
| Stein | R. H. Stein, *An Introduction to the Parables of Jesus* (Philadelphia: Westminster Press, 1981). |
| Stendahl | K. Stendahl, *The School of St. Matthew and its Use of the Old Testament* (Philadelphia: Fortress Press, ²1968). |
| Stonehouse | N. B. Stonehouse, *The Witness of Matthew and Mark to Christ* (London: Tyndale Press, 1944). |
| Tasker | R. V. G. Tasker, *The Gospel according to St. Matthew* (*Tyndale New Testament Commentary.* London: Tyndale Press, 1961). |

| | |
|---|---|
| *TDNT* | G. Kittel and G. Friedrich (eds.), *Theological Dictionary of the New Testament* (E.T. Grand Rapids: Eerdmans, 1964–74). |
| Thompson | W. G. Thompson, *Matthew's Advice to a Divided Community: Mt. 17,22 – 18,35 (Analecta Biblica 44.* Rome: Biblical Institute Press, 1970). |
| *TIM* | G. Bornkamm, G. Barth and H.-J. Held, *Tradition and Interpretation in Matthew* (E.T. London: SCM Press, 1963). |
| Trilling | W. Trilling, *Das wahre Israel: Studien zur Theologie des Matthäus-Evangeliums* (München: Kösel, [3]1964). |
| *TynB* | *Tyndale Bulletin.* |
| Vermes | G. Vermes, *Jesus the Jew* (London: Collins, 1973). |
| Wilkinson | J. Wilkinson, *Jerusalem as Jesus knew it: Archaeology as Evidence* (London: Thames & Hudson, 1978). |

The valuable commentary on Matthew by D. A. Carson in volume 8 of the *Expositor's Bible Commentary* (ed. F. E. Gaebelein. Grand Rapids: Zondervan, 1984) appeared too late to be noticed in this commentary.

# INTRODUCTION

## I. MATTHEW AMONG THE GOSPELS

Modern readers of the Christian Gospels usually have their favourite. Some are drawn to John for its explicit presentation in simple language of profound truths about Jesus; some prefer the vivid, action-packed narrative of Mark; others relate most easily to the human interests and sympathies of Luke. But how many feel most at home in Matthew? It begins with a forbidding list of unknown names, and it deals at length with matters of law and tradition, of the fulfilment of the Jewish Scriptures and of Jesus' confrontations with the Jewish leaders of his day. It seems somehow remote both from modern culture and from modern literary tastes. It is, in one modern commentator's words, 'a grim book'.[1] Many, perhaps, are surprised to find it placed at the beginning of the New Testament, thus causing the unsuspecting new reader to plunge straight into a series of apparently irrelevant 'begettings'!

Why then did the early Christians place Matthew first? For it is a remarkable fact that, among the variations in the order in which the Gospels appear in early lists and texts, the one constant factor is that Matthew always comes first.

Probably the main reason was the belief that it was the first Gospel to be written, a belief which only a minority of scholars would support today. We shall have more to say on this shortly. But it may also be worth remembering that the early Christians were conscious, in a way few Christians are today, that their faith had its roots in Judaism. The issue of the relation between

[1]Beare, p. viii.

15

the Christian church and the Jews remained a vital one both for the Christians' self-understanding and for their presentation of Christ to the non-Christian world. And it is Matthew's Gospel which more fully than the others provides a Christian perspective on this issue. In its constant reference to the Old Testament, its strong Jewish flavouring, its explicit discussions of the conflict between Jesus and the Jewish authorities, it forms a fitting 'bridge' between Old and New Testaments, a constant reminder to Christians of the 'rock from which they are hewn'.

Whatever the reason, Matthew's Gospel was in fact more quoted in Christian writings of the second Christian century than any other. Its careful structure made it particularly suitable for use in the growing churches, both for the instruction of converts and for the training of church leaders, and its wide-ranging collection of Jesus' teaching on the ethical demands of Christian discipleship (most obviously, but not only, in the Sermon on the Mount) ensured it a 'best-seller' rating among the earliest Christian writings.

But despite the preference given to Matthew, from quite early in the second century Christians agreed almost unanimously[1] that 'the gospel' had been given to the church in four authoritative versions, not just in one. Even Mark's Gospel, however little it may have been used compared to the fuller Gospel of Matthew, was accepted alongside it. Many other 'gospels' were written in the second century and beyond, but none of them achieved acceptance alongside Matthew, Mark, Luke and John.

Each of the four has a distinctive contribution to make to our knowledge and understanding of Jesus. It will be the main aim of this introduction, and a major concern of the commentary which follows, to draw out Matthew's special place in the total witness to Jesus, both in his selection of material and in the way he has presented it. Prolonged study of Matthew constantly reinforces the impression that he was a skilful and imaginative writer, who both had clear convictions to convey to his readers and also was adept at communicating them through the medium of a written document. In studying Matthew's Gospel, therefore, while our aim will always be, as Matthew would wish

---

[1]The heretic Marcion, who accepted only an 'expurgated' version of Luke, is the exception which proves the rule!

it to be, to learn about Jesus through the record of his life and teaching, we should not forget that it is *Matthew's* version of the record which we are reading, and that it will therefore not be the same as that of Mark, Luke or John. In accepting that God intended his church to have four Gospels, not just one, Christians have also recognized that each has something different to say about Jesus. It is only after we have listened to each in its individuality that we can hope to gain the full richness which comes from the 'stereoscopic' vision of Jesus as seen through four different pairs of eyes!

## II. SOME CHARACTERISTICS OF MATTHEW'S GOSPEL

### A. A Jewish Christian Gospel

We shall consider in a later section the main theological interests of Matthew. All of them are those one would expect of a Jewish Christian: Jesus as the fulfilment of Old Testatment hopes, the application of Old Testament texts to various aspects of his ministry, his attitude to the Old Testament law, and to the traditions of Jewish scribal teaching, his controversies with the official representatives of the Jewish religion and nation, the nature of the Christian church *vis-à-vis* Judaism. These are the issues which must have been uppermost in the minds of those Jews who had recognized Jesus as the Messiah, and who now needed both to work out their own self-understanding in relation to their Jewish roots and to learn to present and defend the gospel among non-Christian Jews.

It therefore seems likely that the Gospel was written by a Jewish Christian, and that Jewish Christians formed at least a large proportion of its intended readership. Various more detailed features of the Gospel confirm this impression.

There is a distinctly 'Semitic' touch to some of Matthew's Greek, such as a Jewish reader would appreciate.[1] Untranslated Aramaic terms such as *raka* (5:22, see RSV mg.) or *korbanas* (translated 'treasury' in 27:6), and unexplained references to Jewish customs, such as hand-washing traditions (15:2; contrast Mark's explanation for his presumably Gentile readers, Mk.

---

[1]See C.F.D. Moule, *The Birth of the New Testament* ([3]1981), pp. 276–280.

7:3–4) or the wearing of phylacteries (23:5), suggest that Matthew expected his readers to be familiar with Jewish culture. His explanation of the meaning of the name 'Jesus' (1:21) assumes his readers know its Hebrew meaning. He begins his genealogy from Abraham, the father of the Jewish race (1:1–2), and records frequent references to Jesus as 'Son of David'. He regularly uses the more Jewish phrase 'kingdom of heaven' where Mark and Luke use 'kingdom of God'. It is only Matthew who tells us that Jesus' mission (and, initially, that of his disciples) was limited to 'the lost sheep of the house of Israel' (10:5–6; 15:24), and it is remarkable that the explicit prohibition of going among Samaritans in 10:5 is the only mention of Samaritans in this Gospel, in contrast with the favourable attitude to them in Luke. One or two passages suggest an acceptance in principle of the authority of Jewish scribal teaching (23:3,23), though in the context of the Gospel as a whole this cannot be taken as a blanket endorsement of scribal tradition (see comments *ad loc.*). Many of the specific issues discussed would be of primary interest to Jewish readers, such as fasting (6:16–18), the sabbath (12:1–14; 24:20), temple offerings (5:23–24), the temple tax (17:24–27).

Such details reinforce the impression that the Gospel is directed in the first instance towards Jewish concerns. For this reason it is often suggested that Matthew, along with Hebrews, is the 'most Jewish' book in the New Testament. But that is only one side of the picture.

## B. A Gospel for all nations

The same Gospel which records an initial limitation of the Christian mission to 'the lost sheep of the house of Israel' finishes with Jesus triumphantly sending the eleven out to make disciples of all nations, and many hints of this ultimate aim of his mission have occurred in the course of the Gospel (see comments on 28:19, and references given there). Thus the ministry of Jesus, for all its clearly Jewish roots, and its comprehensive fulfilment of the hopes and destiny of Israel, has broken out of the confines of Judaism and in so doing has brought to an end the exclusive privilege of the Jews as the people of God.

We shall discuss this theme of the church and Israel more

fully below. The point of mentioning it here is that in presenting this aspect of Jesus' ministry Matthew's Gospel sometimes seems not so much 'Jewish' as 'anti-Jewish', using language comparable with the sustained polemic against 'the Jews' in John's Gospel. For Matthew is not content to state the positive aspect, that God now calls non-Jews to share the privileges of Israel; he also makes clear the negative aspect, the failure and consequent rejection of Israel, particularly as embodied in its official leadership, and its replacement by Jesus, who in himself sums up all that Israel was intended to be, and by the community of those, whether Jew or Gentile, who through their response to his ministry have now become the true people of God.

This paradox, that the 'most Jewish' Gospel can contain such apparently hostile language in relation to the Jewish nation as we find in 8:10–12; 21:43; 23:29–39; 27:24–25, *etc.*, has led some scholars to suggest that two mutually incompatible elements have been rather clumsily combined into a single book. Thus it is suggested that originally Jewish-Christian material has been revised and expanded by a strongly anti-Jewish editor, himself probably a Gentile.[1]

But it is hardly realistic to expect all Jewish Christian authors to be 'pro-Jewish' and all Gentile Christians to be 'anti-Jewish'. What we see in Matthew is rather the uncomfortable tension in the mind of one who, brought up to value and love all that Israel has stood for, has come to the painful conclusion that the majority of his people have failed to respond to God's call to them, and that it is in a 'remnant', the minority group who have followed Israel's true Messiah, that God's purpose is now centred. Such a conclusion carries with it the recognition that what counts for membership in the true people of God is no longer a person's national identity, but his response of repentance and faith towards God, a response which is open to Gentiles as well as Jews. The 'anti-Jewish' tone of such a writer would spring, then, from the recognition that, as another Jewish Christian put it, 'not all who are descended from Israel belong to

[1]So *e.g.*, with different nuances, P. Nepper-Christensen, *Das Matthäusevangelium: ein judenchristliches Evangelium?* (1958); G. Strecker, *Der Weg der Gerechtigkeit* (1962); S. Van Tilborg, *The Jewish Leaders in Matthew* (1972).

Israel' (Rom. 9:6). When the followers of Israel's Messiah find themselves suspected, persecuted and ostracized by the official leadership of Israel, it is no wonder that an element of 'anti-Jewishness' can be detected, and that it may come to sharper expression than might be expected of a Gentile Christian for whom it was not such a painfully existential issue.

## C. A Gospel for the church

Matthew's Gospel is sometimes described as 'the ecclesiastical Gospel'. This arises in part from the fact that this Gospel is the only one to include the term *ekklēsia* (16:18; 18:17). The use of this term is taken to indicate that the author was writing in and for a formal Christian organization (and therefore probably towards the end of the first century, when 'the church' was becoming a more institutionalized body).

By itself this argument is very weak. In 18:17 the reference is not to a single world-wide body, but to the local 'congregation'. In 16:18 'my church' does refer to the Christian community as a whole, but as early as the fifties Paul, who normally spoke of 'the churches' in the sense of local congregations, could also speak of 'the church' (*e.g.* 1 Cor. 15:9; Gal. 1:13); and when the Old Testament background of the term is taken into account there is no need to read into it all the later ideas of a formal 'ecclesiastical' structure (see comments on 16:18).

It is true, however, that there is much in Matthew's Gospel which would prove very suitable for, and may well have been designed for, the use of church leaders, both in instructing their members in the faith and in determining their own pastoral role. It deals with such practical issues as the sabbath (12:1–14) and divorce (5:31–32; 19:3–9; note in both cases the explicit recognition, not found in the other Gospels, that 'unchastity' terminates a marriage; see on 5:32). More generally it includes extended discussion of the right ethical use of the Old Testament law (5:17–48), and the misuse of scribal tradition (15:1–20), while the onslaught on the scribes and Pharisees in chapter 23 adds up to a wide-ranging presentation, by way of contrast, of what true religious leadership involves. Chapter 10 deals with the church's response to persecution, and chapter 18 concentrates almost entirely on relationships within the Christian community, with special attention given to the proper procedure for dealing with an offender (18:15–20). Warnings against false prophets and pseudo-Messiahs occur in 7:15–20 and 24:4–5, 11,23–26, and there are several reminders that there is need for discrimination between true and false disciples within the professing community (7:6,13–27; 13:24–30,36–43,47–50; 22:10–14). All this suggests that the Gospel of Matthew would have proved particularly valuable to church leaders, and the large quantity of carefully-structured teaching on the nature and demands of discipleship would be very suitable for catechetical use. Such an observation does not, of course, entail a developed ecclesiastical structure, merely a Christian community aware of its distinctive existence and role.

On this basis Matthew's Gospel has been viewed as a sort of 'Manual of Discipline', like the Community Rule of Qumran (1QS).[1] But this is to overstate the difference between Matthew and the other Gospels. While agreeing that Matthew designed his Gospel to be of practical value in the teaching and leadership of a church, one must still recognize that it is essentially a 'life of Jesus', and that most of its contents, however valuable for teaching, are not framed directly as catechetical material, still less set out in the form of an instruction manual.

## D. A carefully-constructed Gospel

We shall consider the structure of the Gospel at the end of this introduction, and I shall then propose a detailed analysis. At this point we need only note that, whatever disagreements there may be about which is the dominant structural pattern, all who have studied Matthew's Gospel in detail have been impressed by the care and literary artistry involved in its composition.[2] We shall see that both in the overall structure of the Gospel, with its dramatic development and its clearly-marked sections and repeated formulae, and also in the grouping of material in such a way that one episode throws light on another, Matthew has set about his task with skill. Symmetrical groups of teaching sections make for easy memorization, and sometimes a

[1]So esp. K. Stendahl, *The School of St Matthew* (1954).
[2]The subtitle of Gundry's commentary, 'A Commentary on his Literary and Theological Art', properly places emphasis on this aspect of the Gospel.

striking dramatic effect is achieved by the balancing of contrasting sections. We shall note such features in the commentary from time to time. To approach Matthew's Gospel as a haphazard collection of unconnected stories and sayings is to miss much of what Matthew wants to communicate.

Careful communicator as he is, Matthew frequently omits incidental details which he regards as inessential to his purpose. Thus stories which in Mark are told in a lively, expansive style, with plenty of picturesque detail, regularly appear in Matthew in a much more concise form, boiled down to the bare essentials which are needed to convey the message Matthew wishes to draw out of the story. (*E.g.*, the stories which make up the 43 verses of Mark 5 take up only 16 verses in Matthew 8:28–34; 9:18–26.) The effect is that Matthew is less immediately attractive as a story-teller, but that the cumulative impression of his more taut narratives is very powerful in its portrayal of the overwhelming authority of Jesus.

*E. A scripturally-based Gospel*
All the Gospels contain frequent quotations of and allusions to the Old Testament, but in Matthew this feature is more pronounced. We shall consider below some of the more prominent features of Matthew's appeal to the Old Testament, particularly his famous 'formula-quotations', and we shall consider them in the context of his overriding theological concern to present Jesus as the fulfilment of all the hopes and patterns of Old Testament Israel. No-one can doubt the importance of this theme for Matthew, nor can any attentive reader fail to notice his delight in drawing attention, either openly or by more subtle allusion, to what may sometimes seem to us rather obscure links between Jesus and the Old Testament.

The study of the distinctive nature of the use of the Old Testament by Matthew has led to some interesting discussions in recent years. K. Stendahl's work, already referred to, was written in the early days of the application of the Qumran discoveries to New Testament studies, and drew close parallels between Matthew's technique and that of the Qumran 'commentaries' on the Old Testament, particularly that on Habakkuk. He pictured the Gospel as the product of an 'exegetical school' like the community of Qumran, a school which had worked out its own distinctive hermeneutical principles and methods. With the rise of redaction-criticism there has since been more tendency to speak of Matthew's Gospel as the product of an individual author rather than of a school, and it has been generally acknowledged that the literary parallel between the Qumran commentaries on scriptural texts and Matthew's scriptural comments and colouring in the course of narrative of the life of Jesus is far from convincing.[1] But the attention drawn by Stendahl to the peculiarities of Matthew's method, in particular to the freedom of his handling of the Old Testament text in his 'formula-quotations', has been important for later studies.

R. H. Gundry replied to Stendahl in his *The Use of the Old Testament in St. Matthew's Gospel* (1967), emphasizing in particular Stendahl's neglect of the numerous Old Testament allusions, which must be taken together with the more formal quotations in an analysis of Matthew's method.[2] Gundry noted that the mixed text-form (*i.e.* use of independent and free renderings of the Hebrew instead of or along with the Septuagint) noted by Stendahl was not confined to the 'formula-quotations', but was found throughout the Gospel except where Matthew was taking over formal quotations from Mark (these being predominantly Septuagintal). He argued that Matthew's free use of the Old Testament text was the result of a deliberate and responsible study of the Scriptures in the trilingual milieu of first-century Palestine, sometimes utilizing various textual traditions already in existence, sometimes translating independently from the Hebrew. The principles of interpretation employed were not arbitrary or atomizing but part of a new hermeneutical tradition deriving from the conviction of the fulfilment of the Messianic hope in Jesus.

An important new element was introduced into the discussion with the publication of M. D. Goulder's *Midrash and Lection in Matthew* (1974). Part of Goulder's argument is a development from the suggestion of G. D. Kilpatrick[3] that Matthew's Gospel was composed for use in regular liturgical reading, its structure

---

[1]See the brief critique in Hill, pp. 35–38.
[2]See esp. pp. 155–159 of Gundry, *UOT* for direct interaction with Stendahl's thesis.
[3]G. D. Kilpatrick, *The Origins of the Gospel according to St. Matthew* (1946).

being designed to fit the demands of a church lectionary. Goulder sees Matthew as an expansion of Mark for lectionary use, in conjunction with the existing Old Testament festal lectionary in use in the synagogue. This aspect of Goulder's work has not met with widespread acceptance.[1] It carries with it, however, another view of Matthew's method which has given rise to increasing discussion. Matthew's only written source, Goulder believes, was Mark. All his additional material derives not from other existing sources, but from Matthew's own fertile imagination, particularly inspired by his knowledge of the Old Testament. Starting from the Old Testament readings prescribed in the lectionary, he has woven together elaborate patterns of related material, by a process which Goulder calls *midrash*. This process has resulted in the creation of stories about Jesus and teaching attributed to him which derive not from any historically-based tradition, but from a scripturally-inspired imagination. Such 'midrashic' procedures were well known and accepted in the Jewish world to which Matthew belonged, and questions of historicity, it is implied, would not have worried, or even occurred to, his original readers.

This is not the place to attempt an adequate discussion of the debate which has arisen out of the proposal to interpret Matthew's work as *midrash*.[2] Four brief comments may be made, however.

1. The word 'midrash' itself is used in widely different senses by those who apply it to New Testament studies, sometimes in ways which specialists in Jewish literature would not recognize. In Jewish writings it became a technical term for a literary composition which takes the form of an extended 'commentary' on a continuous text from the Old Testament, and in that sense it is clearly not a relevant category for the understanding of the Gospels (unless, with Goulder, one speaks of Matthew as a midrash on *Mark*, not on an Old Testament text). Beyond that technical use it becomes a slippery term, capable of carrying connotations which are not properly derived either from Jewish

---

[1] See the critical review of this and other 'lectionary' hypotheses by L. Morris, 'The Gospels and the Jewish Lectionaries', in *GP* III (1983), pp. 129–156.

[2] The whole of *Gospel Perspectives* III (1983) is devoted to this debate. See also, with special reference to Matthew 1–2, my paper in *GP* II (1981), pp. 239–266.

usage or from the phenomena of the Gospels.[1]

2. By whatever term it is described, it is questionable whether the practice of elaborating historical accounts with fictional details under the influence of Old Testament texts was so widespread among first-century Jews, let alone being the dominant approach to Scripture and history. While Old Testament stories did receive a growing volume of traditional embellishment, there is much less evidence for a similar treatment of recent history. No clear parallel can be adduced from first-century Judaism for such elaboration taking place in the traditions of a religious leader within a generation or two of his death. If Matthew wrote as Goulder suggests, he would have been doing something untypical of his cultural milieu, and it is questionable whether his readers would have recognized and accepted his method.[2]

3. Even if the practice were common in non-Christian Judaism, one cannot therefore assume that Matthew would have felt it appropriate to follow it. It is the text of Matthew, rather than presumed current practice outside Christian circles, which should be our guide to Matthew's aims and methods. In particular we must take into account Matthew's emphasis on 'fulfilment', which we shall study below, which raises the question how far a concept of fulfilment makes sense in the absence of a historical occurrence in which that fulfilment is seen as taking place. In other words, in what way is a scriptural theme or passage 'fulfilled' in a story which is simply made up out of that passage?

4. It should be clearly recognized that a delight in tracing scriptural connections and an intention to relate historical fact are not mutually exclusive. To conclude that Matthew's text is full of subtle allusive references to the Old Testament is not *ipso facto* to conclude that the stories it tells are the product of imagination. The commentary that follows will provide plenty of evidence of Matthew's ingenuity in tracing the Old Testament

---

[1]See, on the question of definition, *e.g.* B.D. Chilton, *GP* III, pp. 9–32; Brown, pp. 557–563.

[2]See my general paper in *GP* III, pp. 99–127, and the more detailed studies of specific Jewish texts in the same volume by R.J. Bauckham (Pseudo-Philo) and F.F. Bruce (Qumran literature).

background and significance of the events he records, but it is inherently more likely in such cases that the event suggested the scriptural comment than that it was meditation on the Old Testament text that inspired the story.[1]

The characterization of Matthew's method as 'midrash', and the proposal that therefore much of his material is unhistorical, has been taken up by Gundry in his commentary (1982). 'Matthew did not write entirely reportorial history. Comparison with midrashic and haggadic literature of his era suggests that he did not intend to do so' (p.629). Gundry does not allow such free creativity as Goulder, in that he believes Matthew drew much of his material (even including the contents of chapters 1–2) from an expanded Q source (on which see below), and he sees Matthew's unhistorical contribution more often in the embellishment of existing traditions than in wholesale creation of stories. He does, however, argue more explicitly than Goulder that Matthew's original readers would have had no difficulty in recognizing his method, and would not have thought of interpreting historically Matthew's 'midrashic' contributions. 'History mixed with nonhistory is still an accepted mode of communication; . . . unhistorical embellishment can carry its own kind of truth alongside historical truth' (p.631). The fact that Gundry argues this case explicitly as an evangelical scholar who holds to a belief in the inerrancy of the Bible[2] has inevitably led to a lively debate, which at the time of writing shows no sign of subsiding![3]

The issue of historicity should not be allowed, however, to distract attention from the subtle and fascinating nature of Matthew's use of the Old Testament. In his blend of traditionally Jewish ('rabbinic') interests and methods with a wholly new and Christian emphasis on the fulfilment of the Old Testament revelation in the historical life and teaching of Jesus of Nazareth, he exemplifies well the parable (sometimes taken as

---

[1] This argument is worked out more fully in relation to Matthew 1 and 2 in my paper in *GP* II, pp. 239–266.

[2] See his 'Theological Postscript', pp. 623–640 of his commentary.

[3] Two early detailed reviews, rejecting Gundry's position, were by D.A. Carson, *Trinity Journal* 3 (1982), pp. 71–91 and P.B. Payne, *GP* III, pp. 177–215. Gundry replied to these in a 'Response', as yet unpublished but widely circulated. Further debate with D.J. Moo and N.L. Geisler followed in *JETS* 26 (1983), pp. 31–115.

Matthew's 'self-portrait') of the 'householder who brings out of his treasure what is new and what is old' (13:52).

## III. THE ORIGIN OF THE GOSPEL

We have looked first at some of the characteristics of the Gospel, because it is these features which must determine our estimate of its probable origin. Given that these are among its main features, where, when and by whom is it likely that such a work would have been written?

### A. Place of writing

The characteristics we have noted make it virtually certain that Matthew's Gospel was written in and for a church which was to a large extent composed of converts from Judaism. This would be generally agreed, but it does not necessarily limit the possibilities very closely, as there were Jews settled in significant numbers all over the eastern part of the Roman Empire, and we know from Acts that the church typically grew at first among the Jewish settlers wherever Paul travelled in Asia Minor and Greece.

Early church tradition from at least the middle of the second century affirmed that Matthew wrote 'among the Hebrews'. This may, however, be no more than a guess based on the clearly Jewish orientation of the work, nor does it specify *the place*, since 'Hebrews' might be found in many areas.

Palestine might seem the obvious place for such a 'Jewish' work to have been produced, but the majority of modern scholars have been impressed by B. H. Streeter's arguments,[1] both from a number of incidental features of the Gospel itself and from the fact of its influence on Ignatius and on the *Didache*, that it in fact derives from Antioch (a church which was at first entirely Jewish, but then became the scene of considerable debate over the relation of the church to Judaism: Acts 11:19–30; 14:24 – 15:35; Gal. 2:11ff.).

For the understanding of the Gospel, however, it makes little difference whether it was written in Palestine or Syria (Antioch),

[1]B.H. Streeter, *The Four Gospels* (1924), pp. 500–523.

or in some other part of the eastern Mediterranean, and the location is never likely to be demonstrated conclusively. What does matter is that we recognize it as written in the context of, and directed to the concerns of, a Christian church, many of whose members were still acutely conscious of their roots in Judaism, and who needed to work out as a matter of existential importance what was the true relation of Jesus to Israel.

## B. Date

Most modern scholars have concluded that Matthew's Gospel was written within the last twenty years of the first century. The main reasons for dating it not earlier than about AD 80 fall roughly in the following areas:

1. If, as is generally supposed, Mark's Gospel was written not earlier than about AD 65, and Matthew used Mark, Matthew must be dated significantly after 65.

2. The destruction of Jerusalem in AD 70 is believed to have influenced the language of such passages as 22:7; 23:38; and various parts of chapter 24.

3. The 'anti-Jewish' tone suits the period around AD 85 when Christians were effectively excluded from synagogue worship by the insertion of a curse on 'Nazarenes and heretics' into the synagogue liturgy (the so-called *Birkat ha-Minim*),[1] rather than an earlier period when the lines were less clearly drawn.

4. The Gospel is said to reflect too 'developed' a theological and ecclesiastical situation for an earlier period.

In response to such arguments it should be noted:

1. The assumption that Matthew used Mark in its final form is not universally accepted (see below on synoptic relationships). Nor is the dating of Mark about AD 65 a fixed point. Most patristic writers believed Mark wrote after Peter's death (AD 64?), but Clement of Alexandria said the Gospel was issued while Peter was still alive in Rome. In any case, since all patristic writers assumed Matthew wrote *before* Mark, their beliefs about the date of Mark can hardly be used to support a *later* date for Matthew.

2. This argument assumes, of course, that Jesus could not

[1] See Bruce, pp. 365–366.

have foreseen the events of AD 70. In addition, however, it should be noted that nothing in the wording of Matthew points to these events as already past, and the words of 22:7 do not directly reflect what occurred then as we know it from Josephus.[1]

3. It is in fact much debated whether the relationship with Judaism reflected in Matthew's Gospel is that of two distinct and hostile communities, as would necessarily be the case after the *Birkat ha-Minim*, or that of a debate *intra muros*, between those who represent traditional Judaism and the 'Nazarene' Jews who claim to be the true Israel, still hoping that the rest of the Jews may be won to recognize Jesus as Messiah. This is a matter of subjective impression, not of demonstration, but it is at least arguable that the painful tension evident in the Gospel is more compatible with the period when church and synagogue were still in close and not necessarily hostile dialogue.[2]

4. If the previous argument was a matter of subjective impression, this is more so. It depends in part on reading into passages such as 16:17–19; 18:15–20 a formal ecclesiastical structure which is not required by the text. It depends also on a presupposed pattern of development in first-century Christian thought which is not easy either to demonstrate or to fit into a chronological scheme. It is a bold scholar who can declare a firm date before which a given aspect of theological thought or language could not have occurred.

If the arguments for a date after AD 80 are far from conclusive, is there any indication of an earlier origin? There is, of course, patristic tradition, which dates Matthew before Mark, so that Irenaeus confidently dates it while Peter and Paul were still preaching in Rome (*Adv. Haer.* iii.1.1). But even within the Gospel itself are some indications of an early date. For instance, references to practices connected with the temple (such as 5:23–24; 23:16–22) would hardly have been worth including after the temple ceased to exist in AD 70, and the discussion of the temple tax in 17:24–27 would have been positively misleading

[1]These arguments are developed by B. Reicke in D.E. Aune (ed.), *Studies in New Testament and Early Christian Literature* (1972), pp. 121–134 and by Robinson, chapter 2.
[2]So *e.g.* G. Bornkamm and G. Barth in *TIM*; R. Hummel, *Die Auseinandersetzung zwischen Kirche und Judentum im Matthäusevangelium* (1963).

after AD 70, when the tax was diverted to the upkeep of the temple of Jupiter in Rome. The respectful attitude towards the office of the scribes in 23:2-3 would hardly be included if the Gospel were written when church and synagogue were totally opposed to each other.

Other such indications are collected by Gundry[1] into a detailed and persuasive argument for a date before AD 70 for Matthew. Indeed Gundry goes further and, after arguing that Luke-Acts, which he dates about AD 63, was influenced by Matthew, concludes that Matthew was written before 63.[2] Whether this latter point be granted or not, there is certainly a good case to be made for a date in the sixties for the final 'publication' of Matthew.

It must be recognized, however, that all such conclusions depend on the relative dating of various writings and events, and that there are few fixed points.[3] Our comments below on the relationships between the Synoptic Gospels will suggest that any 'publication date' can be advanced only very tentatively.

## C. Authorship

Patristic tradition is unanimous that the author was Matthew, and no other 'Matthew' is suggested than the disciple of that name whose call is described in 9:9.

The earliest extant example of this tradition is the statement of Papias, Bishop of Hierapolis (usually dated about AD 140), which is quoted by Eusebius (*H.E.* iii.39.16) to the effect that

'Matthew *compiled* the *oracles* in the *Hebrew dialect*, and everyone *translated* them as best he could'.

That sentence, quoted by Eusebius with no surrounding context (though it is clear that *Eusebius* thought Papias was talking about the Gospel of Matthew), is full of ambiguities. Each of the words in italics can be translated in different ways, which substantially affect the meaning:

*compiled* could be 'composed' or 'arranged';

---

[1]Commentary, pp. 599-609.    [2]*Ibid.*, pp. 608-609.
[3]See a useful summary of this point, with strong support for a date before AD 70 for Matthew, in J.M. Rist, *On the Independence of Matthew and Mark* (1978), pp. 4-7.

*Hebrew* is used either for the Hebrew or the Aramaic language;
*dialect* would normally mean 'language', but has been taken to
 mean 'style';
*translated* could be 'interpreted'.

So far it is clear that Papias may be referring either to the
collection (as an 'editor') of existing material, or to 'composition'
by an 'author', and that while his words would normally suggest that this was done in one of the Semitic languages, with
subsequent translation (into Greek, presumably), it might be
argued that he was referring to a Greek work in 'a Hebrew
style'.

But by far the most significant ambiguity is the word *logia*,
translated *'oracles'* above. It normally means 'sayings' or 'pronouncements'. One suggestion, little favoured, is that it refers
to a collection of Old Testament *testimonia* relating to Jesus.
More usually the question is asked whether Papias could have
referred to a book like our 'Gospel of Matthew' by such a term,
or whether he must be speaking of a collection of 'Sayings of
Jesus', perhaps subsequently incorporated into Matthew's
Gospel.

Papias' evidence, then, proves a very shaky foundation for
patristic belief that the First Gospel was written by Matthew.
Nor is the situation improved by Eusebius' view that Papias was
'a man of very little intelligence, as is clear from his books'!
Three lines of approach to this dilemma may be mentioned.

1. To take *logia* in its normal sense, and to conclude that,
whatever Eusebius thought, Papias was not talking about the
Gospel, but about a collection of Jesus' sayings in Aramaic
(possibly something like the hypothetical Q, on which see later).
In that case this quotation has no direct bearing on the authorship of the Gospel.[1]

2. To accept Eusebius' view that Papias *was* talking about the
Gospel, and to conclude that he was simply mistaken about its
being written in a Semitic language[2] (perhaps being led to this

---

[1]This option, which is the majority view, is presented, *e.g.*, by Hill, pp. 22–27.

[2]Virtually all scholars now agree that our Gospel of Matthew was written in Greek, and is
not a simple translation of an Aramaic original. C.C. Torrey did take this approach in his *The
Four Gospels* (1933), but since then the most that has been proposed is that our Greek Gospel
is based on an earlier Aramaic work. Its use of the LXX and its verbal links with Mark really

guess by noticing the 'Jewish' character of the Gospel[1]).

3. To opt for the meaning 'in a Semitic style', and to conclude that Papias is correctly recording the origin of the *Greek* Gospel of Matthew.[2]

The unanimity of patristic attribution of the Gospel to Matthew is thus weakened by the recognition that it is far from certain that the earliest supposed witness to this tradition really does support it at all. If Eusebius' view may have been based on a misunderstanding of Papias, how much weight is to be placed on the other patristic references, which may well derive from the same traditions which Papias was recording?

What then is the evidence of the Gospel itself? It is, of course, like all the Gospels, an anonymous work, in that its text does not include a statement of who wrote it.[3] Its evidence will rather be of the *sort* of person who would be likely to have written such a work.

From the characteristics of the Gospel noted above we may reasonably infer that its author was a Jewish Christian, with an extensive knowledge of and a strong interest in the Old Testament, familiar with scribal traditions and with the methods of Rabbinic debate, and capable of writing in good Greek, even though his own cultural background was clearly Semitic. Many of Jesus' early disciples, known to us and unknown, could fit this description, given the increasing recognition that Greek was widely used in first-century Palestine, particularly in 'Galilee of the Gentiles'. Undoubtedly Matthew would be likely to fit the description, but is there any reason for seeing him as a more likely candidate than others?

All that we know about Matthew in distinction from the other disciples is that he was a tax-collector, and that he apparently also bore the name of Levi (so Mark and Luke in their parallels

---

demand that it was composed in Greek. See further Guthrie, pp. 46–47; Moule, *The Birth of the New Testament* (³1981), pp. 276–280.

[1]This view is favoured by Guthrie, pp. 33–41.

[2]So Gundry, pp. 609–620. Gundry's discussion is unusual in arguing both for an earlier date for Papias than is usually accepted (about AD 100?), and for his being a direct disciple of John the Apostle. Not many scholars, however, have accepted the understanding of *Hebraidi dialectō* as 'in a Hebrew style'.

[3]The heading *According to Matthew* probably first started being added to the Gospel some time in the first half of the second century AD. On these 'titles' see Guthrie, p. 33.

to Mt. 9:9). Both facts have been used to support his authorship of the First Gospel.

A tax-collector would, by virtue of his office, need to be particularly fluent in Greek. He would also need to be literate, used to keeping records. Gundry, following E. J. Goodspeed, has argued for the possibility that he would even be able to use short-hand, and so could have taken notes of Jesus' teaching, possibly acting as the 'recorder' of the disciple group.[1] C. F. D. Moule has argued similarly that the author was 'a well-educated writer – a scribe in the secular, not the rabbinic sense', and has proposed that 13:52 should be understood in this sense as the self-portrait of the 'tax-collector turned disciple'.[2] It has been further suggested that a number of references to money matters and to tax-collectors which are peculiar to this Gospel may be a pointer to its author.[3]

The name Levi has been taken by some to be not so much a personal as a tribal name, indicating that Matthew was in fact a Levite. As such, it is suggested, he would have been particularly at home in the religious niceties of scribal tradition. At the same time, a Levite turned tax-collector might expect to earn the special disdain of his more orthodox fellow-Levites, and so be liable to record with greater emphasis Jesus' conflicts with 'orthodoxy', as much for his own self-defence as for the guidance of other potential converts.[4]

On such grounds, tenuous as they are, it may be suggested that Matthew fits the description of this Gospel's author at least as well as any other person known to us. The fact that the Gospel was so soon and so generally associated with Matthew, who was not a prominent member of Jesus' disciple group, may also support this conclusion, since he would not have been the obvious author to select if it was simply a matter of guesswork.[5]

[1]Gundry, *UOT*, pp. 182–185.

[2]In F.L. Cross (ed.), *Studia Evangelica* II (1964), pp. 90–99. Moule does not, however, regard the apostle Matthew as necessarily the final author of the Gospel, but as at least the source of much of its content.

[3]*E.g.* Gundry, pp. 620–621.

[4]This argument is developed by Albright and Mann, *AB*, pp. CLXXVII-CLXXXIV.

[5]It is sometimes argued, on the assumption that Mark was a source used by the First Gospel, that an apostle would not make use of a non-apostolic source. This strange argument depends on (a) a modern concept of literary independence, (b) the setting aside of the early tradition that Mark was recording Peter's teaching, and so *was* 'apostolic'.

None of this, however, adds up to anything like proof of authorship. We may safely say that the unanimous tradition of the early church, however uncertain its origin, offers us a candidate who on other grounds is likely to have been the sort of person indicated by the character of the Gospel. But no doubt there were other such people among the early disciples. And even if the patristic association of Matthew's name with the Gospel is given full weight, this does not rule out the possibility of more than one stage in its composition. The later the Gospel is dated, the more likely it becomes that Matthew's contribution was at an earlier stage than the final 'edition'.

So in the end we simply do not know the extent of the role of the apostle Matthew in the composition of the First Gospel, but the tradition of the early church encourages us to believe that it was a major one.

### D. Matthew, Mark and Luke

Roughly 45% of Matthew's Gospel consists of material found in a similar (sometimes verbally identical) form in Mark, and in roughly the same order; a further 20% or so is similarly shared with Luke, and again there is a rough correspondence in the order of many of the shared sections,[1] though not in their place in the overall structure of each Gospel. This leaves only about 35% of the Gospel as Matthew's unique contribution, though of course much of the 'shared' material is presented in a clearly distinctive way by Matthew, to the extent that it is sometimes difficult to say whether or not there is a common tradition lying behind two or more of the Gospel accounts of a given incident or saying.

These are some of the facts which go to make up the 'Synoptic Problem'. How do we account for the large areas of overlap? Did one Gospel derive the material directly from another? Did they use common sources? If so, were these sources written or oral, and did they consist of substantial collections or of isolated fragments?

Until fairly recently there was a widely (though never universally) agreed 'solution' to the problem. Put simply, it was that

[1]See W.G. Kümmel, *Introduction to the New Testament* (1975), pp. 65–66 for a useful chart of the order of the 'Q' material in Luke and Matthew.

Mark wrote first, that both Matthew and Luke made direct use of Mark's Gospel, and that Matthew and Luke both had access also to a document no longer extant, consisting largely of collected saying of Jesus, and known to scholars as 'Q' (possibly derived from the German *Quelle*, 'source'). This classical solution, with the arguments generally used to support it, is conveniently set out by Leon Morris in the volume on Luke in this series (pp. 47–59), and it is unnecessary to repeat that presentation here. Morris' conclusion there was that 'nothing more than a tentative hypothesis is justified', and subsequent discussion has shown that his caution was well placed. The areas of growing uncertainty may conveniently be summarized under three headings.

*(i) Marcan priority challenged.* The view that Mark was the first of our Gospels to be written arose in the first half of the nineteenth century, and became dominant soon after the middle of that century. Before that it had been assumed that Matthew was written first. Now the older view is being strenuously resurrected.

The classical view is the 'Augustinian', represented today *e.g.* by B. C. Butler;[1] this holds that Matthew's Gospel was used by Mark, and that Luke in turn used both. The view more widely promoted today, however, is the so-called 'Griesbach Hypothesis',[2] which is now supported by a significant group of scholars of widely varying traditions. This is that Matthew's Gospel was used by Luke, and that Mark is a deliberate condensing of the contents of the two into a single work.

Those who would declare firmly for Matthaean priority on the basis of either of these views are still a minority, but a larger number of scholars have been sufficiently impressed by their arguments to be reluctant to commit themselves firmly to an overall assumption of Marcan priority.

*(ii) Doubts about Q.* Either of the views mentioned in the last

[1]B.C. Butler, *The Originality of St. Matthew* (1951).

[2]Originally put forward by J.J. Griesbach in 1783, now best represented by W.R. Farmer's writings (esp. *The Synoptic Problem*, ²1976), and by B. Orchard, *Matthew, Luke and Mark* (1976). For a critical assessment see C.J. Tuckett, *The Revival of the Griesbach Hypothesis* (1983).

paragraph makes Q unnecessary; the common material, whatever the source from which Matthew derived it, was taken by Luke direct from Matthew, not from a third document. Even among supporters of Marcan priority there have been some who find no place for Q; see *e.g.* the view of M. D. Goulder mentioned above[1] that the so-called Q material is in fact Matthew's free creation, which Luke then took over from Matthew. But where Matthew and Luke are regarded as independently using common material, the 'tendency to be less dogmatic about Q' which Morris noted in 1974 has certainly not decreased. While some scholars continue to write books on the theology and composition of Q, regarded as a single document (though possibly composed in different 'editions'), many are prepared only to speak of 'Q material', envisaged not as a single document, but as various units of material, some written, some oral, to which both Matthew and Luke had access.

*(iii) Direct literary dependence questioned.* Can we speak simply of one Gospel writer 'using' or 'copying from' another's work? Is this to assume something like a modern system of publication and distribution of books which is quite inappropriate to the situation in first-century Christianity?[2] While the verbatim agreements among the Gospels seem to demand that there was literary dependence in some form, need we assume that it was on the completed text of, say, Mark that Matthew drew? Was the classical 'Two-Document Hypothesis' just too simple to be realistic?

Various scholars have been asking such questions, and as a result other approaches have been offered. Some have substituted a more complex but no less definite scheme of relationships, postulating successive editions of each Gospel with lines of dependence criss-crossing between the different Gospel traditions in an attempt to account for the many inconsistencies left by the simple two-document scheme.[3]

[1] See pp. 23–24. Goulder's views were influenced by Austin Farrer, who wrote a famous article 'On Dispensing with Q' in 1954.

[2] This point is argued strongly by Albright and Mann, *AB*, pp. XXXVII–XLVIII.

[3] See *e.g.* the scheme proposed by M–E. Boismard in his *Synopse des quatres évangiles en français*, vol. II (with P. Benoit, 1972). A diagrammatic presentation of the scheme, with discussion, is conveniently available in *JTS* 25 (1974), pp. 485f.

At the other extreme J. M. Rist[1] argues for the literary independence of Matthew and Mark, explaining their overlap by the use of common traditions, which were probably more extensive than is generally assumed, and were largely oral, very likely including parallel traditions of similar but separate teaching and events. For Rist, then, to deny that Matthew derived his material from Mark does not, as has generally been supposed, require that Mark derived his from Matthew. No overall 'priority' between the two Gospels can be established; neither had access to the other.

A position somewhere between these extremes seems more plausible. Building on the work of E. P. Sanders,[2] J. A. T. Robinson[3] envisages the origin of the Gospels not in terms of direct dependence of one Gospel on another, nor in terms of complete literary independence, but in terms of the parallel growth of different gospel traditions (resulting ultimately in our four canonical Gospels), with continued contact between these traditions along the way. The 'gospel-writing' activity of the different church centres was not in isolated compartments. As 'proto-gospels' appeared in different churches they would be available to others, so that by the time the Gospels as we know them were written a process of 'cross-fertilization' had taken place which renders any theory of simple one-way dependence of one Gospel on another quite unrealistic. On this view, the formation of the Gospels was too complex and 'living' a process to be tied down into a diagram of dependence, however complicated, and a simple assumption that 'Matthew used Mark' cannot be the whole truth (still less a neat delineation of a single document Q).

If it was once possible to use the classical 'Two-Document Hypothesis' as a non-negotiable framework for the study of the Gospels, that time is now past. But it is difficult, if not impossible, to discuss the relationship between parallel passages without some general presupposition as to which is likely to be the

---

[1] J.M. Rist, *On the Independence of Matthew and Mark* (1978); similarly *AB*, pp. XXXVII–XLVIII.

[2] Sanders' basic study *The Tendencies of the Synoptic Tradition* (1969) is taken further in an article in *NTS* 19 (1972/3), pp. 453–465.

[3] Robinson, pp. 93–117; see esp. the summary on p. 107.

more original. In the commentary that follows, while bearing in mind the salutary warnings against a simple overall scheme, I shall generally work on the assumption that where Matthew and Mark run parallel it is more likely that the Marcan version is the earlier, and that therefore it is possible to discern Matthew's special interests in the differences between his version and Mark's, even if it would be over-simple to speak baldly of his 'altering the Marcan text'. In dealing with 'Q' material, while judgments of 'priority' would be out of place, Matthaean interest may nonetheless be noted where he differs from Luke's version. Distinctiveness can be perceived even where direct literary dependence cannot be assumed.

## IV. CENTRAL THEOLOGICAL EMPHASES OF MATTHEW

### A. Fulfilment

The essential key to all Matthew's theology is that in Jesus all God's purposes have come to fulfilment. This is, of course, true of all New Testament theology, but it is emphasized in a remarkable way in Matthew. Everything is related to Jesus. The Old Testament points forward to him; its law is 'fulfilled' in his teaching; he is the true Israel through whom God's plans for his people now go forward; the future no less than the present is to be understood as the working out of the ministry of Jesus. History revolves around him, in that his coming is the turning-point at which the age of preparation gives way to the age of fulfilment. Matthew leaves no room for any idea of the fulfilment of God's purposes, whether for Israel or in any other respect, which is not focused in this theme of *fulfilment in Jesus.* In his coming a new age has dawned; nothing will ever be quite the same again.

The sections that follow will deal with various aspects of this overriding theme of fulfilment. But first we must note two of Matthew's special ways of drawing out this emphasis.

*(i) The 'formula-quotations'.* Ten times in Matthew we find the formula 'This was to fulfil (or 'then was fulfilled') what was spoken by the prophet, saying . . .', after which comes a quotation from an Old Testament prophet (or, in one case, the

Psalms). The references are 1:22–23; 2:15; 2:17–18; 2:23; 4:14–16; 8:17; 12:17–21; 21:4–5; 27:9–10. The wording of the formula varies slightly, and in five cases the prophet is named. In another case (2:5–6) the setting of the quotation in the narrative causes the formula to be changed to 'for so it is written by the prophet', but this text is usually classed with the formula-quotations. There are, of course, many other verbatim quotations from the Old Testament, but this group stand out by virtue of their stereotyped formula. All but one are quoted only in Matthew. In each case, if the quotation and its formula were removed, the story would flow on without an obvious gap, which suggests that they are comments added to existing stories; and yet in each case the claim to the fulfilment of Scripture seems to be the main point being made by the section of text in which they occur.

There has been much debate about the origin and function of these formula-quotations.[1] Most scholars now regard them as Matthew's own contribution, rather than as traditional elements in the story of Jesus, and the study of their textual peculiarities indicates that behind them lies some quite original and sophisticated study of the Old Testament in order to discover points of correspondence much more subtle than the direct fulfilment of clear prophetic predictions.[2] Sometimes the subtlety results in an application of the Old Testament text which is 'to our critical eyes, manifestly forced and artificial and unconvincing'; but C. F. D. Moule, in a helpful discussion from which those words are taken,[3] goes on to argue that this 'vehicular' use of Scripture 'is a symptom of the discovery that, in a deeply organic way, Jesus was indeed the fulfiller of something which is basic in the whole of Scripture'. In an article[4] which concentrates on the four formula-quotations of chapter 2, I have suggested that what

[1] In addition to the works of Stendahl and Gundry mentioned above, specialized monographs have been written by W. Rothfuchs, *Die Erfüllungszitate des Matthäusevangeliums* (1969), and G.M. Soares Prabhu, *The Formula Quotations in the Infancy Narrative of Matthew* (1976).

[2] See above for Gundry's argument that these peculiarities are found also in other quotations and allusions in Matthew which are not part of the Marcan tradition.

[3] C.F.D. Moule, *The Origin of Christology* (1977), chapter 5, 'The Fulfilment Theme in the New Testament'.

[4] *NTS* 27 (1980/1), pp. 233–251.

may seem to us an embarrassingly obscure and even irresponsible way of handling Scripture is in fact the outworking of a careful tracing of scriptural themes, which in different ways point to Jesus as the fulfiller not only of specific predictions, but also of the broader pattern of God's Old Testament revelation.

*(ii) Typology.* Matthew's view of Jesus as the one who fulfils the whole fabric of scriptural revelation is most strikingly brought to light in the large number of what may be called 'typological' allusions to the Old Testament. These occur both in his records of Jesus' sayings and in his own wording of narratives and his editorial comments. Typology is not peculiar to Matthew, and may properly be seen as an essential element in Jesus' own self-understanding.[1] But in Matthew it is particularly pronounced.

Typology, at least the typology we are here concerned with as it appears in the Gospels, may be defined as 'the recognition of a correspondence between New and Old Testament events, based on a conviction of the unchanging character of the principles of God's working, and a consequent understanding and description of the New Testament event in terms of the Old Testament model'[2] – except that 'events' is too narrow, since Old Testament persons and institutions (such as the temple or the covenant) come in for the same treatment. Put simply, we are talking here about 'fulfilment' not only of Old Testament *predictions*, but of Old Testament *history* and *religion*, including events and institutions which in themselves carried no explicit reference to the future. In commenting on 5:17 we shall note the idea of the law pointing forward to Jesus, who can therefore be said to 'fulfil' it. In chapter 2 we shall see Jesus presented as a 'new Moses', among other varied typological themes, and in the same chapter he will be equated with God's 'son', Israel (see on 2:15). In 4:1–11 the whole story of the testing of Jesus is undergirded by the recognition of a correspondence between his experience and the testing of God's son Israel in the wilderness as recorded in Deuteronomy. Chapter 12 will offer a series of Old Testament 'precedents' as justification for Jesus' assumption of authority

---

[1] This theme is explored in chapter 3 of my *JOT*.    [2] *Ibid*., p. 40.

over the sabbath (see on 12:3-8), focused in the explicit statement that 'something greater than the temple is here' (12:6),
followed later in the chapter by the same formula applied to
Jonah and Solomon (12:41-42) on the basis of an explicit prediction that Jesus was to undergo a parallel experience to that of
Jonah (12:40); see further the comments on 12:41-42. These are
some of the more striking examples of a conviction which runs
throughout the Gospel, that as God worked in Old Testament
times, so he has worked again in the ministry of Jesus, and yet
with a 'something greater' which makes Jesus the 'fulfilment' of
the whole warp and woof of the Old Testament, not just of the
explicit predictions of the prophets. This typology is not so
much a hermeneutical technique as a theological conviction
which expresses itself in various ways in Matthew's presentation of Jesus' life and teaching. Its effect is to show Jesus as the
point at which all the rich diversity of God's relations with his
people in word and deed converges; that is what 'fulfilment'
means for Matthew.

This emphasis on fulfilment will run through the whole Gospel, but it will be announced with particular force in the prologue, chapters 1 – 2, which is devoted to presenting Jesus in the
light of scriptural patterns and prophecy. See the introductory
comments on chapters 1 – 2 in the commentary. The scene is
thus set, so that Matthew's readers will be alert to scriptural
undertones in the story that follows. The fuller their knowledge
of the Old Testament, the richer will be their understanding of
the significance of Jesus as he is presented in Matthew's pages.

## B. Christology

It follows from what has already been said that Christology, the
explanation of *who Jesus is*, must be at the heart of Matthew's
theological task. Virtually every aspect of the Gospel's theology
could be subsumed under this heading. We shall focus here on
four titles of Jesus which are prominent in the Gospel, using
them as a framework into which to build a variety of theological
themes which seem to have been of special importance to
Matthew.

*(i) Christ.* When we use the term 'Messiah' (or 'Christ', its

Greek equivalent[1]) we usually think in fairly general terms of the one through whom God was going to fulfil his purpose of salvation for his people, as promised in the Old Testament. It is important therefore to realize that the breadth of meaning which Christian hindsight sees in the term would not have been its natural connotation for a Jew in Jesus' day. Different strands of Old Testament hope were remembered and prized by different groups, but it seems clear that the title 'Messiah' would, for most ordinary Jews, have pointed to a coming king of the line of David, whom God would send to restore his people to national independence and to their rightful pre-eminence as the people of God. The wide range of 'fulfilment' ideas which we have hinted at in the preceding section, however naturally they may be fitted into *our* idea of 'the Messiah', would not necessarily have been triggered off by the term in the mind of a Jew who had not learnt to see them all brought together in Jesus.

It is not surprising, then, that when the title 'Christ' is used in this Gospel in discussing what Jesus' mission is there is a note of hesitation in his response (see the commentary on 16:16, 20, 21–23; 26:63–64). Much of the Gospel will indicate the differing attitudes of Jews to Jesus, owing at least in part to their differing expectations of 'the coming one'. In the event Jesus' mission of suffering and death, with its aim the forgiveness of sins and the restoration of a broken relationship with God, could not fail to be at least a puzzle, more likely a total disappointment, to those whose idea of the Messiah was along quite different lines.

So while Matthew himself has no hesitation in describing Jesus as the Messiah (1:1, 16, 17, 18; 11:2; 16:20), and no doubt reads into that title the wide range of his own understanding of Jesus' mission of 'fulfilment', he only once (23:10) represents Jesus as applying it to himself. It was, apparently, a term too loaded to be openly encouraged. Only in the light of Jesus' death and resurrection would his followers be able to use it freely without fear of misunderstanding. Even then, the paradox of a Messiah whose role it was to be crucified would prove a continuing stumbling-block for Jews (see 1 Cor. 1:23).

[1] *AB* (p. 194) regards 'the transliteration of the Gr. *Christos* by Christ' as 'inexcusable', presumably because our familiarity with 'Christ' as virtually a 'name' of Jesus obscures for us the fact that it is a title for the Jewish Messiah.

In the light of this it is remarkable that Matthew feels able to record more freely than the other Evangelists the use of the still more clearly nationalistic title '*Son of David*' with reference to Jesus (of the nine uses of the title in Matthew only 20:30–31 is shared with the other Synoptics). For Matthew and his Jewish readers the term would be full of historical and theological associations. It links Jesus more clearly even than the term 'Christ' with the fulfilment of God's plans for his people Israel, and Matthew's emphasis on David in 1:1 and the following genealogy (and *cf.* 1:20) shows how much the term meant to him. But its use during Jesus' ministry, generally with reference to his healing power (9:27; 12:23; 15:22; 20:30–31; see commentary on 9:27), carried a real possibility of misunderstanding his mission in quasi-political terms, and at least in 21:9, 15 it seems that the crowd used it in this sense. It is perhaps for this reason that Matthew, despite his liking for the title, records also Jesus' comments on its inadequacy in 22:41–45.

Among the richly varied Christological insights in Matthew's prologue (chapters 1 – 2) is an explicit statement of the purpose of Jesus' mission: 'he will save his people from their sins' (1:21). Here is a clear pointer both to a mission of liberation (an idea which was central to Jewish Messianic expectation) and at the same time away from a political understanding of that idea. 'Sins' were the concern of John the Baptist's mission (3:6); Jesus claimed the authority to forgive them (9:1–8), and Matthew alone records that he declared the purpose of his death as 'the forgiveness of sins' (26:28). The liberating mission of the Messiah is then, for Matthew, at a quite different level from that of popular expectation.

*(ii) Son of man.* In Matthew, as in all the other Gospels, the title which Jesus uses to describe his own mission is usually 'the Son of man'. Matthew's recording of this title differs little from that by Mark and Luke. None of them use it themselves in narrative or comment, but all agree that Jesus made frequent use of it, and, most remarkably, that when the title 'Christ' was offered to him, he substituted 'the Son of man' (26:64).

This is not the place to give a full account of the voluminous and continuing debate about this title. Even the description of it as a 'title' is controversial, as the phrase 'a son of man' in Hebrew and Aramaic means simply a human being. When God addresses Ezekiel frequently as 'Son of man' (Ezk. 2:1, 3; 3:1; *etc.*) it is as 'man' in contrast with God, almost meaning 'little man'! (*Cf.* also Pss. 8:4; 80:17.) In later Aramaic a similar phrase came to be used sometimes, rather like the English 'one', to refer to oneself or (occasionally) someone else, in contexts where modesty or prudence made a direct statement undesirable. But the phrase '*the* Son of man' seems to demand a more specific content than that, especially when it is seen that Jesus uses the phrase predominantly in discussing the nature of his specific mission, not the lot of men in general.

But there is no clear evidence that the phrase '*the* Son of man' was used thus as a title in any Jewish literature before the time of Jesus.[1] It is therefore likely that Jesus developed this strange usage himself, perhaps deliberately in order to avoid a familiar title (such as 'Messiah') which would already have carried its own meaning for Jesus' hearers.

It *is* a strange usage: the Greek phrase *ho hyios tou anthrōpou* is as unnatural as the English, and the Aramaic phrase *bar-nāšā'* would not normally be used, as Jesus always used it, with a definite article. It seems most likely that Jesus 'coined' the title on the basis of the vision of 'one like a son of man' in Daniel 7:13 (a passage to which he frequently referred in explaining his mission: see on 10:23; 16:27–28; 19:28; 24:30; 25:31; 26:64; 28:18); in Daniel this is no title, simply a description of a human figure (as opposed to an animal) in a vision, but Jesus' definite article functions virtually as a demonstrative, '*that* Son of man', *i.e.* the one described in Daniel 7:13–14, which Jesus clearly saw as a figure for his own mission.[2]

But while the phrase was probably derived from reflection on Daniel 7:13f., Jesus' use of it as a title for himself extends far beyond what that passage suggests. In addition to the future glory and triumph depicted in Daniel 7:13–14, Jesus uses the

[1]It is a prominent title in the Similitudes of Enoch (1 Enoch 37 – 71), but the date of this work is still disputed. Even if it was written before Jesus' time (which many now doubt), it is questionable how widely it would have been known. It is remarkable that while other parts of the Enoch literature have appeared among the Qumran manuscripts, this section has not.

[2]For this understanding of the phrase see C.F.D. Moule, *The Origin of Christology* (1977), pp. 11–22.

phrase particularly in predicting his own rejection, suffering and death, a theme which Daniel 7 alone would not have required. Further, he speaks of his ministry on earth, both in its humiliation (*e.g.* 8:20) and in its authority (*e.g.* 9:6; 12:8), under this title. It is, then, a wide-ranging term whose content is fixed not by any predetermined meaning as a title (for it had none), but by the breadth of Jesus' own understanding of his unique mission.

*(iii) King.* The title 'King of the Jews' will appear as the charge against Jesus at his trial (27:11, 29, 37, 42), where it is made clear that Jesus is king in a very different sense from what the title conveyed either to the Roman governor and his soldiers or to the Jewish leaders. It might seem then that kingship is a theme better avoided in presenting Jesus' mission. But Matthew cannot set it aside. For him Jesus *is* the true king: in 2:2 he presents him as the real king of the Jews (in contrast with Herod), and in the genealogy of 1:1–17 Jesus' royal ancestry is emphasized. In 20:21 the disciples look forward to Jesus' 'kingdom', and in 21:4–5 Matthew points out explicitly how Jesus' entry to Jerusalem fulfils Zechariah's prophecy of the coming of 'your king'. While Matthew's Gospel, like the other Synoptics, speaks much of the kingdom of *God* (or 'heaven'), he also includes a few references by Jesus to himself ('the Son of man') as having his own kingship (13:41; 16:28; 19:28; 25:31, 34). In 25:31ff. his kingship is described in terms used in the Old Testament for that of God himself. And the Gospel reaches its climax in the declaration of Jesus' universal sovereignty (28:18).

The kingship of Jesus is thus an important theme for Matthew. Jesus 'fulfils' the institution of kingship in the Old Testament: he is the 'son of David', the 'greater than Solomon' (see on 12:3–4, 42). But that kingship, even in the Old Testament, was only a delegated one. The true king is God himself. And the theme of God's kingship (which is what the Greek words traditionally translated 'the kingdom of God' mean) undergirds all Matthew's Gospel, as indeed it was clearly central to Jesus' ministry as all three Synoptic Gospels present it. The mission of Jesus was to establish God's kingship. The phrase 'the kingdom of God' therefore points not to a specific situation or event, but to 'God in control', with all the breadth of meaning that that phrase could cover. Attempts to *define* 'the kingdom of God' inevitably restrict this breadth, and so fail to do justice to the variety of its usage in the Gospels. So, for instance, when the parables of Matthew 13 tell us what 'the kingdom of heaven is like', they are depicting in a variety of contexts what happens when God has his way, when his will is done and his purpose fulfilled. When Jesus tells his disciples to 'seek his kingdom' (6:33) he is telling them to 'put God first', not prescribing a specific line of action, and when he tells them to pray 'Thy kingdom come' this is no less broad in application than the following clause 'Thy will be done'. We shall see in the commentary how important it is to maintain this broad perspective, and not to allow our under-standing of 'kingdom of God' language to be prematurely restricted to a specific area of application.[1]

In the preceding paragraphs I have spoken generally about 'the kingdom of *God*', because this is the phrase we usually find in the Gospels. But it does not take much reading in Matthew to discover that the phrase we find there is usually 'the kingdom of *heaven*' (lit. 'the kingdom of the heavens'), a phrase totally absent from the other Gospels. Matthew's preference for this more typically Jewish form (avoiding direct use of the name of God by a periphrasis: *cf.* Dn. 4:26, 'Heaven rules') is probably due to his predominantly Jewish readership.[2] At any rate, com-parison of Synoptic parallels soon confirms that it is merely a stylistic peculiarity of Matthew, and that there is no difference in meaning. On a few occasions Matthew retains the form 'king-dom of God', perhaps where there is emphasis on a personal response to God (see commentary on 12:28; 21:31, 43; these, together with 19:24, are the only instances of 'kingdom of God' in Matthew, but *cf.* also 'my Father's kingdom' in 26:29, 'Thy kingdom' in 6:10, 'his kingdom' in 6:33).

If Jesus is king, then, it is because God's kingship has been established through his ministry, so that, as 28:18 declares with reference to Daniel 7:14, God has given him all authority in

---

[1] I have developed this argument more fully in D.A. Carson (ed.), *Biblical Interpretation* (1984), pp. 30–44.

[2] Schweizer (p. 47) adds the suggestion that the expression is intended to accommodate the kingship of Jesus along with that of God.

heaven and on earth. In thus sharing God's kingship, he also shares his function as the judge of men (13:41; 16:27; 19:28; 25:31ff.). And in that judgment the criterion will be how men have responded to *him* (7:21–23; 25:34ff.). Such language takes us well beyond any normal idea of Messiahship such as the title 'King of the Jews' might have suggested.

*(iv) Son of God.* Jesus' language about himself as God's Son, which is so familiar to us from the Fourth Gospel, is not nearly so prominent in the Synoptic Gospels. But it is there, sometimes slightly veiled in parable (21:37–39), sometimes explicit (11:25–27, on which see comments; 24:36). Generally, however, language about Jesus as Son of God occurs not in his own words but in what is said about him, whether by God himself (3:17; 17:5), by Satan echoing the voice of God (4:3,6), by demons with their supernatural knowledge (8:29), or by the disciples as their understanding of Jesus begins to deepen (14:33; 16:16–17). Eventually the title comes into the centre of Jesus' confrontation with the Jewish leaders (26:63; 27:40, 43); but while they reject it with mockery, Gentile soldiers perceive its truth (27:54). Several of these references are peculiar to Matthew, and the importance of this title for his Christology is shown as early as 2:15, where he applies to Jesus Hosea's 'son of God' language about Israel. But its full significance comes out only at the end of the Gospel, where 'the Son' stands alongside the Father and the Holy Spirit as the object of a disciple's allegiance (28:19).

Such language takes us far beyond the category of a Jewish Messiah. In various ways the Gospel keeps hinting that this Jesus who fulfils the hopes of the Old Testament is more than just a man sent by God. His coming is the coming of God (see on 3:3). He is one who has no need to repent of sin (3:14–15; *cf.* Matthew's careful avoidance in 19:16–17 of the implication that Jesus does not share the unique goodness of God). He is one who has heaven's armies at his command (26:53–54). At his death and resurrection supernatural portents take place (27:51–54; 28:2–4). Even during his earthly life it is appropriate for him to be 'worshipped' as 'Lord' (see esp. 14:33, and see on 2:2; 7:21; 8:2, *etc.* for the implications of Matthew's use of *kyrios* and of the verb *proskyneō*; the former occurs with reference to

Jesus 44 times in Matthew, as compared with only about 6 in Mark; see further, *TIM*, pp.41–43, 229).

This highest level of Matthew's Christology is effectively summed up in two verses which are often regarded as a 'framework' around the Gospel. Near its beginning, Jesus is seen, in Isaiah's words, as 'God with us' (1:23), while the Gospel closes with an assurance from the Son, whose name stands with those of the Father and the Holy Spirit, 'I am with you always, to the close of the age' (28:19–20).

## C. *The law*

If Matthew is to present Jesus as the fulfilment of the hopes of Israel, one subject he cannot overlook is Jesus' relation to the Old Testament law. Israel prided itself as the people to whom God had given his law; it was the focus of their life and religion. It was concern for the law which had led the scribes to develop in ever-increasing complexity the detailed rules for correct life and worship which eventually went to make up the Mishnah, and it was the meticulous observance of these rules which was the chief distinguishing mark of the 'scribes and Pharisees' who figure so prominently in Matthew's Gospel. How then does Jesus relate to this law? In what sense, if at all, is it possible to speak of 'fulfilment' here?

It is clear even from the narrative content of the Gospel that this was a major concern of Matthew. We see Jesus in debate with the scribes and others over such questions as fasting, table-fellowship with 'sinners', the use of the sabbath, obligation to parents, ritual defilement, obligation to pay the temple tax, the grounds of divorce, imperial taxation, and which is the greatest commandment. These were all issues of Rabbinic interest, and in such controversies Jesus consistently stands out as one who is not content simply to endorse existing interpretations of the law, but who calls for a more radical obedience which, while it may be less literal, is never less demanding.

In 15:1–9, for instance, Jesus attacks scribal tradition on the grounds that its casuistry allows men to escape the demands of true obedience to the law. This is explicitly a defence of the commandment of God against the tradition of men. In the following verses, however, Jesus enunciates a principle which will eventually undermine the conception of defilement which was the foundation of the food-laws of the Old Testament itself. But while Mark 7:19b boldly draws this conclusion, Matthew does not, and it is suggested that Matthew 15:20 represents a significant refusal on Matthew's part to accept the radical implications of Jesus' teaching (see comments *ad loc.*).

Is Matthew then more cautious than Mark in accepting that Jesus' teaching in any way weakened the force of the Old Testament law? Does he cast him rather as a defender of the law against scribal misinterpretation? Indeed one could go even further and find in two passages peculiar to Matthew (23:2–3, 23) even a reinforcement of scribal tradition itself, making Matthew an enthusiast for legalistic observance. I believe that this is not the force of those verses (see commentary), and that even in regard to the continuing validity of the Old Testament commandments Matthew's Jesus is not so 'conservative' as is sometimes suggested.

The main discussion of this issue is the long section 5:17–48, the framework of which is peculiar to Matthew, even though some of its specific contents have parallels in Luke and to a much lesser extent in Mark. This passage indicates a much less 'conservative' picture of Jesus than that suggested above. It begins with a Jesus who finds it necessary to rebut the charge that his mission was to abolish the law (5:17)! In repudiating this charge, verses 18–19 seem at first sight to go back to endorsing the rigid legalism of the scribes, but further study of the passage shows that this cannot be so. Rather this ringing affirmation of the God-given authority of the law is set under the rubric of its 'fulfilment' by Jesus, and that fulfilment points not to a continued literal observance of all its regulations, but rather to a 'greater righteousness' (v. 20), which is explicitly set over against the legalism of the scribes and Pharisees, and which will culminate in the most radical demand imaginable: 'You must be perfect, as your heavenly Father is perfect' (v. 48).

The examples of Jesus' relation to the Old Testament law which lead up to this staggering conclusion will include instances where he reinforces its authority and where he apparently sets it aside. But all the time what he is opposing is essentially an attitude which sees its function as the mere provision of regulations to be observed to the letter – and no more! Even when his prescriptions are such as the scribes might have regarded as a weakening of the law's literal application, the effect is to make a far more searching ethical demand. In all this, there is a sovereign freedom in Jesus' willingness to penetrate to the true will of God which lies behind the law's regulations. The primary impact of the passage is not in terms of a new understanding of the law, but in terms of the significance of Jesus. 'It therefore becomes apparent that it is not so much *Jesus'* stance towards the law that Matthew is concerned to depict: it is how the *Law* stands with regard to him, as the one who brings it to fulfilment and to whom all attention must now be directed . . . The true solution lay in understanding "fulfilment" in terms of an affirmation of the whole of the Law, yet only through its transformation into the teaching of Christ which was something new and unique in comparison with it.'[1]

The presentation of Jesus and the law is thus part of Matthew's Christology of fulfilment. And its effect is the very opposite of legalistic. It is incredible that such a label could ever have been attached to an Evangelist who twice quotes Hosea 6:6 against Pharisaic objections (9:13; 12:7), who frequently emphasizes the priority of love over mere external piety (5:43ff.; 7:12; 19:19; 22:35–40; 25:31ff., *etc.*), and whose Gospel demands a righteousness which exceeds that of the scribes and Pharisees, not by beating them at their own game, but by exemplifying the more far-reaching principles taught by the one of whom 'all the prophets and the law prophesied' (11:13).

## D. The people of God

Fundamental as the law was to Israel's self-understanding, Matthew's presentation of fulfilment in Jesus goes still deeper. He is also the 'fulfilment' of Israel itself. His coming has brought a decisive change to what it means to be the special people of God.

We have seen above that Matthew writes from the point of view of a Jewish Christian, to whom Jewish interests are impor-

---

[1] Banks, pp. 226, 234. Banks's important discussion will be drawn on in the commentary on 5:17–48, which will be in agreement with his basic approach, though I shall wish to demur in detail at some points.

tant, and yet who finds himself obliged to distance himself decisively from the majority of his nation. In this section we shall consider this tension particularly from the point of view of the Christology which gives rise to it. This is, of course, not a concern which is peculiar to Matthew. It was necessarily a central issue in the ministry of the one who presented himself as the Jews' Messiah, but whom the Jews as a whole rejected. All the Gospel writers, even Luke the Gentile, are clearly aware of the importance and the difficulty of the issue. John in particular highlights it. But in Matthew it comes before us in sharper focus. Several of the most telling statements on the subject appear only in his Gospel.

*(i) The failure of Israel.* John the Baptist called Israel to repentance in the light of coming judgment (see on 3:1–12). His new type of baptism symbolized what he explicitly proclaimed (3:7–10), that this judgment threatened the 'children of Abraham' themselves, whose deeds had not matched up to their privileged status. And Matthew takes care to show Jesus' ministry as in direct succession to that of John, as the bringer of 'Holy Spirit and fire', the one who is to implement the judgment (3:11–12).

So we hear repeatedly Jesus' condemnation of 'this generation' for its failure to recognize God's messengers and to respond to his call (11:16–24; 12:38–45; 16:4; 17:17), culminating in the clear warning that now the rebellion of Israel has gone too far, and that the time for judgment has come (23:29–36), which leads on in its turn to the prediction of the destruction of the temple (23:37–39; 24:2ff., leading up to 24:34, 'this generation'). No wonder Jesus was seen as a second Jeremiah (see on 16:14)!

Of course Israel had experienced judgment (including destruction of the temple) before, as in the time of Jeremiah. But there is a note of finality this time which is particularly pronounced in Matthew's account. The section where this comes to the fore is chapters 21 – 23, where Matthew has brought together a variety of sayings and incidents which together add up to a clear repudiation of the official leadership of Israel. Jesus' demonstration in the temple and his symbolic cursing of the fig-tree

(Matthew emphasizes the *immediacy* of the effect), the challenge to Jesus' authority and his deliberate endorsement of John the Baptist's ministry of warning, the sequence of three polemical parables, which add up to a scathing indictment of the nation's failure to produce 'fruit' and the threat of replacement by 'another nation', the series of theological and other debates in which Jesus progressively worsts his opponents (22:46), after which they remain silent throughout chapter 23 while he ruthlessly exposes their 'hypocrisy' and expresses God's repudiation of their empty worship, and warns that the long-delayed judgment must now fall – all this amounts to a powerful climax to the confrontation which has built up throughout the Gospel.

Jesus' strictures are focused on the leaders of the nation, and particularly on its religious leaders ('scribes and Pharisees'). But the parables of 21:28 – 22:14 point to more than a change of leadership, with 21:43 speaking explicitly of a new 'nation'; and the threatened judgment on Jerusalem will affect more than just the leaders. The terrible cry of 'all the people' in 27:24–25 makes it clear that Jesus is rejected by the nation as a whole, not just by its leaders, and the point is underlined by the use here not of *ochloi* ('crowds') but *laos*, the term particularly used for Israel in its privileged status as the people of God. In the rejection of Jesus that status has been forfeited; God will find elsewhere 'a nation which produces the fruit' (21:43).

This perspective is summed up in the saying of Jesus which Matthew has recorded in the context of a Gentile whose faith is greater than any found in Israel: 'Many will come from east and west and sit at table with Abraham, Isaac, and Jacob in the kingdom of heaven, while the sons of the kingdom will be thrown into the outer darkness' (8:11–12). In speaking not only of the rejection of the 'sons of the kingdom', but also of their replacement by others, this saying captures the balance of Matthew's approach to the subject. For the loss of Israel's privilege is not so much an end as a new beginning, opening the way for a true people of God to be constituted in which Jew and Gentile alike may be members, not now on the basis of their nationality, but of their response to Jesus.

*(ii) The true Israel.* C. H. Dodd suggested that in Jesus' view

'The Messiah is not only founder and leader of the Israel-to-be, the new people of God; he is its "inclusive representative". In a real sense he *is* the true Israel, carrying through in his own experience the process through which it comes into being.'[1]

Matthew also seems to present this idea that Jesus himself is the true Israel. Perhaps it is already implicit in his presentation of Jesus as 'King of the Jews' (see above), but it comes to more obvious expression in some of the typological references to the Old Testament. The use of Hosea 11:1 in 2:15 makes sense only if Jesus, as God's son, is equated with Israel as 'God's son'. The same typology underlies the references to Deuteronomy 6 – 8 in the account of Jesus' testing in the wilderness (4:1–11; see commentary *ad loc.*). The parable which most clearly speaks of the failure and replacement of Israel (21:33–43) concludes with Jesus' reference to Psalm 118:22, a passage about Israel's unexpected vindication but now transferred to Jesus in his vindication over against Israel's rebellion.

In discussing Matthew's typology above we noted his remarkable concentration in chapter 12 of Jesus' sayings about 'a greater than the temple/Jonah/Solomon', the effect of which is to place Jesus as the 'fulfilment' of the main pillars of the institutional life of Old Testament Israel. The implication is that the focus of the true Israel is not now in the cult, the prophet, or the king, but in Jesus.

But the theme of Jesus as the true Israel is not the dominant one in the Gospel. For the result of Jesus' ministry was the creation of a community of those who responded to his message. There is evidence in Matthew that it was not only in Jesus himself, but also in this disciple group, in distinction from unbelieving Israel, that the true people of God was now to be found.

Jesus seems to have thought of them as a sort of 'righteous remnant' of Israel, such as the prophets often spoke of. Thus in 13:10–17 he speaks of the majority of his hearers in words taken from Isaiah's call to preach to unresponsive Israel, but contrasts them with his disciples, to whom the privilege of understanding God's secrets has been given. They are the 'meek' who in the

---

[1] C.H. Dodd, *The Founder of Christianity* (1971), p. 106.

Psalms represent God's true servants (5:5). They are called to fulfil the special calling of Israel to be holy, as God is holy (see on 5:48). They are the true flock of God as described in Zechariah (26:31). They will constitute Jesus' *ekklēsia*, a prominent Old Testament word for the congregation of God's people (16:18).

The focus of Israel's national life in the Old Testament had been the covenant made at Sinai, but now Jesus' blood will seal a new covenant such as Jeremiah had predicted (26:28); and a new covenant means a new basis of existence for the people of God. In speaking of the temple destroyed and rebuilt (see on 26:61, and *cf.* the implications of the saying of 12:6 and the repudiation of existing temple worship in 21:12–13) Jesus looked forward to a new basis of worship for the true people of God, and one which envisaged the literal destruction of the old order (24:2).

Such pointers towards a new people of God are given further substance by Jesus' deliberate choice of *twelve* disciples as the leadership of his new community, and the implication is spelt out in 19:28, which envisages them sitting 'on twelve thrones, judging the twelve tribes of Israel'.

Matthew records no explicit description of the disciples as 'Israel', 'the true Israel' or the like, but the indications listed above point unmistakably towards the idea, as do a number of passages where Old Testament prophecies relating to Israel are applied to the disciples of Jesus (see comments on 8:11; 24:31).

Through its rejection of God's final appeal the nation as such has forfeited its claim to be the people of God. Jesus now represents all that Israel should have been, and in those who belong to him the purposes of God for Israel find their fulfilment.

*(iii) The nature of the new community.* Both John and Jesus called on Israel to repent (3:2; 4:17), to recognize that mere membership of the nation was not all that God required. It was 'sins' that stood in the way (3:6), and Jesus came to offer forgiveness of sins (1:21; 9:6; 26:28). Those who responded to this message thus became a community of the forgiven (a fact which must underlie their reaction to one another: 6:14–15; 18:21–35). Their

lives would necessarily become conspicuously different from those around them (5:3–16, *etc.*), so that they, unlike the nation as a whole, would produce the 'fruit' God expected of his people (see comments on the three parables of 21:28 – 22:14).

Membership in the people of God is thus no longer a matter of belonging to the right social or ethnic group. What matters is the response to Jesus' message (7:24–27; 12:41–42), the establishment of a proper relationship with him (7:21–23; 25:31–46). And that response can be made by those outside Israel as well as by those within, even though for the time being his appeal must be made to 'the lost sheep of the house of Israel' (15:24). The faith of the Gentile centurion is therefore significant, not only because it is greater than that of any in Israel, but because it points forward to the coming of many from east and west to join the Israelite patriarchs at the Messianic banquet (8:11–12); those who share the centurion's faith are thus not merely saved in addition to Israel – they become part of the true Israel. It can therefore no longer be a national entity. The universal mission of 28:19 is thus the necessary outcome of the whole basis of membership of the people of God which has emerged throughout the Gospel. It is in Jesus, the true Israel, that the people of God now finds its coherence.

But to recognize that Matthew records Jesus' creation of a new community does not entail reading into his Gospel all the institutional paraphernalia which the word 'church' tends to suggest to us. Indeed, when this Gospel is compared with the letters of Paul, mostly written before even the earliest date suggested for Matthew, it is remarkable how lacking it is in 'church' terminology. No church officers are mentioned, even in 23:8–10 which might seem to invite specific application. 'One never reads: you are "the true Israel", the "saints", the "elect", the "church of the new covenant".'[1] The impression one gains is that Jesus looked forward to, and Matthew is writing for, a community conscious of its own distinctive existence and calling as the people of the Messiah, but not yet formally structured as an institution. It is a community aware of its difference from unbelieving Israel, and of its potentially universal scope, but far

[1] G. Bornkamm, *TIM*, p, 39. He sees in Matthew 'only the most meagre beginnings of a real ecclesiology'.

from wishing to repudiate its Old Testament roots, it is anxious to affirm that in Jesus and his people Israel's destiny is fulfilled.

## V. THE STRUCTURE OF MATTHEW'S GOSPEL

I shall propose in the next section an analysis of the contents of the Gospel which will form the basis of the commentary that follows. But it must be recognized that no two commentators ever agree on the right way to analyse the text in detail, even if they agree on the main divisions. In the case of Matthew even the main divisions are still debated.

This might suggest that the Gospel is an untidy and illogical jumble of disconnected bits. But most readers have been impressed by the careful arrangement of at least some sections of the book, and we shall see that the disagreement over the overall structure is the result of too many pointers rather than of too few.

Among the more obviously deliberate structural patterns in detail, most of which are peculiar to Matthew (the exceptions are marked*), we might note:

    three groups of fourteen generations (1:1–17)
   *three temptations with quotations in reply (4:1–11)
    eight beatitudes (5:3–10)
    six 'antitheses' (5:21–47)
    three types of religious observance (6:1–6, 16–18)
   *three symbolic actions (21:1–22)
    three polemical parables (21:28 – 22:14)
    seven woes on scribes and Pharisees (23:13–36)
   *three prayers and returns to sleeping disciples (26:36–46)
   *three denials by Peter (26:69–75)

Most of these are marked by clearly-repeated phrases or more extensive formal correspondence between the sections, and the effect is to make them easily memorable. Groups of three are particularly frequent, and can be traced very often in the Gospel even where there is no formal correspondence of the members.[1] Such repeated phrases as 'Do not fear' in 10:26, 28, 31, 'is not

---

[1] For a much longer list of such groupings, mainly in threes, see *ICC*, p. lxv.

worthy of me' in 10:37–38, 'little ones' in 18:6, 10, 14, and such memorably structured sayings as 5:22; 7:7–8, 13–14, 24–27 similarly serve to aid memory. They reflect, no doubt, the skill of Jesus as a teacher, but it is a skill which Matthew seems to have learnt in good measure.

On a rather larger scale, most commentators agree that there is evidence of careful construction of at least some major sections of the Gospel, even though the precise rationale of the structure is not so generally agreed. Thus the five formula-quotations of 1:18 – 2:23 serve as a framework for this entire section; chapters 8 – 9 relate ten miracles, which are often seen as structured in three groups of three;[1] chapter 13 is a carefully-arranged sequence of parables with interspersed comments and interpretation;[2] and the strangely-repeated introduction of the guard at the tomb suggests a deliberately chiastic structure in 27:57 – 28:20.[3]

In discerning such structural patterns there is, of course, unlimited scope for the imaginative commentator to 'discover' patterns of which the text gives no hint, and which are more likely to be in the mind of the modern reader with his love of neat 'tables of contents' than in that of Matthew. In the analysis that follows there are several sections where, while an overall theme of the section may be suggested in very general terms, the component parts neither fit into a clear structural pattern nor do they closely relate to one another in theme.[4] But when due allowance has been made for the fact that Matthew may not have felt obliged to fit each section neatly into an overall scheme, there is sufficient evidence of careful arrangement both in detail and in broader outline to mark Matthew out as a careful compiler rather than a haphazard collector of unconnected bits of tradition.

Turning to the structure of the Gospel as a whole, at least three different ways of approaching it need to be noticed.

[1]See below, pp. 150–151, for details.
[2]See below, p. 216.
[3]See below, p. 402.
[4]See *e.g.* sections IIɢ, IIIᴀ, IVᴀ in the scheme below. In each of these, while there is a clear link between some sub-sections, others seem not to have any obvious connection with their context.

*(i) The 'Marcan outline'.* This approach relies more on subject-matter than on explicit 'markers' in the text. It notes that the progression of the story basically follows that of Mark's Gospel. This could be set out roughly as follows:

| | | |
|---|---|---|
| INTRODUCTION | Mk. 1:1–13 | Mt. 1:1 – 4:11 |
| MINISTRY IN GALILEE | Mk. 1:14 – 6:13 | Mt. 4:12 – 13:58 |
| WIDER MINISTRY IN THE NORTH | Mk. 6:14 – 8:26 | Mt. 14:1 – 16:12 |
| TOWARDS JERUSALEM | Mk. 8:27 – 10:52 | Mt. 16:13 – 20:34 |
| CONFRONTATION IN JERUSALEM | Mk. 11:1 – 13:37 | Mt. 21:1 – 25:46 |
| PASSION AND RESURRECTION | Mk. 14:1 – 16:8 | Mt. 26:1 – 28:20 |

This structure may be understood in two ways. Firstly, it is a clear geographical itinerary, from Galilee to Jerusalem, the two phases being totally separate (in contrast with John's Gospel, which records frequent visits to Jerusalem).[1] But secondly, parallel with the geographical movement is a dramatic development from the enthusiasm of the Galilean crowds to the hostility of the Jerusalem authorities, which leads inevitably to the dramatic dénouement of the passion story. In this development the episode at Caesarea Philippi (Mk. 8:27ff.; Mt. 16:13ff.) is the vital turning-point, for it is here that the varying responses to Jesus in Galilee are brought to a head, both in Peter's recognition of Jesus as the Messiah and in Jesus' consequent revelation that his mission will be one of rejection and death. After this the whole tone of his teaching changes, and the movement towards the cross gathers speed and inevitability like the river above a waterfall.

This powerful dramatic structure is undoubtedly at least part of Matthew's plan for his Gospel. Occasional pointers in the text suggest that he not only shares this structure with Mark, but has deliberately emphasized it. See, *e.g.*, the geographical notices, and mentions of Jesus' 'withdrawals'[2] in 4:12–16; 4:23–25; 14:13; 15:21; 16:13; 16:21; 17:22; 19:1; 21:1. Whatever else may be concluded about Matthew's literary structure, the 'Marcan outline' must form an essential part of our understanding of the plan of his work.

[1]See below, on 28:7, for the suggestion that there is a theological symbolism in this geographical pattern.

[2]See below, on 4:12.

*(ii) 'From that time Jesus began . . .'.* Building on an earlier suggestion by N. B. Stonehouse, J. D. Kingsbury has argued[1] that Matthew has given us a more specific pointer to the major sections of his Gospel in the repetition in 4:17 and 16:21 of the phrase 'From that time Jesus began . . .'. In each case it marks a decisive new phase of Jesus' ministry, in 4:17 the beginning of public preaching in Galilee, and in 16:21 the beginning of private instruction of the disciples on the true nature of his mission and its destined end in his death in Jerusalem. On this basis Kingsbury proposed the following overall scheme:

| | |
|---|---|
| 1:1 – 4:16 | The Person of Jesus Messiah |
| 4:17 – 16:20 | The Proclamation of Jesus Messiah |
| 16:21 – 28:20 | The Suffering, Death and Resurrection of Jesus Messiah. |

As far as it goes, this is a valuable observation, which has the advantage of focusing on what does look like a deliberate transition formula. But these three sections should not be regarded as entirely self-contained and/or as conferring a complete thematic unity on all the material within each section. The last in particular covers a very wide range of material, containing within itself verses like 19:1 and 26:1 which seem to point as clearly to a new phase in the story as does the formula of 4:17 and 16:21.

It is worth observing, moreover, that the transition-points in Kingsbury's scheme are virtually the same as two of those noted in the 'Marcan outline'. This means that this formula serves to point up two of the major developments in the story which in any case may be discerned from the subject-matter. In other words, Kingsbury's scheme is not in competition with, but rather serves as a further refinement of, the structural pattern shared with Mark.

*(iii) 'When Jesus had finished these sayings . . .'.* Kingsbury's observation of a transition-formula in 4:17 and 16:21 was made in deliberate contrast to what has been the more traditional way to divide up Matthew's Gospel. This was on the basis of a formula repeated five times, which reads literally (with slight

---

[1]Kingsbury, pp. 7–25.

variations), 'And it happened, when Jesus had finished these sayings, that he . . .', after which a new phase of the story begins (7:28; 11:1; 13:53; 19:1; 26:1). The wording of the formula is unusual in Matthew (the Semitic introduction 'and it happened' followed by a main verb occurs elsewhere only in 9:10, and the verb *teleō*, 'complete', only in 10:23; see further on 7:28), and its standard form, more impressive in the Greek than in RSV, indicates a deliberate structural marker. In each case it concludes a major section of teaching by Jesus, after which the narrative is resumed, and these sections have therefore been identified as the five major discourses of Matthew. Each shows evidence of Matthew's editorial activity in bringing together various sayings of Jesus on a given subject (in each case on the basis of a shorter section of teaching preserved in Mark or Luke),[1] and the result is a fairly clearly defined subject area for each discourse, as follows:

| | |
|---|---|
| Chapters 5 – 7 | Jesus' teaching about discipleship |
| Chapter 10 | Jesus' teaching about mission |
| Chapter 13 | Jesus' teaching in parables (the overall subject being 'the kingdom of heaven') |
| Chapter 18 | Jesus' teaching about relationships among disciples |
| Chapters 24 – 25 | Jesus' teaching about the future. |

For each of these individually see the introductory comments in the commentary *ad loc*.

To observe that Matthew has included in his Gospel five major discourses does not, however, in itself determine the structural pattern of the Gospel as a whole. This further step has been taken most notably by B. W. Bacon,[2] who described the Gospel as 'The Five Books of Matthew against the Jews', a deliberate 'Christian Pentateuch' to replace that of Moses. Each 'book' then consists of a section of narrative succeeded by a discourse. The resultant structure is as follows:[3]

---

[1]These are, respectively, for chs. 5 – 7, Lk. 6:20–49; for ch. 10, Mk. 6:7–13; for ch. 13, Mk. 4:1–34; for ch. 18, Mk. 9:35–48; for chs. 24 – 25, Mk. 13.

[2]B.W. Bacon, *Studies in Matthew* (1930).

[3]For a modified analysis along similar 'pentateuchal' lines see also Hill, pp. 44–48.

|  |  | *Chapters* |
|---|---|---|
| PREAMBLE |  | 1 – 2 |
| BOOK ONE: | DISCIPLESHIP |  |
|  | Narrative | 3 – 4 |
|  | Discourse | 5 – 7 |
| BOOK TWO: | APOSTLESHIP |  |
|  | Narrative | 8 – 9 |
|  | Discourse | 10 |
| BOOK THREE: | THE HIDING OF THE REVELATION |  |
|  | Narrative | 11 – 12 |
|  | Discourse | 13 |
| BOOK FOUR: | CHURCH ADMINISTRATION |  |
|  | Narrative | 14 – 17 |
|  | Discourse | 18 |
| BOOK FIVE: | THE JUDGMENT |  |
|  | Narrative | 19 – 22 |
|  | Discourse | 23 – 25 |
| EPILOGUE |  | 26 – 28 |

Bacon's analysis has been frequently discussed, notably by Davies (pp.14–25). It has been particularly objected that (i) the internal coherence of the narrative and discourse which make up each 'book' is not usually obvious; (ii) the neat chapter division above conceals some awkward decisions, such as the place of chapter 23;[1] (iii) the formula explicitly concludes a collection of sayings, not a 'book' including narrative; (iv) the description of the whole passion narrative as an 'epilogue', incidental to the main structure of the Gospel, hardly fits its actual function as the dramatic climax of the whole story!

A recent article by D. W. Gooding[2] has modified Bacon's theory by rejecting the division of each 'book' into narrative + discourse, seeing the formula rather as a conclusion to the preceding section as a whole, not just the discourse, and especially by observing that the formula serves not only to conclude but also to introduce the section which follows; *i.e.* it is not a concluding formula but a transition formula.

[1]See below, p. 333.    [2]*Revue Biblique* 85 (1978), pp. 227–252.

Clearly an analysis of the Gospel on the basis of this formula will produce a different scheme from that proposed by Kingsbury. The key question is which of the two more effectively displays the development of the story, and from this point of view the fact that the formula of 4:17 and 16:21 more directly corresponds to the Marcan outline is in its favour. It is preferable, therefore, to understand the formula of 7:28, *etc.* not as a pointer to the overall structure of the Gospel, but as indicating the end of Matthew's 'interludes' of collected teaching, after which the narrative is resumed. The 'discourses' therefore fit within the overall narrative structure of the Gospel, but do not determine it.

The analysis that follows attempts to take into account the insights into the structure of the Gospel which have been discussed above. At many points I am fairly confident that it reflects Matthew's conscious purpose in putting his material together in the way he did. But it must be stressed that my headings and subheadings have no more authority than the traditional chapter and verse divisions. They are simply attempts to guide the reader through a text which itself carried no such indications of sections, and which was probably designed in the first instance to be read aloud to the congregation, quite possibly in much larger sections than my analysis suggests. Indeed perhaps the best way to appreciate the structure of a Gospel is not so much to sit down to analyse it in detail, but rather to read it as a whole (or better to hear it read), if possible at one sitting, and thus to allow it to make its own impact as its author intended.

# ANALYSIS

## I. THE BIRTH AND PREPARATION OF JESUS (1:1 – 4:16)

A. THE BIRTH AND CHILDHOOD OF JESUS (1:1 – 2:23)
  (i)   *The genealogy of Jesus the Messiah (1:1–17)*
  (ii)  *The origin and name of Jesus the Messiah (1:18–25)*
  (iii) *The visit of the Magi (2:1–12)*
  (iv)  *The flight to Egypt and the return (2:13–23)*

B. THE PREPARATION FOR JESUS' PUBLIC MINISTRY (3:1 – 4:16)
  (i)   *The ministry of John the Baptist (3:1–12)*
  (ii)  *The baptism of Jesus (3:13–17)*
  (iii) *The test (4:1–11)*
  (iv)  *The withdrawal to Galilee (4:12–16)*

## II. PUBLIC MINISTRY IN AND AROUND GALILEE (4:17 – 16:20)

A. INTRODUCTION TO THE PUBLIC MINISTRY (4:17–25)
  (i)   *Summary of Jesus' preaching (4:17)*
  (ii)  *The call of four disciples (4:18–22)*
  (iii) *Summary of the public ministry (4:23–25)*

B. JESUS' TEACHING ON DISCIPLESHIP (5:1 – 7:29)
  (i)   *Introduction (5:1–2)*
  (ii)  *The advantages of discipleship (5:3–10)*
  (iii) *The distinctiveness of the disciple (5:11–16)*
  (iv)  *Jesus' attitude to the Old Testament (5:17–20)*
  (v)   *Examples of Jesus' radical ethic (5:21–48)*
  (vi)  *Teaching on religious observance (6:1–18)*

# COMMENTARY

## I. THE BIRTH AND PREPARATION OF JESUS
## (1:1 – 4:16)

The analysis of the Gospel given above (pp.63–67) has shown that 4:17 marks the beginning of the first main phase of Jesus' public ministry. In these preceding chapters Matthew introduces the Jesus whose ministry he is going to describe. Who is this Jesus, and where does he come from? So chapters 1 – 2 explain his origin, and 3:1 – 4:16 outlines his preparation immediately before he appeared in public.

In all this, Matthew is primarily concerned to show Jesus as the one in whom the hopes of the Old Testament find their fulfilment. Six times in these chapters we find the formula 'This was to fulfil what the Lord had spoken by the prophet' or the like, introducing the 'formula-quotations' (see pp.38–40) which are a special feature of Matthew's Gospel; and the quotations so introduced do not relate to specific things which Jesus did, but to more general characteristics, his name and birth (1:22–23) and the geographical location of his birth, childhood and ministry (2:5–6, 15, 17–18, 23; 4:14–16). Matthew thus demonstrates that the overall framework of Jesus' preparation for his ministry corresponds to the pattern laid down in the Old Testament. Moreover, as the commentary will make clear, every section of these chapters, whether it includes a formula-quotation or not, is heavily weighted to showing the correspondence of Jesus' preparation to the Old Testament pattern.

Alongside this very striking concentration on introducing Jesus as the fulfilment of the Old Testament runs a higher note:

Jesus is the Son of God. This, one of the main themes of Matthew's Gospel as a whole, is clearly implied by his stress on the conception of Jesus by the Holy Spirit (1:18, 20), and by the name Immanuel, 'God with us' (1:23), and becomes explicit in 2:15 and 3:17, from which it is taken up to become the central theme of the testing of Jesus in 4:1–11.

Thus by the time the reader comes to 4:17 he is well prepared to see this Jesus not just as a preacher of God's message, but as the Messiah to whom the whole Old Testament revelation pointed forward, and even more than that, as the Son of God. There is no literary suspense; in these opening chapters Matthew has laid his theological cards on the table, and he expects the reader to come to the account of Jesus' ministry with this orientation already decided.

## A. THE BIRTH AND CHILDHOOD OF JESUS (1:1 – 2:23)

The subject-matter of these chapters is, as the heading indicates, the beginning of Jesus' life. But a better description of their aim and contents would be 'scriptural proofs of the Messiahship of Jesus'. The genealogy concentrates on linking Jesus to David, whose 'son' the Messiah was to be, and fits him into the whole development of God's purpose of salvation in the Old Testament. Then the remaining 31 verses, dealing with Jesus' birth and childhood, contain no less than five of Matthew's eleven formula-quotations, as well as a sustained parallel between the origins of Jesus and of Moses, and other allusions to Old Testament passages.

The very deliberate scriptural orientation of Matthew in these chapters is seen when they are compared with the infancy narratives of Luke (1 – 2). Luke tells delightful stories, with living characters, in whom he is clearly interested for their own sake. He sets the scene for Jesus' life in the history and expectations of the Jewish people, provides a sketch of his family background, and gives us such meagre information as we possess on his growth as a child. Matthew, by contrast, provides merely the basic facts of Jesus' birth, the visit of the Magi, and his family's geographical movements, only so far as is needed to show the historical application of his chosen scriptural texts.

Even the visit of the Magi, Matthew's most elaborate story, is in fact, as we shall see, carefully related to bring out the theme of Jesus' fulfilment of prophecy. His striking emphasis on geographical locations in chapter 2 leads in each case directly to an appropriate Old Testament text.[1]

So obvious is Matthew's preoccupation with Scripture-fulfilment in these chapters that it is sometimes suggested that the 'facts' that he relates are themselves the product of his own imaginative study of the Scriptures (and, in Gundry's view, his free adaptation of an earlier form of the stories of Luke 1 – 2), so that the virgin birth, the Magi, the flight to Egypt and the slaughter of the children are fictitious stories suggested to Matthew's lively imagination by the texts around which he relates them. This seems the more plausible when it is noted that none of the events recorded in chapter 2 is mentioned in the rest of the New Testament (unless Gundry is right in deriving them from the Lucan stories) or independently anywhere else, beyond the location of Jesus' birth in Bethlehem and his later residence in Nazareth, and the basic historical datum of Archelaus' succession to his father, Herod the Great.

It cannot be maintained, however, that there is any improbability in the basic features of these stories in the light of the historical circumstances of the time. What we know of the cult of astrology, of Herod's character and his political vulnerability, and of the rule of Archelaus fits in well with Matthew's narrative, and the choice of Egypt as a place of refuge by a suspect Jewish family is entirely probable. It is in such details as the moving star and the angelic warnings, not in the outline of the stories themselves, that historians are likely to find difficulties.

The suggestion that Matthew created these stories out of the Old Testament texts around which they are woven is not easy to maintain when it is noted that several of the Old Testament texts explicitly quoted are not ones which would naturally be associated with Messianic fulfilment. Indeed their character is such

---

[1]This aspect of chapter 2 is well summed up in K. Stendahl's important article in W. Eltester (ed.), *Judentum, Urchristentum, Kirche* (1960), pp. 94–105. The title of the article is 'Quis et Unde?', the argument being that chapter 1 is designed to show from Scripture *who* the Messiah is (*Quis?*), and chapter 2 *where* he comes *from* (*Unde?*).

that it is hard to see why they should ever have been introduced into a Christian account of Jesus' origins unless the facts themselves suggested them. Hosea 11:1 and Jeremiah 31:15 (Mt. 2:15, 18) in particular have in themselves no obvious reference to Jesus, and there is no indication that either was interpreted Messianically at the time; and the 'quotation' in Matthew 2:23 does not appear in the Old Testament at all! The only conceivable reason for introducing these texts is that it was already known that Jesus went to Egypt, that there was a slaughter of children, and that Jesus' home was in Nazareth, and that scriptural justification was desired for these elements in his background.

In fact the aim of the formula-quotations in chapter 2 seems to be primarily apologetic, explaining some of the unexpected features in Jesus' background, particularly his geographical origins. It would be a strange apologetic which invented 'facts' in order to defend them![1]

*(i) The genealogy of Jesus the Messiah (1:1–17)*
To us, a genealogy may seem a very tedious way to begin a book, and a waste of space. To the Jewish world in which Matthew belonged it was a matter of importance, as a glance at the numerous genealogies of the Old Testament makes clear. But Matthew is not merely conforming to Jewish literary convention. The way he presents his genealogy shows that it introduces several important strands into his presentation of Jesus as the Messiah. 1. It places Jesus fully in line with the history of Old Testament Israel, as one famous name after another reminds the reader of the forward movement of God's saving purpose. 2. By organizing that history into a regular scheme of three groups of fourteen generations (see on 1:17), it indicates that the time of preparation is now complete, and that in Jesus the time of fulfilment has arrived. 3. By tracing Jesus' descent through the royal line of Judah, it stakes his claim to the title 'King of the Jews' (see p.45). 4. It establishes his status as 'son of David', not only by emphasizing David's place in the genealogy (see on 1:6), but, perhaps, by a play on the name of

[1] I have discussed the historical value of these two chapters more fully in *GP* II, pp. 239–266.

David in the use of the number fourteen (see on 1:17). 5. The mention of certain 'irregularities' in the ancestry of the royal line of Judah serves to counter objections to the manner of Jesus' birth (see on 1:3–6). The genealogy is thus a vital part of the conception of Matthew's introductory section. It is 'a résumé of salvation history, of God's way with Israel'.[1]

Luke's version of the genealogy of Jesus (Lk. 3:23–38) differs considerably from that of Matthew, not only in that it goes further back (to 'Adam, the son of God', thus putting Jesus in the context of the whole human race, not just the Jewish nation), but in the names it includes. From Abraham to David there is close agreement, but from David the two lists diverge, as Matthew follows the line of succession to the throne of Judah from Solomon, whereas Luke's list goes through Nathan, another son of David, and converges with Matthew's only for the two names of Shealtiel and Zerubbabel until Joseph is reached. That either Matthew or Luke simply invented the names he records is neither consistent with their known concern for detail, nor is there any obvious motive for it. We do not know what source Matthew used for the period after Zerubbabel, nor Luke for the whole period from David to Joseph; we can only assume that the family had preserved records, or at least memories, of its ancestry.[2] But how could family records supply two genealogies so different?

The suggestion that Luke's list is in fact the genealogy of Mary, the real human parent of Jesus, is unlikely. Not only does Luke state quite clearly that he is giving the genealogy of Joseph, the 'supposed' father of Jesus (3:23), but it was not the practice to trace a genealogy through the female line (as distinct from occasionally mentioning the mother in a patrilineal genealogy). A more probable explanation of the difference is that while Luke records the actual physical genealogy of Joseph, Matthew records the line of succession to the throne, the 'official' genealogy.[3] This would not necessarily pass from father to son, but would remain within the family. (The verb he uses for

[1] W. B. Tatum, *JBL* 96 (1977), p. 527.

[2] For the likelihood of such records, see M. D. Johnson, *The Purpose of the Biblical Genealogies* (1969), pp. 99–108. Josephus traced his own genealogy in 'public records' (*Vita* 6).

[3] For the probability of such a list being available, see Brown, pp. 87–88.

beget (*gennaō*) is used of a relationship which is not genetic in 1 Cor. 4:15; Phm. 10, and the same metaphor was used of the relationship between a Rabbinic teacher and his pupil. *Cf.* also Ps. 2:7.) It is certainly not impossible that the lines should converge at two points (Shealtiel and Joseph) in a period of 1,000 years. But any solution must remain tentative.[1]

**1.** *The book of the genealogy* (*biblos geneseōs*) would remind a Jewish reader of Genesis 2:4; 5:1, where the same phrase is used in the Greek Old Testament. (The similar phrase 'these are the generations (*geneseis*) of' occurs also in Gn. 6:9; 10:1; 11:10, 27, *etc.* introducing both formal genealogies and narratives.) Matthew's use of *genesis* would therefore suggest that the coming of Jesus is a new beginning, a new creation. (See Davies, pp. 67–73.) The phrase serves here to introduce vv. 2–16. Verses 1 and 17 (which again highlights the three key names of Abraham, David and Christ) thus provide a formal framework for the genealogy, picking out its main relevance: Jesus is *son of Abraham*, a true Jew; he is *son of David* (see on 9:27), and as such he is the *Christ* (see pp. 41–43; in this context of introducing Jesus as the fulfilment of Old Testament hopes it must carry its full theological meaning, 'the Messiah'). It is possible that, like some of the similar formulae in Genesis, v.1 is intended to introduce not only the formal genealogy but also the following narrative, as far as 1:25, 2:23, or even 4:16. It is sometimes regarded, less plausibly, as the superscription to the whole Gospel. But its primary function is to provide with v. 17 the framework for the genealogy. In v. 18 the story proper is introduced, with the same word *genesis* (now in the different sense of 'origin') used to link it to the formal opening in v. 1.

**2.** The list as far as v. 6a follows that of 1 Chronicles 1:34; 2:1–15. *Cf.* Ruth 4:18–22. The *brothers* of Judah are mentioned probably to show Jesus' solidarity with the twelve patriarchs of Israel.

**3–6.** The mention of a mother alongside a father occurs also in Old Testament genealogies; *cf.* 1 Chronicles 1:32; 2:17–21, 24, 26, *etc.* The mention of *Tamar* as the mother of *Perez and Zerah* is in fact derived directly from 1 Chronicles 2:4, and that of Bathsheba in v. 6 from 1 Chronicles 3:5. But the four mothers selec-

[1]See further, 'Genealogy of Jesus Christ', *NBD*, pp. 410–411.

ted for mention form a striking group. Probably all four were non-Jews (Tamar was a local girl, so presumably a Canaanite, Gn. 38:11, 13–14; Bathsheba was the wife of a Hittite), indicating Matthew's interest in the universal relevance of Jesus' coming (*cf.* the Magi of 2:1–12); and in each case there were at least suspicions of some form of marital irregularity, though all four were in fact vindicated by God's subsequent blessing. They form an impressive precedent for Jesus' birth of an unmarried mother from an obscure background. *Rahab* is otherwise unknown as mother of *Boaz*; presumably the harlot of Jericho (Jos. 2:1, *etc.*) is in Matthew's mind, though this identification poses chronological problems.

**6.** David's status as *the king*, the one in whom the family first achieved royalty, is stressed. *Cf.* vv. 1 and 17 for the emphasis on David as the key figure in Jesus' genealogy.

**7–12.** The list follows 1 Chronicles 3:10–17 and Ezra 3:2. Three kings are omitted in v. 8, probably Ahaziah, Joash and Amaziah, though the same Greek form (*Ozeias*) is used in some MSS of the Greek Old Testament for both Ahaziah and *Uzziah* (=Azariah). Confusion based on the similarity of the names may account for the omission, but Matthew's scheme of three times fourteen generations (v. 17) suggests that it was deliberate. The lists must in any case be deliberately selective, like many Old Testament genealogies (which also use the verb 'beget', here translated *was the father of*); Jehoiakim is omitted between Josiah and Jehoiachin (*Jechoniah*), and the following 600 years are covered in only thirteen generations. Matthew has only 27 generations after David, compared to Luke's 42.

**16.** *Joseph*'s father according to Luke 3:23 was Eli. *Jacob* was presumably his adoptive father, or, if we are right in seeing Matthew's as the list of the throne succession, a relative to whom Joseph 'succeeded' in the absence of a son of his own. After Joseph the regular formula 'begat' (*egennēsen*) is dropped, and Joseph is listed simply as *the husband of Mary, of whom* (the Greek pronoun is unambiguously feminine) *Jesus was born* (*egennēthē*, passive). This new phraseology makes it clear that Matthew does not regard Jesus as Joseph's son physically, and vv. 18–25 will explain this at length. The genealogy is thus clearly intended to be that of Jesus' 'legal' ancestry, not of his physical descent. This reading of the text is attested by practically all Greek manuscripts. A few MSS and versions carry a later reading designed to emphasize the virgin birth still further: 'Joseph, to whom being betrothed the virgin Mary gave birth to Jesus' (*egennēsen* can also be used of the mother's 'giving birth'). Only a single MS of the Old Syriac version reads 'and Joseph, to whom the virgin Mary was betrothed, begat Jesus . . .'. This is in fact verbally very close to the previous reading, and in the absence of other support is now generally regarded as a corruption of it.[1] It could hardly have been written by the Matthew who went on to write vv. 18–25!

**17.** Here is the first example of Matthew's tendency to arrange his material in groups, usually of three or seven (see pp. 56–57). The genealogy is arranged in three groups of twice-seven. (In fact the first and last groups contain only thirteen generations; Matthew's observation here is theological rather than statistical!) One purpose is certainly to highlight two essential turning-points in the history of Israel, and of the Davidic line: the accession of David to kingship, and the loss of that kingship at the Babylonian exile; now in the coming of Jesus, son of David, that kingship is to reach its appointed goal. The rounded symmetry of the scheme indicates that the period of preparation is now complete. But there may well be a further nuance in that the numerical values of the Hebrew letters of the name David add up to fourteen (D = 4, W = 6, D = 4). Revelation 13:17–18 is the only clear New Testament parallel to this sort of calculation, known as *Gematria* (but see also Epistle of Barnabas 9:8, a very early Christian work), but it is well attested in Rabbinic circles, and the clear emphasis on David through the genealogy suggests it may be in Matthew's mind. If he did not do it deliberately, he would probably have been delighted to have it pointed out to him![2]

*(ii) The origin and name of Jesus the Messiah (1:18–25)*
These verses do not relate the *birth* of Jesus, but explain his origin (the virgin conception) and his name in relation to a

[1]See B. M. Metzger in *Supplement to NovT* 33 (1972), pp. 16–24; Brown, pp. 61–64.
[2]See further, Davies, pp. 74–77. I have referred to other suggestions of symbolic significance in the three fourteens in *GP* II, pp. 263–264, n. 23.

specific Old Testament prophecy. They concentrate entirely on the experiences of Joseph rather than those of Mary (as do also 2:13-23). Even the miraculous conception of Jesus is related only as its discovery affected Joseph. This remarkable concentration, compared with the complete silence on Joseph elsewhere, may indicate that Matthew's infancy material (except for 2:1-12, where Joseph is noticeably absent from v. 11) derives from special traditions originating with Joseph (whereas Luke's very different account is clearly dependent on Mary's reminiscences). It may also be a result of Matthew's concern to establish Jesus' legal lineage through Joseph, *i.e.* to explain how the preceding genealogy applies to Jesus the son of Mary.

That Jesus was conceived by a virgin mother without the agency of Joseph is clearly stated throughout this section, and is the basis for the introduction of the quotation in vv. 22-23. It is not so much argued or even described, but assumed as a known fact. There may be an element of apologetic in Matthew's stress on Joseph's surprise, his abstention from intercourse, the angel's explanation of Jesus' divine origin, and the scriptural grounds for a virgin birth, due perhaps to an early form of the later Jewish charge that Jesus' birth was illegitimate (see Brown, pp. 534-542). But the account reads primarily as if designed for a Christian readership, who wanted to know more precisely how Mary's marriage to Joseph related to the miraculous conception of Jesus, and who would find the same delight that Matthew himself found in tracing in this the detailed fulfilment of prophecy.

The suggestion that the virgin birth tradition is an imaginative creation by Matthew or his predecessors on the basis of Isaiah 7:14 is precluded not only by this assumption of it as a known fact in Matthew's narrative, but also by its appearance in a completely different form in Luke 1:26-56; 2:5. Further, vv. 22-23, where Isaiah 7:14 is introduced, are clearly an explanatory addition to the narrative, which would flow smoothly from v. 21 to v. 24 without these verses, and not the inspiration for it. Suggestions that the tradition derives from pagan stories of gods having intercourse with women ignore both the quite different tone of such stories, and the impossibility of their being accepted in a Palestinian Jewish setting; yet the Gospel accounts are both intensely Jewish in their contents and expression.

**18.** The reading in RSV mg., omitting the name Jesus, is very likely the original. (It derives from the early Latin and Syriac versions; the substitution of the more familiar title 'Jesus Christ' in the Greek MSS would be natural.) It emphasizes the Messiahship of the one whose 'origin' (*genesis*) Matthew now records. Jesus' conception took place when Mary was *betrothed to Joseph*. In Jewish law betrothal, which lasted about one year, was much more than our engagement. It was a binding contract, terminable only by death (which left the betrothed a 'widow') or by a divorce as for a full marriage. The man was already the *husband* (v. 19), but the woman remained in her father's house. The marriage was completed when the husband took the betrothed to his home in a public ceremony (v. 24; *cf.* 25:1–13); thus they *came together*, and sexual intercourse could begin. That the *Holy Spirit* was the agent in Jesus' conception (*cf.* v. 20) is stressed also by Luke (1:35). In the Old Testament the Spirit of God appears as the agent of God's activity, especially in creation and the giving of life (Gn. 1:2; Ezk. 37:1–14; *etc.*); thus the divine initiative is made clear. The agency of the Spirit in bringing the Messianic age (Is. 11:2; 42:1; 61:1; Joel 2:28; *etc.*) is also in view.

**19.** In Old Testament law the penalty for unchastity before marriage was stoning (Dt. 22:13–21), but by this time divorce, based on Deuteronomy 24:1, was the rule (see further on 5:32; 19:3ff.). Joseph, as *a just* (*i.e.* law-abiding[1]) *man*, could, and perhaps should, have done so by an accusation of adultery resulting in a public trial, but his unwillingness to *put her to shame* (the same uncommon Greek word is used in Col. 2:15 of Christ's 'making a public spectacle' (NEB, NIV) of the principalities and powers) led him to consider the permitted alternative of a private divorce before two witnesses (Mishnah, *Sotah* 1:1, 5).[2]

**20.** As *son of David*, it was necessary for Joseph to *take Mary* (to his house, *i.e.* complete the marriage) in order to establish Jesus' legal Davidic lineage. Similarly, to name him (vv. 21,25) was

---

[1]Brown (pp. 125–128) argues convincingly for this meaning.

[2]See, however, Gundry (pp. 21–22) for the view that his intention was to dispense with witnesses altogether.

formally to acknowledge Jesus as his son, and thus to constitute Jesus also as 'Son of David'; Brown, pp. 138–139. The conveying of God's instructions *in a dream* is a striking feature of the infancy narratives (see also 2:12, 13, 19, 22 – all but one are to Joseph), the more so as the only other occurrence in the Gospel is at 27:19 (to Pilate's wife). Moreover, three of these dreams involve *an angel of the Lord* (*cf.* 2:13, 19), who appears again only at 28:2. But there is no trace here of the elaborate angelology and sensational revelations of some contemporary Judaism; we are in the world of Old Testament piety, where an 'angel of the Lord' frequently conveyed God's instructions to his people (Gn. 16:7ff.; 22:11ff.; 31:11ff.; *etc*). The Greek word *angelos* originally means 'messenger' (so, *e.g.*, in Mt. 11:10; Lk. 7:24; 9:52), and while the angel Joseph saw was presumably a spiritual being, his function was that of a messenger of God. This guidance of Joseph's movements by direct revelation emphasizes God's direction of Jesus' birth and childhood to conform to the scriptural pattern, which is the focus of Matthew's thought in these chapters.

**21.** The language reminds us of similar revelations in the Old Testament (Gn. 16:11; 17:19; *etc.*), as well as of Isaiah 7:14, soon to be quoted. Names, especially divinely revealed names, are full of meaning, and this is often revealed by a word-play which need not always correspond to the actual etymology of the name. In the case of *Jesus* (the Greek form of *Joshua* or *Jeshua*, a common name: see on 27:16) both the sound (*cf.* Heb. *yôšî'a*, 'he will save') and the probable etymology ('Yahweh is salvation', or 'O save, Yahweh') contribute to the explanation *for he will save his people from their sins. His people* will be in the first instance the Jews (Matthew uses this term *laos* particularly for the chosen race), but the man who wrote 28:19 must have expected a wider application ultimately. Salvation *from sins* is an element in the Old Testament hope (*e.g.* Is. 53; Je. 31:31–34; Ezk. 36:24–31) and in later Messianic expectation (Psalms of Solomon 17:28–29, 41; *etc.*), but not the dominant one. Its isolation here warns the reader not to expect this Messiah to conform to the more popular hope of a national liberator, and sets the scene for the unfolding understanding of Jesus' mission in the Gospel.

**22–23.** See pp. 38–40 for the formula-quotations, of which this is the first example. Luke 1:31 probably alludes to the same verse, Isaiah 7:14, indicating that it was not only Matthew who saw its relevance to the birth of Jesus; by the middle of the second century (Justin) it was an important Christian weapon in defence of the virgin birth tradition. But its relevance is often disputed on two grounds. First, it is argued that Matthew depends on the Greek word *parthenos* (*virgin*), whereas the Hebrew *'almâ* means only 'young woman'. *'Almâ* is in fact used only seven times in the Old Testament, of girls or young women, at least two of whom were unmarried (Gn. 24:43; Ex. 2:8). It is not used elsewhere in connection with childbirth (or even marriage), so that its use in Isaiah 7:14 is remarkable, when *'iššâ* ('woman', 'wife') would have been the normal term. It was perhaps this indication that Isaiah was thinking of a birth outside the normal pattern of childbirth within marriage which led the LXX to use *parthenos.* It is a reasonable, if not a necessary, translation. The second objection is that Isaiah 7:14 promises a sign specifically referring to the immediate historical situation in the reign of Ahaz, not to the distant (Messianic) future. The immediate historical reference is clear in vv. 14–17, but it is also clear from the wider context that the prophet's thought is, as often in Old Testament prophecy, not confined to that primary reference. The reintroduction of 'Immanuel' in Isaiah 8:8, 10, and the recurrent theme of a child to be born as deliverer (9:6–7; 11:1ff.), indicate that 7:14 is to be seen as preparing the way for a developing Messianic theme in this section of Isaiah. Clearly the LXX translators, with their striking use of *parthenos*, understood it to refer to more than an ordinary birth, and the choice of *'almâ* in the Hebrew as well as the symbolic name 'Immanuel' suggest that they were right.[1]

Isaiah 7:14 is seen as fulfilled not in the naming of Jesus (v. 21), but in the whole account of his origin and naming in vv. 18ff. (*all this*, v. 22). The point is not that Jesus ever bore *Immanuel* as an actual name, but that it indicates his role, bringing God's presence to man. This meaning is related to that of his actual name, Jesus, in that it is sin which separates man from God's presence, so that salvation from sin results in 'God with

[1]See further, Gundry, *UOT*, pp. 226–227.

us'. But Matthew's stress on the meaning of the name (he gives explicit translations elsewhere only in 27:33, 46) suggests that he saw in it a clue to Jesus' person as well as his work. Jesus was himself 'God with us'; and the assurance of the continuing presence of Jesus in 28:20 forms with this verse a theological framework for the Gospel.

**24–25.** The marriage was thus formally completed, but not consummated before the birth of Jesus. The Greek expression for *not until* would normally suggest that intercourse did take place after the end of this period, and that therefore Jesus' 'brothers' (12:46, *etc.*) were subsequently born of Joseph and Mary in the normal way. There is no biblical warrant for the tradition of the 'perpetual virginity' of Mary.

*(iii) The visit of the Magi (2:1–12)*
This story, peculiar to Matthew, underlines several themes in Matthew's presentation of Jesus the Messiah. It again makes explicit reference to the detailed fulfilment of Scripture, in his place of birth (vv. 5–6), as well as alluding to another Messianic passage (Nu. 24:17). It presents Jesus as the true 'king of the Jews' (v. 2) in contrast with the unworthy king Herod. It begins to draw a parallel between Moses and Jesus which will be further developed in the rest of the chapter (see pp. 85–86). And it shows Jesus as the Messiah of all nations, opposed by the leader of the Jewish nation but recognized as the fulfilment of the hopes of the Gentiles; this too is seen in the light of Old Testament expectation (see on v. 11). The whole episode recalls the story in 1 Kings 10:1–13 of the visit, homage and gifts of a foreign dignitary to the son of David, king of the Jews, a theme which will be taken up more explicitly in 12:42.[1]

Objections to the historicity of this story have been made mainly on two grounds. 1. It is regarded (like the rest of 1:18 – 2:23) as an artificial construction around chosen Old Testament texts. But while several Old Testament passages are apparently in mind, only one is explicitly cited, and that in what appears to be an insertion into the narrative (vv. 5b–6 could be removed without breaking the flow of the narrative), suggesting that it

[1] See further, J. E. Bruns, *CBQ* 23 (1961), pp. 51–54.

was fitted into an already existing story rather than the story was derived from it. 2. The account is said to bear all the marks of pious legend. But in fact, with the exception of the moving star in v. 9, there is nothing historically improbable in the account (see the detailed comments below), and the fact of a comparable visit by eastern Magi to Nero in AD 66 (Dio Cassius 63.7; Suetonius, *Nero* 13) vouches for the probability of this story rather than otherwise. It may perhaps be added that a church which soon found itself in serious conflict with astrology is not likely to have invented a story which appears to favour it.

**1.** *Jesus was born* before the death of *Herod* the Great, which is probably to be dated in 4 BC; the exact date of Jesus' birth is unknown.[1] Various indications in this chapter suggest that the visit of the Magi took place some time after the birth of Jesus: he is now a 'child' (vv. 9, 11), not a 'babe' (Lk. 2:12, 16, though 'child' is used in Lk. 2:27 of Jesus forty days after his birth); v. 7 suggests that the appearance of the star, and therefore the birth, was some time ago; and Herod's murder of all children under two (v. 16) would hardly be necessary if the birth was known to be very recent. The *wise men* are, more correctly, 'Magi', originally the name of a Persian priestly caste, but later used widely for magicians and astrologers (*cf.* Acts 13:6), a numerous class in most countries in Western Asia at the time (see further, Brown, pp. 167–168). Astrology had been developed into a sophisticated science especially in Babylonia, and there is evidence for its influence also in Palestine (see *AB*, p. 14). From what part of *the East* these Magi came can only be guessed; their gifts (v. 11) are most likely of Arabian origin, but would be available to and used by the Magi of Babylonia, and this is perhaps their most likely place of origin. Their reference to 'the king *of the Jews*', and their need to enquire about the birthplace of the Messiah, imply that they were Gentiles, though with a limited knowledge of Judaism (which was well established in Babylonia). For astrological interest in 'the Westland' (Palestine and Phoenicia) see *ICC*, p. 11.

**2.** There are several ancient accounts, pagan and Jewish, of stars heralding the birth of great men (see Brown, pp. 170–171).

---

[1] See, however, E. L. Martin, *The Birth of Christ Recalculated!* (1978) for an attempt to date Herod's death in 1 BC, and Jesus' birth in the late summer of 2 BC.

But probably Matthew had particularly in mind Balaam's prophecy of the rising of a star out of Jacob (Nu. 24:17), which was understood to refer to the coming deliverer.[1] The Magi saw the star 'at its rising' (this is almost certainly the correct translation of *en tē anatolē*, which RSV renders *in the East* here and in v. 9 (see BAGD, p. 62a); the noun *anatolē*, 'rising', provides a verbal allusion to Nu. 24:17).

Attempts to identify the 'star' as a regular astronomical phenomenon have generally focused on three possibilities: 1. A planetary conjunction (of Saturn and Jupiter) in 7 BC.[2] 2. A comet, usually Halley's, which unfortunately appeared too early, in 12/11 BC. 3. A nova (a star which, owing to an explosion, appears temporarily with extraordinary brightness).[3] But no known astronomical phenomena account for the movement of the star as described in v. 9,[4] and this indicates that what Matthew describes is guidance by a miraculous occurrence, even if the initial interest of the Magi was aroused by a nova (or a planetary conjunction – or both!); see further, Finegan, pp. 238-248.

The verb *worship* (*proskyneō*) need mean no more than to pay homage to a human dignitary, but Matthew frequently uses it in contexts where Jesus' more-than-human status is recognized (*e.g.* 14:33; 28:9, 17), and the same implication may be present here. For the title *king of the Jews* see above, p. 45, and on 27:11 below.

**3-4.** Herod's concern is understandable: as an Edomite (*cf.* Mal. 1:4) and a Roman appointee, he was vulnerable to the claims of a king of the true Davidic dynasty. His later years were

---

[1]Brown (pp. 193-196) argues that much of Matthew's story is intended to echo the story of Balaam, not just his prophecy of the star. For Messianic interpretations of Nu. 24:17 see Gundry, *UOT*, pp. 128-129; and *cf.* the 'Messianic' guerrilla leader Simon Ben-Kosiba, who adopted the title Bar-Kokhba, 'son of a star'. Testament of Levi 18:3 predicts the appearance of the Messiah's star in heaven.

[2]So E. Stauffer, *Jesus and his Story* (1960), pp. 36-38; R. A. Rosenberg, *Biblica* 53 (1972), pp. 105-109; Brown, pp. 172-173. E. L. Martin (*op. cit.*) dates it in 3/2 BC.

[3]Thus in the *Quarterly Journal of the Royal Astronomical Society* 18 (1977), pp. 443-449 three astronomers identified it as a nova which Chinese astronomers observed for 70 days in 5/4 BC (the same phenomenon had already been noticed by F. Münter, *Der Stern der Weisen* (1827), p. 29, and by others since: see Finegan, pp. 246-248).

[4]Though E. L. Martin's theory mentioned above includes an attempt to account for this in terms of the movement and 'standing still' of Jupiter.

plagued by the fear of rivals.[1] The phrase *chief priests and scribes* suggests an *ad hoc* gathering, not a formal meeting of the Sanhedrin, with which Herod was on bad terms, and which would also include lay elders. The concern of *all Jerusalem*, while it could well be based on unhappy experience of what Herod might be driven to by fear of a rival, probably also points forward to Jerusalem's later rejection of the true 'king of the Jews' (*e.g.* 23:37, and see below, on 28:7).

**5–6.** The answer to Herod's question was well known; *cf.* John 7:41–42. Matthew introduces here his second formula-quotation (see pp. 38–40; the absence of the phrase 'that it might be fulfilled' is due to the insertion of the quotation into the Jewish leaders' answer rather than into a narrative of the birth in Bethlehem). The text cited differs considerably from the Hebrew and other known versions of Micah 5:2. The ancient name of Bethlehem, *Ephrathah*, is replaced by a currently recognizable term, *in the land of Judah* (differentiating it from Bethlehem in Galilee, Jos. 19:15, but more significantly emphasizing Jesus' origin from the royal tribe). Micah's statement of Bethlehem's insignificance is reversed by the addition of *by no means*, and the 'thousands' (or clans) of Judah become its *rulers*. The following description of the one who *shall come* is a paraphrase of the rest of Micah 5:2, with an allusion to the shepherd theme in v. 4 (*poimainō, govern* in RSV, means 'to shepherd'), but its actual words are drawn from 2 Samuel 5:2, the description of David's role as shepherd of Israel. Not all these changes involve much difference in Hebrew ('are little to be' could become *are by no means least* by the substitution of *l'hyyt* for *lhywt*, and *rulers* is a legitimate translation of the same Hebrew consonants as for 'thousands' or 'clans', *'lpy*), but taken together they show clearly that Matthew is quoting freely, in such a way as to point out the application of the text. His addition of *for* after *rulers of Judah* makes it clear that he regards Jesus' birth in Bethlehem as conferring on it an importance in contrast with its insignificance in Micah's day, hence the change to *by no means least*. (This reversal of fortunes was of course the point of Micah's reference to Bethlehem's insignificance; Matthew has merely made it

---

[1]See my discussion in *NovT* 21 (1979), pp. 114–116.

explicit.) And the introduction of words from 2 Samuel 5:2 makes clearer the status of Jesus as son of David, born in the city of David, to rule like David over the people of God.

**7–8.** It is sometimes alleged that the historical Herod was too cunning and ruthless a man to depend on the co-operation of these foreigners, and that he would have sent his troops with them. But he had no reason to doubt that they would return with the information he needed, and the sight of soldiers with them would have jeopardized their chances of finding the child. His hypocritical motive for desiring the information would not perhaps have deceived his subjects, but might be expected to work with foreigners.

**9–10.** *Went before* (*proēgen*) could mean that it 'led them on' without itself moving, but the words *came to rest* mean literally 'came and stood', and can mean only that the star itself moved to guide the Magi. It is not said to indicate the precise house, but the general location *where the child was*. How it did so can only be left to the imagination, and the search for astronomical parallels to a divine communication is unlikely to be profitable (see on v. 2). To the Magi it brought not critical embarrassment but *great joy*!

**11.** For *the child*, see on v. 1, and for *worshipped*, v. 2. The homage of these learned Gentiles is intended to indicate the fulfilment of such passages as Psalm 72:10ff.; Isaiah 60:1ff. (these passages probably account for the later Christian tradition that these Magi were 'kings'), and two of the gifts are specifically mentioned in Psalm 72:15 (gold); Isaiah 60:6 (gold and frankincense). They are gifts fit for a king, as is also myrrh (Ps. 45:8; Song 3:6), and they remind the reader of the homage of the Queen of Sheba to the son of David, with her gifts of spices and gold (1 Ki. 10:2). The use of *myrrh* in the crucifixion (Mk. 15:23) and burial (Jn. 19:39) of Jesus has led to the tradition that it symbolizes his suffering, but in the Old Testament it is rather a symbol of joy and festivity (see references above, and Pr. 7:17; Song 5:5).

**12.** For the *dream*, see on 1:20. Revelation by dreams was a regular feature in the culture to which these Magi belonged. God's use of their astrological and cultural background to communicate with them does not imply his endorsement of astrology, but indicates his care in meeting individuals where they are.

## (iv) The flight to Egypt and the return (2:13-23)

This section consists of three brief narratives, each leading up to a 'formula-quotation' (see pp. 38-40). Each narrative is concisely worded so as to explain the relevance of the quotation, and the focus throughout is on the fulfilment of Scripture, particularly in the geographical locations of Jesus' childhood.[1]

But alongside this theme another, already hinted at in vv. 1-12, here comes out clearly, the parallel between the childhood of Jesus and the experiences of Moses. This theme is in the nature of a sub-plot, emerging in the details of the narrative, but not in the explicit quotations (which focus on Jesus as the true Israel and the Davidic Messiah). This Moses typology forms a very minor theme in the Gospel as a whole, but here in the infancy narrative it is clearly suggested, particularly for readers who were familiar with non-biblical Jewish traditions about Moses. Josephus (Ant. ii. 205ff.; see also Exodus Rabbah 1:18) records a tradition that a 'sacred scribe' (= astrologer?) foretold to Pharaoh the birth of the deliverer of Israel;[2] Pharaoh in alarm ordered the destruction of all young male children; Moses' father, however, was told in a dream that it was his son who was destined to deliver Israel, and so rescued him from the massacre. A Jewish reader, aware of this expansion of the Exodus tradition, would the more quickly see Jesus as a second Moses in the narratives of chapter 2. But Matthew also alludes to the text of Exodus itself in vv. 13-14 (Ex. 2:15) and 20-21 (Ex. 4:19-20), with reference not to Moses' birth but to his subsequent escape from Pharaoh and return. These allusions, with the mention of Egypt and of the slaughter of the children, would alone suffice to alert the reader. There is not a neat point-for-point correspondence, but rather a series of echoes throughout the chapter which builds up to a deliberate depiction of Jesus as

---

[1]See above, pp. 69-71, for this emphasis throughout chapter 2, and see further my article in NTS 27 (1980/1), pp. 233-251.

[2]According to Targum Pseudo-Jonathan to Ex. 1:15 the 'magicians' Jannes and Jambres gave this interpretation to a dream of Pharaoh.

the new Moses.[1]

**13-14.** For the *dream*, see on 1:20. Again the effect is to emphasize the divine initiative in the details of Jesus' origin. The choice of *Egypt* as a place of refuge was natural; it was the haven for other Israelites in political trouble in Old Testament times (*e.g.* 1 Ki. 11:40; 2 Ki. 25:26; Je. 26:21) and later (see Bruce, p. 5), and was now safely outside Herod's jurisdiction. But for Matthew it held extra meaning as the place where Israel's history as the people of God began.

**15.** In Egypt, then, God now kept his Son safe, as he had preserved Israel there long ago[2] and *out of Egypt* he would soon call him to his work of redemption as he had liberated Israel from Egypt to fulfil their role as his people – indeed, as Hosea 11:1 explained, as his *son*. Hosea's words are not a prediction, but an account of Israel's origin. Matthew's quotation thus depends for its validity on the recognition of Jesus as the true Israel, a typological theme found elsewhere in the New Testament, and most obviously paralleled in Matthew by Jesus' use of Israel-texts in the wilderness (see on 4:1-11); there too it is as God's *son* that Jesus is equated with Israel. Israel's exodus from Egypt was taken already by the Old Testament prophets as a prefiguring of the ultimate Messianic salvation, and Matthew's quotation here thus reinforces his presentation of the childhood history of Jesus as the dawning of the Messianic age.

**16.** The ruthlessness of *Herod*'s later years, particularly where a potential rival was concerned, is well documented; the victims included three of his own sons (Josephus, *Ant.* xvi. 392-394; xvii. 182-187), as well as several large groups of actual or suspected conspirators (*Ant.* xvi. 393-394; xvii. 42-44, 167), in one case with their families (*Ant.* xv. 289-290). It is thus not improbable that his fear of a potential rival should lead him to kill a few babies in Bethlehem. (The number of boys under two, if Bethlehem's population was about 1,000 – and *AB*, p. 19, estimates only 300 – would not be more than twenty.) It was a

[1]See my discussion of this typology in *NovT* 21 (1979), pp. 105-111. Further points of comparison are conveniently set out in Brown, pp. 112-116. (For Daube's alternative proposal of a Jacob-Laban typology see my comments in *NovT* 21, pp. 106-107.)

[2]Gundry (*UOT*, pp. 93-94) sees this preservation rather than the exodus as the point of Matthew's quotation.

minor incident in a period full of atrocities, and the absence of clearly independent accounts in secular history is not surprising.[1]

**17-18.** But here too Matthew sees the fulfilment of a scriptural pattern. Not that God, or Scripture, should be held responsible for Herod's action: Matthew's formula here does not as elsewhere use a final conjunction (*hina* or *hopōs*, 'in order that'), but (as in 27:9, where again a wrong action is seen as fulfilling prophecy) the neutral *then was fulfilled.* The quotation is a slightly abbreviated but correct translation (independent of the LXX) of Jeremiah 31:15. The following verses in Jeremiah go on to assure Rachel that her lost children (the reference is to captives taken into exile) will return, so that 'there is hope for your future'. Perhaps Matthew intends us to see also in Bethlehem's mourning a temporary sorrow, out of which God will bring joy and deliverance through Bethlehem's Messiah, returning from a foreign land; there is no precise correspondence, but the relevance lies in the perception of God's working through disaster to blessing, through death to life. It is possible that the later tradition of *Rachel*'s burial near Bethlehem[2] influenced Matthew's choice of the text, but as the text explicitly locates Rachel's weeping at *Ramah* (in Benjamin, the earlier traditional site of Rachel's tomb, and the place where the exiles, including Jeremiah, were gathered for the march to Babylon in 586 BC, Je. 40:1), this is certainly not the main point. The relevance is not in Ramah or in Rachel (Bethlehem was not in one of the 'Rachel' tribes), but in bereavement as a prelude to blessing.[3]

**19-21.** *Herod died* in 4 BC; how long Joseph and his family had then been in Egypt can only be guessed. Their movements here and in v. 22 are again directed by revelation in a dream (see on 1:20). The words of v. 20 are modelled on Exodus 4:19 (see above, p. 85), even to the extent of preserving the plural, *those who sought . . . are dead*, which is not strictly applicable to Herod.

**22.** *Archelaus* succeeded only to the southern part of his father's kingdom, and his character was quickly shown to be no

---

[1]See my discussion of the historical credibility of the event in *NovT* 21 (1979), pp. 114–119.
[2]Gn. 35:16–20 and 48:7 say she was buried *on the way to* Ephrath (Bethlehem), but 1 Sa. 10:2 shows that the actual site was in Benjamin.
[3]I have discussed other possible nuances in *NTS* 27 (1980/1), pp. 244–246.

better than his father's, until he was deposed for misrule in AD 6. *Galilee*, ruled by his half-brother Herod Antipas, was more likely to be a safe place for the upbringing of the Messiah (it was soon to gain a reputation as a fertile source of 'Messianic' liberation movements).

**23.** Matthew, with his typical avoidance of unnecessary detail, does not mention that Nazareth had already been the family home before the birth of Jesus (Lk. 1:26; 2:4). What interests him is the significance of the choice of Nazareth in the light of Scripture. The Messiah was expected to come from Bethlehem (2:4–6), and Jesus' coming from Nazareth, an insignificant village with a partly Gentile population and outlook, could well be an embarrassment (*cf.* Jn. 1:46; 7:41–42, 52); it must be scripturally defended. Now Nazareth is not mentioned in the Old Testament (or in any other contemporary Jewish literature), and the words *He shall be called a Nazarene*[1] do not occur in the Old Testament. How then does Jesus' upbringing in Nazareth *fulfil what was spoken by the prophets*? Matthew does not explain, and numerous suggestions have been made (see Gundry, *UOT*, pp. 97–104). The two most favoured Old Testament passages are Isaiah 11:1, where the Messiah is described as a 'branch' (*nēṣer*) from the root of Jesse (a similar image, though not the word *nēṣer*, is used in other Messianic passages, *e.g.* Is. 4:2; 53:2; Je. 23:5; 33:15; Zc. 3:8; 6:12), and Judges 13:5, where Samson is presented as a Nazirite (Heb. *nᵉzîr*, LXX *naziraios*). The disadvantage of the former is that the word-play is not obvious in Hebrew, and would be completely lost in Greek; and of the latter that Matthew uses *Nazōraios* not *naziraios*, and that Jesus was never a Nazirite anyway. Neither passage provides Matthew's actual wording. (The 'shall be' of Jdg. 13:5 would have fitted well here; that Matthew instead wrote 'shall be called' suggests that that was not his source.) It should be noted, however, that the formula introducing the quotation differs from the regular pattern (see pp. 38–39) in two ways: it refers not to a single prophet but to *the prophets*, and it concludes not with 'saying' (*legontos*) but with 'that' (*hoti*). This suggests that it is not meant to be a quotation of a specific passage, but a

---

[1] The Greek word is *Nazōraios*, the common New Testament title for Jesus as the man from Nazareth; Mark uses *Nazarēnos*, hence the English *Nazarene*: see *NBD*, pp. 818–819.

summary of a theme of prophetic expectation. Thus it has been suggested that Matthew saw in the obscurity of Nazareth the fulfilment of Old Testament indications of a humble and rejected Messiah; for Jesus to be known by the derogatory epithet *Nazōraios* (*cf.* Jn. 1:46) was not compatible with the expected royal dignity of the Messiah, and thus fulfilled such passages as Psalm 22; Isaiah 53; Zechariah 11:4–14. (Gundry, *UOT*, pp. 103–104, points out that a play on the word *nēṣer* in Is. 11:1 would also convey this same message, as the shoot from the cut-down stump is a symbol of lowly origin (and *cf.* the despised plant image in Is. 53:2), and was so understood in contemporary Judaism.[1])

## B. THE PREPARATION FOR JESUS' PUBLIC MINISTRY (3:1 – 4:16)

*(i) The ministry of John the Baptist (3:1–12)*
John's title, 'the Baptist', can obscure what was in fact the main thrust of his ministry, an announcement of the imminent judgment of God and of the coming of the 'greater one'. In the light of this expectation he called men to repentance, to prepare them for the coming test, and it was in token of this repentance that he administered baptism.

John was an important figure in his own right. His preaching created a widespread revival movement (see v. 5), and his followers constituted a significant group within Judaism which maintained its separate existence beyond the New Testament period. His ministry is recorded by Josephus (*Ant.* xviii. 116–119) more amply than that of Jesus. But for Matthew his significance lay only in his relation to Jesus, and his account of John lays emphasis on the connection (see on v. 2). Wherever John is mentioned in the Gospel it is to throw light on the mission of Jesus. Here his preaching prepares the way for Jesus' ministry, and provides the setting for the launching of Jesus' mission.

**1.** *In those days* relates directly to 2:23, the days of Jesus' residence in Nazareth. It is a vague expression (compared with Luke's precise dating, 3:1), and conceals a lapse of some thirty

---

[1] I have developed this argument further in *NTS* 27 (1980/1), pp. 246–249.

years since the events of chapter 2. A modern biographer could not pass over the bulk of his subject's life in silence, but Matthew hastens deliberately to his true subject, the public ministry, death and resurrection of the Messiah. *John* is introduced abruptly, distinguished by his regular title, *the Baptist* (so also Mark, Luke and Josephus), since he was apparently the first to baptize others (proselyte baptism and the 'baptisms' at Qumran were self-administered). The *wilderness of Judaea* is the land which drops steeply down from the Judaean hills to the Dead Sea, not all of which is 'desert', though it provides only rough pasture; the lower Jordan valley adjoins the *wilderness* proper. In this area John would be likely to have some contact with the monastic sect of Qumran, and his ascetic life as well as his eschatological preaching (see also on vv. 8, 11) and his baptism (see on v. 6) suggest to some that he was brought up as a member of the sect (*cf.* Lk. 1:80). If this is so (and it cannot be more than a guess), he had certainly broken with them by the time of his prophetic ministry, which called all to repentance instead of recruiting for a closed and ritual-bound community, and which saw the eschatological crisis of which they dreamt as already present.

**2.** Matthew (alone) summarizes John's preaching in the same words as that of Jesus (4:17; *cf.* also 10:7 for the preaching of Jesus' disciples). For other parallels see on vv. 7, 8, 9, 10 and 12. For Matthew, therefore, John is not a rival of Jesus (*cf.* Jn. 3:22–26; 4:1) but a preacher of the same message. *Repent* means more than 'be sorry' or even 'change your mind'; it echoes the Old Testament prophets' frequent summons to Israel to 'return' to God, to abandon their rebellion and come back into covenant-obedience. This radical conversion is necessary in the light of the coming of the *kingdom of heaven* (see pp. 45–46), which here means the establishment of God's rightful sovereignty in judgment and in salvation, *i.e.* the Messianic age. This time has now come: *is at hand* does not do justice to the perfect tense of *engizō*, which means literally 'has come near'. The perfect is used also in 26:45 and 46 (*cf.* Lk. 21:8, 20) and introduces a state of affairs which is already beginning and which demands immediate action. Even *AB*'s 'is fast approaching' is too remote. John's summons is urgent: the time for decision has already come.

**3.** While not strictly a 'formula-quotation' (pp. 38–40; it is shared with Mark and Luke, and lacks the 'fulfilment' terminology), this quotation of Isaiah 40:3 serves a similar function. John's location in the *wilderness* provides the immediate reference, but it is his function as a 'preparer of the way' which most interests Matthew. In Isaiah the 'voice' preceded the coming of God; here the phrase *his paths*, instead of Isaiah's 'a highway for our God', allows the reader to see *the Lord* as Jesus. It is one of several places in Matthew (and throughout the New Testament) where Old Testament passages about the coming of God are seen as fulfilled in Jesus (see, *e.g.*, my *JOT*, pp. 150–159). The passage referred originally to the release of Israel from exile; now it is applied to a greater act of salvation. (The Qumran sect saw in this same passage a blueprint for their own withdrawal to the wilderness in preparation for God's coming: 1QS 8:12–14; 9:19–20.)

**4.** John's ascetic clothing is modelled on that of Elijah (2 Ki. 1:8), whom John also resembles in his sudden appearance, his solitary life, his uncompromising message and his eventual clash with the 'king' and his wife. The implications will be drawn out in 11:14; 17:12–13. His diet, though limited, was nutritious and readily available in the wilderness. (Locusts are still eaten in the Middle East: see Bonnard, p. 34, for culinary directions!)

**5–6.** John's baptism was an innovation. The nearest contemporary parallels are the self-baptism of a Gentile on becoming a proselyte, and the repeated ritual washings (also self-administered) at Qumran. Neither accounts adequately for John's baptism, which was apparently a once-only rite, administered by John in the river, and applied to Jews (for this last point see further on v. 9); and neither carried the note of urgent preparation for the coming crisis which was the main point of John's baptism. John's 'converts' were not seeking ceremonial purification, but 'fleeing from the wrath to come' (v. 7). Their baptism was a token of repentance (see on v. 2), involving *confessing their sins*. Matthew does not say, however (as do Mark and Luke), that it was 'for the *forgiveness* of sins'; this he will attribute only to the death of Jesus (26:28).

**7.** The *Pharisees and Sadducees* are mentioned as acting together again only in 16:1. They are better known for their mutual hostility, and they are mentioned here not as a united front, but as the two most prestigious among the varied groups who came to John. They came 'to the *baptism*' (RSV *for baptism* is misleading), whether to seek baptism themselves or to see what was going on we are not told; John's ironical comments indicate that he doubted their genuineness as converts, and 21:25, 32 shows that the priestly authorities as a whole rejected John. *Brood of vipers* (hardly calculated to welcome potential converts!) may have been suggested by Jeremiah 46:22, which pictures Egypt as a snake escaping from tree-fellers (*cf.* v. 10). Jesus was later to take it up in his own attacks on the Pharisees (12:34; 23:33).

**8.** *Cf.* 7:16–20 for Jesus' use of the *fruit* metaphor. John consistently attacks reliance on ceremony or status (v. 9) and insists on a personal repentance which is more than superficial. A strong emphasis on the same point is found at Qumran (1QS 2:25 – 3:12), with reference to ritual washing.

**9.** What John attacks here is not reliance on race (Gentiles too became *children of Abraham* when they became proselytes), but on status as members of the covenant community (*cf*, Jn. 8:33, 39), within which the merits of Abraham were believed to guarantee God's blessing. Jesus attacked the same false security (see 8:11–12), and Paul concludes that 'not all are children of Abraham because they are his descendants', but only those who share Abraham's faith (Rom. 9:6–8; *cf.* Rom. 2:17–29; 4:16–25; Gal. 3:7–29). Isaiah had referred to Abraham as 'the rock from which you were hewn' (Is. 51:1–2), but John says that any other stones would serve God's purpose. The close similarity of the Hebrew words for *stones* and *children* completes a devastating play on words.

**10.** *Cf.* 7:19 for Jesus' use of the same metaphor, in the same words.

**11.** *Coming after me* does not refer to one coming 'later' (*opisō*, 'behind', is not used of time elsewhere in the New Testament), but is a regular description of a follower or disciple. (*Opisō* is so used, *e.g.*, in 4:19; 10:38; 16:24; Lk. 21:8; Jn. 12:19, though this is not obvious in RSV.) Jesus first appeared as a follower of John when he came to his baptism, but John already knew that in fact he was *mightier*, and that he himself was not worthy even to do the lowest slave's task for this 'disciple'. A Rabbi's disciple was expected to act virtually as his master's slave, but to remove his shoes (*carry* implies 'take away' – see MM, *s.v. bastazō*) was too low a task even for a disciple (*Ketuboth* 96a). John's preparatory and symbolic baptism will soon give way to an effective 'baptism' (the verb, apart from its ritual use, signifies 'plunge' or 'drench'; in metaphorical use it implies 'flooding', 'overwhelming') 'in Holy Spirit and fire' (lit.). The prophets looked forward to a purifying 'outpouring' of the Spirit of God in the Messianic age (Is. 32:15; 44:3; Ezk. 36:26–27; 39:29; Joel 2:28–29); the men of Qumran also looked forward to purification by God's 'sprinkling' man with a 'spirit of holiness' and 'spirit of truth' (1QS 4:20–22). Purification by *fire* was also a prophetic hope (Is. 4:4; Zc. 13:9; Mal. 3:2; *cf.* Is. 1:25). John therefore predicts a real cleansing, in contrast with his own merely outward token. If we come to this verse in its own context, and not in the light of later use of such language, we thus find that the 'drenching' John promises is not a specific rite or experience (still less a post-conversion crisis). Rather it points to the purifying effect of the Messiah's work, making effective that return to the holiness of the people of God which John's water-baptism could only symbolize.

**12.** The *fire* that purifies will also destroy all that is worthless. Jesus too talks of this destructive element in his mission, using very similar words (13:30). The judgment is in both passages selective. The *wheat* is separated off as it is thrown up with the *winnowing fork* (better 'shovel') for the wind to blow away the *chaff*, which is then gathered and burnt in fire which is *unquenchable*, because its fierceness will destroy all that is put in it (the word is not, and does not necessarily imply, 'everlasting', which would not fit the threshing-floor imagery). The fear of judgment is thus a prominent element of John's preaching which should lead his hearers to repentance (v. 7). But the judgment, no less than the dawning salvation, is focused in Jesus.

*(ii) The baptism of Jesus (3:13–17)*

**13.** Matthew's account focuses on the encounter between

Jesus and John, and on the personal experience of Jesus, so that it might suggest a purely private baptism. But the setting (see vv. 5-6) and the wording of Luke's account (Lk. 3:21) indicate that Jesus was one among many who were baptized by John, whether by a personal act or by self-immersion together under John's direction (so Jeremias, *NTT*, p. 51). *To be baptized* indicates that Jesus deliberately chose to accept John's baptism, and vv. 14-15 will emphasize this further. Jesus thus intended to identify himself with John's message and with the revival movement it had created, to enrol as a member of the purified and prepared people of God. It is this, rather than any need for forgiveness (which Matthew has deliberately not mentioned as the purpose of John's baptism; see on v. 6), which brought him to join the crowd.

**14.** Matthew does not explain how John recognized Jesus as different from the rest of the crowd, but Luke (ch. 1) relates the revelations which would be part of their joint family traditions. (Jn. 1:31 and 33 perhaps indicate that John's grasp of the *nature* of Jesus' mission was as yet imperfect.) John thus saw Jesus as one of superior status and authority (this, rather than a moral comparison, is the point of his hesitation; see Bornkamm, *TIM*, p. 36); he cannot agree to this voluntary humiliation of the 'mightier' one he had predicted (v. 11), and his words, in the light of v. 11, probably mean 'I need your Spirit-and-fire baptism, not you my water-baptism'. John recognizes that Jesus brings a new situation, eclipsing his own preparatory ministry.

**15.** Jesus' reply accepts John's point, but insists that *now*, for the time being, it is right for Jesus to accept the lower place, because in this way he and John (*us*) will *fulfil all righteousness*. This puzzling explanation uses two words which are prominent in Matthew. *Fulfil* is used mainly of Jesus' relation to the predictions and patterns of the Old Testament (see on 5:17); a paraphrase such as 'bring to reality' or 'accomplish' indicates its essential meaning for Matthew. *Righteousness* in Matthew is not so much 'being good', still less legal correctness, but rather a synonym for the Christian life, viewed as a relationship with God focused in obedience. It was this relationship which John's baptism demanded (*cf.* 21:32), and which now requires Jesus to identify himself with the penitent people of God in order to fulfil his mission. So Jesus regards his baptism among repentant Israel as a necessary step in his accomplishment of God's purpose of salvation. Some have seen here the influence of the Servant figure in Isaiah, who represents his people and bears their sins. This is not explicit, but may be hinted at in the term *righteousness*, which is a prominent feature in Isaiah 53:11, particularly as v. 17 will clearly introduce the Servant theme.

**16.** The experience following Jesus' baptism was crucial to his future ministry, parallel to the 'call' of many of the Old Testament prophets. Mark's account, and less clearly Luke's, suggests that it was a purely private experience; John (1:32–34) indicates that John at least saw *the Spirit descending like a dove*, though the accompanying revelation to him was not the divine pronouncement recorded in the Synoptics. Matthew's account is similar to Mark's (especially if the reading 'opened *to him*', found in many later MSS, is original, though this is not likely). The third-person form of the proclamation in v. 17 suggests a public revelation, but this is hard to reconcile with the fact that Jesus' Messianic status was not publicly stated throughout his ministry, and was only grasped by his closest disciples much later (16:13–20); Matthew therefore, while assimilating the words to those at the transfiguration (17:5), probably intends them to be understood as addressed to Jesus only. The whole focus of the account is on Jesus' 'commissioning', not on a public revelation of his mission.

*The heavens were opened* echoes Ezekiel's inaugural vision (Ezk. 1:1), also by a river (*cf.* also Ezk. 2:2 for the coming of the Spirit). The descent of *the Spirit of God* may indicate the return of the long-absent gift of prophetic inspiration, but more obviously indicates the promised endowment of the Messiah (*e.g.* Is. 11:2; 42:1; 61:1). We need not assume that Jesus had no previous experience of the Spirit; the vision symbolizes his commissioning for his Messianic work, not a new spiritual status. The *dove* as a symbol of the Spirit (Lk. 3:22 indicates that the reference is to the visible 'shape' of the vision, not to the gentle mode of the Spirit's descent) was not common in Jewish thought, but is found in some later Jewish writings, based probably on the Spirit's 'hovering' over the waters in Genesis 1:2.

**17.** The *voice from heaven* (*i.e.* from God) speaks in the second person (*You are* . . .) in Mark and Luke, and Western MSS have the same reading here; but it is more likely that scribes altered an original third person to agree with the Synoptic parallels than that a second person was altered to conform to 17:5. Apparently, then, Matthew has deliberately put it in the third person to remind his readers of the parallel pronouncement in 17:5. The words are generally understood to be drawn from Psalm 2:7, which addresses the Davidic king as God's son and was understood of the Messiah, and Isaiah 42:1, which introduces the Servant as God's chosen on whom he has put his Spirit.[1] RSV mg., which is more literal, makes the allusions clearer. (*Beloved*, Matthew's rendering of 'chosen' in Is. 42:1 here and in 12:18, suggests an 'only' son: *cf.* LXX Gn. 22:2, sometimes also thought to be in mind here.) Jesus' Messianic mission, already symbolized in the vision of v. 16, is thus spelt out around three key concepts; he is the Davidic Messiah, the Son of God, and the Servant whose mission is to bear the sins of his people. Again there is no suggestion that Jesus *became* Son of God at his baptism. It was a pivotal experience, not in that it made Jesus anything which he was not already, but in that it launched him on the mission for which he had long prepared, and defined that mission in terms of Old Testament expectation.[2]

*(iii) The test (4:1–11)*

To refer to this episode as the temptation of Jesus is doubly misleading. Firstly, the verb *peirazō* (vv. 1, 3) in Matthew always signifies testing (and in its 36 New Testament occurrences it clearly indicates tempting to do wrong only in 1 Cor. 7:5; Jas. 1:13–14); see also John 6:6; 2 Corinthians 13:5 for some clear examples of this primary sense. Satan's intention was, no doubt, to persuade Jesus to do wrong, but the initiative was with God (see on v. 1), and the whole emphasis of the story is on the testing of Jesus' reaction to his Messianic vocation as Son of God. Secondly, to speak of '*the* temptation' is misleading

[1] A reference to Is. 42:1 alone is argued by Jeremias (*NTT*, pp. 53–55), and Matthew's third-person form certainly reduces the similarity to Ps. 2:7, but Gundry (*UOT*, pp. 29–31) convincingly defends the combined reference; see also I. H. Marshall, *NTS* 15 (1968/9), pp. 326–336.

[2] For possible echoes also of the exodus theme in these verses (*cf.* p. 85) see, cautiously, Davies, pp. 35–45.

because Matthew does not suggest (and Lk. 4:13, 'until an opportune time', clearly denies) that this was the sum-total of Jesus' struggle against Satanic suggestions (*cf.* Heb. 4:15); it is rather a specific examination of Jesus' newly-revealed relationship with God. The true sense of the passage is well summed up in the title of B. Gerhardsson's monograph, *The Testing of God's Son*.

The source of the account (as for the experience at his baptism) can only be Jesus himself. Its recording by Matthew and Luke differs only in some details and in the order of the second and third temptations. Explanations of the different order, on both literary and theological grounds, are as many as commentators, and all are conjectural, but most agree that Matthew's order, with its focus on the 'Son of God' theme (vv. 3, 6), after which Satan 'drops his disguise' (Schweizer) to reveal his true purpose, is more probably the original. Clearly the chronological order was not felt to be important.

The focus of the story, as of each part of Matthew's introductory section, is on the Old Testament. There are implied parallels between Jesus' experience and that of Moses (see on vv. 2, 8) and Elijah (see on vv. 2, 11); and Psalm 91, quoted by Satan in v. 6, is probably echoed again in v. 11, while its theme of humble expectation of God's protection underlies much of the account. But the primary focus is on Deuteronomy 6 – 8, three times quoted by Jesus in answer to Satan's suggestions (v. 4 = Dt. 8:3; v. 7 = Dt. 6:16; v.10 = Dt. 6:13). It is a description of the lessons God put before the Israelites in the wilderness before their mission of conquest of the promised land, when he tested them (Dt. 8:2) as a man disciplines his son (Dt. 8:5). Israel failed to learn its lessons, but now the true Son of God, at the outset of his mission, faces the same tests in the wilderness and succeeds. The conception of Jesus as the true Israel, already affirmed by Matthew in 2:15, here comes to fuller expression.[1]

**1.** *Then*, a favourite connecting word in Matthew, does not always convey a definite chronological or even logical connection. Here, however, it marks an important sequence, from the confirmation of Jesus' status and mission at his baptism, to the

---

[1] See further, my *JOT*, pp. 50–53; J. A. T. Robinson, *Twelve New Testament Studies* (1962), pp. 53–60.

testing of his response to that experience. Matthew stresses that he was *led up by the Spirit* (*cf.* 3:16) with the express intention of being tested (*cf.* 'to be baptized', 3:13). *The devil* was the agent; he appears in Matthew as a real and powerful rival, the one whose authority is threatened by Jesus' inauguration of the kingdom of heaven (12:24–29; 13:19,39; 16:23; see Kingsbury, pp. 149–152). But his hostile intention is here shown to be put to the service of God's deliberate purpose of testing his Son. The testing in *the wilderness* already recalls the experience of Israel (Dt. 8:2).[1]

**2.** Jesus' fast for *forty days and forty nights* recalls that of Moses at Sinai (Ex. 34:28; Dt. 9:9, 18) and that of Elijah on the way there (1 Ki. 19:8); the mountain (v. 8) perhaps reinforces these allusions. But in view of the explicit reference to Israel's wilderness experiences throughout the narrative, the forty years of Israel's hunger (Dt. 8:2–3) are probably more directly in mind. There is no indication whether Jesus' fast was a total abstinence from food, or merely the privation of living on what little could be found in the wilderness, but it was sufficiently serious to cause real hunger. The Son of God was not exempt from human physical needs.

**3–4.** But the *Son of God* has no need to be hungry, suggests the devil. (*If* does not necessarily express doubt, but takes up the revelation of 3:17, and examines its implications.) He has the power to satisfy physical need by miraculous means. Later miracles prove this was true: see 14:15–21; 15:32–38. The act was thus not in itself wrong. But Jesus recognized in his hunger an experience designed by God to teach him the lesson of Deuteronomy 8:3. His mission was to be one of continual privation, for the sake of his ministry of the word of God; a concern for his own material comfort could only jeopardize it. As Son of God, he must learn, as Israel had failed to learn, to put first things first. And that must mean an unquestioning obedience to his Father's plan. Note that there is no suggestion either in the devil's proposal or in Jesus' reply of a temptation to present himself to others as an 'economic Messiah'. The emphasis is

[1] For the wilderness as the expected site of the Messiah's début see J. A. Kirk, *EQ* 44 (1972), pp. 17–21. Kirk's article proposes an interpretation of the temptation as directed more to Jesus' Messianic activity than to his position as Son of God.

entirely on his own relationship with God.

**5–7.** Whether *the devil took him*, here and in v. 8, literally or in a vision is not clear. The physical impossibility of a mountain commanding a world-wide view (v. 8) may suggest the latter (*cf.* Ezekiel's visionary 'visit' to the temple at Jerusalem while he was in Babylon, Ezk. 8:1–3; 11:24). The *pinnacle* (literally 'small wing') *of the temple* would be some projecting part of the temple buildings; the main temple building was some 180 feet high. The devil's suggestion (and Jesus' reply) again makes no reference to the effect of this spectacular leap on bystanders, giving Jesus instant success as 'Messiah'. Rather the focus is again on his relationship to God. As Son of God, he could surely claim with absolute confidence the physical protection which God promises in Psalm 91:11–12 (and throughout that Psalm) to those who trust him. So why not try it by forcing God's hand (and thus silence any lingering doubts about his relationship with God)? But this would be to *tempt* God (see above, p. 96, on the verb), as Israel did in the wilderness at Massah (Dt. 6:16), when they 'put the LORD to the proof by saying, "Is the LORD among us or not?"' (Ex. 17:2–7). The Son of God can live only in a relationship of trust which needs no test. Christians perplexed by the apparently thin line between 'the prayer of faith' and 'putting God to the test' should note that the devil's suggestion was of an artificially created crisis, not of trusting God in the situations which result from obedient service.

**8–10.** The view from the *mountain* recalls Moses' view of the promised land from Mount Nebo (Dt. 34:1–4). The devil's dominion over all the world, implied here and explicit in Luke 4:6, is stated also in John 12:31 (*cf.* 2 Cor. 4:4; 1 Jn. 5:19). It was this dominion which Jesus had come to contest, and the contest would be fierce. To avoid it by compromise with the devil was not a very subtle temptation, but it provided a crucial test of Jesus' loyalty to his Father, even where it meant renouncing the easy way of allowing the end to justify the means. (After all, Jesus' mission *was* to achieve world-wide dominion: Dn. 7:14; *cf.* Mt. 28:18.) Israel had fallen to this temptation again and again, and had renounced their exclusive loyalty to God for the sake of political advantage. At the entry to the promised land the temptation met them in an acute form (Dt. 6:10–15; Jesus' reply

99

quotes v. 13). But the true Son of God cannot compromise his loyalty, and sharply dismisses the devil, using now for the first time the name which reveals his true purpose, *Satan*, 'the enemy' (of God and of his purpose of salvation).

**11.** The angelic help of Psalm 91:11, which Jesus refused to call for illegitimately (vv. 6–7), is now appropriately given. *Ministered* implies particularly the provision of food, and again the experience of Elijah seems to be recalled (1 Ki. 19:5–8). The lessons of the period of hunger have been well learnt, and God's messengers break the fast that Jesus himself would not break (vv. 3–4).

### (iv) The withdrawal to Galilee (4:12–16)

This section, like 2:13–23, reveals Matthew's special interest in Jesus' geographical movements and their scriptural justification. It bridges the gap between Jesus' experiences in the Jordan valley and the wilderness (3:13 – 4:11) and the opening of his public ministry in Galilee. The Gospel of John records Jesus' early activity (both in Judaea and Galilee) while John the Baptist was still active (Jn. 1:35 – 4:42; N.B. 3:24); this activity, if it is intended to be chronologically arranged in John, must presumably be fitted in after Matthew 4:11, the 'retreat' of 4:12 being that of John 4:3.

**12.** John's imprisonment (see further, 14:3ff.) provides not only the occasion but the reason for Jesus' 'tactical withdrawal' *into Galilee* (for *withdrew*, *cf.* 2:12, 14, 22; 12:15; 14:13; 15:21, all following indications of official hostility). The move entailed a change not only of location but of the style of Jesus' ministry, from a baptizing movement by the Jordan (Jn. 3:22ff.; 4:1–2) to an itinerant preaching and healing ministry (vv. 23–25), less likely to be associated with that of John.

**13.** While *Capernaum* is mentioned in the other Gospels as a scene of Jesus' ministry, only Matthew makes explicit that Jesus now made it his home (*cf.* 9:1; 17:24–25; but see 8:20, suggesting that it was only a 'base' to which Jesus and his disciples returned from time to time from their itinerant ministry). Matthew's reason for mentioning this may be due to his own connection with the town, 9:9 (if the apostle Matthew is the author; see pp. 30–34); or there may be a more theological motive in stressing the unique opportunity offered to this town which yet failed to believe (11:23–24). Capernaum, as a busy lakeside town, ensured a wider audience for Jesus' teaching than Nazareth; *leaving Nazareth* may also reflect the rejection of Jesus by his own people recorded in Luke 4:16–30.

**14–16.** The geographical details given in v. 13 provide the setting for a quotation of Isaiah 9:1–2 (8:23 – 9:1, Heb.). Matthew gives his own translation, abbreviating the text in v. 15 so as to pick out the geographical features alone as a list grammatically unconnected with what follows. *Toward the sea, across the Jordan* in Isaiah describes Galilee from the perspective of the Assyrian invader, as the land west of the river. *Galilee of the Gentiles* was now an even more appropriate description than in Isaiah's day, as successive movements of population had given it a pre-dominantly Gentile population until a deliberate Judaizing policy was adopted by the Hasmonaean rulers, resulting in a thoroughly mixed population. That such an area should be the place of revelation of the Jewish Messiah needed to be justified (*cf.* 2:23), and that justification Matthew finds in Isaiah's prediction of new light dawning in Galilee after the devastation caused by the Assyrian invasion. That Isaiah himself was here, as in 7:14 (see on 1:23), thinking of more than the immediate historical situation is seen by reading on a few verses, where the dawning light is focused in the birth of the divine child of 9:6–7. Galilee, so often the underdog both in political fortunes and in the eyes of official Jewish religion, was in fact destined to play a crucial role in the unfolding of God's plan of salvation. (*Cf.* the Magi, and the women of 1:3, 5–6, for Matthew's interest in the place of 'outsiders' in the purpose of God; and *cf.* on 2:23.)

# II. PUBLIC MINISTRY IN AND AROUND GALILEE
## (4:17 – 16:20)

This long section describes what Matthew regards as the main period of Jesus' public ministry, beginning from his first appearance as a preacher and extending to his disciples' recognition of his unique status and mission. This whole period is set in Galilee and its immediate environment: ministry in Judaea will come later as the climax to Jesus' mission. No indication is given of the length of this period of ministry, nor is the material set out in any clear chronological order. Rather it is arranged thematically, and the subdivisions given below attempt to isolate the main groupings (see the Analysis, pp. 63–65). Some are clear, such as the teaching on discipleship (chs. 5 – 7, the 'Sermon on the Mount'), the two chapters of miracles (chs. 8 – 9), the mission of the disciples (ch. 10), and the collection of parables (ch. 13). The remainder (our subdivisions E and G) does not so clearly fall into large sections on single themes, but often a logical progression is found between individual subsections, and the interest throughout these less homogeneous sections is focused on the varying response of different groups to Jesus, with the growing faith of the disciples and the mounting hostility of the religious authorities as two contrasting sub-plots developing throughout. So while it is not realistic to insist on deliberate logical connections at every point, Matthew was clearly conscious of the importance of a coherent framework, and his arrangement of his material is seldom if ever haphazard. The result is a many-faceted portrayal of the character of Jesus' public ministry which led up to the final clash with the authorities.

### A. INTRODUCTION TO THE PUBLIC MINISTRY (4:17–25)

*(i) Summary of Jesus' preaching (4:17)*
*From that time* indicates a fresh start, a new phase of Jesus' activity (see p. 59 for the importance of this verse in the struc-

ture of the Gospel). At the heart of this new ministry is proclamation of a message identical with that of John the Baptist (3:2), and later to be echoed by Jesus' disciples (10:7). Jesus calls for a decisive response (see on 3:2 for *repent*) to a new situation, the arrival in his ministry of *the kingdom of heaven* (again see on 3:2; and pp. 45–46).

*(ii) The call of four disciples (4:18–22)*
The inclusion of this short narrative in the introduction to the Galilean ministry is necessary not only for the literary purpose of providing the primary audience for the teaching in chapters 5 – 7 (see on 5:1–2), but also because the disciples form an essential element in many aspects of Jesus' ministry to be described in the following chapters. Only the call of Matthew is separately described later (9:9); otherwise these four are intended to be taken as typical of the disciple group. Three of them also formed the 'core group' who were to share some particularly intimate experiences with Jesus (17:1; 26:37; Mk. 5:37; 13:3). Luke 5:1–11 gives a fuller and independent narrative of this incident, of which Matthew typically gives only the details relevant to his immediate purpose.[1]

**18.** The *Sea of Galilee* (*cf.* 15:29), elsewhere in Matthew called simply 'the sea', is more correctly referred to by Luke as the 'lake': it is only some 13 miles by 7 (21 km by 11). Its fishing industry was prosperous, and its *fishermen* not necessarily poor (Zebedee's family employed workers, Mk. 1:20). *Simon* and *Andrew* were from Bethsaida (Jn. 1:44), but had settled in Capernaum (8:5,14). Simon's name is Jewish but Andrew's (like that of Philip, also of Bethsaida, Jn. 1:44; *cf.* Jn. 12:20–22) is Greek, reflecting the mixed culture of Galilee. Simon's 'nickname', *Peter*, is also Greek, but reflects an original Aramaic *Kêpā'*, 'rock' (Jn. 1:42; 1 Cor. 9:5; Gal. 2:9; *etc.*); it was given to him by Jesus (Mk. 3:16; Jn. 1:42).

**19.** *Follow me* (literally 'come behind me') would immediately suggest the disciples of a Rabbi (see Davies, pp. 422–423), who literally followed him around to absorb his teaching, though this was by their own choice, not by his summons. A good teacher

[1]See, however, L. Morris, *Tyndale Commentary* on *Luke* (1974), p. 112, for the view that Luke records a separate incident.

would be expected to have a group of such 'followers'. But Jesus calls his disciples not only to listen and learn, but to take an active part as *fishers of men*. Jeremiah 16:16 had spoken of fishing for men, but this was to catch them for judgment (*cf*. Am.4:2); Jesus' 'fishermen' will save men from judgment.

**20.** The ready response of the fishermen here and in v. 22 indicates the authority of Jesus' summons. It was not their first meeting (Jn. 1:35–42; *cf*. Lk. 5:3), but it was the first time Jesus had demanded their literally leaving home to join him in his itinerant ministry. It did not involve disposing of home and property or a severing of family ties (*e.g*. 8:14; Jn. 21:3), but it would bring a complete disruption of their normal way of life (*cf*. 19:27–29).

**21–22.** *James and John* were partners with the other two (Lk. 5:10), and John may have been one of those who had already met Jesus by the Jordan (the unnamed disciple of Jn. 1:35–40). By adding *immediately* and mentioning the abandonment of *the boat* and *their father* separately (*cf*. Mk. 1:20) Matthew emphasizes the extent and the readiness of their renunciation.

*(iii) Summary of the public ministry (4:23–25)*

Short summaries are a feature of Matthew's Gospel. *Cf*. 9:35 (verbally almost identical with 4:23); 8:16; 12:15; 14:35–36; 15:30–31; 19:1–2. This rather longer summary establishes the general pattern of Jesus' activity into which the incidents in following chapters will fit. It also shows again Matthew's interest in the geographical extent of Jesus' activity,[1] distinguishing the extent of his actual movements (v. 23), of his reputation (v. 24), and of the area from which crowds came to him (v. 25).

**23.** Jesus' own activity in this period was confined, according to Matthew (with few exceptions: 8:28; 15:21; 16:13), to *Galilee* alone. The mention of *synagogues* and of *the* (Jewish) *people* (see on 1:21) suggests that it was concentrated on the Jewish part of Galilee's mixed population (*cf*. 10:5–6; 15:24); two accounts of healing of Gentiles in this section both emphasize the exceptional nature of the occasion (see on 8:5–13; 15:21–28). His minis-

---

[1]*Cf*. 2:13–23; 4:12–16, and see my article in *NTS* 27 (1980/1), pp. 237–240.

try is summarized under three headings: *teaching in their synagogues* (*i.e.* biblical exposition, as in Lk. 4:16ff.), *preaching the
gospel of the kingdom* (*i.e.* public proclamation, as in 4:17), and
*healing*, in which the power of the kingdom of heaven was
actually brought into operation (*cf.* 12:28); John had preached the
same message, but in Jesus' ministry what for John was future
became present, and God's kingdom became a reality. *Gospel*
means 'good news', and *gospel of the kingdom* is used by Matthew
here and in 9:35; 24:14 (*cf.* 26:13) as a summary of the message of
Jesus and of his disciples, that in him the kingdom of heaven
has arrived (*cf.* Kingsbury, pp. 128ff.).

**24.** While Jesus remained in Galilee, his reputation spread
*throughout all Syria* (probably in the Old Testament sense meaning the regions neighbouring Israel to the north and north-east,
not the much larger Roman province of Syria). The variety of
healings specifically recorded in the Gospels amply justifies this
list of *various diseases*. The exorcism of *demoniacs*, usually distinguished from physical healing (see on 8:16), is here included as
an aspect of the practical effect of the coming of the kingdom of
heaven.

**25.** Jesus' following was drawn not only from *Galilee*, the area
of his actual activity, but also from *Judea* to the south, and to the
east from both *Decapolis* (a largely Gentile confederacy) and
Peraea (*beyond the Jordan*, now in its normal Jewish sense, in
contrast with 4:15), which together covered the Old Testament
Gilead; thus the whole ancient 'holy land' (with the exception of
Samaria, which Matthew nowhere mentions except to exclude
it; see on 10:5) responded to the coming of the Messiah.

### B. JESUS' TEACHING ON DISCIPLESHIP (5:1 – 7:29)

The 'Sermon on the Mount' is a collection of Jesus' teaching
bearing in different ways on the theme of discipleship. Much of
it is found only in Matthew, but roughly a half of it has parallels
in Luke, which are, however, located in various parts of his
Gospel. Some of these are verbally identical; others differ radically in wording while retaining the same sense; while others
are superficially similar in form, but convey a different message.
All this suggests that these chapters do not represent a single

actual sermon. But the sermon recorded in Luke 6:20–49, while very much shorter than Matthew 5 – 7, is mostly paralleled in these chapters, much of it in the same order; each 'sermon' begins with a set of 'beatitudes' (though with very different orientation, as we shall see), and each ends with the parable of the two house-builders (though the form and wording of the parables is strikingly different). It is likely, therefore, that Matthew's collection has been structured around an existing sermon 'outline' which Luke also knew (just as each of the other 'discourses' is an expansion of a shorter section of teaching found in Mark). See above, pp. 59–60, for Matthew's major collections of Jesus' teaching.[1]

On this understanding of the nature of the 'sermon', the teaching is throughout the teaching of Jesus, but much of the structure derives from Matthew. Much may therefore be learnt of Matthew's special emphases and of his understanding of Jesus' teaching by studying the way he has put the various sayings of Jesus together.

The theme of this, Matthew's longest and most wide-ranging collection of Jesus' teaching, is indicated by the stated audience (see on 5:1–2); it deals with the character, duties, attitudes and dangers of the Christian disciple. It is a manifesto setting out the nature of life in the kingdom of heaven.

The Sermon thus makes no claim to present an ethic for all men; indeed much of it would make no sense as a universal code. It is concerned not with ethics in general, but with discipleship, with man in his obedience and devotion to God, not with a pattern for society. To interpret it legalistically as a set of rules is to miss the point; it represents a demand more radical than any legislator could conceive, going far beyond what human nature can meet, a demand for perfection (5:48). And central to it is the person of Jesus himself: for his sake the disciples are to be persecuted (5:11); he sets before them his own interpretation of the will of God (5:17–48: 'I say to you . . .'); their eternal destiny depends on their relation to him (7:21–23) and their response to his teaching (7:24–27). The Sermon is thus far from being just a collection of moral precepts. It presents the radical

[1]On the literary character and origin of chapters 5 – 7 see further, Guelich, pp. 33–36.

demand of Jesus the Messiah on all who respond to his preaching of God's kingdom. 'The Sermon on the Mount compels us, in the first place, to ask who he is who utters these words.'[1]

### (i) Introduction (5:1–2)

*The mountain* is not a specific place, but a general term, as we might say 'into the hills' (cf. 14:23; 15:29; 28:16, none of which specifies the exact place; contrast 4:8; 17:1, where 'a high mountain' indicates a specific, though unidentified, peak). It indicates the steeply rising ground to the west of the lake of Galilee. Such 'retreats' to the quiet of the hills, for prayer and teaching, are a regular feature of Jesus' ministry. It is therefore unlikely that any allusion is here intended to Moses' ascent of the specific peak of Sinai to receive the law, thus portraying Jesus as a new lawgiver like Moses. The parallels drawn with Moses in chapter 2 and, perhaps, in 4:1–11, and the later mention of Moses on the 'high mountain' in 17:3, show that the relation of Jesus to Moses was a live issue, but this is in his character as a deliverer and prophet, and thus a type of the Messiah. The Sermon on the Mount will present Jesus as much more than another lawgiver, and its explicit comparison of Jesus' teaching with the Mosaic law will stress newness as much as continuity (5:17–48).[2] Jesus is depicted sitting (the correct posture for formal teaching: cf. 13:2; 23:2; 24:3; 26:55; Lk. 4:20), with *his disciples* round him. *The crowds*, apparently here left behind, are found in 7:28–29 to have been also listening, but that can only be as a more remote audience, for passages like 5:11–16 are clearly addressed only to disciples. Perhaps a rigid distinction between disciples and crowd should not be pressed: there were varying degrees of commitment. But the primary audience is clearly the 'insiders'.

### (ii) The advantages of discipleship (5:3–10)

'Beatitudes' (*i.e.* statements of the type 'Blessed is/are . . .') are found elsewhere in Matthew (11:6; 13:16; 16:17; 24:46) and more frequently in Luke. They are based on a common form of expres-

---

[1]Davies, p. 435. For the nature and purpose of these chapters see further Guelich, pp. 27–33.
[2]See Davies, pp. 25–93, with summary pp. 92f.; Banks, pp. 229–235.

sion in the poetical books of the Old Testament (*e.g.* Pss. 1:1; 32:1-2; 40:4; 119:1-2; 128:1), but nowhere in the Old Testament or other Jewish literature is there so long and carefully constructed a series as here. (Ecclus. 25:7-9 is the nearest parallel, but it does not match the formal structure of this passage.) Psalm 15, listing the qualities required for admission to the 'hill of the Lord', is similar in its conception, but not in its form. The finely balanced structure of these eight sayings is one of the best examples of the way Jesus designed his teaching for easy memorization (note the rhythmical structure, and the correspondence of the second clause in the first and last beatitudes). An element of alliteration in the Greek (the first four qualities all begin with *p*) must presumably be attributed to the translator of the original Aramaic, where no such alliteration can be reconstructed.

The beatitudes of Luke 6:20-22 are often regarded as a variant of the same original saying. But not only are they only four in number, and balanced by four 'woes' not found in Matthew; they are also cast in a second-person form, unlike the third-person form of Matthew and of the Old Testament parallels. Moreover, the contents of Luke's beatitudes, while superficially similar to Matthew's first, second, fourth and eighth, are significantly different in emphasis, as they (and the 'woes') concentrate on the material distress of Jesus' disciples at the time ('you'), while Matthew's deal with the spiritual qualities of all who enter the kingdom of heaven. In view of the many Old Testament precedents, there is no improbability in Jesus' use of the beatitude form on separate occasions and with different emphases. Certainly neither of these distinctive sets of beatitudes is best served by interpreting it as a variant of the other; their aims are clearly different.

'Blessed' is a misleading translation of *makarios*, which does not denote one whom God blesses (which would be *eulogētos*, reflecting Heb. *bārûk*), but represents the Hebrew *'ašrê*, 'fortunate', and is used, like *'ašrê*, almost entirely in the formal setting of a beatitude. It introduces someone who is to be congratulated, someone whose place in life is an enviable one. 'Happy' is better than 'blessed', but only if used not of a mental state but of a condition of life. 'Fortunate' or 'well off' is less ambiguous. It is not a psychological description, but a recommendation.

The beatitudes thus outline the attitudes of the true disciple, the one who has accepted the demands of God's kingdom, in contrast with the attitudes of the 'man of the world'; and they present this as the best way of life not only in its intrinsic goodness but in its results. The rewards of discipleship are therefore spelt out in the second half of each verse. The tenses are future, except in the first and last, indicating that the best is yet to come, when God's kingdom is finally established and its subjects enter into their inheritance. But the present tense of vv. 3 and 10 warns us against an exclusively future interpretation, for God rewards these attitudes with their respective results progressively in the disciple's experience. The emphasis is not so much on time, present or future, as on the *certainty* that discipleship will not be in vain.

**3.** *Poor in spirit* warns us immediately that the thought here is not (as it is in Lk. 6:20) of material poverty. The phrase alludes to an Old Testament theme which underlies all the beatitudes, that of the 'poor' or 'meek' (*'ānî* or *'ānāw*) who occur frequently in the Psalms and elsewhere (N.B. Is. 61:1–2, alluded to in v. 4, and Ps. 37, alluded to in v. 5), those who humbly trust God, even though their loyalty results in oppression and material disadvantage, in contrast with the 'wicked' who arrogantly set themselves up against God and persecute his people. The emphasis is on piety and suffering, and on dependence on God, not on material poverty as such. In later Jewish writings, particularly the Psalms of Solomon and the Qumran literature ('poor in spirit' occurs in 1QM 14:7), 'the poor' continues to denote the faithful and persecuted people of God, whom he will ultimately vindicate. This humble, 'unworldly' attitude, which puts its trust only in God (G. Barth, *TIM*, pp. 123–124, uses the phrase 'empty before God') is the mark of the disciple; the kingdom of heaven belongs to (perhaps better 'consists of') such men. They are God's people.

**4.** *Those who mourn* are not necessarily the bereaved, or even the penitent. They are the suffering, those whose life is, from a worldly point of view, an unhappy one, and particularly those who suffer for their loyalty to God (see on v. 3). The verse echoes Isaiah 61:2, which promises consolation as a part of the

Messiah's work. In God's salvation they will find a happiness which transcends their worldly condition. The use of the passive *they shall be comforted* is a Semitic idiom for what God will do. So also in vv. 6, 7, 9.

**5.** *The meek* echoes the same Old Testament idea as the 'poor in spirit'. They are those who do not throw their weight about, but rely on God to give them their due. Meekness as a characteristic of Jesus' own ministry is stressed by Matthew (11:29; 12:15–21; 21:5). The promise to the meek is quoted from Psalm 37:11 (a psalm concerned throughout with the contrasting attitudes and destiny of the 'meek' and the 'wicked'). The possession of 'the land' there refers primarily to Palestine, though the idea is more generally of the meek supplanting the wicked. Jesus applies it not territorially, but in terms of the ultimate vindication of the meek. God will give them the high place they would not seize for themselves.

**6.** For spiritual *hunger and thirst cf.* Psalm 42:1–2; Isaiah 55:1–2. For *righteousness* in Matthew see on 3:15; the meaning here will be that their one desire is for a relationship of obedience and trust with God. It is thus a personal aspiration, not a desire for social justice. The idea of 'vindication' (a regular meaning of ṣᵉḏāqâ, 'righteousness', in the Old Testament), or of 'justification' (*dikaiosynē*, 'righteousness', often carries this sense in Paul, but probably not in Matthew) may be implied in the promise that this desire *shall be satisfied*, but the ultimate satisfaction of a relationship with God unclouded by disobedience is chiefly in view.

**7.** The importance of *mercy*, and its reciprocal nature, is stressed in Matthew (6:12, 14–15; 9:13; 12:7; 18:21–35; 23:23). For the reciprocal principle *cf.* Psalm 18:25–26, and conversely Job 22:9–10; Proverbs 21:13; *etc.* For the practical character of mercy see on 9:27.

**8.** *Cf.* Psalm 24:3–4. *Pure in heart* should not be restricted to moral, still less sexual, purity; it denotes one who loves God with all his heart (Dt. 6:5), with an undivided loyalty, and whose inward nature corresponds with his outward profession (*cf.* Is. 29:13). 'Such is the generation of those who seek him' (Ps. 24:6), and they receive the promise that *they shall see God*. This can only fully be realized in heaven, when 'we shall see him as he is' (1 Jn. 3:2); then 'we shall be like him', and the longings of v. 6 will be finally satisfied. But in a lesser sense the vision of God is already the experience of his true lovers on earth, who persevere in his service 'as seeing him who is invisible' (Heb. 11:27).

**9.** In a world characterized by conflict and rivalry, a keeper of the peace is rare, a *peacemaker* still rarer. The absence of selfish ambition which has marked the earlier beatitudes provides the only basis for this quality, which is particularly pleasing to God (Ps. 34:14). God is the supreme peacemaker (*cf.* Eph. 2:14–18; Col. 1:20) and this quality marks disciples out as his *sons*, for the son shares the characteristics of the father.

**10.** *Righteousness*, as in v. 6, is more than just 'being good'. It indicates a whole orientation of life towards God and his will. Such a life is conspicuous (*cf.* vv. 14–16), and so attracts persecution, as vv. 11–12 will explain further. *For theirs is the kingdom of heaven* echoes v. 3, thus rounding off the series, and marking it as one composite whole, not a list of optional additions. This God-like character, in its entirety, should be progressively seen in all true disciples, because only where it is found is *the kingdom of heaven*, God's control, really effective.

*(iii) The distinctiveness of the disciple (5:11–16)*
From a general description of the disciple character, the Sermon now turns to a direct address to Jesus' disciples, and indicates the effect that character is to have in their life and witness. (See Davies, pp. 249–251, 289–290, for the possibility that a specific contrast with Judaism is intended, portraying the disciples as the true Israel.)

**11–12.** This saying is formally distinct from the beatitudes, despite the opening *makarioi*. It is an expansion (possibly based on Is. 51:7) of the thought of the last beatitude, but now applied directly to the listening disciples, and introducing the contrast between them and other men which is the theme of vv. 13–16. Insult and slander are the forms which persecution of Christians has often taken from the earliest times (see, *e.g.*, 10:24–25; 1 Pet. 3:16; 4:4, 14–16). Since Jesus himself was abused and slandered, it should be no surprise that his followers receive the same treatment *on my account* (*cf.* 10:18; 24:9). Indeed it should make

111

them *glad* (*cf.* the same verb in 1 Pet. 1:6; 4:13), because it shows that they are in the true succession of God's faithful servants. See 23:29-37 for the theme of persecution of *the prophets* (and *cf.* 13:57; 17:12; Lk. 13:33); the saying does not necessarily view the disciples as prophets, but places them, with Jesus himself, in line with those whose stand for God has incurred the hostility of the world. On *reward*, see Jeremias, *NTT*, pp. 215–217; the idea is frequent in Jesus' teaching (it was already implicit in 5:3–10), not in the sense of an earned payment (this idea is excluded, *e.g.*, by Lk. 17:10) but of a freely given recompense, out of all proportion to the service (19:29; 25:21,23). *In heaven* means not so much 'after death' as 'with God'.

**13.** *Salt* serves mainly to give flavour, and to prevent corruption. Disciples, if they are true to their calling, make *the earth* a purer and a more palatable place. But they can do so only as long as they preserve their distinctive character: unsalty salt has no more value. Strictly, pure salt cannot lose its salinity; but the impure 'salt' dug from the shores of the Dead Sea could gradually become unsalty as the actual sodium chloride dissolved.[1] In any case, Jesus was not teaching chemistry, but using a proverbial image (it recurs in *Bekhoroth* 8b). The Rabbis commonly used salt as an image for wisdom (*cf.* Col. 4:6), which may explain why the Greek word represented by *lost its taste* actually means 'become foolish'. (Aramaic *tāpēl*, which conveys both meanings, was no doubt the word used by Jesus.) A foolish disciple has no influence on the world.

**14–16.** *Light*, like salt, affects its environment by being distinctive. The disciple who is visibly different from other men will have an effect on them. But the aim of his *good works* is not to parade his own virtue, but to direct attention to the God who inspired them. By so doing the disciple will *give light to all* (*cf.* Phil. 2:15). Jesus is pre-eminently *the light of the world* (Jn. 8:12), as Isaiah had prophesied of the Servant (Is. 42:6; 49:6), but this role passed to his disciples (*cf.* Acts 13:47). The *city set on a hill*, rather awkwardly introduced among the sayings about light, reinforces the importance of being conspicuously different.[2] A

[1] See Jeremias, *PJ*, pp. 168–169; J. R. W. Stott, *Christian Counter-Culture* (1978), p. 60.
[2] G. von Rad, *The Problem of the Hexateuch* (1966), pp. 232–242, finds here the brightness of the eschatological city of God on Mount Zion, but this is to complicate a simple illustration.

*bushel* (grain measure of about 9 litres) put over an oil lamp would probably put it out, so that the meaning could be that a lamp is not lit only to be put out again (Jeremias, *PJ*, pp. 120–121); but the emphasis of the passage is on non-concealment (*cf.* Mk. 4:21; Lk. 8:16, 'under a bed'), so again the 'scientific' implication need not be pressed. A secret disciple is no more use in the world than one who has lost his distinctiveness (v. 13). *Your Father who is in heaven* is a favourite expression in Matthew (*cf.* 5:45; 6:1, 9; 7:11; *etc.*), and reflects a major emphasis in Jesus' teaching. In earlier Jewish thought God was generally the Father of Israel rather than of individuals, though this phrase was coming into use by the first century AD in the latter sense (see *ICC*, p. 44).

*(iv) Jesus' attitude to the Old Testament (5:17–20)*
This controversial passage is a general statement of Jesus' attitude to the Old Testament, especially (but not only: see on v. 17) in its legal provisions, designed to introduce the detailed examples of Jesus' ethical teaching in relation to the Old Testament law in vv. 21–48, and indeed at many points throughout the Gospel. The controversy centres on whether these words affirm the permanent validity of the details of the Old Testament law *as regulations*, or whether they express more generally the God-given authority of the Old Testament without specifying just how it is applicable in the new situation introduced by the coming of Jesus. We shall return to this central issue after dealing with the detailed exegesis.

**17.** It is not unlikely that more legalistically inclined Jews, scandalized by Jesus' radical attitude to, *e.g.*, the sabbath or the laws of uncleanness, accused him of setting out to *abolish the law and the prophets*. The charge, and its rebuttal, would be the more worth recording if Matthew's church included Christians who, like the heretic Marcion in the second century (and like some today), disparaged or completely repudiated the Old Testament. But the emphasis of the saying lies not on the negative but on the positive (*cf.* 10:34 for a similar rhetorical construction): Jesus has come *to fulfil the law and the prophets*. Among the many nuances suggested for *plērōsai*, 'fulfil', the following are the main options: (a) to accomplish, obey; (b) to bring out the full meaning; (c) to complete ('to bring to its destined end', Davies, p. 100), by giving the final revelation of God's will to which the Old Testament pointed forward, and which now transcends it (*cf.* the double meaning of Rom. 10:4, 'Christ is the *end* of the law': he both completes and transcends it). It is doubtful if any single translation or even paraphrase can do justice to *plērōsai* here, but (c) points in the right direction. (a) may be immediately rejected: it is not a normal meaning of the verb; it hardly fits 'the prophets'; and it does not suitably contrast with *abolish*, which was a matter of teaching not of action. (b) is true to what Jesus will do in vv. 21ff., but is inadequate as a translation of *plērōsai*, which is normally used in Matthew (as in the LXX) of bringing into being that which was promised. This Matthaean usage, seen especially in the introductory formulae to the formula-quotations (see pp. 38–40), and in 26:54, 56, must surely be determinative for its use here. This is reinforced by the mention of *the prophets*, whose writings are 'fulfilled' when what they looked forward to happens. *The law and the prophets* is a regular Jewish name for the entire Old Testament (*cf.* 7:12; 22:40; Acts 24:14; 28:23; Rom. 3:21) and occurs again in 11:13, with the verb 'prophesied'. So the whole Old Testament, the law as well as the prophets, pointed forward to what Jesus has now brought into being. His ministry brings them to full measure (*cf. plēroō* in 23:32), by supplying the final revelation of the will of God (see Jeremias, *NTT*, pp. 84–85). In the background may be the Jewish expectation (based on, *e.g.*, Is. 2:3; Je. 31:31ff.) that the Messiah's role would include the definitive exposition of the law, sometimes amounting virtually to the promulgation of a new law (see Davies, pp. 183–190). This complex of ideas then lies behind *plērōsai*: Jesus is bringing that to which the Old Testament looked forward; his teaching will transcend the Old Testament revelation, but, far from abolishing it, is itself its intended culmination.[1]

**18.** *Truly* (Greek *Amēn*), *I say to you* is Jesus' own signature: no other teacher is known to have used it. Matthew records it 31 times, John (with a double *Amēn*) 25 times. It serves, like the prophets' 'Thus says the LORD', to mark a saying as important

---

[1]See further, Barth, *TIM*, pp. 67–69; Banks, pp. 208–210.

and authoritative. The saying so introduced is similar to Luke 16:17, and affirms that *the law* (possibly, in the light of v. 17, meaning the whole Old Testament, though v. 19 will speak specifically of 'commandments') will remain intact *till heaven and earth pass away*. (Jesus' own words will remain even longer: 24:35! But the expression is probably less a specific note of time than an idiom for something inconceivable.) The *iota* (the letter *yôḏ*) is the smallest Hebrew letter, and is often optional in spelling; the *dot* (*keraia*, 'horn') may be either the similar letter *wāw* (which is equally optional), or the 'serif' which distinguishes some similar Hebrew letters. The Rabbis discussed at length the destructive effects of such minute alterations to a single letter of the law (*Leviticus Rabbah* 19:2). It is inconceivable that the law should be altered *until all is accomplished*. Three interpretations are possible. (a) 'Until the end of the world'; but this would be a unique use of the phrase, and would merely repeat the earlier part of the verse. (b) 'Until all its requirements are met'; but *is accomplished* (*genētai*) means literally 'happens', and is used of events, not of things 'being done'. (c) 'Until what it looks forward to arrives'; this both does justice to *genētai* (N.B. 24:34, where virtually the same clause has this meaning), and links this verse with the thought of v. 17 (and the *for* with which it opens demands such a link). It is, then, Jesus' 'fulfilment' of the Old Testament which is in view here. The law remains valid until it reaches its intended culmination; this it is now doing in the ministry and teaching of Jesus.[1] This verse does not state, therefore, as it is sometimes interpreted, that every regulation in the Old Testament law remains binding after the coming of Jesus. The law is unalterable, but that does not justify its application beyond the purpose for which it was intended.

**19.** Like the previous two verses, this one warns the disciples against altering or setting aside any part of the law, however small. (*Relaxes* is from the same root as *abolish* in v. 17, and means to 'set aside' or 'teach against' a commandment, rather than to disobey it; 'loose' in 16:19; 18:18 is the same verb. NIV 'breaks' is therefore inappropriate.) That this is Jesus' teaching for his own disciples, not a traditional Jewish saying, is indicated by

---

[1]W. D. Davies argues in *Mélanges Bibliques rédigés en l'honneur de André Robert* (1957), pp. 428–456, that the reference is more specifically to the death of Jesus.

*the kingdom of heaven*: disrespect for the Old Testament makes a poor Christian. (*Least* is used chiefly for its rhetorical effect echoing the *least* commandment, though clearly within the kingdom of heaven there are those who are more or less consistent and effective in their discipleship; the thought is of quality of discipleship, not of ultimate rewards.) The good disciple will *do* and *teach* the commandments: he will go beyond lip-service, to be guided by them in his life and teaching. Does this mean literal observance of every regulation? Not if we may judge by vv. 21–48 and, *e.g.*, Jesus' attitude to the laws of uncleanness (15:1–20; *cf.* Mk. 7:19). The question of interpretation and application remains open: it is the attitude of respect and obedience which is demanded, and to this no single commandment can be an exception. (Banks, pp. 220–223, avoids the apparent legalism of the verse by interpreting *these commandments* as the teaching of Jesus, not the Old Testament law; but *commandment* (*entolē*) elsewhere in Matthew always refers to the Old Testament law, and *the least of these commandments* would certainly be so understood here, following the reference to the details of the law in v. 18 which is linked to this verse by an inferential *then*.)

**20.** This verse dispels any suspicion of legalism which v. 19 might have raised. The *scribes* (professional students and teachers of the law) *and Pharisees* (members of a largely lay movement devoted to scrupulous observance both of the Old Testament law and of the still developing legal traditions), whose obedience to 'the least of these commandments' could not be faulted, do not thereby qualify for *the kingdom of heaven* (whereas the disciple who relaxes the commandments does belong to it, though as the 'least'). What is required is a greater *righteousness* (see on 3:15; 5:6, 10), a relationship of love and obedience to God which is more than a literal observance of regulations. It is such a 'righteousness' which fulfils the law and the prophets (v. 17), and which will be illustrated in vv. 21–48 (in contrast with the legalism of the scribes) and in 6:1–18 (in contrast with the superficial 'piety' of the Pharisees).

The main points of vv. 17–20 may now be paraphrased as follows:

'¹⁷I have not come to set aside the Old Testament, but to bring the fulfilment to which it pointed. ¹⁸For no part of it can ever be set aside, but all must be fulfilled (as it is now being fulfilled in my ministry and teaching). [19]So a Christian who repudiates any part of the Old Testament is an inferior Christian; the consistent Christian will be guided by the Old Testament, and will teach others accordingly. [20]But a truly Christian attitude is not the legalism of the scribes and Pharisees, but a deeper commitment to do the will of God, as vv. 21ff. will illustrate.'

This passage does not therefore state that every Old Testament regulation is eternally valid. This view is not found anywhere in the New Testament, which consistently sees Jesus as introducing a new situation, for which the law prepared (Gal. 3:24), but which now transcends it. The focus is now on Jesus and his teaching, and in this light the validity of Old Testament rules must now be examined. Some will be found to have fulfilled their role and be no longer applicable (see especially Hebrews on the ritual laws, and Jesus' teaching on uncleanness, Mk. 7:19), others will be reinterpreted. Matthew 5:21ff. will be dealing with this reinterpretation, and vv. 17–20 can only truly be understood as an introduction to vv. 21ff. To assert, as these verses do, that every detail of the Old Testament is God-given and unalterable, is not to pre-empt the question of its proper application. If the law pointed forward to a new situation which has now arrived, that question arises with new urgency, and vv. 21ff. will go on to indicate some answers to it. Their answers will be the opposite of legalism (the literal and unchanging application of the law as regulations), as v. 20 has already indicated.

*(v) Examples of Jesus' radical ethic (5:21–48)*
This long section is clearly designed to be read as a whole, consisting of six units of teaching each introduced by 'You have heard that it was said . . . But I say to you . . .', and rounded off with a summary of Jesus' ethical demand in v. 48. It is neither a complete ethic, nor a theological statement of general ethical principles, but a series of varied examples of how Jesus' principles, enunciated in vv. 17–20, work out in practice. And this practical outworking is set in explicit contrast with the ethical rules previously accepted: it is in each case more demanding, more far-reaching in its application, more at variance with the ethics of man without God; it concerns a man's motives and

attitudes more than his literal conformity to the rules. In this sense, it is radical.

In Rabbinic literature 'I (might) hear' is a formula to introduce a literal but misleading understanding of the law, to which is then opposed what you must 'say', a less literal but truer interpretation (see Daube, pp. 55–62). *Cf.* John 12:34 for 'we have heard' introducing a theme of scriptural teaching. *It was said* (*errethē*) is not used elsewhere in the New Testament as a quotation formula (except in Rom. 9:12, where it introduces direct speech from the Old Testament, meaning 'God said'), but the participle *rhēthen* ('what was spoken') introduces Matthew's formula-quotations, and 'it was said' is commonly used to introduce biblical quotations in Rabbinic literature. The audience to whom *it was said* is twice specified (vv. 21, 33) as *the men of old*, which, followed immediately in v. 21 by a direct quotation from the Decalogue, could only mean those to whom the law was given at Sinai; it certainly cannot refer to Jesus' contemporaries. Thus Jesus' repeated formula, unique to this passage, seems to introduce a literal understanding of the Old Testament law. To this he then contrasts his own more discerning exegesis: *but I say to you* (*cf.* the Rabbinic terminology mentioned above). The emphatic and repeated use of *I* is striking, and is rightly regarded as a mark of Jesus' assumption of an authority overriding that of the scribes. This is not a new contribution to exegetical debate, but a definitive declaration of the will of God. It demands (and receives, 7:28–29) the response, 'Who is this?' Thus this passage contributes another aspect to the presentation of Jesus as the Messiah which is Matthew's overriding purpose.

The question is often raised whether Jesus is here merely reinterpreting the Old Testament law (by pointing to its fundamental implications, in contrast with current legalistic application) or going so far as to abrogate it (this is suggested particularly with reference to vv. 31–32, 38ff.). This will be discussed in the detailed exegesis, but we should not expect a simple answer to such a general question from six quite varied pieces of teaching. The introductory formula introduces sometimes a literal Old Testament quotation, sometimes a summary or expansion or even apparently a perversion of an Old Testament law. The treatment varies from a radical intensification of the laws against murder and adultery but with no suggestion of weakening their literal force (vv. 21ff., 27ff.), to an apparent setting aside of the law of equivalent retribution in favour of forgoing legal rights (vv. 38ff.). No consistent pattern of argument need therefore be discerned, beyond the formal contrast of Jesus' radical ethic with what was previously taught. The emphasis is on Jesus' teaching rather than on his relationship to either the Old Testament law or scribal tradition. It is to legalism as a principle, not to a specific code of law, that he is stating his opposition. How this attitude will relate to the application of Old Testament regulations can therefore be expected to vary from one case to another, as we shall see that it does. Jesus' radical ethic takes its starting-point from the Old Testament law, but does not so much either confirm or abrogate it as transcend it. (Cf. the conclusions on 5:17–20, above, pp. 116–117.)

(a) *Murder and anger (5:21–26)*. **21.** The prohibition of murder (Ex. 20:13; *kill* is inadequate to translate *phoneuō*, which, like its Hebrew counterpart, refers to criminal killing) is expanded by a clause, not itself from the Old Testament, which summarizes the Old Testament teaching on the penalty for murder (*e.g.* Gn. 9:6; Ex. 21:12–14; Nu. 35:16–34). *Liable to judgment* can therefore only imply the death-penalty, but the term *judgment* is used perhaps to differentiate this judicial killing from the murder it punishes. The reference is probably, in the light of the Old Testament background, to judgment by a human court, but the next verse will go beyond this to the divine judgment.

**22.** Jesus goes behind the act of murder itself to declare that the anger and hatred which give rise to it, though not capable of being examined in a human court, are no less culpable in the sight of God. The continued validity of the sixth commandment is assumed, but a legalistic interpretation which restricts its application to the literal act alone is rejected. The three parallel statements of v. 22, the first part of each indicating the attitude Jesus condemns and the second its due penalty (each deliberately echoing v. 21, *liable to . . .*), are making the same point in different ways, and should not be interpreted as dealing with different sins. Anger against a *brother*[1] was already condemned in, *e.g.*, Leviticus 19:17–18 (the 'neighbour' there being a fellow-Israelite; *brother* in the New Testament often indicates a fellow-disciple, but Jesus did not encourage parochial loyalty: Lk. 10:29ff.). It expresses itself in such insulting language as 'Raca' (*insults* is literally 'says Raca to'; *Raca*, literally 'empty', is an Aramaic term of abuse, 'idiot') and *You fool!* These are not uncommon or particularly vulgar words (Jesus himself used the latter, 23:17; *cf.* Jas. 2:20), but they suggest an attitude of angry contempt. This attitude renders a man *liable to judgment* (here the judgment of God; it is a favourite word of Matthew in this sense, and does not elsewhere refer to a human court except in v. 21 where it echoes Old Testament language), *to the council* (*synedrion*, either the supreme Jewish council or a local court, *cf.* 10:17, but in this context probably used to symbolize a more ultimate judgment) and *to the hell of fire* (*gehenna*, the name of the place where Jerusalem's rubbish was burnt, used regularly by Jesus, as by Jewish writers, for the place of ultimate punishment). So, in contrast with the human court's verdict on murder in v. 21, Jesus here threatens ultimate divine judgment on anger, even as expressed in everyday insults. As often, Jesus exaggerates to make his point. Anger was condemned in the Old Testament, but never equated with murder; Jesus makes it just as bad! Insulting language was punished at Qumran with periods of penance (1QS 6:25 – 7:9), but Jesus says it deserves hell. This is not an injunction merely to avoid certain abusive expressions (that would be another form of legalism) but to submit our thoughts about other people, as well as the words they give rise to, to God's penetrating scrutiny.

**23–24.** If God will punish anger, we cannot worship him with grudges unsettled. The prophets made much of the futility of worship without a corresponding purity of life (*e.g.* Is. 1:10–17; Je. 7:8–11; Am. 5:21–24; Mi. 6:6–8; *cf.* Ps. 24:3–4). Jesus elsewhere demanded a forgiving attitude of those who sought God's forgiveness (6:14–15; 18:21–35). Here it is the worshipper himself who is at fault, and who therefore has it in his power to put matters right. Only so is his worship acceptable. The *gift* is

---

[1] *Without cause*, RSV mg., is apparently an early insertion to soften Jesus' strong condemnation.

presumably an animal sacrifice, to offer which a layman was allowed to enter the Court of the Priests where the *altar* stood. Jesus' instruction to interrupt such a solemn occasion indicates the importance of the demand. Its application is of course far wider than the specific occasion of a sacrifice in the temple in Jerusalem, which would be a very rare, and therefore significant, experience for his Galilean audience.

**25–26.** A further illustration stresses the urgency of reconciliation. A grievance unsettled can lead, in human terms, to court and to prison. But in this context it is improbable that Jesus was giving no more than prudential advice. The solemn *truly, I say to you* (see on 5:18) suggests a less trivial purpose; the parallel in Luke 12:58–59 is in a context of eschatological urgency, and the other parable of debt and imprisonment (Mt. 18:23–35) is also concerned with God's punishment of the unmerciful. Following the stress on God's judgment on anger in v. 22, this short parable (it should not be taken as a detailed allegory) warns that neglected grievances can have irrevocable consequences, and time may be short. *The last penny* (the *quadrans*, the smallest Roman coin) indicates that God's judgment, if not forestalled by repentance and reconciliation, knows no half-measures.

*(b) Adultery (5:27–30).* **27–28.** The seventh commandment is treated like the sixth: not only the act of adultery but the lust which causes it is condemned. *Woman (gynē)* is used almost always of married women, and often means 'wife'; Jesus' intention is therefore to prohibit not a natural sexual attraction, but the deliberate harbouring of desire for an illicit relationship. (*Lustfully* is literally 'in order to desire her', 'desire' being used generally of desire for something forbidden.) Exodus 20:17 had condemned coveting another man's wife; Jesus here emphasizes that such coveting is not only implicit theft (Ex. 20:17 includes the wife among other items of property!) but implicit adultery. Other Jewish teachers made similar statements both before and after Jesus (Banks, p. 190), but did not parallel the severity of the following verses.

**29–30.** Thus the *eye*, which should keep us from stumbling, can in fact 'trip us up' (the basic meaning of *cause to sin, skan-*

121

*dalizō*, which is always used metaphorically in the New Testament). The parallel saying about the *right hand* is included more for emphasis than to make a separate point (a very similar saying in 18:8–9 includes the foot as well). As in v. 22, Jesus makes his point memorable by exaggeration; the self-mutilation is not to be taken literally, but indicates that the avoidance of temptation may involve drastic sacrifices (the *right hand* is the more valuable), which may include the severing of relationships or the renunciation of favourite activities. The alternative is the loss of the *whole body* (*i.e.* the complete person) in *gehenna* (see on v. 22 and on 10:28).

(c) *Divorce (5:31–32)*. The question of divorce recurs in 19:3–9, and the commentary there should also be consulted.

**31.** The words are based on Deuteronomy 24:1, but are not an exact quotation of it. In Deuteronomy 24:1–4 the main clause is not reached until v. 4, the prohibition of the reunion of a divorced couple after the woman has remarried and her second marriage has ended (by divorce or the husband's death). The original divorce, with its formal certificate (v. 1), is simply assumed, but neither here nor elsewhere in the Old Testament is divorce explicitly approved. This passage was, however, universally accepted among Jesus' contemporaries as permitting a husband to divorce his wife (not vice versa); 19:7 shows that not only the certificate (as here) but the divorce itself was regarded as 'commanded' by Moses. This hardening of the Mosaic acceptance of divorce as a *fact* into a legal precept was a logical deduction, legalistic but not illegitimate. The permissible grounds for divorce were debated: while the school of Shammai restricted the 'some indecency' of Deuteronomy 24:1 to refer only to a sexual misdemeanour authenticated by witnesses, actual practice was governed by the school of Hillel, who reputedly took it of any cause of complaint, even including burning the dinner. (Mishnah *Gittin* 9:10. For actual practice, see Josephus, *Ant*. iv. 253; *Vita* 426.) No court decision was required, only unilateral action by the husband.

**32.** Jesus, by contrast both with current scribal practice and with the implied permission of Deuteronomy 24:1–2, regards the remarriage of a divorced woman[1] as adultery both on her part and on the part of her new husband. Notice that the blame for this adultery is placed firmly on the man whose action caused it, not on the woman. Matthew 19:9 will add that remarriage by the original husband is also adultery. This radical refusal to recognize the validity of divorce will be grounded in 19:3–9 on God's original purpose in creation: marriage is for ever.

*Unchastity* translates *porneia*, the root meaning of which is 'fornication', but it is used more widely, so that it could include premarital unchastity, subsequently discovered. The more natural meaning here is adultery by the wife, and the word is used in this sense, *e.g.*, in Ecclesiasticus 23:23; Hermas, *Mandate* iv. 1.5.[2]

*Except on the ground of unchastity* (*cf.* 19:9, 'except for unchastity') qualifies what is otherwise an absolute prohibition, and this fact, together with the absence of any such qualification in the other reports of Jesus' teaching on divorce in Mark 10:11; Luke 16:18; 1 Corinthians 7:10–11, is generally taken to indicate that the exception in both Matthaean passages is a later legislative addition to Jesus' absolute ideal, with the aim of accommodating it to the harsh realities of the real world. But if, as has just been argued, *unchastity* here means adultery by the wife, the Matthaean clause merely spells out what was taken for granted in current thinking, and is therefore assumed in the other versions, *i.e.* that adultery automatically annuls a marriage by creating a new sexual union in its place. In fact current Jewish law (*e.g.* Mishnah *Yebamoth* 2:8; *Sotah* 5:1) *demanded* the termination of a marriage if either premarital unchastity or adultery was discovered (see on 1:19); in Old Testament times the penalty in either case was death (Dt. 22:20–22), but under Roman rule this could not be enforced. *Cf.* 1 Corinthians 6:15ff. for the idea, based on Genesis 2:24, that sexual union creates a per-

---

[1] *Makes her an adulteress* implies her remarriage, because this was often the only way a divorced wife could survive; Dt. 24:2 expects divorce to be followed by the woman's remarriage.

[2] *Porneia* would not naturally refer, as Bonnard (pp. 68–70) argues, to marriage within the prohibited degrees set out in Lv. 18:6ff.; in 1 Cor. 5:1 it apparently refers not to *marriage* within the prohibited degrees, but to intercourse, which if the father was still alive was in fact adultery.

manent bond. To repudiate a wife after she had committed adultery was therefore simply the recognition that the marriage had already been terminated by the creation of a new union, and as such was mandatory. But 'divorce' proper, the breaking of a marriage which is still intact, is absolutely forbidden. The Matthaean exceptive clause is not therefore introducing a new provision, but making explicit what any Jewish reader would have taken for granted when Jesus made the apparently unqualified pronouncements of Mark 10:9–12. The application of this radical ideal in a society which regards divorce as normal will inevitably raise serious pastoral problems, and will call for great sensitivity. But the problems are not to be escaped by failing to take seriously Jesus' absolute declaration of the will of God – unbroken marriage 'till death us do part'.

*(d) Swearing (5:33–37)*. Oaths and vows were not only permitted but, in certain circumstances, commanded in the Old Testament (*e.g.* Nu. 5:19ff.). Discussions of the relative validity of different forms of oath and vow occupied the Rabbis to the extent of filling several tractates of the Mishnah. But an oath is needed only if a person's word alone is unreliable; it is an admission of failure in truthfulness. Jesus therefore goes behind the whole structure of legislation on oaths to the ideal which it has replaced. The passage, while on the surface concerned with oaths, is thus essentially on truthfulness, focusing on v. 37 rather than v. 34a (Jeremias, *NTT*, p. 220). As with divorce, the accommodating legislation, both in the Old Testament and in later Judaism, is bypassed to return to the ideal which makes it unnecessary.

**33.** The two clauses summarize Old Testament teaching rather than quote it explicitly. *You shall not swear falsely* echoes Leviticus 19:12 (and Ex. 20:7 may also be in mind); *you shall perform to the Lord what you have sworn* takes up the teaching of Numbers 30:2 (v. 3, Heb.); Deuteronomy 23:21 (v. 22, Heb.); Psalm 50:14; Ecclesiastes 5:4 (v. 3, Heb.). All these last are concerned with vows, but Numbers 30:2 mentions oaths as parallel, and the distinction between oaths and vows was generally not kept clear (see Davies, p. 240). The Old Testament thus prohibited both false oaths and unfulfilled oaths or vows.

**34–36.** Jesus' total rejection of oaths (*not . . . at all*) is not paralleled even by the Qumran literature, strict as it was on this issue (Davies, pp. 241–244), and contrasts starkly with the Rabbinic casuistry which he goes on to expose in these verses (*cf.* 23:16–22). That this ideal should not be taken as a rigid rule, *e.g.* with reference to oaths in court, is suggested by Jesus' own response when the High Priest 'put him on oath' (26:63–64), and by occasional 'oaths' in the New Testament (2 Cor. 1:23; Gal. 1:20; *cf.* 1 Thes. 5:27); even God can use an oath (Heb. 6:13–17). But Jesus goes on to repudiate the use of 'second-class' oaths which avoid the name of God (and therefore are not binding). Firstly they do not in fact exclude God, as *heaven*, *earth* and *Jerusalem* are all inseparably linked with God (as Jesus shows by references to Is. 66:1 and Ps. 48:2 (v. 3, Heb.)), and even *your head* is God's creation and under his control. And secondly, as v. 37 shows, they should be unnecessary.

**37.** *Simply 'Yes' or 'No'* is literally 'Yes yes, no no'. The repetition is not a new formula, but a Semitic way of indicating that 'Yes' and 'No' are to be used (alone) on each occasion. (*Cf.* 'two two' in Mk. 6:7 for 'two at a time'.) James 5:12, which is clearly based on this passage, has correctly interpreted the meaning: 'Let your yes be yes and your no be no.' All words are binding, and the Christian's word should need no buttressing. Any addition *comes from evil*, or *the evil one* (RSV mg.): the Greek genitive *ponērou* could be either masculine or neuter, here as often; it makes little difference to the general sense whether the need for safeguards against falsehood is traced to the wickedness of the world in general or to the 'Father of lies'.

*(e) Legal rights (5:38–42).* **38.** The principle of proportionate retribution (here quoted from Ex. 21:24–25; Lv. 24:20; Dt. 19:21) was older and more widely recognized than the Mosaic law, being found already in the Code of Hammurabi (eighteenth century BC) with the same examples of *eye* and *tooth*. Its intention was not to sanction revenge, but to prevent the excesses of the blood-feud by stating that the legal punishment must not exceed the crime. By the time of Jesus physical penalties had generally been replaced by financial damages. What Jesus is opposing here is not therefore brutality, or even physical retaliation, but

the principle of insisting on even legitimate retribution.

**39.** *Do not resist* is wider than 'do not retaliate'; it involves acceptance of ill-treatment, even, as the following examples will show, willing compliance. The verb *anthistēmi* is sometimes used for 'take legal action against'. These verses are not, therefore, a prescription for non-violent resistance (as they are often interpreted), but for no resistance at all, even by legal means. A comparison of the wording of vv. 39-40 with Luke 6:29-30 shows that Matthew's concern is particularly with cases of litigation rather than with violence, and v. 41 is also concerned with legal rights. All the examples deal with the individual's response to other individuals (*one who is evil* represents the same ambiguous phrase as in v. 37, but the context here, with the following series of *if any one . . .* clauses, suggests that RSV is right to take it of an individual wrongdoer rather than of 'evil' as a principle, still less of 'the Evil One'), and there is no warrant for applying these principles to social ethics, still less to politics. A willingness to forgo one's personal rights, and to allow oneself to be insulted and imposed upon, is not incompatible with a firm stand for matters of principle and for the rights of others (*cf.* Pauls's attitude in Acts 16:37; 22:25; 25:8-12). Indeed the principle of just retribution is not so much abrogated here as bypassed, in favour of an attitude which refuses to insist on one's rights, however legitimate. Jesus is not reforming the legal code, but demanding an attitude which sits loose to personal rights. Verses 39b-42 are illustrations of that attitude, not rules to be legalistically applied.

To *strike on the right cheek* was 'a blow with the back of the hand, which even today in the East expresses the greatest possible contempt and extreme abuse' (Jeremias, *NTT*, p. 239); as such it was punishable by a very heavy fine (Mishnah *BK* 8:6). The situation envisaged is thus one of insult rather than of physical violence, and it is possibly to be seen as an aspect of religious persecution (Jeremias, *loc. cit.*). The same verb is used in 26:67 of the ill-treatment of Jesus as a blasphemer, and the words of this verse recall Isaiah 50:6, the Servant's acceptance of insult and ill-treatment. Such acceptance Jesus requires of his disciples, rather than recourse to either retaliation or the law.

**40.** In contrast with the eager litigation of his opponent, the disciple should not only willingly be deprived of his *coat* (the undergarment), but should add his *cloak* (the more valuable upper garment) as a bonus, despite the fact that the law (Ex. 22:25–27) forbade its confiscation on humanitarian grounds. The principle here is not primarily the avoidance of lawsuits (as in 1 Cor. 6:1–8, where v. 7 is probably based on this passage), but a radically unselfish attitude to one's rights and property.

**41.** *Forces you to go* (*angareuō*) is a specific term for the Roman soldier's practice of 'commandeering' civilian labour in an occupied country. (It is used similarly in 27:32.) Here enforced service as a porter is envisaged. The Jews fiercely resented such impositions, and Jesus' choice of this example deliberately dissociates him from militant nationalists. Rather than resisting, or even resenting, the disciple should volunteer for a further *mile* (the Roman term for 1,000 paces, rather less than our mile).

**42.** This free and unselfish attitude to rights extends also to property. Luke's version (6:30) is more far-reaching: 'Give (regularly: present imperative) to every one who begs from you.' Matthew envisages a specific instance (*give* is aorist imperative, normally of a single act). Literal application of this verse as a rule of life would be self-defeating: 'there would soon be a class of saintly paupers, owning nothing, and another of prosperous idlers and thieves'.[1] But the principle is that the need of others comes before my convenience (*cf.* Dt. 15:7–11). The suggestion that *begs* means 'asks for a loan' (Hill), or the reconstruction of the verse into an attack on usury (involving the insertion of a negative for which there is no textual authority; *AB*) is unnecessary if this is not a pragmatic rule but a radical expression of the disciple's unselfish concern for others.

*(f) Love (5:43–47).* **43.** *You shall love your neighbour* is from Leviticus 19:18, which Jesus quotes in a fuller form at 19:19 and 22:39. The prominence of the commandment to love in Jesus' teaching, and especially in Matthew's presentation of it (*TIM*, pp. 75–85), is well known. Here the question is the extent of its application (as in Lk. 10:25–37, where the parable of the Good Samaritan is also introduced as a comment on Lv. 19:18). The

---

[1] L. Morris, *Tyndale Commentary* on *Luke* (1974), p. 130.

*neighbour* of Leviticus 19:18 was the fellow-Israelite, but a very different attitude was required towards those of a hostile community (Dt. 23:3–6; *cf.* Ps. 139:21–22), even though a personal enemy was to be treated with consideration (Ex. 23:4–5; 1 Sa. 24:19; Pr. 25:21) and an individual non-Israelite was to be made welcome (Lv. 19:34; Dt. 10:19). *Hate your enemy* is not a quotation from the Old Testament, and it is hardly fair to regard it as a summary of Old Testament thought on the basis only of such passages as Deuteronomy 23:3–6. But it is an inference which was easily drawn from the clear Old Testament distinction between the attitude required towards fellow-Israelites and towards foreigners, and which appears strongly in the Qumran Manual (1QS 1:3–4, 9–10; 19:21–22, 'that they may love all the sons of light . . ., and hate all the sons of darkness'. *Cf.* Josephus, *BJ* ii. 139, on the Essenes' attitude. Jesus' words are not so much a direct attack on Qumran as on a popular attitude which they shared and perhaps intensified. See further, Davies, pp. 245–249). It must be remembered, however, that *hate* often signifies 'not love' or 'love less' (Mt. 6:24; Rom. 9:13; Lk. 14:26 with Mt. 10:37; Gn. 29:30–31), and need not denote a positive hatred; thus Jeremias translates, 'You shall love your compatriot but you need not love your adversary' (*NTT*, p. 213 n. 3). Certainly the Old Testament, and Judaism as a whole, expected a greater love for fellow-members of the people of God than for those outside.

**44.** Jesus rejects this distinction in favour of an undiscriminating love. The *enemy* will be primarily one who is outside and opposes the community of God's people (see on v. 43, and the reference to *those who persecute* in this verse; see also on brethren, v. 47). The disciple's attitude to religious persecution must go beyond non-retaliation to a positive *love*. But an exclusive application to cases of religious persecution would introduce the very legalism Jesus repudiates; there is no-one the disciple need not love. There is a sweeping universality in the love Jesus demands which has no parallel in Jewish literature (Banks, pp. 200–201). And this love will issue in prayer for the persecutors; it is not just a sentimental feeling, but an earnest desire for their good.[1]

---

[1] *Cf.* Luke's 'do good to those who hate you', 6:27; this and other phrases from the fuller parallel in Luke have found their way into many MSS here and hence into the AV, but do not appear in the older MSS of Matthew.

**45.** Undiscriminating love will mark disciples out as *sons of your Father*, for the son shares the father's character, and it is the character of God to dispense his natural blessings on all alike. Nothing is said here, of course, about spiritual blessings; the verse gives no warrant for a belief in universal salvation. There is no incompatibility between a recognition that some are saved and some lost and a practical kindness which embraces all men, even the persecutor.

**46-47.** A parochial concern is characteristic of the world. If a disciple is to find his *reward* (see on 5:12), he must not just be on a level with other men; he must *do more* (*cf.* v. 20, where the same root *perisson* is used, and the ultimate development of this *more* in the *perfect* of v. 48). *Tax collectors* and *Gentiles* (see on 6:32) are bracketed together again in 18:17. The (Jewish) tax collectors, as an ostracized minority (see on 9:9–11), formed a close-knit group. Jesus' positive attitude elsewhere to tax collectors (9:9–13; 11:19; 21:31-32) and Gentiles (8:10–11) contrasts with the pejorative use of the terms here and in 18:17; their use as colloquial expressions, readily understood in current Jewish society, for 'outsiders' or 'undesirables' cannot therefore be pressed into an endorsement of the very type of discrimination which it is the aim of these verses to condemn. *Brethren* will in context denote primarily fellow-disciples, as generally in Matthew: the love Jesus requires extends outside the 'in-group' to its opponents.

*(g) Summary (5:48).* The 'greater righteousness' demanded in v. 20 has been illustrated in vv. 21ff., and is now summed up (*therefore*) in one all-embracing demand. The demand is that disciples (*you* is emphatic, in contrast with the tax collectors and Gentiles of vv. 46–47 and the scribes and Pharisees of v. 20) must be *perfect* (*teleioi*). This is the 'more' required in v. 47. *Cf.* 19:20–21, where again *teleios* (its only other use in Matthew) indicates God's requirement which goes beyond legal conformity. (There too Lv. 19:18 is superseded by this more radical demand.) *Teleios* is wider than moral perfection: it indicates 'completeness', 'wholeness' (*cf.* Paul's use of it for the spiritually 'mature' in 1 Cor. 2:6; 14:20; Phil. 3:15), a life totally integrated to the will of God, and thus reflecting his character. It is probably

derived here from the LXX of Deuteronomy 18:13, which, with the repeated formula of Leviticus 11:44–45; 19:2; 20:26 ('You shall be holy, for I am holy'), is echoed in Jesus' words. The conformity to the character of God, to which Israel was called in their role as God's special people (see especially Lv. 20:26), is now affirmed as the goal of the disciples of Jesus. It is an ideal set before all disciples, not a special status of those who claim to have achieved 'sinless perfection' in this life; neither here nor in 19:20–21 is there a suggestion of a two-level ethic for the ordinary disciple and the 'perfect'. (*Cf. TIM*, pp. 96–97.)

## (vi) Teaching on religious observance (6:1–18)

The 'righteousness which exceeds that of the scribes and Pharisees' (5:20) is to be seen not only in a new radical approach to the legal and ethical questions which concerned the scribes (5:21–48), but in a new attitude to the scrupulous religious observance which was the hallmark of the Pharisees (6:1–18). The new attitude consists not in a repudiation of the main aspects of Jewish piety, but in an avoidance of ostentation in their performance. Religious observance is to be directed towards God, not to gaining the approval of men.

Almsgiving, prayer and fasting are selected as examples of religious observance. These three were (and are) the most prominent practical requirements for personal piety in mainstream Judaism (see Davies, pp. 307–315). The same three activities, together with the specifically Islamic requirements of the Hajj and recitation of the creed, constitute also the Five Pillars of Islam. Jesus accepts them as central also to the religious life of his disciples. They are treated in three passages of closely parallel structure (vv. 2–4, 5–6, 16–18), with a general introduction (v. 1); a long digression on prayer (vv. 7–15) interrupts the carefully balanced structure, and is perhaps an insertion by Matthew, made up of independent sayings of Jesus, into a characteristically memorable unit of Jesus' teaching.

**1.** The overall theme of the section is stated simply, in words which superficially seem to conflict with 5:16. But what is condemned here is ostentation, particularly in the practice of religious duties. (*Piety* is a good translation for *dikaiosynē* (normally 'righteousness') in this context: it picks up the 'right-

eousness' of 5:20, but with special application to religious observance rather than to ethical obedience, and so acts as a general
term to cover the specific references to almsgiving, prayer and
fasting which follow.) The disciple's life is inevitably, and
rightly, public, but that does not entitle him to show off his
religious devotion; there is a world of difference between living
a conspicuously good and godly life (5:13-16) and striving to
gain a reputation for piety. The difference lies not only in the
motive, but in the result: the former brings glory to God, the
latter only to the performer.

There is also a difference in *reward*. See on 5:12 for the concept
of rewards, which recurs twice in each of the three subsections
that follows (vv. 2, 4, 5, 6, 16, 18). The show-off gets what he has
earned, the approval of men, and so misses the true *reward*
which comes only from *your Father who is in heaven* (see on 5:16;
this view of God dominates ch. 6 particularly).

**2.** Almsgiving was a religious duty, not a philanthropic
option, in Judaism (*cf.* Dt. 15:7-11; Ps. 112:9) and by the first
century AD poor relief based on such almsgiving was impres-
sively well-organized. Jesus expects his disciples to give generously, but not conspicuously. *Sound no trumpet* is probably metaphorical for calling attention to oneself, as in other ancient
literature, since no literal use of trumpets in connection with
almsgiving is clearly attested. *Hypocrite* is a favourite word in
Matthew, used particularly, as here and in vv. 5, 16, to characterize the Pharisees in their ostentatious piety. In chapter 23 it
has become a stereotyped epithet for the scribes and Pharisees.
The Greek word means originally an 'actor', and here that sense
is not far from the surface: they are performing to an audience. It
is this rather than any conscious insincerity which is the point
of the word here, though elsewhere insincerity (22:18), or at
least inconsistency between words and deeds (7:5; 15:7), is in
view. The aim of such play-acting is *that they may be praised by
men*, and in that praise it finds its full *reward* (*misthos*, literally
'wages', that which has been earned). *Have* (*apechō*) is a commercial term for receipt in full, and therefore implies there is no
more to look forward to (*cf.* its use in Lk. 6:24, and the similar
*apolambanō* in Lk. 16:25).

**3-4.** In contrast, the secrecy of the disciple's almsgiving will result in a *reward* (not an earned remuneration, but the disproportionate return of God's grace: see on 5:12), not from men, but from *your Father who* (alone) *sees in secret*. The stress is on the source (and therefore the quality) of the reward in comparison with the hypocrite's 'wages', not on the manner of its giving, as in the late reading reflected in AV 'openly'. The older text does not indicate that the Father's reward is either public or even earthly.

**5–6.** The structure is closely parallel to vv. 2–4, and uses the same key words and phrases, on which see above. The prayers *in the synagogues* were led by a member who stood at the front; to be invited to do so was presumably a mark of distinction in the congregation. Prayer was not normally practised *at the street corners*, but Jeremias suggests that one who strictly observed the afternoon hour of prayer could deliberately time his movements to bring him to the most public place at the appropriate time (*NTT*, p. 187)! The disciple, by contrast, is to pray in the 'storeroom' (*tameion*; *cf.* Lk. 12:24). This was an inner room, secluded, probably windowless, and possibly with the only lockable door in the house; it is thus proverbial for a secret place (Lk. 12:3; *cf.* Mt. 24:26). The clause is modelled on Isaiah 26:20 (where *tameion* occurs in the LXX), as a prescription for hiding away. Jesus is not here forbidding public or communal prayer as such, but the ostentation to which it is too easily prone. The essence of prayer is the communion of the disciple with his Father.

**7–8.** The subject of prayer is expanded with other sayings – a warning against mechanical praying (vv. 7–8), the Lord's Prayer (vv. 9–13), and a comment on it (vv. 14–15) – before the third part of the teaching on religious observance in vv. 16–18. The first saying is aimed not now against the 'hypocrites', but against praying *as the Gentiles do*. Prayer in the non-Jewish world was often characterized particularly by formal invocations and magical incantations, in which the correct repetition counted rather than the worshipper's attitude or intention. *Heap up empty phrases* translates the Greek *battalogeō*, a word otherwise unknown in contemporary literature, and perhaps coined as an onomatopoeic term for empty 'babbling'; its resemblance to the Hebrew *bāṭel* ('vain, idle') would sharpen the point. The stress is

132

apparently on the quality rather than the quantity of the utterance. This is not a prohibition either of repetition in prayer (AV 'vain repetitions' is unwarranted; Jesus repeated himself, Mt. 26:44) or of set forms of prayer (vv. 9–13 go on to give one!), but of thoughtless, mechanical prayer. It is not *many words* that God responds to, but an attitude of prayerful dependence.

**9–13.** The Lord's Prayer occurs in a shorter form in Luke 11:2–4; it is generally assumed that Matthew's version represents the first stage of its expansion in Christian liturgical use, to be completed by the later addition of the doxology (see on v. 13), though there is no improbability in Lohmeyer's view that Jesus taught the prayer in different forms on two separate occasions; the context in Luke is a specific request for instruction on how to pray, while in Matthew it is part of a more general discourse on the nature of prayer.

It has become fashionable in recent interpretation to take the Lord's Prayer, even in the Lucan version, as primarily eschatological, concerned with the disciple's longing for and preparation for the consummation of God's kingdom. Practically every clause can be interpreted in that way. But the fact that Christians have used the prayer throughout the centuries without a specifically eschatological intention suggests that it also has an application to the disciple's daily concerns (which should of course *include* the looking forward to God's victory), even that this application is the primary one.

It is a prayer for *disciples*, who alone can call God 'Father'. It is also a prayer for disciples *as a group* (all the first person pronouns are plural). This, together with its marked similarity to several Jewish liturgical prayers of the period (for examples see McNeile, p. 77), suggests that at least part of its purpose was a liturgical use in Christian worship. This does not exclude, however, its use also as a summary or model for our own prayer, both corporate and private, and its use in this way has preserved many Christians from the self-centred approach which easily characterizes our prayer without such a model.

**9.** *Then* indicates that the following prayer is an expression of the understanding of God's fatherly care in v. 8, in contrast with the practice of the Gentiles (v. 7); an emphatic 'you' in the Greek points the contrast. The address 'Father' found in the Lucan version represents the bold 'Abba' which was a hallmark of Jesus' unique intimacy with God (Mk. 14:36).[1] The boldness is blunted in Matthew's *Our Father who art in heaven*, a more reverent formula found (unlike the simple 'Abba') in some Jewish prayers. This address does, however, express forcibly the tension in the disciples' attitude to God, who is at the same time *in heaven*, transcendent, all-powerful, the Lord of the universe and yet *Our Father*, concerned for the needs of each disciple, and entering into an intimate relationship with them.

Three parallel clauses follow, the first two closely echoing the synagogue prayer known as the *Qaddish*: 'Exalted and hallowed be his great name in the world which he created according to his will. May he let his kingdom rule in your lifetime . . . speedily and soon.' *Hallowed be thy name* is asking for more than reverent speech. (*Hallow* means 'make holy', or better 'treat as holy, reverence', BAGD, p. 9a.) The *name* represents God himself as revealed to men (so frequently in the Old Testament, *e.g.* Dt. 28:58; Is. 30:27). This clause may thus express both a desire to see God truly honoured as God in the world today, and an eschatological longing for the day when all men acknowledge God as the Lord.

**10.** *Thy kingdom come* is the most clearly eschatological clause in the prayer. It must at least include an aspiration for the final establishment of God's rule over all his creation (see pp. 45–46 for the idea of 'kingdom of God/heaven'). But in the ministry of Jesus the kingdom of God had in a sense already come (see on 3:2) and its progressive establishment no less than its final consummation should be the constant concern of disciples. Similarly *Thy will be done* can apply both to men's obedience to God's will in the world today (*cf.* the very personal use of the same phrase by Jesus in 26:42) and to the ultimate working out of God's purpose for the world. To view these three petitions as purely eschatological is to defuse one of the most demanding prayers disciples can be called on to offer, with far-reaching consequences for the daily conduct of their lives; to view them as purely ethical is to ignore the 'blessed hope' which is the mainspring of New Testament discipleship. The three clauses

---

[1] See especially J. Jeremias, *The Prayers of Jesus* (1967), pp. 11–65; more briefly, *NTT*, pp. 62–68, 197.

are rounded off with the phrase *on earth as it is in heaven*, which, in view of the careful balance of the three preceding clauses, is probably to be taken with all of them rather than as an extension of the last. It too allows the double application of these clauses, which have a fulfilment not only in the worship and harmony of heaven but also on earth, progressively as the consummation approaches and completely when it comes. The prayer embraces the whole scope of this outworking of God's purpose, but its focus is not on either present or future, but on God himself, whose glory must be the disciples' first and deepest concern, before they consider their own needs.

11. The three clauses of prayer for God's glory are now balanced by three petitions for the disciples' needs. Material needs are represented by *our daily bread*, but the meaning of *daily* is uncertain. *Epiousios* occurs nowhere else except perhaps in a fragment of an Egyptian account book, published in the last century but since lost! Of the many suggested translations, based on different speculative etymologies, three seem possible. (a) 'For the day (in question)', hence *daily*, possibly with a reminiscence of the daily provision of manna in the wilderness. (b) 'Necessary' for survival, *cf.* Proverbs 30:8, 'feed me with the food that is needful for me'; in the account-book fragment it probably referred to a daily 'ration'. (c) 'For the coming day', which is currently the most favoured translation, supported by Jerome's report of this interpretation in an early Aramaic version of the Gospel. (a) and (b) come to much the same thing, a prayer for the day's material needs to be met. (c) could either carry a similar meaning, asking for tomorrow's food to be provided, or an eschatological sense 'food for the Coming Day', with reference to the expected Messianic banquet (see on 8:11). If the whole prayer is taken eschatologically, this last meaning seems required (see Jeremias, *NTT*, pp. 199–201). But the fact that this bread is required *today* (and still more the Lucan version, which asks for it 'each day') suggests that the thought is of daily provision, and if so it makes little difference whether the request is for today's or tomorrow's bread. Such a request is not in conflict with vv. 25ff., for it is the fact that these needs have been committed to God in prayer that makes anxiety unnecessary.

**12.** *Debts* represents the regular Aramaic term for sin, which literally denoted money debt, here put literally into Greek (Luke has the more ordinary term for 'sins', but retains the idea of debt in the second clause). The thought is of sins in general, as the explanation in vv. 14–15, using the very general term *trespass* (literally 'false step', *i.e.* wrongdoing), makes clear. *Have forgiven* seems clearly to be the correct text in Matthew, though many MSS have substituted the present tense (used here by Luke) to avoid the implication that God's forgiving us depends on our prior forgiveness of others. In fact the Aramaic perfect, which probably lies behind Matthew's aorist tense, could be used with a present sense ('as *herewith* we forgive our debtors', Jeremias, *NTT*, p. 201), so that Luke's present is more idiomatically correct, Matthew's aorist more 'Semitic'. The point lies not in the time-sequence, but, as vv. 14–15 will explain, in the insincerity of a prayer for forgiveness from an unforgiving disciple.

**13.** After material provision and forgiveness for past sins comes a prayer, in two clauses, for protection from future sin. *Temptation* (*peirasmos*) is better 'testing' (*cf.* p. 96, above). God, while he does not 'tempt' men to do evil (Jas. 1:13), does allow his children to pass through periods of testing. But disciples, aware of their weakness, should not desire such testing, and should pray to be spared exposure to situations in which they are vulnerable. If they do find themselves in such a situation, however, they must pray to be *delivered from evil* (or 'the Evil One' – as in 5:37 either translation is possible, and the sense is not greatly affected by the choice). The stress in both clauses is on the vulnerability of disciples and their consequent dependence on God for avoiding sin, though the ultimate threat of the eschatological conflict cannot be excluded from the prayer's perspective.

The familiar doxology, which is absent from all texts of Luke, occurs in slightly varying forms in a good number of early MSS and versions of Matthew at this point, but its absence from several of the most important early witnesses, representing the text of Matthew in use in various parts of the church from the second century, convinces most scholars that it was not in the original text (though in use very early and over a wide area). The prayer is likely to have been originally given and used with the form of a concluding doxology (an essential element in most Jewish prayers) left free, probably as a congregational response. The form we now know (modelled on 1 Ch. 29:11–12?) gradually became standardized as a part of the prayer itself, probably during the second century. Whether it, or something like it, goes back to the time of Jesus we cannot be sure. (For an unusually positive estimate see Davies, pp. 451–453.)

**14–15.** This comment on v. 12 adds little to what was implicit in the prayer itself. It in turn may be interpreted from 18:23–35, where the connection between our forgiving and being forgiven is graphically expounded. The point is not so much that forgiving is a prior condition of being forgiven, but that forgiveness cannot be a one-way process. Like all God's gifts it brings responsibility; it must be passed on. To ask for forgiveness on any other basis is hypocrisy. There can be no question, of course, of our forgiving being in proportion to what we are forgiven, as 18:23–35 makes clear.

**16–18.** After the digression on prayer, the third example of religious observance is presented with the same structure and the same key words as vv. 2–4, 5–6 (see on vv. 2–4). Fasting was a prominent element in Jewish religious life, both at statutory times (Day of Atonement, and other prescribed fasts with historical significance) and occasionally, either by corporate or individual decision (see 'Fasting', *NBD*, p. 373). Strict Pharisees fasted at least twice a week (Lk. 18:12), and made sure that others knew it. *Disfigure* (*aphanizō*) is literally 'make invisible' (it is translated 'consume' in vv. 19–20), a vivid expression for making unrecognizable, either by covering the head or by smearing with ash and dirt. In contrast, the disciple who fasts must look quite normal, clean and happy (anointing with oil was a common cosmetic, not necessarily a sign of special celebration: to put on a show of exceptional gaiety would be as ostentatious as the 'hypocrites'!). Jesus assumes that fasting will continue to be practised among his disciples, as indeed it was, after his death (see further on 9:14–15; *cf.* Acts 13:2–3; 14:23).

*(vii) The disciple's attitude to material possessions (6:19–34)*
The last two long sections have presented Jesus' teaching largely in contrast with the teaching and practice of the scribes and

Pharisees. Now in 6:19 – 7:12 there is a more direct and positive presentation of the true disciple's attitudes, the 'greater right-eousness' which is going to make him conspicuous among other men. First a series of sayings which were apparently originally independent (their parallels are found in Lk. 12:33–34; 11:34–35; 16:13; 12:22–31) are brought together into an impressive demand for detachment from material concerns, and for a prior loyalty to God.

**19–20.** The contrast between earthly and heavenly reward in vv. 1–18 leads naturally to this memorable poetic saying contrasting earthly and heavenly treasure. The use of similar language in 19:21 might suggest that the thought is specifically of almsgiving (*cf.* Lk. 16:9 for the idea of using money with a view to a reward in heaven), but the scope here may also be wider. *Treasures in heaven* are 'stored up' by obedience to God in all areas of life; they are the reward of the disciple who puts God first. *Treasures on earth* give no permanent security or satisfaction; they can be destroyed by *moths* and other vermin (*brōsis*, a general term for 'eating', probably refers to damage by rats, woodworm, *etc.*, rather than to *rust* (Gk. *ios*)), and removed by *thieves*.

**21.** It is not so much the disciple's wealth that Jesus is concerned with as his loyalty. As v. 24 will make explicit, materialism is in direct conflict with loyalty to God. And the danger of amassing possessions is that the *treasure* will command the disciple's loyalty, that material affluence will breed materialism.

**22–23.** This enigmatic saying is included here to reinforce the message of both vv. 19–21 and v. 24, the call for an undivided loyalty to God. *The eye is the lamp of the body* either in that it is the 'window' through which light enters the body (hence RSV *full of light, full of darkness*, for the adjectives 'light' and 'dark') or, more probably, in that it enables the body to find its way. In either case its effectiveness depends on its being *sound* (*haplous*). *Haplous* is literally 'single', but is used in the LXX to translate the root *tm*, 'complete', 'perfect', which is often used of 'undivided' loyalty. So the 'single eye' is primarily a metaphor for a life totally devoted to the service of God. But *haplotēs* is also used in the New Testament with a connotation of generosity (Rom. 12:8;

2 Cor. 8:2; 9:11, 13; *cf.* Jas. 1:5) and such a nuance here is suggested by the contrasting 'evil eye' (RSV *not sound*), a regular expression not only for jealousy but for niggardliness (*e.g.* Dt. 15:9; Pr. 22:9; Mt. 20:15, and often in Jewish literature). There seems to be a deliberate *double-entendre* here, with *haplous* taking up not only the theme of undivided loyalty but also that of detachment from material concern, hence of generosity. The two themes intertwine throughout this section.

The result of such a *sound eye* is a well-illuminated *body*. The body here represents the whole person, and if the idea of the lamp was of that which enables the body to find its way, the thought is of a purposeful life, directed towards its true goal. The alternative is a life in the dark, like a blind man, because the 'evil eye' of selfish materialism gives no light to show the way.

**24.** *Serve* is literally 'be a slave of'; a man could satisfactorily have two employers, but not two owners. So the same theme of undivided loyalty is stressed again. *Hate* here, as often in the Bible, carries a comparative sense, not necessarily of active dislike so much as of displacement by a higher loyalty (*cf.* on 5:43). The rival owner is *mammon*, Aramaic *māmōnā'*, which means essentially 'possessions'. It was not a personal name (as Milton makes it, drawing on its 'personification' in this passage). While it sometimes carried the connotation of wealth wrongly acquired, this is usually indicated in the Targums by the addition of *dišᵉqar* ('of falsehood'; *cf.* Lk. 16:9, 11). *Māmōnā'* alone is more neutral, as in the Targum to Proverbs 3:9, 'Honour God with your mammon' or even the Palestinian Targums to Deuteronomy 6:5, 'You shall love Yahweh your God with . . . all your mammon'. The same neutral connotation is found at Qumran and in the Mishnah. The rival loyalty then is not that of ill-gotten gains, but of material possessions however legitimate. They can be used to serve God, but they can also themselves claim a man's allegiance. *Mammon* thus here represents the principle of materialism, and this is in direct conflict with loyalty to God.

**25.** The remainder of the chapter deals with 'anxiety'. *Merimnaō* ('to be anxious') refers essentially to a state of mind ('be overconcerned about', *AB*). This will no doubt be revealed in frenzied activity, but Jesus' focus is primarily on the mental attitude rather than its practical outworking (*pace* Jeremias, *PJ*, pp. 214–215), for it is here that the conflict with faith arises. To forbid 'anxiety' does not rule out a responsible concern and provision for one's own and others' material needs, nor does Jesus here forbid us to work (see on v. 26). His concern, as in the preceding verses, is with priorities, and the essential message of this passage is 'First things first', which means in fact 'God first'. Given that prior emphasis, concern for material needs will not be able to usurp the first place which it too often occupies in a disciple's interests. The objects of our anxiety, food, drink and clothing, are to be seen as less important than the *life* and the *body* which they supply, and subsequent verses will draw out the moral that, since God provides the latter, he can be trusted for the former. The two concerns of this verse, food and clothing, will be picked up respectively in the illustrations from nature in vv. 26 and 28.

**26.** If this light-hearted illustration were pressed too literally, it might suggest that the disciple has no need to grow and harvest food. But the point is that God sees that even the birds are fed, and a disciple is more valuable to him than a bird. What is prohibited is worry, not work. Even the birds have to spend a lot of energy in hunting or searching for their food, but the point is that it is there to be found. And it is provided by *your heavenly Father*; a true understanding of that phrase is the ultimate antidote to anxiety.

**27.** Anxiety in any case achieves nothing. It cannot add even a little time to our life-span. (Indeed it may shorten it!) *Hēlikia* normally means 'age', 'life-span'. In Luke 19:3 it clearly means 'height', and the fact that *cubit* is a measure of physical length apparently supports this meaning here (so AV, RV, NEB and some other versions). But a cubit (46 cm) would not be a slight (or even desirable?) addition to a man's height, as the context here seems to require, and Luke 12:26 demands. For a similar linear measure applied to length of life *cf.* Psalm 39:5, and indeed our 'life-*span*'.

**28–30.** This second illustration parallel to v. 26 is again not to be pressed into a recommendation of passivity and idleness, but is another argument from the less to the greater to indicate God's care for his children. The *lilies* should probably not be identified with a single species, as they are taken up in v. 30 as *grass*, the dead weeds used as fuel for an *oven*. It is wild vegetation in general which shows the prodigality of God's provision for the adornment of his creation, and thus forbids anxiety about our own clothing. Such anxiety indicates *little faith*, a word used elsewhere in Matthew for the disciples when they failed to trust Jesus in a situation of physical need (8:26; 14:31; 16:8; 17:20). Faith is, for Matthew, a very practical reliance on the care and power of the Father and of Jesus (*cf.* 8:8–10; 9:2, 21–22, 28–29; *etc.*). Anxiety is therefore its opposite, and is ruled out for the disciple.

**31–32.** A primary concern with material needs is characteristic of *the Gentiles*. As in 5:47; 6:7, the word seems to be used to make not so much a racial as a religious distinction; they are men without God. Such men have no knowledge of a *heavenly Father*, and so they have no antidote to anxiety and a consequent materialism in their outlook. The disciple by contrast realizes that his Father *knows that you need them all*, and his faith assures him that he both can and will provide them. As in vv. 7–8 this awareness is the basis for an attitude in striking contrast with the 'Gentile', who not only worries himself but worries his gods by his aggressive and unbelieving prayer.

**33.** This verse is the climax of vv. 25ff. Instead of emphasizing the negative ('Do not be anxious') it now sets out the positive attitude required of disciples, without which they will inevitably be subject to anxiety. They are to direct their attention consistently (*seek* is present imperative, implying a continuing obligation) towards *his*[1] *kingdom and his righteousness*. For 'kingdom of God/heaven', see pp. 45–46, above; here the primary emphasis is on submission to God's sovereignty here and now, *i.e.* obedience to his will, though the idea of looking forward to, and working for, the ultimate establishment of his kingdom cannot be ruled out. Similarly *his righteousness* (which is absent from the parallel in Lk. 12:31, but serves here to focus Matthew's special concern with practical discipleship) will refer, as in 5:6, 10, 20, to the kind of life which God requires in the present age, rather than to his ultimate act of 'vindication' or 'salvation'. What this

---

[1] Many MSS specify 'God's', but the meaning is in any case unambiguous.

verse demands is, therefore, a commitment to find and to do the will of God, to ally oneself totally with his purpose. And this commitment must come *first*. It is not to be crowded out by material concerns. Moreover, we are assured that if we thus put God first, our material needs (*all these things*, echoing v. 32) will be provided. Material concern is therefore not only distracting, but unnecessary.

This positive climax makes it clear that vv. 25ff. are not prescribing an irresponsible, happy-go-lucky optimism, or a fatalistic acceptance of the *status quo*, nor are they decrying the body and its concerns as sordid and unworthy of our attention. They call the disciple to an undistracted pursuit of his true goal, to which lesser (though legitimate) concerns must give way; and they assure him that if he will put first things first, God will take care of the rest.

**34.** While the call not to *be anxious* links this verse with what precedes, its theme is rather different in that it deals with *trouble* ahead, while vv. 25–33 envisaged full provision, not trouble. It is a salutary reminder that God's sure provision of our needs does not guarantee a life without problems. But they need not be multiplied by worrying about them before they occur; God knows about these too, and can be trusted to deal with them when the time comes. *Cf.* James 4:13–15.

### (viii) The disciples' attitude to one another (7:1–6)

**1–2.** *Judge* (*krinō*) often carries the connotation 'condemn', and it is in that sense that it is used here. The use of our critical faculties in making value-judgments is frequently required in the New Testament, as in vv. 6 and 15–20 of the present chapter. There may be a place for verbal rebuke and even stronger measures: 18:15–17. This passage, however, is concerned with the fault-finding, condemnatory attitude which is too often combined with a blindness to one's own failings. The least that such an attitude can expect is to *be judged* with equal harshness by other men. But the passive, as often in Matthew, probably conceals God himself as the agent. Just as he will forgive those who forgive (6:14–15), he will condemn those who condemn. The parable of the unforgiving debtor (18:23–35) illustrates the point clearly. *Cf.* Romans 2:1, 21–23; James 4:11–12. The proverbial saying, *the measure you give will be the measure you get*, occurs in Mark 4:24 in a different sense, with reference to care in receiving Jesus' teaching, and in Luke 6:38 with reference probably to generosity in giving. It occurs commonly in Jewish literature to indicate divine retribution (*e.g.* Mishnah *Sotah* 1:7). Here too it expresses the reciprocal principle in judgment, and so reinforces the previous clause.[1]

**3–5.** This grotesque illustration, drawn from the carpenter's workshop, exposes graphically the hypocrisy of the sort of criticism condemned in vv. 1–2. The *speck* (*karphos*, a tiny splinter of wood or straw; the word is used in secular Greek metaphorically for something minute) and the *log* (more literally a beam or rafter) in the eye are found also in two Rabbinic sayings, perhaps derived from Jesus' illustration (*Arakhin* 16b; *BB* 15b). *Hypocrite* (see on 6:2) is only here applied to a disciple rather than to Jesus' Jewish opponents. *AB* here translates by 'Casuist!', but the English usage of 'hypocrite' is not far from the sense of inconsistency intended here. Unless v. 5 is to be read as sarcastic (when the beam is removed, the speck will be found to be imaginary), it indicates that there is in fact a fault in the *brother*; the *hypocrite*'s error is not in his diagnosis, but in his failure to apply to himself the criticism he so meticulously applies to his brother.

**6.** This enigmatic saying stands alone, but comes appropriately here in that it qualifies the apparently absolute prohibition of 'judgment' in v. 1. *What is holy* refers probably to consecrated food, which was to be eaten only by the priests and their families (Ex. 29:33–34; Lv. 22:10–16; Nu. 18:8–19); to give it to *dogs*, which were regarded as unclean animals to be fed with unclean food (Ex. 22:31), was unthinkable.[2] It is equally unthinkable that something as valuable as *pearls* should be given to *swine*, another unclean animal (*cf.* 2 Pet. 2:22 for a similar contemptuous linking of dogs and pigs). The use of *dogs* in a racial

[1] The Jewish idea of God's two 'measures', mercy and judgment, may also be in view (see Jeremias, *PJ*, pp. 213–214); the saying would then recommend disciples to exercise mercy if they are to receive this 'measure' from God. But the proverbial saying is independent of this idea.

[2] The suggestion that *what is holy* is a mistranslation of the Aramaic *qᵉdāšā'*, 'ring' (see Black, pp. 200ff.) gives an attractive parallel to *pearls*, but makes the mention of *dogs* less apposite.

context in 15:26, although the word is different, has been taken to suggest an overtone of Jewish exclusivism here, but the context does not indicate this. Holy and valuable things (the reference is primarily to teaching, probably) must be given only to those who are able to appreciate them. *Cf.* Paul's emphasis that only the 'spiritual' can understand spiritual teaching (1 Cor. 2:13–16). God's gifts are not to be laid open to abuse, or his truth to mockery. There is a right discrimination which is different from the censorious judging of vv. 1–2. The early Christian application of this saying to eucharistic discipline (Didache 9:5) is too narrow a definition of a general principle.

*(ix) The disciple's attitude to God (7:7–11)*

**7–8.** The three balancing clauses in each of these verses add up to a strong exhortation to persistent prayer. *Seek* and *knock* are metaphors for prayer, not separate exhortations ('knocking' is found also in Rabbinic sayings as a metaphor for prayer). All three imperatives in v. 7 are present tense, which indicates continuous, persistent prayer. It is such prayer that will find an answer (*cf.* the parables of Lk. 11:5–8; 18:1–8). This is, as Jeremias puts it (*PJ*, pp. 159–160), 'beggar's wisdom': 'If the beggar, although harshly repulsed at first, knows that persistent appeals will open the hands of his hard-hearted fellow men, how much more certain should you be that your persistence in prayer will open the hands of your heavenly Father.'

**9–10.** The reason for this confidence is explained by a consideration of fatherhood. A human father will not meet his son's request for food (*bread* and *fish* would be the commonest food around the Lake of Galilee; *cf.* 14:17) with useless or even harmful substitutes. (The round loaf would look not unlike a stone, and a snake might be taken for a fish, particularly the eel-like catfish of Galilee, *Clarias lazera.*)

**11.** Yet human fathers are *evil* (a strong word, the same as for the 'Evil One' in 6:13, *etc.*); man's essential sinfulness is assumed, but the claims of true fatherhood prevail even over this. *A fortiori*, therefore, *your Father who is in heaven* (the phrase provides the key to this passage) can be expected to provide the best for his children. Thus any suggestion of reluctance on God's part which might have been derived from the call for persistence in vv. 7–8 is set aside, and the disciple can come to his Father in full confidence of his willingness to respond. The *good things* appear more specifically in Luke (11:13) as 'the Holy Spirit', who is the source of blessing in the disciple's life (see Rom. 8). Matthew's wording would include this theme, but is more general, and the position of these verses suggests that the material provision of 6:25–34 is also in mind. There is no warrant for applying the phrase only to the blessings of the age to come (as does Jeremias, *PJ*, p. 145).

### (x) Summary of Jesus' ethic (7:12)

Verses 13–27 will constitute a general conclusion on the demands of discipleship. The specific ethical teaching of the Sermon on the Mount therefore comes to its climax in this verse. *So* links the verse not with the immediately preceding verses but with the whole teaching of the Sermon so far, as it relates to our attitude towards other men, and the rule which follows presents in a nutshell the 'greater righteousness', the distinctive behaviour and attitude expected of the disciple. This 'Golden Rule' (the Emperor Alexander Severus reputedly had it written in gold on his wall – not a bad example to follow!) is often compared with the negative principle (Do not do to others what you yourself dislike) which is found in a wide variety of ancient literature from the Athenian Isocrates to Rabbi Hillel (*Shabbath* 31a; *cf.* Tobit 4:15). In this form it found its way into early Christian teaching from the second century, and appears in some early texts of Acts 15:29. Some earlier Jewish maxims (Ecclus. 31:15; Letter of Aristeas 207) point towards the more comprehensive positive form of the rule, but Jesus was apparently the first to formulate it explicitly, and he elevates it to a place of new importance: *this is the law and the prophets*, a summary of the revealed will of God. A similar formula is used of the double commandment to love in 22:40, and Matthew undoubtedly intends us to understand this rule as spelling out what it means to 'love your neighbour as yourself'. It is interesting that Hillel made a similar claim for his negative version: 'This is the whole law; all else is commentary' (*Shabbath* 31a). As a general principle to guide us in specific ethical decisions, the Golden Rule has not been bettered. In the positive form propounded by Jesus it makes a very far-reaching demand for unselfish love in action.

*(xi) Warnings against spurious discipleship (7:13-27)*
The radical demands of Jesus have been set out in the main body of the 'Sermon on the Mount', culminating in the all-embracing principle of 7:12. Now the Sermon is concluded with a group of four short sections (vv. 13-14, 15-20, 21-23, 24-27), each of which is at least partially paralleled in Luke, the last three being similarly grouped together at the end of the sermon in Luke 6:20-49. Together they constitute a striking call for genuineness in the disciple's response to the demands of Jesus. Each presents a contrast between the genuine and the spurious, and this genuineness is found not in the disciple's profession but in his performance. A professed adherence to Jesus and his teaching may be very impressive so as to deceive others, and even the professed disciple himself, but Jesus here gives warning that it will not deceive God, who looks for practical results. The teaching of the Sermon on the Mount is not meant to be admired but to be obeyed.

**13-14.** *Life* (*i.e.* eternal life: the idea is parallel to entering the kingdom of heaven in v. 21) is not found by following the crowd, but by a deliberate and costly decision. A similar metaphor is used in Luke 13:24, 'Strive to enter by the narrow door', in answer to the question, 'Will those who are saved be few?' The imagery here is different and more elaborate, but the essential message is the same. True discipleship is a minority religion. The image of the *narrow gate* here is expanded to include also the common Jewish teaching of the two ways, of life and of death (*cf.* Je. 21:8; it is developed at length in the early Christian manual, the Didache). Precisely how the two images are to be related is not clear – is the 'narrow gate' at the beginning or the end of the 'hard way'? Or is the hard way to be seen perhaps as the way through the gate, so that the two images coalesce? This last is the more likely if we accept (as I think we should) the reading of RSV mg. in v. 13 'For the way is wide and easy', which envisages a wide way with no gate (no need for decision) from which it is necessary to step aside through a narrow gate to find life. (The later introduction of a gate on the wide way would be a natural 'improvement' to balance the structure of the verses.) *Easy* and *hard* are not the best translations of *euruchōros* and *tethlimmenē*, which reinforce 'wide' and 'narrow', rather than introduce a new idea; 'roomy' and 'restricted' would be better, contrasting the popularity or availability of the two ways rather than the ease of travelling on them; but the latter idea may also be implied in v. 14, since nouns from the same roots as 'narrow' and 'hard' are used together in Romans 2:9; 8:35 for 'tribulation and distress'.

**15.** The second section (vv. 15–20) focuses on *false prophets*, a phenomenon already well known in the Old Testament (*e.g.* Dt. 13:1–5; Je. 23:9–32), but increasingly found also in the New Testament church, within which prophecy was an honoured gift (Acts 11:27–28; 21:9–11; 1 Cor. 12:10, 28; 14:1ff.; *etc.*). We hear of false prophets already active in 2 Peter 2:1; 1 John 4:1–3; Revelation 2:20, as well as in Jesus' warning in Matthew 24:11, 24. By the end of the first century they were a serious problem (Didache 11:8–12). The connection of thought with vv. 13–14 may well be that, like the false prophets in the Old Testament (Je. 6:13–14; Ezk. 13:1–16) they would offer an easier alternative to the narrow way of Christian discipleship.[1] Their teaching would be plausible, enabling them to pass as true disciples (*sheep*), but in fact their effect would be destructive (*cf.* Acts 20:29–30 for a similar use of *wolves* for false teachers from within the congregation).

**16–18.** The plausibility of this false teaching demands that some test be found (*cf.* 1 Jn. 4:1–3). Here Jesus sets out not a doctrinal but an ethical test: *You will know them by their fruits.* The *fruits* are not specified, but the idea is clearly that profession must be tested by practice. The image derives perhaps from the bad fruits of God's vineyard in Isaiah 5:1–7 (*cf.* Je. 2:21). The same image is applied in 12:33 to the Pharisees. Here it relates specifically to false prophets, but the principle would apply equally to any Christian profession. Profession is easy, and even Christian behaviour may be counterfeited, but what a man really is will inevitably show itself by the way he lives. The metaphor should not be pressed to the point of denying that a

---

[1] G. Barth (*TIM*, pp. 73–75) identifies them as antinomians.

person can change; but if the change is to be real, it must be radical, resulting in a new kind of person, not just a new profession or behaviour pattern.

**19–20.** The principle of v. 16a (repeated in v. 20) will determine men's final destiny. Profession of discipleship alone will be no protection against the coming judgment. Jesus here reinforces John the Baptist's attack on superficial repentance (v. 19 is a verbatim repetition of 3:10). This Gospel frequently emphasizes the danger of a purely nominal discipleship, and warns that there will be professed disciples who will be rejected at the end (*cf.* 7:21–23, 24–27; 13:37–43, 49–50; 25:31–46).

**21.** The third section (vv. 21–23) makes more explicit the point of v. 19, the ultimate rejection of those whose discipleship was only superficial. It relates not only to the false prophets of v. 15, but to any spurious profession of discipleship. The criterion for entry to *the kingdom of heaven* (*cf.* 'entering into life' in vv. 13–14) is, as vv. 16ff. have shown, practical obedience, not an appeal to Jesus as *Lord*, however urgent (*cf.* 25:11 for equally urgent and equally fruitless repetition). While *kyrie* (*Lord*) is sometimes in the Gospels no more than a polite form of address ('Sir': *e.g.* 13:27; 21:30; 25:20), in Matthew it is generally used in contexts which indicate a deeper and more religious meaning, recognizing Jesus' authority and his exalted status; it is thus the characteristic form of address to Jesus by disciples (often substituted by Matthew where the other Synoptics have 'Teacher' or 'Rabbi': see *TIM*, pp. 41–42). Here it is therefore a deliberate claim to a master/disciple relationship; it is an emphatic profession of faith. Nor is there any suggestion in vv. 21–23 that it is insincere; they are self-deceived, unaware (like the 'goats' of 25:44) that their discipleship does not match up to Jesus' criteria of obedience (v. 21) and personal relationship (v. 23).

**22.** The judgment theme becomes more explicit in the phrase *on that day* (a standard phrase for the final day of judgment; see 24:36; Lk. 10:12; 17:31; 21:34; *cf.* the Old Testament 'day of Yahweh'). Not only the profession of discipleship, but even miraculous activity in the name of Jesus, is not enough to prove a genuine disciple. For the use of Jesus' name by exorcists outside the disciple group *cf.* Mark 9:38; Acts 19:13ff. Prophecy, exorcism and miracles can be counterfeited. 'Charismatic' activity is no substitute for obedience and a personal relationship with Jesus. Nor, indeed, are any other 'good works' – *cf.* Bengel's searching comment on this verse: 'Add also: we have written commentaries and exegetical notes on books and passages of the Old and New Testaments, we have preached fine sermons, *etc.*'

**23.** Notice that in vv. 21–23 Jesus presents *himself* as the judge at 'that day', when his hearers would have expected *God* to be mentioned. The claim is all the more striking for being assumed, not argued. Moreover, the criterion of judgment is their relationship with *him*. For *I never knew you* as a formula of repudiation see also 25:12, and *cf.* Peter's denial, 26:70, 72, 74. *Depart from me, you evildoers* is a quotation from Psalm 6:8, where it is the words of the pious sufferer to his persecutors.

**24–27.** The well-known parable of the two builders, which constitutes the last section of the Sermon on the Mount, occurs in Luke in totally different words, and in a different form (the difference lies in the depth of the foundations, not, as here, in the site chosen), but with the same function of emphasizing the importance of the hearer's response to the Sermon. Both men represent those who *hear these words of mine* (note the same casual assumption of *Jesus'* ultimate significance, as in vv. 21–23); the difference lies in *doing* them. (*Poieō*, 'to do', is a key word in each of the sections 15–20, 21–23, 24–27.) On this practical response (as opposed to the enthusiastic but superficial allegiance of vv. 21–23) depends the ability of the disciple to survive the *floods* and *winds*, which probably symbolize both the pressures of life in this world and, particularly in connection with vv. 21–23, the ultimate test of God's judgment (*cf.* Is. 28:14–19 for God's judgment as a flood, against which only a God-given foundation (v. 16) can stand; also Ezk. 13:10–16). The result of a spurious or superficial discipleship will be total collapse – both versions of the parable (and therefore of the Sermon) end with the word *great*: this is not a warning to be taken lightly.

*(xii) Conclusion (7:28–29)*
The opening words of v. 28 (literally, 'And it happened when Jesus had finished . . .') are repeated verbatim in 11:1; 13:53; 19:1

and 26:1, in each case with a reference to the teaching just concluded. This clause uses Old Testament language (see, *e.g.*, LXX Jos. 4:11; 1 Sa. 13.10) not used in this way elsewhere in Matthew, and is apparently a deliberately formal transition formula to mark the end of the five great collections of teaching in Matthew and to lead back into the narrative (*cf.* the formulae of Nu. 16:31; Je. 26:8, which in Hebrew (not in LXX) are very close to Matthew's wording). See above, pp. 59–62, for the use of this formula as an indication of a basic fivefold structure of the Gospel. Without endorsing that view, the formula is clearly important as a signpost to the development of Matthew's theme (see Kingsbury, pp. 2–7). The collected teaching on discipleship is finished, and we return in 8:1 to the narrative of the first public phase of Jesus' ministry begun in 4:17 and summarized in 4:23–25.

But first Matthew notices the popular reaction to Jesus' teaching. For *the crowds* as a secondary audience to Jesus' teaching to his disciples, see on 5:1–2. Their astonishment (*cf.* 13:54; 22:33) was not so much at the content of his teaching, but his *authority* (an important word, applied to Jesus' deeds as well as his words; *cf.* 8:9; 9:6–8; 10:1; 21:23ff.; 28:18). In contrast with the careful quoting of authorities by the *scribes*, Jesus interpreted (and even went beyond) the law on the authority of his own direct perception of the will of God. That is why he could make response to *his* words the criterion of judgment (vv. 24–27). He was clearly very much more than a teacher of the law, as the scribes. '*Their* scribes' may indicate Matthew's awareness of a growing hostility between church and synagogue by the time he wrote his Gospel (*cf.* '*their* synagogues', 4:23; 9:35; *etc.*), but perhaps is no more than a necessary distinction from Christian 'scribes', who appear in 13:52; 23:34.

### C. A SELECTION OF JESUS' MIRACLES (8:1 – 9:34)

The preceding section (chapters 5 – 7) has introduced the reader to the *teaching* of Jesus, which has impressed the crowds with his *authority* (7:29). Now that authority is further seen displayed in his deeds. The careful collection of teaching in the previous three chapters is balanced by an equally deliberate collection of narratives, concentrating especially on Jesus' healing ministry. The whole complex of chapters 5 – 9 thus forms an impressive 'anthology' illustrating the pattern of ministry spelt out in 4:23 and repeated at the end of the section in 9:35 – teaching, preaching and healing. The dominant impression throughout is of the unparalleled authority of Jesus the Messiah (see Davies, pp. 90–91).

The section contains ten miracles (all but one acts of healing or exorcism), all except one paralleled in different places in Mark, and all in Luke, but here brought together into an arrangement peculiar to Matthew. The first three healings clearly form a deliberate group leading up to a summary in 8:16–17 (see commentary there), and this has led many to see the whole section as designed in three groups of three miracles each (the two miracles intertwined in a single story in 9:18–26 counting as one), divided by two incidents relating to discipleship in 8:18–22 and 9:9–17. Some have suggested common themes for the three groups; *e.g.* three miracles of healing (8:1–17), three miracles of power (8:23 – 9:8), three miracles of restoration (9:18–34) – so *ICC*; Guthrie, p. 32; or three healings of excluded persons (8:1–17); three signs of power (8:23 – 9:8); three double healings (9:18–34) – so Green. But the last two groups at least do not suggest such themes naturally, and the threefold structure itself is not compelling after 8:1–17. It is in the anthology as a whole rather than in its detailed structure that we should discern Matthew's purpose.

A comparison with the accounts of these same events in Mark and Luke shows that Matthew's versions are considerably shorter. This is achieved, as elsewhere in Matthew, by eliminating most of the less essential (though interesting) narrative details provided by Mark, so as to concentrate attention on the miracle itself, and particularly on the words of Jesus. The effect is to heighten the emphasis on the uniqueness of Jesus as seen in his authority over illness, the natural elements and spiritual powers, as well as over men and their destiny; the exclamation of the crowds in 9:33 thus fittingly brings the section to a climax.

*(i) The leper (8:1–4)*

**1.** For the *mountain* and for the *crowds*, see on 5:1–2. The crowds who have been impressed by the authority of Jesus' words (7:28–29) are now to be the witnesses also of his deeds (cf. 9:8, 33).

**2.** The *leper* was an outcast from normal society. It is probable that the 'leprosy' of the Bible was a term covering various skin complaints as well as the much more serious 'true' leprosy (called by the Greeks *elephantiasis*).[1] Not all were in fact serious or contagious, but all were lumped together and covered by the strict 'quarantine' regulations of Leviticus 13 – 14. The sufferer was not only potentially a health hazard, and likely to be physically objectionable; he was also ceremonially unclean. While other diseases are 'healed' in the New Testament, a leper is 'cleansed' (see, *e.g.*, 10:8), and it is the religious authorities who must certify this. The disease was regarded as incurable (2 Ki. 5:7); that the leper approached Jesus with the conviction of his ability to help is therefore an indication of an awareness of the authority of Jesus like that of the centurion (see vv. 8–9). It is therefore likely that Matthew's use of the two significant terms *knelt* (*proskyneō*, normally translated 'worship'; see on 2:2) and *Lord* (*kyrie*, which need not mean more than 'Sir', but see on 7:21) indicates that he sees here more than polite deference. His omission in the following verses of any reference to Jesus' emotions (Mk. 1:41, 'moved with pity'; 1:43, 'sternly charged', a word implying indignation) also concentrates attention on Jesus' power rather than his human character.

**3.** Jesus frequently *touched* those whom he healed (8:15; 9:25, 29; *etc.*), but the additional expression *stretched out his hand* here focuses attention on the act, which is specially significant in the case of a leper. To touch an unclean person was to contract defilement oneself (Lv. 5:3); Jesus' disregard for this ceremonial point should be seen in the light of his attitude to the law in 5:17–48 and such passages as 12:1–14 (on sabbath observance) and 15:1–20 (on ceremonial defilement). The mission of Jesus and the demands of love clearly took precedence. The immediacy of the cure further highlights the authority of Jesus (contrast Nu. 12:9–15).

**4.** Jesus' command to *say nothing* (which suggests that the

[1] See S. G. Browne, *Leprosy in the Bible* (1979), especially pp. 13–15.

crowds, mentioned in v. 1 to introduce the whole collection of miracles, were not in fact present on this occasion) is paralleled in 9:30; 12:16; 16:20; 17:9, and more frequently in Mark. This motif of secrecy, which is often regarded as an apologetic device of Mark to explain why so few responded to Jesus during his ministry, is better understood as reflecting a real danger that Jesus could achieve unwanted popularity merely as a wonder-worker, or worse still as a nationalistic liberator, and so foster a serious misunderstanding of the true nature of his mission. See further on 16:20–21. In directing the man to present himself with the prescribed offering (Lv. 14:10ff.) to the priest in Jerusalem, Jesus was following the provisions of the law of cleansing in Leviticus 14. Several interpretations are here possible of the phrase *for a proof to the people* (literally 'for a testimony to them'): (a) this act will give public proof that the leper is cured and may return into society; (b) it will prove to the (presumably already hostile) priests that Jesus respects the Old Testament law (*cf.* 5:17); (c) it is a witness to Jesus' Messianic mission, as the conqueror of disease (*cf.* 11:5 for this implication of the healing of leprosy). The same phrase recurs in 10:18 and Mark 6:11 (*cf.* Mt. 24:14), so that it has a wider application than to this incident alone (where it fits uncomfortably after a command to tell no-one), and this favours the third view. Matthew clearly sees the incident as significant for the understanding of who Jesus is. The 'testimony' of this miracle may be both negative (a witness *against* those who reject Jesus; so in Mk. 6:11) and positive (a call to belief; see 24:14 and probably 10:18). See further, Banks, pp. 103–104.

*(ii) The centurion's servant (8:5–13)*

**5.** After the leper, excluded from the congregation by his physical condition, comes the centurion, excluded by his race. *Capernaum* was now Jesus' home (see on 4:13), and is the scene for much of the narrative of chapters 8 and 9. (The similar story of Jn. 4:46–54 relates to a royal 'official' of Capernaum, but is located at Cana; it probably relates to a separate incident, and certainly derives from an independent tradition.[1]) The *centurion*

---

[1] See the list of differences in L. Morris, *The Gospel according to John* (1971), p. 288.

was a junior officer in the auxiliary forces under the command of Herod Antipas, which were non-Jewish, drawn largely from Lebanon and Syria. His sympathy for the Jewish religion (Lk. 7:3–5) was therefore that of an interested neighbour. Luke tells us that he approached Jesus through his Jewish friends; Matthew typically omits this detail as not essential to the story, and represents him as approaching Jesus directly in the first instance. The racial element in the confrontation is thus more emphatic in Matthew's version.[1]

**6.** *Lord*, as in v. 2, need mean no more than 'Sir', but probably to Matthew it was indicative of an awareness of the unique authority of Jesus, further evidenced in the centurion's words in vv. 8–9. The *servant* was probably a personal attendant: Luke mentions that he was 'dear' to the centurion. The Greek word *pais* could also mean 'child', and is so used in John 4:51 (otherwise that passage uses the normal word for 'son'). It is therefore sometimes suggested in the light of John 4:46ff. that this story originally related to the centurion's *son*. But Luke, who uses *pais* in 7:7, calls him unambiguously a 'slave' in vv. 2, 4 and 10; 'servant' is a regular meaning of *pais* in the New Testament, while nowhere except John 4:51 does it denote a 'son' as opposed to a 'child' (unrelated to the speaker). See above for the independence of this incident from that of John 4:46–54.

**7.** Jesus' reply, using the unusually emphatic first person pronoun, should probably be read as a question (NEB mg., 'Am I to come and cure him?'). Verse 6 contained no explicit request, and Jesus thus draws out its implications. The stress falls on the personal pronoun. Such an approach by a Gentile officer to a Jewish preacher was at least unusual. If Jesus' 'astonished or indignant question' (Held, *TIM*, pp. 194–195) does not express a real reluctance to contract ritual defilement by entering a Gentile's house (there is no record that he ever entered a Gentile's house, or healed a Gentile except at a distance), it at least probes the genuineness of the man's faith. Does he realize what he is asking? It is thus closely parallel to his response to another Gentile request for healing in 15:23–26; indeed the two stories run parallel at many points, both involving the trial and the

[1] See further in I. H. Marshall (ed.), *New Testament Interpretation* (1977), pp. 254–255. Much of the detail that follows is more fully presented in my exegesis of 8:5–13, *ibid.*, pp. 253–264.

triumph of a Gentile's faith. Jesus' words in vv. 10–12 will make it plain that he recognizes no racial barrier to faith; his question here is designed to elicit the centurion's recognition of the same truth.

**8.** The centurion does not argue the question of whether a Jew should enter his house; he simply treats it as irrelevant. His diffidence is based not on racial grounds but on a sense of personal unworthiness before one whose authority he recognizes as far greater than his own. In any case a personal visit is unnecessary. His faith goes beyond that of the leper in expecting a cure at a distance, simply by a *word*.

**9.** His conception of Jesus' power over illness is expressed in terms of the absolute authority of a military command. There is no reason to press the comparison to the point of asking under what authority Jesus is.[1] The point is simply that on the analogy of his military experience he is confident that what Jesus says will be done.

**10.** This verse is the key to the whole incident. The *faith* of this Gentile is superior to that of any Israelite, so much so that Jesus *marvelled*, a strong word used of Jesus only here and in Mark 6:6 (where it was caused by *lack* of faith among his own people!). *Truly, I say to you* (see on 5:18) draws attention to the significance of the verdict. Matthew's wording, 'with no one in Israel',[2] stresses more strongly than that of Luke the total inability of Israel to match this standard. *Faith* should not be interpreted here in the light of later theological discussion; it is defined by vv. 8–9 as an absolute practical reliance on Jesus' power.

**11.** Matthew now drives home the implications of this event by adding (vv. 11–12) a saying of Jesus on membership in the kingdom of heaven which was apparently originally spoken in a different context, since it occurs in a similar form in Luke 13:28–29, but not in Luke's story of the centurion. The saying emphasizes in very strong terms that the kingdom of heaven is not a Jewish preserve, but is open to Gentiles like this centurion, and further that Jews will in fact find themselves excluded. Thus

[1] It was probably this question which led to the alteration of the text in some early versions to read 'in authority', thus eliminating the statement of the centurion's subordinate status.

[2] See RSV mg.; the more familiar *not even* in the text, which occurs in many MSS, is clearly derived from Lk.

faith, not race, is the criterion for membership of God's kingdom.

*Sit at table* represents the Greek word for 'recline', which was the normal posture for meals, especially more formal ones (*cf.* Jn. 13:23). The imagery is that of the Messianic banquet (*cf.* 26:29; Lk. 14:15; 22:30), a prominent theme in Jewish eschatological expectation, derived from Isaiah 25:6 (N.B. 'for all peoples'), but narrowed down in both apocalyptic and Rabbinic writings to be an exclusively Israelite blessing, under the presidency of the Hebrew patriarchs, *Abraham, Isaac, and Jacob*. The *many* who will join the banquet are not explicitly Gentiles, but they are clearly set in contrast with the 'sons of the kingdom' in v. 12, who are certainly Jews. For a Jew to sit at table with a Gentile was to contract ritual defilement, yet Jesus here envisages the patriarchs themselves sitting down with Gentiles as fellow-guests at the banquet. Worse still, in describing their coming *from east and west*, he uses words which in the Old Testament relate to the world-wide gathering of *Israel* (Ps. 107:3; Is. 43:5–6; 49:12: see my *JOT*, p. 63).

**12.** The affront to Jewish exclusivism in v. 11 was pointed enough. Now the shocking converse is presented: even Jews themselves are not assured of a place at the Messianic banquet. *Sons of the kingdom* means those to whom the kingdom belongs by right, its heirs by birth (*cf.* the Rabbinic phrase 'sons of the age to come' echoed by Luke in 16:8; 20:34–35). 'It was the current belief that no descendant of Abraham could be lost.'[1] But Jesus says that they will be; not all of them presumably, since Abraham, Isaac and Jacob at least will be there, but the point is that membership in the kingdom of heaven will not be on the basis of race, that believing Gentiles will take the place of unbelieving Jews. *Outer darkness, weeping* and *gnashing of teeth*, which were symbolic Jewish descriptions of the fate of 'the ungodly' (see *ICC*, p. 78), are to be, incredibly, the experience of the 'sons of the kingdom'. There could hardly be a more radical statement of the change in God's plan of salvation inaugurated by the mission of Jesus.

**13.** After the inserted saying, Matthew concludes the story

[1] J. Jeremias, *Jesus' Promise to the Nations* (1958), p. 48.

quickly. The healing word which the centurion asked for is recorded, and it takes up the central theme of faith from v. 10. Such faith is unanswerable, and the cure, though distant, is immediate (*cf.* v. 3; 9:22).

The centurion's story has thus highlighted faith as the 'one thing needful'. It is a practical faith which expects and receives results. Such faith renders tradition and heredity meaningless, and 'of such is the kingdom of God'. Schweizer draws an appropriately uncomfortable moral: 'The warning in this story may be especially urgent in an age when Africans and Asians in the community of Jesus may well be called on to show to "Christian" Europe what Christian life really is' (p. 216).

*(iii) Peter's mother-in-law (8:14-15)*
The third 'excluded person' healed is a woman. It has even been suggested that in touching a woman's hand Jesus infringed the law (Hill, p. 160, citing SB, I, p. 299), but it is not likely that this single tradition preserved in a late collection (*Kallah* 50b) represents an accepted ruling of the time of Jesus. The cure is related with a minimum of detail (Mark's meagre 44 words are cut to 30 in Matthew!); even the disciples are omitted in Matthew's version. The *fever* may have been malarial, but the different causes of fever were not differentiated. Peter was a native of Bethsaida (Jn. 1:44), but Capernaum (some two miles away) was his home during Jesus' ministry (*cf.* 17:24-25); his *house* was probably where Jesus lived in Capernaum, and thus the site of much teaching and healing (*cf.* 9:10, 28; 13:1, 36; Mk. 2:1ff.; 9:33). It was a sizeable establishment, the home also of Andrew (Mk. 1:29) and of Peter's mother-in-law. The fact that Peter kept this home (and, apparently, his fishing equipment: 17:27; Jn. 21:3) indicates that the demand of 19:21, Luke 12:33, *etc.* did not apply literally to all disciples. Indeed the hospitality of such homes (*cf.* Lk. 10:38-42) was the essential condition of Jesus' chosen homeless way of life (v. 20); *served* also indicates literal provision of food, *etc.* (*cf.* 4:11, the same word).

*(iv) Summary of Jesus' healing ministry (8:16-17)*
These verses are the climax of 8:1-17, a carefully composed section (see Held, *TIM*, pp. 253-255) in which three specific

healing miracles lead up to a general summary which is then capped with an Old Testament quotation relating to Jesus' healing ministry in general. The three healings reveal Jesus' compassion in meeting the needs of despised and rejected people, and above all his authority in curing instantly three serious diseases of varied character.

**16.** The summary widens the perspective to include *all who were sick* (*cf.* 4:24, with a fuller specification), and also those *possessed with demons*, the first specific case of which is still to be recorded (8:28ff.). Here, as usually in the Gospels (and more clearly in Mark's parallel, 1:32–34), sickness and demon-possession are differentiated, as are their cures. *Spirits* are *cast out with a word* (never by a touch) without the conscious participation of the 'victim', while the sick are *healed*, often by a touch, and almost always in response to the patient's faith. Mark's vivid scene of the sabbath evening 'surgery' is again drastically reduced to a more formal summary, primarily designed to lead into Matthew's own climax in v. 17.

**17.** Matthew's primary interest in the healing miracles is in their revelation of the mission of Jesus. They are a fulfilment of Isaiah 53:4, here quoted by Matthew in what appears to be his own literal rendering of the Hebrew, which speaks of 'sick-nesses' and 'pains' (see RSV mg. at Is. 53:4), whereas the LXX (and the Aramaic Targum) spiritualized the meaning into 'sins'. The following verses in Isaiah 53 do in fact deal with *spiritual* deliverance through the Servant's suffering, with recurrent references to 'transgressions', 'iniquities', *etc.*, and it is likely that the 'diseases' and 'pains' of vv. 3–4 were intended to be understood in this light, as Christian thought (and translation) has always done. Physical suffering and sin were always closely linked in Jewish thought. Matthew was well aware of the Servant's role in Isaiah 53 as one of redemptive suffering (see on 20:28), and this was the dominant use of the passage in Christian circles.[1] But this did not prevent him noticing that the literal applicability of Isaiah 53:4 to the healing ministry of Jesus added another dimension to his fulfilment of the mission of God's Servant (*cf.* 12:18ff. for another non-redemptive application of a

---

[1] See my *JOT*, pp. 110–132, for the origin of this use with Jesus himself.

'Servant' passage). It is in the totality of his life and ministry, not only in its redemptive aspect, that Matthew delights to trace Jesus' fulfilment of the scriptural pattern.[1]

### (v) Two would-be followers (8:18–22)

**18.** In order to introduce the miracles of the calming of the storm and the healing of the Gadarene demoniacs (on the east side of the lake), Matthew mentions Jesus' decision to leave Capernaum, apparently to escape from the growing crowds (a frequent necessity in Jesus' Galilean ministry). This decision inevitably results in a separation of his true followers, who will accompany him, from less committed supporters, and thus Matthew introduces in vv. 19–22 two case-studies illustrating the demands of committed discipleship. The same incidents are related at a later point in Luke's narrative (9:57–60, with a further similar example added in vv. 61–62). They are introduced not for any interest in these two individuals, whose response to Jesus' challenge is not even mentioned, but as object-lessons, and the repetition of the key words 'disciples' and 'followed' in v. 23 suggests that the following narrative should also be seen as a lesson on discipleship (*TIM*, pp. 54–55, 201–203). Thus the overall emphasis on the authority of Jesus' Messianic works in chapters 8 – 9 (and *cf.* the authoritative *gave orders* here) is shown to have a corollary in the necessary response of discipleship.

**19.** The first example is a *scribe*, for while the scribes as a class are normally mentioned as in opposition to Jesus, as individuals they were potential disciples. The phrase in v. 21 'another of the disciples' may imply that this scribe was already a disciple, but if so it was only in a loose sense, since he addresses Jesus as *Teacher*, a term used only by outsiders in Matthew (see *TIM*, p. 41; contrast *Lord* in v. 21), and seems to think of discipleship as volunteering to *follow* a Rabbi as his pupil (see on 4:19). *Wherever you go* is literally 'wherever you may be departing', and probably refers only to the proposed journey across the lake, not to a

---

[1]The Greek words for *took* and *bore* might refer either to undergoing them himself (the primary meaning of the Hebrew) or to removing them (presumably Matthew's thought: he does not suggest that Jesus became sick), but as in Is. 53 the overall concept is of the removal of the people's troubles by the Servant's suffering, the ambiguity is justified.

life-time commitment. He is an academic dilettante disciple.

**20.** Jesus' reply shows that he is not a typical Rabbi, and that following him is no light matter. His chosen style of life is one of homelessness and insecurity (many homes, like Peter's, were open to him, but he had none of his own), and his disciples were called to share this style of life. This was a matter of choice, not of necessity, as Jesus' family was probably a comfortable, if not affluent, 'middle-class' one.[1] On *Son of man*, used here for the first time, see pp. 43–45. The suggestion that here it is used in its basic sense to mean 'man' in general makes nonsense of v. 20 as a reply to v. 19: it is Jesus' insecurity, not that of mankind (would this even be true?), which is relevant.[2]

**21.** If the condition of the previous 'volunteer' was uncertain, this one is explicitly a *disciple* (note his use of *Lord*; see on 7:21). What is in question is his degree of commitment. If his father was already dead, his request was a natural, even essential, one. The dead must be buried within 24 hours (though the subsequent ceremonies could last a week), and this duty was incumbent on the son (Gn. 50:5; Tobit 4:3; 6:14). It was so important that it took precedence over essential religious duties (Mishnah *Berakoth* 3:1), and even justified priests in contracting ritual defilement (Lv. 21:2). It has been suggested, however, that the father was not yet dead, so that what was requested was an indefinite postponement.[3]

**22.** The reasonable request meets a peremptory refusal. Following Jesus takes precedence over even family obligations (*cf.* 10:35–39; 12:46–50; 19:29). If the consecration of a Nazirite or of the High Priest did not allow him to attend even to his father's funeral (Nu. 6:6–7; Lv. 21:11), Jesus' demand is no less absolute. The urgency of discipleship will be emphasized further in 10:5ff. *The dead* can only mean those outside the disciple group, who lack spiritual life, and who in the absence of a higher calling can be left to deal with mundane matters. The reply seems needlessly stark, even offensive. Black (pp. 207–208) has therefore sug-

[1]See my article in *EQ* 51 (1979), pp. 6–7.

[2]For a possible political angle to this saying, contrasting Jesus with the Romans ('birds') and their puppets ('foxes'), see K. E. Bailey, *Through Peasant Eyes* (1980), pp. 24–25.

[3]K. E. Bailey (*ibid.*, pp. 26–27) gives ample evidence of the colloquial use of 'to bury' in the sense of 'to look after until death', which was a son's clear duty to his father. To fail to do so would be to fly in the face of the expectations of society.

gested that the original Aramaic was 'Let the *waverers* bury their dead', the words 'waverers' and 'dead' sounding very similar. But even so the refusal would be no less absolute, and the use of 'dead' for the godless is in fact found in rather later Judaism (SB, I, p. 489). The epigrammatic form of the saying as it stands is typical of the shock-tactics with which Jesus' radical demand is presented.[1]

### (vi) Calming the storm (8:23–27)

The evidence for Jesus' unique authority is now taken a stage further by the first record of a 'nature-miracle' – 'even winds and sea obey him' (v. 27). This, in the context of chapters 8 – 9, must be the main significance of this incident for Matthew, and his telling of the story, eliminating again a lot of inessential detail so that the calm authority displayed by Jesus leads without distraction to the climax in v. 27, makes this clear. Since Bornkamm's famous article of 1948 (see *TIM*, pp. 52–57), it has been generally agreed that Matthew's placing of the incident after vv. 19–22, together with some details in his wording, shows it was for him 'a kerygmatic paradigm of the danger and glory of discipleship'. This may indeed be granted, though whether we should therefore assume that Matthew deliberately presented the ship as an allegory of the church and the storm as its eschatological conflicts is less certain. At least we may be sure that for him it was still primarily, as for Mark and Luke, a record of Jesus' supernatural power, with the trial of the disciples' faith as a sub-plot (*cf.* the centurion's servant (8:5–13) for a similar blending of themes).

**23–24.** See above on v. 18 for the link with vv. 18–22. The word for *storm* usually means 'earthquake' – literally a 'shaking'; Matthew's use of this unexpected term is more likely designed to highlight the seriousness of the physical danger than to suggest a reference to eschatological upheavals (as in 24:7; Rev. 6:12; *etc.*). The lake is notorious for sudden, violent squalls. That Jesus was none the less *asleep*, even on a voyage which would normally take only an hour or two, certainly indicates that he like other men could be exhausted by constant activity; the contrast with the disciples' anxiety underlines his calm control of the situation.

[1] See further, Banks, pp. 97–98, and more fully M. Hengel, *The Charismatic Leader and his Followers* (1981), esp. pp. 3–15.

**25.** The contrast is heightened by the words of their request, which in Matthew takes the form of a prayer, the two words *save* and *Lord* (see on 7:21, and note its frequent repetition in this chapter, vv. 2, 6, 8, 21, 25) being as appropriate to the situation of Christian worship as to the disciples on the lake.

**26.** Jesus' rebuke (even before he acts; in Mark and Luke he acts first) further emphasizes that discipleship involves a *faith* which is a practical trust (*cf.* on vv. 8–10), and which excludes anxiety (*cf.* 6:25ff.). The phrase *little faith* (rather less derogatory than Mark's 'Have you no faith?') is a favourite for Matthew in such situations (see on 6:30). *Rebuked* indicates graphically the personal authority of Jesus, as master of the created order.

**27.** This authority is recognized by *the men*; the phrase would normally mean 'men' in general, and Matthew's use of this term is probably intended to indicate the reaction of a wider group than only the disciples who were present. In the Old Testament it was a mark of the sovereignty of God himself that the sea obeyed his orders (Jb. 38:8–11; Pss. 65:5–8; 89:8–9; *etc.*); a passage like Psalm 107:23–32 must surely have been in Matthew's mind as he narrated this story and recorded the response of amazed recognition. He does not draw out the implication explicitly, but in the light of the Old Testament passages above it is clearly revolutionary. Jesus is being progressively revealed as the Messiah – and more.

*(vii) The Gadarene demoniacs (8:28–34)*

**28.** Gadara was a city of Decapolis, 6 miles (10 km) south-east of the lake, but controlling territory up to the shore of the lake east of the Jordan outflow (Josephus, *Vita* 42). In all three Synoptic Gospels there are variant readings. Mark and Luke probably wrote 'Gerasenes', perhaps referring to the modern *Kursi*, on the eastern shore, rather than to the Roman city of Gerasa, over 30 miles (50 km) from the lake.[1] *Gadarenes* is probably Matthew's original reading. There is no means of deciding whether the site of the incident was near the Jordan outflow (Matthew) or on the eastern shore (Mark/Luke). Both sites offer a 'steep bank' (v. 32) and both had largely Gentile populations, as the presence of a

[1] The reading 'Gergesenes' was apparently introduced by Origen because neither Gadara nor the Roman Gerasa was by the lake.

large herd of pigs requires. The 'city' of v. 33 need not be Gadara itself, but a local settlement near the lake within Gadarene territory. The *two demoniacs* are only one in Mark and Luke. For similar 'doublings' by Matthew see 20:30 (*cf.* 9:27), the second animal in 21:1ff., and the specification of two false witnesses in 26:60. No single explanation is likely to suit these rather different cases (see commentary on 21:2; 26:60). Here and in 20:30 it is suggested that this is Matthew's way of compensating for his omission of another exorcism (Mk. 1:23ff.) and healing of the blind (Mk. 8:22ff.) respectively. This not only envisages an incredibly mechanical style of composition; it also fails to account for the further double healing of the blind in 9:27. R. Bultmann[1] mentions the introduction of twos for the sake of symmetry as a 'popular folk motif'; but neither here nor in 20:30 is such an effect achieved. Did Matthew then double the patients to increase the magnitude of the miracle, or to indicate a more general ministry of exorcism? Or did he simply have a different tradition of the incident which remembered a second and less memorable demoniac whom Mark and Luke ignored? There is no agreed solution, but one interesting suggestion[2] is that those healed in 8:28ff.; 9:27ff.; 20:30ff. in each case confess Jesus as Son of God or Son of David, and since Jewish law required *two* witnesses, Matthew confirms this testimony by mentioning two witnesses (this would then parallel Matthew's specification of *two* witnesses in 26:60). This verse summarizes five verses of description in Mark, and the whole incident in Matthew is less than half its length in Mark. Matthew's interest is in showing the authority of Jesus, and so he concentrates on his confrontation with the demons, not on the men who were the battleground; personal details are thus almost entirely omitted.

**29.** Literally 'What to us and to you?': they want nothing to do with the *Son of God*, a phrase generally restricted to those who confess their faith in Jesus, but used also by the devil (4:3, 6) and his associates, who recognize the authority they will not accept. Their eventual *torment* (*cf.* Rev. 14:10; 20:10) was thought to be reserved for the time of the final judgment (so much Jewish apocalyptic, *e.g.* 1 Enoch 12 – 16; Jubilees 5:5–10; 10:1–13), but

[1]R. Bultmann, *The History of the Synoptic Tradition* (1963), pp. 314–316.
[2]J. M. Gibbs, *NTS* 10 (1963/4), pp. 456–457.

Jesus' presence, even *here* (in Gentile territory), indicates that it is already beginning *before the time* (*cf.* 12:28). (In 26:18 *kairos* ('time') is used for the cross as the decisive moment of Jesus' conflict, but in this context the common Jewish expectation is the more likely reference.)

**30–31.** Matthew does not mention the dialogue of Mark 5:8–10, but goes straight to the main point, the exorcism itself. The *swine*, however, still feature prominently, for it is their behaviour which emphasizes the spectacular nature of the exorcism, as does also perhaps Matthew's addition that they were *at some distance* away. Jesus' command to come out (Mk. 5:8) is assumed; the *if* does not convey uncertainty. Once expelled, the demons will need a 'home' (see 12:43ff.), and pigs, as unclean animals, are clearly suitable.

**32.** The panic stampede provides visible proof of the exorcism to the bystanders (note that their report was of 'what had happened to the demoniacs' (v. 33), not 'to the pigs'!) as well as to the men themselves. Similar visible confirmations are recorded both for Jewish (Josephus, *Ant.* viii. 48) and pagan exorcisms (Philostratus, *Vita Apoll.* iv. 20). But these were deliberately designed as proofs, whereas nothing in this incident or in Matthew's wording suggests that this was Jesus' intention. Matthew's grammar may indicate a different understanding of the incident – the herd *rushed* (singular), and 'they perished' (plural). Does he mean that the *demons* were thus destroyed? (In Mark and Luke it is clearly the herd that is the subject of the verb 'were drowned'.) No attention is given to the economic morality, still less the humaneness, of the destruction of a large herd of pigs, but we may assume that for Jesus the liberation of two men took precedence over such considerations.

**33–34.** The local reaction is thoroughly understandable; Jesus was not a comfortable person to have around! P. P. Levertoff's comment is telling, if perhaps too cynical about their motives: 'All down the ages the world has been refusing Jesus because it prefers its pigs.'[1] No mention is made of the cured men and their mission to their own people (Mk. 5:18–20); Matthew is interested in the mission to Gentiles rather as a post-resurrection develop-

---

[1] P. P. Levertoff, *St. Matthew* (1940), p. 26.

ment (see on 10:5–6). The incident has been recorded only to show the authority of Jesus even over supernatural powers.

*(viii) The paralytic (9:1–8)*

**1–2.** *His own city* is Capernaum (see on 4:13), the scene of the earlier miracles in 8:5–17. Verse 8 will reveal the presence of large crowds again, and Mark 2:1–2 describes them graphically, but Matthew again omits descriptive details, even the unforgettable picture of the hole in the roof (Mk. 2:4). This time, however, it is not the miracle itself to which he is thus drawing attention, but (as in 8:5–13) the dialogue which accompanies it, which will introduce a new aspect of Jesus' authority. So right at the outset we have his declaration, *Your sins are forgiven.* To us this seems scarcely relevant to a case of paralysis, but in a culture where disease was generally traced to sin (see Jn. 9:2) this was not so. Jesus himself does not state here or anywhere else that a given illness is the result of sin (*cf.* Jn. 9:3), but to the patient the assurance of forgiveness was real cause to *take heart* (*cf.* v. 22: in both cases Matthew alone includes this word). For Jesus' response to the faith of others than the patient himself (*their faith*), *cf.* 8:5–13; 15:22–28.

**3.** This is the first mention of opposition to Jesus, which will be a recurrent theme. It derives from *the scribes*, now seen (unlike 8:19) in their typical role as representatives of the official religion which necessarily reacted against the radical claims of Jesus. How Jesus is *blaspheming* need not be stated (as it is in Mk. 2:7): Jewish religion of the time had no room for a personal declaration of forgiveness, still less for this to be uttered by a mere man, on his own authority.

**4–5.** For Jesus' awareness of *their thoughts*[1] *cf.* 12:25; 22:18. While effective forgiveness is no easy matter, it is certainly easier to *say* 'Your sins are forgiven' than to say 'Rise and walk', as the former requires no visible result while the latter lays one open to ridicule if nothing happens. If then Jesus' word is effective for the latter, they may assume that he was not bluffing about the former. If it was assumed that the illness was the result of sin (see on v. 2), the logical connection of healing with

[1]The more vivid reading *seeing* (RSV mg.) is likely to be original, parallel to his 'seeing their faith' in v. 2

forgiveness was of course even more direct. The use of *eukopōteron* ('easier') for an *a fortiori* argument occurs in Greek only in sayings of Jesus (*cf.* 19:24 parr.; Lk. 16:17).

**6.** The command to the paralytic in fact proves more than that his sins are forgiven; it indicates the *authority* of the forgiver. For *the Son of man* see pp. 43–45. Here, as in 8:20, it makes nonsense in context to take it as meaning 'man' in general; Jesus is not claiming that anyone can pronounce forgiveness (nor would his act of healing in any way indicate that), but that he himself has this special authority. The term 'Son of man' could not by itself convey this, even if it were understood to have a Messianic connotation, for Jewish expectation did not include forgiveness among the Messiah's functions. It was rather a part of God's eschatological blessings (*e.g.* Is. 33:24; Je. 31:34; Mi. 7:18–19). Yet here *on earth* Jesus is claiming this authority: *cf.* 16:19; 18:18 for forgiveness 'on earth' as an extension of the authority of God 'in heaven'. Jesus therefore brings *on earth* the authority of God (*cf.* 12:28 for this idea of 'realized eschatology').

**7–8.** The cure is, as always in Matthew, immediate. The fear of the crowd (Mark and Luke here mention only amazement) indicates the supernatural impact of Jesus, as in 17:6; 27:54 (*cf.* Mk. 4:41; 5:15; 10:32; 16:8). The emphasis is again on his *authority*, seen in his teaching (7:28–29), his power over illnesses as varied as 'leprosy', paralysis and fever (8:1–17), his demand for undivided allegiance (8:18–22), his control over natural forces (8:23-27), over supernatural powers (8:28–34), and now his right to pronounce God's forgiveness. In all these Jesus stands out as different from other men. The general term *men* in v. 8 is therefore unexpected. It may be generic (their surprise was that Jesus *as man* had such authority); or it may look forward to the extension of Jesus' authority to his disciples in 16:19; 18:18.

*(ix) The call of Matthew (9:9–13)*

**9.** *Matthew*, later to be included in the Twelve (10:3), is named in the parallel passages in Mark and Luke as Levi. It seems clear that the same man is concerned (*cf.* Simon/Cephas for two Semitic names for the same individual). The *tax office* at Capernaum would be concerned with tolls on goods crossing the frontier of Antipas's tetrarchy either across the lake from

Decapolis or across the Jordan from Philip's tetrarchy. Matthew was thus apparently a customs official in the service of Herod Antipas rather than a collector of direct taxes, but the two distinct occupations (see Jeremias, *NTT*, pp. 110–111) are both represented by the Greek *telōnēs*, and were generally linked together in Jewish writings, often bracketed with thieves and 'sinners' in general. Both occupations were despised as unpatriotic and inevitably involving contact with ritual uncleanness, quite apart from the extortion which was an inevitable result of the economic system. There is no evidence of any previous direct contact between Matthew and Jesus (*cf.* on 4:20), but Jesus was by now well known in Capernaum. That this popular 'Rabbi' (*cf.* 8:19) should take the initiative in calling an outcast to be his disciple was a sign of acceptance to which Matthew understandably responded readily.

**10.** For *sat at table*, see on 8:11. Luke specifies that the meal was in Levi's house. The main point is that Jesus was prepared to sit at table with *sinners*, a term which could apply to the *'am haāreṣ*, the common Jewish people who could not or would not keep the scribal rules of tithing and purity (among whom the *tax collectors* were prominent), but is used more widely of the immoral (Lk. 7:37ff.), heretics (Jn. 9:16ff.) and Gentiles (Gal. 2:15), as well as of tax collectors. To share a meal was a sign of intimacy, and Jesus' notorious willingness thus to identify himself with the undesirable is a prominent feature of the Gospel portrait (see especially Lk. 15:1–2; 19:1–10).

**11.** The reaction is inevitable. After the objection of the scribes to Jesus' 'blasphemy' comes that of the *Pharisees* to his behaviour, for practical observance of the law was the main concern of Pharisaism. To be the guest of an *'am haāreṣ* disqualified a man from being a *ḥābēr*, one recognized as observing all the rules of tithing and purity (Mishnah *Demai* 2:2–3). While the customs officer as such was probably not ritually unclean (though the *tax collector* was, and rendered unclean any house he entered, Mishnah *Tohoroth* 7:6), this gathering of *sinners* would certainly involve the breach of the very detailed scribal regulations relating to food. From the Pharisaic point of view Jesus was undoubtedly in the wrong, as their question implies.

**12.** Jesus replies with a proverbial saying; similar sayings, portraying the philosopher as a healer, occur in several Greek writings;[1] *cf.* Lk. 4:23. The difference between Jesus and the Pharisees lies in their conception of priorities in the will of God: for the Pharisees the first priority is obedience to regulations, for Jesus a mission to people. A healer must get his hands dirty.

**13.** Two further sayings reinforce this difference of perspective. The first is a quotation of Hosea 6:6, introduced by a typically Rabbinic formula, *Go and learn what this means.* It is a call to reflection, for Jesus is pointing not to the surface meaning of the text (the validity of *sacrifice* is not the point here or indeed anywhere in Jesus' teaching; *cf.* 5:23–24) but to Hosea's underlying concern, the danger of a religion which is all external, in which ritual demands have taken the place of love (*mercy* represents Heb. *ḥeseḏ*, normally and appropriately translated 'steadfast love' by RSV). Jesus' table-fellowship to which they object is in fact the supreme fulfilment of God's *desire*, while in their censorious indifference is a rebirth of the superficial religion which Hosea deplored. The second saying returns more directly to the present situation, and has the same shocking effect as 8:11–12; those who are to be *called* (not only to this meal but to the Messianic banquet) should surely be *the righteous*, but Jesus reverses the standards of formal religion, and invites only the disqualified. *Righteous* is not entirely ironical: in their sense of the word they *were* 'righteous' (*cf.* Phil. 3:6), but it is precisely the adequacy of such righteousness that Jesus constantly calls in question (see on 5:20; also on 3:15; 5:6, 10). *Sinners* who 'hunger and thirst for righteousness' are closer to true righteousness than the self-satisfied.

## (x) The question about fasting (9:14–17)

**14.** After the hostile questioning by scribes (v. 3) and Pharisees (v. 11), a third group now appears in opposition to Jesus' practice, *the disciples of John.* Cf. 11:2; 14:12; Luke 11:1 for John's disciples, and Acts 18:25; 19:3 for the continued existence of such a community. John 3:25ff. and 4:1 suggest that they saw Jesus and his disciples as rivals. For Jewish *fasting*, see on 6:16–18. John's disciples presumably joined the Pharisees in

[1]See H. B. Swete, *Mark*, p. 42; M.-J. Lagrange, *Marc*, p. 44.

observing not only the one fast enjoined in the Old Testament law (the Day of Atonement) and other prescribed fasts of a commemorative nature, but a regular routine of weekly fasts. The probable addition of *much* (RSV mg.) reinforces the point. *Cf.* 11:18 for John's own asceticism. We have no evidence beyond 6:16–18 and this passage for Jesus' attitude to fasting, but v. 15 and 6:16–18 together with the continued use of fasting in Acts 13:2–3; 14:23 (for special purposes, not as a routine) show that he did not repudiate fasting as such, while this verse indicates that his practice was not rigorous. He presumably observed the Day of Atonement at least, but not the Pharisaic routine. Mark 2:18 suggests that the occasion here was a regular Pharisaic fast, but it is not clear whether the question related to Jesus' general practice or specifically to the meal of v. 10.

**15.** A *wedding* is a time of joy, not of asceticism. That Jesus saw his ministry in this light may reflect the idea of the Messianic banquet (see on 8:11), already anticipated in his table-fellowship with sinners (9:10). *Cf.* 25:1ff. for Jesus as the *bridegroom*, the one who is the centre and cause of the joy of his disciples. John's disciples had lost their 'bridegroom', who was already in prison (4:12), so they had reason to *mourn*. The same would be true one day for Jesus' disciples. While the saying need mean no more than that Jesus will not always be present, *taken away* (echoing Is. 53:8 ?) suggests a violent end, and the beginnings of official opposition in this chapter would give an early intimation of this eventual outcome. Jesus and official Judaism were scarcely compatible, as vv. 16–17 will go on to indicate.

**16–17.** These verses do not relate directly to the situation of vv. 14–15 and were probably an independent saying, referring to Jewish tradition in general, not specifically to John's disciples. But they express an important general truth of which the question of fasting was a specific example. Jesus has brought something new, and the rituals and traditions of official Judaism cannot contain it. The explosive exuberance of the new era (for wedding, garment and wine as all symbols of eschatological salvation, see Jeremias, *PJ*, pp. 117–118) must break out of the confines of legalism and asceticism. The Greek for *tear* is *schisma*, which is also often used metaphorically; combining incompatible religious attitudes is a recipe for schism. What form the *fresh wineskins* will take is not spelt out, but they at least indicate that Jesus looked for some formal structure in religion, not for anarchy: ' "Free" thought that recognizes no authoritative control, is as useless as spilt wine' (McNeile). *Both are preserved* is probably only the conclusion of the 'story' of the wineskins, not a deliberate prescription for the perpetuation of unreformed Judaism alongside the new life of the kingdom of heaven.

*(xi) The ruler's daughter and the woman with a haemorrhage (9:18–26)*

**18–19.** This double healing story is one of Matthew's most spectacular abbreviations: his nine verses correspond to 23 in Mark. Descriptive details, extra characters and sub-plots are ruthlessly pruned away, and the two healings recast into the simplest possible form. The father (Jairus in Mark) is not named, and is simply a *ruler* (a general term for an official or important person, not necessarily in a political sense, and therefore appropriate to the synagogue leader, as Mark specifies). More important, Matthew's telescoping of the two stages of the story (first Jairus' appeal, then the news of his daughter's death, after which the appeal is not withdrawn) results in the appeal being made when the girl is already dead, not just dying. It therefore appears from the beginning as what it ultimately became, an appeal for a raising of the dead, a much more startling act of faith than a request for help *in extremis*. That she was really dead, not only apparently as v. 24 suggests, is made clear by Luke (8:53, 55) and is presupposed in the mention of the raising of the dead in 11:5. While faith is not mentioned explicitly in this story, the ruler's practical confidence in Jesus' healing power is closely parallel to the 'faith' depicted in 8:8–9; 9:2. For *knelt* (*prosekynei*) see on 2:2; 8:2.

**20–21.** The *haemorrhage* (a menstrual disorder) rendered her, and anything she touched, ceremonially unclean (Lv. 15:25ff.), hence perhaps her approach from *behind*, and her touching only the *fringe*, though even that should have made a pious Jew recoil in horror. But her determination and her conviction of Jesus' healing power outweighed the risk. To expect to be healed by touching Jesus' clothes (*cf.* 14:36) may suggest a rather 'magical' conception of his healing role, but one which he did not rebuke. In wearing the *fringe* (or 'tassel') Jesus was faithful to the Old

Testament law (Nu. 15:38–39; Dt. 22:12); his objection in 23:5 is to the misuse of it for ostentation.

**22.** Matthew (unlike Mark and Luke) presents the healing as the direct result of Jesus' word, rather than of the previous touch; any impression of a 'magical' element in the cure is thus removed (and *cf.* his omission of Jesus' awareness 'that power had gone forth from him', Mk. 5:30). The key, as always, is *faith*, of the same practical kind as in 8:8–9; 9:2 (*cf.* 9:29; 15:28). The sonorous declaration *hē pistis sou sesōken se* ('Your faith has made you well') was apparently a favourite pronouncement of Jesus (*cf.* Mk. 10:52; Lk. 7:50; 17:19), leaving no doubt of the condition of his healing ministry. *Take heart* (*cf.* on 9:2) was specially appropriate to one who had good reason to hesitate in approaching Jesus.

**23–24.** Professional mourners were hired even by the poorest families (Mishnah *Ketuboth* 4:4 specifies 'not less than two flutes and one wailing woman'); for the *flute players*, *cf.* Josephus, *BJ* iii. 437: Matthew's addition of this peculiarly Jewish touch in his economical account is noteworthy. *Not dead but sleeping* must presumably be taken as indicating that her (real) death is not to be permanent. *Katheudō* ('sleep') is normally used literally in the New Testament, or metaphorically for spiritual inertia, not death (in contrast with *koimaomai*, also literally 'sleep', which regularly refers to death), so that Jesus' words ought to suggest that she was only in a coma. But see on v. 18 for the reality of her death, and Daniel 12:2 (and probably 1 Thes. 5:10) for this sense of *katheudō*. No doubt *they laughed at him* because they took his words literally, and knew they could not be true (so Luke).

**25–26.** The presence of Peter, James and John (so Mark and Luke) is not mentioned, and Jesus seems to go in alone with the corpse, like Elijah (1 Ki. 17:19ff.) and Elisha (2 Ki. 4:32ff.). The report in *all that district* (*cf.* v. 31) prepares for the climax of v. 33, and for the corollary drawn in 11:2–5.

### (xii) Two blind men (9:27–31)

Matthew has two very similar accounts of the healing of two blind men. The other, 20:29–34, is parallel to the story of Bartimaeus in Mark 10:46–52. This one has no parallel in the other Gospels (the other healing of a blind man in Mark (8:22–26) is quite different, and is not related by Matthew). Unless we are to credit Matthew with simply duplicating his own story, and there is no obvious motive for his doing so, nor are the stories the same in detail, we must assume that he here relates a separate incident, using standard ideas and terminology common to these and several other miracle stories. The narration is as usual economical and unconcerned with personal details (though Wellhausen's 'nicht mit Liebe', 'without love', was a bit strong!).

**27.** For the *two*, see on 8:28. The appeal for *mercy* (*eleēson*) is repeated in 15:22; 17:15; 20:30–31, in each case asking for practical help; *cf.* also 18:33, and the regular use of *eleēmosynē* for 'alms'. Mercy is not an emotion, but a practical response to need. The fact that not only here but also in 15:22; 20:30–31 it is linked with *Son of David* (see above, p. 43) suggests that such 'mercy' was expected to characterize the Davidic Messiah, and 11:4–5, with its use of Isaiah 35:5–6 and 61:1, indicates that there was sufficient popular awareness of the Messiah's healing role to justify this explicit appeal.

**28.** Presumably *the house* is that of 9:10, at Capernaum. It seems that Jesus did not respond to their first request. *Cf.* 15:23 for a similar lack of response, which eventually resulted in a striking illustration of persistent faith (and *cf.* on 8:7, above). Here too faith is tested, and indeed explicitly questioned, so that, like the leper, the centurion, the ruler and the woman with the haemorrhage, they must explicitly confess it. Again, as throughout these two chapters, faith is shown to be a practical confidence in the power of Jesus.

**29.** The two regular elements of touch and healing word come together, but the focus is on the latter (*cf.* on v. 22). The words are virtually those of 8:13 (and *cf.* 15:28), and their effect, like that of the parallel declaration of v. 22, is to emphasize *faith* as the one essential condition of Jesus' healing ministry. *According to* does not mean 'in proportion to', but rather implies 'in response to'; the deed matches the faith.

**30–31.** For Jesus' desire for secrecy, see on 8:4. *Sternly charged* represents an emotional term implying indignation. Jesus was acutely concerned to avoid misguided enthusiasm, but his vehement prohibition was ignored; indeed it would be hard for formerly blind men to conceal their cure! Jesus' healing miracles, thought not designed to excite curiosity, were nevertheless too spectacular to pass unnoticed (*cf.* v. 26).

*(xiii) A dumb man (9:32-34)*
The miracle itself is only a minor element in these verses; it acts as the 'text' around which Matthew constructs a concluding paragraph drawing out the significance of the collection of miracles in chapters 8 – 9. The varied demonstration of Jesus' unique authority in these chapters provokes either wonder or opposition, depending on the viewpoint of the observer. The whole paragraph is closely parallel to 12:22-24, except that the complaint in that case includes blindness, and the crowd's reaction is more explicitly Messianic. The relationship is parallel to that between the last paragraph and 20:29-34 (on which see above).

**32.** *Kōphos* means both 'deaf' and 'dumb', the two complaints being naturally linked together. Here v. 33 indicates that the latter meaning is primarily in mind, as in 12:22; 15:31. In view of the careful distinction normally drawn between illness and demon-possession (see on 8:16), it is surprising that here and in 12:22 a physical complaint is attributed to demonic influence: *cf.* Mark 9:17ff., the only other such instance, again in a case of dumbness. The fact that the language here is entirely that of exorcism (*demon cast out*; no mention of faith or of touching the patient), whereas elsewhere the deaf and dumb are healed normally (15:30-31; Mk. 7:32ff. – but see 12:22, where the blind and dumb *demoniac* is 'healed') indicates that this case was regarded as primarily one of possession, with the dumbness as a 'byproduct'.

**33.** For *in Israel*, *cf.* 8:10; here again the implication is that the nation under its official leadership has fallen short. The authority inherent in Jesus' deeds, displayed cumulatively in a variety of spheres in chapters 8 – 9 (see on 9:8), provided, like the authority of his words in chapters 5 – 7 (see on 7:28-29), a striking contrast with the existing leadership, and people noticed it. 'The scribes taught and nothing happened. Jesus spoke and demons fled, storms were settled, dead were raised, sins forgiven . . . His authority in deeds and words was nothing less than the presence of the Kingdom of God' (Ladd, p. 166).

**34.** Predictably, this popular response was not welcome to *the Pharisees*. The accusation will be repeated in 12:24 (see comments there), and this may be the reason why this verse is omitted here by a few important MSS. But its appropriateness here as the climax to the mounting opposition seen in this chapter (vv. 3, 11, 14 – and *cf.* Jesus' dismissal of the old forms of religion in vv. 16–17) supports its genuineness. It is not so much an anticlimax after v. 33, as a parallel climax showing the other side of the polarization resulting from the impact of Jesus' authority.

### D. THE PARALLEL MINISTRY OF THE DISCIPLES (9:35 – 11:1)

The authority displayed by Jesus in word and deed (chapters 5 – 9) is now seen extended to his disciples (see comments on 9:35–38; 10:1); their ministry is carefully presented as parallel to and derived from that of Jesus in this second collection of Jesus' teaching (see the introductory comments on chapters 5 – 7, above, and Introduction, pp. 59–60). The material found in chapter 10 is almost all paralleled in Mark and/or Luke (all except verses 5–8, 16b, 40–41), but occurs in a bewildering variety of different contexts. It is all connected by the theme of the mission and consequent suffering of the disciples, and thus, like chapters 5 – 7, bears the marks of a deliberate collection by Matthew of separate units of Jesus' teaching bearing on this question. Its basis is the mission charge recorded in Mark 6:7–13 and Luke 9:1–6, but the sayings added to this emphasize further the urgency of their mission, and the certainty of persecution for those engaged in it.

*(i) Summary and introduction (9:35–38)*

These verses fill a dual role, both as a summary of the ministry of Jesus in chapters 5 – 9 and an introduction to the parallel mission of the disciples in chapter 10. The wording is carefully designed to look both back and forward, and to emphasize the continuity between these two sections of the book.

**35.** The words are almost identical with 4:23 (see notes there). Chapters 5 – 9 are thus enclosed in a framework which draws out the threefold nature of Jesus' ministry revealed in them, a ministry of *teaching, preaching* and *healing*. At the same time the repetition of the words *healing every disease and every infirmity* in 10:1, with reference to the *disciples'* commission, shows that the authority revealed in Jesus' ministry in chapters 5 – 9 (see on 9:33) is passed on to them. There is a note of restless activity in this verse which will also be taken up in 10:5ff. The reference to *all the cities and villages* confirms that the activity of chapters 8 – 9, which was largely located in Capernaum, was only a typical selection of Jesus' ministry, not an exhaustive account.

**36.** The cause of Jesus' ceaseless activity is traced to his *compassion* on *the crowds*. The vivid verb 'have compassion' (literally referring to a 'gut reaction'!) is always in the New Testament used of Jesus himself (except in three parables: 18:27; Lk. 10:33; 15:20); like his 'mercy' (see on 9:27) it regularly issues in action to meet the need which evokes it. Here that need is expressed in the Old Testament metaphor *sheep without a shepherd*, a phrase which referred especially to lack of political leadership (Nu. 27:17; 1 Ki. 22:17; Ezk. 34:5) but which here presumably denotes a lack of spiritual care and guidance as well (*cf.* Zc. 10:2–3). *Harassed and helpless* is literally 'torn and thrown down', continuing the metaphor of sheep unprotected from predators, or even suffering from unscrupulous shepherds (*cf.* Zc. 11:16). The ordinary people of Israel are 'lost sheep' (10:6; 15:24) awaiting the Messianic shepherd (Ezk. 34:23; Mi. 5:4; Zc. 11:4ff.; *etc.*).

**37–38.** If the need of Israel is one spur to urgency, another is the opportunity. *The harvest is plentiful*, and it is ripe.[1] *Harvest* is used in the Old Testament as a picture of the coming judgment (Is. 27:12; Ho. 6:11; Joel 3:13); John the Baptist had taken this up (3:12), and Jesus does so elsewhere (13:39–40; *cf.* Mk. 4:29). Here, however, as in John 4:35, his thought is rather of men's readiness now to respond to the gospel by 'fleeing from the wrath to come'. The context shows that the *labourers* here are not angels sent out to execute final judgment on the nations, as his Jewish hearers would expect, but men sent out to rescue others *from* judgment, and beginning within Israel itself (10:5–6). For

---

[1]The violent change of metaphor suggests that these verses were not originally connected with v. 36; in Lk. 10:2 they occur as part of the mission charge to the seventy.

this task the disciples were, and have always been, too *few*, and the command to ask the *Lord of the harvest* (probably representing an Aramaic term for 'chief harvester' (see *AB*, p. 114); but clearly God is intended) for reinforcements has never been superseded. The mission is God's, and under his control. Chapter 10 will spell out what that mission is, and what it will involve for those who are 'sent out'.

## (ii) The twelve (10:1–4)

**1.** As an immediate practical solution to the need for workers (9:37–38), Jesus now summons *his twelve disciples*. This is not an account of their selection (as in Mk. 3:13–15; Lk. 6:13, to which Matthew has no parallel), but of their commissioning. They appear here for the first time as an already defined group, whose function is here seen to be that of mission (*cf.* on *apostles*, v. 2), though in 19:28 a continuing leadership role is also in view; that passage also indicates that the number *twelve* was chosen as a deliberate reference to the twelve tribes of Israel, and this tallies with several other indications that Jesus saw this inner circle of his followers as representing the true people of God. For *authority* see above, on 9:6–8 (and *cf.* 7:29; 8:9); in those cases the authority displayed was that of Jesus himself, and the word described a central aspect of his ministry. That authority he now vests also in his disciples, whose healing mission is described in the same words used for his mission in 4:23 and 9:35. *Cf.* on 10:7–8 for the close parallel between the missions of Jesus and of his disciples. The disciples are therefore here given *authority* for mission, not institutional leadership. *Unclean spirits* (*cf.* 12:43) are generally called 'demons' in Matthew (*cf.* 9:32–34), or occasionally simply 'spirits' (8:16; 12:45).

**2.** *Apostles* occurs only here in Matthew; elsewhere he speaks of 'the twelve (disciples)': 11:1; 20:17; 26:14, 20, 47. While Luke (like Paul) uses 'apostle' of an office, the other Gospels use it, as Matthew does here, only in a context of mission. It means one who is 'sent' ('sent out' in v. 5 is the verb from the same root). For *Simon* and *Andrew* (and for Philip, v. 3), see on 4:18. *First* would be unnecessary simply to mark the beginning of a list, and indicates Peter's prominence in the group, which will be spelt out more explicitly in 16:16–19; all four Gospels agree in presenting Peter as the leader of the disciples; he and the two *sons of Zebedee* formed a specially trusted inner group (17:1; 26:37; cf. Mk. 5:37; 13:3).

**3–4.** Little is known of the remaining members of the twelve, except Judas Iscariot. *Bartholomew* is traditionally identified with Nathanael, who appears only in John, but Nathanael is nowhere said to be one of the twelve. *Matthew*'s occupation is mentioned to identify him as the one whose call was previously described (see on 9:9), and *James*' father and *Simon*'s nickname to distinguish them from their better-known namesakes in v. 2. *Thaddaeus* is mentioned nowhere outside the lists of Matthew and Mark; Luke (6:16 and Acts 1:13) replaces him with 'Judas the son of James' (cf. John's 'Judas (not Iscariot)', 14:22), and some MSS in Matthew and Mark read instead 'Lebbaeus'. The cases of Matthew and Peter (see on 4:18) show that a man could be known by more than one name, but it is possible that the membership of the inner circle was not entirely fixed, or that there was some uncertainty as to the identity of the obscure twelfth member of the group. For *Cananaean* Luke has 'Zealot', and the name probably represents the Aramaic term for a Zealot, *qan'ana'*. This was not yet at the time of Jesus a technical term for the revolutionary political party, but Matthew and Luke would have known it as such. Probably Simon's nickname originated from a 'zeal' for the law (cf. Paul's use of 'Zealot' in this sense, Acts 22:3–5; Gal. 1:14; Phil. 3:6), but this would be likely to make him sympathetic to the ideals of the later Zealot party. The inclusion of this man together with the government employee Matthew is evidence of the breadth of Jesus' appeal. *Iscariot* is usually thought to mean 'man of Kerioth' (a city in southern Judaea), but has also been explained as meaning 'traitor', 'assassin', 'carrier of the leather bag', or 'redhead'!

*(iii) Instructions for their mission (10:5–16)*
This first part of the collection of Jesus' teaching in chapter 10 relates more directly to the immediate mission of the disciples as Jesus sent them out during his ministry in Galilee, whereas the subsequent part of the chapter deals more generally with the nature of the Christian mission in the world.

**5–6.** This startling restriction of the disciples' mission to Israel is found only in Matthew, where it is matched by an equally restricted statement of Jesus' own mission (15:24). Yet this same Gospel not only recognizes a deliberate mission to Gentiles at a later period, after the resurrection (28:19-20; *cf.* 24:14), but also includes sayings of Jesus which include other nations in God's plan of salvation (8:11-12; 21:43; 25:32), and we have seen in the early chapters a clear interest in the significance of Jesus for the Gentiles (2:1-12; 4:14-16, 24-25).[1] Matthew cannot then be accused of anti-Gentile bias. Rather this saying reflects the historic fact that with very few exceptions (8:5-13 deals with a Gentile in Jewish territory; 15:21-28 is clearly presented as exceptional) the mission of both Jesus and his disciples before the resurrection was in fact limited to Israel; the time for the Gentile mission was later.[2] The emphasis of the saying lies not primarily on the prohibition of a wider mission, but on the priority of the mission to Israel. To call Israel to repentance was the primary focus of Jesus' ministry; the call was urgent and demanded total concentration (*cf.* 10:23). They were *lost sheep*, a common Old Testament metaphor (Je. 50:6; Ezk. 34:1-16; *cf.* Is. 53:6); the reference, as in these Old Testament passages, is apparently to Israel as a whole, not to a specific group. *Go* in v. 5 is literally 'go away', *i.e.* digress; in the historical situation of the Galilean mission this effectively restricted them to Galilee, which was completely surrounded by Gentile and Samaritan territory. This is Matthew's only reference to *Samaritans* (even 4:25 pointedly omits them). Luke, by contrast, includes three mentions of them in his Gospel (9:52ff.; 10:29ff.; 17:11ff.), each time in a way which opposes the traditional Jewish hostility to them (and *cf.* Jn. 4:4-42; Acts 1:8; 8:5-25); Matthew apparently reflects a more traditionally Jewish outlook.

**7-8.** Their mission consists of both preaching and healing; the two go together as complementary aspects of the announcement of the kingdom of heaven (as in Is. 61:1-2, quoted in 11:5 and in Lk. 4:18-19 with reference to Jesus' own mission), and each confirms the validity of the other. The healing activity of Jesus and his disciples was more than kindness; it was itself a part of

[1] *Cf.* my article in *NTS* 27 (1980/81), pp. 237-240.
[2] See the discussion by M. D. Hooker, *ExpT* 82 (1970/1), pp. 361-365; also J. Jeremias, *Jesus' Promise to the Nations.*

the proclamation of God's kingdom (*cf.* 12:28).

There is a striking parallel between the mission of the disciples and that of Jesus himself (*cf.* on 9:35, and also the parallel between 10:5–6 and 15:24). The words they are to preach are the same as those of Jesus in 4:17, and the acts of healing listed in v. 8 cover practically all the types of Jesus' healing miracles recorded in chapters 8 and 9. *Cf.* also the description of Jesus' ministry in 11:5.[1] Their mission is an extension of his, for which they are vested with his authority. *Raise the dead* is introduced in such a matter-of-fact way that some commentators have doubted whether it is to be taken literally, despite the two records of such miracles later by disciples (Acts 9:36ff.; 20:7ff.), and appeal has been made to the metaphorical use of 'dead' in 8:22; 'raise the dead' would then be a command to arouse the spiritually indifferent.[2] Such an understanding is plausible, however, only if the other commands of this verse are also taken metaphorically (as Fenton proposes), and in the light of the literal miracles of chapters 8 – 9 this seems impossible. It is fairer to the text, though certainly it calls for a bolder faith, to accept that Jesus did not exclude the raising of the dead from his disciples' share in his own authority to heal.

Their ministry must be *without pay*, unlike that of the mercenary prophets who plagued the church by the end of the first century (Didache 11–12). Their status as apostles of Jesus, and their authority to heal, were a gift, not bought or earned, and must be exercised in the same spirit. Paul made much of this principle (1 Cor. 9:18; 2 Cor. 11:7). But see further on v. 10b.

**9–10.** *Take* is literally 'obtain' (and *in* is more correctly 'into' or 'for'). The saying in its Matthaean form thus does not so much specify the appropriate equipment for travelling, but rather assures the disciples that no previous fund-raising is necessary, nor need special equipment be acquired. They can go just as they are, and the mission is urgent. The principle is that of 6:25ff.; they can leave the provisions to God. This is not a call to asceticism, for due provision of food and lodging is assured (vv. 10b–11 and *cf.* 6:30–33); it is a call to put first things first. This spirit of sitting light to material provision is good both for the

[1] See further, Held, *TIM*, pp. 250–251.
[2] So especially J. C. Fenton, *ExpT* 80 (1968/9), pp. 50–51.

179

disciple's own attitude in his mission, as he trusts God for practical provision, and for his credibility in an age aware of the possibility of using religion for profit (*e.g.* Mishnah *Aboth* 1:3; *Bekhoroth* 4:6). A church whose members are preoccupied with material concerns still finds it hard to convince the world that it should take God seriously. The *bag* may be either one for carrying food (no packed lunch required), or the beggar's bag, such as itinerant Cynic preachers carried (see BAGD, p. 656b); the former seems more appropriate to the theme of no prior provision. The second *tunic* may have been a spare, or intended for extra warmth during a night spent in the open (and therefore not needed, see v. 11). *Sandals* and *staff* were normally essential for travelling (see, *e.g.*, Ex. 12:11); the forbidden *sandals* were perhaps, like the second tunic, a spare pair procured for the journey (Mk. 6:9 allows them to *wear* sandals, and the gesture commanded here in v. 14 presupposes some sort of footwear which could hold dust). The well-known discrepancy over the *staff* (Mk. 6:8 specifically allows them to carry one) may arise from the difference in the verbs: the Matthaean version forbids the acquisition of a staff for the journey, while the Marcan allows them to take (only) the one they already possess. Clearly there is some variation in the details of the different versions of the relevant sayings (Luke indicates that there were at least two separate such injunctions: 9:3 and 10:4; *cf.* 22:35–36), but the essential theme of an urgent mission which does not require or even permit elaborate provision is not affected. These injunctions have assumed that the disciples will be provided for in some other way, and this assumption is drawn out in the following saying, that *the labourer deserves his food*. He deserves it, and it will be provided (v. 11 will explain how); therefore he need not provide for himself. This principle, so important to later Christian thought (1 Cor. 9:14; 1 Tim. 5:17–18; *etc.*), is not in conflict with v. 8b: the principle of the Christian worker deserving his keep and accepting hospitality is not the same thing as requiring 'payment for services rendered', difficult as it may sometimes be to separate them in practice.

**11.** *Worthy* suggests to us a test of character, but this is not essential to its meaning (*AB* translates 'suitable'). They are to look for someone able and willing to accommodate them, and this would normally be someone open to their message, though not necessarily already committed to their cause. The expectation of free hospitality, which seems so bold to our culture, is in accord with eastern tradition, where the guest, who might be a complete stranger, has unquestioned rights to provision and protection (*cf.* Gn. 18:1–8; 19:1–8; Jdg. 19:15–24).

**12–13.** The salutation (*peace* is the standard greeting still today in both Hebrew and Arabic) is no mere formality. *Cf.* the blessing given by Isaac, which once uttered was a potent force (Gn. 27:33–38), and other Old Testament statements of the efficacy of a word (Ps. 147:15, 18; Is. 9:8; 45:23; 55:10–11; *etc.*). The *peace* which they wish to the household goes out and is effective; but it is not automatic, and a wrong attitude in the receiver will result in its return, like an uncashed cheque.

**14–15.** Jesus fully expected his message, and his messengers, to meet with rejection as well as acceptance: see vv. 17–39. The result would be a division among men which they were not to gloss over, but rather to emphasize: *shake off the dust from your feet*, a dramatic gesture of repudiation still in use in the Middle East.[1] The *house* or *town* which is thus marked out as in opposition to the message of Jesus faces a judgment more severe even than that of *Sodom and Gomorrah*, the most notorious centres of iniquity of the Old Testament, destroyed by fire and brimstone (Gn. 19:24ff.; *cf.* Lk. 17:28–30). They have had the benefit of a clearer call to repentance, God's last word, and so the guilt of their failure to respond is greater. '"Post-Christian" man is a different man from the heathen, to whom the Word of Jesus has not yet come' (Schweizer, pp. 240–241).

**16.** This verse, while clearly appropriate for the initial sending out of the disciples, also serves to introduce the theme of persecution which will dominate the next section. *Sheep in the midst of wolves* are in constant danger, and have no capacity for self-defence; they depend on the shepherd (*cf.* Jn. 10:12–15). Initially perhaps the *wolves* would be particularly the Pharisaic establishment, but the principle is relevant to Christians in all ages who must live and witness in a hostile world. Jesus did not envisage

---

[1] G. Dalman, *Arbeit und Sitte in Palästina*, I, p. 522. The later Jewish view that earth from heathen territory brings uncleanness (*Shabbath* 15b; *Nedarim* 53b) may be in the background, but the basic symbolism is that of repudiation.

his people as a power-group. But they are not to be like sheep in their attitude. Their vulnerable position demands that they be *wise* (*phronimos* is better 'sensible', 'prudent'; it is the word used in LXX for the 'cunning' of the *serpent* in Gn. 3:1). *Cf.* Luke 16:1–8 with its commendation of the 'prudence' (*phronimos* again) of the steward. Christians are not to be gullible simpletons. But neither are they to be rogues. *Innocent* is literally 'unmixed', *i.e.* pure, transparent; it demands not naivety, but an irreproachable honesty. The balance of prudence and purity will enable Christians both to survive and to fulfil their mission to the world.

*(iv) Warnings of conflict and persecution (10:17–39)*
This collection of sayings centres on a single theme, but it may be subdivided for convenience.

*(a) Persecution predicted (10:17–23).* The setting is the mission of the Twelve in Galilee, but the principles are general ones relevant to Christians facing persecution in any situation; after v. 23 the immediate situation recedes further from view. Jesus assumes that his heralds will meet with rejection and persecution – he gives instruction for their response when opposed, but not for dealing with the converts of a successful mission!

**17.** While the immediate concern is with persecution by Jews, the Christian can expect opposition from *men* in general (*cf.* 16:13 for this general sense). The book of Acts shows the variety of groups who actively opposed the Christian mission. The *councils* (literally 'sanhedrins') may refer to the councils of 23 members who were responsible for discipline in the local synagogue, but the word could apply to any formal body (*cf.* Hare, pp. 102–104). *Flogging in synagogues* (*cf.* 23:34; Acts 5:40; 22:19; 2 Cor. 11:24) was a punishment for disobedience or breach of the peace (by preaching an unpopular message) rather than for heresy as such (Hare, pp. 43–46, 105).

**18.** The mention of *governors and kings* suggests a wider canvas than the purely Israelite mission of vv. 5–6, 23. The Roman prefects of Judaea (the same word for 'governor' is used in 27:2, 11, 14) and 'king' Herod of Galilee with his later successors as kings of the Jews would fit the description, and there were Gentiles in Palestine, but the specific mention of the *Gentiles* suggests that the wider mission of the post-resurrection period is already in view. Acts supplies several examples of Christians arraigned before the Gentile authorities by hostile Jews (17:5-7; 18:12-17; 24:1-9; 25:1ff.). *For my sake* does not necessarily imply that the charge was explicitly that of following Jesus, but that it resulted from their Christian obedience. The trial would thus turn out *for a testimony* (literally; it is the same phrase as in 8:4, where see discussion) by confronting the authorities and the Gentiles in general with the truths they stood for, as Jesus' own trial was to confront Pilate with the truth (Jn. 18:33-38).

**19-20.** The prospect of trial before governors and kings would naturally terrify the humble disciple. But this situation too is covered by the *do not be anxious* of 6:25-34. In both cases God will provide what is needed (in this case words, in ch. 6 material needs, but the principle is the same); here in addition *the Spirit of your Father* (a unique expression in the New Testament) will speak through them. Elsewhere in Matthew the activity of the Spirit is related to Jesus himself; but here, where the disciple publicly represents Jesus, the Spirit is active for him too. Perhaps Joel's prophecy of Spirit-inspired speech by God's people is in mind (Joel 2:28-29; *cf.* Acts 2:15-21).

**21.** The words reflect Micah 7:6, which will be more explicitly alluded to in vv. 35-36, but the family divisions which in Micah indicated the breakdown of social order here assume a more radical meaning; this is religious persecution ('for my name's sake', v. 22) which extends even *to death*, and even the closest family ties will give way to it. Jesus' thought here extends beyond the immediate Galilean situation, where martyrdom at the hands of close relatives was not yet likely, to the passionate and all-consuming opposition which loyalty to his cause has evoked through the ages since.

**22.** That this hatred is *for my name's sake* (see on v. 18) differentiates Jesus' prediction from the general apocalyptic expectation of social strife in the last days (see *ICC*, p. 106); it is Jesus' followers as such who will meet with general rejection (*by all*). *To the end* is the adverbial phrase *eis telos*, 'right through' (see BAGD, p. 812a), not a specific reference to the eschatological consummation. An identical promise occurs at 24:13, also in a context of persecution and mission. The nature of that 'salvation' promised is not spelt out here, but it is clearly not escape from persecution; rather it depends on faithfully holding out through it.

**23.** This verse is a centre of controversy.[1] Any proper exegesis must take it in its context: the Christian missionary's response to Jewish persecution must be to move on, for there will always be further scope for the mission to Israel until 'the Son of man comes'. The emphasis is therefore on the unlimited scope for the mission to Israel, in the light of which the Christian must not be cowed into giving up his mission, nor must he waste time 'flogging a dead horse'. The command to move on when opposed reflects that of v. 14 (and *cf.* the principle of 7:6); the book of Acts shows how the application of this principle contributed to the rapid spread of the gospel. The restriction of the mission here to Israel reflects that of 10:5–6 (see discussion there).

Does this verse envisage the parousia within the lifetime of Jesus' hearers (or even, as Schweitzer believed,[2] during the Galilean mission of the Twelve, a hope whose failure led to Jesus' own disillusionment)? Two questions are involved: what does it mean to 'complete the towns of Israel' (literally), and what is the 'coming of the Son of man'?

*The towns of Israel* is a geographical expression and can hardly mean 'all Jewish communities' (including the Diaspora); in this context of the Galilean mission it apparently means Palestine. But it is not clear what it means to 'complete' these towns: suggestions include the preaching of the gospel in each town, the conversion of 'all Israel' (as in Rom. 11:26), or the exhausting of possible places of refuge from persecution. The interpretation given above assumes the first of these.

*The Son of man comes* is an echo of the language of Daniel 7:13, which does not speak of the 'son of man' coming to earth, but rather coming to God to receive authority, and Jesus' frequent uses of such language show that he applied it to his own future glory in times and situations varying from his vindication after the resurrection (26:64; *cf.* 28:18, echoing Dn. 7:14) to the final

---

[1] See L. Sabourin, *BTB* 7 (1977), pp. 5–11, for a recent brief survey of interpretations.
[2] A. Schweitzer, *The Quest of the Historical Jesus* ([2]1911), pp. 357–358.

judgment (25:31; *cf.* 19:28). See further, below, on 16:28; 24:31, and the discussion in my *JOT*, pp. 139–148, especially p. 145 section 2. *AB* (p. 125) sees this saying as referring to 'the exaltation of the Messiah in passion-resurrection', while others see it as pointing forward to the manifestation of his authority in the climactic events of AD 70 ((*JOT*, p. 140, with references there). Perhaps it is better to think of the fulfilment of the vision of Daniel 7:13–14 in the authority of Jesus without reference to a specific time (Sabourin, *BTB* 7, pp. 9–10); at any rate, it is far from clear that any reference to the parousia is intended. Certainly the context is not concerned with chronological predictions, but with the continuation of the mission, and the mention of the coming vindication of Jesus functions as a spur to their preaching.

(b) *Like master, like servant (10:24–25).* The principle of vv. 24–25a recurs in Luke 6:40; John 13:16; 15:20, in the last case again with reference to persecution. It is expressed as a general truth, but its application to Jesus' own disciples is obvious. The disciple who has the privilege of sharing Jesus' work (see above, pp. 174, 176, 179) and representing him (see below, v. 40), must also expect to share his unpopularity. More specifically, they will face the same insults (*will they malign* is not in the Greek). *Beelzebul* will recur in 12:24, 27 as the name of the demon to whose power Jesus' enemies attributed his miracles. Here it is applied as an insult to Jesus himself (as Jesus himself called Peter 'Satan', 16:23!). It probably derived from the Canaanite god mentioned in 2 Kings 1:2 in the form *Baal-zebub* ('lord of flies'), whose official title may have been *Baal-zebul*, 'Baal the prince' or possibly 'Lord of the height' or 'of the dwelling'; but in popular Jewish usage it had become the name of a senior demon; 12:24ff. shows that it could be used as a synonym of 'Satan'. It is thus an insult which carries a hint of the charge of satanic inspiration brought in 9:34 and 12:24, a charge Christians themselves have not been slow to throw at other Christians from whom they differ.

(c) *Whom to fear (10:26–33).* 'Fear' is the key word of this section (see vv. 26, 28, 31). There are right and wrong fears for the disciple of Jesus, and true discipleship depends on distinguishing them.

**26–27.** The *fear* very naturally engendered by the sort of conditions described in vv. 17–25 could put a stop to the disciples' mission. These verses therefore emphasize how essential, and indeed ultimately inescapable, is their duty to bear witness to what they have seen and heard; this duty must override their natural reluctance to incur men's hostility. The idea in v. 26, that everything must come to light, occurs not only in the parallel passage, Luke 12:2, but in connection with the saying about the lamp under the bushel in Mark 4:22; Luke 8:17. In each case the context shows that it is a statement of the duty of witness rather than a general observation (which would in any case be hard to justify). Verse 27 then puts the same duty into an explicit command: Jesus' private teaching is to be publicly proclaimed (the flat *housetops* form a natural platform for a public announcement). The parallel in Luke 12:3 is phrased in terms of the inevitability of the teaching becoming public; in Matthew this becomes the disciple's deliberate intention.

**28.** Two types of *fear* are here contrasted: fear of men is a self-interested cowardice, but fear of God is a healthy response of awe and obedience in the face of the Almighty, and one which is positively commended throughout the Bible.[1] *Psychē*, here translated *soul*, also means 'life'. The intention is not to separate man into two parts, 'body' and 'soul', but to point out that there is more to man than his animal existence; men may terminate that, but they cannot touch his real self. But God, who made them, can also *destroy both soul and body in hell* (*gehenna*: see on 5:22). 'Soul' and 'body' are again not two separable parts of man; each one alone, and both together, can be used to indicate the whole person. The emphasis here is on the total and final destruction in hell, as opposed to the limited nature of merely physical death. *Destroy* (*apolesai*) carries the connotation of 'loss' and 'ruin' as well as of literal destruction, so that the expression does not necessarily, though it may, imply a view of the annihilation of the impenitent as opposed to eternal punish-

---

[1] That *him* here must mean God is now generally accepted; see I. H. Marshall, *ExpT* 81 (1969/70), p. 278. No such power is attributed to Satan in the Bible, nor is the Christian bidden to fear him.

ment.[1] Compared with the fate which awaits the disobedient and apostate, martyrdom is a far less fearful prospect.

**29–31.** If the argument of v. 28 against fear of persecution was a grim one (the alternative is worse!), the following verses present a more attractive reason. The God who can destroy in hell is also the God who cares for the sparrow. In his hands there is nothing to fear. *Sparrows* (or small birds – the precise species is not important) were a cheap food for the poor (though also pets for the rich; Catullus, *Carmina* ii, iii); they are listed as the cheapest of the birds sold for food in a third-century AD decree.[2] *Penny* here is the *as*, one-sixteenth of a *denarius* (see on 20:2). Yet even their death is not *without your Father*;[3] nothing in God's world is outside his concern or control. Yet sparrows, and Christians, do die. This saying does not promise escape from suffering or even death, but the knowledge that the time of its coming is in the hands of your Father, whose intimate knowledge of and concern for his children is spelt out in vv. 30 and 31.

**32–33.** The fear of men, which from three different angles has formed the subject of vv. 26–27, 28 and 29–31, could cause the disciple to fail to *acknowledge* Jesus *before men*, which is effectively to *deny* him. These verses reinforce the warning of v. 28 that there is a worse fate than human persecution, that is to be repudiated by Jesus himself before the Father. The 'acknowledgment', whether of Jesus by the disciple or vice versa, is one of solidarity – 'we belong together'. To be denied is to be excluded from this fellowship. A man's standing before God is thus explicitly made to depend on his relationship to Jesus, and Jesus himself stands in the role of arbiter of a man's ultimate destiny.[4] This 'egocentricity' is a striking characteristic of the teaching of Jesus. 'It is without parallel in the world of Jesus' (Jeremias, *NTT*, pp. 250–255). Even more remarkably, the saying is patterned on 1 Samuel 2:30, where the one honoured or

---

[1] See *ICC*, p. 109, for Jewish beliefs about hell.

[2] See A. Deissmann, *Light from the Ancient East* (1927), pp. 272–275.

[3] *Will* in RSV is not in the Greek, but is probably the right interpretation.

[4] In Lk. 12:8 the subject of the second 'acknowledge' is 'the Son of man', but to make this refer to someone other than the 'me' who is the object of the first 'acknowledge' not only violates Jesus' regular use of 'Son of man' to refer to himself, but also destroys the balance of reciprocal acknowledgment on which the saying depends, and which comes out more forcefully in Matthew's version; *cf.* Mk. 8:38.

despised is God himself (see Gundry, *UOT*, pp. 77, 209). The Christological implications of this saying are therefore important. So the disciple must choose which solidarity be prefers, that with men in this life, or that with Jesus *before my Father who is in heaven*. The inevitability of this choice dominates the rest of the chapter up to v. 39.

*(d) Jesus' divisive mission (10:34–36).* **34.** Anyone who recognized Jesus' mission as Messianic might properly *think that I have come to bring peace on earth*, on the basis of Isaiah 9:5–7; Zechariah 9:9–10; *etc*. That *was* his mission, as Luke 2:14 declares, and his disciples' message, as v. 13 has shown. But the peace the Messiah brings is much more than the absence of fighting, which men dignify with the name of 'peace'; it is a restored relationship with God. And in the bringing of such 'peace', paradoxically, conflict is inevitable, as not all will accept it. The *sword* Jesus brings is not here military conflict, but, as vv. 35–36 show, a sharp social division which even severs the closest family ties. (For this figurative use of *sword*, *cf*. Lk. 2:35; 22:36 (probably); the parallel in Luke (12:51) has 'division' for 'sword'.) Jewish Messianic expectation often included a period of conflict before the Messiah's triumph, but Jesus speaks here, as in the preceding and following verses, more of a division in men's personal response to him. As long as some men refuse the Lordship of God, to follow the Prince of peace will always be a way of conflict.

**35–36.** These verses paraphrase Micah 7:6, already alluded to in v. 21 (see commentary there); but what was in Micah a general prediction of social disruption, and in v. 21 was applied to religious persecution, is now presented as the direct (and intended) result of Jesus' own mission. The verb translated *set against* is more literally 'separate': Jesus does not come to poison family relationships, but rather he brings a division, regrettable but inevitable, between those who respond to his mission and those who reject it. Christian experience down the ages confirms that genuine love and obedience to the fifth commandment do not rule out the possibility of the choice reflected in v. 37, and of the consequent division of the family.

*(e) The cost of discipleship (10:37–39).* Verse 37 spells out the cost to the disciple of the division forecast in vv. 34–36, and vv. 38–39 go on to add other aspects of the debit side of discipleship. Those who followed Jesus did so with their eyes open.

**37.** Because of the division which Jesus provokes within families (vv. 34–36), true discipleship may bring a conflict of loyalties, and in that case, following Jesus must take precedence over the natural love of family (the Greek word is *phileō*, natural affection, not *agapaō*, the loving commitment which is a Christian characteristic). The Christian may even have to leave his family (19:29). The Lucan parallel (Lk. 14:26) calls for 'hatred' of the family, but Matthew's version correctly interprets this Semitic idiom (*cf.* Gn. 29:31; Dt. 21:15; Mal. 1:2–3) as an expression of prior loyalty or of choice rather than of actual dislike. Jesus calls not for an unloving attitude, but for a willingness to put him first in the concrete situation where the calls of Jesus and of family conflict. For the Rabbis too the claims of the teacher came before those of the father (Mishnah, *BM* 2:11). For *worthy*, see on v. 11; 'not the right sort to be my disciple'.

**38.** Worse still, the disciple will find that in following Jesus he must *take his cross* (*cf.* 16:24 for a positive command to do so). After Jesus' own crucifixion, the meaning would be obvious – the public obloquy of the walk through Jerusalem to Golgotha, and the painful and unjust death, if they were not the disciple's literal fate, vividly illustrated what he could expect from 'men' – like Master, like servant (*cf.* vv. 24–25). But could his disciples have understood this during his ministry? He had not yet taught them about his coming death, but already the opposition experienced and predicted made it a clear possibility. And crucifixion itself was not an uncommon sight in Roman Palestine; 'cross-bearing' language would have a clear enough meaning, even before they realized how literally he himself was to exemplify it.

**39.** The paradox of this verse recurs frequently in the Gospels in slightly varying forms (16:25; Mk. 8:35; Lk. 9:24; 17:33; Jn. 12:25); clearly it was a keynote of Jesus' call to discipleship. *Finds* here corresponds to 'would save', 'seeks to gain', 'loves' in the parallel passages; for *life* (*psychē*) see on v. 28. *AB* (p. 129) helpfully translates 'grasps at self . . . rejects self'. True life, real fulfilment, is found neither by the line of least resistance nor by aggressive self-assertion. But this is not a general philosophical maxim; it is the loss of life (not necessarily literally, though it *may* be) *for my sake* which achieves the goal. The disciple puts Jesus before his own natural inclinations and interests as well as before those of his family. As throughout this passage, Jesus' demand centres on loyalty to himself (*cf.* on vv. 32–33), in full awareness of the conflict this may entail.

*(v) The privileged status of the disciple (10:40–42)*
The debit side of discipleship has dominated vv. 17–39. But there is also a credit side, the privilege of being recognized as Jesus' representative.

**40.** To *receive* (into one's house, primarily, as in vv. 11–14; but the acceptance of their teaching is also implied) the disciple who is entrusted with the authority to do Jesus' work (v. 1, *etc.*) is to receive Jesus, for in Jewish thought 'a man's agent is like to himself' (Mishnah, *Berakoth* 5:5; *cf. TDNT*, I, pp. 414ff.). Davies (pp. 97–98) sees in this verse the equivalent concept to Paul's 'in Christ' language; the disciple is identified with Jesus. But the verse goes further (*cf.* Jn. 13:20): to receive Jesus is to receive *him who sent me*. 'God himself enters the house with Jesus' messengers. What a statement!' (Jeremias, *NTT*, p. 239). Thus the reception afforded to Jesus' disciples becomes the test of a man's relationship to God, as will be spelt out more fully in 25:31–46.

**41.** Those who pass this test will receive a reward (*cf.* on 5:12). The phrase *a prophet's (righteous man's) reward* could mean a reward given by the prophet, or one equal to that which a prophet receives, or more probably a reward proportionate to the importance of a prophet. *Cf.* the rewards given to those who 'received prophets' in 1 Kings 17:8–24; 2 Kings 4:8–37. The *prophet* and the *righteous man* represent God, as v. 40 has explained, whether they be those of the Old Testament period (*cf.* 13:17) or the Christian prophet and the man who exemplifies the righteousness set out by Jesus in 5:20; 6:1–18. Here it is apparently parallel to the 'you' of v. 40, rather than distinguishing specific classes of men of God. *Because he is* is literally 'in the name of', *i.e.* 'in his capacity as'.

**42.** To *give a cup of cold water* was and is an essential act of courtesy and hospitality in the East. It is taken for granted, and deserves no *reward*, yet even this act of acceptance will receive one; God's rewards go beyond our deserts (see on 5:12). Again it is not philanthropy which is in view, but reception of a disciple *because he is a disciple* (again literally 'in the name of'). On the *little ones* see further on 18:6, 10, 14 (and *cf.* the 'least' of 25:40, 45). While they may include children, as 18:1–6 makes clear, the term probably designates more generally God's special people, *i.e.* the disciples.[1]

Thus these verses place the disciple in the privileged position of the one who, representing Jesus, also represents God, and whose reception is therefore the test of a man's attitude to God himself, leading to either reward or the loss of it. This is solid comfort for those who find the world against them because they belong to Jesus.

*(vi) Conclusion (11:1)*
The formal conclusion (for which see on 7:28–29) again acts as a transition from the collection of sayings, here specified as *instructing his twelve disciples*, to a resumption of the narrative of the itinerant ministry of teaching and preaching (*cf.* the formulae of 4:23; 9:35, the third member in which – healing – is mentioned here in the following verses, 11:2–5).

### E. VARYING RESPONSE TO JESUS' MESSIANIC ACTIVITY (11:2 – 12:50)

'The deeds of the Christ' (11:2), which have been set out in chapters 5 – 10, provoked different responses from different groups. These responses, most of which consist of misunderstanding if not outright rejection, will be examined in chapters 11 – 12, and explained in the parables of chapter 13. Further examples of the response to Jesus will occur in chapters 14 – 16, until the true response is found in Peter's confession in 16:13–20, which will bring the second main part of the Gospel to its climax. This is the thread which runs through these chapters with their apparently miscellaneous selection of incidents. Through them we are led from a view of Jesus as others saw him

---

[1] See E. Schweizer, *NTS* 16 (1969/70), pp. 222–223.

to the true confession of his Messiahship which eluded most of his contemporaries, conditioned as they were by false or inadequate ideas of the Messiah.

### (i) John the Baptist (11:2–19)

The Forerunner, whose proclamation introduced Matthew's presentation of the Messiah (3:1–12), is now appropriately called as the first witness to the meaning of his ministry. His response is equivocal, positive but uncertain, and Jesus' comments on his role go on to point out the contrast between his preparatory role and the true time of fulfilment. John remains the one who points forward.

*(a) John's question (11:2–6).* **2–3.** John's arrest was mentioned in 4:12; the full story of his imprisonment will wait until 14:3–12. No doubt he had anxiously followed the career of the one whom he had recognized as his superior (3:14–15) and had probably already taken to be the 'mightier one' for whose coming he had prepared (3:11–12). *The Christ* is Matthew's description of Jesus, and sums up the impression he has aimed to convey in chapters 5 – 10 (its use in narrative is very unusual – 1:17 is the only near-parallel in Matthew – and clearly deliberate); John, as his question shows, was not yet ready to be so positive, though he would have liked to be. His hesitation was probably due (as v. 6 suggests) to a discrepancy between his expectations for 'the coming one' (*i.e.* the one he had predicted in 3:11; 'the coming one' was not a recognized Messianic title in Judaism) and what he actually heard about Jesus. The ministry so far recorded does not match up with the expectations of 3:11–12, and the miracles which are its most obvious feature were not a part of the common Messianic expectation. John may also have found it difficult to accept a Jewish 'Messiah' who failed to fast as his own followers did (9:14ff.)., and who kept the sort of company which a careful Jew would avoid (9:9ff.).

**4–5.** The evidence to which Jesus points is not immediately conclusive, as it does not chime in with the popular (and probably John's) idea of the Messiah's work. But his words are an unmistakable allusion to passages in Isaiah which describe God's saving work (Is. 35:5–6; *cf.* 29:18), and the mission of his anointed servant (Is.61:1). If these did not form part of the general expectation, and of John's, they should have done. In Jesus' own understanding of his mission, Isaiah 61:1-2 looms large (Lk. 4:18ff.; and *cf.* above on 5:3-4). The relief of suffering, literally fulfilled in his healing miracles recorded in chapters 8 – 9 (though lame and deaf are not included there), reaches its climax in *good news* to *the poor*, the godly minority described in the beatitudes of chapter 5 (see on 5:3 for the concept of the *ʿanāwim*, which causes *AB* to translate *poor* here as 'humble'). If this is too gentle a mission for John's Messianic hopes, he has missed the biblical pattern on which Jesus' mission is founded.

**6.** *Take offence* is the same verb as in 5:29-30, 'be tripped up by'. Many were 'put off' by Jesus, when his style of ministry failed to tally with their expectations, and even offended against accepted conventions. 'Good news to the poor' was an offence to the establishment, while a mission of the relief of suffering and the restoration of sinners would be at best irrelevant to those who fought for national liberation. It took spiritual discernment not to be 'put off' by Jesus, and such perception was enviable (for *blessed*, see above, on 5:3-10). While it applies directly to John's state of uncertainty, this beatitude is also a key to the theme of this section of the Gospel, which will introduce many who found Jesus hard to take.[1]

*(b) Jesus' verdict on John (11:7-15).* **7-9.** John's preaching had created a sensation (see 3:5), and the movement *into the wilderness* had been a remarkable phenomenon. Jesus now examines its motives, to show the real significance of John. The series of three questions and answers (whose punctuation is not certain, see RSV mg.; but the sense is not affected) suggests motives progressively closer to a true understanding of John. *A reed shaken by the wind* might be literal (You did not go just for the scenery!), but in context is more likely to be a metaphor for a weak, pliable person; John was not such a person, and the implied answer is 'Of course not'. It was John's rugged independence which attracted a following. Nor was he *clothed in soft raiment*; far from it, as 3:4 shows. It was as a man conspicuously

[1]See an excellent exposition of v. 6 in the light of the characteristics of Jesus' ministry by C. L. Mitton in *ExpT* 82 (1970/1), pp. 170-172.

separate from the establishment (*kings' houses*) that they were attracted to him. (There may be an ironical reference to his present residence in a 'king's house' – as a prisoner of conscience in Herod's fortress!) His rough clothing in fact points to his real role, as *a prophet* (see on 3:4), and the crowds would gladly have accepted this description of John. But even that is not enough.

**10.** *John* is not just *a* prophet, but the *messenger* of Malachi 3:1. In Malachi the wording is 'before *me*', and his role is to prepare for the coming of God for judgment. Jesus' application of this text to John implies that his own (Jesus') coming, for which John prepares, is the coming of God himself, an implication which is the more staggering for being so calmly assumed (see further, my *JOT*, pp. 91–92, 155). But the wording is adapted to that of Exodus 23:20,[1] so as to give a second person in place of the first, which eases the reference to John as sent by God to precede Jesus. The same combined quotation is used by Mark in his editorial description of John (Mk. 1:2–3), and was probably a well-known *testimonium* in early Christianity.

**11.** John is thus the greatest of prophets, indeed of all men up to his time – *great*, that is, in his place in God's purpose, not necessarily in his personal worth. But that purpose was leading to a new order, *the kingdom of heaven* (see pp. 45–46), of which John was only the herald, and which is the fulfilment of all that went before. To be *in* that kingdom, even as the *least*, is to be *greater* (in the same sense) than the great man who proclaimed its coming, but remained as yet outside it. For *least*, *cf.* 5:19, with the warning of 18:1–4 and 20:25–28 against worldly calculations of status in the kingdom of God.

John is thus seen, in his capacity as the forerunner, as standing outside the kingdom of heaven. He is the last of the old order, as the subsequent identification with Elijah (v. 14) will make clear. In v. 12 his 'days' are seen as the time when God's kingdom begins to be a reality, but his own place is rather with the Old Testament (v. 13). It was not his privilege to be involved in the ministry of Jesus, with its new perspective and dynamic. To speak of him as 'outside the kingdom of heaven' in this sense

[1] 'Angel' in Ex. 23:20 is the same Hebrew word as 'messenger' in Mal. 3:1; the two passages were apparently taken together in Jewish exegesis: see Stendahl, pp. 49–50.

is not of course to pronounce on his personal salvation (any more than that of any of the Old Testament saints), but on his place in the development of God's plan.

Verse 11 suggests, as v. 12 will make explicit, that now with the ministry of Jesus the kingdom of heaven which John proclaimed is already a reality. The old order has been superseded.

**12.** John's coming precipitated a new situation, described here in terms of *violence*. *Men of violence* is an unusual word which always conveys a bad sense. This makes RSV mg. very unlikely, as it assumes a good sense for the cognate verb (the similar saying of Lk. 16:16 has the same verb in the sense of 'coming violently' but with 'men', not 'the kingdom of heaven', as subject). Here the verb is probably to be read as passive, not middle: it refers to violence inflicted on the kingdom of heaven, which Jesus condemns (*take by force, harpazō*, normally means 'plunder' or 'seize'[1]). This violence began with the time of John's preaching, because that was when the kingdom of heaven began to be proclaimed, even if John himself was not 'in' it. The saying is thus not concerned with violence in general, but with a specific violence directed at 'the kingdom of heaven'. Among many suggested interpretations of this *violence*, two seem more likely than others. (a) P. W. Barnett argues[2] that Jesus refers to the political activists among his (and John's) followers who tried to divert his mission into one of national liberation, a movement which reached its climax after the feeding of the 5,000 (see especially Jn. 6:14–15, using the same verb *harpazō*). It is not clear, however, why this issue should be introduced here, unless (and this must be speculation) John's followers had moved increasingly in a political direction, causing Jesus, while endorsing John's message, to dissociate himself from his 'violent' followers. (b) More commonly Jesus is understood to refer to the violent opposition encountered by 'the kingdom of heaven', already seen in the arrest and imprisonment of its herald, and more ominously foreshadowed in the growing official opposition to Jesus himself. In the context of John's question from prison this seems the more relevant sense.

So while John was the last of the old order, his fate was the

[1] For a different view see Ladd, pp. 159–164.
[2] *Reformed Theological Review* 36 (1977), pp. 65–70.

foretaste of the conflicts which are already beginning to affect the new order. Here again God's kingdom is clearly seen as already present, as a force sufficiently dynamic to provoke violent reaction.

**13.** John's status as the last of the Old Testament prophets is reinforced. *Until* could include or exclude John, but the following verse will make clear his inclusion among the prophets, just as v. 11 showed his exclusion from the subsequent kingdom of heaven. He belongs to the forward-looking (*prophesied*) era of the Old Testament. The prophets are (unusually) mentioned before the law, but the whole Old Testament is regarded as pointing forward to the kingdom of heaven. *Cf.* on 5:17, above.

**14.** Whereas Mark is content to leave the returning Elijah unidentified (9:11–13), Luke records the identification only in a private revelation to John's father (1:17), and John portrays the Baptist himself as rejecting it (1:21), Matthew here and in 17:12–13 records an open declaration that John was Elijah, and suffered the fate of Elijah. The hope of Elijah's return to prepare for God's coming was raised by Malachi 4:5–6 (3:23–24, Heb.) and had developed into a popular expectation by the time of Jesus (see *TDNT*, II, pp. 931–934). He was identified with the 'messenger' of Malachi 3:1 (see on v. 10, above). If John fulfils this role as the herald of God's coming, he is indeed 'more than a prophet'. But, despite his outward resemblance to Elijah (see on 3:4), John's ministry did not in every way correspond to the popular expectation; his role, like that of the one who came after him, was discernible only by those *willing to accept it*.

**15.** This formula is used by Jesus after sayings which require special insight (see 13:9, 43; Mk. 4:23; Lk. 14:35). It is a call for more than superficial understanding, an invitation to explore the implications of what has been said.

*(c) The response to John and Jesus (11:16–19).* **16–17.** Unresponsiveness to the voice of God is the characteristic of *this generation* (see on 12:39), and will be its downfall (see especially 23:29–36). The accusation in v. 19 is that which the religious leaders rather than the crowds levelled against Jesus, and it is they rather than the crowds of v. 7 who are pictured in the *children*'s game of weddings and funerals. Jesus and John are the ones who *piped*

and *wailed*, but neither dance-music nor dirge evoked a response, only a sulky refusal.

**18–19.** In their different ways both John and Jesus were strikingly unconventional. So they attributed John's dour asceticism and preaching of judgment to demonic influence, but were no less scandalized by Jesus' free mingling with the unrespectable (see 9:9–13). They refused to hear God's voice in either form, the sombre or the joyful, in judgment or in mercy, if it did not accord with their conventions. There was no pleasing them.

The final sentence puts the religious leaders in their place. *Wisdom* is God's wisdom, almost a periphrasis for God himself. 'God is his own interpreter', and in his superior wisdom both the contrasting appeals of John and Jesus have their appointed place. His wisdom is *justified* (vindicated) by the very *deeds*[1] which scandalize those who will not respond (*cf.* v. 6). The proof of the pudding is in the eating.

*(ii) Towns which rejected Jesus' appeal (11:20–24)*

**20.** The failure of 'this generation' to respond to Jesus' appeal (vv. 16–19) is matched by the failure of the *cities* (in fact small lakeside towns) to respond to his *mighty works*. These alone, even without a verbal message, should have revealed that God was at work (as Jesus had indicated to John, vv. 4–6), and so should have caused them to *repent*, *i.e.* to turn from their rebellious attitude towards God. *Then*, as often in Matthew, marks not so much a chronological link (in Luke the same passage occurs in a different context, 10:12–15) as a logical one; this is a further example of the rejection of Jesus' ministry which is the theme of chapters 11 – 12. *Most of* could perhaps mean 'very many', but Capernaum is in fact the principal scene of the Galilean ministry in Matthew (see on 4:13), and therefore had an exceptional opportunity to repent. For repentance of a whole community, *cf.* Jonah 3; individuals had responded, but there had been no general change of attitude.

**21–22.** *Chorazin* and *Bethsaida* were not specially important towns. Matthew in fact records no miracles in either (but, for

---

[1]The reading *children* (RSV mg.) has in fact earlier support, but is usually assumed to be due to assimilation to Lk. 7:35. It would denote those who, unlike 'this generation', are responsive to God's wisdom, and so prove whose children they are.

Bethsaida, *cf.* Mk. 8:22ff.; Lk. 9:10ff.), which emphasizes how selective the Gospel records of Jesus' ministry are; *cf.* 4:23; 9:35 for general summaries covering this wider ministry. *Tyre and Sidon* were attacked by the Old Testament prophets for their rejection of God and his will (Is. 23; Ezk. 26 – 28; Am. 1:9–10; *etc.*) and symbolized the arrogance of the pagan world. But the failure of the Galilean towns to respond to the direct evidence and appeal of Jesus and his mighty works was worse even than the paganism of Tyre and Sidon. They had not the excuse of ignorance. *Cf.* on 10:15, where *the day of judgment* has been mentioned in a similar context.

**23–24.** *Capernaum* is denounced in words which echo Isaiah's oracle against the king of Babylon (Is. 14:13–15); its arrogant self-sufficiency, like that of Israel's great enemy of the past, will lead to its downfall. And if to be compared with Babylon was not sufficiently offensive to Jewish pride, Jesus puts even *Sodom* (see on 10:15) on a level above the people of his own town. Arrogance and immorality will be punished, but not so severely as the rejection of God's direct appeal. 'Only the rejection of forgiveness is unforgivable.'[1]

*(iii) The true response to Jesus' appeal (11:25–30)*
In contrast with the misunderstanding and rejection which have dominated this chapter so far, these verses show us who can truly appreciate Jesus' mission, and what he offers to them.

**25–26.** *At that time*, like 'then' in v. 20, points to a close connection with the verses that precede. This is Jesus' response (*declared* is literally 'answered') to his rejection especially by the religious leadership, *the wise and understanding*, those who, if they had lived up to their reputation and responsibility, should have been the first to recognize *these things*, *i.e.* the significance of Jesus' mission. Instead, it was the *babes*, the humble, unlearned, simple people, who understood (*cf.* 21:15–16). Jesus uses children, as elsewhere, as the paradigm of those whom the world regards as insignificant; but in this context they also represent those who are free from false preconceptions and so are open to the new light now being revealed to them. It was such people,

[1]Jeremias, *NTT*, p. 150.

rather than the theologians, who became Jesus' disciples. But this was not the product of some natural law; it was the *gracious will* of the *Father*, who has *hidden* and *revealed*, and it is this revealing will of God (not just the incomprehension of the wise) which calls forth Jesus' formal thanksgiving, expressing his dependence on and delight in his Father's will. For *Father* as Jesus' special address to God, see above, on 6:9. The reversal of the world's standards expressed here echoes Isaiah 29:14, 'the wisdom of their wise men shall perish', and is picked up again in 1 Corinthians 1:18ff. Spiritual understanding does not depend on human equipment or status. It is the gift of God, and so is given to those in whom he is well pleased (the verb in 3:17 is from the same root as *gracious will* here). It depends on the sovereign purpose of the *Lord of heaven and earth*, and his choice falls on those the world would never expect.

**27.** This verse stands out as a more explicit statement of Jesus' relationship with the Father than any other in the Synoptic Gospels. It has therefore often been dubbed 'Johannine', with the implication that Jesus himself could not have spoken it. But, as Hill sanely remarks, 'Is it a legitimate canon of criticism that any Synoptic saying which has a parallel in John must *ipso facto* be spurious? . . . Without such points of departure in the Synoptic tradition it would be an eternal puzzle how Johannine theology could have originated at all!' (Hill, p. 205). In particular, the description of Jesus as simply *the Son* is paralleled in 24:36, and the idea of Jesus as Son of God is, of course, central to this Gospel (2:15; 3:17; 4:3; 6: 8:29; 14:33; 16:16–17; 17:5; 21:37; *etc.*), while the address to God as 'Abba', Father, agreed to be a unique characteristic of Jesus, attests that this relationship was central in his own consciousness.[1]

The relationship implied by the 'Father' of v. 25 is here spelt out. There are no secrets between Father and Son (though see 24:36 for an apparent exception). *All things* refers here (in the light of vv. 25–26) to the knowledge they share; in 28:18 there will be a similar claim in respect of authority. The past tense of *have been delivered* may indicate the Son's eternal relationship with the Father before his incarnate life, though this is not

[1]For fuller defence of the authenticity of the saying, see A. M. Hunter, *NTS* 8 (1961/62), pp. 244–245; Jeremias, *NTT*, pp. 56–59; Dunn, pp. 27–34.

explicit here. The rest of the verse is about the mutual *knowledge* of Father and Son. 'Know' in the Old Testament is much more than a mental acquaintance; it is an intimate relationship. The exclusive communion between Father and Son is of the essence of their relationship. For anyone else to share in this knowledge, however, is a matter of revelation, and as such is not a natural right, but a matter of divine choice. Thus God's sovereign initiative in revelation, set out in vv. 25–26, is applied specifically to our knowledge of God: it does not come naturally (see 1 Cor. 2:6–16 for a spelling out of this theme). It depends on God's choice, or, more specifically, *the Son*'s choice. Thus Jesus unequivocally describes himself and his will as the key to men's approach to the Father; there is no other.[1]

**28.** The last three verses of the chapter contain many echoes of the invitation of Jesus Ben Sira in the appendix to his wisdom book (Ecclus. 51:23–27; *cf.* also Ecclus. 6:24–31) to men to come and learn from him and take up wisdom's yoke, so that they may find rest. No doubt Jesus and his hearers knew and valued this book, but Jesus' invitation reveals a higher authority: it is his own yoke that he offers, and he himself gives the rest which Ben Sira had to win by his 'little labours'.

Jesus issues his invitation to *all who labour and are heavy laden*. The last word is unusual, and reminds us of 23:4, where the scribes and Pharisees are accused of making the people carry 'heavy burdens' by their legalistic demands. Scribal religion was meant to honour God, but its effect was to condemn the ordinary Jew to hard labour. The *rest* Jesus offers instead is not a release from all obligations; 5:20 shows that his demands are greater. But because of who he is (v. 29), his demands are such that to respond to them is *rest* ('relief' would be an equally good translation). As with the beatitudes of 5:3–10, while there is an eschatological aspect to this promise (*cf.* the 'rest' of Heb. 4:1–10), to interpret it as wholly eschatological would deprive it

[1]Jeremias (*NTT*, pp. 59–61) has argued that the definite articles before 'Father' and 'Son' should be read as generic, making the saying an observation on human relationships – only a father and his son have true mutual knowledge. Linguistically this is possible, though it may be questioned whether it would be a true observation. But if so the point of such an observation in this context could only be to illustrate the mutual knowledge of Jesus and his Father. The Christological implications of the saying would be the same, though more parabolically expressed.

of its practical value to those who are burdened by legalism. Even here and now discipleship to Jesus, for all its stern demands, is *rest* as compared with all human religion.

**29–30.** The *yoke* was sometimes in the Old Testament a symbol of oppression (Is. 9:4; 58:6; Je. 27 – 28), but was also used in a good sense of the service of God (Je. 2:20; La. 3:27). Later it came to be used commonly in Jewish writings for obedience to the law - the 'yoke of the law' is one every Jew should be proud to carry.[1] Such a yoke should not be oppressive, for after all the function of a yoke (the sort worn by humans) is to make a burden easier to carry. But through 'the arbitrary demands of Pharisaic legalism and the uncertainties of ever-proliferating case law' (*AB*, p. 146) the law had itself become a burden, and a new yoke was needed to lighten the load.[2] Jesus' yoke is *easy* (*chrēstos* normally means 'good', 'kind'), not because it makes lighter demands, but because it represents entering into a disciple-relationship (*learn from me*) with one who is *gentle and lowly in heart* (*cf.* 2 Cor. 10:1 for these as recognized qualities of Jesus). The words echo the description of God's servant in Isaiah 42:2–3; 53:1–2, and specially the words of Zechariah 9:9 which Matthew will pick up again at 21:4–5; it is also the character Jesus expects, and creates, in his disciples (5:3ff.). This attractive aspect of Jesus is a vital counterbalance to the sterner side seen in 7:13–27; 10:34–39; *etc.* To emphasize either to the exclusion of the other is to miss the real Jesus. *You will find rest for your souls* is an echo of the Hebrew text of Jeremiah 6:16 (LXX is different), where it is the offer of God to those who follow his way; Jesus now issues the invitation in his own name!

### (iv) Objections to Jesus' free attitude to the sabbath (12:1–14)

The unfavourable responses to Jesus' ministry (see above, introduction to section E, pp. 191–192) are now focused in ch. 12 on the Pharisees. This follows appropriately after 11:28–30, showing the 'rest' brought by taking Jesus' 'easy yoke' in contrast with Pharisaic legalism. The opposition of scribes and Pharisees to Jesus has already come to light (9:3, 11, 34), but now their contrasting approaches to the will of God are more sharply

[1] *E.g.* Mishnah *Aboth* 3:5; *Berakoth* 2:2; see further, M. Maher, *NTS* 22 (1975/76), pp. 97–103.
[2] On 'yoke' in Judaism and in this verse, see especially *NIDNTT*, III, pp. 1161–1164.

revealed in the question of the sabbath, which was to the Jews not just a ceremonial regulation, but a witness to God's creation, a sign of Israel's special covenant relationship with God, a gift of God to make Israel more holy, and a promise of the joys of the world to come. It was thus, in theory, a blessing not a burden. Pharisaic concern for the detailed regulation of religious duty was in danger, however, of putting the rules before the good purpose for which they were given. The regulation of sabbath activity soon reached the point where it required considerable erudition to know what was and was not permissible, and virtually nothing was left to private judgment.[1] Underlying the conflict in this passage over the interpretation of the sabbath commandment is the more fundamental question of who has the authority to interpret it; ethics is focused in Christology.

1–2. To *pluck heads of grain* was not in itself illegal (see Dt. 23:25), but to do so constituted reaping, one of the 39 areas of work explicitly forbidden on the sabbath according to Mishnah *Shabbath* 7:2. Jesus nowhere disputes that the disciples' action was, in Pharisaic terms, *not lawful*. It is sometimes suggested that Matthew's addition of the fact that they *were hungry* is intended to legitimate the action, on the grounds of need. But the only need which could override sabbath regulations was danger of death, and there is no suggestion of that here. The mention of hunger serves rather to prepare for the mention of David's action in v. 3.

3–4. This, the first of four arguments against the Pharisees' attitude, refers to the incident in 1 Samuel 21:1–6, which is not said to have occurred on the sabbath, though later Jewish exegesis assumed this, as it was on the sabbath that the bread was changed (1 Sa. 21:6; *cf.* Lv. 24:8). This possibility, and the element of hunger, are not sufficient, however, to make the two actions significantly parallel; David's 'law-breaking' was of a different character. Unless the argument is simply that if the law can be broken once it can be broken again – and few have been satisfied with such an interpretation! – its force must lie in the persons concerned. David, it is assumed, could break the law because he was David, and the implication is that 'a greater than

[1]See Mishnah *Shabbath* and *'Erubin* for the regulations of the second century, many of which go back to the time of Jesus.

David is here' (cf. vv. 6, 41, 42 for this argument in explicit form). The argument lacks any cogency unless it is based on the claim to a Messianic authority at least equal to that of David himself (cf. my JOT, pp. 46-47).

**5-6.** The second argument is more direct, as it concerns an actual infringement of sabbath law which the Old Testament itself sanctioned. It is usually assumed that the priests' action in view is the offering of the sabbath sacrifices (Nu. 28:9-10), and perhaps the changing of the shewbread (Lv. 24:8). In fact there were other temple duties which were held to supersede the sabbath regulations (see Mishnah 'Erubin 10:11-15; Pesahim 6:1-2). E. Levine[1] has argued that a more clearly parallel action would be the reaping of the offering of the first sheaves, which the Pharisees regarded as required on the sabbath, while the Sadducees did not allow it (Mishnah Menahoth 10:3, 9). Such an appeal to a point of honour for the Pharisees would certainly be a powerful *argumentum ad hominem*, but again the point of the argument is not so much in any precedent for the disciples' action as in the question of authority. If the service of the temple could legitimate sabbath 'work', how much more can *something greater than the temple*. The *something* (the Greek is neuter) is not necessarily to be seen as an impersonal 'thing' (*e.g.* the kingdom of God) rather than Jesus himself, for in the parallel formulae of 12:41 and 42 the neuter is used in a comparison of Jesus with a *person* in the Old Testament. In Jesus and his ministry a new work of God, transcending the temple ritual of the Old Testament, has begun. As the temple has been the focus of God's presence among his people, so now it is in Jesus and his new community that God is to be found.[2] Such typological comparisons are a feature of this chapter, and are more fully developed in the Letter to the Hebrews. Its implication is not so much the rejection of the temple as its anticipatory role, pointing forward to the *greater* embodiment of God's presence in the Messiah (whose role included the restoration of the temple: see on 21:12-13; 26:61).

**7.** The third argument repeats the appeal to Hosea 6:6 already found in 9:13. Its aim is not, any more than in Hosea, to repudi-

[1]NTS 22 (1975/6), pp. 480-483.
[2]See B. Gärtner, The Temple and the Community (1965), pp. 114-116.

ate ceremonial observance, but to establish God's order of priorities. God cannot be quoted in support of the attitude which condemns before it understands, which puts demands before consideration. 'God is no longer primarily understood as the demanding one, but as the gracious one, the merciful one' (*TIM*, p. 83). This scriptural argument in Matthew thus achieves the same effect as the pronouncement 'The sabbath was made for man, not man for the sabbath' (Mk. 2:27), which it replaces. The disciples were *guiltless* not in that they had not infringed the scribal regulations, but in that they did so on their Master's authority; hence the *for* which begins the next verse.

**8.** The fourth argument draws out the implications of the first and second: Jesus, as Messiah, has authority over the sabbath. (On 'Son of man' see pp. 43–45). This Christological point is completely lost in the suggestion sometimes made that *Son of man* is here a mistranslation for 'man'; this would make this verse closer in meaning to Mark 2:27, but would quite destroy the consistency of the argument here in Matthew. As Son of man Jesus does not abrogate the sabbath law, but claims the right to interpret it in a way which effectively undercuts Pharisaic legalism.

**9–10.** The second conflict is located in *their synagogue*, the use of *their* (*cf.* 4:23; 9:35; 10:17; 13:54; 23:34) serving to highlight the gulf which was developing between Jesus and the Jewish establishment. The *withered hand* was literally 'dry', *i.e.* lifeless, perhaps paralysed; the man was thus not in imminent danger of death, which alone justified treatment on the sabbath according to Mishnah *Yoma* 8:6. He could as well be healed the next day. He is therefore made into a test case by the Pharisees, whose question Matthew records as a direct challenge in general terms (contrast Mk. and Lk., where the issue is not brought into the open until Jesus challenges their unspoken thoughts). In terms of Pharisaic law, there could be only one answer.

**11–12.** Jesus' response this time is not to assert his own authority directly, nor to quote an Old Testament example, but to point to the inconsistency of their own practice. They were strict in prohibiting another man's healing, but not where their own property was concerned. The Qumran sect specifically forbade rescuing an animal from a pit on the sabbath (CD 11:13–14), but clearly general practice at that time was more lenient. Later Rabbis discussed the issue, some allowing articles to be thrown in the pit to allow the animal to climb out, others saying it should be fed until it could be lifted out on a weekday; but the Talmud concludes that the avoidance of animal suffering should override regulations (*Shabbath* 128b). Yet they could not waive the rules for a *man*! (*Cf.* 6:26; 10:31 for Jesus' estimate of the value of men compared with animals.) The concluding principle, *it is lawful to do good on the sabbath*, is, says Bonnard (p. 175), 'disturbing, for, if generalized, it would make all organized church life impossible: there is always some "good" to undertake in preference to a religious duty'. But if we can avoid such convenient generalization, the principle embodies well the message of Hosea 6:6. It is better to err on the side of 'goodness' than on that of heartless adherence to regulations.

**13.** The healing is almost incidental to the main point of the story, but the command to stretch out an unmovable hand neatly illustrates the faith which was the correlative to Jesus' healing power.

**14.** A single infringement of scribal regulations was hardly sufficient to warrant Jesus' liquidation, but these incidents have illustrated the irreconcilable difference between Jesus' radical approach to the question of obedience to God's will and the rule-bound religion of the establishment. This first mention of their plans to destroy him shows the breach is now irreparable.

*(v) Jesus' response to opposition (12:15–21)*
Matthew's longest Old Testament quotation is introduced here to emphasize the contrast between the violent opposition of the Pharisees and the gentleness of the Lord's Servant portrayed in Isaiah 42. Yet in his lowliness and his concern for the helpless is manifested the true authority of God's chosen one, whose ultimate victory is assured.

**15–16.** For Jesus' 'tactical withdrawals', *cf.* on 4:12. Here the cause is his awareness of the Pharisees' plots, which only Matthew mentions here, perhaps in order to stress Jesus' mastery of the situation, despite his non-aggressive attitude (v. 19). Verses 15b–16 are a drastic abbreviation of Mark's summary of Jesus' healing ministry (3:7–12), though the substitution of *all* for Mark's 'many' highlights Jesus' power. Jesus' demand for silence is the cue for the Isaiah quotation, which serves to explain the 'Messianic secrecy' (on which see on 8:4) not as the result of weakness and timidity, but as the deliberate and authoritative (*ordered* is a strong verb of warning or rebuke) fulfilment of the role of the Servant.

**17ff.** As in 8:16–17 a summary of Jesus' healing ministry introduces a formula-quotation drawn from the portrait of God's Servant in Isaiah. See on 8:16–17 for this unusual use of the Servant theme. But whereas there the fulfilment was seen in the healings themselves, here it is rather in the character of the healer (meekness, v. 19; gentleness, v. 20), and in the ultimate goal of his work ('justice to the Gentiles', vv. 18d, 20c, 21). The text of the quotation differs from all known versions, and appears to be an independent translation from the Hebrew, with the words adapted to emphasize how Jesus' ministry fulfilled the spirit of the Servant's mission, which is first outlined by these verses in Isaiah 42:1–4.

**18.** Jesus is described as God's *servant* elsewhere only in Acts 3:13, 26; 4:27, 30, though the idea of his fulfilment of Isaiah 42 and 53 is common in the New Testament. Matthew's version of the second line, *my beloved with whom my soul is well pleased*, provides a clear echo of the voice at Jesus' baptism (see on 3:17; *cf.* also 17:5), and the mention of the bestowal of the *Spirit* in the next line (*cf.* 3:16) reinforces the reminiscence. The mission then inaugurated is now being fulfilled.

**19.** The verbs in vv. 19–20 are mostly negative. It was in what Jesus did *not* do that the distinctiveness of his mission was most clearly seen in contrast with the aggressive Messiah of popular expectation. The unassertive character of Jesus' ministry accords with his description of himself in 11:29 as 'gentle and lowly'. *Wrangle* is Matthew's interpretation of the Hebrew 'cry out', a verb often used of complaining of injustice; Jesus did not 'shout back' at the Pharisees when they plotted against him.

**20.** The weak and vulnerable (the *smouldering wick* is one in danger of going out altogether) are the special object of his mission, and he deals with them with all the gentleness offered to the over-burdened in 11:28–30. Far from letting them be broken and quenched, he will lead them *to victory*, for in him they will find *justice*, a word whose scope in the Old Testament is wider than mere legal vindication, denoting rather the setting right of whatever is not as it should be, 'the complete establishing of the will of God' (*TIM*, p. 141). The paradoxical *victory* of the meek and gentle Servant is brought out by Matthew's paraphrase (which also includes the thought of Isaiah 42:4a-b, which Matthew omits).

**21.** The LXX wording of Isaiah 42:4c serves to bring out the universal scope of the Servant's mission, already indicated in v. 18. For Matthew's emphasis on a gospel for the Gentiles see Davies, pp. 327ff.

*(vi) Jesus accused of collusion with the devil, and his response (12:22-37)*

The preceding verses have revealed Jesus as the healer whose mission is empowered by God's Spirit (v. 18). This paragraph now shows how this activity was interpreted by observers at the time, and draws out the significance of the Spirit's activity in Jesus' ministry. The relationships of this passage to material in Mark and Luke are complex, and it seems probable that this is a collection of Jesus' sayings brought together because they all relate to exorcism and the Spirit. As such it forms a deliberate unity, in which it is important to interpret the parts in relation to the whole. In particular, to take vv. 31-32 out of the context in which Matthew has recorded them is to invite dangerous misunderstanding.

**22.** The account of the healing and of the response to it (vv. 22-24) is closely parallel to 9:32-34; see notes there, especially on the unusual linking of demon-possession with a physical ailment. Here, unlike 9:33, the cure is described as 'healing' not as 'casting out', but it is the latter explanation which forms the basis of the following dialogue (vv. 24-28), so that while the visible effect was of physical healing, the underlying cause was clearly understood to be demonic both by Jesus and by the onlookers.

**23.** *Amazed*, used only here in Matthew, is a stronger word than the more conventional term translated 'marvelled' in 9:33, and suggests a public reaction to Jesus' authoritative action strong enough to require an alternative explanation (found in v.

24) from those who could not accept him as *Son of David*. While popular thought would concentrate on the role of the *Son of David* as Israel's ideal king and liberator (see above, pp. 42–43), Matthew also indicates his role as a healer (see on 9:27). Jesus fulfilled that role, but was conspicuously not the conquering and ruling Messiah of popular expectation; hence the crowd's puzzlement – the question is introduced by *mēti*, which formally suggests the answer 'No', but leaves open the possibility that it may be 'Yes' (*cf.* its use in 26:22, 25; Jn. 4:29).

**24.** The reality of Jesus' power was undeniable, so, as in 9:34, it is its source that is questioned. The Pharisees' accusation amounts to a charge of sorcery, one which continued to be levelled against Jesus in later Jewish polemic. It was a serious charge, for sorcery was a capital offence (Mishnah *Sanhedrin* 7:4). For *Beelzebul*, see on 10:25, where the name is applied directly to Jesus himself, no doubt with the same implication as here. In this context (see vv. 26–27) it is apparently used as a synonym for Satan. In Mark 3:22 the charge is that it is because Jesus is himself possessed by Beelzebul that he can exorcize by his power; Matthew has retained the charge, but perhaps felt the explanation too offensive to repeat.

**25–26.** The charge was not only offensive, but ridiculous, as Jesus points out. Assuming that *Satan* (see on 4:10) and other demons form a united front against God, the defeat of one demon is a blow to Satan's power, and cannot therefore be Satan's work. As a debating-point it is effective; but it also reveals Jesus' vivid awareness of the reality and the concerted power of the spiritual forces of evil, of which an individual case of demon-possession is but a small local manifestation. There is a *kingdom of Satan* as well as a kingdom of God, and this passage reveals the two as locked in mortal conflict in the ministry of Jesus. The Pharisees could not have been more wrong!

**27.** A second debating-point concerns Jewish exorcists (*your sons* applies generally to 'your own people'), of whom we have records, *e.g.*, in Acts 19:13 (*cf.* Mk. 9:38); Josephus, *Ant.* viii. 46–48; *BJ* vii. 185 (*cf.* Tobit 6:7, 16–17; 8:2–3).[1] The argument assumes that Jewish exorcism was real and effective, and that it

---

[1] Vermes (pp. 63–68) gives further examples.

was acceptable to the Pharisees. The next verse will claim a unique significance for Jesus' exorcisms; they were differently executed, lacking the magical techniques generally used and depending on a simple irresistible authority, and the concentration of such activity in Jesus' ministry contrasts with the relative scarcity of references to exorcism in non-Christian Jewish literature. But if exorcism as such was accepted in Jewish society, why should Jesus' practice of it be suspect?

**28.** The unique character of Jesus' exorcisms (see on last verse) is to be attributed to the *Spirit of God*, rather than to any demonic spirit.[1] In his work of deliverance, they may see God's victory over Satan. The unusual use of *kingdom of God* (instead of Matthew's regular 'kingdom of heaven') serves not only to echo 'Spirit of God', but also to point out the contrast with the 'kingdom of Satan' (see on v. 26). Jesus thus claims the arrival in his ministry of that to which the Old Testament and Judaism had looked forward. It is already present (*ephthasen*, 'has come upon', is reminiscent of *ēngiken* in 3:2; 4:17; 10:7; see on 3:2), but its character is not that of popular expectation; it is a spiritual victory, not a national or political one – the enemy is Satan, not Rome. *Ephthasen* perhaps therefore suggests an arrival which catches unawares (*cf.* 1 Thes. 2:16). Thus the Pharisees have failed to recognize the arrival of the new age, which is already challenging them to decision. Jesus here warns them of the seriousness of the position they are adopting; vv. 31–32 will spell out the consequences.[2]

**29.** Thus Jesus destroys Satan's kingdom not from within (as the Pharisees alleged: see vv. 25–26) but by direct assault on the *strong man*. The figure may be drawn from Isaiah 49:24–26, where the 'prey' rescued is God's people; so the *goods* here may represent people in Satan's power, but more likely they are merely a part of the metaphor of conquest and plunder. The 'binding of Satan' was a feature in Jewish apocalyptic hope (Testament of Levi 18:21; *cf.* 1 Enoch 54:3–5; 69:27–28) and became also part of Christian eschatology (Rev. 20:1–3). *First*

---

[1] Luke has, more vividly, 'finger of God' (11:20), echoing Ex. 8:19, another case of clearly supernatural power. See R. G. Hamerton-Kelly, *NTS* 11 (1964/5), pp. 167–169, for the close relation of God's 'hand' and his 'Spirit' in the Old Testament.

[2] See Ladd, pp. 139–145, for a good discussion of this key verse.

may refer back to an earlier binding by Jesus (*e.g.* the defeat of Satan in 4:1ff.), but more likely is part of the overall metaphor. Satan is powerless before the victorious incursion of God's kingdom in Jesus' ministry of deliverance.

**30.** In this conflict neutrality is impossible. To be *against* Jesus (as the Pharisees were showing themselves to be) is to be on Satan's side. *Gather* and *scatter* do not represent specific actions (*e.g.* gathering God's people – so Bonnard), but constitute a vivid metaphor to reinforce the 'slogan' of the first half of the verse. The reversed form of this slogan in Mark 9:40 (though its effect is, in context, less polemical) equally excludes the middle ground.

**31–32.** Matthew has here brought together two related and puzzling sayings found in Mark 3:28–29 and in Luke 12:10, so that the interpretation of each is governed by the other. The saying in Mark contrasts *blasphemy against the Holy Spirit* (which is unforgivable) with all other sins and blasphemies (which may be forgiven); that in Luke specifies the forgivable blasphemy as speaking *a word against the Son of man*. Blasphemy against the Holy Spirit (*i.e.* against the manifest activity of God, as seen in v. 28) is more serious than other forms of slander and abuse (*blasphēmia* is usually speech against God in the LXX, but in secular Greek it is used also of slander generally; so also in Rom. 3:8; 1 Cor. 10:30); it indicates a deliberate refusal to acknowledge God's power, a totally perverted orientation, like that of Isaiah 5:20 ('those who call evil good and good evil'). This was what the Pharisees were doing in attributing Jesus' healings to Satanic power. Is the *Son of man* then on a lower level, less than divine, that he can be slandered with impunity? Rather the *incognito* character of Jesus' ministry means that failure to recognize him for what he was might be excusable (*cf.* Acts 3:17); even Peter 'spoke against' him (26:69–75) and was forgiven. The difference is then between failure to recognize the light and deliberate rejection of it once recognized; *cf.* Numbers 15:30–31 for unforgivable blasphemy in contrast with unwitting sin in vv. 27–29. At Qumran slander of one's fellow was forgivable after penance, but slander against the community brought permanent expulsion from it (1QS 7:15–17). But the punishment for blasphemy against the Holy Spirit is not only on earth, but extends to *the age* *to come*; it indicates a hardening against God which is deliberate and irreversible.

Early Christian interpretation took the blasphemy against the Son of man as that of the unbeliever, but blasphemy against the Holy Spirit as that of the Christian – hence the idea that sin after baptism is unforgivable. But this is too rigid, and the text makes no such distinction. The Pharisees, after all, would hardly be regarded as believers, yet it is their blasphemy against the Spirit which is here condemned. These verses have been made the ground of much unnecessary fear for over-sensitive Christians whose supposed 'unforgivable sin' bore no resemblance to the deliberate stance adopted by these Pharisees; for a striking example see George Borrow, *Lavengro*, chapters LXXV–LXXVII. Ultimately only God can know when an individual's opposition to his work has reached this stage of irreversible rejection.

**33–35.** These verses use different metaphors to make the same point, that what you say and do depends on, and reveals, what you are. The Pharisees' abuse of Jesus could not therefore be treated as a thoughtless passing remark; it revealed their true nature. In terms of the radical division of v. 30, it showed them to be against rather than for. This same radical division, between *good* and *evil*, is illustrated from the *tree* and *fruit* metaphor of 7:16–20 (see notes there; *make* here is not a command to be given literal application, but an idiomatic way of stating the situation: 'suppose . . .'). John the Baptist's metaphor of the *brood of vipers* (*cf.* 3:7, and see on 3:2 for Matthew's careful linking of Jesus' preaching with that of John) is used here to indicate their basically wrong orientation; *cf.* 15:17–20 for the theme that the root of evil words and deeds is in what a man is in himself. The principle that like produces like underlies this passage. Its application is not to suggest that no-one can be changed, but that as long as they remain unchanged at heart, their words and behaviour will show it.

**36–37.** The principle of the previous three verses explains why *your words* are a sound basis for judgment: they reveal what you really are. That is why the harsh judgment of vv. 31–32 could be pronounced on the basis of the Pharisees' verbal abuse; it showed them to be fundamentally against God's purpose. *Argon* ('careless') is literally 'work-less' (see, *e.g.*, 20:3, 6).[1] The word may imply 'ineffective' (*cf.* the 'useless' faith of Jas. 2:20), hence 'a careless word which, because of its worthlessness, had better been left unspoken' (BAGD, p. 104b). It may also imply 'untrue';[2] but the point is that what might appear an idle quip, and therefore quite innocuous, may, because of what it reveals about the person who says it, be the basis for a severe condemnation. The reference to v. 24 is clear, but the principle applies more widely.

*(vii) Jesus' verdict on 'this generation' (12:38–45)*
The phrase 'this generation' which occurs in vv. 41, 42, 45, and is prepared for by 'an evil and adulterous generation' in v. 39, holds this section together as a condemnation of the negative attitude of Jesus' contemporaries, and especially of their religious leaders, which the preceding verses have highlighted.

**38–39.** This exchange with the Jewish leaders recurs in an expanded form in 16:1–4. The *sign* they require is some authentication of Jesus' message and claims which will be more impressive than the healings and exorcisms they have seen and rejected (see v. 24). In 16:1 they require a sign 'from heaven', *i.e.* one which is clearly the work of God. *Cf.* Exodus 4:8–9; Isaiah 7:11; 38:7–8 for such signs; similar signs were required to authenticate some Rabbis according to *Baba Metzia* 59b (R. Eliezer, *c.* AD 90) and *Sanhedrin* 98a (R. Jose b. Kisma, *c.* AD 110). As a *teacher* (see on 8:19) Jesus might then expect such a demand. This sceptical search for tangible evidence is rejected by Jesus, for 'the demand for a sign spells the end of faith' (Schweizer). It thus indicates a *generation* which, instead of being humbly responsive to God's call, is *evil and adulterous* (a regular Old Testament metaphor for rebellion against God). Jesus' condemnation of 'this generation' is a prominent theme in Matthew; see, apart from this passage, 11:16–19; 16:4; 17:17; 24:34, and especially 23:29–36, which shows that it refers to his contemporaries, not just Jews or men

---

[1] G. B. Caird (*The Language and Imagery of the Bible* (1980), p. 22) says they 'are not . . . "thoughtless" words, such as a carefree joke, but deedless ones, loafers which ought to be up and busy about what they say, the broken promise, the unpaid vow, words which said, "I go, sir" and never went'.

[2] So Jeremias, *NTT*, p. 220; *cf.* JB, 'unfounded'.

in general, as those in whom Israel's age-long rebellion has culminated, and on whom judgment must therefore fall. In Mark 8:12 the refusal of a sign is unqualified. The exception here, *the sign of the prophet Jonah*, is, as v. 40 will make clear, one reserved for the future, when Jesus' ministry is over; until then, there will be no sign.

**40.** It is commonly asserted that the 'sign of Jonah' is Jesus' preaching. This exegesis can be sustained only by dismissing v. 40 as a later interpolation giving a new and incompatible sense to the phrase. (Against this view see my *JOT*, pp. 80–82, and against the probability that the sign consists in preaching, *ibid.*, p. 44.) Jewish interest in the book of Jonah focused on the fish episode in chapters 1 – 2, not on the preaching to Nineveh in chapters 3 – 4 (which will be taken up in v. 41), so the 'sign of Jonah' would naturally be interpreted, as this verse demands (*cf.* Jon. 1:17 (2:1, Heb.) ), in terms of Jonah's deliverance, even where, as in Luke 11:30, the parallel is not explicitly drawn out.[1] The point is, then, that Jesus, like Jonah, will undergo an experience which will be a 'sign' of his divine commission; the preaching of the early church duly drew this conclusion from the resurrection (Acts 2:22–36; 4:10–11; *etc.*). *Three days and three nights* was a Jewish idiom appropriate to a period covering only two nights (see my *JOT*, p. 81, n.2.). *The heart of the earth* probably refers to Sheol, the place of the dead (*cf.* Jon. 2:2, 'the belly of Sheol' – Jonah was rescued from the prospect of death, Jesus from death itself).

**41–42.** A separate point, though again involving *Jonah*, contrasts the scepticism of Jesus' hearers with the response of pagans to men of God in the past. Neither *the men of Nineveh* nor *the queen of the South* (*i.e.* of Sheba, in South Arabia – see 1 Ki. 10:1–13) might have been expected to take seriously the words of an Israelite. Because they did, their response will, by contrast, *condemn* 'this (Jewish) generation'. *Cf.* the contrasts drawn in 10:15; 11:21–24, again in the light of *the* (day of) *judgment*. The contrast is not simply that the pagans responded to God's messenger while 'this generation' did not; their offence is compoun-

[1]Bonnard argues that Matthew's version refers to imprisonment rather than deliverance, to the cross rather than the resurrection; but the mention of the three-day period points to the end of the ordeal, and no Jewish reader could hear Jonah 1:17 without thinking of 2:10.

ded by the fact that they are rejecting *something greater than* an Old Testament prophet, wise man, or king. For this repeated phrase see on v. 6, where the Old Testament reality transcended was the temple (and its priesthood); taking the three verses together we see Jesus as greater than temple (priesthood), prophet and king (wise man), a comprehensive list of those through whom God's message came in the Old Testament. There is thus a striking note of finality about the use of this formula; the one in whom all these are transcended is surely God's ultimate revelation. It is not that Jesus was visibly more impressive than the temple, Jonah or Solomon, but that in his Messianic role he brought the reality to which all pointed forward.

**43-45.** This little parable takes up a number of points from the preceding verses: the exorcism scene echoes vv. 22-29, the application in v. 45 takes up 'this generation' from vv. 39, 41-42, and the point of the parable could be summed up in the words of v. 30 – there is no room for neutrality. It is shown by the end of v. 45 to be a parable, not an objective psychiatric observation. It warns of the danger of half-hearted repentance: *this evil generation* might be 'cleansed' by Jesus' ministry among them, but a repentance which does not lead to a new allegiance leaves a void which the devil will exploit; he who is not positively with Jesus must inevitably end up against him.

The parable gives a vividly humorous account of the experiences and tactics of the expelled *unclean spirit*, but its point is in the condition of the *house*. Verse 44 is not a statement of the inevitable outcome of exorcism; there is an implied 'if' – if he finds it *empty* he will return; therefore it must not be left empty. The *seven other spirits* (seven is the number of perfection!) are needed to help him effect entry to the inhospitable territory of a clean 'house', and to make it unclean enough to live in again!

*(viii) Jesus' true family (12:46-50)*

**46.** Matthew does not tell us how Jesus' family responded to his teaching (contrast Mk. 3:21); but the contrast between their *standing outside* and the inner circle of his 'true' family suggests their lack of whole-hearted response.[1]

**48–49.** Jesus' words have been taken to imply a lack of proper respect for his mother; but see his remarks on the subject, 15:3–6. The point here is, as in 10:34–37, that there is a tie which is closer even than that of family.

**50.** The *disciples* (v. 49) who are thus privileged are described as *whoever does the will* of God. The emphasis, as in 7:15–27, is not on intellectual assent but on practical obedience; that is the essence of discipleship, and here, as in 7:21–23, it is the test of the reality of a relationship with Jesus.

Here then, in contrast with the various wrong responses to Jesus set out in chapters 11 – 12, is the response for which he looked, and the section closes with Jesus, rejected by most of 'this generation', surrounded by the select group of the true family of his *Father in heaven*.

## F. JESUS' TEACHING IN PARABLES (13:1–53)

The word 'parable' has not so far occurred in Matthew's Gospel, though several short sayings are in effect little parables (*e.g.* 5:25–26; 11:16–19; 12:43–45). Now he has brought together eight parables, together with detailed interpretations of three of them and some teaching on the purpose of parables, to make up the third of his great collections of Jesus' teaching (see pp. 59–60, above). It is a more varied collection than the similar one in Mark 4, with its parables of growth, but there is a clear connection both in the thought of the various sections and in the careful structuring of the chapter.

Chapters 11 – 12 have illustrated the growing divisions among men in their attitude to Jesus, culminating in the sharp contrast between true disciples and all others in 12:46–50. Division, and the problem of how some could reject Jesus' message while others responded, are the underlying themes of this chapter too; the parables thus provide some explanation of the attitudes revealed in the preceding narrative.

Division is seen in the structure of the chapter. The parable of

---

[1]The addition of v. 47 in most of the later MSS is apparently due to the pedantic desire to provide an antecedent to 'the man who told him', v. 48, and to the presence of a similar statement in Mk. and Lk.; it adds nothing to the content.

the sower is spoken in public to 'great crowds' (vv. 1–3), but its explanation and the teaching about parables are spoken only to the disciples (vv. 10–11). More parables are then spoken to 'the crowds' (v. 34), but the crowds are again left behind (v. 36), and the second explanation and further parables are spoken to the disciples in 'the house' (which Jesus had left in v. 1). The unresponsive crowds are thus clearly distinguished from the disciples to whom alone explanation is given, and this distinction is spelt out in vv. 11–17.

This division and contrast runs also through the contents of these parables. They are often referred to as 'parables of the kingdom', and indeed all of them are explicitly about 'the kingdom of heaven' (on which see pp. 45–47). But it is men's response to the preaching of God's kingdom which is their theme, and in this response there is a division between fruitful soil and unproductive, good grain and weeds, good fish and bad, while those who find the treasure and the pearl are remarkable precisely because they act so differently from other men, and the scribe of v. 52 is distinguished from other householders who can produce only what is old. The kingdom of heaven, for all its growing power (vv. 31–33), is a 'secret' (v. 11), and a secret is a secret only if not everyone is in the know. That so crucial a revelation is offered to men, and so powerful an agent is at work, and yet there are some who remain unresponsive and unaffected – this is the great mystery which these parables are designed to explain. The parables are grouped thus:

Introductory parable: the sower (1–9)
  Interlude: the purpose of parables (10–17)
          explanation of the sower (18–23)
    Three parables of growth: weeds (24–30)
                      mustard seed (31–32)
                      yeast (33)
  Interlude: the purpose of parables (34–35)
          explanation of the weeds (36–43)
    Three further parables: treasure (44)
                      pearl (45–46)
                      net (47–50)
Concluding parable: the householder (51–53).

*(i) and (iii) The sower (13:1–9 and 18–23)*
The explanation of the parable does not follow immediately after
it, but is preceded by vv. 10–17 which explain why an explanation is necessary, and to whom it may appropriately be given.
While this order is clearly logical (and is repeated in the case of
the parable of the weeds, vv. 24–30 and 36–43), it will simplify
our study if in each case we deal with parable and explanation
together.

It is often argued that the original intention of the parable was
different from that drawn out in vv. 18–23, and that the explanation therefore does not derive from Jesus but from a later Christian reapplication of his story. Parables are, in the nature of the
case, capable of being applied in different ways, but many of the
parables in the Gospels are accompanied by some indication of
their purpose, either in the wording itself or in the way they are
introduced, quite apart from the three in this chapter which
have detailed explanations attached (see P. B. Payne, *GP*, I,
pp. 171–172); and Matthew makes it quite clear that Jesus did
help his disciples to understand his parables (13:10–18, 36, 51;
15:15ff.).

The authenticity of this particular explanation is defended in
detail by P. B. Payne (*ibid.*, pp. 163–207). It can be attributed to
Jesus, of course, only if it is consistent with the apparent meaning of the parable, and this will be our concern in the following
exegesis. We may note here, however, the carefully demonstrated conclusion of B. Gerhardsson,[1] that 'the parable and the
interpretation fit each other as hand fits glove'.

The explanation is sometimes described as 'allegorizing'. But
more recent scholarship has moved away from Jülicher's insistence that only one main point should be sought in each parable, and it is now accepted that the details may sometimes be
intended to be significant. And if any parable was so intended,
surely the sower must be, for its fourfold structure places the
emphasis on the differing fate of the seed, not merely on a
contrast between fruitful and unfruitful. In drawing out the
significance of these deliberately drawn cameos, vv. 19–23 are
not searching arbitrarily for allegorical opportunities (such

[1] *NTS* 14 (1967/8), pp. 165–193.

promising material as the sower himself and the harvest receive no identification), but are echoing the structure of the parable itself.

The overall purpose of the parable is best discussed after we have considered some details.

**1–2.** *The house* (presumably that of 8:14; 9:10, 28) serves here and in v. 36 to make clear the distinction between the public teaching which follows and the private explanation and further teaching (see introduction to this chapter). The impressive scene, with Jesus seated to teach (see on 5:1–2) and the *great crowds* on the shore was probably typical of this phase of Jesus' ministry, and shows graphically the authority of Jesus which was recognized by ordinary Jews outside the disciple group (*cf.* 7:28–29).

**3–8.** There is nothing abnormal about the conditions which the sower encountered (see Jeremias, *PJ*, pp. 11–12), and all may have occurred within the same field; the apparently high rate of wastage (though the four types are not said to be equal in quantity!) may however be deliberately exaggerated to make the point of the parable. The same may be true of the rates of yield of the successful seed; the experts differ as to what was a typical yield, depending on the method of reckoning,[1] but the point of the parable does not lie in the size of the yield, but in the variety in the fate of the seed. This is not a general description of Palestinian agriculture, but a story designed to teach a specific lesson.

**9.** See on 11:15. Here, as elsewhere, the formula conveys a challenge not only to understanding but to life.

**18.** The 'title' of the parable can be misleading. *The sower* himself is not the focus of attention, nor is he identified in what follows. It is the seed and the soils which are the subject.

**19–23.** There is some awkwardness in the spelling out of the application. This arises not from a difference of focus between the parable and its interpretation, but within the wording of the interpretation itself. The description of the four types focuses, as surely the parable intended, on their varying receptiveness to what they hear; all *hear the* same *word*. Yet each type is identified

[1]Jeremias (*PJ*, p. 150), following Dalman, sees thirty- to a hundredfold as abnormal, 'surpassing all human measure', while P. B. Payne (*GP*, I, pp. 181–186) argues that it was 'not at all fanciful', but 'suggested the blessing of God'; *cf.* Gn. 26:12.

as *what was sown* in a certain place (*i.e.* apparently the seed, not the ground which received it). This introductory phrase (or conclusion, in the first case) serves as a short-hand reminder of the appropriate scene in the story, rather than being logically integrated into the interpretation.[1] But this awkwardness does not obscure the application, which in any case rests on the interaction of the unvarying seed with the various types of ground.

**19.** For *the word of the kingdom*, a phrase used only here by Matthew, see on 'gospel of the kingdom' (4:23). To *understand* is more than an intellectual grasp of the message; *cf.* the contrast in 7:24ff. between hearing and 'doing' the word. The word which is only *heard* is easy prey for the *evil one*. It is a non-starter.

**20–21.** But to start is not necessarily to finish. Here the word is *received* (not 'understood') *with joy*, but joy without understanding and commitment cannot last: *endures for a while* is literally 'is temporary'. *Tribulation* is a general term for suffering which comes from outside; *persecution* is deliberately inflicted, and usually implies a religious motive. *Falls away* is literally 'is tripped up' (*cf.* 5:29–30); it is not a gradual loss of interest, but a collapse under pressure.

**22.** This time the soil is good, but it is already taken up. The *world* (*aiōn*, the present age, the secular concerns of earth as opposed to the kingdom of God) offers both *cares* (*cf.* 6:25–34, where 'anxious' is from the same root) and *delight* (the normal meaning of this word, *apatē*, is 'deceit'; RSV has preferred its later sense of 'pleasure', but either sense suggests the seductive effect of wealth, which offers what it cannot deliver), but both can be equally engrossing.

**23.** Now at last hearing is matched by *understanding* (*cf.* on v. 19). The *fruit* is unspecified, but is presumably that practical acceptance of God's sovereignty which is the goal of the 'word of the kingdom'.

In the context of Jesus' ministry the parable serves to explain why it is that the 'good news of the kingdom' meets with such a varied response as we have seen in chapters 11 – 12, from

---

[1]The passive participle 'sown' *could* be applied to the ground on which the seed falls, though this is not normal in Greek; so JB, and see P. B. Payne (*GP*, I, pp. 172–177) for an argument for this as the sense of the original Aramaic.

enthusiastic acceptance to outright rejection. The fault lies not in the message, but in those who receive it. Men are both inadequate in themselves to respond as the 'word of the kingdom' requires (trampled and shallow soil), and also exposed to competing pressures from outside (tribulation and persecution, worldly cares and delights, and behind them all the evil one himself). The wonder is not that some do not produce fruit, but that any do. But here lies the parable's encouragement both to Jesus' followers then and to all who since then have preached this same gospel; not all will respond, but there will be some who do, and the harvest will be rich. The theme is thus closely related to that of the verses which divide the parable from its explanation, the division between those to whom the 'mysteries of the kingdom of heaven' are revealed and those who can hear the same message but will never understand it.

Yet the parable is probably more often employed today as a call to members of the church to examine themselves in their response to God's word. And this application, though secondary, is surely also within the parable's intention, for the careful spelling out of the causes of the seed's failure is surely not mere scenery. Unreceptiveness, shallowness, preoccupation with the world are not faults confined only to 'those outside', nor does the parable's division between fruitful and unfruitful necessarily correspond to the limits of church membership.

*(ii) The purpose of parables (13:10–17)*
While these verses are formally an interlude between the first parable and its explanation, they are crucial to the conception of the chapter as a whole, as they set out the division between the enlightened disciples and the unresponsive crowd which is the focus both of the structure of the chapter and of much of its contents.

**10.** This, unlike the preceding parable, is a private conversation; perhaps Matthew wants us to see it as taking place in the boat away from the crowd on the shore, but it is the privacy not the place which matters. The disciples' question arises not only from the fact that Jesus has just addressed the crowds in a parable, but also from the contents of that parable, which shows that Jesus knew that some of his hearers would be unable to grasp his message; in that case why use this cryptic form of teaching rather than plain statement? It is not a question only about the sower, but about the new method of teaching which it heralds. Verse 34 will spell out what the rest of Matthew's Gospel will reveal, that after this point, while crowds continue to follow Jesus, he will no longer teach them except in parables. (The only significant exception is ch. 23, most of which is hardly 'teaching'!) From now on open teaching will be given only to the disciples, and that in increasing measure.

The Greek *parabolē* is wider than our 'parable'; in the LXX it translates *māšāl*, which includes proverbs, riddles and wise sayings as well as parables. Matthew uses it for instance for Jesus' cryptic saying about defilement (15:10–11, 15), and in 24:32 ('lesson') it indicates a comparison. Speaking *in parables* is therefore enigmatic, and requires careful interpretation.

**11.** To know the truth about *the kingdom of heaven* is to *know secrets*. The Greek *mystērion*, used only here in the Gospels, became important for Paul to indicate that God's truth comes only by revelation, not by natural insight. That is the sense here too – only those to whom *it has been given* (by God) can understand the nature of God's kingdom proclaimed by Jesus, and therefore the facts about its growth, membership, demands and privileges which these parables convey. Parables, which to the hostile and the merely curious were simple stories, would yield their riches only within this context, to those who *know the secrets*. Thus there is an inevitable division between *you* (the disciples) and *them* (specified in Mark's version as 'those outside'). The carefully antithetical structure of this verse, as of v. 12 and of vv. 13 with 16, reinforces the division of men into two groups.

**12.** The laws of capitalist economics (capital breeds income; lack of capital spells ruin) serve as a 'parable' of spiritual enlightenment. The 'secrets' of God's kingdom can be grasped only by those who already have the spiritual capacity to receive them, *i.e.* the disciples as opposed to 'those outside'. Thus the division of v. 11 is here reinforced. Logically, that which one *has not* cannot *be taken away*, but the paradox is vivid and effective. It is probably unwise to be too specific in applying the details of an epigram of this nature which occurs in different contexts (*cf.*

25:29, and the different position in Mk. 4 and Lk. 8), but perhaps the 'taking away' refers here to the ultimate uselessness of a 'religion' which is not that of the kingdom of heaven.

**13.** The latter part of the verse is an allusion to Isaiah 6:9-10, which describes Israel's failure to respond to the prophet's message. Jesus sees himself in a similar prophetic role, meeting a similar unresponsiveness in those of his hearers who are not disciples, and it is this situation which makes parables an appropriate method of teaching. In terms of the division of vv. 11 and 12, the same form of words can reveal 'secrets' to 'those who have', but convey nothing but riddles or mere everyday stories to those to whom 'it has not been given'. It is the appropriateness of parables to this situation which is the point of this verse (as of vv. 11-17 as a whole); it does not spell out either their purpose or their result. Thus the common view that Matthew with his *because* is deliberately 'softening' Mark's statement of purpose ('so that'), making parables a means of overcoming their unresponsiveness rather than causing it (for which see Gundry, *UOT*, pp. 33-34), is beside the point. Verse 13 alone could be read in that sense, but in the context of the paragraph as a whole this is impossible: the division between the disciples' enlightenment and the crowd's dullness is repeatedly affirmed and emphasized as the essence of the disciple's privilege, and parables are explained as appropriate to this situation (on the principle of 7:6?), not as designed to change it. For the verb *understand* here and in vv. 14 and 15, see above, on v. 19: anyone can *hear*, but only a disciple can *understand*.

**14-15.** The same passage in Isaiah which inspired v. 13 is now quoted in full in the LXX version. The arguments often advanced for these verses being a later addition to the text of Matthew are unconvincing.[1] It is likely that they are Matthew's own addition, along the lines of his formula-quotations (see pp. 38-40), to underline the allusion in Jesus' words. The wording of the introductory formula is not that of the formula-quotations, but it conveys the same idea of fulfilment. Isaiah 6:9-10 was not in fact a prediction for the distant future but rather for Isaiah's own

[1] See Gundry, *UOT*, pp. 116-118; there is no textual evidence for the absence of these verses.

experience, but this experience formed a typological pattern which is now *fulfilled* as Jesus re-enacts the role of the Old Testament prophet. Perhaps a statement of fact, *with them indeed is fulfilled*, is used rather than the usual purpose clause to show that the spiritual dullness was the situation within which Jesus taught rather than itself the product of his teaching. It is similarly notable that in v. 15 the LXX, which is here followed, substitutes for the Hebrew imperatives ('make fat', 'make heavy', 'shut') a passive verb ('has been made fat') and two active ones (the Greek reads literally 'with their ears they have heard heavily and their eyes they have closed'), thus placing the blame for their unresponsiveness not on the prophet (here Jesus) but on the people themselves. Thus, as we saw in v. 13, the emphasis is not on either the purpose or the result of Jesus' speaking in parables, but rather on the existing situation within which it took place.

**16–17.** Verse 16 forms a striking counterpart to v. 13, contrasting 'you' with 'them'. (As in the case of Matthew's other formula-quotations, vv. 14–15 could be removed without breaking the flow of thought; they are the Evangelist's comment.) This beatitude (see on 5:3–10 for the term) is recorded in Luke 10:23–24 after the great thanksgiving for the special revelation to the disciples (= Mt. 11:25–27). Both contexts stress the same theme of a division between the enlightened disciple and other men. The disciples are thus privileged (*blessed* = to be congratulated; see on 5:3–10) above their unbelieving contemporaries, but v. 17 adds a further dimension; even the men of God in the Old Testament period (*prophets and righteous men*, as opposed to those who refused the prophets' message) did not share the privilege of seeing *what you see*. Jesus thus claims again that in his ministry the time of fulfilment of the hopes of Israel has come.

The theme of esoteric revelation in vv. 11–17 is sometimes dubbed 'predestinarian'. But the passage describes an existing division (one which was a constant feature of Jesus' ministry as this Gospel records it), and explains why speaking in parables is appropriate in that situation. It does not discuss how one *becomes* a disciple, *i.e.* how one may move from one side of that division to another. Still less does it say that such a transfer is impossible – after all, presumably the disciples were themselves once 'outside'. What it does make clear is that natural insight is not enough; spiritual enlightenment is *given* (v. 11). But how and to whom it is given is not the theme of these verses.

*(iii) Explanation of the sower (13:18–23)*
See above, with *(i) The sower (13:1–9)*.

*(iv) and (vi) Three parables of growth; and explanation of the weeds (13:24–33 and 36–43)*
As with the sower, so now we shall deal with the second extended explanation together with the parable it explains, even though it is again separated from it in the text by a statement on the purpose of parables.

*(a) The weeds (13:24–30, 36–43)*. On the question of the authenticity of the explanations given in this chapter, see above, on vv. 18–23. The explanation of the weeds, like that of the sower, takes up the details of the story in a way which has been dubbed 'allegorizing'. Here again, however, it is hard to explain why the parable was told in this form if it was not intended that these details (as with the sower, not all details of the story receive an application) should be noted. The identification of the details in vv. 37–39 does not involve any departure from what is apparently the intended theme of the parable, and should not therefore be dismissed as illegitimate. If Jesus did not intend the story to be so understood, what *did* he intend by it? There is no other obvious answer.[1] It is true that the latter part of the explanation (vv. 40–43) focuses on the final division rather than on the call for patience which is prominent in the story, but it is precisely in the expectation of this ultimate division that the call for patience is grounded.

The parable is usually understood as depicting the mixed character of the church, in which true and false believers coexist until the final judgment. But in Jesus' own ministry this was not yet an issue, and in v. 38 the field is identified as 'the world' rather than the church. So the canvas is broader than the specific

---

[1] 'The point of the interpretation is exactly that of the parable itself': Hill, p. 235.

issue of church discipline. Jesus announced God's kingdom, and this would lead many of his hearers to expect a cataclysmic disruption of society, an immediate and absolute division between the 'sons of light' and the 'sons of darkness', as the men of Qumran put it. Yet things went on apparently as before. It was to this impatience that the parable was primarily directed. God's kingdom does bring division, and that division is final, but while it is already present in principle, its full outworking is for God to bring about in the final judgment, not for man to anticipate by human segregation. Of course this has its practical application to the search for a 'pure church' here on earth, but the perspective is wider. It is, as in the two following parables, that of the contrast between the present hiddenness of God's kingdom and its future consummation, when the 'righteous', who are now barely distinguishable from the 'sons of the evil one', will 'shine like the sun' (v. 43).

This consummation will come at the final judgment, which comes into focus in vv. 40–43. Here the explanation moves from the simple identification of details to develop more fully the brief climax of the parable. It thus brings into focus the fundamental division of men into two classes which we have seen to be basic to the whole chapter, and which was implicit in the parable.

**24.** *May be compared to* (*cf.* 'is like' in vv. 31, 33, 44, 45, 47 and similar formulae introducing other parables about *the kingdom of heaven*); the point of comparison in all these cases is not strictly the noun which follows but the parable as a whole: it is not the *man who sowed* who is compared to the kingdom of heaven, but the situation resulting from his sowing. We might paraphrase, 'This is what it is like when God is at work.'

**25–30.** The *weeds* are probably darnel, a poisonous plant related to wheat and virtually indistinguishable from it until the ears form. To sow darnel among wheat as an act of revenge was punishable in Roman law, which suggests that the parable depicts a real-life situation (*NBD*, p. 948). A light infestation of darnel could be tackled by careful weeding, but mistakes would easily be made. In the case of a heavy infestation the stronger roots of the darnel would be tangled with those of the wheat, making selective weeding impossible.[1]

**36.** For the significance of *the house*, see introductory remarks on ch. 13.

**37-39.** This detailed 'lexicon' to the parable provides a handy guide to its interpretation without focusing on any one point or drawing out the overall application. The following verses will expand the role of the *Son of man* to be not only the sower, but the chief harvester, and owner of the kingdom (*cf.* 25:31ff., where similarly divine functions are accorded to the Son of man). For *the world*, see introduction to this section. For *sons of the kingdom*, see on 8:12; here it is not ironical.

**40.** The remaining verses develop the final scene of the story into a portrayal of the final judgment similar to that of 25:31-46 (and *cf.* 13:49-50). It focuses on *the close of the age*, the ultimate turning-point when the period of the secret growth of God's kingdom alongside the continued activity of *the evil one* will be brought to an end, and the new age which was inaugurated in principle in Jesus' earthly ministry will be gloriously consummated.

**41.** Compare 24:31, where *the Son of man* sends out *his angels* (*cf.* also 16:27; 25:31) to gather the chosen. The two missions are necessarily complementary where there is an absolute division into two classes. *Out of his kingdom* does not necessarily imply that the 'sons of the evil one' were once in it, but that they will have no place in it when it is fully consummated (*cf.* 8:12). The *kingdom* which is here ascribed to the Son of man (as in 16:28; *cf.* 20:21) is in v. 43 'the kingdom of their Father'. These are not two separate kingdoms (one on earth, the other in heaven, according to some commentators); the sharing of attributes between God the Father and the Son of man is typical of the judgment scenes of this Gospel (*cf.* 16:27-28; 25:31ff.).[2] *All causes of sin* (literally 'stumbling-blocks') *and all evildoers* echoes the Hebrew text of Zephaniah 1:3 (see RSV mg. there), where it describes the objects of God's eschatological judgment; here it corresponds to the 'sons of the evil one' (v. 38). The *causes of sin* are not things, but people, as in 16:23, where Peter is described by the same word (*cf.* the use of the cognate verb in 18:6).

[1]See further, Jeremias, *PJ*, pp. 224-225.
[2]See J. D. Kingsbury, *The Parables of Jesus in Matthew 13* (1969), p. 98.

**42.** The image of the *furnace of fire* derives from the parable itself (v. 30 – the darnel was useful fuel where wood was in short supply); it is not in its own right a New Testament image for hell (though *fire* alone is, of course, often so used). For *weep and gnash their teeth*, cf. 8:12.

**43.** The ultimate glory of the 'sons of the kingdom' is described in imagery which reflects Daniel 12:3, and which contrasts strikingly with their previous 'hiddenness' during the period of 'growing together'. For *he who has ears, let him hear*, see on 11:15.

*(b) The mustard seed (13:31–32).* For *is like*, here and in v. 33, see on 13:24. The point of comparison is not the seed in itself, but what happens when it is sown. *Mustard seed* was proverbially minute (*cf.* 17:20, and Mishnah *Niddah* 5:2, *etc.*), though of course it is not literally the smallest known seed. The point of the parable lies in the contrast between this insignificant beginning and the *greatest of shrubs* which results. The expression is literally 'greater than the vegetables' and contrasts the full-grown shrub (it normally grew to about 3 metres) with other edible garden produce. It is an exaggeration to call it a *tree*, but the language suggests that Jesus was thinking of the Old Testament use of the tree as an image for a great empire (see especially Ezk. 17:23; 31:3–9; Dn. 4:10–12; *etc.*). From these passages also comes the picture of the *birds . . . in its branches*; there the birds represent the nations gathered under the protection of the empire (Ezk. 31:6; Dn. 4:20–22), and it is possible that Jesus' words here envisage the coming of the Gentiles into the kingdom of heaven.[1] But the main point lies simply in the huge extent of this kingdom which has developed from such unimpressive beginnings.

*(c) The yeast (13:33).* The theme is again of contrast between the tiny quantity of yeast and the size of its effect. *Three measures of meal* would be about 40 litres, which would make enough bread for a meal for 100 people, a remarkable baking for an ordinary *woman*, but it makes the point vividly! *Leaven* (yeast) is

---

[1] *Cf.* T. W. Manson, *The Teaching of Jesus* (1935), p. 133n.

usually in the Bible a symbol for the pervasive power of evil, but it is its pervasiveness, not its metaphorical connections, which is in view here. *Hid* is not the natural verb here, and must be designed to emphasize the secret, inconspicuous way the kingdom of heaven begins to take effect.

So the three parables of growth all focus on the paradox of insignificant or hidden beginnings and a triumphant climax. In Jesus' ministry this was a real issue: for those outside the disciple group it affected the credibility of an announcement of God's reign which had apparently little to show for it; for the disciples there was the natural impatience to see God's kingdom in all its glory, and the total eradication of all that opposed it. To them, and to us today who may expect God to act dramatically and without delay, Jesus points out that the full growth (harvest, mustard plant, leavened dough) is assured from the moment the seed is sown, however unpromising its appearance and whatever opposition it may meet in its development. The way of God is not that of ostentation but of ultimate success. Little is great where God is at work.

*(v) The purpose of parables (13:34–35)*
The theme of vv. 10–17 is here briefly resumed in a second interlude before the second set of three parables (see earlier comments on the structure of the chapter as a whole). The remaining sections will be addressed only to the disciples. For the concentration on parables in public teaching from now on, see on 13:10. This practice, which was previously explained from Isaiah 6:9–10, is now seen as the fulfilment of Psalm 78:2. The psalm title ascribes it to Asaph, who was regarded as a prophet (1 Ch. 25:2; 2 Ch. 29:30); but Matthew's mention of *the prophet* reflects his belief that all the Old Testament was 'prophetic' (*cf.* 11:13) and awaited 'fulfilment' (*cf.* 5:17).[1] The psalm describes only the writer's own intention, but as in 12:40–41 and 13:13ff., Jesus' role is seen as 'fulfilling' that pattern on a typological principle (see on 13:14–15). It is the word *parables*

---

[1] For the attribution to Isaiah in some important MSS (see RSV mg.) see Gundry, *UOT*, p. 119n.; the 'prophet' is unspecified also in 1:22; 2:5, 15; 21:4, and Isaiah was a popular candidate for scribal attribution, rightly or wrongly!

(Heb. *māšāl*; see on 13:10) which makes the connection, but *what was hidden* (translating Heb. *ḥîḏôṯ*, 'riddles', sayings requiring insight or explanation to be understood) appropriately sums up Matthew's earlier explanation of Jesus' procedure in telling parables to the crowds but explaining their significance only to the disciples. See further, on v. 52.

*(vi) Explanation of the weeds (13:36–43)*
See above, with *(iv) Three parables of growth (13:24–33).*

*(vii) Three further parables (13:44–50)*
The first two of these parables belong closely together, developing the theme of whole-hearted response with which the parable of the sower concluded. The third is closely related to the parable of the weeds, and emphasizes again the division which the preaching of God's kingdom brings.

*(a) The treasure (13:44).* For 'is like', here and in vv. 45 and 47, see on v. 24. Valuables such as coins or jewels were often *hidden* in a jar in the earth (*cf.* 25:25), and discoveries of such *treasure* trove were a favourite theme of popular stories. The *man* is probably a day-labourer; on the legal and moral justification of his action towards his employer see Derrett (pp. 1–16), but that is not the point of the parable. It lies rather in both the *joy* which a disciple experiences in 'finding' the kingdom of heaven (*i.e.* in a relationship with Jesus who brings it), and in his willingness to give up everything else for this (*cf.* 10:37–39; 19:27–29). But it is wrong to describe this 'giving up' as 'sacrifice'; the man sold from self-interest, in order to buy something far greater. The disciple's 'giving up' is in the context of *joy*!

*(b) The pearl (13:45–46).* The message is the same. *Pearls* were highly valued in the ancient world (see Jeremias, *PJ*, p. 199 for the fantastic prices they could fetch). The action of the *merchant* (a substantial trader, not a local retailer), while more economically improbable than that of the finder of the treasure, immediately catches the imagination.[1] In the face of the 'wealth that

---

[1] See R. Schippers in *Studia Evangelica* II (1964), pp. 236–241 for an excellent exposition in the light of the decision which faced the rich man in 19:21–22.

demonetizes all other currencies',[1] prudent calculation gives way to extravagant action.

*(c) The net (13:47–50).* This is the third parable with a formal explanation (vv. 49–50). The fact that most of the explanation is repeated verbatim from vv. 40–42 (even though the *furnace* is less appropriate to the disposal of fish than of darnel) indicates how closely the parables of the weeds and the net are linked in their theme. More precisely, the net echoes the last 'act' of the parable of the weeds, the sorting out of good from bad. The *net* is the large 'dragnet' which is drawn between two boats or by ropes from the shore, collecting all fish and other creatures within the area covered, which must then be *sorted* out to remove the *bad*, *i.e.* those unsuitable for eating. The reference, as in the weeds, is not primarily to a mixed church, but to the division among mankind in general which the last judgment will bring to light. See further, on vv. 40–42.

*(viii) Concluding parable: the householder (13:51–53)*
While v. 52 is not normally listed as one of the parables of this chapter, it resembles them in the formula 'is like', the concern with the kingdom of heaven, and the homely illustration; structurally it stands in parallel with the introductory parable of the sower.[2]

**51.** In v. 36 the disciples had asked for explanation. Jesus now checks that the teaching given specifically to them and not to the crowds has been effective. It has produced *understanding*. For this key word see vv. 13, 14, 15, 19, 23, above: it is the special prerogative of the disciple to whom the mysteries are revealed.

**52.** *Therefore* ought to refer back to v. 51; in that case the parable of the householder relates to the fact of the disciples' understanding. This, and the fact that it speaks of *every* scribe, tells against the view that it is the Evangelist's description of his own role.[3] While *grammateus* normally denotes a *scribe* in the technical sense of a professional teacher of the Jewish law (5:20;

---

[1] A. M. Hunter, *The Parables, Then and Now* (1971), p. 79.

[2] For its classification as a parable see further D. Wenham, *NTS* 25 (1978/9), pp. 516–517.

[3] So especially Bonnard (pp. 210–211), following von Dobschütz's view that the Evangelist was a converted scribe.

7:29; 8:19; *etc.*), this literal meaning seems hardly relevant to this context, and it is more likely that Jesus is designating his disciples (who had no formal training) as the 'scribes' of the kingdom of heaven. The teaching he has given has *trained* them. (*Mathēteutheis* is from the same root as 'disciple', but in the passive is more naturally translated 'instructed' than 'made a disciple'.) In comparing them to a *householder who brings out of his treasure* . . ., Jesus is not merely describing them, but as usual in parables is challenging them to fulfil a role: they have received 'treasure' through his instruction; now they are to 'bring it out' in teaching others. *What is new and what is old* as a description of Christian teaching may include a dig at the *Jewish* scribes, who could produce only what was old! It also refers back to v. 35, where Jesus' new teaching is identified as going back to 'the foundation of the world'. It is new and revolutionary, but its validity lies in that it is grounded in God's eternal truths, now at last brought to light.

**53.** Like the parallel formulae at the end of the other major collections of teaching (see on 7:28–29), this verse both concludes the teaching and leads into the following narrative; there is no clear paragraph break, and the following verses will describe a mixed reaction to Jesus' teaching which amply illustrates much of the teaching in the preceding parables about men's response to the kingdom of heaven.

### G. VARYING RESPONSE TO JESUS' TEACHING AND MIRACLES (13:54 – 16:20)

In chapters 11 – 12 Matthew has presented a collection of incidents which reveal Jesus' Messianic activity, and the varying reactions to it. A further similar collection now follows, closely modelled on Mark 6:1 – 8:30. There is a subtle change of emphasis, in that in place of a relatively settled ministry in the lakeside towns of Galilee, we find Jesus more on the move and travelling in more isolated regions. Perhaps this is more than a change of scene, for the section begins with the last record of Jesus' teaching in a synagogue (13:54), and his rejection in Nazareth leads into increasingly hostile responses to his teaching. The theme of division which ran through the parables of chapter 13 is now therefore illustrated by an increasing polariz-ation in people's views of Jesus. Throughout the section, from the rejection at Nazareth and Herod's wrong identification to Peter's confession, the central question is, 'Who is Jesus?'

### (i) Nazareth rejects Jesus (13:54–58)

**54.** Jesus's *own country*, while not named, is clearly here only the village of Nazareth, not Galilee as a whole. (The 'parallel' passage, Lk. 4:16–30, is more explicit.) This is the last recorded visit of Jesus to a synagogue, which suggests that the pattern of ministry outlined in 4:23; 9:35 will now no longer be possible; this episode shows why. The people's *astonishment* is for the same reason as in 7:28 (indeed every use of *ekplēssomai* in the Gospels relates to the effect of Jesus' teaching and miracles). It is again a question of authority: such *wisdom* and such *mighty works* require a more than human origin. The same question has already led to the accusation of demonic power (9:34; 12:24), and will arise again in 21:23.

**55–56.** It is the very ordinariness of Jesus' home background that causes the astonishment (*cf.* Jn. 6:42). Mark here describes Jesus himself as 'the carpenter'; Matthew perhaps felt this too low a description for the Messiah, but *the carpenter's son* would share his father's occupation. The family trade is not mentioned elsewhere in the New Testament. It was a skilled craft, probably involving a thriving local construction business; for details see *AB, ad loc.,* where it is better translated 'builder'. We know no more details of the family than are given here. *James* became a leader in the church (Gal. 1:19; *etc.*) and *Judas* may be the 'brother of James' of Jude 1. No more is heard of the other brothers and sisters.

**57.** For *took offence,* see on 11:6. The same word was used in 13:21. It is the opposite to the positive response of faith. Jesus' saying has become proverbial; it is expanded in the Gospel of Thomas 31, with the curious and slightly incongruous statement that a doctor does not cure those who know him. Several similar observations about philosophers or famous men have been pre-served from the ancient world, on the theme 'Familiarity breeds contempt'. The *prophet* of Jesus' saying was not a purely hypo-thetical illustration, for Jesus' own role as prophet was already a matter of public discussion (16:14; *cf.* 21:11, 46).

**58.** Matthew omits Mark's statement that Jesus was 'amazed' at their unbelief and 'could not' work 'any' miracle there. Perhaps he felt the expressions to be unsuitable for the Son of God, but he is, as usual, abbreviating Mark's version throughout, and the connection between unbelief and the lack of miracles remains. Jesus' power is neither magical nor automatic, and the importance of faith in this connection has already been stressed (*cf.* 8:10, 13; 9:2, 22, 28–29).

*(ii) Herod Antipas thinks Jesus is John the Baptist revived (14:1–12)*
The famous story of the death of John, drastically abbreviated from the version in Mark, finds its place here as a footnote to Matthew's account of what Herod Antipas thought of Jesus; the official ruler of Galilee thus joins the list of responses to Jesus. Indeed he even, despite himself, testifies to Jesus' true significance, as the one to whom John's mission pointed forward. At the same time the fate of the prophet John (v. 5) foreshadows what awaits Jesus the prophet among his own people (13:57); *cf.* 17:12 for the parallel.

**1–2.** *At that time* is one of Matthew's connecting phrases (*cf.* 11:25; 12:1) which is not to be pressed chronologically, since vv. 13ff. will go on to record Jesus' action on hearing news of John's death, an event which is presupposed in these verses as already in the past. *Herod* Antipas is mentioned only here in Matthew, correctly designated *tetrarch* (minor local ruler) unlike his father, the 'king' of 2:1. (Antipas petitioned unsuccessfully for the title 'king', and popular usage probably continued to accord him his father's title, as in v. 9; *cf.* Mk. 6:14.) His execution of *John* provoked widespread disapproval (so Josephus, *Ant.* xviii. 116–119), and v. 9 indicates that he himself was not happy about it; hence no doubt his superstitious belief in John's 'resurrection'.[1]

**3–4.** Besides unjustly divorcing his first wife (and thus pro-

---

[1] One of the more remarkable eccentricities of 'scholarship' is the view of Enoch Powell M.P., that it was in fact John, not Jesus, who rose from the dead, and that the records of Jesus' ministry are in fact corruptions of earlier accounts of the risen John. Matthew 14:2 is the foundation of this theory; perhaps Antipas would have been flattered to be taken so seriously!

voking war with her father, the king of Petra) in order to marry
Herodias, Antipas broke Jewish law by marrying his half-
brother's wife (Lv. 18:16). John's protest would therefore represent orthodox Jewish opinion, and would be damaging to Antipas' prestige among his Jewish subjects. It was, moreover, perhaps more than a passing remark: *said* is in the imperfect tense,
which may indicate a continuing 'campaign'. Josephus' view
that Antipas executed John for 'sedition' (*Ant.* xviii. 118) may
not therefore be entirely unconnected with the motive the Gospels record. *Philip* is so named in Mark, but Josephus names him
as simply 'Herod' (*Ant.* xviii. 109), and records that Philip the
tetrarch was married to Salome, Herodias' daughter (*Ant.* xviii.
136–137). For the possibility that Herodias' husband was also
called (Herod) Philip, see H. W. Hoehner, *Herod Antipas* (1972),
pp. 131–136.[1]

**5.** That Antipas *wanted to put him to death* is confirmed and
more fully explained by Josephus (*Ant.* xviii. 117–118). Verse 9
records that he was nonetheless *sorry* to do so, perhaps because
of the way it was done, his hand forced by a trick, but also
because of the ambivalent attitude of a man threatened by one
whose integrity he must respect; see more fully Mark 6:20. For
John's popular appeal see 3:5–6; 11:7–9. Jesus would also be
protected by the same popular reputation (21:46, a verse which
deliberately echoes this, further underlining the parallel
between John and Jesus).

**6–11.** An unedifying story, told with a bald realism which
conveys the atmosphere of a licentious oriental court. For *the
daughter of Herodias* (Salome), see on vv. 3–4, and further Hoehner, *op. cit.*, pp. 151–157. *Girl* (v. 11) is a term which can be used
of those of marriageable age; she was at least a teenager. John's
execution was against Jewish law, both in that he had no trial
and that he was *beheaded*.

**12.** The report to Jesus indicates a continuing close link
between the two movements. Matthew thus underlines the
relationship set out in 11:2–19, where Jesus' ministry, for all its
contrasts, is seen as the legitimate sequel to that of John. It is
this continuity to which Antipas' bizarre conjecture in v. 2 has

[1] Hoehner's book provides an exhaustive study of the various problems in this story, pp.
110–171.

234

now again borne witness, and Matthew will continue to make the point as his story goes on.

### (iii) Jesus feeds a large crowd (14:13–21)

Attempts to reformulate this story into a naturalistically acceptable form (*e.g.* that many members of the crowd produced and shared their lunch-packs, or that Jesus distributed only minute token fragments of food) clearly do not do justice to the text. Matthew intends us to see this as a miraculous event, and as one that really happened, not as a 'parable'. The fact that all four Evangelists record it (and Matthew and Mark both record a second such incident) indicates that it was important to their understanding of Jesus.

But what was its importance? It was a proof of Jesus' miraculous power, certainly, but few Gospel miracles are recorded (or were performed) for that purpose only. John in particular, by the discourse which follows this incident in chapter 6, indicates that it had symbolic value, and Matthew too indicates (16:9) that it contained lessons for the disciples, and that to interpret it merely at the level of material provision is to miss the point.

Two Old Testament passages come to mind: the miraculous provision of bread in a 'lonely place' (literally 'desert') recalls the manna of Exodus 16, and the details of the story throughout echo Elisha's miracle of feeding a hundred men with twenty 'loaves' (2 Ki. 4:42–44). In both cases a prophet provided literal food, and Jesus the great prophet does likewise (though on a vastly increased scale in comparison with Elisha); Jewish expectation of a return of manna when the Messiah comes (2 Baruch 29:8; *cf.* Rev. 2:17) suggests it was a Messianic gesture.

But there is more to this meal than physical sustenance (see on v. 15); eating together is a symbol of unity. Instead of being dismissed and dispersed (v. 15), the crowds are welcomed into a new community. See on v. 19 for Jesus' role as 'head of the family'. Many regard this as a foretaste of the 'Messianic banquet' (see on 8:11); while a meal of bread and fish with no wine is hardly a 'banquet', it symbolizes the gathering of the people of God which will be consummated then. John clearly saw in this event a eucharistic element, and while this specific connotation belongs to the period after the Last Supper, it is not surprising that the incident came to be seen in the light of the Last Supper, itself a symbol of communion, and a foretaste of the Messianic banquet (26:29).

**13.** Chronological sequence is again not exact – Jesus could hardly withdraw from Nazareth (13:53–58) *in a boat*! What is important is the move *to a lonely place* as a result of the news of John's death. For such 'tactical withdrawals', see on 4:12. Jesus' movements recorded for the remainder of his 'Galilean' ministry include a much higher proportion of time spent *apart*, particularly in areas outside Antipas' province. Away from the threat of political suppression, and relieved of the pressure of the Galilean crowds, he is thus able to concentrate more directly on the private instruction of his disciples. Luke tells us that the 'lonely place' was near Bethsaida, across the lake in Philip's tetrarchy, about four miles from Capernaum by land. It was not 'desert' in our sense (see the 'grass' in v. 19 and the nearby villages, v. 15). For the motive of *the crowds* in following Jesus, see on v. 22.

**14.** For Jesus' *compassion* and its result, see on 9:36. Here Matthew mentions healing, Mark teaching, and Luke both! Jesus' ministry was an integrated whole, in which physical and spiritual need were met together.

**15–16.** *The day is now over* is literally 'the hour has already passed by', referring to the normal time for the evening meal. To miss one day's meal would not cause great hardship, and Jesus' determination to provide a meal is to be accounted for more in terms of its significance (see above) than of physical necessity. The command to the disciples (echoing 2 Ki. 4:42–43) deliberately involves them in the action (see also their active part in vv. 19–20), so that they will remember and learn from it.

**17–19.** Bread and fish were basic Galilean rations; it was a very ordinary meal. But the command *to sit down* (*anaklinomai*, literally 'recline'), while it may only reflect the effect of being on the ground rather than at table, may also be a hint of the more formal banquet at which guests reclined on couches. This is not a casual snack, but a formal occasion; see above for the possible connotation of the 'Messianic banquet'. *Blessed* is the normal giving of thanks before a meal, the responsibility of the head of the Jewish family. (He 'blesses' God for the food, rather than 'blessing' the food.) The actions and words are the same as those in the meal at Emmaus (Lk. 24:30), and no doubt in other meals where Jesus presided over the disciple 'family'. It is striking that the four verbs 'take', 'bless', 'break' and 'give' occur with minor variations not only in all six accounts of the two miraculous feedings and in that of the Emmaus meal, but also in all four accounts of the Last Supper (including 1 Cor. 11:23–24). It was a daily Jewish ritual, but in Christian memory it became filled with fuller meaning, as both these experiences in the 'lonely place' and the last meal in the upper room pointed forward to that great feast at which Jesus would be host to all his people of every race.

**20.** *Baskets* were regularly used for carrying food and equipment, so that their availability among a crowd out for the day is not surprising. There is no reason to see the number *twelve* as symbolic; that each of the twelve disciples who 'served' could fill his basket with left-overs merely emphasizes the abundance of the food provided.

**21.** *About* is literally 'as if'; the number is thus impressionistic rather than exact. Matthew's mention of the *women and children* is perhaps not just pedantry; it may reflect the similar rider added to the tally of the old people of God in Exodus 12:37. No group is excluded from Jesus' new community, whatever the conventions of society.

### (iv) Jesus walks on the water (14:22–33)

This episode is closely linked with the preceding story of the miraculous feeding in Matthew, Mark and John (Luke does not record it) not only in an unbroken narrative sequence, but also in that both incidents fulfil the dual role of revealing the supernatural power of Jesus (so that v. 33 appropriately summarizes the impact of the two events together) and of teaching symbolically the nature and privilege of discipleship. This symbolic aspect is more strongly emphasized by Matthew's inclusion (vv. 28–31) of an independent tradition about Peter's attempt to copy Jesus' act, a vivid lesson on the role of faith in following Jesus. At the same time there are strong reminiscences of the equally symbolic event of Jesus' stilling of the storm (8:23–27). *Cf.* the transfiguration (17:1–8) for a similarly 'numinous' experience which reveals Jesus' supernatural status.

**22.** *Made* is literally 'compelled', an unusually strong word. John 6:14–15 tells us that the popular response to the feeding miracle was to hail Jesus as 'the prophet' and to try to force him into a role of political leadership. If the disciples shared this dangerous misunderstanding (and 16:5–12 shows that they had failed to see that the true significance of the miracle was not at the level of material provision), Jesus needed to despatch them urgently to prevent their being affected by the popular enthusiasm. *The other side* would normally mean the west side of the lake, from which they had come that same day, and that is where we find them arriving in v. 34. This is strange, since the object of the journey seems to have been to escape from Antipas' territory (14:12–13); it has therefore been suggested that what was intended was a move to another part of the eastern shore (*cf.* Mk. 6:45, 'to Bethsaida'), but that the wind of v. 24 forced them off course and across to the west (McNeile, p. 217). John 6:17 however suggests that the intended destination was the western shore.

**23.** *Dismissed the crowds* sounds more orderly than John's account suggests, where a likely reading of 6:15 is that Jesus 'fled' into the hills! The situation was serious, and this was a major turning-point in Jesus' relation with the Galilean crowds. Hence no doubt the importance of Jesus' solitary prayer, recorded by Matthew only here and in Gethsemane. *When evening came* is literally 'when it was late' – very late, to judge by all that had happened since v. 15, and by v. 25.

**24–26.** The marginal reading 'out on the sea' is literally 'in the middle of the sea'; either reading therefore excludes the suggestion that they were close to the shore, and saw Jesus walking either on the shore or in shallow water. What they saw in the pre-dawn dimness (*the fourth watch* is 3 to 6 a.m.) was a physical 'impossibility', and in such circumstances, after a mind-stretching evening and a gruelling sleepless night, it is no wonder that they registered a *ghost* (literally 'apparition', used of any unnatural vision, *e.g.* of a spirit).

**27.** *Take heart* is, as in 9:2, 22, an assurance for those who have good reason for fear: it does not indicate that the crisis is not real, but that in the presence of Jesus fear can be dismissed. *It is I* (*egō eimi*) is an expression used by Jesus at other moments of revelation (Mk. 14:62; Lk. 24:39; Jn. 8:58; 18:5-6), and it may not be fanciful to see in it an echo of the divine name in Exodus 3:14, here connecting the one who has power over the sea with the God who made it.

**28-31.** Matthew elsewhere introduces Peter as the spokesman of the disciples, or as the typical disciple, in whom we may see ourselves, and it seems clear that this story is told with the same purpose. It is an object-lesson about faith. At the same time the episode, reflecting Peter's own impulsive yet vulnerable personality, rings true as his actual experience, not merely as a cautionary tale.

Interpreters differ over whether Peter's proposal is intended as an object for imitation. If it is, it teaches the disciple to expect to share his Master's power, and in obedience to his call (note that Peter will not try without an explicit 'command', vv. 28-29) to do that which is naturally impossible. This depends on faith, and Peter's loss of faith (*of little faith* is *oligopistos*, a favourite word of Matthew used elsewhere in 6:30; 8:26; 16:8; 17:20, in all of which it denotes rather *un*belief than inadequate belief) consists in allowing the material facts (*the wind*) to weigh more heavily than the power of Jesus. *Doubt* is literally 'be divided in two'; true faith is single-mindedly focused on Jesus.

Others suggest that far from being, temporarily at least, a hero of faith, Peter is here revealed as foolhardy and childish, an example of the wrong approach to discipleship. His desire to imitate Jesus is presumptuous (*cf.* on 4:5-7, 'testing God'), and Jesus' acceptance of his request is intended to teach him by his mistake.[1] Verse 31 seems to imply, however, that Peter's fault was in his loss of confidence, rather than in his initial proposal, so the story should preferably be read as an example of true faith which did not survive the crisis.

**32-33.** For *worship*, see on 2:2; in this context it is clearly more

---

[1]Tasker (pp. 145-146) suggests that the attempt was a failure from the start; he interprets 'walked' (v. 29) as an inceptive aorist, 'began to walk', and instead of 'and came' in the same verse he adopts the variant reading 'to come' (so AV, RV). Most modern scholars and versions however regard the reading 'and came' as original; in that case Peter's attempt was initially successful.

than social convention. While Matthew's readers would have seen in the phrase *Son of God* a statement of Jesus' unique relationship with God (as no doubt Matthew intended them to), in the original context, as in the use of the same words in 27:54, it represents more the instinctive reaction to a display of supernatural power (*cf.* Mk. 6:51, which speaks of their being 'astounded', but records no words). As the disciples groped for adequate words to express their awareness that Jesus was more than an ordinary man, this phrase came to mind, perhaps because of its Messianic connotations (see on 3:17; there is some evidence for the idea of the Messiah as Son of God in first-century Judaism). The disciples' reaction here does not upstage Peter's deliberately Christological use of the title in 16:16, but prepares the way for it.[1]

*(v) The popularity of Jesus as a healer (14:34-36)*
*Gennesaret* was a region (not just a town) on the western shore south of Capernaum. See on v. 22 for the surprising return to Antipas' territory. It was an area where Jesus was well known, and these verses show that it was especially as a healer that he was still welcomed by ordinary people (contrast the official hostility in the next section). The impression given by these verses (as by 4:23-24; 8:16; 9:35; 12:15; 15:30-31) is of a mass healing (*all that were sick*; *as many as touched*), which contrasts with the very individual character of the healings which are specifically recorded elsewhere. The method, too (to *touch the fringe of his garment*), sounds impersonal and almost mechanical in contrast with the personal interest and faith usually described. But a brief summary cannot go into such detail, and the story of the woman healed by just this means in 9:20-22 shows that in the individual case it was far from impersonal. What Matthew emphasizes is Jesus' healing power, and the widespread recognition and response it evoked, and the fact that Jesus' compassion extended to the people at large to whom he proclaimed God's kingdom.

[1] See further, Stonehouse, pp. 214-219.

*(vi) Dispute with Pharisees and scribes over defilement (15:1–20)*
Jesus' involvement with crowds of common people, and even being touched by some who would, because of their illness, be ceremonially unclean, forms a fitting introduction to the Gospel's major treatment of the question of defilement. The debate arises out of a specific issue, that of ceremonial washing before meals, but the sayings to which it gives rise have a far wider application, going to the root of the whole issue of the sort of purity God requires. Mark draws out clearly the effect of Jesus' teaching on the Old Testament laws of purity ('Thus he declared all foods clean', Mk. 7:19). Matthew, however, is careful to restrict the explicit discussion to the issue of washing, which was one of later Jewish tradition, not of Old Testament law. Even on this level Jesus' teaching is bold and radical, in deliberate confrontation with the authoritative rulings (halakah) of scribal law. The issue of the scriptural laws of purity was a more far-reaching one still, and the continuing debate on this in the apostolic church makes it unlikely that Jesus had made an explicit pronouncement on the subject. Certainly Matthew records none, and Mark's enigmatic clause is an editorial comment, grammatically independent of the saying in which it is set. But if the issue was not yet directly broached, the principles set out by Jesus' words in vv. 11 and 17–20 made the ultimate abandonment of the Old Testament food-laws by the church inevitable.

**1.** For *Pharisees and scribes*, see on 5:20. They are not to be identified, but on an issue such as this their interests would be closely similar. The wording suggests an official deputation to test Jesus' conformity to the law, and the addition of *from Jerusalem* may suggest concern in the capital, with its stricter legal standards, over an apparently heterodox movement in Galilee.

**2.** The particular issue they raise was occasioned, Mark tells us, by what they saw of Jesus' disciples' practice. A Rabbi was responsible for his disciples' life as well as their theology, and their practice is correctly taken to indicate that Jesus had taught them to *transgress the tradition of the elders*. This phrase refers to the oral law, a continuing elaboration of rules for living based on the Old Testament law but going far beyond it, which developed eventually into the incredibly detailed regulations of the Mishnah. For the Pharisees (to which party most of the scribes belonged) this tradition was an authority alongside the Old Testament law. The relative weight of these two authorities will be the focus of the first part of the passage. The Old Testament required a ritual washing of hands in certain cultic situations (*e.g.* Ex. 30:18ff.; Dt. 21:6), but the regular washing before meals described by Mark 7:3–4 seems to have been introduced only shortly before the time of Jesus. It was probably not yet expected of the common people, but Jesus, as a 'Rabbi', should have known better!

**3.** As in 12:1-8, Jesus does not deny the charge, but undermines its significance. They *had* transgressed the tradition of the elders, but what was that tradition worth? The actual issue of defilement is not broached until v. 11; before that the question of authority must be resolved. So this verse sets up a sharp contrast between the *commandment* and the *tradition*, and between the two authorities from which they derived (*of God . . . your*). Jesus' defence takes the form neither of a rejection of all rules in favour of a free antinomian position, nor of a rejection of all 'tradition' as such (which was the position of the Sadducees), but of a question of priority. A tradition which presumes to override the authority of *the commandment of God* deserves no respect.

**4–6.** The two commandments, from Exodus 20:12 (*cf.* Dt. 5:16) and Exodus 21:17 (*cf.* Lv. 20:9) are attributed explicitly to *God* (Mark has 'Moses') to emphasize the seriousness of Jesus' counter-charge. Notice that Jesus' interpretation of the *honour* due to parents includes the financial responsibility of the child. This responsibility was being evaded with the approval of the scribes by a convenient 'extension' of the Old Testament provisions for oaths. The developed legislation relating to the formula *Korban* (Mk. 7:11, here represented by *given to God*) or *Konam* fills a whole tractate of the Mishnah (*Nedarim*). In Josephus it is used both for an oath dedicating a person to God (*Ant.* iv. 73, based on Lv. 27:1–8, where the term does not yet occur) and for a simple oath formula like that criticized in Matthew 23:16–17 (*Apion* i. 167). It has been suggested that it is this latter use which lies behind Jesus' charge here: if a man asserted on oath (*Korban*) that he would not honour his responsibilities to his parents, he was bound to keep his oath. But more probably it is the man's own property which is declared *Korban*, dedicated to God, and therefore unavailable to his parents. This convenient declaration apparently left the property actually still at the disposal of the one who made the vow, but deprived his parents of any right to it. Later Rabbinic legislation allowed for such an oath to be waived in favour of obedience to the fifth commandment (Mishnah *Nedarim* 9:1), but clearly it was not always waived in Jesus' day. Such a pious fraud is in direct conflict with the will of God as expressed in the fifth commandment. A *tradition* which thus *made void the word of God* had no authority for Jesus.

**7–9.** For *hypocrites*, see on 6:2. The dominant idea here is of the inconsistency which professes to aim to please God, but in fact opposes his will. *Isaiah*'s words (29:13) related originally to the people of his own day, but Jesus sees a correspondence ('typology') between their false religion and that of his own contemporaries which makes his words in effect a 'prophecy' about them too.[1] The LXX form of the quotation, with the idea of emptiness (*in vain*) of such a religion, gives added point to Jesus' charge, though the Hebrew text is quite sufficient to make the point that a religion of merely formal worship and obedience to rules and regulations is useless if *their heart is far from me*.[2] The thought is typical of Jesus' constant opposition to legalistic religion, as seen already, *e.g.*, in 6:1–18; 12:1–14, and brought to a climax in chapter 23.

**10.** *The people* is the same word translated 'crowd(s)' in 13:2, 34, 36. There the crowd was given parables without the explanation which was reserved only for the disciples. Here *the people* stand midway between the religious leaders and the disciples, in that they are given new teaching in opposition to the scribal position, but this teaching (v. 11) remains only a 'parable' (see on v. 15) which again is explained specifically to the disciples.

**11.** This epigram, which is the sum of Jesus' public teaching on this issue, states a principle of inward religion which was destined in time to undercut for the Christian church the whole

[1] For other such instances, see my *JOT*, pp. 68–70.
[2] On the text-form, see further my *JOT*, pp. 248–250.

elaborate system of ceremonial purification of the Old Testament and of later Judaism. It remains sufficiently cryptic not to be perceived immediately in all its radical newness, and to need further explanation for the disciples. The focus on words is reminiscent of 12:33–37; words which *come out of the mouth* form an appropriate contrast to defilement from *what goes into the mouth*. As in his exposition of Christian obedience in 5:21–48, Jesus goes behind the outward act and the literal observance of regulations to what 'proceeds from the heart' (v. 18). His words suggest a view of 'original sin', *i.e.* that sin springs from what a man is in himself, not from his environment.

**12–14.** It is hardly surprising that *the Pharisees were offended* by a saying which cut at the roots of their understanding of religion. Far from apologizing, Jesus declares their rejection as leaders of God's people. Israel was described as God's *plant* in, *e.g.*, Isaiah 60:21; 61:3, and the same metaphor was taken up at Qumran (CD 1:7; 1QS 8:5; 11:8), and by the Pharisaic author of Psalms of Solomon 14:2–3. The implication of Jesus' words is therefore that the Pharisees' claim to be God's true people is false. It echoes the condemnation by John the Baptist in 3:10, 12. The true Israel is located elsewhere. *Blind guides* neatly reverses the Jewish claim recorded by Paul (Rom. 2:19) to be 'a guide to the blind'. Their failure to perceive the true nature of God's will is disastrous not only to themselves but to those who follow their teaching and share their approach to religion.

**15–16.** *The parable* is the cryptic saying of v. 11. *Parabolē*, used elsewhere in Matthew in the more restricted sense of our word 'parable', also covers the meaning of the Hebrew *māšāl*, a proverb or epigram, usually one which requires wisdom to understand and apply. As such, like the parables of ch. 13, it calls for further explanation for those who are privileged to belong to Jesus' 'inner circle'. The surprise in Jesus' reply suggests either that he had already given them teaching on this subject, or, more likely, that the general approach to religious observance underlying his teaching as a whole should by now have been plain enough for this saying to cause them no problem.

**17–18.** The purely physical effects of *whatever goes into the mouth* are earthily indicated (*passes on* is a euphemism for the literal meaning 'is expelled into the latrine'). In contrast *the heart* is the source of a man's true character, and therefore of his purity or impurity. For *the heart*, *cf.* on 5:8; it is not merely the seat of emotion, but the true person as he really is, not just as he appears outwardly (*cf.* the use of the word in 6:21; 11:29; the heart is what 'makes a person tick').

**19.** This unflattering account of some of man's basic instincts (see on v. 11 for comment on 'original sin') is partly modelled on the second part of the Ten Commandments, but the inclusion of *evil thoughts* makes plain again Jesus' concern with what lies behind the outward act. *Slander* is literally 'blasphemies' (see on 12:31), so that perhaps the attitude to God as well as to men is included, thus taking in the first part of the Ten Command- ments; it reinforces the emphasis on impurity in words already noted in v. 11 and expounded in 12:33–37.

**20.** The last clause is not in Mark's version, and it is sometimes suggested that by thus deliberately focusing on the issue of washing before meals (a matter of scribal tradition, not of Old Testament law) Matthew is avoiding the wider and more radical implications of Jesus' teaching in relation to the Old Testament food-laws. His striking omission in v. 17 of Mark's 'declaring all foods clean' is taken to point in the same direction. But Matthew's careful restriction to the original issue of v. 2 may well represent the debate as it took place in Jesus' time; the principle for the abandonment of the food-laws is there, but there is as yet no explicit pronouncement on that subject. Mark's clause correctly points out the inevitable outcome of Jesus' words, but the issue was still to be raised directly.

### (vii) A Gentile woman's faith (15:21–28)

A comparison with Mark 7:24–30 shows that Matthew has com- pressed the story of the exorcism to the barest minimum, and at the same time expanded the dialogue which is for him the important feature of the story. It remains a miracle-story, but, as in the case of the centurion's servant (8:5–13), where also the dialogue takes precedence over the story, the main interest is in the question of Jesus' response to the faith of a Gentile. Indeed the two accounts are closely parallel in many ways, not only in being the only Synoptic accounts of healing at a distance, but in the racial issues involved, with Jesus' apparent reluctance to respond to a Gentile's request met by the persistent faith which ensures his response in the end. The question raised by 15:1–20 of Jesus' attitude to Jewish ideas of purity, with all its crucial implications for the Gentile mission, is here put to the practical test of a Gentile's desire to share in the benefits brought by the Jews' Messiah.

**21–22.** For Jesus' 'withdrawals', see on 4:12. This brief visit to Gentile territory was not, as v. 24 makes plain, for the purpose of evangelism, but rather in the nature of a 'retreat' after the pressures of controversy and popularity.[1] *Canaanite* is not used elsewhere in the New Testament, and has a faintly old-fashioned ring, perhaps intended to emphasize that she belonged to the pagan peoples who opposed Israel in Old Testament times. *Cried* is in the imperfect tense, indicating a constantly repeated appeal (as the disciples' reaction in v. 23 confirms). *Lord*, as in 8:2, *etc.*, need be no more than a polite address, here and in vv. 25 and 27, but the appeal to Jesus as *Son of David* is striking in the mouth of a Gentile. Perhaps she had heard vaguely of Jewish Messianic speculation about Jesus (*cf.* on 12:23), and thought the title would please this Jewish visitor; but the developing dialogue (esp. v. 27) suggests a more sophisticated awareness of the significance of Jesus' role as the *Jewish* Messiah.

**23.** See on 8:7 for Jesus' apparent reluctance to respond to a Gentile request for healing. Here it is more emphatic, as the discouraging silence of this verse is reinforced by the strongly negative statements of vv. 24 and 26. The disciples' request, *Send her away*, while clearly motivated by a desire for peace and quiet (*cf.* 19:13?), need not imply that they disapprove of her request, but rather that to grant it will be the easiest way to get rid of her. (The same verb in Lk. 2:29 applies to a dismissal with desire satisfied. *Cf.* Mt. 14:22; 15:39; Lk. 14:4.) If they are thus endorsing her request, Jesus' emphatic statement of his objection in v. 24 follows more cogently than if they too opposed her request. There is a principle at stake here which must be worked out rather than ignored in favour of the line of least resistance.

---

[1] *Came out* does not indicate that Jesus did not actually go into the Gentile area, for v. 21 reads literally *'into* the district'; she 'came out' either from her house to meet him, or from the remoter hinterland.

**24.** The principle is the same as that of 10:5–6, of a mission restricted to Israel. There it was an injunction to the disciples; here it is given as Jesus' own pattern of working. See on 10:5–6 for the relation between this limitation in the period of Jesus' earthly ministry and the subsequent widening of the Christian mission to all nations. The statement here is Jesus' explanation to the disciples of his unexpectedly unwelcoming response to a woman in need; she herself need not have heard it, as it is only in v. 25 that she approaches him closely.

**26.** F. W. Beare describes this as an 'atrocious saying', expressing 'incredible insolence' and based on 'the worst kind of chauvinism'. *Dogs* was a current Jewish term of abuse for Gentiles, and the suggestion that the Greek term *kynaria*, a diminutive, is an affectionate reference to dogs as pets, while it appeals to modern Western sentimentality, falls foul of the lack of any such idea in Judaism, or of a known diminutive form to express it in Aramaic. So Jesus is expressing the contemptuous Jewish attitude to Gentiles in order to explain why her request does not fit into his mission to Israel. But written words cannot convey a twinkle in the eye, and it may be that Jesus was almost jocularly presenting her with the sort of language she might expect from a Jew in order to see how she would react. The point is a serious one, that a mission to Israel must have its limits, but the tone need not have been a humourless rudeness.

**27.** *Yes, Lord* is not a meek acceptance of Jesus' harsh words, but rather an objection ('Yes, it *is* right . . .', or 'Yes, do help me'); *yet* is literally 'for', and explains why she is not prepared to accept Jesus' 'It is not fair'. But her argument that dogs do at least get the *crumbs*, while it rejects the implied refusal of her request, accepts Jesus' basic position, that his primary mission is to Israel. But that mission allows others to share in Israel's blessings, if only as a secondary effect. If she is only a 'dog', at least let her have the dog's rations! The response is surely no less tongue-in-cheek than Jesus' teasing challenge.

**28.** No-one else receives from Jesus the accolade *Great is your faith!* (though again the centurion is the nearest equivalent, see 8:10). Was it merely her persistence in expecting a response despite apparent refusal ('by faith, not by sight')? Or is there also the idea of her spiritual perception in recognizing *both* the

247

primary scope of Jesus' mission to Israel *and also* the fact that that was not to be its ultimate limit? She thus, like the centurion, foreshadows the time when the true Israel will transcend the boundaries of culture and nationality.

## (viii) Healing ministry among the Gentiles (15:29–31)

Jesus' return to *the Sea of Galilee* is not to a Jewish area, but round the north shore to the Gentile area to the east of the lake (reference to *the God of Israel* in v. 31 surely demands a Gentile crowd, and Mark's parallel specifies that he came to the Gentile Decapolis, Mk. 7:31). For *the mountain, cf.* on 5:1, where the same Greek phrase is used. At this point Mark reports only a single healing, but Matthew follows up his account of Jesus' response to one Gentile's faith by one of his occasional general summaries of Jesus' wider healing ministry (*cf.* 4:23–24; 8:16; *etc.*), culminating in the Gentile crowd's astonished tribute to the power of *the God of Israel*. It is as if he is anxious that Jesus' apparently reluctant response to one Gentile should not be seen as the whole story. Presumably, however, the principle of 15:24 requires that this healing ministry too must be seen as exceptional; it may be significant that neither these verses nor the following story refer to Jesus' teaching among the Gentiles, only to his meeting physical need. The list of complaints cured echoes Isaiah 35:5–6 (*cf.* Mt. 11:5); it is the Messianic blessings of Israel in which these Gentiles are privileged to share.

## (ix) Second feeding of a crowd (15:32–39)

Both Matthew and Mark record this as a separate event from that of 14:13–21, and 16:9–10 emphasizes that there were two such incidents. While the basic shape of the stories is similar, the details differ, both in all the numbers involved, and in the dialogue leading up to the miracle. Matthew and Mark then want us to understand that two such miracles occurred. Why should they make a point of this, when so many other miracles are passed over in general summaries? Perhaps it is enough that tradition remembered two such events, and that the fact that such a remarkable miracle, as opposed to the large numbers of 'routine' healings, occurred twice was sufficiently striking to be worth recording. But the fact that this second feeding follows on from two accounts of Jesus' ministry to Gentiles, and apparently involves the same Gentile crowd who have just 'glorified the God of Israel' (v. 31), suggests that we have here a deliberate indication that the benefits given to Israel by their Messiah were also to be available outside the Jewish circle. In that case 15:21-39 as a whole forms a brief 'manifesto' for the extension of the Christian mission to the non-Jewish world.

For the general characteristics and significance of the narrative, see on 14:13-21.

**32-33.** A crowd which stayed with Jesus *in the desert* (*i.e.* away from civilization) for *three days* must have been remarkably impressed with his power and 'charisma'. Did they, like the Jewish crowd of 14:13-23, hope for some dramatic development under this popular leader? (See on 14:22.) In contrast to the previous occasion, it is Jesus who here takes the initiative in suggesting to the disciples that some provision is needed. It is also remarkable that after their previous experience they still seem to think only in terms of regular sources of supply (unless their *we* is emphatic, to indicate their own helplessness and to leave the way open for Jesus to make provision again). But perhaps they had taken Jesus' words in 15:24 too literally, and so neither cared so much, nor expected Jesus to use his Messianic power, when the crowd was a Gentile one.

**34-38.** Significant differences from the previous occasion include (a) the different numbers of loaves, baskets and people, though the overall scale of the miracle is still fantastic; (b) the use of *eucharistēsas* (*having given thanks*), which makes the foreshadowing of the Lord's Supper even more obvious; and (c) the appropriate use in this Gentile context of a different word for *baskets*, these being a general-purpose flexible basket (used also for lowering Paul from the wall in Acts 9:25 !), whereas the wicker baskets of 14:20 were of a type specially associated with Jews (see BAGD, p. 447b). For other details of the wording, see on 14:17-21.

**39.** *Magadan* is unknown (as is the 'Dalmanutha' of Mk. 8:10), and that is, no doubt, why some early texts witness to the substitution of 'Magdala', presumably the home of Mary the Magdalene. Magdala was on the west side of the lake, in Jewish territory, as the sequel here requires. Whether Magadan was an alternative name, or a neighbouring area, or results from a textual error, can only be speculation.

*(x) Jesus' repudiation of Pharisees and Sadducees (16:1–12)*
After the brief account of Jesus' visits to Gentile territory, Matthew now returns us to the disputes with the Jewish leaders from which Jesus 'withdrew' in 15:21. The unexpected co-operation of the two bitterly opposed groups, *Pharisees and Sadducees*, found together only here and in 3:7 (where see comment), perhaps indicates a pragmatic 'unholy alliance' to deal with a teacher who in different ways threatened each of them.

**1–4.** The immediate demand of the Jewish leaders for a *sign from heaven* contrasts sharply with the Gentile crowd's response to Jesus' miracles (15:31). If such signs mean nothing to them, what would be the point of any more? But in any case, the request was not sincere, but *to test him*, a trap designed to discredit Jesus if he refused (as they knew he would, after 12:38ff.). On vv. 1 and 4, see comments on 12:38–39, where a similar request is met by the same response, and the mysterious *sign of Jonah*, here unexplained, is spelt out in 12:40–41. Verses 2–3 are not found in many of the important early MSS and versions, and are generally agreed to be a later addition to the text, perhaps inspired by Luke 12:54–56, where different weather signs are used in a similar way.[1] It is interesting that this dubious text is the only New Testament occurrence of the phrase *signs of the times*, often used today in relation to eschatological predictions, but here referring to discerning the significance of Jesus' earthly ministry (particularly such 'signs' as have just been recorded in 15:21–39).

**5–12.** This dialogue is not easy to follow, because in it two separate themes are interwoven: first, the disciples' entirely material concern about the shortage of bread (vv. 5,7), which Jesus dismisses by reminding them of how much greater shortages have recently been more than adequately met (vv. 8–10), and secondly, Jesus' warning against the 'leaven of the Pharisees and Sadducees' (v. 6), which the disciples failed to grasp at

[1] The case for these verses as part of the original text is argued by B. C. Butler, *The Originality of St. Matthew* (1951), pp. 141–142, and, on different grounds, by Gundry, pp. 323–324.

first because of their concern with actual bread (vv. 11–12). It is not clear whether Jesus deliberately used their concern with literal bread to introduce his warning on metaphorical 'leaven', or whether the two subjects were quite unconnected, and confused only because of the disciples' preoccupation with their physical need.

**8–10.** For *little faith*, see on 6:30. It is a favourite term of Matthew, here substituted for the charge of lack of understanding and hardness of heart in Mark 8:17–18. Not only have they failed to grasp Jesus' metaphorical teaching because of their preoccupation with their material problem, but even at the material level they have failed to learn the lesson of the miracles of feeding (*cf.* comments on 14:22). *Cf.* 15:16 for their failure to *perceive*, to see beneath the surface.

**11–12.** What then is *the leaven of the Pharisees and Sadducees,* against which Jesus is warning them? It is specified as their *teaching*, but this is puzzling, as the teaching of these two groups was at most points sharply opposed. Morever in Mark 8:15 the reference is to 'the leaven of the Pharisees and the leaven of Herod' – and Herod was not renowned for his 'teaching'! Perhaps one point at which the 'teaching' of Pharisees and Sadducees (and Herod) might coincide would be in their view of the proper credentials of the Messiah, and it was this issue which prompted the dialogue of vv. 1–4. What is at issue is essentially their attitude of hostility to Jesus' claims and their failure to perceive God's working in his ministry. *Leaven* is here a symbol of the penetrative power of evil (see above, on 13:33, and *cf.* 1 Cor. 5:6–8; Gal. 5:9), and it was the insidious effect of the attitude revealed in the request for a sign that Jesus warned his disciples against.

*(xi) Jesus is the Messiah (16:13–20)*
Peter's confession of Jesus as the Messiah forms the climax to the long section of the Gospel which began in 4:17 with Jesus' public teaching in Galilee. Throughout this section the question which Jesus poses in v. 13 has been increasingly in view. While Matthew has made clear in the first part of the Gospel (1:1 – 4:16) his own conviction that Jesus is the one in whom God's purposes are fulfilled, and has recorded the clear declarations of

who Jesus is by God (3:17), and by the demons (8:29), he has not so far recorded any explicit declaration by Jesus of his role as Messiah (though of course much of the recorded teaching points unmistakably in that direction). Rather we have seen the frequent amazement of the crowd at his authority in word and deed (4:24–25; 7:28–29; 9:8,26,31,33; 13:54; 15:31), which has led to speculation whether he is the son of David (12:23; the title is also offered to him by suppliants in 9:27; 15:22), which no doubt gave rise to the authorities' repeated demand for a sign to authenticate his supposed claims (12:28; 16:1). Moreover, John the Baptist has pointed forward to a 'coming one' (3:11–12) and has tentatively identified Jesus in this 'Messianic' role (11:2–6), while Herod has confused Jesus' ministry with that of John (14:1–2). In this situation it is time for the issue to be clarified, but it is significant that, in accordance with the principle set out in 13:11–17, it is to the disciples in private that the clarification is given, here and in 17:1–13. The crowds remain in a state of uncertainty, and this, as v. 20 will vividly show, is quite deliberate.

**13–14.** The setting for this private gathering is appropriately in *the district of Caesarea Philippi*, a non-Jewish area near the headwaters of the Jordan, where there was no Galilean crowd in attendance. In Jesus' question Matthew has *the Son of man* where Mark and Luke have simply 'I'; this substitution confirms the view set out above (pp. 43–45) that 'the Son of man' was understood to be Jesus' special way of referring to himself, but not a title with a ready-made content, thus leaving open the question 'Who is this Son of man?' (*cf.* Jn. 12:34). The reply reveals a growing consensus in interpreting Jesus as *one of the prophets*, for all the individuals mentioned come into this category. For *John the Baptist*, see on 14:1–2 (and for John's prophetic role, 11:9–14); for the expectation of a return of *Elijah*, see on 11:14. *Jeremiah* was a plausible identification, especially in that he, like Jesus, was a prophet of judgment, declaring God's impending destruction of his own nation, and therefore opposed and persecuted by its leaders.[1] But if a prophetic role was inadequate even to understand John the Baptist (11:9), it

---

[1] So J. Carmignac in G. Jeremias (ed.), *Tradition und Glaube* (1971), pp. 283–298.

falls far short of the truth about Jesus.

**15-16.** The disciples' awareness has already progressed beyond that point, despite the rebuke just delivered in 16:8-11. Their experience of Jesus' authority has led them to a much higher assessment of who he is (8:27; 14:33). Moreover Jesus' teaching has been geared towards a fuller revelation to them than that available to the crowds (13:11-17). Jesus' second question therefore expects, and receives, a more adequate response. *Simon Peter* articulates a conviction that was no doubt at least embryonic in all of them. On *the Christ*, see pp. 41-43. The title has occurred so far only in Matthew's editorial words (1:1,16,17,18; 2:4; 11:2), not in reported speech. In 11:2 it indicates the significance behind John's reference to the 'coming one', but this is the first time it has been openly spoken. The words *the Son of the living God* are added only in Matthew's version (where they lead on to a long section addressed to Peter, vv. 17-19, occurring only in Matthew); apparently Matthew wants us to grasp that Peter's confession, despite the potentially misleading nature of Messianic language (see pp. 41-43) and Peter's own failure to grasp its practical implications (see vv. 22-23), went beyond a merely nationalistic fervour to an awareness of Jesus' special relationship with God. For the title 'Son of God', see on 3:17 and 14:33. The adjective *living* (which has, of course, a good Old Testament pedigree) may perhaps have been included to contrast the one true God with the local deities (Caesarea Philippi was a centre of the worship of Pan).

**17.** Verses 17-19, addressed to Peter, have been regarded as a late addition designed to support an early claim to the primacy of the bishop of Rome. Whether or not they give any such support, there is no textual evidence for their addition to the Gospel after its original composition, and the strongly Semitic character of the language throughout these verses points to a relatively early origin in a Palestinian environment.[1]

Jesus' 'beatitude' (see on 5:3-10 for the meaning of *blessed*) is pronounced on Peter alone; the other disciples may have shared his insight, but Peter, characteristically, expressed it. Matthew often illustrates Peter's place at the head of the disciple group;

[1]For a defence of the originality of these words as sayings of Jesus during his ministry see Ladd, ch. 10 (with special reference to the idea of the 'church') and Meyer, pp. 186-197.

*cf.* 10:2 ('first'); 14:28ff.; 15:15; 17:24–27; 18:21, all peculiar to Matthew. He is the spokesman, the pioneer, the natural leader. His God-given grasp of the truth about Jesus underlines his key position, and thus forms the basis for the remarkable declarations of vv. 18 and 19.

**18.** *And I tell you*, with the pronouns standing out emphatically in the Greek, marks out the following words as Jesus' reciprocal response to what Peter has just said. Peter has declared Jesus' true significance; now Jesus in turn reveals where Peter stands in the working out of God's purpose. And as Peter's confession was encapsulated in a title, 'Messiah', so Jesus now sums up Peter's significance in a name, *Peter*. It is not now given for the first time, for Matthew has used it throughout in preference to 'Simon' (which never occurs without 'Peter' until v. 17), and Mark 3:16 and John 1:42 indicate that it was given at an earlier stage. What Jesus here reveals is its significance. It was apparently an original choice by Jesus, for no other use of *Petros* (or the underlying Aramaic *kêpā'*, 'Cephas')[1] as a personal name is known before this; now he reveals why he chose it. It describes not so much Peter's character (he did not prove to be 'rock-like' in terms of stability or reliability), but his function, as the foundation-stone of Jesus' church. The feminine word for *rock*, *petra*, is necessarily changed to the masculine *petros* (stone) to give a man's name, but the word-play is unmistakable (and in Aramaic would be even more so, as the same form *kêpā'* would occur in both places). It is only Protestant overreaction to the Roman Catholic claim (which of course has no foundation in the text), that what is here said of Peter applies also to the later bishops of Rome, that has led some to claim that the 'rock' here is not Peter at all but the faith which he has just confessed. The word-play, and the whole structure of the passage, demands that this verse is every bit as much Jesus' declaration about Peter as v. 16 was Peter's declaration about Jesus. Of course it is on the basis of Peter's confession that Jesus declares his role as the church's foundation, but it is to Peter, not to his confession, that the rock metaphor is applied. And it is, of

---

[1] With one exception, in Egypt in the fifth century BC; see J. A. Fitzmyer in *Text and Interpretation. Studies presented to Matthew Black*, ed. E. Best and R. McL. Wilson (1979), pp. 126–130.

course, a matter of historic fact that Peter was the acknowledged leader of the group of disciples, and of the developing church in its early years. The foundation-stone image is applied in the New Testament primarily to Christ himself (1 Cor. 3:10ff.; 1 Pet. 2:6–8; *etc.*), but *cf.* Ephesians 2:20; Revelation 21:14 for the apostles as foundation.[1]

One of the chief objections to the authenticity of this passage is that talk of 'building a church' betrays an ecclesiastical interest which would be impossible during Jesus' ministry. But this is to read all the later connotations of *ekklēsia* ('church') into a word which in terms of its Old Testament background (where LXX used it to translate Heb. *qāhāl*, one of the regular terms for the 'congregation' or 'community' of God's people) would be completely appropriate to describe the 'Messianic community' of the disciples of Jesus. Indeed, 'a Messiah without a Messianic Community would have been unthinkable to any Jew' (*AB*, p. 195). The building metaphor is the natural one to use in connection with the name *Petros*, and does not demand the idea of a full-blown hierarchical structure. (It may also reflect the expectation that the Messiah would rebuild the temple, for which see on 26:61.) The new community of the purified people of God was at the heart of John the Baptist's mission, and was the necessary outcome of Jesus' ministry, with its effect of dividing men according to their faith or unbelief (see esp. introduction to ch. 13, above, pp. 215–216). What is striking is not so much the idea of 'building a community', but the boldness of Jesus' description of it as *my* community, rather than God's.

The *gates of Hades* (RSV mg.) occurs in Isaiah 38:10 (representing Heb. 'gates of Sheol'); Wisdom 16:13 and other Jewish sources, where it means the same as 'the gates of death' (Ps. 9:13; 107:18; *etc.*), the place of the dead. To say that *the powers of death* (so RSV, correctly) *shall not prevail against* the community is thus to say that it will not die, and be shut in by the 'gates of death'. The words do not indicate an attack by the 'powers of evil', but simply the process of death. Still less does the text support the picturesque idea of an attack on death's gates by the church. (What could this mean? A sort of *descensus ad inferos* by the

---

[1]See O. Cullmann, *Peter: Disciple, Apostle, Martyr* (1962), pp. 220–228 for a careful discussion of the significance of this imagery.

church?!) So Peter is to be the foundation-stone of Jesus' new community of the restored people of God, a community which will last for ever.

**19.** Not only is Peter to have a leading role, but this role involves a daunting degree of authority (though not an authority which he alone carries, as may be seen from the repetition of the latter part of the verse in 18:18 with reference to the disciple group as a whole). The image of *keys* (plural) perhaps suggests not so much the porter, who controls admission to the house, as the steward, who regulates its administration (*cf.* Is. 22:22, in conjunction with 22:15). The issue then is not that of admission to the church (which is not what *the kingdom of heaven* means; see pp. 45–47), but an authority derived from a 'delegation' of God's sovereignty. That authority is exercised in *binding* and *loosing*, which were technical terms for the pronouncements of Rabbis on what was or was not permitted (to *bind* was to forbid, to *loose* to permit). This verse therefore probably refers primarily to a 'legislative' authority in the church, though clearly such decisions must have direct implications as to what may or may not be forgiven, and this application will be taken up in 18:18. (It is this latter aspect which is expressed in the apparently similar saying of Jn. 20:23.) An early instance of Peter's exercise of this authority was when he was chosen to pioneer and authorize the church's acceptance of Gentile converts (Acts 10 – 11; *cf.* Acts 15:7–11). *Shall be bound* and *shall be loosed* are literally future perfects ('shall have been bound' and 'shall have been loosed'), and as the future perfect sounds as stilted in Greek as in English, the tense is apparently deliberate. In that case it is not that heaven will ratify Peter's independent decisions, but that Peter will pass on decisions that have already been made in heaven.

**20.** For Jesus' commands to silence, see above on 8:4. Here the subject is specifically his Messiahship. Verses 21–23 will show how even Peter had not yet grasped the true nature of Jesus' mission, as one of rejection and suffering rather than popularity and triumph. The danger of misunderstanding in a wider circle was much greater (see on 14:22), and the explicit use of the nationalistically loaded term *Christ* ('Messiah') could only foster such misguided enthusiasm and so hinder Jesus' true mission. Peter's confession, properly understood, was true and God-given, but the title 'Christ' alone, without the interpretation which v. 21 gives to it, was worse than inadequate.

# III. PRIVATE MINISTRY IN GALILEE: PREPARING THE DISCIPLES (16:21 – 18:35)

As in 4:17, the formula 'From that time Jesus began . . .' marks a new phase of ministry. 4:17 indicated the character of the first phase as open preaching and exposure to the Galilean crowds, with an increasing insistence on the question 'Who is this?', leading to the climax of 16:13–20. Now both the style and the content of Jesus' teaching enter a new phase. It is focused on the private instruction of his disciples, and its content is the true nature of his Messianic mission as one of suffering and rejection, in which they are to follow him. See above, p. 59, on the structure of the Gospel.

## A. TEACHING ON JESUS' MISSION (16:21 – 17:27)

*(i) First announcement of Jesus' suffering and death (16:21–23)*
From the literary point of view 16:21 marks a new beginning, and Jesus' teaching now enters a decisively new phase, but these verses continue directly from vv. 13–20, and can be understood only against that background. The Messiahship Peter has triumphantly declared is to be very different in character from what he imagined. Peter remains at the centre of attention, in his failure to understand Jesus' mission as much as in his readiness to proclaim it. Here too he is typical of the disciple group, for whom he is no doubt still the spokesman. We see now why the confession which Jesus welcomed in 16:16–17 had to be followed by a command to 'tell no one'. If the disciples had so little idea of his mission as 'Christ', what would the crowds have made of it? Peter's 'gaffe' vividly illustrates how radically new and difficult to grasp Jesus' idea of the role of the Messiah must have been for any Jew, however favourably disposed.

**21.** For *Jesus* some of the oldest MSS read 'Jesus Christ', a title unusual in Matthew (only 1:1,18; *cf.* 1:16; 27:17,22 for 'Jesus who is called Christ') but which may well be the true reading here, where it takes up the title from Peter's confession in v. 16 and (perhaps with a touch of irony?) fills it out with a meaning Peter cannot accept. The reason why these things *must* happen is not spelt out here, but from Jesus' teaching elsewhere it is clear that the pattern he here sets out is that which he saw laid down for his mission in the Old Testament (see my *JOT*, pp. 125–132, 148–150). *The elders and chief priests and scribes* were the three groups who together made up the Sanhedrin, Israel's highest court; Jesus is to be officially executed. The estrangement between Jesus and the official Jewish leadership is thus already irrevocable. The prediction that he must *be raised* (note the passive verb – Jesus' resurrection is almost always in the New Testament described as what God did for him, rather than what he himself achieved) does not directly arise from any one Old Testament prediction, though the theme of God's vindication of his suffering servant may be a part of the background (see *e.g.* Is. 52:13–15; 53:10–12; *cf.* Pss. 16:10–11; 118:17–18,22). *On the third day* (which is idiomatically equivalent to Mark's 'after three days' – neither phrase is as much concerned with precise timing as with the shortness of the interval) is often seen as derived from Hosea 6:2–3, where the 'resurrection' in view is that of Israel's national life. This may well be so (see my *JOT*, pp. 54–55), but if so the reason is not that Jesus spoke only of a metaphorical resurrection of Israel, which his disciples later interpreted in the light of the Easter event as a prediction of his own resurrection (so, *e.g.*, Lindars, pp. 60–61), but rather that here, as in 4:1–11, Jesus saw his mission as the 'fulfilment' of Israel's hopes and destiny, and so understood this Israel-text as a pointer to his personal destiny. (*Cf.* his similar typological use of Jon. 1:17 in 12:40, and comments there.) It is Jesus' own fate, not Israel's future, which is the subject of this announcement.

**22–23.** *Rebuke* (*epitimaō*, the same verb as some MSS have in v. 20) does not necessarily convey a note of censure, so much as of stern warning, 'to give someone a talking to'. Peter is horrified both by the unorthodox character of Jesus' notion of Messiahship and by its unacceptable implications for the fate of his master (and his own?). *God forbid* represents a Greek idiomatic expression probably meaning 'May God be gracious to you', *i.e.* spare you this fate. Peter cannot grasp that such a 'disaster' could be God's purpose. Jesus *turned* to face not only Peter but the other disciples behind him (see Mk. 8:33), as they too needed to learn from Peter's mistake. His rebuke contrasts strikingly with the blessing pronounced in vv. 17–19: as Peter's former pronouncement was inspired by God, this one was from *Satan*, to the extent that Peter himself is cast in Satan's role as the tempter (*cf.* 4:10); and as Peter was there declared a rock to build on, now he is a rock to stumble over (*hindrance* is the word for a 'stumbling-block' – see on 13:41, and on the cognate verb used in 5:29–30; 11:6; for similar rock-imagery applied to Christ as both foundation and stumbling-block, *cf.* Rom. 9:33; 1 Pet. 2:6–8). *On the side of* is an odd paraphrase of a verb which means simply 'think'; Peter's attitude of mind is human, not divine. If his confession in v. 16 was inspired by God, his subsequent words reveal an interpretation of that confession in terms of natural human considerations.

## (ii) Discipleship will also involve suffering (16:24–28)

If discipleship means identification with the Master, they must expect to share the fate he has just outlined for himself. The point is made by an expanded version of the saying already recorded in the charge to the disciples in 10:38–39, together with a reminder that the ultimate stakes are high.

**24–26.** See on 10:38–39 for much of the detail of these verses. If 'cross-bearing' was a vivid metaphor there, after v. 21 it has here become a painfully real possibility. The 'loss of life' may therefore be as literal for the disciple as it will be for his master. Of course a more general application to the radical demands of discipleship, as set out above on 10:38–39, is also appropriate here too, but in the context of ch. 16 the literal application of Jesus' words is now brought into focus. In such a context *deny himself* must not be trivialized into a call for a mild asceticism; it means to renounce his right to life. This sort of discipleship is not the result of an easy compliance, but of a deliberate and irrevocable decision: *would* in v. 24 is a verb of choice – 'has resolved to'. In vv. 25–26 the ambiguity of *psychē* ('soul/life') is exploited as in 10:39; whatever the gain (including the saving of your physical *life*), if the price is your *life* (your true self, seen *sub specie aeternitatis*), it is too high. These verses then call for a true sense of values, and remind the disciple that he is faced with a fundamental choice of where his true allegiance is to lie, with God or the world (*cf.* on 6:24).

**27.** The seriousness of the choice is indicated by the coming judgment by *the Son of man* (*cf.* on 13:41). In the Old Testament judgment is God's prerogative, and the words from Psalm 62:12 (*cf.* Pr. 24:12) which form the second part of this verse are words about God. Taken together with the ascription of a *kingdom* to the Son of man in the next verse, this is a quite remarkable assumption of a divine role for Jesus in his future glory. His coming will be *in the glory of his Father*, in the sense that he shares that glory and authority. It is in the light of this ultimate authority that the disciple's allegiance must be decided.

**28.** Verse 27 referred to Jesus' future 'coming' as judge; this verse specifies, with all the solemn assurance of Jesus' *Truly, I say to you* (see on 5:18), that that 'coming' (as *king*, hence his authority to judge) will be witnessed by some of his audience before they die. This raises the same problem as in 10:23, of an apparent prediction of the parousia within the first century. See the discussion at 10:23, to which it may be added that here the 'coming' is more specifically one of judgment and kingly authority. Another distinctive feature of this saying is that it immediately precedes the account of Jesus' transfiguration, which has led some to conclude that that event, with its 'proleptic vision' of Jesus' glory, was the specific 'seeing' here predicted. (Does 2 Pet. 1:16–18 suggest this identification?) But the transfiguration hardly amounts to a fulfilment of the Son of man's 'coming with his angels to repay every man' (v. 27), even though it may be a foretaste of such a coming. It is better not to look for a specific event, but to see the fulfilment of this prediction, with its unmistakable echo of Daniel 7:13–14, in the authority of the risen Jesus which will be proclaimed (again in terms drawn from Dn. 7:14) in 28:18. There is no more reason here than in 10:23 to interpret the 'coming' as a coming *to earth*; as in Daniel 7:13–14 it is a coming *to God* to receive *his kingdom*. It will be 'seen' not so much in a single event as in the perception that Jesus, risen and vindicated at God's right hand, is now in the position of supreme authority, an authority which will reach its culmination when Jesus, *the Son of man*, is revealed as judge in the final assize (see further, on 25:31ff.).

*(iii) A vision of Jesus' glory (17:1–13)*

The 'transfiguration' is closely linked in all three Synoptic Gospels with Peter's confession and the subsequent first teaching of Jesus' role of suffering and death. The sequence is instructive: the euphoria suggested by the acknowledgment of Jesus as Messiah has been shattered by the revelation of what that Messiahship will involve, both for Jesus and for his followers; but now this apparent failure at the human level is balanced by a revelation of the supernatural reality which lies behind it. The one who is to suffer is God's chosen Messiah, his Son, whose true nature is revealed in divine glory. So the *theologia crucis* and the *theologia gloriae* are boldly brought together; neither is complete without the other.

The disciples' experience is described in v. 9 as a *vision*, *horama*, a noun used elsewhere in the New Testament (all in Acts) only for apparently 'inward' experiences. It is probably not useful to enquire how 'physical' the experience was; at least it impressed Peter as sufficiently real to require the erection of booths! But the whole scene is clearly 'numinous' – light, brilliance, the cloud (see on v. 5), a voice from heaven, the disciples' fear, and the appearance and sudden disappearance of men of long ago. Nothing like it occurs elsewhere in the Gospels (not even in the post-resurrection appearances of Jesus); it is a brief glimpse behind the scenes.

A subsidiary theme is that of the revelation of Jesus as the new Moses (see above, on 2:13–23; 5:1–2), suggested by several echoes of the account of Moses' meeting with God on the mountain in Exodus 24 and 34, and by the allusion to Deuteronomy 18:15 in v. 5, all of which will be noted below.

**1.** *After six days* is unusually precise. It stresses the continuity of this episode with the preceding scene in 16:13–28, and perhaps echoes Moses' mountain experience in Exodus 24:15–18. *Peter, James and John* as an 'inner circle' of disciples appear again as Jesus' chosen companions in a moment of private communion with God in 26:37 (*cf.* Mk. 5:37); Moses also had three special companions on the mountain (Ex. 24:1,9). The *high mountain* was presumably, as this incident follows the 'retreat' to the district of Caesarea Philippi, one of the lonely peaks of the neighbouring Hermon range, though tradition has located the incident on Mount Tabor in Galilee (which, however, was not so much *apart*, having a settlement on the top).

**2.** The traditional translation *transfigured* (from the Latin) represents a verb elsewhere translated 'transformed' (Rom. 12:2) or 'changed' (2 Cor. 3:18). Its meaning here is spelt out by the clauses that follow. *His face shone like the sun* recalls Moses in Exodus 34:29–35, and the *garments white as light* suggest a heavenly being (*cf.* 28:3; Lk. 24:4); *cf.* the description of the ultimate glory of 'the righteous' in 13:43.

**3.** The significance of *Moses and Elijah* here has been variously understood as (a) representing the law and the prophets (though the fact that Elijah is not represented among the pro- phetic writings of the Old Testament is against this); (b) two of the three Old Testament men of God who traditionally did not die (Enoch was the other; according to Dt. 34 Moses did die, but his burial by God had developed by the first century AD into a belief in his 'assumption'); (c) two great leaders who talked with God at Mount Sinai (Gundry); (d) the two whose 'return' was expected in connection with the Messianic age.[1] The last seems most relevant in this context, where their appearance underlines the Messianic role of Jesus, though none of the others is thereby ruled out. It may also be relevant that both Moses and Elijah in their God-given missions experienced rejection and suffering. Jesus is thus indicated as the one in whom the pattern of God's Old Testament servants reaches its ultimate fulfilment.

**4.** Peter's proposal to build shelters for Jesus and his august visitors may be no more than a spontaneous and rather inept attempt to rise to the occasion with proper hospitality. Or per- haps he wants to 'institutionalize' the fleeting vision (as Moses set up the 'tent of meeting' in Ex. 33:7–11); if so he has again misunderstood Jesus' mission, which is not to stay on the holy mountain but to go down to the cross. The *booths* (the word normally means 'tents') would be temporary shelters of branches, such as were erected for the Feast of Tabernacles, but

---

[1] For this belief about Elijah see above, on 11:14, and below, on vv. 10–12; for Moses see the promise of a coming 'prophet like Moses' in Dt. 18:15–18, and the evidence cited in *TDNT*, IV, pp. 856–864 for later Jewish beliefs; an expectation that both Moses and Elijah would return together is found in *Deuteronomy Rabbah* 3:17, though this is later than the New Testament period.

there is nothing else in the context to suggest that the incident happened during that festival.

**5.** A *cloud* is often in the Old Testament a sign of God's presence (*e.g.* Ex. 24:15–18; 40:34–38), and by adding *bright* Matthew emphasizes that this is no ordinary cloud, but the *Shekinah* of the visible glory of God (see *NBD*, pp. 1101–1102). As in Exodus 24:16, God speaks out of the cloud. The first part of the declaration is the same as that in 3:17, on which see comments. The added words *listen to him* are probably to be seen as an echo of Deuteronomy 18:15,19, where the same demand is made in reference to the promised prophet like Moses. In this context there is perhaps an implied rebuke of Peter's recent failure to grasp Jesus' teaching about the Messiah's role (16:21–23).

**6–8.** The understandably terrified reaction of the disciples (*filled with awe* is literally 'very much afraid') in response to such a supernatural experience is gently relieved by Jesus' familiar *have no fear* (*cf.* 14:27), and by the sight of, literally, 'Jesus *himself* alone' – *i.e.*, perhaps, Jesus as they knew him.

**9.** See on 8:4; 16:20 for Jesus' commands to silence. Now they had something even more spectacular than a mere verbal claim to talk (and boast?) about, and the danger of popular Messianic fervour was increased by the involvement of Moses and Elijah. This silence is to be maintained only until after the resurrection, because no interpretation of Jesus' claims in terms of national politics would be possible when the predicted rejection and death were a reality, and he was no longer there to lead an insurrection.

**10.** The vision of Elijah has raised the question of how his expected return relates to Jesus' Messianic role. *Then* may also suggest a closer connection with v. 9; if Elijah has now come (as we have just witnessed), why may we not now proclaim your Messiahship? Possibly also the mention of resurrection (and therefore death) seems to them inconsistent with Elijah's role in 'restoring all things' (v. 11). Altogether, their eschatological time-table is confused![1]

**11–13.** Jesus endorses the scribes' expectation (v. 11), but goes

---

[1]For Elijah expectations, see on 11:14; Ecclus. 48:10 says he will 'restore the tribes of Jacob', and for scribal expectations see *e.g.* Mishnah *Eduyoth* 8:7; *BM* 3:4–5, where his role is especially seen as one of solving legislative problems.

on to show that the reality is so different from the way they pictured it that *they did not know him* (v. 12). *Is to restore all things* (the future tense is that of the scribal hope, not Jesus' prediction of a still future coming of Elijah) reflects Malachi 4:6 (3:24, Heb.), where the same verb is used only of Elijah's 'turning' the hearts of fathers to children; see on v. 10 for the more universal 'restoration' he was now credited with. Hence the failure to recognize John the Baptist as the returning Elijah (see on 11:14); and his fate points to a similar fate for *the Son of man*, who similarly fails to match up to the way popular expectation has developed.

*(iv) The power of faith (17:14-20)*

When Moses came down from the mountain he was confronted by Israel's apostasy (Ex. 32); so on Jesus' return from the mountain he enters a scene of spiritual conflict (v. 18) and unbelief (vv. 17,20). The story, which in Mark is a vivid account of a spectacular healing, is pared down to the barest essentials (becoming almost prosaic by comparison), so that attention is focused on what is for Matthew the main point, the unbelief of the disciples, and Jesus' teaching on the power available to those who have faith. Even the remarkable account of the father's faltering faith (Mk. 9:21-24) is omitted so that the disciples' failure stands in stark contrast with the authority of Jesus.[1]

**14-15.** If the 'mountain' of v. 1 was Hermon, the *crowd* is unexpected here. Had Jesus and the three disciples returned separately to Galilee, where they found the other disciples already in difficulties? Or is this episode, for all the appropriateness of its contrast with the glory of vv. 1-13, not in chronological sequence? *Is an epileptic* is an interpretation of the rare verb *selēniazomai* (lit. 'to be affected by the moon'), which in secular Greek would more normally be translated 'lunatic'. The symptoms recorded here (esp. in the fuller account in Mark) resemble what we would call epilepsy, but v. 18 will indicate that this is in fact a case of demon-possession.[2]

**16.** The disciples should have been able to deal with the case:

[1] See H.-J. Held, *TIM*, pp. 187-192 for a full account of Matthew's editorial work on this story.

[2] See further *ISBE*, I, p. 959.

265

see 10:1,8. Their failure illustrates the too-frequent combination of a divinely-given authority with a lack of the faith needed to exercise it.

**17.** For Jesus' sayings condemning 'this *generation*' for its failure to respond to his mission, see on 12:38–45. There is an allusion here to Moses' verdict on his own contemporaries in Deuteronomy 32:5,20. It is the disciples' 'little faith' (v. 20) which provokes this complaint, but they alone do not constitute the faithless generation. In their failure to trust God in this practical test they are typical of the attitude of Jesus' contemporaries as a whole; even within the disciple group the unbelief of 'this generation' is reflected. This expression of exasperation is a rare insight into the frustration of Jesus' appeal to an unresponsive world.

**18.** See on vv. 14–15 for the nature of the complaint. The description is clearly of an exorcism, but the addition of *the boy was cured* suggests that a physical disorder (probably epilepsy) was involved as well as demon-possession; accounts of exorcisms do not usually refer to 'healing' of the person concerned (*cf.* 'heal' in v. 16, the same verb as here).

**19–20.** For *little faith*, see on 6:30; 14:31. Here again, as Jesus' following words show, it points not even to a faith which is small but real, but rather to *faithlessness*. For even the smallest *faith* (see on 13:31 for the proverbial significance of *mustard seed*) can *move mountains* (again a proverbial expression, for the most improbable occurrence; see Is. 54:10; 1 Cor. 13:2; *cf. Baba Bathra* 3b). A similar promise of the unlimited possibilities for those who have faith will occur at 21:21. It is a striking illustration of the fact that faith is, for Jesus, not a matter of intellectual assent, but of a practical reliance on a living God. It is important to observe here that it is not the 'amount' of faith which brings the impossible within reach, but the power of God, which is available to even the 'smallest' faith.[1]

*(v) Second announcement of Jesus' suffering and death (17:22–23)*
With 16:21 and 20:17–19 this short passage forms part of the

---

[1]Most later MSS here add v. 21, taken from Mk. 9:29, where it is the answer to the question which in Matthew is answered by v. 20; it is not in the earliest witnesses to the text here, and was clearly not originally a part of Matthew.

insistent emphasis on this new aspect of Jesus' teaching, which serves to increase the tension as the narrative approaches the final confrontation in Jerusalem. The word *gathering* is unusual, and suggests a rendezvous, perhaps after the return of the small group from the mountain, but more probably the assembling of the group of disciples who were together to make the pilgrimage to Jerusalem for the Passover, where Jesus' predictions would be fulfilled. (The journey will begin, after further teaching, in 19:1.) The content of the prediction is similar to 16:21 (see comments there), but now includes the idea of being *delivered*. It is the same word which will later be used for Judas's betrayal (26:15-16,21, *etc.*) and which is often used in New Testament descriptions of Jesus' mission of suffering (Acts 3:13; Rom. 4:25; 8:32; 1 Cor. 11:23; *etc.*). While it certainly is appropriate to the action of men (as in 27:2), the passive here may also echo the frequent Old Testament references to God delivering someone *into the hands of* an enemy (Ex. 21:13; 23:31; Nu. 21:2-3, 34; Dt. 1:27; *etc.*), thus picking up the divine necessity of Jesus' suffering from the 'must' of 16:21.

### (vi) The question of the temple tax (17:24-27)

An annual half-shekel tax (based on Ex. 30:11-16, though it was not there a regular payment) was paid for the upkeep of worship in the temple by most adult male Jews, whether resident in Palestine or not. Unlike the Roman taxes, to be discussed in 22:15-22, it was a matter of patriotic pride. It was, however, also a matter of controversy, as the Sadducees disapproved of the tax, and the men of Qumran paid it only once in a lifetime. So what was Jesus attitude? Would he in this, as in other matters, take an independent line, and thus alienate the majority of patriotic Jews? The answer is characteristically (*cf.* 22:21) independent without being offensive – Jesus asserts that he is not obliged to pay it, but is prepared to do so to avoid 'scandal' which might unnecessarily prejudice his mission (see further, Banks, pp. 92-94).

After AD 70, when the temple was destroyed, the Romans diverted this tax to the temple of Jupiter in Rome, after which it ceased to be a matter of patriotism and became a symbol of their subjection to a pagan power; the fact that the story is none the less recorded is one of the incidental indications that Matthew's Gospel should be dated before AD 70.

**24.** This is the last visit to *Capernaum*, and again the group is apparently living at Peter's home (v. 25; see on 4:13; 8:14–15), so that *the collectors* naturally approach Peter, as head of the house, even though Jesus is recognized to be the *teacher*, the leader of the group. Rabbis were exempt from paying this tax, and so were the priests in Jerusalem; would Jesus claim a similar exemption? The question assumes that he does pay regularly, and Peter agrees. Payment could be made in person at the Passover festival in Jerusalem (hence the money-changers' stalls in 21:12, as only the special Tyrian coinage, which was not in common circulation, was acceptable), but collections were made in other areas of Palestine and abroad a month earlier. This incident therefore takes place about a month before Passover.

**25–26.** Perhaps Jesus had heard the question and answer outside; at any rate he knew a question had been raised in Peter's mind. His analogy does not equate the temple tax with the *toll or tribute* exacted by an imperial power, but simply explores the basis of any taxation. No ruler taxes his own family. But this is God's tax, so God's Son is not obliged to pay it. That appears to be the logic of the argument, though the claim to be God's Son is not here made in so many words. Underlying the argument is the principle hinted at in 12:5–6, that the temple ritual points forward to 'something greater', the principle on which Christians soon came to abandon the temple worship and its sacrifices as having been superseded by Christ.

**27.** But Jesus will pay the tax to avoid giving *offence*. See above on 11:6; 13:57; 15:12 for this meaning of *skandalizō*. Jesus was quite prepared to 'give offence' where the issue was central to his mission, but a premature assertion of independence from Jewish ritual would have served no useful purpose. So Peter is told to go and find the money[1] in a fish's mouth! But we are not told that he did so, and it has been plausibly suggested that Jesus' words were merely a playful comment on their lack of ready money. Both pagan and Jewish literature provide popular stories of wealth found in a fish that was caught,[2] and Jesus may

---

[1] A *stater* is the equivalent, in the acceptable coinage, of two 'half-shekels'.

[2] Herodotus iii. 41–42; *Shabbath* 119a; *Genesis Rabbah* 11:4 as cited in SB, I, p. 614.

not have intended his 'command' to be taken any more literally. (See on 15:26 for the possibility that what looks in cold print like a serious statement may have been spoken in a less serious vein.) At any rate, this 'miracle' is not the point of the story. We are left to assume that, by whatever means, Jesus did pay the tax. The story is thus an illustration of Jesus' willingness to comply with the conventions of the society to which he belonged rather than cause unnecessary offence, a principle which has wider application than the specific issue of the temple-tax.

## B. TEACHING ON RELATIONSHIPS AMONG THE DISCIPLES (18:1–35)

The fourth major collection of Jesus' teaching, which is concluded by the usual formula in 19:1 (see pp. 59–60), is concerned with relationships among Jesus' followers, who are clearly seen as a distinct community (as 16:18 has led us to expect). Within such a community there is opportunity both to harm and to care for others, and the health and effectiveness of the group will depend on the attitudes to one another which are fostered. While all that is in this chapter would be relevant even in the period of Jesus' ministry, Matthew has clearly brought it together in this compact form with a view to the needs of the developing church. It is not so much a 'Manual of Discipline', with regulations parallel to those of the so-named document from Qumran (see Davies, pp. 221ff.), as a guide to relationships: it is only in vv. 15–17 that specific procedures are set out, and those are not so much 'disciplinary' as pastoral.

As in chapters 10 and 13, a shorter section of teaching in Mark (9:35–48) is taken as the basis of the collection, but is expanded by the addition of other sayings of Jesus, some of which are paralleled in Luke, but most are peculiar to Matthew. For convenience of discussion the chapter may be divided into sections where different themes come to the fore, but there is a continuity of thought throughout the chapter which makes such divisions artificial, and causes commentators to divide over whether, *e.g.*, v. 5 belongs with the preceding or the following section.

The sayings are addressed to 'the disciples'. Some interpreters see this as including only the Twelve, a view which has important implications especially for the application of vv. 18–20. But it is more probable that all disciples are in mind, not just a leading élite. (See Thompson, pp. 71–72, 83–84.)

## (i) True greatness (18:1–5)

Mark 9:33–34 records a dispute among the disciples over their relative importance, which gives rise to Jesus' teaching on true greatness. In Matthew the issue is presented as a more 'academic' question, but the principle is drawn out more explicitly.

**1.** The disciples' question begins in the Greek with a particle meaning 'so'. Jesus' words in 17:25–26 have opened up a new vista: if Jesus claims a special relation with the 'king' of heaven, how do the authority structures of this new *kingdom of heaven* relate to those of 'the kings of the earth'?[1] It is not, then, a question merely about church hierarchies, still less about grades of importance in heaven after this life, but about the whole principle of the evaluation of importance in God's sight. (See above, pp. 45–47, on 'the kingdom of heaven'.) Human societies treat questions of rank very seriously;[2] how then are they to be treated in God's society?

**2–3.** Jesus' answer is typically graphic and radical. It amounts to a total reversal of human value scales. A *child* was a person of no importance in Jewish society, subject to the authority of his elders, not taken seriously except as a responsibility, one to be looked after, not one to be looked up to. To *turn and become like children* is therefore a radical reorientation from the mentality of the rat-race to an acceptance of insignificance. The AV translation 'be converted' is not correct if it suggests a technical theological meaning for the verb *strephomai* ('turn'), but it points appropriately to the radical nature of the change involved (*cf.* Jn. 3:3 for a similar image). It is, then, the status of the child that is the point, rather than any supposedly characteristic quality of children, such as humility, innocence, receptiveness or trustfulness (and how many parents would regard at least the first two as characteristic of children?).

**4.** The emphasis we have seen in vv. 2–3 is here made explicit. True greatness is to be found in being little, true importance in

[1]See Thompson, pp. 95–99, for the train of thought.
[2]See Davies, p. 228, for attitudes at Qumran.

being unimpressive. That is what the *kingdom of heaven* does to the world's scale of values. *Humbles himself* does not refer to an arbitrary asceticism or a phoney false modesty; it does not describe a character-trait (*ICC* says children are 'untempted to self-advancement' – really?), but the acceptance of an inferior position (as Jesus did, Phil. 2:8, where the same phrase is used).

**5.** The 'child' of vv. 2–4 represents the 'little ones' (insignificant believers) of vv. 6,10,14, and in this verse the transition has already begun. *One such child* therefore is not a reference to children as such, but to those who as Jesus' followers (*in my name*), whether young or adult, have accepted the child's status. The 'greatness' of such 'children' (v. 4) lies in their relationship to Jesus. (*Cf.* 25:31–46 for the principle of receiving Jesus in receiving his 'little ones'.) One application of this principle might be, as Gundry (p. 361) suggests, to 'acceptance of little people, "average" Christians and especially youth, by ecclesiastical leaders'.

### (ii) On stumbling-blocks (18:6–9)

These sayings are linked together by the words *skandalizō* ('cause to sin', vv. 6,8,9) and *skandalon* ('temptation (to sin)' 3 times in v. 7), a 'stumbling-block', something which trips someone up. For these words see above, on 5:29–30; 11:6; 13:41; they occur also in 13:21,57; 15:12; 16:23; 17:27; 24:10; 26:31,33, and form an important theme of Matthew's presentation. Disciples are vulnerable, and stumbling-blocks are a real danger. They can be found both in ourselves (vv. 8–9) and in other members of the disciple-group (vv. 6–7), hence the relevance of this section in ch. 18. The RSV and NIV paraphrases are too narrow – one can be 'tripped up' as much by a disparaging attitude, a lack of concern and pastoral care, or a refusal to forgive, as by a 'temptation to sin'.

**6.** The transition from the child who formed the illustration in vv. 2–4 to the *little ones* is now complete (see on v. 5). Similar language has been used of Jesus' disciples in 10:42 and 11:25, and it will be taken up in the 'least' of 25:40,45. This is how they appear in the world's eyes, weak and insignificant; *cf.* the 'poor in spirit', 'meek' and 'persecuted' of 5:3–12.

So the *little ones* here are not necessarily only the less important or more vulnerable members of the congregation, though what is said here applies particularly to them. Anyone who trips a fellow-disciple, whether by attitude or by action, or even by failure to act, incurs such judgment that by comparison a quick drowning would be merciful! (*It would be better for him to . . .* might suggest only that it would benefit the congregation to be rid of him, but the Greek makes it clear that it is preferable from his point of view too.)

**7.** The apparent 'fatalism' of this verse is an echo of the realism of 13:37–43 which accepts that *skandala* (13:41) will remain in the world until the final consummation. Until then we are all vulnerable. This is the *woe* of the world in general, and of every disciple, whose life will never be free of *skandala*. But this fact does not remove the responsibility of those who are the cause of others' stumbling – for them there is a further *woe*. (See on 23:13–36 for the meaning of 'woe'.) This paradox of individual responsibility within a world governed by 'necessity' will be graphically illustrated in the case of Judas Iscariot.

**8–9.** Virtually the same saying has been recorded in 5:29–30; see comments there. Apart from superficial variations in the way the point is made, and the inclusion of the *foot* as well as *hand* and *eye*, the main difference is that here the fate of those who 'stumble' is specified as *eternal fire*, a phrase which will recur in 25:41 (see comments there), and which develops the idea of 'destruction in hell' found in 10:28. In 5:29–30 the point was a warning against things in the disciple's own life which will trip him up. In this context of relationships that seems out of place, and some have suggested that the *hand*, *foot* and *eye* here refer to other disciples who are a danger to you and who must be 'cut off' either by expelling them from the congregation or by avoiding them. But the repeated *your, you, from you* surely points to the same personal application as in 5:29–30, perhaps with the thought that your own sin may be the cause of another's stumbling, and so must be avoided at drastic cost.[1]

### (iii) Care for the 'little ones' (18:10–14)

The 'little ones' have already emerged in the preceding verses as ordinary Christians, who in their vulnerability need the care of

[1] So Thompson, pp. 116–117, 119–120.

their fellow-disciples. That message is now backed up with the thought that God's care extends to every one of them. It is in this connection that Matthew includes the parable of the straying sheep. It is, as in Luke 15:3–7, a parable of God's 'pastoral' care. Verses 15ff. will show how disciples are to imitate his concern in their care for their straying fellow-disciples.

**10.** To *despise* even *one of these little ones* (and one individual can conveniently be ignored in one's care for 'the church') is to show that you have not grasped the principle of true greatness (vv. 1–5). It is also to part company with *my Father*, to whom every one is important. *Angels* are found in Daniel 10 and 12:1 as the heavenly representatives of nations, and in Revelation 1:20 as representatives of churches. Here even individuals have their heavenly representatives, who *always behold the face of* God, a phrase derived from courtly language for personal access to the king. So even the least of the 'little ones' enjoys constant personal access to God.

**12–13.** In Luke this parable is aimed at Jesus' opponents, who objected to his 'evangelistic' concern with undesirables; here it is addressed to disciples, to remind them that God's 'pastoral' care is extended to all his 'little ones'. The fact that the same shepherd image can so effectively apply to both situations perhaps reveals the artificiality of our categories. It is appropriate to its application here that the sheep is not yet 'lost' as in Luke (and v. 14 assures us that it will not be), but only *astray*. For a fascinating account of shepherds' habits to fill in the story, see Jeremias, *PJ*, pp. 133–134.[1] It is interesting that the Gospel of Thomas has completely missed (and indeed reversed) the point of the parable, by making the straying sheep the 'largest' which the shepherd 'loves more than the 99'!

**14.** The moral is clear, and the implication for the disciple is presumably that he must share God's concern for each 'little one', and not despise any (v. 10). Verses 15ff. will show what this means in practice.

---

[1] The picture of God as the shepherd searching for his wandering sheep echoes Ezk. 34:1–16, the passage which also lies behind Lk. 19:10; it is no doubt this association which accounts for the insertion in many later MSS of a version of Lk. 19:10 as v. 11 here, where it breaks the flow of the argument.

*(iv) 'If your brother sins . . .' (18:15–20)*

While it is probably true that vv. 15–17,18, and 19–20 were originally separate sayings, they are brought together here into a close connection in which the overall flow of thought is important. This passage is often seen as a guide to church leaders on disciplinary action. But vv. 15–17 are addressed to 'you' (singular), the individual disciple, and their concern is not with the punishment of an offence but with the attempt to rescue a 'brother' whose sin has put him in danger. The passage is thus a practical guide to how a disciple can imitate his Father's concern for the wandering sheep (vv. 10–14).

**15.** The words *against you* are missing from several important MSS, and are probably not an original part of the text (see Thompson, pp. 176–177). In that case, while vv. 21–22 are concerned with the disciple's reaction to a personal offence against himself, the concern here is with the *brother's sin*, of whatever kind, rather than with a personal breakdown of relationships. The disciple is not to ignore a fault he sees in his fellow-disciple, but to confront him with it, with the hope that he will repent, and so will be *gained* (*cf.* 1 Cor. 9:19–22; 1 Pet. 3:1 for this verb referring to the conversion of an outsider; here it is of a disciple who is rescued from spiritual ruin). This pastoral concern easily degenerates into a destructively critical spirit (see on 7:1–5); but one of its marks is that it is exercised, if possible, *between you and him alone*. Only if that fails is a wider 'exposure' needed. (*Tell him his fault* is the same verb, *elenchō*, as in, *e.g.*, Lk. 3:19, 'reprove'; Jn. 3:20, 'expose'; Jn. 8:46, 'convict'.)

**16.** The next recourse must be to involve *one or two others*. Their function is to add force to the persuasion; if he will not listen to one, he may be convinced by *two or three witnesses* (Dt. 19:15). The law in Deuteronomy 19 relates to a 'judicial' trial, but there is no such scene here (nor would the 'one or two others' be witnesses of the original offence in any case). The offender is not 'on trial' (contrast the use of the same text in 2 Cor. 13:1; 1 Tim. 5:19). The point of the Old Testament reference is the principle that multiple testimony is more convincing, not the specific judicial application.

**17.** Finally, and only if necessary, the disciple may inform *the church* (*i.e.* the congregation of disciples; see on 16:18 for the word, which there envisaged the community of Jesus' people as a whole, but here is used more practically of the local group). But still the object is not that 'the church' should take disciplinary action, but that the offender should listen; *i.e.* this is the ultimate level of persuasion to lead to repentance. The church meets not to adjudicate a dispute, but for a pastoral appeal.[1] If the appeal fails, this verse says nothing about excommunication or other disciplinary action by the church, but prescribes the attitude *you* (singular) should then take to the impenitent offender. *A Gentile and a tax collector* were proverbially people from whom a good Jew kept his distance. While Jesus rejected this attitude in its literal application (*e.g.* 8:5–13; 9:9–13; *etc.*), he can still use the expression metaphorically for someone to be avoided ('ostracized', Gundry; 'put in quarantine', Bonnard), just as we can speak of 'sending someone to Coventry' without necessarily having any personal dislike of Coventry as a city! After all persuasion has failed, a cold shoulder may still bring him to his senses; at any rate there can be no real fellowship with someone who has so blatantly set himself against the united judgment of his fellow-disciples.

**18.** The introductory formula (on which see on 5:18) and the change to the plural *you* in vv. 18–20 suggest that Matthew has added a saying of an originally wider application because he saw its relevance to the pastoral issue of vv. 15–17. Apart from the plural verbs it is almost identical with 16:19 – Peter's legislative authority is therefore here vested in the disciple group as a whole. The basis of the church's appeal to the sinner in v. 17 was their united conviction of what was right or wrong conduct for a disciple; this verse assures them that they have a right to such a conviction, and that therefore their refusal to allow the brother's sin to pass without rebuke carries the prior endorsement of *heaven* (see on 16:19 on the future perfect construction). *Bind* and *loose* here, as in 16:19, have neuter objects (*whatever*, not 'whoever'), and refer to the pronouncement of what is or is not sin, rather than directly to the condemnation or forgiveness of the sinner, though the latter will clearly follow. Bonnard pertinently remarks that such a divine authority, against which

[1] For this whole pastoral orientation of vv. 15–17, over against the commonly-held 'disciplinary' interpretation, see esp. Thompson, pp. 176–188.

there is no appeal, must be used by the church with care and compassion! There is, of course, no indication in this verse of how, or by what agency, this authority of the congregation is to be exercised; no church leader or elders are mentioned (and *cf.* 23:8–12 for some pertinent cautions).

**19–20.** The repeated introductory formula indicates another independent saying of Jesus, but the flow of thought is maintained not only by the *two or three* echoing v. 16, but also by the repetition of the promise that decisions *on earth* will be ratified *in heaven*. The promise is not confined to 'the church' as a whole, but extends to the agreed request of *two of you*, because if their gathering is *in my name* then Jesus himself is part of that gathering. Davies (p. 225) calls this 'a Christified bit of rabbinism', as it echoes a Rabbinic belief that 'if two sit together and words of the Law (are) between them, the Shekinah (God's presence) rests between them' (Mishnah *Aboth* 3:2). But now the 'divine presence' is Jesus himself. The Jesus who could speak the words of 28:20, and of whom the name Emmanuel could be used (1:23), here assures his disciples that that great universal truth applies also at the personal level. And that gives a whole new dimension to an apparently insignificant gathering of two or three concerned disciples. No doubt the primary application is to their prayer for the sinner of vv. 15–17, but the principle of Jesus' presence among his people, and therefore of the efficacy of their agreed request, can hardly be confined to that specific situation (even though, like other such promises in 17:20; Jn. 14:12–14; *etc.*, it is not to be regarded as an automatic formula for success where prayers are agreed which are not compatible with the one in whose name they are uttered).

## (v) Forgiving personal offences (18:21–35)

The concern about a brother's sin in vv. 15–17 was not necessarily motivated by injury to oneself, but rather by a pastoral concern for the brother's own discipleship, which might even require an attitude of ostracism. But this response must not be motivated by personal retaliation (*cf.* on 5:38–42); so vv. 21–35 now emphasize the priority and the unlimited application of forgiveness in the area of a disciple's personal relationships. It is a different subject from that of vv. 15ff., but one which is an essential complement to those verses; the proper severity of v. 17 must be balanced by a forgiving attitude which reflects the disciple's own experience of much greater forgiveness.

**21–22.** The Rabbis discussed the question, and recommended not more than three times (see *ICC, ad loc.*). Peter's *seven times* is therefore generous, but Jesus' reply does away with all limits and calculations. His allusion to Genesis 4:24 neatly contrasts Lamech's unlimited vindictiveness with the unlimited forgiveness of the disciple. The Hebrew of Genesis 4:24 clearly means *seventy-seven times* (as RSV mg.), and this is also the most natural rendering of the Greek (Gundry, *UOT*, p. 140); but to be concerned as to whether the figure is 77 or 490 is to return to the pedantic calculation which Jesus rejects!

**23–34.** The reason why forgiveness must be unlimited is explained in a vivid parable. The unimaginable size of the original debt (the *talent* was the highest unit of currency, and *ten thousand* the highest Greek numeral – 'a billion pounds' would convey the impression) is picked up in the emphatic *all that debt* of v. 32. If that is the measure of the forgiveness the disciple has received, any limitation on the forgiveness he shows to his brother is unthinkable. The fact that the second servant's debt is one six-hundred-thousandth of the first emphasizes the ludicrous impropriety of the forgiven sinner's standing on his own 'rights'. The whole forms an unforgettable commentary on Luke 6:36.

Derrett (pp. 32–47) explains the details of the story, including the huge sum involved, in terms of the accountability of the chief minister of an oriental emperor for the tax returns of a large province. In that case the request of v. 26 would not be unrealistic, but would be for permission to carry over one year's assessment into the next. But even so the king's response in v. 27, which is not to defer the payment but to cancel the debt, goes far beyond the request, and no doubt Jesus included this feature to emphasize the free basis of God's forgiveness. (*Out of pity* is the same word as is used for Jesus' 'compassion' in 9:36, on which see notes.)[1] *Jailers* in v. 34 is an unjustifiable euphemism; the Greek word means *torturers*, whose job is to put pressure on the

[1]For other details of the background to the story see Derrett's article, and also Jeremias, *PJ*, pp. 210–214.

defaulter and his family to produce the money. This is, of course, part of the scenery of the parable, and is not meant to depict God as sanctioning brutality.

35. Jesus' application picks up specifically the last scene of the parable, but it is based on the parable as a whole. Those who will not forgive cannot expect to be forgiven. The point was made strongly in the Lord's Prayer and the comment which follows it (6:12, 14–15), and the use of 'debts' for sins there is illuminated by the emphasis on debt here (vv. 24,28,30,32,34 all use the same word or its cognates). If the church is the community of the forgiven, then all its relationships will be marked by a forgiveness which is not a mere form of words, but an essential characteristic; *from your heart* excludes all casuistry and legalism.

# IV. MINISTRY IN JUDAEA (19:1 – 25:46)

Section III (16:21 – 18:35) has seen Jesus, still in Galilee, preparing his disciples for the coming conflict with the leaders of the nation, culminating in his rejection, suffering and death. Now the scene shifts to Judaea, the place of the final conflict. In 19:1 – 20:34 we see Jesus *en route* for the capital, teaching and acting with an authority which cannot be ignored; in chapter 21 the gauntlet is thrown down, and the confrontation comes into the open, leading up to the inevitable climax in the passion narrative of chapters 26 – 28.

## A. ON THE WAY TO JERUSALEM (19:1 – 20:34)

### (i) Introduction (19:1–2)

We know from the Gospel of John that Jesus made several visits to Jerusalem before his final Passover visit, but Matthew has not mentioned these, and tells us only of the one climactic journey to Israel's capital. The resultant simple progression from Galilee to Jerusalem is highly effective as a dramatic plot, and it is the intervening journey which forms the scene for the next two chapters. (Luke has expanded this journey to fill no less than ten chapters between the Galilean ministry and the entry into Jerusalem.) *The region of Judea beyond the Jordan* seems to point to Peraea, the part of Transjordan east of Judaea, but as this was not properly a part of Judaea the expression perhaps serves as a general indication of a movement southwards which will bring Jesus eventually into Jerusalem (20:17; 21:1) from the east via Jericho (20:29). Mark at this point mentions Jesus' teaching the crowds, while Matthew (as in 14:14) substitutes his healing them; the two were, of course, inseparable aspects of his ministry (*cf*. 4:23; 9:35).

### (ii) Teaching on divorce and marriage (19:3–12)

The question of divorce has already been discussed in 5:31–32. See the commentary there for the background in scribal debate, and for the essential position of Jesus in relation to this debate. It is important to remember that the issue was not 'divorce' in the modern sense of a legally approved annulment of a marriage on the initiative of either partner (or both), but the right of the Jewish man (*not* the woman) to repudiate his wife by a simple unilateral declaration against which there was no appeal.

**3.** For *tested*, *cf.* on 4:1,3; 16:1, where the same verb is used. Knowing Jesus' views, they could expect him both to incriminate himself by apparently making light of the 'law' of Deuteronomy 24:1-4, and to lose popular support by condemning the divorce which was freely practised by his contemporaries. Moreover, among those contemporaries was Antipas, whose recent divorce had already drawn the fire of John the Baptist, with disastrous results (14:3-12). So it was an explosive question. The question is in Matthew's version about the permissible grounds of divorce ('Will *any* cause do, or are there limits?')[1] But underlying this is the whole question of whether divorce is permissible at all (which is how the question reads in Mark), and it is at this level that Jesus answers it.

**4-6.** The discussion as Mark records it is restructured by Matthew, while leaving the contents intact, so as to produce a more 'logical' order: statement of basic scriptural principle (vv. 4-6) – objection from another scripture (v. 7) – explanation of how scripture B relates to scripture A (v. 8) – resultant pronouncement (v. 9). Matthew thus presents Jesus as more a prophet than a Rabbi (so Bonnard, p. 281), going behind scribal debate to the essential principle of God's will. The principle is drawn from Genesis 1:27 and 2:24, which show not only that sexual union is God's creation purpose for man, but also that that union is exclusive and unbreakable. *One flesh* vividly expresses a view of marriage as something much deeper than either human convenience or social convention, and this is drawn out by Jesus' ringing pronouncement (rightly and magnificently emphasized in the marriage service), *What God has joined together, let not man put asunder*. To see divorce as *man* undoing the work of *God* puts the whole issue in a radically new perspective.

---

[1] See above, on 5:31, and *cf.* Josephus, *Ant.* iv. 253, paraphrasing Dt. 24:1: 'He who desires to be divorced . . . for whatsoever cause – and many such may arise – . . .'!

**7–8.** It was this sort of radical pronouncement which the 'test' (v. 3) was designed to elicit. Now the trap is sprung: Jesus, they imply, has just repudiated what *Moses commanded*. Deuteronomy 24:1–4 does not of course explicitly command or even approve divorce, but it certainly accepts it as a real possibility, and this was taken as divine sanction for the practice. But Jesus picks up the Pharisees' verb: divorce was not *commanded* but *allowed*, and that concession was an accommodation to human *hardness of heart* (the thought is not so much of the cruelty of men to their wives, as of their unresponsiveness to the mind and will of God). Jesus therefore refuses to allow a necessary concession to human sinfulness to be elevated into a divine principle. The ideal is rather to be found in going back to first principles, to what was *in the beginning*. An ethic which is truly to reflect God's will must be built, not on concessions, but on basic principles. This is a crucial element across the whole field of ethical discussion, and one which has not always been observed when Christians have failed to distinguish which are the 'weightier matters of the law'. Jesus' appeal to first principles has the effect of apparently setting one passage of Scripture against another, but this is not in the sense of repudiating one in favour of the other, but of insisting that each is given its proper function, the one as a statement of the ideal will of God, the other as a (regrettable but necessary) provision for those occasions when human sinfulness has failed to maintain the ideal.

**9.** As in 5:32, the implication is drawn that divorce and remarriage is *adultery*, since it substitutes a new sexual union for that indissoluble union which God has created. In 5:32 it was the remarriage of the divorced wife which was labelled as adultery; here it is the husband's remarriage.[1] But here again an exception is made in the case of a divorce which is the result of the wife's *unchastity* (see on 5:32 for the rationale of this exception and its relation to the absolute form of the prohibition in Mark and Luke; a 'divorce' in such a case is only to recognize that the marriage has already been broken, not to initiate a break where the marriage is still intact). The wording of the saying suggests that in the case of a divorce on the grounds of unchastity the

[1] The variations in the text shown in RSV. mg. represent attempts to assimilate this verse to 5:32.

husband is allowed to remarry.[1] In that case, despite the ideal of an unrepeatable union of 'one flesh' set out in vv. 4–6, Jesus, like Moses in Deuteronomy 24, has made allowance for the hardness of men's hearts. There is an undeniable tension between the absolute idealism of vv. 4–8 and the acceptance of a reality which falls short of the ideal in v. 9 (in its Matthaean form), and the danger is that we will do as Jewish legalism had done and build our expectation on the concession rather than the ideal. But Christian ethics in a fallen world will always be subject to such tensions; sinful situations sometimes make it impossible to implement the ideal, and in such cases we may have to choose between courses none of which leaves no room for regret. What is important is that in so doing we do not lose sight of the ideal, and that we accept the 'lesser evil' for what it is, an 'evil', even where it is the best course open to us in the circumstances. It is at this point that Jesus' emphasis differs from that of the scribes, even of the more rigorous school of Shammai.

**10.** Jesus' reaffirmation of the ideal of unbreakable marriage provokes the disciples to reflect rather weakly that such a demanding commitment might be better avoided by not marrying at all! (Was this a serious suggestion, or were these words spoken with a wry smile which the printed word cannot convey?)

**11–12.** Jesus' reply is often interpreted as endorsing the disciples' suggestion, and recommending celibacy. In that case it is at odds with vv. 3–9, which clearly present marriage as a God-given institution, so highly prized that it is not to be violated by divorce; nor does Jesus elsewhere suggest celibacy as an ideal. *This saying* is literally 'this word', which can be taken as referring to either (a) the disciples' comment in v. 10 or (b) Jesus' teaching about marriage in vv. 3–9, especially its practical culmination in v. 9. On interpretation (a), these verses would apparently be saying that the disciples' proposal of celibacy is a good one, but that not all are able to remain celibate; in that case celibacy becomes a 'higher' ideal for those who can attain it. On interpretation (b), on the other hand, the disciples' comment is set

---

[1]This has been disputed esp. by Roman Catholic exegetes, following the disciplinary code of the post-apostolic church; but the idea of a 'divorce' without right of remarriage seems not to have been current in the first century.

aside, with the statement that the ideal of marriage (vv. 3–9) is indeed a demanding one, to which not everyone is called, but that it is a responsibility not to be evaded by those whom God calls to it. This second interpretation is preferable, as it avoids setting vv. 10–12 against vv. 3–9. In that case v. 11 and the last sentence of v. 12 agree with the disciples that only those *to whom it is given* (*cf.* 13:11 for the same idea of a special privilege for disciples) can *receive* (lit. 'find room for', 'cope with') the demand of true Christian marriage. For 'a man' (v. 10; the word is *anthrōpos*, a human being, not *anēr*, man as opposed to woman) on his own it *is* too hard; but where God's 'gift' makes it possible, it is to be *received*. The rest of v. 12 then adds (as a sort of parenthesis) a list of those to whom it is not 'given', *i.e.* those whose calling is not to be married. Celibacy was most unusual in Jewish society, and it is not unlikely that Jesus himself was abused as a *eunuch* (always a term of disparagement, if not of abuse) because he was not married;[1] this verse may then reflect an element of apologia for his own condition, as he points out that physical incapacity (whether natural or man-inflicted) is not the only legitimate reason for celibacy, but that some may be called to voluntary celibacy (*made themselves eunuchs*, not literally of course) because of the special demands of their role in *the kingdom of heaven*. Jesus himself was one such. But these verses emphasize that whether one is married or not is not a matter of 'better' and 'worse', but of God's gift, which is not the same for all disciples.

### (iii) The blessing of the children (19:13–15)

It was a Jewish custom to bring a child to the elders on the evening of the Day of Atonement 'to bless him and pray for him' (Mishnah *Sopherim* 18:5). This may well be the background to this incident. The disciples' objection may then be to the popular assumption that Jesus is to be identified as a regular 'elder', as well as to the feeling that their Master has more important concerns than to be bothered by children.[2] For the

---

[1] See J. Moloney, *JSNT* 2 (1979), pp. 50–52.

[2] *The people* is not in the Greek, which reads simply 'them'; if, as the grammar in Matthew's version suggests, it was the children themselves who were 'told off', the contrast of attitudes is heightened.

generally low estimate of the importance of children, see on 18:2–3; here, as there, Jesus reverses conventional values, and accepts as important those whom society (and even his own followers) despised. *To such belongs the kingdom of heaven* is another way of stating the principle of true greatness set out in 18:1–5. While it is the children themselves whom Jesus welcomes for their own sake, *such* also points beyond them to all those of whatever age whose acceptance of a childlike status makes them great in Jesus' new value-scale, where the insignificant and rejected – the sick, outcast, Gentiles, women, children – achieve a new acceptance and importance. To *lay hands on* someone is normally in the Gospels associated with healing (several times in Mark, and *cf.* Mt. 9:18) but here it is more generally an act of identification and acceptance, not to mention a naturally affectionate response to children.

### (iv) The rich young man (19:16–22)

In a culture where wealth was regarded as a sign of God's blessing and where a religious teacher was therefore expected to be at least moderately wealthy, the lifestyle of Jesus and his disciples was conspicuously different. The relation of wealth to discipleship was therefore an important issue, not least to the disciples themselves. This story serves to introduce the discussion of the question in the following section.

**16.** Only Matthew tells us that the *one* was young (vv. 20,22); Luke adds that, as his wealth suggests, he was a leading member of society (lit. 'ruler'). His question, in which there is no indication that he was not sincere, is rightly concerned with *eternal life* (*cf.* 25:46), but reflects the common assumption that it is to be found by what I *must do* rather than by what I *am*. Indeed *what good deed?* suggests that he had in mind some specific act to earn the favour of God, perhaps a spectacular act of charity, instead of a life of consistent obedience. For reasons which will emerge in the next verse, Matthew has transferred the adjective *good* from the address 'Teacher' to the content of the question.

**17.** Jesus' reply picks up the word *good* and explores its implications. The man's question had located 'goodness' in his proposed 'good deed', and so had made it a human quality, as if man were morally self-sufficient. But in absolute terms, only

*One is good*; *i.e.* human 'goodness' is relative to the goodness of God, and so goodness is to be found not in our own resources, but in accepting his standards, and reflecting his character. So it is through *keeping* God's *commandments*, not through 'good deeds' of our own devising, that we may *enter life* (*cf.* 7:13–14 for this phrase). The commandments thus function not as an automatic passport to life, but as a pointer to the absolute goodness of the one who gave them.

On Matthew's alteration of both question and answer as they appear in Mark, see N.B. Stonehouse, *Origins of the Synoptic Gospels* (1963), chapter V. Mark's wording might allow (though of course it did not require) the inference that Jesus differentiated himself from God in a way which was embarrassing to a more developed Christology. We might have averted this possible false inference by adding a footnote; Matthew achieves this by an adaptation of the wording which, however, does not affect the main flow of the dialogue (which is not concerned with Christology), and in particular preserves the crucial statement that only in God is true goodness to be found.

**18–20.** The fifth to the ninth of the Ten Commandments are concerned primarily with the way we treat other people, and are thus appropriately summed up in Leviticus 19:18, *You shall love your neighbour as yourself* (*cf.* 22:39 for a similar use of it). These commandments (unlike the tenth) are primarily concerned with observable actions, and therefore it is relatively easy to check one's performance against them (though Jesus has shown in 5:21–28 that this is an inadequate view of 'keeping' them). It is on this basis that the man can claim, probably quite sincerely, to have *observed all these*, though the claim betrays a woefully superficial understanding of the commandment to love one's neighbour as oneself, which is thus 'rendered innocuous' (*TIM*, p. 102). But he is himself aware that this is not good enough, and there is no reason to doubt that the question *What do I still lack?* denotes a genuine perception that the mere observance of external rules falls short of true 'goodness'. Tasker (p. 187) suggests that he has noticed Jesus' omission of the tenth commandment, and it is on this that 'his conscience is troubling him . . . He has become a slave to his possessions. There is much wealth in his house, but leanness in his soul.'

**21–22.** The term *perfect* was used in 5:48 (where see comments), in that case also in contrast with a legalistic misuse of Leviticus 19:18. It indicates an approach to goodness which exceeds the righteousness of the scribes and Pharisees (5:20) by going behind the rules to the will and character of God, who himself is 'perfect' (5:48). This verse does not teach a 'higher level' of discipleship ('perfection') to which only a few attain by extraordinary self-sacrifice, while others may remain content with 'entering life' by mere legal obedience (v. 17). *All* disciples are called to the 'greater righteousness' of 5:20, and to be 'perfect' (5:48). By this more searching demand Jesus shows the man how inadequate his supposed righteousness (v. 20) really was; it did not touch him at the point of his real interests. To obey 'perfectly' the command of Leviticus 19:18 will involve him in a practical renunciation for which he is not prepared. So he went away, and there is no suggestion that he ever returned, or that his supposed 'keeping of the commandments' brought him the 'life' he was looking for.[1]

Jesus' further demand includes two elements, first selling and giving, and then following Jesus. The two must not be separated as if 'charity' alone could make 'perfect'. While the selling and giving will be a practical application of Leviticus 19:18 (Jeremias, *NTT*, pp. 221–223), it is primarily the necessary counterpart of following Jesus, as vv. 27–29 will make clear, and it is *discipleship*, not just charity, which is the issue.

But is poverty then an essential condition of discipleship for all? Verse 26 will allow that the rich can be saved, and among Jesus' followers there were some who were wealthy, and indeed on whose wealth he and his closest companions apparently depended for their living (see on 8:14–15 for Peter's home and possessions). The demands of discipleship will vary for different individuals and situations. But they will never be less than total availability to the claims of Jesus, however differently these apply in practice. 'That Jesus did not command all his followers to sell all their possessions gives comfort only to the kind of people to whom he *would* issue that command' (Gundry, p. 388).

<hr />

[1]On 'perfection' in 5:48 and 19:21, see further, *TIM*, pp. 95–99; Davies, pp. 209–215; J. Piper, *Love Your Enemies* (1979), pp. 146–148.

*(v) Wealth and rewards (19:23–30)*
The rich man in the preceding section illustrates a general principle: contrary to popular expectation, wealth is a hindrance in relation to 'the kingdom of heaven', where earthly ideas of priorities and rewards are turned upside down.

**23–24.** If *the kingdom of heaven* demands the total renunciation of personal rights and possessions seen in v. 21, then wealth is a handicap (*cf.* 13:22). Typically, Jesus illustrates the point with a ludicrous parallel (*cf.* 7:3–5): the *camel*, the largest common animal (*cf.* 23:24), trying to squeeze through the smallest imaginable hole. Various wooden attempts to make it less ludicrous (*e.g.* the later reading *kamilos* = 'cable', or an imaginary postern-gate called 'The Needle's Eye'[1]) not only fail to appreciate Jesus' sense of humour, but also miss the point that humanly it *is* 'impossible' (v. 26).

**25–26.** By current Jewish thinking the disciples were right to be *astonished*. The rich were those whom God had blessed; if they cannot *be saved*, who can? *Sōzō*, 'to save', normally in the Gospels refers to rescue from danger or illness, but here, where it parallels 'to enter the kingdom of God', it anticipates the later 'theological' meaning. Jesus' reply echoes the thought of Genesis 18:14, and places 'salvation' firmly in the category of the supernatural work of God (in contrast with the young man's hope of attaining eternal life by 'doing'). On this basis, while wealth may be a handicap, no earthly circumstances can determine a man's fate.

**27.** Peter's question sounds almost mercenary, and perhaps it was. But while his attitude may be questionable, the idea of rewards, even 'compensation', is one which is not inappropriate, as indeed Jesus' reply will make clear; see on 5:12, above.

**28.** The first 'reward' that Jesus mentions is *in the new world* (*palingenesia*, lit. 'rebirth'; the only other New Testament use is in Tit. 3:5). The word itself is more typical of Stoic philosophy than of the Jewish milieu, but it effectively conveys the Jewish eschatological hope of 'new heavens and a new earth' in the Messianic age (Is. 65:17; 66:22; *etc.*). Jesus sees that hope fulfilled

[1]On these see K. E. Bailey, *Through Peasant Eyes* (1980), pp. 165–166.

when *the Son of man* is enthroned as king (*cf.* 25:31–34, and for the language *cf.* 1 Enoch 62:5; 69:27–29; *etc.*). The thought is derived from Daniel 7, where not only are the themes of thrones, glory, judgment and kingship associated with 'one like a son of man' (vv. 9–14), but that kingship is also given to 'the people of the saints of the Most High' (vv. 22,27). So here the followers of the Son of man share his kingship; but whereas in Daniel 7 it is *Israel* who thus rules over *the nations*, here it is Jesus' *twelve* followers (see on 10:1 for the significance of the choice of twelve) who *judge* (probably in the Old Testament sense of ruling, Jdg. 3:10, *etc.*) *the twelve tribes of Israel.* This remarkable transfer of imagery graphically illustrates the theme of a 'true Israel' of the followers of Jesus who take the place of the unbelieving nation, a theme which runs through much of the teaching of Jesus in this Gospel (*cf.* 8:11–12; 21:43). For further development of the theme of the disciples' share in Jesus' kingship, see 1 Corinthians 4:8; 6:2; Ephesians 2:6; Revelation 20:4. It also lies behind the request of Zebedee's wife in 20:21.

**29.** In Mark 10:30 the promise is of *a hundredfold* compensation 'now in this time', while *eternal life* is 'in the age to come'. Does Matthew's omission of these phrases suggest that he sees the reward as entirely other-worldly? (So, *e.g.*, *TIM*, p. 29.) He does not say so, and the use of two different verbs (*receive, inherit*) suggests that there is still a distinction. But if Mark's text could have been taken as a promise of very literal 'compensation', Matthew's version allows us both to understand the 'hundred-fold' in a wider sense (how many would *want* a hundred houses, fathers, mothers and children?) and to realize that *eternal life* is not something totally separate from the blessings of discipleship here and now. The point is not a sequence of stages of reward, but an assurance that the losses which discipleship may involve will be handsomely repaid.

**30.** This 'slogan', which occurs also in 20:16 and Luke 13:30 (*cf.* also Mk. 9:35), expresses vividly the general effect of Jesus' teaching in turning upside-down the world's values. Here it appropriately refers back to the discussion of wealth in vv. 23–26, and to the case of the rich man who failed to make the grade (vv. 16–22), perhaps also to the reversal of conventional values in vv. 13–15. But it may also contain a warning to Peter not to imagine that his 'sacrifice' (vv. 27–29) has earned him a place of special honour; this will be the theme of the following section, after which the slogan is repeated. The verse therefore functions here both as a conclusion to 19:13–29 and as the first member of the 'framework' enclosing 20:1–15.

*(vi) The parable of equal wages for unequal work (20:1–16)*

F. W. Beare appropriately entitles this story 'The Eccentric Employer'. It is not meant to reflect normal economic practice, nor to be a pattern for labour relations. In an age of unemployment (*cf.* Josephus, *Ant.* xx. 219–220), when there was no state security to fall back on and no trades union power to protect the worker, when an employer could literally 'do what he chose with what belonged to him' (v. 15), the employer's action in taking on additional workers whose productivity could not possibly match the wage they were paid may be understood as 'the behaviour of a large-hearted man who is compassionate and full of sympathy for the poor' (Jeremias, *PJ*, pp. 37, 139). The essential point of the parable is that God is like that; his generosity transcends human ideas of fairness. No-one receives less than they deserve, but some receive far more. But this generosity is offset by the very natural resentment of those who received only a fair wage. To whom then is this parable addressed? Can we identify those represented both by the lucky late-comers and by the jealous regular workers?

Parables are characteristically open-ended, and a general rule for their interpretation is, 'If the cap fits, wear it!' But sometimes it is possible and helpful to envisage the situation which originally gave rise to them. In this case an important clue may be the similarity of this parable to that of the Prodigal Son, which is also structured around the contrast between the one who receives (and deserves) fair treatment and the one who deserves nothing but is given everything, and the jealousy which results. As that parable was aimed at the religious leaders who objected to Jesus' acceptance of tax collectors and sinners (Lk. 15:1–3), the same could well be the original aim of this parable; God's grace to the undeserving should be a cause for joy, not for jealousy. At a later date the same message would properly apply to the acceptance of Gentiles into the people of God, and at a more personal level, cases like the penitent thief of Luke 23:39–43 might be understood on the same basis as compared with those whose lives had been devoted to the service of the gospel.

But Matthew has given us a more specific clue, by the way he has introduced the parable. It follows (and is concluded by) the statement that *Many that are first will be last, and the last first*, suggesting that the message is, in general terms, that God's standards are not those of strict reward for services rendered, so that none of us has a claim as of right on his goodness. More specifically, this follows on the discussion of rewards in 19:27–29; Peter's (valid) assumption that God will be no man's debtor must not be taken to suggest that loyal service guarantees a greater reward, that the first disciples 'who have borne the burden of the day' will have precedence over those who come in after. The 'rewards' God gives are not calculated like that (see on 5:12), and from the viewpoint of human justice they may sometimes look unfairly generous.

It is a measure of our failure to share God's values that we feel a natural sympathy with the complaint of v. 12, however much we accept the cool logic of vv. 13–15. 'It is frightening to realize that our identification with the first workers, and hence with the opponents of Jesus, reveals how loveless and unmerciful we basically are. We may be more "under law" in our thinking and less "under grace" than we realize. God is good and compassionate far beyond his children's understanding!' (Stein, p. 128).

**1–7.** In a twelve-hour day from sunrise to sunset, the times represent roughly 6 a.m., 9 a.m., noon, 3 p.m. and 5 p.m. The *denarius* was a normal day's wage for a labourer.[1] *Whatever is right* (v. 4) would be assumed to be the appropriate fraction of a denarius. There is no need to explain the hiring of additional workers at various stages in the day as normal practice – this is a parable, not a sociological study! Nor need we decide whether the explanation in v. 7 was genuine or a lame excuse for laziness. The point is not their motivation, but the fact that, for whatever reason, they are 'workless' (the literal meaning of *argos*, RSV 'idle', which is not necessarily pejorative) and

---

[1] *Cf.* Tobit 5:14, the 'drachma' being the equivalent Greek coin; attempts to give a modern monetary value vary from 9½ old pence (McNeile) to 25 cents (Gundry), but any such 'equivalent' is ludicrously inappropriate to its actual buying power.

therefore likely to go hungry.

**15.** RSV margin is the literal meaning of the Greek. See on 6:22–23 for 'evil eye' as an expression for jealousy and niggardliness.

*(vii) Third announcement of Jesus' suffering and death (20:17–19)*
The earlier announcements in 16:21 and 17:22–23 have already set out the pattern of what awaits Jesus in Jerusalem; but now that the final climactic journey is under way (since 19:1), the sense of urgency is increased, and the specific and repeated mention of *Jerusalem* as the goal in vv. 17 and 18 points insistently towards the ultimate drama now about to begin. The main elements of the passion have already been included in 16:21 and 17:22–23 (on which see comments), but this final announcement is more specific. It makes explicit what was implied in 16:21, that he will be *condemned* in a trial which gives formal expression to his nation's rejection of its Messiah. But at the same time it also involves *the Gentiles* in the process, and not only goes into more detail on the nature of his suffering (*mocked* and *scourged*; see on 27:26–31), but also for the first time specifies the mode of his death, to be *crucified* (*cf.* the sayings about 'taking the cross' in 10:38; 16:24, which, however, stopped short of saying explicitly that this would be literally the fate of their Master). The effect is to emphasize not only the totality of the rejection (Jewish leaders and Gentiles), but also the humiliation and the harrowing pain; this is to be no glorious martyrdom, but an ugly, sordid butchery. It is thus all the more striking to read yet again here that *he will be raised on the third day*; the contrast, and the miraculous power which creates it, are more marked than ever. Verse 28 will go on to explain the paradox: this apparently tragic death is in fact an act of service, a source of life for 'many'.

*(viii) James and John: greatness in service (20:20–28)*
While this constitutes an episode in its own right, it also serves to bring together graphically the messages of the preceding paragraphs. The idea of heavenly rewards (19:27–29) and the theme of the first being last (19:30, illustrated in 20:1–15, and repeated in 20:16) are here taken up in a specific request for a

reward in terms of 'being first', and this in the context of Jesus' 'kingdom' (19:28). In contrast with this natural ambition is the example of Jesus, the result of whose 'service' has been outlined in 20:17–19 in terms of suffering and rejection; but whereas vv. 17–19 left that outcome unexplained, v. 28 now shows that it was not to be a meaningless sacrifice: through death comes life.

**20.** *The mother of the sons of Zebedee* was a regular member of the disciple group who accompanied Jesus (27:56), so her involvement in her sons' ambitious ideas is hardly surprising. Mark does not mention her, because James and John were clearly the focus of the story. *Cf.* on 8:5, where Matthew similarly omitted the spokesmen to concentrate on the person from whom the request originated. The suggestion that her involvement is a fiction designed by Matthew to present the two apostles in a more favourable light 'is interesting solely as an example of ignorance of the ways and manners of mothers anxious for their sons' (*AB*)! For *kneeling before*, see on 2:2 and 8:2.

**21.** The promise of 19:28 forms the background to this request; the 'thrones' are already assured, leaving only the question of precedence. And since James and John formed with Peter the 'inner circle' (see on 17:1), the request was humanly quite natural. It may even be that the 'snubbing' of Peter in 16:23, and the implied rebuke of him in 19:30, seemed to offer a chance for them to take precedence over him (*cf.* Jn. 21:20ff. for another possible indication of some rivalry between Peter and John).

**22-23.** For the *cup* as a metaphor for destined suffering, *cf.* 26:39, and many Old Testament uses (*e.g.* Is. 51:17; Je. 25:17ff.; Ezk. 23:31ff.). The necessary connection between the cup and the throne, between suffering and glory, is one which becomes increasingly clear throughout the New Testament, but already Jesus has been teaching it since 16:21–28. So the brothers' claim, *We are able*, like Peter's in 26:33,35, was not made in ignorance; they meant it, even though in the event they did not live up to it (26:56). And one day they would drink it, James in Acts 12:2, John perhaps in his imprisonment on Patmos. But even so, their 'place' in Jesus' kingdom is not to be earned, but is *prepared by my Father* (*cf.* 25:34).

**24.** The *indignation* was that of 'jealousy not of holy humility' (Bonnard) – *the ten* are no more free of ambition than *the two* *brothers*.

**25–27.** While there may be a note of disapproval in the verbs *katakyrieuō* and *katexousiazō* ('lord it over' and 'exercise authority over'), because human authority is seldom, if ever, exercised without an element of selfishness, the verbs themselves are not necessarily pejorative, and these verses do not suggest that human society has no need of properly structured authority. The point is that the values of secular society do not apply *among you*; authority and 'greatness' among the disciples of Jesus are the reverse of what the world is used to; true greatness is in service. In this, as in other areas of human values, Jesus has turned the world upside down. (*Cf.* above, on 18:1–5; 19:13–15, 23–30; 20:1–16; *etc.* For other teaching on 'greatness', *cf.* 5:19; 11:11; 18:1–5; *etc.*) Self-importance, the desire to be noticed and respected, the ambition to make one's mark and to impose one's will on others, this is the value-scale of the rat-race, not of the kingdom of Christ.

**28.** In this *the Son of man* is an example, not in that his disciples can also give their lives as a ransom, but in the attitude of service (putting others first) which inspired his unique self-sacrifice. The form of our service will be different from his, but its motivation must be the same, *not to be served but to serve*. It was his special mission to fulfil the role of God's *servant* in Isaiah 52:13 – 53:12, whose life would be given for the sins of his people.[1] The phrase *to give his life as a ransom for many* is one of the clearest statements in the New Testament of the saving effect of Jesus' death. *Lytron* ('ransom') and the preposition *anti* ('for', literally 'instead of') point clearly to the idea of his 'taking our place', as the payment of an equivalent sum of money procures the release of the captive (or, in the Old Testament, the 'redemption' of what was dedicated to God: see Lv. 27 for relevant legislation).[2] There is of course no exact analogy between Jesus' death and such ransom-language, so that the passage does not require us to ask to whom payment is made, or how the 'equivalent' is calculated. The point is that a 'payment' was needed to

[1] See my *JOT*, pp. 116–121, for a discussion of the authenticity of this saying and of its basis in Isaiah 53.

[2] For the 'substitutionary' implications of such language see L. Morris, *The Apostolic Preaching of the Cross* (1965), pp. 29–35.

achieve the 'release' of *many*, and that Jesus' death provides it. The servant's vicarious death in Isaiah 53 provides the closest model for this spiritual release, just as from another angle the same passage had pointed to Jesus' physical 'bearing of diseases' (see on 8:17). From the same passage too comes the unexpected term *many* (*cf.* Is. 53:11–12), which will be repeated in 26:28, again in a context of vicarious suffering echoing Isaiah 53. At Qumran and in some Rabbinic writings 'the many' is a term for the covenant community, derived probably from the use of the word in Isaiah 53:11–12 and Daniel 12:2–3, 10;[1] but the clear influence of Isaiah 53 in these two sayings sufficiently accounts for Jesus' use of the term. Thus Jesus' mission to 'save his people from their sins' (1:21) is now revealed as one of vicarious death on the pattern of the Servant of God in Isaiah 53.

*(ix) Two blind men (20:29–34)*

This short story occupies a strategic place in the Gospel: it is the end of the account of Jesus' itinerant ministry, and its setting *as they went out of Jericho* points forward to the next town on the road, Jerusalem. The Messianic mission revealed in the preceding chapters is now reaching its climax, and it is with the open acclamation of his Messiahship (v. 30, to be taken up by the crowd in 21:9) that Jesus approaches the city. But it is typical of Jesus' Messiahship that it expresses itself in an act of 'service' (see vv. 25–28) which the crowd regards as beneath his dignity (see on v. 31). The pre-Jerusalem ministry appropriately concludes with a miracle of healing.

A similar healing of two blind men was recorded in 9:27–31; see comments there on the relation between the two accounts. Here Matthew is telling, in his usual concise way, the story of the man whom Mark names as Bartimaeus (Mk. 10:46–52). But, as in 8:28–34, Matthew mentions two people where Mark tells of only one (see on 8:28 for possible explanations). Here the fact that Mark names the man many indicate that he was known in the Christian community as a disciple, in which case it is possible that Mark has omitted to mention his unnamed partner so as to concentrate attention on the better-known Bartimaeus.

[1]Hence *AB* translates 'the community' here; see the discussion in *AB*, pp. 243–247.

**29–31.** The *great crowd*, no doubt composed largely of other pilgrims bound for Jerusalem for the Passover, will become quite a cavalcade by 21:9. On *Son of David*, see above, p. 43, and on 9:27; it has been suggested that the fact that it is blind men and Gentiles who recognize and appeal to Jesus as such is meant to be seen as a rebuke to the Jewish leaders who failed to grasp a fact which was so obvious![1] The crowd clearly see Jesus in the same light (*cf.* 21:9), and therefore do not want their 'Messiah' troubled with so everyday a problem as a beggar's blindness.

**32–34.** To *stop* when accompanied by such an enthusiastic crowd cannot have been easy. Jesus is again deliberately over-turning the popular sense of priorities for the Messiah. Even at this stage of the impending confrontation, when one might expect his mind to be on 'higher things', he is motivated by *pity* (the same verb as in 9:36; 14:14; *etc.*). 'In this mere "stopping" of the Son of David, on the way up to Jerusalem, is all the difference between Jesus and a political or triumphal Messiah, or also between Jesus and a religious genius absorbed in his own meditation; even the nearness of his own decisive suffering does not get in the way of his service (v. 28) for men' (Bonnard, p. 301). The word for *eyes* in v. 34 is unusual and poetic, sometimes used of the 'eyes of the soul'; perhaps Matthew's use of it, and the mention that they *followed him*, suggests that this physical healing points to a greater blindness which Jesus can dispel, one which was seen in the ambition of James and John (20:20–28), and which will become increasingly clear in the Jewish leaders he is now going to meet in Jerusalem.

## B. ARRIVAL IN JERUSALEM (21:1–22)

Matthew has not recorded any earlier visit by Jesus to Jerusalem, though we know from the Fourth Gospel that he had been there several times during the course of his ministry, and there are hints of this earlier ministry also in Matthew (see 23:37; 26:55).[2] But from 16:21 on Matthew has been preparing us for this climactic visit, when the confrontation between Jesus and the Jewish leaders must come to a head (*cf.* 19:1; 20:17–18). Now

[1] J. M. Gibbs, *NTS* 10 (1963/4), pp. 463–464.
[2] *Cf.* L. Morris, *Studies in the Fourth Gospel* (1969), pp. 40–45.

Jericho is behind, and Jesus and his disciples have reached the final ridge of the Mount of Olives where the city comes into sight. But they do not come alone, for it is Passover season when thousands of other Galilean pilgrims would arrive in Jerusalem by the same route. Among this crowd, and with their vocal support, Jesus' arrival is a deliberately staged 'demonstration', a sequence of symbolic actions designed to have an unmistakable impact on the already suspicious Jerusalem authorities (see on 15:1). The 'triumphal entry' and the demonstration in the temple together constitute a clear and public challenge to them to face up to a Messianic claim which was the more impressive for being presented in deeds rather than words. Together with these two public acts Matthew records an equally symbolic miracle witnessed by the disciples, whose meaning is closely related to the events in the temple. 21:1-22 therefore sets the scene irrevocably for the confrontation between the Jewish leaders and their Messiah which is to follow.

### (i) The entry (21:1-11)

Jesus had walked all the way from Galilee, and surely did not *need* to ride a donkey for only the last two miles. Verses 2-3 may well suggest a pre-arranged plan, but even if that was not the case, the use of a donkey now (the only time Jesus is ever recorded as travelling other than on foot) can only have been a deliberate gesture.[1] Matthew will draw out its Messianic implications in vv. 4-5, and various other details of the story which will be noticed in the following comments reinforce the impression that Jesus is here presenting himself as the King of the Jews.

Some details of the story have led scholars to suggest that, despite the apparently direct sequence from chapter 21 through to the passion story in chapters 26 – 28, this event in fact took place at the Feast of Tabernacles[2] or at that of the Dedication.[3] This would mean that the events of what we have come to know

---

[1]Mishnah *Hagigah* 1:1 suggests that pilgrims who were capable of arriving on foot were expected to do so.

[2]T. W. Manson, *BJRL* 33 (1950/1), pp. 271-282.

[3]B. A. Mastin, *NTS* 16 (1969/70), pp. 76-82.

as 'Holy Week' in fact took place over a period of several months, and that the dramatically swift build-up of the confrontation with which we are familiar owes more to the literary skill of Mark than to historical fact. The Fourth Gospel, however, is quite explicit in dating all these events during the week leading up to Passover (Jn. 12:1,12),[1] and while the shout of Hosanna, the palms (only in John!) and other features would be appropriate to the other festivals, there is no reason to regard them as exclusively tied to those festivals, or as improbable also in the 'carnival' atmosphere of the build-up to Passover, and in connection with the arrival of the Messianic king.

**1.** *Bethphage* was a 'suburb', technically part of Jerusalem, but separated from the city by the steep valley of the Kidron. While the route over the *Mount of Olives* was the normal route from the east, Jesus' use of the donkey at that point may also have been intended to remind the pilgrims of the peaceful yet triumphant return of King David back over the Mount of Olives by which he had fled during Absalom's rebellion (2 Sa. 15:30), when he too presumably rode on a donkey (2 Sa. 16:1-2).

**2-3.** How did Jesus know what they would find? Was this an example of his supernatural knowledge? Or did he assume that any village street would have donkeys tied up in it? In the latter case it was a matter of commandeering the first suitable animals they found, using the right of *angareia* ('requisitioning') which belonged to royalty and was claimed also by Rabbis,[2] a right which would follow from Jesus' description of himself as 'the Lord'.[3] On the other hand it is suggested that Jesus had planned the whole thing, and that the donkeys were ready to be released when the agreed 'password' was given (in much the same way as the room for the Last Supper was apparently pre-arranged: Mk. 14:12-16); we know that he had friends in nearby Bethany (v. 17; Jn. 11:1-3; 12:1). It is impossible to be sure of the circumstances, and therefore we cannot build much on what would be a unique description of himself by Jesus as *'the Lord'*. The term

[1]The 'cleansing of the temple' is of course related in Jn. 2:13ff., not as part of the passion story, but that too is explicitly dated at the Passover (2:13).

[2]So J. D. M. Derrett, *NovT* 13 (1971), pp. 243-249.

[3]Or, according to Derrett, 'their owner', taking 'of them' with *kyrios* ('Lord' or 'owner') rather than with 'need', a possible though not necessary understanding of the Greek.

would normally mean 'God', and the disciples' response could therefore mean 'They are needed for divine service'. But *ho kyrios* could also mean 'the owner' (of the donkeys), which might refer either to Jesus, the 'real' owner (as in Derrett's view above), or to the actual owner, who may have been in the group accompanying Jesus. *He will send* may refer either to 'any one' at the beginning of the verse (so most English versions) or to 'the Lord' (in which case this would still be part of the disciples' response, as in Mark 11:3, 'The Lord . . . will send it back here immediately').

Only Matthew mentions two animals, and it is sometimes supposed that he has deliberately exploited the double mention of the donkey (by Hebrew parallelism) in the Zechariah quotation which follows in order to introduce a second (fictitious) animal. It can hardly be supposed that Matthew of all New Testament writers failed to recognize Hebrew parallelism, and it is hard to see what he would gain by deliberately separating the two parts of the poetic description to produce two animals. But if he had reason to think there were in fact two animals, then to notice a 'hint' of this in the poetic repetition would be in character.[1] Morever, Mark tells us that the colt had never before been ridden (Mk. 11:2), so that it would be only prudent to bring its mother as well to reassure it among the noisy crowd.[2]

**4-5.** The formula-quotation (see above, pp. 38-40) is drawn mainly from Zechariah 9:9, but the first clause comes from Isaiah 62:11, a passage which also promises the coming of a saviour. The king promised in Zechariah 9:9-10 is one who is (literally) 'vindicated and saved' (Matthew omits these words), humble and peaceful, all in striking contrast with the aggressive militarism of popular Messianism. The emphasis in Matthew's version falls on *humble* (the same word as 'gentle' in 11:29 and 'meek' in 5:5; *cf.* the portrait of the Lord's servant in 12:18-21; see further, *TIM*, pp. 125-131), a trait which is demonstrated by the use of a donkey, not because it is beneath his royal dignity (see on v. 1, above) but because it is contrasted with the war-horse of the military leader. Matthew thus emphasizes what surely Jesus' symbolic act was designed to show, that he is

---

[1]So Stendahl, p. 200; *cf.* Lindars, p. 114.   [2]See further, Gundry, *UOT*, pp. 197-199.

Messiah indeed, but a Messiah whose triumphal route leads to suffering and humiliation, not to a show of force (see further, my *JOT*, pp. 105–106).

**6–7.** *Garments* serve as improvised saddle-cloths, placed on both animals, but there is no need to understand *thereon* (literally 'on top of them', where 'them' could refer as well to the garments as to the donkeys) as meaning that Jesus rode on both animals in turn. The mother was brought to help to control the colt as Jesus rode on it, and both animals were therefore decked appropriately for the festive occasion.

**8.** *Most of the crowd* is better translated 'the very great crowd'; Matthew wants us to realize that this was an impressive event, not a passing recognition by a few people. The improvised 'red carpet' (*cf.* 2 Ki. 9:13 for a similar use of *garments*) marks the arrival of a great dignitary.

**9.** While Matthew's version of the shouts of the crowd does not include an explicit mention of kingship (contrast Mk. 11:10; Lk. 19:38; Jn. 12:13), perhaps in order to avoid too 'political' a note, there is no doubt that their enthusiasm derived from a recognition of his acted allusion to the 'king' of Zechariah 9:9, and the use of *Son of David* in this context points the same way. However carefully Jesus had selected the prophecy which he enacted, it was inevitable that popular ideas of what Messianic kingship meant would be quickly aroused. *Hosanna* is a Greek form of the Hebrew words translated 'Save us' in Psalm 118:25, a phrase which had already come to be used, more as an exclamation of praise than a prayer, in Jewish worship.[1] From the next verse of Psalm 118 come also the next words, *Blessed is he who comes in the name of the Lord!* This is the last of the Hallel Psalms (113 – 118), which were chanted antiphonally at all the great festivals of Israel, these two verses forming a climax in the performance. As an expression of religious enthusiasm these exclamations would come naturally to a crowd of Passover pilgrims.

**10–11.** When the Magi came looking for the King of the Jews, 'all Jerusalem' was troubled (2:3). Now when the king arrives *all the city* is *stirred* (literally 'shaken', the word from which we get 'seismic'!). Whether this is a stirring of enthusiasm or of

[1] See Gundry, *UOT*, pp. 41–43.

apprehension is not clear. Indeed the impression is that the people of the city did not know what to make of this dramatic arrival, and it was the Galilean pilgrims accompanying Jesus who enlightened them. *The prophet from Nazareth* sounds almost an anticlimax after the positively Messianic fervour of the preceding verses (see on 16:13–16 for 'prophet', and on 2:23 for 'Nazareth'), but it is not unlikely that, as well as identifying the stranger to the people of Jerusalem, the phrase alludes to the hope of the coming of 'the prophet', based on Deuteronomy 18:15–18, which was a significant factor in the eschatological expectation of many Jews (*cf.* Jn. 6:14).

## (ii) The demonstration in the temple (21:12–17)

While the traditional designation 'the cleansing of the temple' contains an important truth, it misses much of the significance of this event. It is the sequel to and culmination of the deliberately symbolic entry to the city; we see now how the Messiah stakes his claim in the central shrine of his people. 'Planned for prime time and maximum exposure, it was a "demonstration" calculated to interrupt business as usual and bring the imminence of God's reign abruptly, forcefully, to the attention of all . . . It was at once a demonstration, a prophetic critique, a fulfilment event, and a sign of the future' (Meyer, p. 197).

Malachi 3:1 has already been cited in 11:10 to identify John as the 'messenger' who prepares the way for the Lord who is coming to his temple to purify its worship (vv. 1–4). Zechariah 14:21 promised the coming of a day when 'there shall no longer be a trader in the house of the LORD of hosts'. Jewish Messianic expectation included the belief (based on the visions of Ezk. 40 – 48, and focused by Zc. 6:12–13) that the Messiah would renew and purify the temple, which had been desecrated not only by pagan conquerors (Antiochus Epiphanes in 167, Pompey in 63 BC) but also by the false worship of God's own people. These and other hopes are triggered by Jesus' action when he comes as Lord of the temple to purify it. His demonstration thus speaks not only of the corruption of the current Jewish approach to the worship of God, but also of his own Messianic authority. It is as deliberate and unmistakable a challenge as the donkey-ride into the city, and its location in the focal point of Israel's religion makes it impossible to ignore.[1]

**12.** Matthew does not feel it necessary to mention the interval of one night which Mark 11:11–15 records between Jesus' first arrival in the temple and his action. He thus makes the direct connection between the events of vv. 1–11 and 12–13 more obvious, but Mark's note is important in discounting the notion that Jesus' act was one of spontaneous anger rather than of deliberate design. The scene is not in the temple building itself, but in the Court of the Gentiles, a huge enclosure around the temple proper, where the market in sacrificial necessities was established, under the colonnades around the court. The market performed a useful and indeed necessary role in providing the animals needed for sacrifice by those who had travelled from a distance, and the Tyrian currency which was required for temple dues (see on 17:24), and the market's location in the Court of the Gentiles was sanctioned by the priestly authorities. Nor is it clear that the traders necessarily took unfair advantage of their privileged position. Jesus' action is not directed against the traders as such (and therefore as a protest on behalf of exploited pilgrims), but against *all who bought* as well as *all who sold*, *i.e.* against the pilgrims who had come to sacrifice as well as the traders. It seems, then, that it is not any specific malpractice that Jesus rejects, but the whole system of sacrificial worship which had developed into big business, and particularly the temple authorities who had allowed its commercial aspect to become enshrined within the temple precincts (see v. 13 for this emphasis). In so doing, Jesus not only clearly sets himself above the existing religious authorities of his nation, but also claims the right (which surely can only be Messianic) to declare that the whole system of sacrificial worship, for all its scriptural origin, has developed into something which is no longer acceptable to God.

It was a dramatic gesture, an acted parable, for those with eyes to see, that 'something greater than the temple is here' (12:6). There is no indication, nor is it likely, that any lasting reform was achieved; no doubt the tables were back for the rest

[1]See further, on the Messianic significance of the event, B. Gärtner, *The Temple and the Community* (1965), pp. 105–111; Meyer, pp. 197–202.

of the week, and Jesus took no further action. But the point had been made, and it was not lost on the authorities.

**13.** *My house shall be called a house of prayer* comes from Isaiah 56:7, where it is part of God's promise that in the time to come there will be a place for outcasts and foreigners to worship God with his people. Mark continues with the words 'for all the nations', and the location of the market in the Court of the Gentiles suggests Jesus had this aspect of the text in mind. But his main point is that the temple was to be a place of unhindered worship, not of commerce. Jeremiah's description of the temple of his day as a *den of robbers* (Je. 7:11) referred not so much to what went on inside the temple as to how its worshippers behaved in daily life; but Jeremiah's accusation of a misplaced confidence in hypocritical worship, and the consequent threat of judgment on the defiled temple (7:1–15), form a proper ground for Jesus' predictions of the coming destruction of the temple (23:38; 24:2; *etc.*).

**14.** According to 2 Samuel 5:8, *the blind and the lame* are excluded from (God's) house by David's decree. But the Son of David (v. 15) welcomes and heals them *in the temple*. As the only recorded healing by Jesus in the temple this is surely significant of his bringing a new era in which the old ritual barriers give way to God's purpose of universal blessing (*cf.* on Is. 56:7 previous verse).

**15–16.** *The children* have picked up the shouts of the crowd in v. 9. After the events of vv. 12–14 it would be surprising if Jesus did not have a noisy following, even if there was not much theological depth to the acclamation. But *cf.* 11:25 for the ability of children to perceive spiritual truth which the learned fail to grasp. For the unusual combination of *chief priests and scribes*, *cf.* 2:4. Hitherto opposition to Jesus has come from scribes and Pharisees, but his high-handed action in the temple has now brought the priestly authorities into the alliance against him. Jesus' defence of the children's enthusiasm is drawn from the LXX version of Psalm 8:2.[1] But Psalm 8 talks of praise offered to *God*, not of the acclamation of the Messiah or any other man, indeed in explicit distinction from 'mere man' (v. 4). Is it then

[1]See my *JOT*, pp. 251–252, for the relation of this LXX text to the Hebrew.

only the idea of the acceptability of children's praise to which Jesus refers, or is there implied here a claim to a status even higher than that of 'Son of David'?

**17.** During Passover week most pilgrims had to find sleeping accommodation outside the city, and Jesus and his party apparently did so for the whole of this week (*cf.* Lk. 22:39).

*(iii) The lesson of the fig-tree (21:18–22)*

Matthew's purpose in including this story is clearly that there are spiritual lessons to be drawn from it, hence the inclusion of vv. 21–22. Few readers have been able to find much value in the story in itself, indeed many have been embarrassed by its destructiveness and even apparently petty vindictiveness. It is generally seen more as a symbolic act, not only in the use the Evangelists make of it, but also in the original intention of Jesus. As such it relates to the two great symbolic actions in vv. 1–17, and Mark has made the connection the more obvious by interweaving the successive episodes of Jesus' treatment of the temple and of the fig-tree (Mk. 11:11–25). This symbolism is fully explored in W. R. Telford's book, *The Barren Temple and the Withered Tree* (1980); the temple with its barren ritual is as fruitless as the tree, and is ripe for destruction. Matthew has disentangled Mark's interwoven narrative, giving the impression that each event took place all at once, and by so doing has produced a more striking miracle story (hence his double use of *at once* in vv. 19 and 20); the symbolic nature of the tree as a picture of the temple or of Judaism is thus less emphasized, but still remains to be inferred from the sequence of the stories.[1]

**18–19.** Micah 7:1, with its image of a fruitless fig-tree introducing a picture of Israel's moral and religious failure (*cf.* Je. 8:13), may have inspired Jesus' 'acted parable' of the failure of the Judaism of his day. As Mark 11:13 reminds us, ripe figs would not normally be expected at Passover time, but Jesus may have hoped for the small and unpalatable early (male) fruit which appear on some trees with the first leaves at this season (see *NBD*, p. 377). At any rate, a tree which promises fruit but provides none is an apt symbol of a religion without godliness,

[1] See further, *NIDNTT*, 1, pp. 724–725.

and the summary destruction of the tree can only point in the same direction as Jesus' demonstration in the temple (see on v. 13, and *cf.* Jesus' parable of the barren fig-tree in Lk. 13:6–9).

**20–21.** It is not the symbolism which the disciples notice, but the power of Jesus' word, and their response implies the question, 'Can *we* do such marvels too?' To *have faith* and *never doubt* are really synonyms rather than a description of a particularly strong kind of faith, for the very similar reply in 17:20 has already said that even the 'smallest' faith suffices. *This mountain* could refer either to the Mount of Olives or to the temple hill, but there is no ground for seeing specific reference either to the eschatological splitting of the former (Zc. 14:4) or to the coming 'removal' of the latter;[1] it is rather a graphic presentation of the proverbial idea of moving mountains (see on 17:20), *i.e.* a pictorial way of saying that for God nothing is impossible.

**22.** The lesson is summed up in words reminiscent of 7:7–11, but with the important qualification that this *carte blanche* is offered only to those who *have faith*. And 'faith' is always in Matthew not a quality of the one praying, but a relationship of practical trust with the one to whom prayer is offered (8:10; 9:2,22,29; 15:28; 17:20).

## C. CONTROVERSIES WITH THE JEWISH LEADERS (21:23 – 23:39)

Jesus' arrival in Jerusalem has been marked so far by provocative and symbolic *actions*; now (v. 23) he turns to teaching in the colonnades around the Court of the Gentiles, from which he has just expelled the traders. But Matthew tells us nothing of his teaching in itself, for what now follows is a long series of dialogues between Jesus and the official leaders of the nation, leading up (in ch. 23) to a prolonged and violent denunciation of those among them who professed to be the guardians of the nation's religious and moral conscience, the scribes and Pharisees. The confrontation which began in 21:15–16 is thus carried forward to the point of total mutual rejection, which must quickly lead to the elimination of Jesus as a disturber of the peace.

[1]So Telford, *op. cit.*, ch. 4.

Throughout this section Jesus' opponents are variously described as chief priests and scribes (21:15), chief priests and elders of the people (21:23), chief priests and Pharisees (21:45), Pharisees and Herodians (22:15–16), Sadducees (22:23), Pharisees (22:34,41). The various power groups in Judaism, who in other respects could not be expected to see eye to eye, are thus all in their different ways drawn into active opposition to Jesus. But these are only the *leaders*, and the ordinary people are explicitly set over against them, as being 'astonished at his teaching' (22:33) and accepting Jesus as a prophet, to the chagrin of the authorities (21:46; *cf.* 21:26). In 23:1–12 Jesus appeals to the crowds over the heads of their supposed religious mentors. It is thus the leadership of Israel, not Israel as a whole, which is here clearly on a collision course with Israel's Messiah. (But see further, on 27:20–25.)

## (i) The question of authority (21:23–27)

**23.** *The chief priests and elders* together with the scribes made up the Sanhedrin, which was responsible for maintaining order in civil and religious affairs. This was, then, a high-level deputation. *These things* are presumably Jesus' actions in vv. 1–13, but underlying the question are the ummistakable claims which those actions involved, which had led to the explicitly Messianic reaction of the crowd (vv. 9,15) to which they had already objected.

**24–25.** Jesus' reply, evasive as it appears, actually uses an approved Rabbinic method of debate by counter-question. Nor is this a 'clever' trick question irrelevant to the issue, for the authority of Jesus was closely bound up with that of *John*, who had spoken of the 'one to come', and whose mission Jesus had publicly endorsed. To believe John would properly lead to the acceptance of Jesus as sent by God. John's *baptism*, besides being the most distinctive feature of his ministry, was the one most obviously offensive in its radical implications for membership of the true Israel (see on 3:5–6,9). At this point too Jesus' message was in line with that of John, as the following parables will make very clear.

**26–27.** The leaders' dilemma was not one of genuine uncertainty (they did *not* accept John's credentials) but of diplomacy.

But by declining to pronounce an 'official' verdict on John, whose ministry was so clearly in line with that of Jesus, they had forfeited the right to challenge publicly the authority of Jesus.

*(ii) Three polemical parables (21:28 – 22:14)*
While these parables are distinct from one another, the placing of the three together as this point in Matthew's Gospel adds greatly to their impact, and is an important point to note in interpreting each one individually. All are clearly directed against the Jewish leaders, and all are concerned with the question of who is really acceptable to God, who are his true people. The theme of the failure and rejection of official Israel which runs through these parables is one which recurs more prominently in Matthew's Gospel than in the others, achieving its most explicit expression in 21:43. We have noted this theme already in such passages as 3:7–10; 8:11–12; 12:38–42; 13:10–17; 15:1–9; 16:5–12. It is also implicit both in the growing tension between Jesus and the establishment and also in some of his teaching, which suggests that the true Israel is now to be found in himself and in those who follow him. It has been vividly enacted in this chapter both in the demonstration in the temple and in the symbolic destruction of the fig-tree; and it will appear with new force in the denunciations of ch. 23, culminating in the prediction of the destruction of the temple which will also form the main theme of ch. 24. It is within this sustained build-up that these three parables occupy an important place.

*(a) The two sons (21:28–32).* **28–31.** The story is clear and simple, and its point is obvious, that what counts is not promise but performance. As in 7:15–27, the emphasis is on what we *do* (v. 31; *cf.* on 7:24–27). Its application is to the contrast between *you* (the chief priests and elders, v. 23) and *the tax collectors and the harlots*, those whom they most despised and regarded as furthest from pleasing God (see on 9:9–10). In the background of this parable lies the scandalized reaction of the religious leaders to Jesus' association with such outcasts (see 9:9–13, *etc.*), which also gave rise to another parable about two sons in Luke 15. The paradox is deliberately sharp and uncomfortable; as in 8:11–12 the tables are turned, and the unlikely are accepted while the

'religious' are excluded. (*Go in before*, while it clearly states the *priority* of the tax collectors and prostitutes, does not explicitly either include or exclude the religious leaders from the kingdom of God; but the clearly opposite attitudes of the sons in the parable, and the even clearer message of vv. 41–43, suggest that the verb points to displacement and not only precedence.) The connection of the parable with the preceding dialogue in vv. 23–27 indicates that the leaders' failure was not merely in terms of moral and religious sincerity, but in the fact that they, the leaders of God's people, had failed to recognize and welcome God's saving action in the ministry of Jesus, to which the outcasts had eagerly responded. It was this that excluded them from the *kingdom of God*. (This phrase, rather than Matthew's regular 'kingdom of heaven', is used here and in v. 43, both in connection with the rejection of the religious leaders, perhaps to emphasize the personal nature of that response to and relationship with God in which they have failed.)

**32.** This verdict is illustrated in the reaction of the two groups to *John*. The leaders could not recognize for themselves *the way of righteousness* (Semitic for 'right way'; *cf.* Pr. 8:20) which he both preached and exemplified, and *even when* they *saw* how the tax collectors and prostitutes were changed by his message, even this was not enough to convince them. As in vv. 25–27 (and see above, on 3:2), Jesus here firmly endorses and aligns himself with the message of John. If they had believed John, they would also have accepted Jesus.

*(b) The tenants of the vineyard (21:33–46).* This parable is usually described as 'allegorical', since its story is clearly to be understood as corresponding to the different phases of God's dealings with Israel, the application being made explicit in v. 43. Most commentators regard this allegorical use of the story as a later adaptation of an originally simple parable of Jesus, which is variously reconstructed as a vindication of the offer of the gospel to the poor,[1] an attack on the strong-arm tactics of the Zealots,[2] a commendation of resolute opportunism similar to that of the unjust steward,[3] and many more. All such reconstruction is

[1]Jeremias, *PJ*, pp. 70–77.     [2]J. E. and R. R. Newell, *NovT* 14 (1972), pp. 226–237.
[3]J. D. Crossan, *JBL* 90 (1971), pp. 451–465.

speculative; there can be no doubt that the parable as we have it *is* about Israel's failure in its duty to God and its consequent danger, and Trilling (pp. 55–65) has argued cogently that this was its original sense, with v. 43 as the logical conclusion in Jesus' proclamation, not just in Matthew's interpretation. Even in its simplest form, as found in the Gospel of Thomas, the parable appropriately conveys this message, even though nothing is said about reprisals after the killing of the son. Derrett (pp. 286–312) has helpfully filled in the social and economic background to the story, and argues that all the details ring true and need not be ascribed to the demands of allegory, though his reconstruction of the situation involves a lot of reading between the lines.

**33.** A new *vineyard* was a major and long-term investment, from which no returns could be expected for at least four years (Derrett, pp. 289–290). The *householder* is, then, a man of capital and an absentee landowner, while the *tenants* are the actual growers, responsible to pay him a fixed proportion of the proceeds. The language of this verse clearly echoes Isaiah 5:2, another famous story of a disappointing vineyard. The reason for failure here is different (the tenants, not the vines), but no Jewish hearer could fail to recognize in the owner and the vineyard a picture of God and his people Israel. (For similar imagery *cf.* Ps. 80:8ff.; Je. 2:21; Ezk. 19:10ff.)

**34–36.** All the versions of the story differ slightly over the details of how many servants were sent and how they were treated, but the theme of God's repeated appeal, particularly through his prophets, is clear in all.

**37.** The Gospel of Thomas says that the owner (generously) attributed the rejection of the first servant to the tenants' failure to recognize him. But with *his son* there can be no such excuse; he comes with the full authority of his father. *Cf.* Hebrews 1:1–2 for the Son as God's last word in succession to the prophets. While the point is not explicitly applied, it is hard to believe that after the revelations of 3:17 and 17:5, and after his use of language like 11:27, Jesus could have used the word *son* in his story without intending it to point to his own relationship with God. If so, this would be, according to Matthew, his first *public* claim, even if not explicit, to be Son of God, and may well lie behind

Caiaphas' charge in 26:63.

**38–39.** Unless the tenants believed the father to be dead (as Jeremias suggests, *PJ*, pp. 75–76), how could they expect the murder of the heir to give them the title to the vineyard? Derrett argues (pp. 300–306) that the owner's failure to obtain rent for four years would forfeit his title to the property. But the story smacks more of instinctive rejection and unthinking greed than of careful legal reasoning; and the rejection of God's sovereignty, and therefore of his Son, by his people is more a matter of 'gut reaction' than of reasoned policy.

**40–41.** As in v. 31 (and *cf.* vv. 25–27), Jesus' opponents are made by a question to pronounce what turns out to be their own condemnation, just as David was made to do by Nathan (2 Sa. 12:1–7). The *other tenants* will be explained in v. 43, but both there and here it is stressed that their tenure too will depend on their producing *the fruits*; there is no room for complacency on the part of the new people of God (*cf.* Paul's argument in Rom. 11:20–22).

**42.** From the rejected son of the story we turn to the rejected *stone* of Psalm 118:22–23, perhaps helped in Jesus' original words by the well-known assonance between the two words (*ben* and *'eben*) in Hebrew (see on 3:9). The psalm referred originally to the deliverance of Israel from a situation where it seemed their enemies had triumphed, a deliverance which could be ascribed only to the miraculous intervention of God on behalf of his chosen people. Jesus, and other New Testament writers following his lead (Acts 4:11; 1 Pet. 2:4,7), saw in this a prefiguring of his own rejection and subsequent vindication when God raised him from the dead and set him at his right hand.[1] The quotation here serves to round off the parable by providing the missing element in its presentation of the Jews' rejection of Jesus, *i.e.* his subsequent vindication in the resurrection. It is not certain whether *the head of the corner* is to be understood as the key-stone in the foundation (so apparently Eph. 2:20) or in the top of the wall (see *NIDNTT*, III, pp. 388–390); either way it is the stone on which the structure depends.

[1] *Cf.* my *JOT*, pp. 55–59, for such a use of several psalms by Jesus.

**43.** *Therefore I tell you* indicates a solemn pronouncement, and there follows the most explicit statement in Matthew of the view that there is to be a new people of God in place of Old Testament Israel. It is expressed in terms of the transfer of *the kingdom of God*; Trilling (p. 85) suggests that the personal form of the expression is used here (rather than 'kingdom of heaven'; *cf.* 21:31) to indicate '*the presence of God* in his people's history and his gracious saving work': *i.e.* the sphere in which we must look for God at work in salvation is no longer the nation of Israel but another *nation*. This is not the Gentiles as such (that would require the plural *ethnesin*, not the singular *ethnei*), but a people of God derived from all nations, Jew and Gentile, who now, as 1 Peter 2:9 makes clear, constitute the 'holy nation, God's own people', which was Israel's prerogative according to Exodus 19:5–6. There is thus both continuity and discontinuity: the reign of God continues, and remains focused on a 'nation', but the composition of that 'nation' has changed, not just by the replacement of its leaders, whose failure the parable has highlighted, but by the new principle of belonging which has been set out in 3:8–10; 7:15–23; 8:11–12; 12:39–42; 21:28–31, *etc.*; it is a nation which *produces fruits*, not one whose membership is automatic.

**44.** The verse given in RSV mg. is practically the same as Luke 20:18, which adds to the stone metaphor of Psalm 118:22 two further allusions to Old Testament 'stone'-passages, Isaiah 8:14–15 and Daniel 2:34–35, 44–45. Since many of the older witnesses to the text of Matthew omit the verse here, it is commonly regarded as a later insertion from the Lucan parallel. The similar collection of 'stone'-passages in 1 Peter 2:4–8 (*cf.* Rom. 9:32–33) shows that these texts were important in early Christological interpretation of the Old Testament.

**45–46.** Both John and Jesus had a degree of popular support that baffled the religious leaders (*cf.* v. 26). The theme will recur in 26:3–5 (*cf.* 26:55) and provides the situation which made Judas' betrayal a necessity for them.

*(c) The wedding feast (22:1–14).* Commentators spend much time discussing what was the original form and purpose of this parable. Comparison with Luke 14:16–24 and Gospel of Thomas

64 leads most to conclude that these versions are closer to an original simple story about a supper party where the invited guests all excused themselves and previously uninvited people from the streets took their place. The moral of the story was then a warning to take up God's invitation while it was still open (so esp. Thomas) and/or a justification of Jesus' acceptance of social and religious outcasts in place of the respectable (so esp. Luke). But Matthew, it is usually concluded, has transformed this simple story by turning the householder into a king, the supper into a wedding feast, and the (one) servant into a series of deputations, by virtually ignoring the excuses of those previously invited and by adding instead the quite incongruous theme of the killing of the messengers, resulting in a military expedition to burn down the offenders' city (while the supper goes cold?); then, to complicate matters still further, Matthew has added an originally separate parable about an improperly dressed guest (which hardly fits the situation described in v. 10). In so doing, we are told, Matthew has made Jesus' simple moral tale into an allegory of the history of salvation to match 21:33–43, with in v. 7 an explicit *ex eventu* reference to the destruction of Jerusalem in AD 70 to make the application unmistakable.

Underlying this view is the assumption that all three versions stem from a single original form, even though they are too different to be traced to the same immediate source. It is a questionable assumption. Most preachers will use a good story more than once, and in different forms to suit different contexts, and there is no improbability in Jesus' doing likewise.[1] At any rate, it seems a better method to examine Matthew's text as it stands, and see whether it makes sense in its own terms, rather than as a supposed adaptation of a lost original.

And in Matthew's text the context is important. As part of Jesus' running dialogue with the religious leaders, and in succession to the two parables in 21:28–43, it would be strange if this story did not have something to say about their failure to meet God's requirements and about a consequent change in the composition of the people of God. In other words, the 'allegorical' content of the story is likely to be in this case, as in

[1] See H. Palmer, *NovT* 18 (1976), p. 255.

21:33–43, essential to the function of the parable. If the story sometimes verges on the absurd, why not? It is, after all, a parable, not a sober historical narrative, and parables are designed to convey lessons, not to be mirrors of real life.

**1–5.** As in 8:11 and in 25:1ff., a banquet symbolizes the blessings of God's salvation. *Those who were invited* would already have received and accepted an earlier invitation; it was customary to send again to tell them when the meal was ready,[1] and it is this second invitation which is given in v. 3 and repeated in v. 4. Their double refusal is therefore going back on their previous promise, as in the case of the disobedient son in 21:30, and of the tenants in 21:35–36, whose original contract implied a promise to deliver the produce. This parable too, then, is aimed at the already religious, not at outsiders who reject God's invitation at the first hearing. They give a higher priority to their *farm* and *business*, for they cannot serve both God and mammon (6:24). The Gospel of Thomas version of the story stresses this by concluding, 'The buyers and the merchants shall not come into the places of my Father.'

**6–7.** Here the application has stretched the story beyond the bounds of real-life probability, though Derrett (p. 139) points out that to refuse a king's wedding-invitation could be tantamount to political insubordination. The treatment of the servants recalls that in 21:35–36, and it seems probable that Israel's rejection of the prophets (and of Jesus' disciples?) is in view. *Their city*, which reads very oddly in the context of the story (did all the invitees live in one city, which was not that of the king?), is clearly intended in that case to refer to Jerusalem, and this verse must then refer to the destruction of Jerusalem in AD 70. This has often been taken as proof of an origin late in the first century for at least this feature of the parable, but Robinson (pp. 20–21) argues that it is stock language which not only does not require a knowledge *ex eventu*, but in fact does not correspond precisely to what happened in AD 70, since the *city* was not burnt, only the temple. 23:37–38 and 24:2 (*cf.* 26:61?) make it clear that Jesus expected Israel's rejection of God's message to result in the destruction of the temple.

[1] See K. E. Bailey, *Through Peasant Eyes* (1980), pp. 94–95.

**8–10.** The theme of a different, and unexpected, people of God to take the place of those who failed to respond has concluded both the preceding parables (21:31–32, 41–43). As the gospel is preached to a wider circle (which, as in 21:43, is not necessarily *only* Gentile) it will attract *both bad and good*, and it is this problem which necessitates a further expansion of the story in vv. 11–13, leading up to the overall summary in v. 14.

**11–13.** A *wedding garment* is not a special type of garment, but the clean clothes (preferably white) which would normally be worn on a special occasion; to come in dirty clothes is an insult to the host.[1] Each guest was responsible for his own clothing. Augustine's theologically motivated suggestion that the host provided special garments is supported by no relevant evidence. It was prompted by the question how a man just brought in from the street could have had opportunity to go home and change; but this is simply another feature where the parable departs from real-life probability in order to draw out a lesson. And that lesson is that, though entry to God's salvation is free for all, it is not therefore without standards, or to be taken lightly. The warning that the new tenants must produce the fruit (21:41,43) is here reinforced. It was the claim to belong without an appropriate change of life which characterized the old Israel and brought about its rejection; the new people of God must not fall into the same error. The *garment* should probably not be pressed further than this to represent specifically repentance, or justification, or any specific 'works'; it is simply a life appropriate to one of God's new people. Without it, there can be no guarantee of security, as 7:13–27 has already made clear. The treatment of the offender is, of course, also described in terms which reflect more the application of the story than the real-life situation; for the terms used, see 8:12; 13:42,50. As in the parables of the weeds and the net, it is only the final judgment which will reveal who are the true guests at the banquet.

**14.** This well-known epigram sums up in different ways the message of both parts of the parable. Those who went to their farm and business had been *called*, but were not *chosen*. And even among those *called* in from the streets, we have seen one

[1] So Derrett, p. 142, and *cf.* the interestingly similar but later parable of Johanan ben Zakkai in *Shabbath* 153a (see Jeremias, *PJ*, p. 188).

(representative of many) who turned out in the end not to be *chosen*, despite his response to the invitation. But in each case the fault was their own, whereas *chosen* suggests to us that their fate depended on someone else's (God's) 'choice', thus raising all the familiar problems of the doctrine of election. Jeremias (*NTT*, p. 131) sees *eklektoi* ('chosen') as 'a technical term for the messianic community of salvation', the emphasis being on the fact of membership, not on the means of achieving it. Certainly this suits the context, and the fact that *eklektoi* can be used in relation to this parable suggests that our tidy logical distinction between divine 'selection' and culpable human rejection of God's offer is not easy to impose on the New Testament. The message of the verse is that of the parable of the sower: there is many a slip between initial response to the gospel and ultimate fruitfulness.

*(iii) The question of imperial taxes (22:15-22)*

It was the imposition of direct Roman taxation that had sparked off the revolt of Judas of Galilee in AD 6, and Judas' ideology was the mainspring for many of the resistance movements which we conveniently label collectively as 'Zealots'. To approve of Roman taxation was to come out openly against this militant nationalism which enjoyed strong popular support, and it was no doubt the hope of Jesus' questioners that he would thus forfeit much of his following. But the opposite answer would be a convenient proof of Jesus' treasonable attitude, to be used in persuading the Roman governor to act against him. The question was therefore a clever 'trap' (the literal meaning of *entangle* in v. 15). If ever there was a time when the Pharisees were open-minded about Jesus, it has now clearly passed.

**15-16.** The *Herodians*, who appear only here in Matthew, were presumably partisans of the Herodian family (and therefore of Antipas in particular), whose political allegiance was therefore indirectly to Rome. Their rather unlikely collaboration with the *Pharisees* here represents therefore the two sides of Jesus' dilemma, for the Pharisees, while not usually noted for political activity, are unlikely to have approved whole-heartedly of the Gentile rule over the people of God. The address to Jesus, while it contains an element of flattery, reflects what was surely his actual reputation, that of a fearless teacher and controversialist. All that has happened since his arrival in Jerusalem amply illustrates his willingness to speak his mind. (*Regard the position of* is literally 'look at the face of', an idiom taken up in the word translated 'partiality', *e.g.*, in Acts 10:34; Rom. 2:11; Eph. 6:9; Jas. 2:1,9; *cf.* NEB, 'truckling to no man'!)

**17.** The *tax* (the Greek is singular) is specifically the poll-tax levied on all Jews and paid direct to Rome. There were other indirect taxes on sales, customs, *etc.*, but this tax was the primary mark of their political subjection to a foreign power. *Lawful* does not refer to Roman law (there was no question about that!), but to the law of God; is it permissible for the people of God to express allegiance to a pagan emperor?

**18–21.** For *hypocrites*, see on 6:2. Here it is the idea of insincerity rather than inconsistency which is prominent. The *money for the tax* was the Roman denarius (see on 20:1–7), a coin which strict Jews found objectionable because it bore a portrait of the emperor (and the Decalogue forbade the making of images) and also an inscription describing him as 'son of a god' (see Derrett, pp. 329–331). For normal commerce special copper coins were minted without these features, out of deference to Jewish susceptibilities; so no Jew need handle the objectionable denarius except to pay his tax, for which it was obligatory. The fact that Jesus' questioners could provide one on demand cut the ground from under their feet – they were using Caesar's money, so let them also pay his taxes! Indeed the verb Jesus uses reinforces this point: *render* generally means 'give back' (whereas the verb they had used in v. 17 was simply 'give'). It is the verb for paying a bill or settling a debt; they owe it to him.

But Jesus' reply does not stop with a simple acceptance of Roman taxation. *To God the things that are God's* has sometimes been regarded as virtually cancelling the previous words, since God's claim is above that of Caesar. But that is to make nonsense of Jesus' argument drawn from the production of the coin. The addition serves rather to put the whole issue in a wider perspective. It was loyalty to God which was the basis for Zealot objections to Roman taxation, but Jesus, without reducing the demands of loyalty to God, indicates that political allegiance even to a pagan state is not incompatible with it. This is not a rigid division of life into the 'sacred' and the 'secular', but rather a recognition that the 'secular' finds its proper place *within* the overriding claim of the 'sacred'. What should happen when the two conflict is not at issue here; in the political situation of Jesus' time he, unlike the 'Zealots', clearly sees no such conflict.

**22.** It was an answer with which no Zealot could be content, if he understood Jesus' meaning, but the words could not be unambiguously construed as firmly for or against the Zealot option. So it *was* a clever answer, at which *they marvelled*. But if the interpretation given above is correct, Jesus did not just evade the trap with slick ambiguity, but laid down an important principle for his followers who would soon face the issue of the legitimacy of secular authority, even though there is no easy rule of thumb by which to apply that principle to each specific situation.

*(iv) The question about resurrection (22:23–33)*

'The Sadducees hold that the soul perishes along with the body' (Josephus, *Ant.* xviii. 16). Their question is therefore, for them, no more serious than that of the Pharisees and Herodians. Indeed it has the air of a stock example, designed to ridicule belief in the resurrection by a *reductio ad absurdum*. But as in the previous case, Jesus turns the trick question into an occasion for positive teaching.

**23.** *The same day* emphasizes to the reader that the whole sequence of debate from 21:23 to 23:39 forms a complete whole, in the light of which each individual argument is to be understood. The *Sadducees'* denial of a *resurrection* was a corollary of their insistence on taking only the Pentateuch as their scriptural authority. Passages like Isaiah 26:19; Daniel 12:2, on which the Pharisees based their belief (see Acts 23:8), were therefore for them a later deviation from the religion of Moses.

**24.** The basis of their 'objection' is the levirate law of Deuteronomy 25:5–6; their summary of this law concludes with some words from Genesis 38:8, an actual example of the application of this principle in the family of Judah. *Marry* is not the normal Greek word, but a technical term for the performance of the levirate duty.[1] *Raise up* (*anastēsei*) echoes *resurrection* (*anastasis*) in v. 23, and may hint that such physical 'continuity' is the only 'resurrection' they recognize.

**25–28.** It seems that the levirate law remained in force, since the Rabbis continued to discuss such cases (Mishnah *Yebamoth*). So the story may not be entirely hypothetical, though its resemblance to that of Sarah in Tobit 3:8–15 may indicate an origin in popular story-telling.

**29.** *You are wrong* applies both to the specific case cited (which Jesus deals with in v. 30) and to the real issue underlying it (which will be tackled in vv. 31–32). Of course the Sadducees did *know the scriptures* (at least those books which they regarded as such) in a superficial sense, but they had not penetrated through to their real meaning and thereby discovered the *power of God*; so there are not here two separate causes of error, but a failure to understand Scripture which leads to an inability to appreciate what God can do. Their outlook was essentially that of secular man, who cannot accept a God whose work goes beyond present human experience; a knowledge of Scripture (even only of the Pentateuch, from which Jesus will argue in vv. 31–32) should have taken them beyond that.

**30.** The specific problem they had cited was inappropriate because it assumed that a resurrection life must be subject to the same conditions as life on earth. But 'the power of God' (v. 29) creates a wholly new kind of life, not a mere reanimation of that which we experience now (see the argument of 1 Cor. 15: 35–50). In this new deathless life there will be no place for procreation, and the exclusive relationship within which this takes place on earth will therefore not apply. It is this aspect of marriage which Jesus' argument excludes from the resurrection life, rather than any suggestion that loving relationships have no place there. The Sadducees' question may have been cynical, but the issue it raises is a real one for those who have married more than once; Jesus' reply points them to a possibility of fulfilment of these relationships in the risen life which the exclusiveness of the marriage bond in earthly life would have rendered unthinkable. Jealousy and exclusion will have no place

[1]On levirate law see further, *NBD*, p. 745.

there.

**31–32.** The real issue for the Sadducees was not the question of marriage but the possibility of resurrection at all. Jesus draws his argument from Exodus 3:6, part of the Scriptures which the Sadducees accepted. It is so compressed as to seem quite unconvincing. But study of the context from which the quotation is taken suggests a deeper theological reasoning than is apparent on the surface. When God spoke to Moses at the burning bush, *Abraham, Isaac and Jacob* had long been dead, and yet God identified himself as their God. But could he be *God of the dead*? As Calvin comments, 'As no man can be a father without children, nor a king without a people, so, strictly speaking, the Lord cannot be called the God of any but the living.' It is in this context that God reveals his name, Yahweh, 'I AM WHO I AM' (Ex. 3:14–16), and the object of that revelation is to assure Moses of the active, saving presence of God with his people to rescue them from Egypt. Could this living, saving, covenant-keeping God establish a relationship with Abraham, Isaac and Jacob only to allow it to be terminated by death? 'To be the God of' implies a caring, protecting relationship which is as permanent as the living God who makes it. 'With unsurpassable brevity this sentence says that faith in God includes the certainty of conquering death' (Jeremias, *NTT*, p. 184).

**33.** We are not told what the Sadducees made of Jesus' argument, except that it 'silenced' them (v. 34). But his argument had not been intended for them alone, and the *crowd* recognized this as something new and remarkable. *Cf.* on 7:28–29 for their being *astonished at his teaching*. Throughout this dialogue with the religious leaders in chapters 21 – 23 this 'crowd' is an important though silent participant (*cf.* 21:46; 23:1). Much of the teaching is intended for public consumption.

*(v) The greatest commandment (22:34–40)*

The combination of Deuteronomy 6:5 and Leviticus 19:18 to form a summary of the requirements of God's law, which forms the heart of this episode, occurs again in Luke 10:25–28 as a lawyer's reply to *Jesus'* question, 'What is written in the law?' – a reply which Jesus approves, and which leads into the parable of the Good Samaritan in order to define the scope of 'neighbour' in Leviticus 19:18. The passages are sufficiently different to indicate two separate occasions when this combination of Old Testament texts played a central role in Jesus' ethical teaching; indeed it is likely that he made frequent use of such a creative summary (cf. 7:12 for an alternative 'summary of the law'). Both texts were frequently referred to in Jewish ethical discussion, but they are not found singled out together in this way in Jewish writings.[1] This teaching of the primacy of love is taken up by Paul in his statement that 'love is the fulfilling of the law' (Rom. 13:8–10; cf. Gal. 5:14; Jas. 2:8), and has remained at the centre of Christian ethics ever since, though the proper balance between love for God and love for the 'neighbour' has been, and remains, a source of tension between the 'other-worldly' and the 'this-worldly' demands of discipleship.

**34–36.** The outcome of this 'discussion' will be richly positive teaching, but its motivation is again hostile. *They came together* probably echoes deliberately the plotting of the heathen against God's anointed in Psalm 2:2 (Gundry, *UOT*, p. 141), and the question is, as in 16:1; 19:3; 22:15–18, a *test*. It was, of course, an entirely legitimate question, and discussions of the relative importance of commandments frequently occupied the Rabbis.[2] Distinction between 'hard' and 'easy' commandments, even between more and less 'weighty' ones, was permissible, but in principle every command (and the scribes distinguished 613 commands in the Old Testament law) was equally binding. An incautious reply by Jesus could suggest that he repudiated some of these commandments, and thus lay him open to a charge of 'annulling the law' (cf. on 5:17).

**37–38.** Deuteronomy 6:4–9, from which this quotation is taken, was repeated twice daily by pious Jews as the opening of the *Shema'*. It therefore already played a key role in Jewish religious life, and Jesus' emphasis on this text could cause no surprise. *Heart*, *soul* and *mind* are not different 'parts' of man, but different ways of thinking of the whole man in his relation to God; no clear distinction can be drawn between them. *Dianoia*

[1] The exhortation to 'Love the Lord and your neighbour' in Testament of Issachar 5:2 (cf. Testament of Dan 5:3) may well be based on these texts; the passage may reflect Christian influence even though there is no direct quotation of the texts.

[2] See Banks, pp. 165–166; for examples, SB, I, pp. 901–905.

('mind') perhaps indicates more our intellectual commitment, but this is also a part of the biblical meaning of the *heart* (see on 5:8; 15:18). The three nouns together indicate the essential nature of man, his ultimate, fundamental loyalty, not just a superficial allegiance.[1]

**39.** Leviticus 19:18 is declared to be *like* Deuteronomy 6:5; *i.e.* the two stand together, on a level of their own, as the guide to all the other commandments of the law. Neither is to be raised above the other; each depends on the other for its true force. This text has already been quoted and interpreted in 5:43–47, where it has been made clear that the *neighbour* is not just, as in Leviticus, the fellow-Israelite, but includes the 'enemy'. *As yourself* assumes, rather than commands, a basically self-centred orientation, which Jesus requires his disciple to overcome.

**40.** The two great commandments do not dispense with all the rest (such an answer *would* have been a dangerous response to the 'test'), but the rest *depend* on them (literally 'hang', a technical term for laws which are derivable from others). They remain commandments of God, but they find their coherence in the overriding principle of the double commandment to love. Jesus' words here are not, then, a recommendation of what has come to be known as 'situationalism', the view that there are no principles for Christian conduct other than to do the most loving thing in the given situation. Rather they direct us to understand and apply the commandments of the law within the context of an obligation to love God and man, an obligation of which the commandments are themselves particular expressions.[2]

### (vi) The Messiah as Son of David (22:41–46)

The series of 'discussions' ends with Jesus taking the initiative. The question he poses is, at least on the surface, one of 'academic' theology – is it correct to describe the Messiah as 'Son of

[1]In the different versions of the Old Testament text, as well as in the New Testament quotations of it, there is considerable variation in the nouns used; for details see Gundry, *UOT*, pp. 22–24. Mark and Luke each have four nouns; Matthew, in returning to the familiar three of the Old Testament text, has omitted 'strength', a Hebrew noun which was rendered in the Targums by the Aramaic *māmōnā'*, for which see on 6:24; he has thus produced a version which concentrates less on the practical implications of love for God than on its inward consistency.

[2]See further, G. Barth, *TIM*, pp. 75–85.

David'? In this context, however, it cannot be merely academic, for Jesus himself has just been hailed as 'Son of David' by the crowds (21:9, 15), and the title has recurred several times in the course of his public ministry (9:27; 12:23; 15:22; 20:30–31). It was, of course, a commonplace of Jewish expectation that a Messiah would come who was David's son and successor on the throne of Judah (see esp. Psalm of Solomon 17), and it is in this light that Jesus' significance has been seen by at least some of his followers. But the title will not be used again, and it is a cross, not a throne, which awaits Jesus. In what sense, then, if at all, is he David's son?

We have seen repeatedly that for Matthew it is important to claim that Jesus is descended from David. (See p. 43 and, *e.g.*, on 1:1,17; 9:27.) Matthew cannot, then, have believed that Jesus here *denied* his Davidic lineage. And if he had done so, the early church could hardly have continued to stress the fact as it did (see Rom. 1:3 for an early Christian confession to this effect). The point here is rather that the title is *inadequate*, if not *misleading*, as a guide to the nature of Jesus' Messianic mission. He is no mere successor or replica of David, but rather he is David's Lord, with an authority far higher than a merely earthly national throne.

The same Old Testament text (Ps. 110:1) will be used to make the same point in 26:64. The method of argument is one familiar in Rabbinic debate, to set up two scriptural themes which are apparently in conflict (an 'antinomy') and to seek for a resolution. The Gospels record only the antinomy (David's son/ David's Lord), not the resolution, but we may fairly assume that it lies in the recognition of two levels of Messiahship, much as in Romans 1:3–4 Jesus is declared 'descended from David according to the flesh' *but also* 'Son of God in power . . .'. They are not mutually exclusive truths, but complementary. So Jesus *is* David's son, but he is *far more*. And the political connotations which 'Son of David' carried made it, *on its own*, a potentially misleading title, which Jesus never claimed for himself, though he defended the right of others to apply it to him (21:14–16).

**41–42.** What is a monologue by Jesus in Mark and Luke appears as a question-and-answer dialogue in Matthew. The title *Son of David* thus appears directly in the mouths of the

Pharisees; it is Jesus' role to question this traditional language. At the same time the explicit question *Whose son is he?* suggests that an alternative account is needed; if he is not David's son, then whose? If he is not 'answerable to' David, from whom is his authority derived? The question is left unanswered, but its implications are obvious.

**43–45.** The conclusion that the Messiah is *David's Lord* is drawn from Psalm 110:1, a verse which became one of the key Old Testament passages for early Christian understanding of the role of Jesus.[1] The argument depends on Jesus' explicit view that the Psalm was written by David, and that it refers to the Messiah, neither of which is endorsed by most modern critical scholarship, but both of which were apparently universally accepted among Jesus' contemporaries.[2] The term *my Lord* (which in Hebrew is not the same as 'the LORD' representing the name of God) clearly implies that the one so described is in a position superior to the speaker, David. And when David used that term he was *inspired by the Spirit* (literally just 'in (the) Spirit'), *i.e.* he spoke as a prophet. So the Messiah is divinely designated as superior to David.

**46.** It is obvious what answer Jesus implies, but *no one was able to answer him a word*, because the question was not just an academic one as posed by Jesus, and to accept his argument would be to recognize him as 'something greater than David' (to use the formula of 12:6, 41, 42; *cf.* on 12:3–4). The fear of further debate suggests that their silence was itself a damaging admission, and they could not risk being manoeuvred into further admissions. Thus the whole sequence of debate which began in 21:23 leaves Jesus in possession of the field. From now on he will not debate with the authorities, but will go over their heads to the crowd.

*(vii) The failure of scribes and Pharisees (23:1–36)*
This long section, while it can conveniently be divided into two sections with regard to the style and the audience addressed, is all on one theme, and as in the case of other such 'discourses'

---

[1] See D. M. Hay, *Glory at the Right Hand* (1973).
[2] For an argument in favour of the validity of these assumptions, see my *JOT*, pp. 163–169; *cf.* Gundry, *UOT*, pp. 228–229.

(chs. 5–7, 10, 13, 18) consists partly of material found in different places in the other Synoptic Gospels. It seems that Matthew has taken the brief denunciation of Mark 12:38–40 as starting-point and has expanded it with other sayings of Jesus independently preserved (esp. some found also in Lk. 11:37–52, there recorded as spoken at a Pharisee's dinner-party!). Chapters 24 – 25 will speak of judgment to come on the nation, and this chapter prepares for that theme by showing the rottenness at the heart of official Judaism; vv. 37–39 will link the two discourses together.

From the debate and parable of chapters 21 – 22 we now move to direct attack, exposing ruthlessly the failings of the religious leaders which have been emerging in the preceding chapters. The tone is harsh, and the attack has been described as grossly unfair, even 'libellous'.[1] Were *all* scribes and Pharisees as bad as this? Mark 12:28–34 at least suggests otherwise. But Jesus' attack here is not only (or even primarily) against conscious hypocrisy, but against the faults inherent in the Pharisaic approach to religion even at its best. Even the most scrupulous of Pharisees followed a system which tended to understand righteousness in terms of more and more minute legal prescriptions, and which could therefore dangerously distort the whole question of what it means to please God. In thus obscuring the way to a 'better righteousness' (see on 5:20), the scribes and Pharisees were thus guilty, however unconsciously, of a more fundamental and damaging failure than simply falling short of their professed standards.

Verses 2–12 are addressed to 'the crowds and his disciples', describing and warning against the scribes and Pharisees in the third person; in vv. 13–36 the style changes to a direct address to them in the form of a series of seven denunciations ('woes'). But the intention throughout is to 'expose' the religious leaders, and so to challenge their claim to leadership; the true target of the whole discourse is the crowds and disciples who need to break free from Pharisaic legalism. (For the combination 'scribes and Pharisees', see on 5:20; 15:1.)

---

[1] See the summary of Jewish reactions to this chapter in Garland, pp. 1–2.

*(a) Address to the crowds (23:1–12).* **1.** For *the crowds*, see on 22:33. While they are differentiated from the more committed *disciples*, they are at least potential followers of Jesus, and this public dialogue is intended to appeal over the heads of the leaders to those who have been attracted to Jesus' teaching as a new and better way.[1]

**2–3.** *Moses' seat* is a figurative expression for the teaching authority (*cf.* our professorial 'chair') or those officially responsible for interpreting and applying the laws of Moses.[2] Jesus thus accepts the legitimacy of the scribes' function, but questions the way they exercise it. The command to *practise and observe whatever they tell you* is surprising in the light of Jesus' attack on scribal tradition in 15:1–20, and specifically on the Pharisees' teaching in 16:6–12 (*cf.* his disputes with them over the sabbath, 12:1–14, on divorce, 19:3–9, *etc.*). Moreover v. 4 goes on to attack their legal regulations. It is probable, then, that v. 3 should be read as a whole, in which the emphasis is on the second half and the first functions only as a foil to it, perhaps spoken with an ironical, tongue-in-cheek tone. One might paraphrase, 'Of course you may do what they *say*, if you like, but don't do what they *do*'.[3]

The focus throughout ch. 23 is on a life which, whether consciously or not (and no doubt some scribes and Pharisees would fall into one category, some into the other), does not match up to their profession of loyalty to God.

**4.** If v. 3a might by itself be taken as a blanket endorsement of scribal teaching, this verse forbids such an interpretation. For the technical sense of *bind*, see on 16:19; 18:18; that sense may lie behind this verse too, the emphasis therefore falling on the *prohibitive* nature of Rabbinic legislation. 'They have multiplied "the number of ways in which a man may offend God", but they have failed in helping him to please God' (Garland, p. 51). Thus 'Jesus here castigates the legalism which can impose regulations but cannot or will not give relief to the lawbreaker' (*AB*, p. 278). The *heavy burdens* laid on *men's shoulders* contrast with

[1] See further, Garland, pp. 34–41.

[2] A later convention of referring to the front seat in the synagogue as *'Moses' seat'* derives from this figurative use, but is not attested as early as the first century.

[3] See further, Banks, pp. 175–177.

Jesus' easy yoke and light burden in 11:28–30, which offers rest to those who are 'heavy laden'.

**5–7.** For Pharisaic ostentation see, more fully, 6:1–18. *Phylacteries* are small leather boxes containing scrolls of texts from Exodus and Deuteronomy. Perhaps *make broad* refers to the size of the straps by which these were (and are) bound on to the forehead and left arm of the Jewish man when at prayer, but it has also been suggested that it refers to wearing the phylacteries (*tefillim*) during the rest of the day, and not only as prescribed at the hours of prayer. The size of *fringes* (see on 9:20) was a matter of debate, the school of Shammai prescribing longer ones than the school of Hillel. These and other practices were designed to cut a more pious figure in Jewish society, in order to achieve the respect expressed in the title *rabbi* (lit. 'my great one'), which was not yet purely a technical term for ordained scribes (like our 'Reverend'!), but was used of a respected teacher (and in Palestinian society of Jesus' day no-one was more important than a leading teacher).

**8–10.** These verses, while still commenting on the practice of the scribes and Pharisees, are addressed directly to Jesus' disciples, warning them against adopting this status-seeking attitude. *Rabbi* (v. 8) and *master* (v. 10) probably act here as synonyms. They are titles appropriate only to the *one teacher* (v. 8), *the Christ* (v. 10), in relation to whom all his followers stand on an equal footing as *brothers*. Jesus thus incidentally asserts his own unique authority: he has the only true claim to 'Moses' seat'. Over against that unique authority his disciples must avoid the use of honorific titles for one another ('Christian rabbinism', Bonnard) – an exhortation which today's church could profitably taken more seriously, not only in relation to formal ecclesiastical titles ('Most Rev.', 'my Lord Bishop', *etc.*), but more significantly in its excessive deference to academic qualifications or to authoritative status in the churches.

In this context it is surprising to find the term *Father* discussed (v. 9). There is no evidence for its use as a title in a similar way to 'rabbi' and 'master', either in Jewish or Christian circles at this period. Acts 7:2; 22:1 illustrate its respectful use collectively for 'elders' in Israel, and it is possible that it thus came to be used individually for major Rabbinic teachers.[1] But in Jesus' teaching 'Father' is always a title for God alone (not even for Jesus, unlike 'rabbi' and 'master'), and its use for any man (except of course in a purely literal sense!) is therefore to be deplored. In a different sense Paul could describe himself as the 'one father' of those whom he had led to Christ (1 Cor. 4:15; *cf.* Phil. 2:22), but this is not used as a title.

**11–12.** The two exhortations to service and humility have occurred separately before (for v. 11, *cf.* 20:26–27; for v. 12, *cf.* 18:4); now brought together they powerfully enforce the totally unconventional attitude which Jesus requires of his disciples, in contrast with the status-consciousness of the scribes and Pharisees.

*(b) Denunciation of the scribes and Pharisees (23:13–36).* This direct denunciation (in the second person) takes the form of seven accusations, all (except v. 16) introduced by the phrase *Woe to you, scribes and Pharisees, hypocrites! because . . .*, after which follows a brief cameo illustrating their failure to live up to their position as guardians and interpreters of God's law (23:2). On *hypocrites*, see on 6:2; 7:5; 15:7; 22:18; the word clearly has a wider range in Matthew than in our usage, and the six uses of it in this chapter illustrate that range. The overall emphasis falls less on conscious insincerity than on their failure to perceive that their religious practice and teaching are in fact inconsistent with the desire to please God, which is their (no doubt sincerely) professed aim. Their whole religious system is so fundamentally misconceived that it amounts to 'a radical subversion of God's will' (Garland, pp. 115–116). The whole passage then is 'not simply an attack on the ethical contradiction in the personal lives of the scribes and Pharisees but a characterization of their failure as the divinely appointed leaders of Israel, particularly as it related to their responsibility in interpretation of the law' (*ibid.*, p. 124).

*Woe* sometimes in Matthew expresses a regretful lament, 'Alas' (see 24:19); sometimes a 'powerful and denunciatory

[1] See R. S. Barbour, *ExpT* 82 (1970/71), p. 139.

judgement akin to a curse' (Garland, p. 87; see his long discussion of 'woes', pp. 64–90), as in 11:21. In 18:7 it seems to be used once in each sense. Such series of 'woes' are familiar from the Old Testament prophets (*e.g.* Is. 5:8–23; Hab. 2:6–19), where the tone is of condemnation, and that is the emphasis here too. The 'woes' function almost as a converse of the 'blesseds' of 5:3–12; as the beatitudes set out the true way to please God, so the woes describe the wrong way, and pronounce judgment on those who follow and teach it.

**13.** The first woe describes the effect of Pharisaic legalism on *entering the kingdom of heaven*, a phrase which has been used in such key verses as 5:20; 7:21; 18:3; 19:23–24 to describe a saving relationship with God. Not only does their own attitude prevent such a relationship, but their teaching makes it impossible for all who, in their sincere desire to please God, adopt the Pharisaic way. Jesus, it is implied, has brought the true way of salvation, and only those who follow him can either enter or give entry.

**14.** The verse printed in the margin comes from Mark 12:40, but is not in the best MSS of Matthew.

**15.** To seek for *proselytes* (religious converts) is not in itself a fault; Jesus will tell his disciples to do just that (28:19). But if the proselytizer is himself a *child of hell* (*i.e.* one destined for hell – see on 5:22; 10:28; it is not so much a term of abuse as a statement of fact), to win converts is only to increase its population. The phrase could more literally be translated 'make him a child of hell more double (*i.e.* devious, hypocritical) than you are', perhaps with reference to the frequent tendency of converts to outdo their converters in (perverted) zeal.[1]

**16–22.** In 5:33–37 the subject of oaths has already been broached, and Jesus has cut through all casuistry to declare all oaths inappropriate for a disciple. But the exhaustive discussion of the relative validity of oaths was a characteristic concern of the kind of legalism he is here attacking, and so it serves now to illustrate their distorted sense of values. The background to this attack lies in the popular tendency (which is still common today) to substitute trivial 'oaths' for serious (and therefore more 'dangerous') ones. Here was fruitful ground for scribal 'nit-picking',

[1]For Jewish proselytism in the first century AD see Hare, pp. 9–10.

and there was much dispute (see Garland, pp. 133–136). But, as in 5:34–35, Jesus again shows how one oath implies another, and (vv. 21–22) all ultimately involve God as the one who is invoked. In ch. 5 the conclusion was drawn that therefore oaths should be avoided altogether. Here the object is not a positive recommendation for disciples, but to expose the absurdity of the scribal debates, and indeed their 'ungodliness'. 'Their virtuoso theology, acutely perceptive, lacks reverence for God' (Jeremias, *NTT*, p. 146). For *blind*, *cf.* 15:14, and for *fools* (v. 17), *cf.* on 5:22; here the word is used neither in thoughtless insult nor with personal bitterness, but as a considered indictment of their lack of discernment.

**23.** The fourth woe does not relate to their meticulous observance of the Old Testament tithing law (Lv. 27:30; Dt. 14:22) in itself, for Jesus accepts this as proper (*without neglecting the others*), but rather to their sense of proportion. They have been so concerned to apply the tithing law in respect of every garden herb that *justice, mercy and faith* have been ignored. This phrase recalls the summary of true religion (in contrast to extravagant sacrifice) in Micah 6:8, especially as *faith* is here probably to be understood as 'faithfulness'. In describing this trio of Old Testament virtues as *the weightier matters of the law*, Jesus thus echoes the prophetic view that an inward righteousness is more important than, and alone gives meaning to, ritual observance. *Cf.* 7:12; 22:40 for similar 'summaries of the law'. It is this focus which makes possible the 'righteousness exceeding that of the scribes and Pharisees' (5:20), for 'they concentrated on the minor and practicable pieties, to the neglect of the broad and inexhaustible principles'.[1] As in 23:3, the acceptance of the scribal rules implied in *without neglecting the others* serves only as a foil to the more important positive prescription of the sentence. Again we could paraphrase, 'Observe your meticulous rules if you like, but don't therefore neglect the things that really matter.'[2]

**24.** This lack of a sense of proportion is delightfully burlesqued in the ridiculous picture of a *gnat* strained out of a drink to avoid impurity (Lv. 11:20–23), while a *camel* (also impure, Lv. 11:4) is

[1] G. B. Caird, *The Language and Imagery of the Bible* (1980), p. 92.
[2] See Banks, pp. 179–180.

swallowed whole. The joke may have been aided by an Aramaic pun on *qalma* (gnat) and *gamla* (camel).[1]

**25–26.** The fifth and sixth woes both focus (as indeed the fourth did in a different way) on the failure to distinguish between external correctness and internal purity. Rabbinic debates on the relative importance of the inside and outside of utensils in matters of ceremonial purification are well documented,[2] but Jesus is not entering into that debate, but rather using it as an illustration for the more important distinction between externals (such as that whole debate was concerned with) and 'internal' moral issues (such as *extortion and rapacity*).[3] The principle enunciated in v. 26 is the same as that in 15:11, 18–20, and renders the whole Rabbinic argument superfluous. Their failure to see this was the root of their 'hypocrisy'.

**27–28.** *Tombs* were whitewashed regularly at festival time to ensure that passers-by did not inadvertently touch them and so become defiled (Mishnah *Shekalim* 1:1; *cf. Ma'aser Sheni* 5:1). This custom is generally assumed to be the background to Jesus' words, but that whitewashing was not a mark of beauty but rather a warning of uncleanness, repulsive rather than attractive. The word *whitewashed* here means literally 'plastered' (with lime), and S. T. Lachs[4] has suggested that the reference is to funerary urns or ossuaries (bone-containers) which were beautified with a marble-and-lime plaster. This view provides a much more appropriate contrast between outward attractiveness and inward defilement.[5] The point is thus the same as in vv. 25–26.

**29–31.** The seventh woe describes the hostility of the scribes and Pharisees to God's true messengers, and goes on to predict its outcome. There was in the first century a great emphasis on building splendid tombs, including some for long-dead worthies (*e.g.* Herod's new marble monument over David's tomb, Josephus, *Ant.* xvi. 179–182). Jesus takes this as symbolic of a desire to honour *the prophets and the righteous*, despite the fact

---

[1]See Black, pp. 175–176.    [2]J. Neusner, *NTS* 22 (1975/6), pp. 486–493.

[3]H. Maccoby in *JSNT* 14(1982), pp. 3–15, helpfully analyses the argument in relation to its Rabbinic background.

[4]*HTR* 68 (1975), pp. 385–389.

[5]*Cf.* Story of Ahikar (Armenian) 2:2 for the same metaphor applied to a beautifully made up but dangerous woman!

that many of them according to the Old Testament (and many more in later tradition) had been persecuted and killed by those in authority. *Cf.* Acts 7:52. But for all their fine words, the current leaders are still *sons* of their *fathers*, as their attitude to God's messengers in their own day shows (v. 34).

**32.** This ironic imperative introduces the idea which will dominate vv. 34-39, that Jesus' own generation is the one in which Jewish rebellion against God reaches its climax and will therefore incur its ultimate punishment. *Cf.* 1 Thessalonians 2:14-16 for this idea of a *full measure* of Jewish rebellion seen in their attitude to Jesus (and, in that context, their opposition to the Christian mission to Gentiles).

**33.** In 3:7 John the Baptist had pictured the Jewish leaders as a *brood of vipers* fleeing from the wrath to come; Jesus takes up the picture and declares the flight is futile.

**34.** *Prophets, wise men and scribes* were God's spokesmen in the Old Testament and in developing Judaism. Now Jesus himself[1] is sending his disciples to them in the same role (*cf.* 5:11-12; 10:40-41 for the continuity between Old Testament prophets and the disciples of Jesus). As he has already indicated in 5:11-12, they can expect no better treatment from the 'sons' (v. 31) than the prophets received from the 'fathers' (v. 30). The inclusion of *crucify* in the list of persecutions is surprising, in that Jews could not and did not crucify, and there is no record of their instigating the Romans to crucify any of Jesus' disciples (Hare, pp. 90-91). It seems that Jesus' own mission is so closely bound up with his disciples' that his fate forms part of theirs. *Persecute from town to town* recalls Jesus' warning in 10:23. Thus Jewish rebellion reaches its climax not only in the rejection of Jesus, but in the persecution of his disciples, and this too will contribute to the coming punishment.

**35.** The cumulative effect of the rejection and murder of all God's spokesmen is graphically traced *from Abel to Zechariah*, who were the first and last martyrs of the Old Testament, since 2 Chronicles was the last book of the Hebrew canon, and Zech-

---

[1]In Lk. 11:49 similar words are ascribed to 'the Wisdom of God'; it may be a quotation from some lost source, but there is no doubt that here it is Jesus' messengers, not God's messengers in the past, that are intended.

ariah's murder is recounted in 2 Chronicles 24:20–22.[1] In both accounts the call for vengeance is explicit (Gn. 4:10; 2 Ch. 24:22), so that the choice of these two examples is doubly appropriate to Jesus' theme of the culmination of blood-guilt. The Zechariah of 2 Chronicles 24 (who is clearly indicated here by the specific mention of the place where he was killed) was son of Jehoiada; *Barachiah* was the father of the post-exilic prophet (Zc. 1:1), but the two Zechariahs were frequently confused in Jewish tradition (see Gundry, *UOT*, pp. 86–88, note).

**36.** The decisive situation of *this generation* has already been noticed (11:16–19; 12:38–45; 17:17; *cf.* Jeremias, *NTT*, p. 135) and the theme will come to its climax in the next chapter, leading up to 24:34. The coming of Jesus, and his rejection by his own people, has brought Israel's rebellion to the point where judgment can no longer be delayed. Verses 37–39 will spell this out more fully.

*(viii) The fate of Jerusalem (23:37–39)*
The passage forms a bridge between the denunciation of official Judaism in chapter 23 and the more explicit prediction of a consequent judgment on the nation in the destruction of its temple, which is the basis of chapter 24. It thus forms an appropriate, if solemn, climax to Jesus' public teaching. These are, in Matthew, his last words to his people.

**37.** *Jerusalem* symbolizes the nation whose capital it is. Israel's treatment of God's messengers (already set out in vv. 29–36) shows that a final choice has been made. It was Jesus' mission to avert the punishment predicted in vv. 35–36 by bringing Israel to repentance; he was willing (*would I* is literally 'I wanted') but they were not (*would not*, the same verb). The image of a *hen* (Greek is simply 'bird') protecting its young is used in the Old Testament for God's protection of his people (Pss. 17:8; 91:4; Is. 31:5; *etc.*); now Jesus has come personally to exercise that divine function. (*Cf.* Is. 30:15 for refusal to accept God's offer of protection.) The note of sorrowful disappointment in this lament is an important counterbalance to the violence of some of the denunciations in vv. 1–36; it gave Jesus no pleasure to pronounce

[1] Fortuitously in English they are A to Z, but Z is not the last letter in either the Hebrew or Greek alphabet!

judgment on those to whom he came to offer salvation.

**38.** While the *house* might refer to Israel as a whole (*cf.* 10:6; 15:24), the context here directly before ch. 24 indicates that the immediate reference is to the temple (where the words are spoken), whose fate will symbolize God's judgment on his people. The verse translates literally 'Behold your house is left (or 'abandoned') to you deserted.'[1] The verb is the one used, *e.g.*, in v. 23 ('neglect') or in 19:27,29. It therefore speaks not so much of the physical condition of the temple, as of the fact that *God has departed from it* (*cf.* Ezk. 10:18–19; 11:22–23). Its physical destruction (24:2) is only the outward completion of God's repudiation of it, which will be symbolized in 24:1 when Jesus leaves it, never to return. The repeated second person pronoun ('to you' is unfortunately omitted in RSV) emphasizes that it is now just that, *'your* house', not God's house. *Cf.* Jeremiah 12:7 for a similar warning, whch preceded the previous destruction of the temple by the Babylonians in 587 BC. The theological background to this theme is set out in 1 Kings 9:6–9. The temple is the symbol of God's relationship with his people; when that relationship is broken, the temple is abandoned.

**39.** *Again* is a weak translation concealing the important Matthaean phrase *ap' arti*, 'from now on', used also in 26:29; 26:64. In each case, together with the introduction *I tell you*, it points to a new situation now beginning, an eschatological change. Jesus is now leaving the scene of Jewish public life, in which he has made his unheeded appeal; the next meeting will be very different. *Blessed is he who comes in the name of the Lord* echoes the greeting (drawn from Ps. 118:26) on his previous entry to Jerusalem (21:9). Does this mean, then, that a time will come when Jerusalem will welcome him again, when Israel will accept him as its Messiah? Is this a hint of Paul's teaching on the future salvation of Israel (Rom. 11:25–26)? Two factors tell against this interpretation. Firstly, the words *until you say* are expressed in Greek as an indefinite possibility rather than as a firm prediction; this is the condition on which they will see him again; but there is no promise that the condition will be fulfilled.[2]

---

[1] The last word is omitted by some MSS, perhaps to harmonize with Lk. 13:35, but is probably part of Matthew's original text.

[2] For the conditional nature of the prediction, see D. C. Allison, *JSNT* 18 (1983), pp. 75–84.

Secondly, a prediction of future repentance would be quite out of keeping not only with the flow of thought throughout ch. 23 (of which this is the climax) and ch. 24 which deals with judgment to come, but also with the perspective of the Gospel as a whole, which has repeatedly spoken of Israel's last chance, and of a new international people of God (8:11–12; 12:38–45; 21:40–43; 22:7; 23:32–36; *etc.*) Even more clearly the *For* with which the verse begins unambiguously links it with God's abandonment of his house in v. 38. All this suggests that this verse, while it expresses the condition on which Israel may again see its Messiah, makes no promise that this condition will be fulfilled.[1]

## D. JESUS' TEACHING ABOUT THE FUTURE (24:1 – 25:46)

This is the fifth and last of the great 'discourses' or collections of Jesus' teaching, marked off by the recurrent concluding formula found in 7:28; 11:1; 13:53; 19:1 and 26:1. Its theme is the future repercussions of his ministry, the ultimate consummation of the kingdom of heaven. Central to this passage is the theme of judgment: judgment on Jerusalem, in 24:1–35; the judgment associated with the parousia, in 24:36–51; two great parables of judgment, in 25:1–30; and the scene of the final judgment, in 25:31–46. As judgment was also a key theme of ch. 23, it is sometimes argued that chs. 23 – 25 form a single discourse on judgment. Certainly there is a continuity of theme, as we shall see on 24:1–2; but the two passages are differently conceived, ch. 23 as public teaching in opposition to the scribes and Pharisees, chs. 24 – 25 as private teaching to the disciples. The pronounced change of scene and of audience in 24:1–3 indicates that Matthew saw chs. 24 – 25 as a separate discourse. Jesus' public teaching is now finished; this (like all the five great discourses, with the partial exception of ch. 13) is instruction for disciples only.

Chapter 24 poses great problems for the interpreter. It begins by talking about the coming destruction of the temple (which was to take place in AD 70 as a result of the Roman repression of

[1] See full discussion in Garland, pp. 204–209.

the rebellion of AD 66), but by the end of the chapter it seems clear that the scene has moved to the parousia, the final 'coming' of the Son of man. Both events are combined in v. 3 in the question of the disciples which sparks off the discourse, and which further specifies that the parousia will mark 'the close of the age'. What, then, is the connection between these two events, and how may we decide which parts of the chapter deal with the one and which with the other? How far is this a prediction of events within 'this generation' (v. 34), and how far is it concerned with the end of all things? Or are the two so closely connected that we must conclude that Jesus mistakenly expected his parousia and the 'close of the age' to take place within 'this generation'? These questions will necessarily underlie the detailed commentary that follows, but a few general remarks at this point may help to indicate the overall perspective of this commentary.[1]

(a) The fact that the destruction of the temple and the 'close of the age' can be dealt with together in this chapter indicates that there is a close *theological connection* between them. Both are aspects of the consummation of Jesus' ministry. Both involve a judgment which will vindicate him as God's true and last word to his people. We have noted previously the way language about the 'coming of the Son of man', derived from Daniel 7:13, can be applied to different phases in the completion of Jesus' mission (see on 10:23; 16:28; and on 26:64, below); this means that we must be prepared to find similar language applied to different historical situations which in their different ways embody the progressive fulfilment of Jesus' mission as the Son of man.

(b) One clear aim of this chapter is to prevent *premature excitement* about the parousia. This theme will recur most clearly in vv. 4–5, 6b,8,14,23–28,36, and the whole chapter seems to aim to damp down rather than to promote an expectation of an immediate 'close of the age'. Such an emphasis would consort very strangely with a declaration that the parousia *must* occur within the generation.

---

[1] Other interpreters take different positions; for a critique of my approach see D. Wenham in H. H. Rowdon (ed.), *Christ the Lord*: Studies in Christology presented to Donald Guthrie (1982), pp. 127ff., esp. pp. 138–142.

(c) A theological connection between the events of AD 70 and the close of the age does not in itself imply that they must take place at the same time. This implication is found rather in such language as 'immediately after the tribulation of those days' (v. 29) and 'this generation will not pass away until . . .' (v. 34). The tension between such words (if they are interpreted as referring to the parousia) and the overall emphasis mentioned in the previous paragraph is striking. Nor is this tension much lessened by speaking, as commentators regularly do, of a 'prophetic perspective' which telescopes nearer and more distant events; if Jesus gave such a specific first-century AD date for the parousia, no amount of 'prophetic perspective' can make a delay of nineteen hundred years acceptable. When we find, however, that v. 36 openly disclaims any knowledge by Jesus of 'that day and that hour', it seems questionable whether Jesus *could* have intended such a specific date.

(d) All this (and much more) points towards the view that the time references of vv. 29 and 34 (and therefore also the content of the intervening verses) refer not, as is generally assumed, to the parousia, but to the coming judgment on Jerusalem. I have argued this case (with reference to the parallel passage in Mark) in my *JOT* (pp. 227–239), and in the commentary that follows I shall attempt to explain it in more detail. In a nutshell, however, this view is that v. 36 marks a deliberate change of subject, where Jesus turns from answering the first part of the disciples' question ('when will this (*i.e.* the destruction of the temple) be?') to the second part ('and what will be the sign of your coming and of the close of the age?'). Verses 4–35 therefore say that the temple will be destroyed within 'this generation', but that that event is not to be identified with the parousia; vv. 36ff. show that the date of the parousia is, by contrast, unknown even to Jesus himself, and therefore calls for constant readiness. However close the theological connection between the two events, they are thus not only implicitly but quite deliberately presented as *historically distinct*.

(e) The whole chapter is deeply indebted to the language of the Old Testament, not by way of direct quotations, but by the constant use of the language particularly of the apocalyptic parts of the Old Testament (esp. Daniel). Sometimes there is a clear allusion to a specific passage; more often the language is reminiscent of recurring apocalyptic themes. It is important in interpreting this chapter to recognize the conventional associations of such language, and not to attempt to interpret literally terms which had an accepted figurative significance in such contexts. In dealing with vv. 29–31 we shall have cause to keep this factor particularly in mind.[1]

On the interpretation here adopted vv. 4–35 form a continuous whole referring to the coming judgment on Jerusalem; but for convenience we may subdivide the chapter into smaller units.

## (i) Jesus foretells the destruction of the temple (24:1–2)

As we have seen on 23:38, Jesus' *leaving the temple* symbolizes the end of its relevance in the purpose of God. The fact that he goes from there to the Mount of Olives (v. 3) may be a further echo of Ezekiel 11:23, where 'the glory of the LORD', on leaving the temple, stops at the same point. The disciples' preoccupation with *the buildings*, therefore, may be due not only to a tourist's fascination (which they well merited – see the description in Josephus, *Ant.* xv. 392–402, 410–420) but also to incredulity that Jesus could be repudiating such a noble structure dedicated to the glory of God and still in the process of completion. But Jesus in response goes beyond the repudiation of the temple to foretell its total destruction. Micah (3:12) and Jeremiah (7:12–14; *cf.* 26:1–19) had dared to make a similar prediction about Solomon's temple, and it had been fulfilled in 587 BC, but Jewish apocalyptic belief in Jesus' time was that the temple was indestructible. Jesus' prediction became known and was quoted in a garbled form at his trial (26:61) and at his execution (27:40). It was the starkest expression of his rejection of Jewish nationalism and of those leaders whose power was focused on the temple and its rituals.

[1]The language is so typical of Jewish apocalyptic that it is often argued that much of the chapter originates not from Jesus but from a non-Christian Jewish apocalypse incorporated (with Christian additions) by Mark into his Gospel and taken over by Matthew with further Christian elaboration. There is no reason, however, why Jesus should not have used standard apocalyptic language, and the contents of the chapter do not in fact agree with the regular themes of Jewish apocalyptic as fully as this theory requires: see, *e.g.*, Jeremias, *NTT*, pp. 125–126. For full discussion of the origins of the chapter see D. Wenham, *The Rediscovery of Jesus' Apocalyptic Discourse* (*GP*, IV, 1984).

*(ii) Warnings against premature expectation (24:3–14)*

**3.** In Mark 13:4 the disciples' question apparently relates only to the date of the destruction of the temple. In Matthew it is expanded to cover not only *this* but also *the sign of your coming and of the close of the age.* This last phrase is governed by a single definite article in Greek, which indicates that the 'coming' (*parousia*) and the 'close of the age' are descriptions of the same event. The effect is to allow Jesus' reply in the remainder of the chapter to distinguish this eschatological event from the destruction of the temple, and this is consistently done. But the linking of the two events by the disciples shows that the destruction of the temple was of such momentous significance that to them (and no doubt to all who heard of Jesus' prediction) it seemed that it must be the beginning of the end. It is Jesus' task, then, to extend their horizons, to make them realize that a continuation without the temple until the 'close of the age' is possible, that the end of the temple (and with it of the special status of Judaism) is not necessarily the end of all things. *Parousia* ('coming') is used only in this chapter in the Gospels (vv. 3,27,37,39), though in the Epistles it is used several times of Jesus' return in glory. Its literal meaning is 'presence' (as in 2 Cor. 10:10), but it was used for official visits by high-ranking persons, state visits, and also for divine visitations, hence its technical use for Jesus' ultimate 'visitation'. The expression *the close of the age* (*synteleia tou aiōnos*) will recur in 28:20; strictly it could refer to the conclusion of any era (not necessarily the final one), and it has sometimes been taken here to refer to the end of the 'Jewish age', *i.e.* the time of transference from a national to an international people of God. But generally in apocalyptic such expressions point to a more 'final' conclusion (for references see Gundry, p. 477), and the phrase has already occurred in that sense in 13:39, 40,49.

**4–5.** Jesus' reply begins immediately with what is to be one of its main themes, the danger of being *led astray*, of jumping too hastily to eschatological conclusions. *In my name* does not mean they come with, or even claim, his authority, but rather that they aim to usurp his place. He is the only *Christ*, and anyone else claiming that role is an impostor. In the years leading up to the Jewish War there were many nationalistic leaders who collected a popular following (Acts 5:36-37; 21:38 mention only a few of them), and while they are not specifically recorded as claiming to be the Messiah, there is little doubt that their followers tended to see them in that light (see Bruce, pp. 320-322).

**6-8.** Similarly, wars and natural disasters could be interpreted, and often were in the ancient world, as 'signs of the end'. But these things are, and always have been, part of human history; they *must take place* as part of God's overarching purpose, not in any specific connection with *the end*. Verse 7 makes the point by echoing Isaiah 19:2, which foretold similar events in Old Testament times. *The beginning of the sufferings* (lit. 'birth-pangs', a technical term in apocalyptic for the period of suffering which must lead up to the new age) suggests that, while all such events have an ultimate connection with the final consummation, they are far from being its immediate precursors, and so cannot be used to plot its nearness. All that is mentioned in vv. 5-8, then, is presented precisely as *not* being 'signs of the end'.

**9-12.** These verses similarly speak in general terms of the sufferings to come, not now in relation to the world at large, but more with reference to Jesus' disciples. They will, as he has predicted already, be persecuted and hated. (*Cf.* 10:17-22, a passage closely related to this, and closer in wording to the parallel passage in Mk. 13:9-13. It is interesting that here, in contrast to both 10:17-22 and Mk. 13:9-13, the persecution is to come from *all nations*, not just from the Jews; in ch. 10 a mission to Jews only was in view (10:5-6, 23), but now an international involvement of the disciples is envisaged, as 28:18-19 will spell out.) This persecution will take its toll, in that *many will fall away* ('be tripped up', the same verb as in 5:29-30; 13:21; 18:6-9; *etc.*; here it echoes particularly Dn. 11:41), and the disciple group itself will be the scene of betrayal, hatred, false prophecy and *wickedness* (lit. 'lawlessness'). And lawlessness will lead to the cooling off of *love*, a connection to be noted. *Most men's love* is literally 'the love of the many', which could mean disciples' love *for* 'the many' outside; but the sequence of thought in these verses, where it is the disciple group itself which is under pressure, suggests that it means that 'the majority' (of the disciples) will cool off in their love, whether for God or for their fellow-men. It is a sombre picture of a church in decline. All this, the context indicates, is part of the history which must run its course before 'the end' comes; but there is no indication as to the temporal relation between such a situation and 'the end'.

**13.** Endurance is a prominent apocalyptic theme (*cf.*, *e.g.*, Dn. 12:12–13). When the majority 'cool off', only those who *endure* will *be saved*, *i.e.* only they will enjoy the blessings of the new age. *To the end* does not necessarily point to the apocalyptic consummation (as though those who have lived earlier cannot be saved!), but is a standard phrase for 'right through' (it lacks the article, which would be needed, as in vv. 6 and 14, to refer to 'the End'). The whole verse is repeated from 10:22, where it clearly related to the contemporary situation of the mission to Israel, not to 'the close of the age'.

**14.** For *gospel of the kingdom*, see on 4:23. Verse 9 ('by all nations') has already hinted at an extension of the disciples' mission beyond the limits imposed in 10:5–6 and 15:24, and now Jesus points clearly to a time when Israel's special priority will be over, and the gospel which Israel (in its leaders – see ch. 23) has largely rejected will be preached to the Gentiles. The *world* is *oikoumenē*, lit. 'the inhabited area', a standard term originally for the Greek world (as opposed to barbarians), then for the Roman Empire, and subsequently for the whole of the then known world; it is thus not so much a geographical term which must include every area and community now known to be on earth, but rather an indication of the universal offer of the gospel *to all nations*, *i.e.* outside the confines of the Jewish community. (This extension does not, of course, imply any cessation of the mission to Israel; see on 10:23.) *Then the end will come* may seem at first sight to allow the calculation of a date for the final consummation; but that would depend on defining a specific time or situation which could be regarded as 'the preaching of the gospel throughout the whole world'. In one sense Paul could claim long before AD 70 to have 'fully preached the gospel' in a large area of Asia and Europe (Rom. 15:19), and at many times since then similar claims could have been made with reference to an area far wider than the *oikoumenē* known in Jesus' time. But Jesus' words allow no such calculation. *The end* cannot come *until* the gospel has reached far outside the Jewish world, but that gives us no warrant for deciding when it *must* come.

### (iii) The coming crisis in Judaea (24:15–28)

Verses 4–14 have been in a sense a digression, indicating what are *not* to be regarded as 'signs of the end'. We now return more directly to the question of v. 3, 'When will this be?' Verses 15–22 describe the crisis which will soon come upon Judaea, and which will be the prelude to the destruction of the temple predicted in v. 2; vv. 23–28 then go on to give further warnings against premature eschatological expectation even in that terrible situation – even then, 'the end is not yet'.

**15.** *The desolating sacrilege* is a literal Greek rendering of the phrase rendered 'the abomination that makes desolate' in Daniel 11:31; 12:11, which itself echoes the similar language of Daniel 9:27. An 'abomination' in Old Testament idiom is an idolatrous affront to the true worship of God, and the reference in Daniel was to the pagan statue which Antiochus Epiphanes set up in the temple at Jerusalem in 167 BC, thus 'desolating' the worship of the temple. Jesus thus looks for a repetition of this act of sacrilege, committed *in the holy place* (which would normally mean the temple itself, not just the city of Jerusalem – *cf.* Acts 6:13; 21:28); the phrase *let the reader understand* calls on those who read Daniel's words to apply them to their own situation (*cf.* Dn. 12:10). Mark 13:14, in defiance of the rules of grammar, makes *standing* a masculine participle, suggesting a personal 'abomination'; Matthew has substituted the more correct neuter, and so probably understands Jesus to have envisaged some 'thing' comparable to Antiochus' statue. Suggestions for the identification of such an 'abomination' in the period before the destruction of the temple include the emperor Gaius' attempt to set up a huge statue of himself in the temple (AD 40–41, and therefore far too early to be an immediate precursor of the crisis, as the context here demands – in any case, the plan was never carried out); the desecration of the temple by the Zealots in the winter of AD 67/8,[1] shortly before the Roman siege began (which is the time to which our text points, but involved no strictly

---

[1] Josephus, *BJ* iv. 150–157, *etc.*

340

idolatrous symbol); or the appearance of the Roman standards (regarded by the Jews as idolatrous) in the temple at its actual destruction in AD 70. This last would clearly be too late to allow escape from Jerusalem itself, but v. 16 speaks not of the city but of Judaea, which was to suffer savage devastation during and after the siege of Jerusalem. Whatever the precise fulfilment of Jesus' warning, it seems clear from what follows that it is in the events of the Jewish War of AD 66–70 that he sees the reappearance of Daniel's *desolating sacrilege*.

**16–18.** Its appearance is the cue for urgent flight; those in the countryside of Judaea must take to the hills as the Romans come to ravage the farmlands and villages. The man of leisure resting on his flat roof will have no time to collect his valuables, and the working-man in the field must make do with his working-clothes. It is a vivid picture of an urgent crisis. Eusebius (*H.E.* iii.5.3) tells us that before the siege some of the Jerusalem Christians, in response to 'an oracle given by revelation', fled to Pella in Transjordan. These words can hardly be that 'oracle' (Pella is not in 'the mountains', nor had anything yet happened to the 'holy place'), but Jesus' warnings may have inspired that later 'oracle'.

**19–20.** A refugee's lot is hard enough without extra impediments. *In winter* roads in Palestine were practically impassable with mud,[1] and *on a sabbath* gates would be shut and provisions unobtainable.[2]

**21–22.** For the horrors of the siege, see Josephus's *Jewish War*, *e.g.*, v. 512–518. Jesus' words recall Daniel 12:1, an eschatological vision which Jesus sees as at least foreshadowed in these catastrophic events. But the destruction will not be allowed to run its full course: the *days* will be *shortened*, perhaps in order to allow *the elect* to survive, or perhaps because the presence of *the elect* in the world mitigates the severity of God's judgment (*cf.* the 'righteous' in Sodom, Gn. 18:23–32). The passive verb ('be shortened') perhaps indicates that even the horrors of human warfare come within the providential control of the God to whom 'the elect' belong.

[1] J. Jeremias, *Jerusalem in the Time of Jesus* (1969), p. 58.

[2] See Banks, pp. 102–103, for this interpretation rather than the expectation that Jesus' disciples would feel obliged not to move on the sabbath for reasons of legalism.

**23–25.** Such a crisis will be a golden opportunity for the sort of Messianic pretenders already predicted in v. 5; in the urgency of Israel's need they will be eagerly welcomed as God's answer to her problems. Often in the church's history (and sometimes today) a period of crisis leaves God's people wide open to plausible perversions of the truth, particularly if they are accompanied by *great signs and wonders.* 'Miraculous' activity is, in the Bible, by no means always the work of God (*cf.* Dt. 13:1–3, on which this passage may be based). In such a situation *the elect* need to be forewarned (v. 25) if they are not to be *led astray* into a premature expectation of 'the end'.

**26.** Popular expectation was that the Messiah would appear *in the wilderness* (hence perhaps some of the excitement about John the Baptist; see on 3:1–3), and several of the rebel leaders of the first century did in fact operate from there (see on v. 5, and *cf.* Josephus, *Ant.* xx.97–99, 167–172). The *inner rooms* (lit. 'storehouses') probably indicates a secret place (as in 6:6), and may reflect the Jewish expectation of a 'hidden' Messiah, who would emerge from obscurity (*cf.* Jn. 7:27). Such notions are easily played on to create a false expectancy in the absence of any evidence, and Jesus insists that his return (unlike his first coming) will be no secret affair which some may fail to recognize altogether.

**27.** On the contrary, it will be as unmistakable and as universally visible as a flash of *lightning.* (Lightning is also sudden, and that may be part of the symbolism; but the preceding verses, and the reference to visibility *from the east . . . as far as the west*, indicate that that is not the main point.) Thus the mention of the parousia here is precisely in order to indicate that it is *not* to be looked for in the chaotic events of the Jewish War, but will be something of quite a different character.

**28.** The same point of the unmistakable coming of the Son of man is made by this proverbial saying, perhaps based on Job 39:30, though similar sayings are found elsewhere in the ancient world.[1] The reference is presumably to vultures rather than to *eagles* (which do not normally eat carrion); precise identification of species is not normally a concern of biblical writers, and in

[1] A. Ehrhardt, *The Framework of the New Testament Stories* (1964), pp. 53–58.

any case Aramaic used the same term for both types of large flesh-eating bird. As the presence of the vultures infallibly indicates where the corpse is, so there will be no need to search for the coming of the Son of man – it will be obvious.

*(iv) Climax of the crisis within 'this generation' (24:29–35)*

Verses 15-28 have spoken of Judaea's crisis, but without describing the climax of that crisis in the destruction of the temple. Yet this was the question which gave rise to the whole discourse (vv. 2–3). When, therefore, v. 29 speaks of a cataclysmic event 'immediately after the tribulation of those days', it is natural to expect that now Jesus is going to complete the account with a specific mention of the fate of the temple. But these verses contain no explicit mention of the temple. Instead, vv. 29–31 consist of a collage of Old Testament apocalyptic language, which to modern ears sounds like a description of the 'parousia and the close of the age' (*i.e.* the second part of the question in v. 3). Yet the events so described are explicitly dated within 'this generation' (v. 34), whereas the parousia cannot be so dated (v. 36); and v. 27 has just explicitly distinguished the parousia from the events of the siege of Jerusalem. All this suggests a need to re-examine the language of vv. 29–31 to see what is the appropriate reference of the Old Testament terminology of which they are composed.[1]

**29.** After the opening phrase (which by itself rules out a reference to an event expected at a time remote from the Jewish War) the words of this verse are drawn from Isaiah 13:10 and 34:4. Of these the first is a description, in the symbolic language of apocalyptic, of the fall of Babylon, and the second of God's judgment on 'all the nations', but particularly on Edom. Similar language is used elsewhere of God's judgment within history on cities and nations (*e.g.* Ezk. 32:7; Joel 2:10; Am. 8:9). While such language may be taken as foreshadowing some final cosmic disintegration, its immediate reference is therefore to temporal judgment, and particularly to the fall of political powers. If such colourful language is appropriate to the fall of pagan nations such as Babylon, it is surely still more suitable for the

---

[1]See above, p. 335, for reference to my discussion of the parallel passage in Mark, on which the following commentary is based.

destruction of Jerusalem, with all the momentous implications that must have for the status and destiny of the people of God. A literal application of this verse to the disintegration of the universe is therefore quite inappropriate. 'Only a pitiful pro-siness could imagine that Christ meant an actual dropping of the stars upon the earth.'[1]

**30.** Language about *the Son of man coming on the clouds of heaven* (the word *parousia* is *not* used here) is clearly an allusion to Daniel 7:13–14, which, as we have seen above (see on 10:23; 16:28), speaks not of a 'coming to earth', but of coming to God to receive vindication and authority. 'The coming of the Son of Man in the clouds of heaven was never conceived as a primitive form of space travel, but as a symbol for a mighty reversal of fortunes within history and at the national level.'[2] Such language therefore fits well with the apocalyptic language in v. 29 in describing the destruction of the temple, viewed as an act of divine judgment, whereby the authority of Jesus is vindicated over the Jewish establishment which has rejected him. (For this understanding of the significance of the destruction of the temple, *cf.* 23:29-39.) The language is allusive rather than specific, and depends for its force on a familiarity with Old Testament imagery which is unfortunately not shared by all modern readers!

*The sign of the Son of man in heaven* has been interpreted in many different ways. From a very early date it was understood as a visible appearance of a cross in the sky, but the text does not say this, and in the light of the symbolic language of v. 29 we should not expect such a literal interpretation. Some argue that the 'sign' *is* the Son of man himself, seen in his triumph. Others point out that *sēmeion* is the LXX translation for the 'standard' or 'banner' referred to in the Old Testament as a signal for the gathering of God's people; see, *e.g.*, Isaiah 11:12; 49:22. The 'standard' and the 'trumpet' (also mentioned here in v. 31) together become fixed in Jewish liturgical language about the 'gathering of the exiles'.[3] At any rate it is clear that we are still in the area of apocalyptic symbolism, and that a literal identifica-

[1]D. Lamont, *Christ and the World of Thought* (1934), p. 266.
[2]G. B. Caird, *Jesus and the Jewish Nation* (1965), p. 20.
[3]See T. F. Glasson, *JTS* 15 (1964), pp. 299–300.

tion of 'the sign of the Son of man' is not likely to be possible.

The triumph of the Son of man will be greeted by the *mourning* predicted in Zechariah 12:10–14.[1] *All the tribes of the earth* is better translated 'all the tribes (families) of the land', for in Zechariah 12:10-14 the mourning is explicitly restricted to the families of Israel.[2] What is in view here, then, is not so much a world-wide lamentation, but the response of Israel when they see the vindication of 'him whom they pierced'. In Zechariah 12 the mourning was one of repentance; does Jesus then here hint at a future repentance of Israel, or is that to read too much into the allusion?

**31.** Again the language is recognizably drawn from the Old Testament.[3] For the *loud trumpet call*, see Isaiah 27:13 (and see on the 'sign' in v. 30, above), and for the subsequent phrases especially Deuteronomy 30:4 and Zechariah 2:6 (LXX). Such passages refer to the regathering of Israel's exiles, but now those to be gathered are described as the *elect* (*cf.* vv. 22, 24, and the same word translated 'chosen' in 22:14). The 'Son of man's people' are no longer merely the members of the nation, but (as in 8:11–12) a chosen remnant, drawn from all corners of the earth. This will be the necessary corollary of the vindication of the Son of man. *Angeloi* might be translated 'messengers' (as it is in 11:10), and referred to human preaching of the gospel throughout the world, or taken in its normal sense of *angels* (as the roughly parallel language of 13:14; 16:27 may suggest), in which case it refers to the supernatural power which lies behind such preaching. But whereas in 13:41 the 'angels of the Son of man' *gather* the evil *out* of his kingdom, here they *gather* the chosen into it. The reference is not, therefore, as in 13:41, to the final judgment, but to the world-wide growth of the church (*cf.* above, on v. 14), which is consequent on the ending of Israel's special status, symbolized in the destruction of the temple.

Thus when the significance of the Old Testament imagery is appreciated, vv. 29–31 may be recognized, as the context virtually demanded, as a highly symbolic description of the theological significance of the coming destruction of the temple and

---

[1]*Cf.* Rev. 1:7 for another combination of Dn. 7:13–14 with Zc. 12:10ff., where the 'piercing' of the one mourned is explicitly taken up, as in Jn. 19:37.
[2]See my *JOT*, pp. 237, 257.      [3]See my *JOT*, pp. 63–64, 256–257.

345

its consequences. The next four verses will go on to emphasize the imminence of 'all these things', before vv. 36ff. go on to distinguish the unknown time of the parousia clearly from the events envisaged in these verses.

**32–33.** Most common trees in Palestine are evergreen, so that the bareness of *the fig tree* in winter is conspicuous. Its large *leaves* do not appear until late in the spring, a sure sign of the approach of summer. *All these things* (*i.e.* probably the conspicuous events of vv. 15ff.) are similarly a sure sign that *it is near*.[1] As Jesus' discourse was prompted by the question when the temple would be destroyed, it is natural to see that reference here; the 'abomination of desolation' and the events which accompany it will surely mark the end of the temple and all that it stood for.

**34.** The time of this catastrophic event is now even more closely specified, and the solemn *Truly, I say to you* marks this out as a pronouncement to be noted. Those who interpret this passage as referring to the parousia must therefore either conclude that it proved to be untrue, or that *this generation* does not here carry its normal meaning. It has, for instance, been taken to mean 'the Jewish race', or 'unbelieving Judaism'. It is unlikely that such an improbable meaning for the noun would have been suggested at all without the constraint of apologetic embarrassment! Nor can *all these things* easily be taken to exclude the events described in the immediately preceding verses. On the natural understanding of this verse either Jesus was wrong (or Matthew has misunderstood him), or the discourse has not yet taken up directly the question of v. 3b, the 'sign of your parousia and of the close of the age', but has rather concentrated entirely so far on the first part of the disciples' question, 'When will *these things* (the destruction of the temple) be?'

**35.** Jesus' words (like *God*'s word, Is. 40:8!) can be trusted totally; another major hurdle, this, for those whose interpretation makes v. 34 at best misleading!

*(v) The unexpected parousia of the Son of man (24:36 – 25:13)*
As Jesus' reply to the disciples' question (v. 3) moves on to 'the sign of your parousia and of the close of the age', the emphasis

---

[1] RSV *'he* is near' is quite gratuitous. The Greek adverb *engys*, 'near', gives no indication of gender, and the subject of the verb is not specified.

falls consistently throughout these verses on the fact that the time of that parousia is not revealed, and that it will come when it is least expected – *i.e.* there is to be *no* 'sign' in the sense of a prior warning. Most will be caught unawares, but disciples must be in constant readiness. 25:13 echoes 24:36, and thus marks out this whole section as an extended discussion of the theme of the unknown 'day' and 'hour', a theme which recurs explicitly also in vv. 39, 42, 43, 44, 50, while its implications are drawn out in the various parables and other short sayings which make up the section. 24:36, 42 have parallels in Mark 13, and most of the rest of 24:37–51 has parallels in Luke 12 and 17, while 25:1–13 appears only in Matthew (though perhaps suggested by Lk. 12:35–37); it seems, then, that this section, like much of the great discourses of Matthew, is a collection of relevant sayings of Jesus brought together to underline the point initially introduced by v. 36.

**36.** *But of that day and hour* marks a deliberate change of subject from 'these things' which have been discussed in vv. 33–34. The time of 'these things' could be given a clear limit (v. 34), but no time is known for 'that day and hour'. As v. 3 has proposed a double agenda for Jesus' discourse, first 'these things' and secondly 'your parousia and the close of the age', it seems likely that it is the latter which is here taken up. This is confirmed by vv. 37 and 39 which specifically speak of the *parousia*, a word which has been conspicuously absent from vv. 4–35 (except to state in v. 27 that the parousia is to be distinguished from the period then under discussion). The date of the parousia, then, is unknown not only to men and even *angels*, but also to *the Son.* This title for Jesus occurs also in 11:27 (where see discussion); its omission from many MSS and early versions of the text (see RSV mg.) is probably due to doctrinal embarrassment at the attribution of ignorance to Jesus, a feature which is certainly unlikely to have been imported gratuitously into the tradition (and which is in any case undoubtedly part of the original text of Mk. 13:32). This is the clearest statement in the New Testament of a limitation of Jesus' knowledge, and it is perhaps significant that it is expressed in Father/Son language, a relationship which combines the ideas both of intimate unity and of filial dependence.[1]

**37-39.** If the time is unknown, it will catch people unprepared. The analogy with *the days of Noah* suggests that judgment is to be a major feature (though it is not the whole picture) of *the coming of the Son of man*. But the main point is the unpreparedness of Noah's contemporaries. Whereas Noah and his family were ready, everyone else carried on oblivious to the threat of judgment, and so, while Noah was saved, they were *swept away*. The implication is that it is possible to prepare for the parousia, not by calculating its date, but by a life of constant readiness and response to God's warnings and introductions. There will apparently be only two categories, the prepared (and therefore saved) and the unprepared (and therefore lost).

**40-41.** This radical division is reinforced by two cameos of ordinary life suddenly disrupted. Both men are involved in the same work in *the field*, both women in the same *grinding at the mill*. It is not a difference in work or situation which causes the separation, but a difference in readiness. (*Cf.* 13:30 for the idea of a coexistence of the 'saved' and the 'lost' until the final judgment.) *Taken* is the same verb used, *e.g.*, in 1:20; 17:1; 18:16; 20:17; it implies to take someone to be with you, and therefore here points to the salvation rather than the destruction of the one 'taken'. No indication is given of where they are 'taken' to; the point is simply the sharp division which the parousia will entail.

**42.** The practical conclusion to be drawn from vv. 36-41 is that of constant readiness, which will also be the focus of the rest of the chapter and of 25:1-13. The parallel verse in Mark (13:35) is the conclusion to a short parable about a door-keeper, which Matthew omits (no doubt because it makes the same point as Matthew's longer parable in vv. 45-51). *Your Lord (kyrios)* is in the Marcan version 'the master *(kyrios)* of the house', referring back to the parable; Matthew has drawn out the latent Christological overtones of the word (*cf.* on 7:21).

**43-44.** The point of vv. 36-42 is summed up in a little parable paralleled in Luke 12:39-40. If house-breakers (*broken into* is

[1] In the Gospel of John both themes constantly intertwine: see, *e.g.*, Jn. 5:19-30; 14:6-11.

literally 'dug through', an easy mode of entry into a mud-walled house) gave prior warning, no-one would be caught out; *the Son of man*, like the burglar, does not advertise the time of his arrival. The only precaution, therefore, is constant readiness. In view of such plain statements as this it is astonishing that some Christians can still attempt to work out the date of the parousia!

**45–51.** Another, longer parable makes a similar point, but also indicates what 'being ready' will mean in practical terms. It describes a *servant* (lit. 'slave') who is given overall authority as a steward during *his master*'s absence (*cf.* the responsibility given to the slaves in 25:14ff.). He can exercise his stewardship well (vv. 45–47) or badly (vv. 48–51). The way in which these options are described helps to give more concrete meaning to 'being ready'; it is not to sit quietly waiting, but to provide for the *household* (vv. 45–46) – *i.e.* it is in service to others that we prepare for the parousia. In contrast, unpreparedness consists in selfish exploitation of others (v. 49). So ' "to watch" means an active, laborious, responsible service'.[1] The reward for faithfulness is a place of higher and permanent responsibility (v. 47; *cf.* 25:21, 23); the punishment for failure is, literally, to be 'cut in pieces' (v. 51 – see RSV mg.), a savage feature of the story-scene which recalls the 'torturers' of 18:34 (*cf.* 1 Sa. 15:33; Heb. 11:37). But as in 22:13 and 25:30, the application also finds its way into the story, and so the slave's punishment is further described in the terms used earlier for the ultimate fate of the wicked (*cf.* 8:12; 13:42, 50). This fate he will share with the *hypocrites;* the unfaithful disciple can therefore expect no better fate than the 'hypocrites' who have been castigated in ch. 23 for not *doing* what their professed position demanded.

**25:1–12.** *The parable of the bridesmaids* is a further reinforcement of the same call for constant readiness for a 'coming' which will be at a time no-one can predict. This theme has already led to emphasis on a *division* between the ready and the unready (24:40–41, 45–51), and this is now drawn out more clearly in the contrasting fates of the *wise* and *foolish* (vv. 2, 8–9) 'in that day'. These terms have already been used to mark a similar division in 7:24–27 and in 24:45, and in each case the 'wise' have been depicted

---

[1] J. Lambrecht, in Didier, p. 328.

as those who are engaged in action appropriate to their professed status. This parable then is also primarily concerned with taking appropriate action in view of the coming 'day', so as not to be caught unprepared. When that happens, it will be too late to prepare, and *the door will be shut*.

It is disputed how far the details of the parable are intended to be given 'allegorical' identifications. To see the bridegroom as Jesus himself seems warranted in the light of 9:15. This would be a bold figure for him to use, as the Old Testament frequently describes *God* (not the Messiah) as the bridegroom, and Israel as the bride (Is. 54:4–5; 62:5; Je. 2:2; Ho. 1 – 3; *etc.*); but this would not be the only instance of Jesus' parables casting him in a role which is characteristically ascribed to God in the Old Testament.[1] In this context, where the focus is on the parousia of the Son of man, this identification seems required; and in that case perhaps it is reasonable to see the wedding feast as the Messianic banquet, as it was in 22:1–14 (*cf.* on 8:11). But to look for specific identifications of the oil (faith? good works?), or the bridesmaids, beyond being representatives of those who are ready or not, seems to be going beyond what the context requires. The story, vividly detailed as it is, is essentially a warning not to be caught unprepared, a warning which may apply to different groups at different times. It is a warning addressed specifically to those inside the professing church who are not to assume that their future is unconditionally assured; all ten are expecting to be at the feast, and until the moment comes there is no apparent difference between them – it is the crisis which will divide the ready from the unready.

**1–4.** *Then* clearly links the parable with the preceding warning; it is not a description of *the kingdom of heaven* in general, but of what will happen when God's sovereign purpose reaches its climax in the parousia of the Son of man. The details of the story are not all clear, as contemporary wedding customs are not fully known. The *maidens* may be attendants of the bride, or servants in the bridegroom's home, or perhaps friends and neighbours. (The term 'bridesmaids' in our heading is not necessarily to be read in a modern cultural context!) They are waiting to escort the bridegroom in festal procession, probably in the last stage of the cere-

[1] See P. B. Payne, *GP*, II, pp. 338–341.

monies as he brings his bride home for the wedding feast. It is apparently a torchlight procession, the *lamps* probably being 'torches' (of oil-soaked rags wrapped on a stick) rather than standing lamps, which are described by a different word in 5:15 and 6:22; the word used here regularly means 'torch'.[1] The addition 'and the bride' at the end of v. 1 (see RSV mg.) has early MSS support, but is more likely to have been added to complete the picture (a wedding without a bride *is* odd – but Jesus is not telling a complete story!), than to have been omitted by a church which had learnt to think of itself as the 'bride of Christ' (Eph. 5:23–32).

**5.** Jeremias (*PJ*, pp. 172–174) argues plausibly that *the bridegroom was delayed* by protracted negotiations over the financial settlement. The theme of a delayed coming has appeared already in 24:48, and will return in 25:19; it was no doubt already an issue when Matthew wrote – how could an 'imminent' coming be so long delayed? This parable, like the last (see 24:50), insists that delay is no excuse for not being ready at any time. That the girls *slumbered and slept* ('nodded off and were sound asleep' would get the sense of the Greek tenses) is no fault in itself, for both 'wise' and 'foolish' did so; during the 'delay' life must go on, and we cannot live on constant alert. The difference was whether they had already prepared for the summons, or had left preparation to the last minute, when it would be too late.

**6–10.** *Trimmed their lamps* is literally 'put their torches in order'. They are lighting them for the procession. A well-soaked torch would burn for a quarter of an hour or so, but those with no oil were no sooner lit than they went out. The rebuff given by the *wise* to the *foolish* (which should probably read more strongly than RSV: 'Certainly not; there will never be enough . . .') is not a charter for selfish unconcern for others, but its presence in the parable may be intended to remind us that no-one can ultimately rely on another's preparedness. The formal finality of *the door was shut* again hardly fits the atmosphere of a village wedding, but effectively makes the point that there is a 'too late' in God's time-table (*cf.* Heb. 3:7 – 4:13).

**11–12.** The application increasingly colours the story. The girls' appeal and the bridegroom's response recall the chilling

[1]Jeremias (*PJ*, pp. 172–174) discusses the story details at length, but relies too much on modern Arab customs! For a more sober discussion see A. W. Argyle, *ExpT* 86 (1975), pp. 214–215. For the 'torches' see further, *NBD*, p. 672.

words of 7:22-23; here, as there, *I do not know you* is a decisive formula of rejection, rather than a mere statement of fact (which could hardly to true of half of the bridal procession!). The formula of 22:14, 'Many are called, but few are chosen', would aptly sum up the point, which is similar to that of 22:11-13: it is not enough to be 'in on the act', to be a professing disciple; the disciple must also be prepared for the ultimate encounter. How we are to prepare, this parable does not specify, but the next one will take up this point.

**13.** This verse summarizes the message of the whole section which began in 24:36. If does not literally fit the story of the parable just told (neither wise nor foolish 'stayed awake' – which is what *watch* literally means), but uses a different metaphor to drive home the call for constant readiness.

### (vi) The parable of the talents (25:14-30)

The theme of 'being ready', which dominated the last section, is still at the centre of this parable, which again portrays a 'coming' and its consequences for those who should have been preparing for it.[1] But this parable takes up the question which that of the bridesmaids left unanswered: what *is* 'readiness'? It is not a matter of passively 'waiting', but of responsible activity, producing results which the coming 'master' can see and approve. For the period of waiting was not intended to be an empty, meaningless 'delay', but a period of opportunity to put to good use the 'talents' entrusted to his 'slaves'.

The English use of 'talent' for a natural (or supernatural) aptitude derives from this parable, and represents a common application of it to the need to 'live up to our full potential'. But of course the Greek *talanton* is simply a sum of money, part of the story-content of the parable, and our interpretation should not be influenced by the subsequent use of the word in English. In the context of Jesus' ministry the sums of money entrusted to the slaves are more likely to represent not natural endowments given to men in general, but the specific privileges and opportunities of the kingdom of heaven. The opportunities open to a disciple may differ in character and magnitude, but they are all to be faithfully exploited before the master returns. 'Readiness', therefore, consists in having already

[1] J. Lambrecht (in Didier, pp. 311ff.) in fact takes 24:36 – 25:30 all as a single section under the heading 'Exhortation to Vigilance'.

faithfully discharged our responsibilities as disciples, whether they have been small or great. It is the master who allocates the scale of responsibility; the slave's duty is merely to carry out faithfully the role entrusted to him.

A similar parable in Luke 19:12-27 makes essentially the same point, though it differs substantially in detail. The two are usually regarded as variant versions of the same original parable of Jesus, though opinions differ as to which might in that case be closer to the original. It is, however, at least possible that Jesus should have told similar stories on more than one occasion, changing the details in order to emphasize different areas of application for different audiences. At any rate, each should be interpreted on its own terms, not by means of the other.

**14-18.** *For* indicates a close link with the theme of 24:36 – 25:13, and particularly with the exhortation of v. 13. Slaves (*servants* is the usual English euphemism for this word) often rose to positions of great influence and responsibility (*cf.* 18:23ff.; 21:34-36; 24:45ff.). Even so, the sums entrusted to them are huge: a *talent* varied from place to place, and depending on the metal used for monetary purposes, but it was generally regarded as equal to 6,000 denarii (for which see on 20:1-7), so that in terms of modern purchasing power it represents thousands of pounds (*cf.* on 18:23-34). The allocation of these huge sums *according to ability* is not only commercial sense, but recognizes that God reckons with his people as individuals whose circumstances and personalities differ. The third servant failed to recognize his master's intention, and substituted security for service. To that (mistaken) end his action was entirely appropriate: 'Money can only be guarded by placing it in the earth', observed a later Rabbi (*Baba Metzia* 42a). But *cf.* 13:44 for the possible result!

**19-23.** For the *long time*, see on 25:5. *Settled accounts* makes it clear that they had been given the money specifically for trading – the profit accruing was no unexpected bonus, but was what was intended from the start (*cf.* the idea of Lk. 17:10). The 'reward' of faithful discharge of this responsibility is 'not a well-endowed pension, but even greater responsibility' (Schweizer, p. 471). It may be significant that both slaves receive identical commendations, despite the different scale of responsibility originally given to them; their achievement has been proportionately the same, however different their original endowment. *Enter into the joy of your master* is hardly commercial language (not even in GNB's more mundane version, 'Come on in and share my happiness'!); here, as in v. 30, the application is again creeping into the telling of the story.

**24–28.** The third servant has simply failed to grasp the nature of his responsibility. His failure is due not so much to laziness as to 'a sort of religious and oriental fatalism' (Bonnard). Underlying this was his view of his master (which the latter accepts with a grim irony in v. 26) as a 'rapacious capitalist' (Beare). Of course this characterization is not an allegorical description of God, any more than the less-than-ideal characters who represent God in other parables (Lk. 11:5–8; 16:8; 18:2–5; *etc.*). Even on this unflattering view of his master, however, his action was irresponsible; it represents a discipleship which consists of playing safe, and so achieving nothing (contrast 10:39), 'a religion concerned only with not doing anything wrong' (Schweizer, p. 473). 'Being ready' consists not only in keeping your slate clean, but in active, responsible, faithful service which produces results.

**29–30.** Verse 29 is a repetition of 13:12 (see comments there). In v. 30, as in 24:51, the story has been 'invaded' by its application, and the traditional description of the fate of the wicked (*cf.* 8:12; 13:42, 50) makes explicit that the parable is to be understood (as vv. 21, 23 had already hinted) in terms of the ultimate basis of salvation or condemnation.

### (vii) The last judgment (25:31–46)

The theme of judgment which has run through chs. 23 – 25 here reaches its superb climax. In particular the call to be ready for the parousia of the Son of man has increasingly raised the question of what constitutes readiness, of how one may be prepared. The preceding section has begun to answer this question; now we are taken further in our understanding of the criteria on which judgment is to be based.

This powerful description of the final judgment is sometimes misleadingly described as a 'parable'. In fact, while vv. 32–33 do contain the simile of a shepherd, otherwise this is a straightforward judgment scene, similar in its conception to the prophetic and apocalyptic visions of the 'day of the Lord' found in the Old Testament and in later Jewish literature, but going far beyond them in at least three ways: (a) the Son of man himself is at the centre, both as judge and as the one to whom men must respond in order to be pronounced 'blessed' (v. 34); (b) 'all the nations' are judged, not only the Gentiles; (c) the criterion of judgment is not their attitude to Israel, or even to God's law, but their treatment of Jesus' 'little brothers'.

Until fairly recently it was generally assumed that this passage grounded eternal salvation on works of kindness to all in need, and that therefore its message was a sort of humanitarian ethic, with no specifically Christian content. As such, it was an embarrassment to those who based their understanding of the gospel on Paul's teaching that one is justified by faith in Christ and not by 'good works'. Was Matthew (or Jesus?) then against Paul?

More recent interpreters have insisted, however, that such an interpretation does not do justice to the description of those in need as Jesus' *brothers*, nor to the use elsewhere in Matthew of language about 'these little ones' (see below, on v. 40). It is therefore increasingly accepted that the criterion of judgment is not kindness to the needy in general, but the response of the nations to *disciples* in need. The passage is sometimes described as an expansion of the theme of 10:40–42, where the gift of a cup of water is specifically 'because he is a disciple', so that 'he who receives you receives me'. Opinions vary as to whether Jesus had in mind specifically Christian *missionaries* (as the context in ch. 10 suggests), or pastors and teachers, or some other special group within the number of disciples (those insignificant ones who are 'greatest in the kingdom of heaven', 18:3–4). But on any of these views the criterion of judgment becomes not mere philanthropy, but men's response to the kingdom of heaven as it is presented to them in the person of Jesus' 'brothers'. It is, therefore, as in 7:21–23, ultimately a question of their relationship to Jesus himself.

This line of interpretation, which seems to be more truly in tune with the theological emphases of the Gospel as a whole, will be assumed in the following comments.[1]

[1] For a useful setting out of the suggested interpretations see G. E. Ladd in R. N. Longenecker and M. C. Tenney (eds.), *New Dimensions in New Testament Study* (1974), pp.

**31.** References to the *coming* of the *Son of man* in *glory* in association with *angels* have occurred already in 16:27–28; 24:30–31; and his *glorious throne* echoes 19:28. In commenting on those passages (and on 10:23) I have suggested that this fulfilment of the visions of Daniel 7 is something which Jesus expects progressively over the whole period from his resurrection to his parousia, as the 'everlasting dominion' predicted in Daniel 7:14 becomes increasingly a reality. Here we see the climax of the progressive fulfilment, for it seems clear from what follows that we are now transported to the ultimate manifestation of that authority in the final judgment associated with the parousia (which has been the focus of the whole discourse since 24:36). But Jesus goes beyond the vision of Daniel 7, for whereas in that passage the throne was that of God the judge, now it is the Son of man himself who sits on it as King (v. 34); moreover *all the angels with him* probably echoes Zechariah 14:5, where they accompany 'the LORD your God' in his coming to judgment. And in v. 32 the language recalls the gathering of all the nations for judgment in Joel 3:1–12, where again it is God who sits in judgment.[1] However, this divine figure still refers to 'my Father' as the one who has pronounced judgment; the context of thought seems close to that of John 5:19–29, where the Father has given to the Son 'authority to execute judgment, because he is the Son of man' (v. 27).

**32–33.** The point of the *shepherd* simile is to emphasize yet again the ultimate *division* among those who up to that point have been mixed up together (as *sheep and goats* regularly are in Palestinian flocks, the goats being hard to distinguish superficially from the sheep, which are not like the white varieties of Europe!); *cf.* the parables of ch. 13 for this emphasis on division, which has also been a key theme since 24:38. There is no middle ground between the saved and the lost. *Sheep* (which are more commercially valuable) are a regular Old Testament image for God's people, and so appropriately symbolize the 'blessed' here. *Right* and *left* in Jewish as in many cultures symbolize favour and disfavour, good and bad fortune.

**34.** For the Son of man as *the King*, *cf.* 13:41; 16:28; 19:28. The

---

191–199; also, more recently, Stein, pp. 130–140.     [1]See further, my *JOT*, pp. 157–159.

title reflects the ultimate destiny of the Son of man according to Daniel 7:14. But if *he* is king, what sort of *kingdom* can the righteous *inherit*? 19:28 suggested that his disciples will share his kingly authority, and 25:21, 23 defined the 'reward' as one of further authority. So the language here may indicate not merely the idea of 'entering *his* kingdom', but of a delegation or sharing of his authority, a 'kingship' of their own, under his. For *prepared, cf.* 20:23, where again it is a sharing in Jesus' authority 'in his kingdom' which is at issue. To know that this kingdom is established *from the foundation of the world*, sure and unalterable, is solid assurance for persecuted disciples in a hostile world.

**35–36.** The hardships listed recall those promised in ch. 10 to Jesus' disciples in their mission, and are strikingly echoed in Paul's description of his experiences as a Christian missionary in 2 Corinthians 11:23–27. The acts of kindness expected in response to these hardships recall Isaiah 58:7; the list is repeated four times in this passage, and is clearly meant to be remembered as a guide to practical discipleship. It is by such acts that one prepares for the judgment.

**37–39.** While *righteous* usually denotes character or behaviour, it can also have a more forensic sense, 'acquitted', and so here it denotes those on whom a favourable verdict has just been pronounced (*cf.* 13:43, 49). Their failure to recognize whom they were helping is eloquent testimony to the condescension of the king who is present incognito in his humblest follower.

**40.** For Jesus' *brethren, cf.* 12:48–50; 28:10. It is a term specially for his disciples, not for men in general. The reference to *the least of these* in this connection reminds us of 'these little ones' in 10:42, which was taken up more fully in 18:6, 10, 14. (See above, on these verses and on 18:5.) In 10:42 the reference is particularly to disciples sent out in the master's name; in ch. 18 it refers more to relationships within the church. It seems, therefore, inappropriate to relate 'the least of these' here to a specific group. It is in *any* brother of Jesus, however insignificant, that Jesus himself is served, and it is *that* service which is therefore the criterion of judgment, as it indicates how one responds to Jesus himself. It is important to note that, in each of the passages which refer to 'these little ones', the point is to declare the importance of such people because of their identifi-

357

cation with Jesus (see esp. 10:40, 42; 18:5). 'It is the nearest that Matthew, or the synoptic tradition generally, comes to the conception of the Church as the Body of Christ' (Green, p. 206).

**41.** As in 7:23, the ultimate sentence is to *depart from me, i.e.* loss of fellowship with Jesus. For *fire* as a picture of hell, *cf.* 5:22; 13:42, 50; 18:8–9. Here, as in 18:8, the fire is *eternal*, a word which may convey either the sense of 'going on for ever' or that of 'belonging to the age to come'. If it is the former, the reference might be either to a fire which never goes out because it is constantly fed with new fuel, even though the fuel does not last for ever, or to an unending experience of burning for the *cursed*. It is clear therefore that the terminology of this verse and of verse 46 does not by itself settle the issue between those who believe that hell consists of endless conscious torment and those who see it as annihilation.[1] Whereas the 'kingdom' in v. 34 was prepared for the blessed, the fire here is not *prepared* for the cursed, but rather *for the devil and his angels;* the cursed are going to a fate that was not meant to be theirs.

**42–45.** As in vv. 37–39, the dominant note is one of surprise. Jesus' way of assessing service is not that which comes naturally; as so often, his teaching here turns the world's standards upside down. The 'guilt' of the cursed arises not so much from doing wrong things as from failure to do right. As in 25:1–12 and 14–30, to do nothing is seen as the road to condemnation.

**46.** Throughout this passage there have been only two classes of people, the blessed and the cursed, those 'for' and those 'against' (*cf.* 12:30). So now there are only two destinies (*cf.* Dn. 12:2). For *eternal*, see the note on v. 41. But whereas 'fire' and *punishment* might carry within them the idea of annihilation, *life* by its very nature excludes the possibility of termination. If 'everlasting' is an 'unfortunate mistranslation' in relation to the fate of the wicked, it is clearly an essential part of what *eternal life* must convey.[2]

---

[1] To translate *aiōnios* as 'everlasting' instead of 'eternal' has the effect of foreclosing this issue by allowing only that sense of *aiōnios* which 'annihilationists' would argue is not required in this context. Hence Tasker's comment (p. 240) on the AV use of 'everlasting' in vv. 41 and 46: 'It would certainly be difficult to exaggerate the harmful effect of this unfortunate mistranslation'!

[2] On the relevance of these verses to discussion of the fate of the wicked, see C. Brown, *NIDNTT*, III, pp. 98–100.

# V. THE DEATH AND RESURRECTION OF JESUS
## (26:1 – 28:20)

We now come to the events which, particularly since 16:21, have been insistently predicted as the climax and indeed the essential purpose of Jesus' ministry. This is no more 'appendix' or 'epilogue' (as has sometimes been suggested by those who see the essential structure of the Gospel in the five 'books' concluded by the five great discourses; see above, pp. 59–62); rather Martin Kähler put the emphasis in the right place when he described the Gospels (with some exaggeration!) as 'passion narratives with extended introductions'.

From now on Matthew follows Mark's narrative very closely (unlike Luke and John, both of whom, while maintaining the same basic order of events, drew on important independent traditions). Virtually everything in Mark 14 – 15 reappears in Matthew 26 – 27 (except for some less essential narrative details), and little is added beyond Matthew's typical allusions to Scripture, and his own distinctive way of telling the same events. The most obvious non-Marcan section in chs. 26 – 27 is the account of Judas' death in 27:3–10, and that, like the narrative in chs. 1 and 2, is really an extended fulfilment-story, structured around one of Matthew's formula-quotations. Most striking is the absence of any teaching of Jesus from these chapters; apart from a few key sayings, Jesus is silent. The time for teaching, and therefore the time for response to Jesus' appeal, is past. There remains only the work he came to do.

Through these chapters run two complementary emphases. On the one hand, Jesus goes obediently to a fate which 'must' happen in fulfilment of the Scriptures. The Son of God is willingly carrying out his Father's purpose. There is no sense of his being the unfortunate victim of forces too strong for him; he is in charge. But at the same time there is equal emphasis on the deliberate and responsible actions of those who are determined to do away with him, primarily the Jewish leaders but also the Jewish crowd, and especially the traitor Judas. Thus God's saving design and man's malevolence are here woven together into an immensely powerful drama, which will conclude in ch. 28 with the ultimate triumph of Jesus as the risen Lord of all.

## A. PREPARATION FOR THE PASSION (26:1–46)

### (i) Introduction (26:1–2)

The last use of Matthew's formula (cf. 7:28; 11:1; 13:53; 19:1) includes now the word all, perhaps to emphasize that this is the end of Jesus' teaching. There may be a deliberate echo of the similar formula which concluded Moses' teaching in Deuteronomy 32:45. Jesus' reminder of his earlier predictions of the passion (16:21; 17:22–23; 20:18–19) serves now to underline that what is about to happen is planned by God (even before it is 'planned' by men in vv. 3–5!), and that Jesus knows and accepts it beforehand. The fact that it is to happen at the Passover is no coincidence; the commemoration of Israel's rescue from Egypt is the appropriate time for the ultimate act of redemption to occur.[1] The significance of the Passover typology will become more obvious in vv. 17–30. After two days probably means 'the day after tomorrow'. 'Passover day' itself was Nisan 14, when the lambs were killed in the late afternoon, but the term was used loosely for the whole festival period, including especially the eating of the Passover meal, which was in the evening which began Nisan 15 (the Jewish 'day' began at sunset). The date could now therefore be either Nisan 12 or 13. The chronology will be discussed on v. 17.

### (ii) The plot against Jesus (26:3–5)

3–4. A meeting of the chief priests and the elders under the chairmanship of the high priest sounds like a semi-formal meeting of at least a sub-committee of the Sanhedrin, in which these two groups were the dominant part. It is striking that the scribes and the Pharisees, who have been the most prominent antagonists of Jesus in the Gospel so far, are not mentioned now that the time for official action has come. Indeed, Pharisees appear again only

[1] Cf. the Palestinian Targums on Exodus 12:42, which identify 'four nights' to be remembered, of which the Passover night is the third, and the night of future Messianic redemption the fourth. See B. D. Chilton in GP, I, pp. 28–32.

in 27:62, and scribes in 26:57; 27:41 (several mentions of 'scribes' in Mark 14 – 15 are omitted by Matthew). They were represented in the Sanhedrin, but here in Jerusalem it is the priestly and aristocratic group who make the running, and Matthew's emphasis on their initiative from now on makes it plain that it is the official representatives of Israel who have now finally rejected the Messiah. *Caiaphas*, who is not named by Mark, was High Priest from AD 18 to 36.

**5.** The fear of *a tumult among the people* was a real one in the light of Jesus' reception in 21:8–11, 15–16. But they could hardly delay until after *the feast*, as Jesus would presumably leave Jerusalem, while an arrest before the feast could hardly help, as the crowd was already there and had already been listening to Jesus' 'inflammatory' teaching for some days. Jeremias (*EWJ*, pp. 71–73) therefore suggested that *en tē heortē* means not 'during the feast' but 'among the festival crowd'; *i.e.* they wanted a less public opportunity to arrest Jesus. This translation is improbable, but it correctly points up their dilemma; an arrest was possible only *during the feast*, and yet it was bound to cause trouble *unless* it could be done *by stealth* (v. 4). It was to this dilemma that Judas' offer provided the unexpected answer (vv. 14–16).

*(iii) The anointing at Bethany (26:6–13)*
Instead of proceeding straight to the answer to the authorities' dilemma, Matthew, following Mark, first relates a story which stands dramatically over against the atmosphere of intrigue and hostility in vv. 3–5, 14–16. (In placing the story here Mark followed his frequent 'sandwich' technique, where one story is inserted into the middle of another to draw attention to the way one interprets or balances the other.) It is a story of anointing, which must inevitably suggest the Messianic mission of Jesus ('Messiah' = 'anointed'); and it shows Jesus prepared for his death in fulfilment of that mission. So behind the human plots of the priests and Judas stands Jesus' deliberate acceptance of Messianic suffering.

All four Gospels have a story of a woman anointing Jesus. Matthew, Mark and John all place it at Bethany in the context of the passion, though John differs from the others in detail (including the date – he places it before the entry to Jerusalem).

Luke 7:36-50, however, differs so much both in setting and in content (it is in Galilee, in a Pharisee's house, it involves a 'sinner', and gives rise to Jesus' teaching on forgiveness and love) that it may well relate to a separate and earlier incident; in that case the action of the woman (unnamed, except in John) here may be in deliberate imitation of that earlier tribute of love.

**6.** *Bethany*, where Jesus had close friends (Jn. 11:1-2; 12:1-2; *cf.* Lk. 10:38-42), was where Jesus and his disciples spent at least the first night during this Passover week (see on 21:17, but also below, on vv. 30, 36). *Simon the leper* is otherwise unknown to us. He was presumably a well-known local figure, perhaps one whom Jesus had cured (as one who was still a *leper* could not entertain guests to dinner) but whose nickname remained as a reminder of his former disease.

**7.** The *very expensive ointment* is identified by Mark and John as 'nard', *i.e.* spikenard, an extremely expensive luxury imported from India, used especially for anointing the dead (*NBD*, p. 855). This last fact gives point to Jesus' comment in v. 12, but there is no suggestion that the woman herself saw it in that light; it was not uncommon for guests at a banquet to be anointed, but the use of such an expensive oil was an act of extravagant devotion. It may well be that she did it to express her belief that Jesus was the Messiah.

**8-9.** The objection is not voiced, as in Mark, by 'some'; still less, as in John, only by Judas; but by *the disciples*. Perhaps by recording this Matthew wishes to warn his readers that it is possible for sincere Christians to adopt such an unbalanced sense of values that they regard as *waste* what is in fact a 'beautiful' act of devotion to Christ. Their concern for *the poor* is admirable, but it is a question of priorities.

**10-11.** Jesus' reply establishes the right priorities for that situation. This was a *beautiful* act (perhaps 'noble' or 'admirable' would better convey the sense of *kalon*), because it recognized the special nature of this occasion when Jesus was still present. The continuing obligation to help *the poor* is not in the least decried; indeed v. 11, with its echo of Deuteronomy 15:11, assumes that that obligation will always apply to Jesus' disciples. But that duty must not be turned into a rigid regulation which allows no room for the spontaneous (and even extravagant) expression of devotion to Jesus.

**12.** Of course a *body* would not normally be anointed *for burial* before it was dead! Rather this was done for the corpse (see Mk. 16:1; Lk. 23:56 – 24:1; Jn. 19:39–40). Jesus' interpretation of the woman's act therefore seems to assume that his death will be that of a criminal, whose body would not be buried with proper ceremony; Matthew will accordingly make no further mention of anointing in connection with Jesus' burial.

**13.** Individual acts of charity to the poor are soon forgotten; not so this loving 'extravagance'. *This gospel* is a remarkable phrase for Jesus to use in this context. The phrase has been used already in 24:14, again with reference to a 'world-wide' preaching (though here the word is *kosmos*, an even more all-inclusive idea than *oikoumenē* – see 24:14), but whereas there the 'gospel of the kingdom' might have been taken to be simply Jesus' teaching, here it is clear that it includes also his life, and particularly the events of his passion.

*(iv) Judas joins the plot (26:14–16)*

**14.** We now pick up from v. 5, and see the answer to the dilemma of *the chief priests. Judas Iscariot*, hitherto mentioned only in the list of the twelve in 10:4, now becomes the central actor in the drama (26:14–16, 21–25, 47–50; 27:3–10 all focus on him). His involvement is on his own initiative, and comes across in v. 15 as a cold business proposition. The reason for his action can only be guessed. John 12:6 tells us that he had an eye for financial gain, and the sum involved (equal to 120 denarii, for which see on 20:2) was not inconsiderable, but few have been able to believe that this was enough to cause such a radical volte-face. If he was the only Judaean in the group (see on 10:4) he may have resented the leadership of the Galilean fishermen, but even cultural pride would hardly turn him against one whom he still believed in. More likely he was disillusioned that Jesus' idea of Messiahship (just graphically confirmed in v. 12) was not that for which he had joined the movement; with the threat of imminent official reprisals instead of the triumphant leadership of Israel he may have been hoping for (*cf.* 19:28), it was time to get out before it was too late. He may even have concluded sincerely (as did Saul of Tarsus) that Jesus was after all a false prophet, who must be destroyed. Whatever the reason, Matthew does not present him as a reluctant informer. For the place of his decision in the purpose of God, see on v. 24.

**15.** To *deliver him* would mean in that situation to inform them, as only one of his constant companions could, of where among all the Passover crowds he could be secretly arrested, to avoid a popular uproar. *Thirty pieces* (shekels) *of silver* was the sum laid down as compensation paid to an owner for the loss of a slave (Ex. 21:32); but Matthew's mention of the specific sum is clearly intended to echo Zechariah 11:12, where that same sum is 'weighed out' (the same word in LXX as *paid* here) as the derisory 'wages' of the rejected shepherd, who was a Messianic figure.[1]

**16.** *From that moment* is the same phrase as was used in the formula of 4:17; 16:21 to mark a new beginning. It implies that the ball has now been set rolling, and all that now remains is to find *an opportunity*.

So the scene is set. 'The calm prediction of Jesus is contrasted with the furtive plottings of the Jewish leaders. The devotion of the faithful woman who prepares Jesus for his death is counterpointed by Judas' calculated betrayal. . . . The section 26:1–16 is a striking overture to the events and themes of Matthew's Passion' (Senior, p. 50).

*(v) The Last Supper (26:17–30)*
Despite the plots of vv. 3–5, 14–16, these verses show us Jesus in charge of the situation. He knew the priests' purpose before they had formulated it (v. 2), and he is already well aware of Judas' role (vv. 21–25). He now initiates the process which will lead without a break throughout these chapters to its climax on the cross. Its context, we are not allowed to forget, is the Passover, and it is with Jesus' 'Passover' meal, giving startling new meaning to a familiar ritual, that the process begins.

**17.** Properly speaking the feast of *Unleavened Bread* ran from Nisan 15 to 21, but Passover day itself, Nisan 14, was loosely included in that period (in fact it was on the evening which began Nisan 14 that leaven began to be removed from the houses: Mishnah *Pesaḥim* 1:1–3), and so it is referred to here as *the first day of*

---

[1] See further, on 27:9–10, for Matthew's use of this Old Testament passage.

*Unleavened Bread.*[1]

*To eat the passover* unambiguously points to the Passover meal, which was officially eaten on the evening which began Nisan 15. (Remember that the Jewish day began at sunset and not, like ours, at midnight.) But the Gospel of John (see esp. Jn. 13:1; 18:28; 19:14) plainly dates the Last Supper on the night which began Nisan 14 (*i.e.* the night *before* the regular Passover meal), so that Jesus in fact died on the afternoon at the end of Nisan 14, the time when the Passover lambs were killed. This date is also suggested by Paul's language about Christ being 'sacrificed as our Passover' (1 Cor. 5:7), and is supported by the independent Jewish tradition that Jesus was executed 'on the eve of the Passover'[2] as well as by the fact that according to astronomical calculations Nisan 15 never fell on a Friday between AD 27 and 34 (Finegan, pp. 292–296).

Is Matthew (following Mark) then wrong in describing this as a Passover meal and in dating its preparation on Nisan 14? The matter is too complex for full discussion here, and has given rise to innumerable theories, many of which depend on the quite unsupported assumption that Jesus operated on a different calendar from that of official Judaism. The simplest solution, and the one assumed in this commentary, is that Jesus, knowing that he would be dead before the regular time for the meal, deliberately held it in secret one day early. Luke 22:15–16 indicates Jesus' strong desire for such a meal with his disciples before his death, and his awareness that the time was short. Of course it was strictly incorrect to hold a 'Passover' at any time other than the evening of Nisan 14/15, but Jesus was not one to be bound by formal regulations in an emergency situation! (This would also explain the lack of any mention of a lamb, the central feature of the Passover meal; the lambs had to be ritually slaughtered in the temple, and this could not be done until the next day. It was therefore a Passover meal in intention, but without a lamb.)

The date of the preparation and eating of the meal was, therefore, as Matthew states, Nisan 14 (*i.e.* the evening which *began* that day; the killing of the lambs would take place later that

---

[1]Josephus also refers to the 14th as 'the day of unleavened bread' (*BJ* v. 99); see further, Gundry, p. 524, for the frequent confusion of Passover and Unleavened Bread in Josephus.

[2]*Sanhedrin* 43a; so also the 2nd-century Gospel of Peter 2 (5).

same 'day', *i.e.* before sunset the next afternoon, as Mk. 14:12 indicates), and not the normal date of Nisan 15. It is our unfamiliarity with the Jewish reckoning of days which has caused most interpreters to think that in speaking of Nisan 14 Mark and Matthew meant the evening *following* the sacrifice, rather than the evening *preceding* it. In Jewish terms, the sacrifice in the afternoon and the regular Passover meal that same evening were on different 'days'.[1]

**18–19.** Matthew has dispensed with Mark's picturesque account of the disciples following the man with the waterpot, by substituting *a certain one*, a Greek phrase which functions like our 'so-and-so' to indicate that Jesus gave full details, but Matthew is not including them. It seems, especially from Mark's account, that Jesus had an existing agreement with the owner of the house for the use of a large room (such a room was unlikely to be available in Jerusalem at Passover time without prior arrangement). *Kairos (time)* often refers to an appointed, climactic moment, the time of fulfilment or consummation (see, *e.g.*, 8:29; 13:30; 21:34). Like the Johannine references to Jesus' 'hour' (Jn. 2:4; 7:30; 12:23; 13:1; *etc.*; Matthew has a similar use in 26:45) it shows Jesus' conscious fulfilment of a predetermined plan.

**20.** *When it was evening* suggests a time shortly after sunset, but the Greek *opsias genomenēs* means more generally 'when it was late'. If Matthew's dating of the preparation of the meal on Nisan 14 (and therefore not before sunset) is to be taken precisely, then the meal itself would have begun some time later. (*Cf.* the use of the same phrase in 14:23 for a period long after 14:15, where *opsias genomenēs* was already used!) *Sat at table* is literally 'reclined', the normal posture by New Testament times at least for a special meal such as the Passover (see Jeremias, *EWJ*, pp. 48–49).

**21–22.** Mark's version of Jesus' words includes the phrase 'one who is eating with me', generally agreed to be an allusion to Psalm 41:9. While we might have expected Matthew to retain so suitable an allusion to the fulfilment of Scripture, perhaps he has felt it unnecessary to do so explicitly, as the whole story of vv. 21–25 (esp. v. 23) inevitably recalls that Psalm to those who knew it. This is the first time Jesus' predictions of his passion have

[1] I have spelt out this understanding of the chronology more fully in *Hokhma* 9 (1978), pp. 9–14.

explicitly included the treachery of *one of you*, though *betray* here is the same Greek word as 'deliver' in 17:22; 20:18; 26:2, where the person responsible was not specified. *Very sorrowful* is a rather weak translation for a phrase which contains Matthew's favourite word for violent emotion, even shock (used in 17:6, 23; 18:31; 19:25; 27:54). They are so shaken that they cannot even trust their own self-knowledge – though the form of their question might be better translated, 'You can't possibly mean me, can you?'

**23.** Since the meal was eaten from a common *dish* into which all those present would frequently *dip* their *hands*, this is no more specific an identification than v. 21. It is hard to imagine that, if Judas had been openly identified as the traitor, he would have been allowed to leave the room unhindered (unless, of course, the disciples thought Jesus was talking about some indefinite time in the future). Jesus' failure to be more specific here is another example of his willingness to let events take their course. (Even Jn. 13:21-30, with an apparently specific identification, finishes with the eleven mystified as to Judas' purpose: Jn. 13:28.)

**24.** Here is the paradox of the whole passion story in a nutshell – the events must happen *as it is written*; but this does not excuse the deliberate betrayal. This same paradox of God's sovereign purpose and man's responsibility runs through the early Christian preaching of the cross (see Acts 2:23; 3:13–19; 13:27–29). *Cf.* 18:6–7 for the same paradox in a wider context.

**25.** Only Matthew records this direct question and answer, and in view of the general lack of clear identification noted on v. 23, we must assume that it was a private conversation. Judas, surely disingenuously, uses the same incredulous form of question as the others (see on v. 22), but it is interesting that instead of *kyrie* ('Lord' – see on 7:21) Judas, here and in v. 49, uses *Rabbi (Master)*, a term appropriate to any Jewish teacher, and not used at all by the other disciples in Matthew. So his question, in comparison with theirs, rings hollow, and Jesus need only turn it back upon him, *You have said so*. In 26:64 and 27:11 there is an element of qualification (not of evasion) in this form of words, in that the charges made, even if true, are not in the words Jesus himself would have chosen; it is thus 'an affirmation modified

only by a preference for not stating the matter *expressis verbis*.[1]
But in all these cases it is clearly affirmative, picking up and
accepting the answer already proposed by the question (like the
American idiom, 'You got it'!).

**26.** J. Jeremias (*EWJ*, pp. 84–88) has helpfully outlined the
normal course of the Passover meal, which (with the exception of
the lamb) we may assume was followed at Jesus' anticipated
'Passover'. The thanksgiving over the bread and the cup
recorded in vv. 26 and 27 will therefore be a regular part of the
main section of the meal (making this the third of the four cups of
the Passover), and we may reasonably assume that Jesus used the
traditional words of thanksgiving. *Blessed* refers, of course, to
blessing God, not blessing the bread; the form of words was
'Blessed art Thou, O Lord our God, King of the Universe, who
bringest forth bread from the earth'. But Matthew, taking these
well-known words for granted, records only the startlingly
unfamiliar words which Jesus added, and which would hence-
forward form the basis for the Christian meal which took the
place of the old Passover. The Passover ritual had its own words
of explanation for the food and drink, relating to the events of the
deliverance from Egypt; but now Jesus gives a new interpretation
in terms of a new and greater deliverance.[2]

In describing the broken bread as *my body*[3] Jesus at least makes
unmistakably clear that he is to be violently killed; any hopes his
disciples may still have cherished, that he did not mean what he
said about going to Jerusalem to die, are now dramatically dis-
pelled. That was no doubt hard enough to accept, but in commanding them specifically to *eat* (and in v. 27 to *drink* – only Matthew
includes these imperatives, making more explicit the 'Do this' of
1 Cor. 11:24–25) he goes further, and introduces the concept of a
personal participation in the effects of that death, a concept more
powerfully spelt out in John 6:48–58. If the eating of the Passover
meal served to identify the Israelite with the redemption from
Egypt, so does this 'eating' and 'drinking' convey the benefits of

[1] D. R. Catchpole, *NTS* 17 (1970/71), p. 217.

[2] For the different forms in which Jesus' words are recorded, and for a proposal for the
original Hebrew or Aramaic form, see Jeremias, *EWJ*, pp. 138–203, and his summary in
*NTT*, pp. 288–292.

[3] The verb *is*, here and in v. 28, should not, of course, be taken in a crudely literal sense; *cf.*
13:19–23, 37–39, where the same verb is used throughout to indicate a symbolic equivalence.

Jesus' paschal sacrifice to those who share his table.

**27–28.** The words over the cup fill out this idea. *Blood . . . poured out* is unmistakably sacrificial language, and the allusive phrase *for many* (for which see on 20:28) identifies that 'pouring out' as that of the Servant of God of Isaiah 53:12, who 'poured out his soul to death', as 'an offering for sin' (Is. 53:10). So the whole idea of vicarious suffering for the sins of God's people which runs throughout Isaiah 53 underlies these words. Matthew makes this even more explicit by adding *for the forgiveness of sins*. And that last phrase, together with the mention of *the covenant*, echoes Jeremiah's prophecy (31:31–34) of a 'new covenant' leading to the forgiving and forgetting of the sins of God's people.[1] The phrase *blood of the covenant* (echoing Ex. 24:8) recalls that God's relations with his people had always depended on the sacrificial shedding of blood, and this new covenant is no exception.

So these words, rich in Old Testament associations, indicate that Jesus' death will inaugurate the new relationship between God and his people to which the prophets looked forward. To speak of a covenant is to speak of a community of the people of God. From now on this community will be constituted by the sacrifice of Jesus, and will consist of those who by 'eating' and 'drinking' are identified with the benefits of his sacrificial death. Here, then, is the theological foundation for the theme, which has emerged throughout this Gospel, of a new basis of membership of the people of God. The Passover which brought about the formation of the nation Israel under the Sinai covenant (*cf.* the allusion to Ex. 24:8) now points forward to a new redemption constituting a true Israel in distinction from the merely national community of the old covenant.

**29.** Jesus' words over the bread and the cup have focused on death. But beyond that death lies life, in *my Father's kingdom*. *Again* represents the important Matthaean phrase *ap' arti*, 'from now on' (for which see on 23:39); it 'serves to mark a point in time which separates the two situations of "now" and "one day" ' (Trilling, pp. 86–87); a new day is now dawning. The words *fruit*

[1] The word 'new' occurs before *covenant* in many early MSS, as it does also in the disputed text of Lk. 22:20, and unquestionably in 1 Cor. 11:25. But even if it was not an original part of the text in Matthew (as seems likely), an allusion to Je. 31 is clearly implied in the words *for the forgiveness of sins*.

*of the vine* were part of the regular thanksgiving which Jesus will have used over the cup (v. 27), for which see Mishnah *Berakoth* 6:1. The next such 'feast' together will be with the *new* wine of the Messianic banquet (see on 8:11). Mark's version of this saying seems to refer only to the joyful prospect for Jesus himself, but Matthew's addition of *with you* makes it clear that that banquet is no private celebration, but an act of fellowship. The companionship of Jesus with his disciples, so soon to be broken by death, will be restored *in my Father's kingdom* (an unusual and lovely phrase, including the Father himself in that future family reunion of Jesus and his disciples). So the emphasis on death in the preceding words leads to a sense not of sombre finality, but of joyful anticipation of new life through death.

**30.** The *hymn* was presumably Psalms 115 – 118, the last part of the *Hallel*, which were sung at the end of the Passover meal. The *Mount of Olives* was *en route* for Bethany (see on v. 6), but Jesus has no intention of going back there for this night. According to Luke 21:37; 22:39 they regularly slept out on the slopes, as many Passover pilgrims did, rather than in Bethany itself.

*(vi) Jesus predicts Peter's denial (26:31–35)*
This short dialogue on the way to the Mount of Olives illustrates Jesus' remarkable concern for his chosen band of followers. Even in the face of his own impending suffering, he is aware that the coming ordeal will be too much for them, and so he continues to devote time to warning, explaining, preparing them. In this way, though they will still fail him at first, it will be possible for them to come to terms with the experience afterwards. As usual, Peter appears in the role of leader, in failure and restoration as well as in loyal service.

**31.** *Fall away* is literally 'be made to stumble', the same verb as in 5:29–30; 11:6; 13:21, 57; 15:12; 18:6–9; 24:10 (see the comments esp. on 11:6 and 18:6–9). It is the opposite to the response of accepting faith. *Because of me* indicates that it is Jesus' own ordeal which will 'trip them up'. Their failure will be due not merely to fear for their personal safety, but to inability to grasp the purpose of Jesus' suffering. This shockingly unheroic expectation of the fate of the Messiah and his followers is then shown to be already *written* in Zechariah 13:7, a rather cryptic passage which is probably to be understood as one of a series of pictures in Zechariah 9 – 14 of a humble rejected Messianic figure, the shepherd-king.[1] In Zechariah 13:7-9 the shepherd who 'stands next to' God is struck by God's sword and the flock is scattered; but eventually one-third of them, refined and purified, are restored to be God's people. So the suffering of the Messiah has its devastating effect also on his people (*the flock*; cf. Lk. 12:32, and see further, my *JOT*, pp. 208-209), but will lead in time to their establishment as the Messianic community.[2]

**32.** This saying, another clear prediction of the resurrection (cf. 16:21, *etc.*), includes the new note of a renewed fellowship with the disciples after the passion. It will be taken up in 28:7, 10 and fulfilled in 28:16-20, where the scattered flock is regathered in Galilee. To *go before* might be a continuation of the shepherd image in the idea of the shepherd leading his flock (cf. the same verb in 2:9); but the verb *proagō* also means to go on ahead and so to get there first (*e.g.* 14:22; 21:31), and the story in ch. 28 suggests this meaning here. When they leave for Galilee, rather than leaving a corpse behind in Jerusalem, they will find a risen Lord is already there ahead of them!

**33-35.** For the idea of *denying* Jesus, cf. on 10:32-33. The alternative, for the follower of a crucified Messiah, is to *deny* oneself (16:24). Peter (and the others, v. 35b) has as yet no understanding of the choice which will be required; to him it is a simple black-and-white issue of principle. But Jesus' prediction in v. 31 was based on a more intimate knowledge of the pressures, both internal and external, which they would have to face. Matthew's omission (together with Luke and John) of Mark's 'twice' with reference to the cock-crow is typical of his tendency to leave out unnecessary narrative details. Cocks were expected to crow at regular times during the night, of which the second (about 1.30 a.m.) was the most important for time-keeping, and so could be spoken of as *the* cock-crowing.[3]

---

[1] For a valuable exploration of this theme, see F. F. Bruce, *This is That* (1968), pp. 100–114.

[2] See further, my *JOT*, pp. 65, 107–109, 154 for the significance of the quotation, and *ibid.*, pp. 241, 246 for its text-form. The first person verb, *I will strike*, which replaces an imperative in the Old Testament text, does not materially change the meaning, as the imperative is addressed by God to his sword; in either case, God is clearly the agent.

[3] See H. Kosmala, *Annual of the Swedish Theological Institute* 2(1963), pp. 118–120; 6(1968), pp. 132–134 for the punctuality of cocks in Jerusalem; cf. also Senior, p. 96 n. 5 To make an

*(vii) Jesus' prayer in Gethsemane (26:36-46)*

This remarkable narrative, which probably lies behind John 12:23-28 and Hebrews 5:7-10 as well as the explicit Synoptic accounts, gives perhaps the most intimate insight into the nature of Jesus' relationship with his Father, as well as into the cost of his Messianic mission. It blends together the reality of his humanity with the uniqueness of his position as Son of God. At the same time it illustrates the weakness of the disciples, and prepares us for their subsequent failure.

Dunn (pp. 17-20) has a useful discussion of objections raised against the historicity of the account, particularly the observation that the disciples could hardly have recorded words spoken while they were asleep! See on this also Gundry (p. 533), to which one might add that Luke's account of forty days of post-resurrection teaching allows plenty of opportunity for Jesus to inform them of what he had gone through on this momentous night. The story is told throughout from Jesus' point of view rather than that of the disciples (in contrast with, say, 17:1-8).

**36.** *Gethsemane* (meaning 'oil-press') was a 'garden' (Jn. 18:1), perhaps an enclosed olive-orchard, on the slopes of the Mount of Olives. It was a regular rendezvous for Jesus and his disciples (Jn. 18:2; *cf.* Lk. 22:39-40), perhaps their overnight bivouac for the festival (*cf.* above, on vv. 6, 30), so that Judas knew where to find them. Jesus could easily have foiled his plan by choosing a different place for this night, but, as we saw on v. 23 above, this was not his intention.

**37-38.** The three who accompanied Jesus at the transfiguration (see on 17:1) are with him now apparently simply for companionship. But it may be significant that it is these three who have explicitly declared their readiness to share Jesus' fate (20:22; 26:35); they are now called to share with him in preparing for it, and even at this level they will fail. *To be sorrowful and troubled* hardly does justice to the Greek verbs which suggest an anguish of wretchedness. *My soul is very sorrowful* (again a weak translation of the uncommon word *perilypos*, 'deeply grieved'; *cf.* Mk. 6:26) is an echo of the LXX translation of the refrain of Psalms 42 – 43,

---

issue of historical harmonization out of this obvious simplification is surely pedantic: see the notorious example in H. Lindsell, *The Battle for the Bible* (1976), pp. 174-176.

'Why are you cast down, O my soul . . .?', the lament of a righteous sufferer who knows his hope in God will ultimately be vindicated. *Even to death* probably indicates the scale of his grief (as in Jon. 4:9), but may also define its cause – it is grief as he approaches death. In this emotional turmoil Jesus wants company (*with me* is added by Matthew to make this plain); that the Son of God should want the 'moral support' of three fishermen (and that he should be disappointed, v. 40) is a supreme illustration of the paradox of the incarnation.

**39.** While others sometimes *fell on their faces* before Jesus (17:6; *cf.* Lk. 5:12; 17:16), this is the only time Jesus is said to have prostrated himself. The posture indicates the strength of the emotion which leads to prayer. But the address *My Father* (*cf.* on 6:9; 11:25–27) lifts the whole episode from that of an abject appeal to the intimate communion of the Son of God with the Father, whose will he delights to do. The issue is not whether or not Jesus should accept the Father's purpose, but whether that purpose need include the horrifying *cup* (see on 20:22) of vicarious suffering, or whether there is some other way. Hence the remarkable blend in this verse of a clear request with the acceptance that that request might not be granted – a blend which could well be imitated in much of our praying, with its often peremptory demands. The only issue that matters is what are the limits of the will of God. Jesus' prayer is an exploration of those limits, but never attempts to break outside them.

**40–41.** *Watch* means simply 'keep awake', and that is certainly its primary sense here and in v. 38. The specific *temptation* facing these three disciples was that of denying Jesus (vv. 31–35), and their failure when the test came was due to their failure now to share in Jesus' preparation for the ordeal. They would be, almost literally, 'caught napping'. But we have seen the same word *watch* used metaphorically in 24:42–43; 25:13, and no doubt Matthew expects the exhortation of v. 41 to be applied beyond the problem of inability to keep awake in this unique crisis. The weakness of *the flesh* is a permanent problem of Christian discipleship, which calls for constant vigilance and for the prayer which Jesus has already prescribed in 6:13.[1]

---

[1] *Spirit* and *flesh* are used here, unusually in the Gospels, for 'the will of man and his physical weakness'; see D. Hill, *Greek Words and Hebrew Meanings* (1967), p. 242.

**42.** Jesus' second prayer is an 'advance' on the first; the 'if it be possible' of v. 39 is now resolved, and so the tentative request gives way to a firm *thy will be done*. This direct echo of 6:10 is the third echo in Jesus' Gethsemane prayer of the Lord's prayer (*cf.* 'Father', v. 39, with 6:9; and v. 41 with 6:13) – Jesus practises what he had preached to his disciples!

**43–44.** Matthew's explicit mention of three prayers by Jesus on this occasion may be intended to contrast with the three denials in vv. 69–75 which will result from Peter's failure to share in Jesus' prayer.

**45–46.** Most modern versions take Jesus' first words here as a question, like that of v. 40. If they are read as imperative, as in the older versions, they must either be heavily ironical, or a significant time-lag must be assumed before the *Rise* of v. 46. For *the hour*, see on v. 18. The time of preparation is over, and the action is about to begin. *Let us be going* could suggest a desire to escape, but the verb implies rather going into action, advance rather than retreat. Jesus goes now willingly to meet the *sinners* through whom his Father's will is to be achieved. The use of the word *sinners*, here alone in Jesus' predictions of his passion, perhaps indicates some of the reasons for his revulsion in the face of 'this cup' (vv. 37–39).

## B. THE ARREST AND TRIAL OF JESUS (26:47 – 27:26)

### (i) The arrest (26:47–56)

Judas' movements have not been mentioned since Jesus let him know that he was aware of his intentions (26:25). Now we see that he has not been idle since then, and his plans are about to materialize. But even though on the surface it is Judas who takes the initiative at this point, the repeated message of these verses is that in fact it is Jesus who is in control. What happens happens only because Jesus deliberately refuses to prevent it, as he could easily do.

**47.** Judas is described as *one of the twelve* not simply to identify him (that is hardly necessary after vv. 14–16, 25), but to emphasize the shocking fulfilment of Jesus' prediction in v. 21. For the composition of the *great crowd*, see Blinzler (pp. 61–70), who concludes that they were a detachment of the 'police' who were at the disposal of the Sanhedrin (supported, according to Jn. 18:3, 12, by 'soldiers' who were in fact the Jewish temple guards), and suggests that the number, while 'great' in comparison with the unprepared disciple group, should not be overestimated – this was, after all, intended to be an 'undercover' operation (vv. 3–5).

**48–49.** For a Rabbi's disciple to *kiss* his master (on hand or foot) was not an everyday greeting, but a mark of special honour. Nor dare the disciple take this initiative uninvited; to do so was a 'studied insult' (*AB*, p. 329). The greeting of Jesus as *Rabbi* in this context is therefore heavily ironical (see on v. 25, the only other use of this address in Matthew, again by Judas). Judas' action thus not only identifies Jesus to the arresting party, but marks his own public repudiation of Jesus' authority.

**50.** Jesus responds with the word *Friend*, sometimes used for a 'table-companion', perhaps to remind Judas of his presence at the supper-table that evening; but in the two other uses of this form of address in Matthew (20:13; 22:12) there is an element of rebuke. The following words (lit. 'for which you are here') are obscurely elliptical, and could be construed as a command (as RSV mg.), a wish ('let what you have come for be carried out'), or even an exclamation ('What an errand you have come on!'). The interrogative construction adopted by RSV is less plausible; Jesus is well aware of Judas' errand, but none the less he does not resist, even encourages, its completion.

**51–52.** John supplies the names of both the disciple (Peter) and the high priest's slave (Malchus), and Luke tells of the restoration of the ear. But Matthew simply tells the bare facts in order to draw out the message of Jesus' rejection of violent resistance, with which he will in vv. 53–54 contrast the supernatural aid Jesus could have used if he so chose. Jesus' sovereign control of the events in which he appears as the helpless victim is thus highlighted. *All who take the sword will perish by the sword* is probably not just a proverbial maxim (it would in any case be untrue as a general observation), but may echo the interpretation of Isaiah 50:11 reflected in the Targum, which interprets the 'kindling of fire' as taking up the sword. Jesus thus lives out the principle of non-resistance which he has required of his disciples in 5:39–42. It is this issue of Jesus' non-resistance which is the context of this statement; a blanket endorsement of pacifism requires wider support than this one specific instance.

**53–54.** The disciple who tried armed resistance had simply misread the situation. Jesus is not a helpless victim, needing any human help available. He is being arrested because he chooses; if he wanted help he could call on far more than a few swords. (A *legion* was made up of 6,000 soldiers. Were the *twelve legions* one each for Jesus and the eleven remaining apostles?) His refusal to thwart his enemies' plans either by evasion (see on v. 36) or by supernatural power derives from his repeatedly voiced conviction that his mission must be one of rejection and suffering (see on 16:21; 17:22–23; 20:17–19, 28). Behind these earlier predictions it has not been hard to discern *the scriptures* as the source of Jesus' conviction; now that source is made explicit. And for Jesus there is no other option but that *the scriptures be fulfilled*. That issue had been settled in Gethsemane.

**55–56.** This attitude of Jesus makes the show of force by the Jewish leaders quite inappropriate. For *robber*, see on 27:38, where the same word is used. Far from leading an insurrection, Jesus has been *sitting teaching* as the Rabbis did. But even in this wrong association too Jesus sees *the scriptures of the prophets fulfilled*, thinking perhaps especially of Isaiah 53:12, 'he was numbered with the transgressors'. The disciples' flight immediately fulfils another prophecy, Zechariah 13:7, as Jesus had predicted in v. 31.

## (ii) The Jewish 'trial' (26:57–68)

Jesus is taken to Caiaphas' house at night, and from there to the governor's residence in the morning (27:1–2). On this all four Gospels agree. John tells us nothing of what took place there except Peter's denial. Luke 22:66 suggests that any legal proceedings were delayed until the early morning, after Peter's denial; but Matthew follows Mark in placing the proceedings during the night, before Peter's denial, with the verdict finally reached in the morning. By later Mishnaic law a capital trial could not be held during the night, and so it is possible that the 'trial' took place in two stages, first an informal, hastily convened gathering to determine the charge against Jesus, followed by a more formal verdict pronounced by the full Sanhedrin in the morning. But perhaps it is more likely that Matthew and Mark are speaking of a single protracted sitting which finally reached its verdict at day-break.[1]

It is uncertain how far this Jewish hearing may be described as, or indeed was intended to be, a formal 'trial'. If it was to result in execution it could in any case be only a preliminary to the Roman governor's official judgment (see on 27:1–2). Several features of the (admittedly very condensed) record do not tally with the rules for capital trials set out in Mishnah *Sanhedrin* 4–7, though it is in any case uncertain whether these late second-century rules were in force as early as the time of Jesus. Formal sessions of the Sanhedrin were not normally held at the High Priest's house (see Blinzler, pp. 112–114), so that while 27:1 suggests that (at least by the end of the hearing) the Sanhedrin as a whole had been assembled, it is probably better to see this not as a 'trial' proper, but as an *ad hoc* gathering to enable the Jewish authorities to agree on, firstly, the need to have Jesus executed (this being a matter of *Jewish* law), and secondly, an appropriate tactic to induce the Roman governor to impose the death penalty (which would, of course, require a charge of which Roman law could take cognizance); so Derrett, p. 407, note. Whatever the official status of the gathering, the Evangelists leave us in no doubt that it was not an unprejudiced hearing, but was convened specifically 'that they might put him to death' (v. 59)!

But Matthew clearly wants us to see more in this episode than a rather sordid manoeuvre by the priests. It is also the occasion of Jesus' climactic declaration, before the supreme authorities of Israel, of his Messianic mission. The apparently helpless victim of official suppression is progressively revealed as the builder of the new temple, the Messiah, the Son of God, and the one now to be enthroned as Lord at God's right hand. A rich irony thus underlies the whole scene, and the reader is enabled to see that it is the 'judges' who are judged.

Meanwhile in the background is the dismal figure of Peter, and Jesus' bold testimony is set in marked contrast with Peter's failure to confess his Lord; see further on vv. 69–75.

**57.** See on vv. 3–4; the similar wording here suggests that the

---

[1]So esp. Sherwin-White, pp. 44–46; *cf.* Blinzler, pp. 145–148.

same group was involved, and the fact that they *had* (already) *gathered* confirms that this is the planned working out of the decision made then. Even if as yet only a minority of the 71 members of the Sanhedrin had been summoned, one-third was recognized as a quorum.

**58.** The two protagonists are now in place; Jesus' ordeal will come first, then that of *Peter*. The introduction of Peter at this point is to enable the reader to hold both plots in mind, and to compare and contrast the performance of the two 'witnesses'.[1] The *courtyard* was the outdoor enclosed area where servants and 'hangers-on' not involved in the hearing would gather; for the limited access see John 18:15–16.

**59–60.** *Two witnesses* in agreement were essential for a legal condemnation to death (Nu. 35:30; Dt. 17:6; 19:15; the rule was fundamental to all Jewish law) and the authorities, despite their clearly hostile purpose, were concerned to have a valid case. Whatever the formal charge before the governor, it was important that Jesus should be known to have been correctly condemned under Jewish law. *Sought* is in the imperfect tense, which suggests a protracted search. Matthew's statement that they *sought false testimony* need not mean that they *wanted* it to be false, but may be a compressed way of saying that they sought any testimony which could be made to stick – and in the event what they were offered was false. But the charge which is offered in v. 61 is not stated (as it is in Mark) to be 'false' witness, and Matthew, by specifying that it came from *two*, seems to want us to conclude that, however malicious and misinterpreted, it does rest on a genuine saying of Jesus.

**61.** None of the Gospels has recorded these precise words as spoken by Jesus, but it is clear that he had more than once used words which could give this impression. The nearest 'equivalent' is John 2:19 (which John interprets as a prediction of the resurrection). That saying contains no 'threat' against the temple, but Matthew has already recorded Jesus' predictions (in a context of deserved judgment) of the destruction of the temple (23:38; 24:2), and his generally 'anti-temple' stance has been illustrated in 12:6 and 21:12–13. Stephen's alleged teaching in Acts 6:13–14 lends

---

[1] For this understanding of Matthew's dramatic composition, see further on vv. 69–75, and more fully B. Gerhardsson, *JSNT* 13(1981), pp. 49–51.

further weight to the probability that Jesus had been understood to be threatening to destroy and replace the temple, and the Sanhedrin must necessarily take a very grave view of such language, both from the point of view of theology and from that of national morale. 'To evoke, even conditionally, the destruction of "this temple" was to touch not just stone and gold and not only the general well being but history and hope, national identity, self-understanding and pride' (Meyer, p. 183). It was both sacrilegious and treasonable.

It is clear from the passage already mentioned that Jesus did believe that as a result of his mission the temple would no longer be at the centre of God's dealings with his people, and that it would be replaced by 'something greater' (12:6). But there is no suggestion anywhere in his teaching that this would be a literal rebuilding (and Mk. 14:58 makes it explicit that the new temple would be 'not made with hands'). See above on 12:6; 16:18 for the nature of the 'something greater', the new congregation of God's people focused not on a building but on Jesus himself. *In three days* is an idiom for a short time (Jeremias, *NTT*, p. 285), and need not be taken literally; but it is not surprising, and probably not unintended, that Jesus' disciples quickly saw in such language (as in the similarly cryptic saying in 12:39-40, a suggestive parallel to this) a prediction of the resurrection, as John records (2:21-22).

The sequence from Jesus' 'threat' against the temple to the question of his Messianic claim (v. 63) is not spelt out, but would be obvious to anyone versed in Jewish Messianic expectation. Zechariah 6:12 said that the (Messianic) 'Branch' would 'build the temple of the LORD', and this, together with Ezekiel's visions in chapters 40ff., led to a widespread expectation that the destruction of the existing temple and its replacement with a new and perfect one would be a feature of the Messianic age (see Senior, pp. 170-171; Meyer, pp. 200-202). The High Priest's question in v. 63 is thus the natural deduction to draw from v. 61.

**62-63.** Jesus' *silence* may be construed as another example of his refusal to prevent the course of events (*cf.* on vv. 23, 36, 53-54) – he could, as far as our evidence goes, have rightly denied having uttered a threat against the temple in the terms cited. But no doubt Matthew saw in his silence also the fulfilment of Isaiah 53:7. His silence allows the High Priest to assume his admission

379

of the charge, and therefore to press the theological implications of such language. *I adjure you* is a rare and formal expression (*cf.* 1 Ki. 22:16 for a similar Old Testament formula), invoking the name of God in order to compel a true answer. This is therefore the climax of the hearing, and Jesus' answer will be the crucial evidence. Even if (on the principle enunciated in 5:34–37) Jesus disapproves of the 'oath' element in the question, he can hardly fail to respond now.

But in any case he would not wish to remain silent, for the form of the High Priest's question goes to the heart of Jesus' own claims for his mission, and offers a suitable basis on which those claims can be reaffirmed and clarified. The question whether Jesus was *the Christ* (Messiah) was already a matter of open discussion, even before the charge in v. 61 (see 12:23; 21:9–11, 15; 22:41ff.), and no doubt Judas had further briefed the authorities on what was being said in private among the disciples. *Son of God*, while not frequently used as a title of the Messiah, was not necessarily introducing a new idea, as 2 Samuel 7:14 had said of David's son, who 'shall build a house for my name', that 'he shall be my son'; and on this basis (together with Ps. 2:7) at least the men of Qumran were familiar with the idea of the Messiah as God's Son (4Q Florilegium; perhaps also 1QSa 2:11–12). In any case, this too had been a feature of Jesus' public teaching, at least by implication (see on 21:37). The wording of Caiaphas' question (esp. in Mark) probably suggests that it did not even sound like a dispassionate enquiry: 'Are *you* the Messiah?' (you, the abandoned, helpless prisoner!); Lohmeyer[1] aptly describes the question as 'sarcastic or furious'.

**64.** However sarcastically intended, the High Priest's words corresponded to Jesus' claims. There is no doubt, then, that *You have said so* is to be understood, as in v. 25 (*cf.* also 27:11), as affirmative, though 'reluctant or circumlocutory in formulation'.[2] The element of reluctance, while perhaps partly attributable to Jesus' disapproval of the oath-formula (see on v. 63), is because what the High Priest understands by the words he has used (and particularly the political implications he can and will draw from them) is far from Jesus' conception of his Messianic role. So,

---

[1] *Das Evangelium des Markus*, p. 328.
[2] D. R. Catchpole, *NTS* 17 (1970/71), p. 226; see further, on v. 25, above.

while not refusing the titles offered, Jesus goes on to qualify their meaning: *But I tell you . . .* And this qualification lifts the whole idea of Messiahship out of the sphere of Jewish earthly politics into that of heavenly authority, while the title 'Christ' is quietly discarded in favour of *Son of man* (for which see pp. 43–45). *Seated at the right hand* echoes Psalm 110:1, already discussed in 22:41–46, but now explicitly applied to Jesus. *Power* is a typically Jewish reverential expression to avoid pronouncing the sacred name of God (which might have laid Jesus open to the charge of blasphemy, though ironically it was precisely that charge on which he was condemned, v. 65!). *Coming on the clouds of heaven* (together with the phrase 'the Son of man') is a clear allusion to Daniel 7:13, already similarly alluded to in 24:30. See above on 10:23; 16:27–28; 24:30 for the meaning of such language. We have seen that its natural application in terms of its Old Testament source is to the vindication and enthronement of the Son of man in heaven, not to a descent to earth. It is therefore in this verse a parallel expression to 'seated at the right hand of Power'; the two phrases refer to the same exalted state, not to two successive situations or events. In this verse the appropriateness of this interpretation is underlined by the fact that this is to be true 'from now on' (*hereafter* is a quite misleading rendering of the more specific phrase *ap' arti*, which, as in 23:39 and 26:29, denotes a new period beginning *from now*). Indeed it is something which Jesus' inquisitors themselves *will see* (an echo of Zc. 12:10, as in 24:30?), for it will quickly become apparent in the events of even the next few weeks (not to mention the subsequent growth of the church) that the 'blasphemer' they thought they had disposed of is in fact now in the position of supreme authority.[1]

Here, then, in Jesus' first open statement of who he is, he makes claims on a different level from those of the 'Christ' as popularly understood, and in so doing 'presents to the High Priest better weapons than he could have dreamed of'.[2]

**65–66.** *Blasphemy* in the Old Testament carried the death penalty by stoning (Lv. 24:10–23); it was therefore in Jewish law a sufficient ground for a capital conviction. The ritual *tearing of robes* (see Mishnah *Sanhedrin* 7:5) marked its seriousness, as this

---

[1] On the significance of this reference to Dn. 7:13 see further, my *JOT*, pp. 140–142.
[2] Gerhardsson, *JSNT* 13 (1981), p. 57.

action was otherwise expressly forbidden the High Priest, even in a context of personal mourning (Lv. 21:10). Just how Jesus' words constituted *blasphemy* is disputed. He had carefully avoided pronouncing the divine name (see on v. 64),which was the later strict definition of blasphemy (Mishnah *Sanhedrin* 7:5). To claim to be Messiah was hardly in itself blasphemous – it might after all be true! But to claim to be God's anointed in such an improbable situation (helpless, deserted by his followers, rejected by the leaders of God's people) might well be seen as 'taking God's name in vain', especially when the title 'Son of God' has been included in the claim, and when the words of v. 64 are added to this (sitting at God's right hand in glory), the total claim does indeed constitute 'an offensive encroachment on the prerogatives of God'[1] – unless, of course, it was true. Jesus' words thus left only two choices open to the authorities, either to accept his claim or to condemn him for this 'blasphemy'. They apparently did not find the choice difficult.

**67-68.** *They* should properly denote the authorities who have just pronounced sentence (though Mark mentions the 'guards', lit. 'servants', as also taking part). If such behaviour seems inconsistent with priestly dignity, Derrett (pp. 407-408) suggests, first, that only by such outward action could they visibly dissociate themselves from Jesus' 'blasphemy', and secondly, that the call to *prophesy: who is it that struck you?* (addressed, as Mk. 14:65 explains, to a blindfolded man) is itself a test of his claim, as the Messiah was expected to be able to do this. In any case we have already noted that the gathering was probably neither a formal 'trial' nor an unbiased group. It is likely that Matthew saw in this ill-treatment, as in the silence of Jesus in v. 63, another fulfilment of the prophecies of God's Servant (see Is. 50:6). It is also an occasion for Jesus to exemplify his own teaching in 5:39.

*(iii) Peter's failure (26:69-75)*
A valuable article by B. Gerhardsson[2] interprets this episode, together with the preceding, as a contrasting pair of examples on the theme of confession and denial. Jesus' bold confession before

---

[1]D. R. Catchpole, *The Trial of Jesus* (1971), p. 126; see *ibid.*, pp. 126-148, for full discussion of the question.
[2]*JSNT* 13 (1981), pp. 46-66.

the highest authorities contrasts with Peter's failure to do the same before their servants. In the background stand Jesus' words about the importance of acknowledging him before men (10:32–33).

Matthew's dramatic skill is further seen in the progressive aggravation of Peter's sin, both in the increasingly public nature of the challenge (one girl – one girl speaking to the bystanders – the bystanders as a group) and in Peter's response (evasion – denial under oath – cursing Jesus).

**69–70.** *A maid* is literally 'one servant-girl' (the latter word being a diminutive form), surely a deliberately ironic description: the bold Peter quails before one single slip of a girl! The description of Jesus as *the Galilean* is probably derogatory on the lips of a Judaean, rather than conveying (as it might have done in official circles) the suggestion of 'revolutionary' (Vermes, pp. 46–48). Peter's first 'denial' (not yet explicit) is *before them all*, thus emphasizing his guilt in the light of 10:33.

**71–74.** A Galilean *accent* was conspicuous, and was a matter of some ridicule in Judaean society (see Vermes, pp. 52–57). Peter's *oath* in v. 72 would be intended to confirm the veracity of his statement (contrary to Jesus' principle in 5:34–37), but the *curse* of v. 74 is different. The words 'on himself' are not in the Greek, and the verb used (*katathematizō*, equivalent to Mark's *anathematizō*, to 'pronounce anathema', for which *cf.* 1 Cor. 12:3; 16:22) does not elsewhere refer to a curse on oneself except where (as in Acts 23:12, 14, 21) this is explicitly stated. Did Peter then actually pronounce a curse on Jesus (as later Christians were required to do as proof of their apostasy)?[1] If Matthew and Mark have understandably refrained from stating this explicitly, it is the probable implication of the words they have used.

**75.** While the other Gospels all at least imply the subsequent rehabilitation of Peter (it is most explicit in Jn. 21:15ff.), Matthew will not mention him by name again. Perhaps, in view of Peter's subsequent history, he assumes that it is obvious; and no doubt he expects his readers to cast their minds back to passages like 16:17–19; 19:27–28. He may even have given deliberate hints to this effect in 12:32 and in the 'acted parable' of 14:28–31. Here,

[1]This is persuasively argued by H. Merkel in E. Bammel (ed.), *The Trial of Jesus* (1970), pp. 66–71, supported by Gerhardsson, *art. cit.*, pp. 54–55.

however, Peter's failure and remorse are unrelieved, and Jesus' shocking prediction in vv. 31–34 is amply fulfilled.

### (iv) Jesus is transferred to the Roman governor (27:1–2)

At the conclusion of their all-night hearing (see on 26:57–68 for the night/morning question) the Jewish authorities must now find a way of having their verdict implemented. The death penalty could be imposed only by order of the Roman governor (Jn. 18:31; Sherwin-White, pp. 35–43 has effectively quashed earlier doubts about this constitutional provision), but a charge of 'blasphemy' would carry no weight with him. It was therefore necessary to *take counsel* over an appropriate charge, and also, no doubt, over appropriate persuasive tactics. They could not expect an easy ride, as *Pilate the governor* (AD 26–36; his official title was apparently 'praefectus') was notorious for his obstinacy in refusing to accommodate to Jewish prejudices, his portrait in non-Christian Jewish sources being considerably less flattering than that in the Gospels![1] He would be resident in Jerusalem at Passover time, thought it is debated whether his residence (the *praetorium* of v. 27) was, as has been traditionally thought, in the fort of Antonia on the north side of the temple area, or in Herod's former palace on the West Hill (so Blinzler, pp. 173–176); most recent commentators favour the latter.[2]

### (v) The death of Judas (27:3–10)

This story interrupts the sequence of Jesus' trial, in the manner of a dramatic interlude. Indeed it can hardly fit chronologically between the decision of 27:1–2 (which is apparently its immediate cause) and its sequel in vv. 11ff., as it shows the priests apparently in the temple, with leisure to debate the buying of a field! But Matthew has appropriately inserted here the tradition of what happened to Judas, perhaps in order to form a suggestive contrast with the fate of Peter. Each is thus seen to have fulfilled Jesus' prediction (26:24 for Judas; 26:34 for Peter), but Peter's bitter weeping (of repentance? see on 26:75) contrasts with Judas' despairing remorse and suicide. Matthew's striking focus on Judas (26:14–16, 21–25, 47–50) is thus brought to its climax in a

---

[1] See esp. Josephus, *Ant.* xviii. 55–62, 85–89; Philo, *Legatio ad Gaium* 299–305. *Cf.* Lk. 13:1.
[2] See further, Wilkinson, pp. 137–141.

grim warning of the results of deliberate apostasy (as opposed to Peter's temporary lapse under pressure).[1]

The passage culminates in a formula-quotation (see pp. 38–40), and as usual there is a mutual interaction of the text and the story, the text being adapted so as to make clear how the events 'fulfilled' it, and the events being narrated in such a way as to allude to the text (see Senior, pp. 392–393, for details). The 'text' cited in vv. 9–10 is basically derived from Zechariah 11:13 but includes also elements derived from the book of Jeremiah (for details, see on vv. 9–10; but in the meantime we need to be aware of the influence of these passages in the telling of the story in vv. 3–8).

It is now widely agreed that the main lines of the story came to Matthew as an independent tradition which then suggested to him (or to earlier interpreters) the relevant texts – rather than the older view that Matthew created the story out of the text.[2] Most recently, D. Moo[3] concludes that 'there is reason to doubt whether any important part of the narrative in Matt. 27:3–8 has been created under the influence of Old Testament passages'.

**3–4.** *Repented* is not the word usually so translated in the New Testament (which usually implies a resulting forgiveness), but means 'regretted', 'changed his mind'; its only other New Testament uses are in 21:29, 32; 2 Cor. 7:8; Heb. 7:21. It is thus appropriate to convey the idea of remorse without suggesting Judas' salvation. For the allusion to Zechariah 11:12–13 in *thirty pieces of silver*, see on 26:15. *Innocent blood* is a familiar Old Testament expression, occurring for instance in Jeremiah 19:4 (see below, on vv. 6–8, 9–10). The question of responsibility for the 'blood' of Jesus will recur in vv. 24–25, where the same words will be used, together with the formula of dissociation, *See to it yourself*. So Judas, despite his remorse, is unable to off-load his guilt; but at the same time the return and use of the blood-money also implicates the *chief priests and elders* (notice the 'official' designation of the leadership, as in 26:3; 27:1), thus adding to the

---

[1] See further, Senior, pp. 347–352, on the role of this story in its setting in Matthew's passion narrative.

[2] See, *e.g.*, Stendahl, pp. 196–197; Lindars, pp. 25, 116–122; and especially the very full discussion by Senior, pp. 343–397 (with summary on this issue, pp. 391–396).

[3] *GP*, III, pp. 157–175.

accumulated blood-guilt already spelt out in 23:29–36.

**5.** *Throwing down the pieces of silver in the temple* echoes Zechariah 11:13; there it was a gesture of defiance by the rejected shepherd against the authorities of the nation, and here too the implication of the word for *temple* (*naos*, properly the inner sanctuary, where only the priests were allowed to go) may be again to implicate the priests, who will now be obliged to pick up the blood-money (see Garland, p. 199, note). *Hanged himself* is a word used nowhere else in the New Testament (hardly surprisingly!), but in LXX 2 Samuel 17:23 it describes the suicide of Ahithophel, David's friend who betrayed him; did Matthew therefore deliberately use it of the betrayer of the Son of David? The question of how far this is physically compatible with the gruesome account in Acts 1:18 has been the subject of much lurid imagination, but Matthew's matter-of-fact statement does not suggest that he was interested in the precise cause of death.

**6–8.** The priests' decision to buy *the potter's field* with the *blood money* is basic to the fulfilment of Scripture in the next verses; but it also provides a suggestive derivation for the traditional name Akeldama, *Field of Blood*, which Acts 1:18–19 also associates with Judas' death, though in a different way.[1] The traditional site of Akeldama is in the valley of Hinnom, which was a source of potter's clay (hence the previous name, 'potter's field'?). If Matthew knew this location, the association with Jeremiah 19:1–13 would be obvious, since that passage is about burials in the valley of Hinnom, which has become a 'place filled with innocent blood', to be called the 'valley of Slaughter', the whole scene being focused on a 'potter's earthen flask'. But the *potter* also appears mysteriously in Zechariah 11:13, as the recipient of the thirty pieces of silver 'in the house of the LORD'. The Syriac version of Zechariah, by altering one letter, reads 'treasury' for 'potter' (RSV has adopted this reading), and it is often suggested that Matthew knew both readings and has exploited the variant in his 'exposition'. But the 'treasury' plays almost no part in his narrative – it is the 'potter' and the 'house of the Lord' (both in the Hebrew text) that form the central features of these verses, and which therefore are the key to the claim of fulfilment. The

---

[1] See *NIDNTT*, I, pp. 93–94.

*treasury*, perhaps the source from which the money had been paid to Judas, would be the natural place to deposit money left in the temple, but its use as *blood money* made it unclean. A burial-ground (itself an unclean place) was a suitable use for it.

**9–10.** By now the echoes of Jeremiah 19:1–13 and of Zechariah 11:13 in the preceding narrative have made Matthew's intention clear to an attentive reader who knows his prophetic scriptures. But now the *fulfilment* is spelt out in a 'quotation' which is basically drawn from the Hebrew text of Zechariah 11:13 (with the order of the clauses drastically rearranged), but which also includes hints of Jeremiah (for such 'combined quotations', *cf.* above, on 2:6; 11:10). Perhaps the mysterious *potter* of Zechariah 11:13 invited attention to Jeremiah, the prophet whose association with the potter was memorable (Je. 18:1–6; 19:1, 11). The various reminiscences of Jeremiah 19:1–13 which we have mentioned above would then be noticed, and in the process the buying of the potter's field might recall Jeremiah's famous buying of a field (though not from a potter!) in Jeremiah 32:6–9; hence the inclusion of *for the potter's field* in the 'quotation'. The whole composite quotation is ascribed to *Jeremiah* as the better-known of the two prophets from whom it is drawn. (*Cf.* the attribution of a combined quotation to Isaiah in Mk. 1:2–3.)[1]

Zechariah 11:4–14 is one of a group of passages in Zechariah 9–13 describing a 'Shepherd-King', God's ruler for his people whom they reject and who as a result is 'pierced' and 'smitten'.[2] Lying behind the Christian use of this passage, therefore, is the image of Jesus as the suffering Messiah; Matthew has previously included references to Zechariah's 'Shepherd-King' in 21:4–5; 24:30; 26:31. Here the clear relevance of the 'thirty pieces of silver' of Zechariah 11:12–13 to the story of Judas has suggested to Matthew a complex sequence of meditation on the fulfilment of Scripture, which to modern readers seems a strange way of writing history. But if we are to do justice to Matthew we must recognize that this is not a collection of unconnected Old Testa-

[1] For less satisfactory explanations of the attribution to Jeremiah, see Gundry, *UOT*, pp. 125–126, note. A further nuance is Senior's suggestion that it is not meant to be an ascription of *authorship*, but rather a reference to a 'Jeremiah-strain' in Old Testament prophecy, *viz.* prophecies of judgment and condemnation, within which this Zechariah text would be classified; so Senior, pp. 367–369.

[2] See F. F. Bruce, *This is That* (1968), pp. 100–114, for the whole concept.

ment ideas thrown together at random, but the result of a careful theological study which takes account not only of superficial verbal 'coincidences', but of underlying themes of prophetic expectation.

*(vi) The Roman trial (27:11–26)*

This is the official trial of Jesus, and yet the description sounds less like a formal judicial hearing than a macabre example of oriental bargaining. Pilate, as prefect of Judaea, had the sole authority to acquit or to condemn, and to determine the sentence. There is a perfunctory attempt at a formal examination of the prisoner, but increasingly the dominant force is not the official role of the governor but the demands of the Jewish leaders, backed by 'the people'. It is here that the focus of Matthew's attention falls, so that Trilling's assessment of Pilate's role, if overstated, is on the right lines: he 'has the function of an "extra" or perhaps a catalyst which helps to define unequivocally the people's stance towards the Messiah' (Trilling, p. 73).

John offers a fuller and independent account of the trial before Pilate (Jn. 18:28 – 19:16), which at several points helps to fill in Matthew's brief description, particularly in explaining the strangely ambivalent attitude of Pilate himself.[1]

**11.** For the location, see on 27:2. The trial probably took place on a raised platform in front of the governor's residence, and thus in public. *Are you the King of the Jews?* presumably repeats the charge presented to Pilate by the Jewish leaders (*cf.* Lk. 23:2). It cleverly incorporates Jesus' admission of his Messiahship in a formula with the maximum political innuendo. The title *King of the Jews* is used in Matthew only by Gentiles (2:2; 27:29, 37; in 27:42 the Jewish leaders substitute 'King of Israel'), and coming from the man who in fact held political authority over the Jews it carries a clearly ironical, even contemptuous, tone. In the sense in which Pilate presumably understood the title, Jesus could quite properly have disclaimed it. But it expressed a theme of Old Testament prophecy which Jesus had come to fulfil, and had indeed deliberately enacted in 21:1–9. He therefore uses again the formula of 'qualified assent' used already in 26:25, 64 (see com-

---

[1] For the significance of some of the details in John's account, see F. F. Bruce, *GP*, I, pp. 7–20.

ments, *ad loc.*). In this case, unlike 26:64, the qualification is not spelt out; if it had been, it would no doubt have been in terms of a totally different conception of 'kingship', as in John 18:33–37.

**12–14.** As in 26:62–63, Jesus' silence is emphasized, no doubt again with Isaiah 53:7 in mind. For Pilate it was not only a matter of surprise (as Holtzmann remarked, 'Silence was certainly not a usual failing on the part of Jewish defendants'!); it was also a judicial embarrassment, as 'Roman judges disliked sentencing an undefended man' (*cf.* Acts 25:16), and the courts established the practice of offering a defendant three opportunities to respond before convicting by default (Sherwin-White, pp. 25–26).

**15.** The existence of this amnesty custom is not attested outside the Gospels, though some have found a hint of it in Mishnah *Pesaḥim* 8:6 (see Blinzler, pp. 218–221). If it was a purely local and perhaps temporary concession (perhaps Pilate's own innovation to try to maintain the goodwill of his difficult subjects), this is hardly surprising. The political expediency of such a recognition of popular feeling can readily be judged from the use of amnesties in the modern world, and their acceptability in the Roman world is well illustrated by Blinzler (pp. 205–208). The account pre-supposes that neither Jesus nor Barabbas was yet formally con-demned; clemency to a condemned man was the sole prerogative of the emperor.

**16–18.** The plural *they had* is surprising; could it refer to 'the crowd' (v. 15), who had their candidate for amnesty already selected? *Barabbas* ('Son of Abbas', but the name sounds in Aramaic very like 'Son of the Father', an irony Matthew may well have noticed) is described by Mark as a 'rebel' involved in a recent violent insurrection (*cf.* v. 38, where the 'robbers' are also prob-ably politically motivated 'brigands'), and his popularity may therefore have been that of a Robin Hood type of folk-hero. *Notorious* represents a word which can have either a good or a bad sense; to the authorities no doubt Barabbas was 'notorious', but to the people he was apparently 'well-known, popular'. In any case Pilate's attempt to relieve himself of responsibility for con-demning an undefended man on a trumped-up charge (which is what v. 18 suggests) was singularly inept. Even if Jesus still enjoyed some popular support (see below, on v. 22), a nationalis-tic crowd is not likely to accept the nominee of the occupying power as a candidate for amnesty; their minds were already made up.

Some readers were understandably shocked when the NEB printed in both vv. 16 and 17 the name Jesus Barabbas (cf. RSV mg.; GNB). But most modern textual critics support this reading on the grounds that this same natural repugnance to the idea of Jesus' name being shared by Barabbas probably accounts for the deliberate removal of the name 'Jesus' from most surviving MSS. Origen, writing before any of our existing Greek MSS were written, wrote that 'in many copies it is not stated that Barabbas was also called Jesus' – which implies that in most this *was* stated! It is very hard to imagine Christian scribes *adding* the name Jesus to Barabbas if this was not already in the text, but very easy to understand their suppressing it (as Origen himself wanted to do), particularly as none of the other Gospels mentions his first name. There is nothing improbable in Barabbas having the very common name Jesus.[1] It is therefore possible that Pilate's *faux pas* sprang from a genuine mistake, if the crowd shouted for Jesus (Barabbas) and he thought they meant the other Jesus. Certainly Matthew's text reads more dramatically with two holders of the same name: 'Which Jesus do you want; the son of Abbas, or the self-styled Messiah?'

**19.** Only Matthew mentions Pilate's *wife* and her *dream*, and nothing is known of her from other sources, but she is hardly the sort of figure legend might be expected to invent. She may have been one of the many Gentile women who had a secret interest in Judaism,[2] hence her interest in the case of Jesus. (Does her knowledge of it suggest that Pilate had prior warning of the Jewish leaders' intentions?) At any rate Matthew has clearly inserted this verse together with vv. 24–25 in order to heighten the impression of Jesus' legal innocence – even a pagan woman can see it! But while she is open to the voice of God (from whom dreams come; cf. 1:20; 2:12, 13, 19, 22), the Jewish leaders are deaf to it. Thus 'Matthew uses the Gentile woman's word as a bright foil whereby the guilt of the Jews stands in darker relief' (Trilling, p. 68).

---

[1] Josephus mentions at least 12 separate holders of the name in the first century AD, including four of the High Priests! For one other holder of the name, see below, on v. 24.

[2] See Blinzler, p. 217 and n. 32.

**20–23.** There is no reason to suppose that the Jewish leaders *persuaded the people* against their will; they merely reinforced an existing preference. In stressing that *they all* called for Jesus' crucifixion Matthew prepares for the terrible climax of v. 25; this is more than a vocal minority. Whereas in the period before Jesus' arrest Matthew seems to have carefully distinguished between the people as a whole ('the crowds') and their leaders (see above, pp. 305, 318, 323–324), there is now no difference; all together are calling for Jesus' death. (*The people* in v. 20 is the same word as 'the crowds' in 21:9, 46; 22:33; 23:1.) There is no reason to suppose that the crowd gathered in front of the residence consists of just the same individuals who welcomed Jesus on his arrival in Jerusalem and who applauded his teaching; indeed it is not unlikely that the Jewish leaders had taken steps to ensure that the crowd on this occasion was sympathetic to their cause. But undoubtedly Matthew intends us to notice a change in the popular reactions to Jesus; those who were previously undecided, even inclined to favour Jesus, have now decided against him, influenced no doubt by the news that their religious leaders had judged him a blasphemer. The call *Let him be crucified* is remarkable on the lips of a Jewish crowd, for crucifixion was a Roman punishment, abhorrent to most Jews (see on vv. 32ff.). But it was the necessary outcome of the decision to bring Jesus before Pilate on a political charge, as this was the regular method of Roman execution for provincial rebels.

**24.** Pilate's dramatic gesture and the corresponding cry of 'all the people' (v.25) are, like v. 19, found only in Matthew. The effect of the whole complex is to underline in the strongest way the responsibility of 'the Jews' for Jesus' death. The symbolic *washing of hands* recalls the ritual prescribed in Deuteronomy 21:6–9, and the metaphorical language of Psalms 26:6; 73:13. *Cf.* 2 Samuel 3:28 for David's similar declaration of his own innocence of a killing which was likely to be attributed to him. It is sometimes argued that this act makes sense only in a Jewish context, and that it has no precedent in Graeco-Roman culture. But the symbolism is obvious enough (remember Lady Macbeth!), and the removal of blood-guilt was a major concern in much pagan literature.[1] In using the same formula of disassociation as in v. 4, *See to it yourselves*, Pilate aims to

[1] See, *e.g.*, Sophocles, *Ajax* 654; Virgil, *Aeneid* ii. 719, for washing the body to remove pollution incurred by killing.

exonerate himself from what he clearly regards as an unjust killing.[1] There is an interesting parallel in Josephus, *BJ* vi. 300–309, where a later procurator, confronted by another Jesus, a prophet of doom denounced by the Jewish authorities, decided to 'pronounce him a maniac and let him go'. Pilate would have gladly done the same; if the Jewish leaders were not prepared to accept this, they must carry the blame.

**25.** Pilate's disavowal of responsibility is balanced by the apparently enthusiastic acceptance of it by *all the people*, '*His blood on us and on our children!*' No verb is expressed in the Greek, and the addition of 'be' in RSV, NEB, NIV, making the declaration into a wish, is unjustified. The sentence is rather a statement accepting what Pilate has just said – 'the responsibility is ours'. Jesus has been 'convicted' under Jewish law, and they will therefore be answerable for his death to Rome or to anyone else. (For a parallel formula of acceptance of responsibility, *cf.* Jos. 2:19; and for the metaphor of 'blood' being 'on' a person, *cf.* Dt. 19:10, 13; Ezk. 18:13; 33:4–6; Acts 18:6.) To read this declaration as an eternal 'curse' on the Jewish race is therefore to press the language beyond its biblical context.[2] In recording these solemn words, and in particular the phrase *and on our children*, Matthew perhaps had particularly in mind the fate of the Jews of 'this generation' in the Jewish War of AD 66–70, a fate already foreshadowed in 23:35–39 as a result of the rejection of God's final messenger. It was a fate which would fall on the nation as a whole, and would signal the end of its privileged status (see on 21:43). It is perhaps for this reason that Matthew attributes the cry to *all the people*, using now not the general term for 'crowds' as in vv. 15, 20, 24, but *laos*, the name particularly used in the LXX for God's chosen people, and so used generally also in this Gospel. The same phrase occurs in the LXX of Jeremiah 26:8–9 for those who attacked Jeremiah and thus risked bringing 'innocent blood' on themselves (v. 15), a parallel Matthew probably had in mind. Of course it was only a small number of the nation who were there, and to

---

[1] The addition of *righteous* to the text in many MSS makes this explicit, echoing vv. 4 and 19; it was probably not in the original text, but correctly interprets Matthew's purpose in recording the incident.

[2] See the full discussion by H. Kosmala, *Annual of the Swedish Theological Institute* 7 (1968/9), pp. 94–126.

read into these words a 'curse' on all Jews for ever is ludicrous (after all, Matthew and his fellow-apostles were Jews!); but Matthew wants his readers to understand that the loss of Israel's special status which is so evident in his Gospel is to be interpreted in the light of their rejection of Jesus.

**26.** For all his gesture and protestation, Pilate was still obliged to give the final word, and he did so in what was probably a characteristically sadistic way: he had this 'innocent' man *scourged* as well as *crucified*! *Scourged* conceals a horrible reality, for this punishment, often used as a preliminary to execution (Sherwin-White, pp. 26–28), was no token beating, but often, as in the case of the other Jesus mentioned above (Josephus, *BJ* vi. 304), meant being 'flayed to the bone'; it was sometimes by itself fatal. In Luke 23:16, 22 and John 19:1 the scourging seems to be an independent punishment imposed before the death sentence is passed, and as an attempt to avert it. This verse in Mark and Matthew therefore apparently covers a more complex (and brutal) sequence than appears at first sight.

## C. THE CRUCIFIXION OF JESUS (27:27–56)

### (i) The mockery by the soldiers (27:27–31)

The Jewish mocking (26:67–68) is now offset by a similar outrage by Gentiles. John 19:1–5 indicates that this took place before Pilate reached his final verdict; in that case Mark, followed by Matthew, has 'tidied up' a complex sequence of events by separating off the physical ill-treatment of Jesus (including the scourging, see on v. 26) from the judicial procedure, in the context of which it in fact occurred.

**27.** For the *praetorium*, see on vv. 1–2. *The soldiers of the governor* were auxiliaries, not Roman legionaries, and would be recruited from non-Jewish inhabitants of the surrounding areas (*e.g.* Phoenicians, Syrians, perhaps Samaritans), who would have no love for the Jews. To have a Jewish 'king' at their mercy would therefore be a welcome opportunity to indulge the same sort of anti-Jewish prejudice which led to a similar incident in Alexandria a few years later (Philo, *In Flaccum* 36–39). Indeed the gathering of *the whole battalion* (about 600 men, if the word is used in its technical sense) for such a rare treat may be no exaggeration. *AB* translates, 'the whole battalion paraded together before him' – a mock 'guard of honour'.

**28–30.** The *scarlet robe* is literally a soldier's red cape, which served to parody the emperor's purple robe. The *reed* represents a royal sceptre, and the *crown of thorns* a royal crown. Jesus is thus enthroned as king, and offered the homage of *kneeling* which a Hellenistic ruler required. *Hail, King of the Jews!* may even be intended to parody the formal greeting, *Ave Caesar*. The whole scene, while it degenerates in v. 30 into physical abuse, is primarily one of mockery rather than of torture. H. StJ. Hart[1] argues that the 'crown' was made to imitate the crown with rays like those of the sun worn by several Eastern rulers, so that the 'thorns' (perhaps the long spikes at the base of the leaf of the date-palm) were designed to stick outward rather than inward.

**31.** Criminals were normally led out naked for crucifixion. Perhaps the return of Jesus' *own clothes* was a regular concession to Jewish sensibility, which found nakedness offensive. The clothes will feature again in v. 35. No indication is given of whether the 'crown' was removed with the other royal regalia; Blinzler (pp. 244–245) argues that it was, because the soldiers would not be allowed to mock the Jews (in the person of their 'king') publicly, and that therefore the traditional inclusion of the crown of thorns in pictures of the crucifixion is incorrect.

## (ii) The crucifixion (27:32–44)

Verses 22–26 have prepared us for the horrible event which this section describes. Crucifixion, while never sanctioned by Jewish law, was a common sight in Palestine from the first century BC on; it was the punishment used by the Romans particularly for political rebels and violent criminals, carried out with maximum publicity so as to be a deterrent to others.[2] It would be easy, and is a frequent practice in Christian preaching, to dwell in harrowing detail on the nature of the suffering inflicted by this barbarous punishment. But the Gospel writers do not do so, and Matthew remarkably passes over the actual fastening to the cross in a bare

[1] *JTS* 3 (1952), pp. 66–75.
[2] For a description of how it was carried out, see Blinzler, pp. 248–251, and for a fuller discussion of its significance, M. Hengel, *Crucifixion* (1977); more briefly, see *NBD*, pp. 253–254.

participle (v. 35a). His interest is more in the meaning of the event, and his emphasis falls again, as in vv. 27–31, on the element of mockery, not now by Gentiles, but by Jews reviling their 'king'. Even more remarkably, in this improbable setting some of the highest Christological titles come to expression: King of the Jews, temple-builder, Son of God, King of Israel, and again Son of God. In their very mockery, they ironically reinforce those titles, for it is in the degrading fate of crucifixion that Jesus' noble mission is accomplished. The shocking paradox of a crucified Messiah could hardly be more sharply underlined.

**32.** It was the cross-beam only which the prisoner carried to the place of execution – the upright was already in position ready to receive it. Even so, the weight was considerable, and not surprisingly was beyond the strength of Jesus after the scourging and ill-treatment. The 'commandeering' of a porter (see on 5:41 for the practice; the same verb is used here) was probably not an uncommon result. *Simon* appears as a chance passer-by, but the memory of his name (and of his family, Mk. 15:21) suggests that he may have joined the disciples of Jesus as a result of this experience.

**33–34.** *Golgotha* was presumably a regular place of execution outside the city, in a prominent public place so that the deterrent effect of crucifixion could operate. While no certainty is possible, the site of the Church of the Holy Sepulchre (which is outside the city wall of Herodian Jerusalem) seems the most likely location.[1] The drink of *wine mingled with gall* ('myrrh' in Mark) is usually understood as a narcotic to reduce the pain of crucifixion, and *Sanhedrin* 43a tells us that such a drink was offered by the noble ladies of Jerusalem to those about to be executed (a practice inspired by Pr. 31:6–7). If so, Jesus' refusal of it might mean that he was determined to undergo his fate in full consciousness.[2] At any rate, for Matthew its main significance lies in the reminiscence of Psalm 69:21 (heightened by his use of the LXX word *gall*, not 'myrrh'), which will be echoed again in v. 48. This psalm, together with Psalm 22, will re-echo throughout the account of the crucifixion, thus presenting Jesus as the fulfilment of the figure of the 'righteous sufferer' of those psalms.

[1] See *NBD*, pp. 161–162, and more fully Wilkinson, pp. 145–150.
[2] See, however, Gundry, *UOT*, p. 202, n. 6 for the view that it was rather a deliberately unpleasant drink, a mockery rather than an act of mercy.

**35-36.** Any belongings of an executed man normally passed to the execution squad. But in this very ordinary circumstance, Matthew sees an echo of Psalm 22:18. Jesus' cry from the cross in v. 46 no doubt first drew attention to this psalm, and several echoes of it occur in the story: see also vv. 39, 43. It was the soldiers' regular duty to keep watch over the crucified men, no doubt to prevent interference and even a possible rescue attempt; but their watch is important to Matthew because it paves the way for their exclamation in v. 54, which forms the theological climax of the story.

**37.** The written *charge* (or *titulus*) was normally carried before a criminal on the way to execution, or hung around his neck, and would then be fixed to his cross, thus reinforcing the deterrent effect of the punishment. *King of the Jews* in such a context is of course ironical, a warning to other would-be liberators; but no doubt Matthew expects his readers to see behind the irony to the paradoxical truth of Jesus' kingship achieved through his death. *Over his head* perhaps indicates that Jesus' cross was of the traditional †-shape, rather than the T-shape frequently used.

**38.** *Robbers* is the word (*lēstēs*) used also in 26:55 and of Barabbas in John 18:40. It can apply to a highway bandit (Lk. 10:30; 2 Cor. 11:26), but is used by Josephus of political insurgents (such as Barabbas), so that these two may have been not so much common thieves as political rebels (which was, of course, the charge against Jesus too). Thus Jesus dies, ironically, as one of a trio of 'Zealot'-type insurgents, the very option from which he had so clearly dissociated himself during his ministry. Matthew probably thought of Isaiah 53:12, 'he was numbered with the transgressors'.

**39-40.** *Derided* and *wagging their heads* suggest another echo of Psalm 22, this time of v. 7, and even more clearly of Lamentations 2:15. The mocking of God's people in their distress by unbelievers is a frequent Old Testament theme; see further on vv. 41-43. The focus of the mockery now is Jesus' alleged threat to *destroy the temple and build it in three days*. Had news of this charge at the Sanhedrin hearing (see on 26:61) already leaked out to ordinary bystanders, or was that charge itself based on what was already commonly believed to be Jesus' declared aim? But another echo of that hearing comes in the title *Son of God* (see on 26:63). Its use here is again clearly ironical, but the total clause 'If you are the Son of God' perhaps also carries a sinister echo of Satan's probing words in 4:3, 6. Here, as there, it would still be possible for Jesus to exploit his privileged status, and so to escape the awful consequences of his mission. The temptation already faced and rejected in Gethsemane is thus repeated. And, with a poignant reversal of what the onlookers meant, it is precisely *because* he is the Son of God that he continues to accept the Father's will, and does not *come down from the cross*. It is this paradoxical truth, unrecognized by his Jewish mockers, which the Gentile soldiers will confess in v. 54.

**41-43.** The full listing of the Jewish dignitaries, as in 26:57 (normally the *scribes* have not been mentioned in chs. 26 – 27), serves to underline the total rejection of Jesus by official Judaism. They can even bear to use the precious title *King of Israel* in mockery of the one in whom they have refused to *believe*; and again the title *Son of God* is used to express their scorn. But this time it carries another nuance, for in Wisdom of Solomon 2:10-20 we read of the plots of the wicked against 'the poor and honest man', culminating in the jibe 'If the just man is God's son, God will stretch out a hand to him and save him from the clutches of his enemies'. Here is another Jewish example of the theme of the persecuted servant of God. But the words of v. 43 in fact echo even more directly yet another part of Psalm 22, this time v. 8, which probably also inspired the passage in Wisdom.

**44.** To the mockery of Jewish bystanders and Jewish religious leaders is added that even of Jewish criminals. The totality of Jesus' rejection by his people is complete.

*(iii) The death of Jesus (27:45–56)*

So far the story of the crucifixion has focused on the theme of the hostility and mockery of both Gentile soldiers and Jewish bystanders, and Jesus has appeared as the passive, apparently helpless, victim who suffers in silence. Now the picture begins to change, as we see both in the accompanying events and in Jesus' own words and attitude something of the true significance of what is happening. As before, Matthew shows no interest in the physical nature of Jesus' suffering, or the medical cause of death, but by a series of clear allusions to Old Testament passages continues to point to Jesus' death as the moment of fulfilment, leading up in v. 54 to a climactic confession of faith from the most unlikely source.

**45.** This is the first specific note of time in Matthew's account of the crucifixion, since he did not, like Mark, state that the crucifixion was effected at the third hour;[1] his readers would therefore probably assume (as John also suggests) that *the sixth hour* (*i.e.* noon) was roughly the time of the crucifixion, the whole morning having elapsed during the trial, scourging, mocking, *etc*. In that case the three hours *until the ninth hour* would be the whole time that Jesus remained alive on the cross. The whole period was marked by *darkness*. There could not be a natural eclipse at the time of the Passover full moon; perhaps it was caused by a dust storm, or heavy cloud cover, but it is more likely to be understood, as Matthew surely intended, as a direct sign of God's displeasure, as in Amos 8:9. *All the land* marks a relatively local phenomenon, like the earthquake of v. 51, rather than a world-wide disruption as suggested in RSV mg. *Cf.* 24:30 for this use of 'the land'; here there is probably a deliberate echo of the similarly threatening darkness 'in all the land of Egypt' in Exodus 10:22.

**46.** The sequence from v. 46 to 50 suggests that this cry was uttered just before Jesus' death. *Cried* (*anaboaō*, used only here in the New Testament) is a strong verb indicating powerful emotion or appeal to God. This is no dispassionate theological statement, but an agonized expression of a real sense of alienation, reflecting the full meaning of Jesus' death as a 'ransom for many' (20:28). This is, remarkably, the only time in the Synoptic Gospels where Jesus addresses God without calling him 'Father'. The words are, of course, a quotation of the first verse of Psalm 22 (on which see above, on v. 35), a psalm which moves from despairing appeal to triumphant faith, and the Christian reader can, with hindsight, see the appropriateness of this total message. But it is illegitimate to interpret Jesus' words as referring to the part of the psalm which he did *not* echo. As throughout the crucifixion scene, it is the suffering of the righteous man in Psalm 22, not his subsequent vindication, which is alluded to. But the fact that Jesus can

---

[1] Mk. 15:25 creates a conflict with Jn. 19:14, where Pilate's verdict is 'about the sixth hour'; Blinzler (pp. 267–269) argues that this embarrassing verse was not in the original text of Mark.

still appeal to '*my* God' places his sense of abandonment poles apart from a nihilistic despair; this is the 'cup' which he has willingly accepted from his Father's hand (26:36–46).

Mark 15:34 presents Jesus' words in an Aramaic form. Matthew's *Eli* (which seems necessary to explain the misunderstanding that he was calling on Elijah, v. 47) is Hebrew, while the following words remain Aramaic; but since the Targum to Psalm 22 similarly uses the 'Hebrew' *Eli* here, Matthew's wording may well reflect the current version.

**47.** For *Elijah* as an important figure in Jewish eschatological expectation, see on 11:14; 17:3, 10–13. Later Jewish piety developed the idea of his appearance from heaven to help in time of need.[1] In interpreting Jesus' cry in this way the bystanders perhaps indicate some awareness that Jesus had presented his mission as bringing in the age of fulfilment, when Elijah was to appear.

**48–49.** The drink of *vinegar* is another echo of Psalm 69:21 (see above, on v. 34). Its immediate availability suggests that it was the '*poska*, wine vinegar diluted with water, the usual refreshing drink of labourers and soldiers' (Blinzler, p. 255) which the soldiers guarding the cross would have for their own use. It was thus offered as an act of kindness,[2] to which others in the crowd mockingly objected that, if any relief was to be given, it should be given by *Elijah* in response to Jesus' supposed appeal.[3]

**50.** The medical cause of death by crucifixion can only be a matter of speculation, in the absence of experimental evidence. What does seem clear from Matthew's account is that in Jesus' case it was not a slow ebbing of consciousness. The *loud voice*, like that of v. 46, suggests considerable remaining strength, and Matthew's unusual expression *yielded up his spirit* probably indicates a deliberate act of will. (This is even clearer in Lk. 23:46.) The parallel expression in Mark and Luke (literally 'breathed out', 'expired') makes it clear that *spirit* here refers simply to Jesus' human 'spirit' (*i.e.* his life); there is no reference to the Holy Spirit

[1] See *TDNT*, II, p. 930.
[2] *Pace* Gundry, *UOT*, pp. 203–204.
[3] The extra words in RSV mg. are taken from Jn. 19:34, where the incident occurs after Jesus' death. They occur here in some important Greek MSS, but are not found in the early versions and patristic citations.

here. Matthew gives no indication whether the 'cry' is the triumphant 'It is finished' of John 19:30, or a further cry of agony like that in v. 46, but the use of the verb *krazō* ('cry') may be a further reminiscence of Psalm 22, where this verb occurs in the LXX of vv. 2, 5, 24.

The time of Jesus' death was presumably still 'about the ninth hour' (v. 46). The events of vv. 57-60 (more fully set out in Jn. 19:31-42) could hardly be accomplished in much less than three hours, and John 19:31-42 makes clear what Matthew assumes, that the burial had to be effected before sunset, when the sabbath began.

**51.** The tearing of *the curtain of the temple* (probably that separating off the 'holy of holies', though there was also a curtain at the entrance to the sanctuary building from the Court of the Priests), while perhaps physically caused by the earthquake, is surely understood as a symbol of the opening of access to God through the death of Jesus.[1] The obverse of this idea is the judgment of God on the old system of worship, and in the light of Jesus' words about the coming destruction of the temple the tearing of the curtain may also be seen as a foreshadowing of the more drastic events to come in AD 70. *From top to bottom* may be added to show that this was the work not of man but of God, 'desecrating' his own temple.[2]

Apart from perhaps explaining how the curtain came to be torn, the earthquake is presented as the means by which the tombs were opened. In the Old Testament an earthquake is a symbol of God's mighty acts (*e.g.* Jdg. 5:4; Ps. 114:7-8), especially in judgment (*e.g.* Joel 3:16; Na. 1:5-6; see further, Senior, pp. 313-314).[3]

**52-53.** The extraordinary sequel to the earthquake (all the more extraordinary in that there is no record of such an event outside Matthew) is presumably also to be seen as symbolic. Jewish theology had developed from such passages as Isaiah 26:19 and Daniel 12:2 a belief in a bodily resurrection in the last days (Ezk.

---

[1] See Heb. 6:19-20; 10:19-20 for the development of this symbolism. *Cf.* also Eph. 2:11-19.

[2] Is there a confused memory of this event in the Rabbinic tradition that 'during the last forty years before the destruction of the temple the doors of the sanctuary would open by themselves' (*Yoma* 39b)?

[3] For the incidence of earthquakes in the Jerusalem area, see D. Baly, *The Geography of the Bible* (1974 ed.), p. 25; also *ISBE*, II, pp. 4-5.

37:1–14 was interpreted of that eschatological resurrection, and the words used here suggest that Matthew had that passage particularly in mind), and John 5:25–29 records Jesus as teaching that 'the hour is coming, and now is' when this hope would be fulfilled through his agency. This account therefore presents that belief in concrete form, apparently as the result of Jesus' death. *After his resurrection*, however, unless it represents an unexplained delay of two days between the rising of *the saints* and their arrival in *the holy city*,[1] perhaps suggests that Matthew has not recorded these events in strict 'chronological' order, and that the rising of the saints is seen as the sequel not so much to Jesus' death as to his *resurreciion*, thus reflecting the view 'that Jesus' resurrection was the beginning of the general resurrection at the end of time' (Dunn, p. 118), a view picked up in, *e.g.*, 1 Corinthians 15:20ff. *The saints* are presumably the people of God in the Old Testament, those who according to Hebrews 11 all died 'in faith' looking forward to resurrection to a better life (Heb. 11:13–16, 35, 39–40); through Jesus that hope now comes to fruition. The theological significance of this event is therefore important for Matthew's analysis of the meaning of Christ's death; its character as 'sober history' (*i.e.* what a cine-camera might have recorded) can only be, in the absence of corroborative evidence, a matter of faith, not of objective demonstration. It was, in any case, a unique occurrence and is not to be judged by the canons of 'normal' experience.[2]

**54.** Verses 51–53 (*cf.* also v. 45) have presented a breathless series of events, natural and supernatural, which build up to a powerful demonstration of the profound significance of Jesus' death (and resurrection). We now read of the effect of this demonstration of divine displeasure on the pagan soldiers at the cross. Mark mentions only *the centurion*; Matthew's inclusion of *those who were with him* provides a confessing group to balance the mocking group of vv. 39–43, 49; and the fact that this second group, unlike the first, is made up of Gentiles points forward to the disciples drawn from all nations (28:19) who will replace the unbelieving 'sons of the kingdom' (8:11–12; 21:43; *etc.*). To be *filled*

[1] The phrase could apply in the Greek only to their 'appearing', but more likely, as in RSV, refers to their 'coming out'.
[2] The question is usefully discussed by D. Wenham in *TynB* 24 (1973), pp. 42–46.

*with awe* (*cf.* 17:6) is a proper reaction to the manifestation of God's power (*cf.* 'afraid' in 9:8; 28:5 – the same verb), and the confession *'Truly this was the Son of God!'* closely echoes the disciples' reaction in 14:33, again in a context of fear in face of divine power. See the discussion on 14:33; here it is even more questionable how much Christian theological content should be read into the phrase from the point of view of those who uttered it (especially as it is expressed in a more 'secular' way in Lk. 23:47), but undoubtedly Matthew intends us to see in this confession the true interpretation of what has taken place. The title *Son of God*, which had been used in mockery in vv. 40, 43, is thus restored to its proper place.

**55–56.** The story of Jesus' death is rounded off by a mention of those who witnessed it. At the same time these verses lead into the next section, for the reappearance of the same people in 27:61 and 28:1, as witnesses also of his burial and of his resurrection, assures us that there was no possibility of mistake as to the reality of the death of the one who subsequently rose from death. Luke 8:1–3 mentions the group of women, including *Mary* of *Magdala*, who had looked after the disciple group in Galilee; they were therefore long-standing members of Jesus' entourage. *Mary the mother of James and Joseph* could be a description of Jesus' mother (see 13:55 for his brothers' names), but 'the other Mary' (27:61; 28:1) seems an unlikely way to refer to Jesus' mother; moreover, Mark 15:40 specifies that her son was 'James the less', which suggests a member of the disciple group (thus distinguished from James son of Zebedee) rather than Jesus' brother who was probably not yet a disciple, but subsequently became the leader of the Jerusalem church.

### D. THE BURIAL AND RESURRECTION OF JESUS (27:57 – 28:20)

The remaining part of the Gospel falls into a balanced structure of great dramatic power, in which the account of the resurrection is the focal point:

27:57–61   Jesus dead and buried
  27:62–66   Setting of the guard
    28:1–10   The empty tomb and the risen Lord
  28:11–15   Report of the guard
28:16–20   Jesus alive and sovereign.

## (i) Jesus dead and buried (27:57–61)

This little section emphasizes two things: first, that Jesus was truly dead, and secondly that, contrary to custom, he was given a decent and reverent burial. The Romans did not normally bury a crucified body, but simply threw it out on the ground. Jewish piety forbade this, but executed criminals were buried in a public plot, without honour, and were not allowed to be placed in their family tombs (Daube, pp. 310–311). Joseph's action, therefore, while not against Jewish law, was exceptional and extravagant.

**57.** Mark and John make it clear that this took place before sunset, when the sabbath began; Deuteronomy 21:22–23 required a hanged man to be buried before dark (cf. Josephus, *BJ* iv. 317, for the same scruple specifically with regard to crucified bodies). We learn from the other Gospels that *Joseph* was a member of the Sanhedrin (Mark) who had opposed the plot against Jesus (Luke) and was in fact a secret disciple (John). That he was *rich* would explain his owning an unused tomb just outside the capital (it is only Matthew who tells us that it was *his own* tomb, v. 60); but perhaps Matthew mentions the fact also because it recalls Isaiah 53:9, 'they made his grave . . . with a rich man'.

**58–61.** The request to Pilate was not unusual – it was the Jewish leaders who might have objected to Joseph's thus 'breaking ranks'. Rock-cut tombs of around the same period may still be seen in the area around Jerusalem (including some actually within the Church of the Holy Sepulchre), often containing more than one chamber, with niches in the sides for several bodies, the whole entered by a low 'doorway' with a trough outside along which a *great stone* is rolled to seal the entrance against animals and grave-robbers.[1] A *new* tomb is not so much one recently completed, as one so far unused, *i.e.* with none of its niches occupied. In mentioning this, and the *clean* shroud (again only in Matthew), Matthew emphasizes the care and reverence of Joseph's treatment of the body. The extremely expensive spices mentioned in John 19:39–40 are further evidence of his extravagant loyalty. For the women's watch, see on vv. 55–56.

[1] See further, Wilkinson, pp. 155–159; *NBD*, pp. 153–154.

*(ii) The setting of the guard (27:62-66)*

The guard, so important in Matthew's account of the resurrection, are not mentioned in the other Gospels. His reason for mentioning them is presumably that a story about the disciples stealing Jesus' body was being used to discredit Christian claims; Justin says that such stories were still being actively disseminated in the middle of the second century (*Dial.* 108). The fact of such propaganda in itself indicates that it could not be denied that the tomb was empty; what was questioned was how it came to be empty.

On the historicity of Matthew's story, see further, on 28:11-15.

**62.** Matthew's clumsy phrase means simply 'on the sabbath'. Such a deputation to Pilate and sealing of the tomb on a festival sabbath was surely not compatible with scribal understanding of the law, but Matthew's avoidance of the word 'sabbath' is strange, for one might have expected him rather to draw attention to this breach of the law by *the chief priests and the Pharisees*. Perhaps he uses this odd expression (based on the phrase in Mk. 15:42, which Matthew omitted in his v. 57), because the important day for *him* was not the sabbath, but the day Jesus died, *the day of Preparation*. Notice the reappearance of the *Pharisees* (see on 26:3), in order to emphasize that the two opposing wings of the Sanhedrin are still united in their fear of Jesus' influence, to the extent of contravening their own sabbath regulations.

**63-64.** *Impostor* and *fraud* are related words in Greek. It is the same charge which Jesus levelled against false prophets in 24:4, 5, 11, 24 ('lead astray'); his opponents see him in the same light, but the facts will prove them wrong.[1] The prediction referred to may be that of 12:40, as that is the only public mention of the *three days* Matthew has recorded. But no doubt Judas or some other informer could have briefed them on Jesus' more explicit private statements (16:21; 17:22-23; 20:17-19). The *first* fraud would be Jesus' Messianic claim, the·*last* a faked 'resurrection' to support it.

**65-66.** *You have a guard* would be permission to use their own (Jewish) temple guards for the purpose. *Take a guard* (RSV mg., an

---

[1] The word *planos* ('impostor') points forward to the charge frequently levelled against Jesus in later Jewish polemic, as found in the Talmud, that he was a *mesith*, one who entices others into idolatry or apostasy.

equally possible translation) would suggest that Pilate gave them a detachment of his (non-Jewish) auxiliary troops. 28:14 shows that they were answerable to Pilate, and it is unlikely that the Jews would have needed Pilate's permission at all to deploy their own police; moreover the word for *guard* is (uniquely in the New Testament) a transliteration of the Latin word *custodia*. It is therefore more likely that it was Pilate's troops who were used; the Jewish leaders are going for maximum security. Pilate by this time must have been thoroughly tired of the whole business, hence perhaps his surprisingly ready (or resigned?) compliance with the leaders he had previously tried to thwart.

### (iii) The empty tomb and the risen Lord (28:1–10)

The New Testament nowhere describes Jesus' resurrection.[1] All we are given is an account of its effects, from two points of view: the tomb was found to be empty, and the disciples met the risen Lord. This central paragraph of Matthew's concluding section includes both these lines of 'evidence' (hence the title given above), while the succeeding paragraphs will take both further, the empty tomb in vv. 11–15 and the risen Lord in vv. 16–20. In all of this there is no doubt an element of Christian apologetic, aiming to supply evidence to support the Christian claim of Jesus' resurrection. But the emphasis throughout (except in the story of the guard) is not on factual proof for the non-Christian world, but on the impact of the incredible truth on Jesus' bewildered and exhilarated followers, on their fear and joy, doubt and assurance. It is with the restoration of their broken relationship with him, with all that this implies for their continuing mission, that Matthew will conclude his book.

The difficulty of harmonizing all the details of the Gospel accounts of both the empty tomb and the resurrection appearance is notorious.[2] A lack of precise agreement in independent accounts of such a bewildering series of events is hardly surprising. How far Matthew's account is independent of that of Mark is much debated. His verses 1 and 5–8 are broadly similar to Mark, but he omits some of Mark's detail (particularly the

[1] For an early example of such a description, see the second-century 'Gospel of Peter'; the contrast with the sobriety of the New Testament accounts is remarkable.
[2] For a recent painstaking attempt to do so, see J. W. Wenham, *Easter Enigma* (1984).

intended anointing and the discussion about the stone), and has included in vv. 2–4 a much more explicitly 'supernatural' account of the 'angel of the Lord' who apparently corresponds to the 'young man' of Mark 16:5. Whether vv. 9–10 represent a tradition unknown to Mark depends on the still unresolved question of whether Mark's Gospel originally ended at 16:8.[1]

**1.** The wording of RSV points clearly to the period about dawn on the Sunday. The first phrase, *opse . . . sabbatōn*, more naturally means 'late on the sabbath', while the verb *epiphōskō*, translated *towards the dawn*, is used in Luke 23:54 for the 'beginning' of a Jewish day in the evening. On this basis Black (pp. 136–138)[2] argues that Matthew is speaking of the Saturday evening. This would be at odds with all the other Gospels, which locate the women's arrival at or just before dawn. But elsewhere *epiphōskō* refers to dawn, and there are clear parallels for *opse* used to mean 'after' as in RSV (see BAGD, p. 610b), so that the RSV translation seems preferable.[3] Mark's 'very early . . . when the sun had risen' is quite unambiguous, and it is hard to understand why Matthew should have wanted to alter such a clear tradition. *To see the sepulchre* is a rather colourless motive compared with that indicated in Mark 16:1–2, particularly as they have already 'seen' it in 27:61, but Matthew's interest is not in the women's intention, but in their unexpected experience. It has often been remarked that the role of *women* as the first witnesses both of the empty tomb and of the risen Lord can hardly be an apologetic fiction, as women were not accepted as witnesses in Jewish society.

**2.** For the *earthquake*, *cf.* on 27:51. There it served to open the graves of the 'saints'; here it is presumably the means by which *the stone* is moved. *The angel of the Lord* now appears for the first time since the two opening chapters of the Gospel (see on 1:20). There he was the mouthpiece for God's messages of explanation and of instruction to Joseph and the Magi. Here too he comes to explain and to instruct in vv. 5–7. There is no suggestion that the opening of the tomb is necessary to allow the risen Christ to come out; indeed in v. 6 it is clear that he has already risen. The women are called not to see him rising (it is this motif which is added by

[1] For a full discussion of the possibility of an independent tradition underlying Matthew's differences from Mark, see D. Wenham, *TynB* 24 (1973), pp. 21–54.
[2] *Cf.* Gundry, pp. 585–586.    [3] *Cf.* M. D. Goulder, *NTS* 24 (1977/8), p. 237.

the 'Gospel of Peter'), but to see that he has risen; the opening of the tomb is thus for their benefit, not for his.

**3-4.** The description of the angel echoes Daniel 10:6 ('his face *like the appearance of lightning*'), and the vision of God himself in Daniel 7:9 ('*raiment white as snow*'). For the reaction of *the guards*, compare again Daniel 10:7-9, and the response in Revelation 1:17 to a vision which was also described in terms partly drawn from Daniel 7:9-10. So the 'angel of the Lord' is seen here, as often in the Old Testament, as more than a mere 'messenger'; the description is not far from that of a theophany. He comes with all the majesty of God, and mortals cannot stand before him (hence also the women's fear in vv. 5, 8).

**5-7.** The guards are ignored for the rest of the paragraph; the angel's message is only for *the women*. The invitation to *see the place where he lay* is appropriately addressed to the same people who had watched the body being deposited (27:60-61) – so there is no possibility of mistake; the one who *has risen* is the same *Jesus who was crucified*. This was *as he said*, for Matthew has recorded several explicit predictions of the resurrection (16:21; 17:23; 20:19, and implicitly 12:40). But the one the angel refers to specifically is 26:32, 'After I am raised up, *I will go before you to Galilee*', a prediction which is about to be fulfilled in vv. 16-20. *There you will see him* confirms our conclusion on 26:32, that *proagō* in this context means 'to go on ahead' rather than 'to lead'. The *disciples* (unlike the women, vv. 9-10) must wait until *Galilee* to see the risen Jesus.

The emphasis on *Galilee* in vv. 7, 10, 16, making it the place where the whole story ends in a triumphant climax, is the culmination of Matthew's tendency throughout to emphasize Galilee as the place where light dawns (4:12-16), as opposed to Jerusalem, the city where Jesus meets rejection and death, and over which he can only lament as he predicts its violent fate (23:37-39). It is often suggested that this 'bias' of Matthew (and Mark) accounts for the fact that he records no appearances of the risen Jesus to the disciples in Jerusalem, whereas Luke and John focus them there (though Jn. 21 adds a subsequent Galilean appearance). On this see Stonehouse (ch. VI); he argues that Matthew's account, besides explicitly recording an appearance to the *women* in Jerusalem, does not exclude Jesus' appearing to the eleven in Jerusalem prior to the Galilee episode of vv. 16-20.[1]

**8.** The addition of *joy* to the *fear* which Mark mentions already begins to prepare for the exultant climax to come in vv. 17-20. The mixed emotion is surely the natural result of what has gone before. *To tell* suggests that, as Luke 24:9-11 records, they did pass on the message immediately. The contrast with Mark's 'They said nothing to anyone' is striking, but Mark can hardly have meant this to be understood as more than a temporary silence, unless he wanted to depict the women as disobedient to the command in his v. 7. In the absence of knowledge of what, if anything, originally followed Mark 16:8, we canot be sure how to interpret their silence.

**9-10.** No appearance of Jesus to the women outside the tomb is mentioned by Luke, and Luke 24:22-24 seems to leave no place for it. Moreover Luke 24:34 seems to suggest that the first appearance was to Peter, and 1 Corinthians 15:5 indicates the same, if Paul's list is meant to be chronological. But in view of the invalidity of women as witnesses, it is hardly to be expected that Paul's all-male list should include them. John 20:11-17, like Matthew, also records the first appearance as experienced by Mary of Magdala (who strangely speaks in the plural in v. 2, and so may not have been alone), and two striking coincidences (touching Jesus, and the message to Jesus' 'brothers') suggest that the same incident may lie behind these verses. In that case Matthew here records an event which Luke omitted, perhaps because he was more concerned with the testimony of the twelve than with that of women.

Dunn (pp. 126-128) suggests that some of the ambiguity in the resurrection accounts with regard to the role of the 'young man', the angel(s) and the risen Lord may be due to the fact that the women, in their 'muddled state of fear and joy', were themselves not quite sure whom or what they had seen. 'They came to recognize the vision as an appearance of Jesus (perhaps on the basis of Peter's experience), but their account of it was so con-fused and confusing that it was not taken seriously by the other disciples. Some ignored it, since the testimony of women did not count anyway; some interpreted it as "a vision of angels"; some

[1]He also believes that the latter episode involved a wider circle of 'disciples' (pp. 168-182). This last point, however, is not widely accepted; see on v. 16.

accepted it as a genuine appearance of the risen Lord.'

'*Hail!*' represents the normal Greek greeting, an almost homely 'Hello!', in contrast with the fearsome appearance of the angel. Their *worship* (see on 2:2; 8:2; *etc.*) and *taking hold of his feet* is an appropriate response of glad and reverent homage, and the physical contact (the occurrence of which perhaps explains Jn. 20:17, 'Do not hold me') is not emphasized in such a way as might suggest that Matthew included it as a deliberate attack on 'docetic' ideas of the resurrection (*cf.* Lk. 24:39–43). Even if not so designed, however, it forms an interesting incidental confirmation of the physical reality of the risen Jesus.

Jesus' words do not simply repeat those of the angel. In addition to the not inconsiderable fact that this time it is *Jesus* himself who confirms his former promise, v. 10 adds a specific command *to go* to Galilee, and most remarkably designates the disciples as *my brethren*, a term which in the light of its use in 12:49–50 and 25:40 must surely mean the disciples rather than the 'brothers' of 12:46; 13:55. For the extent of this group, see below, on 28:16.

*(iv) The report of the guard (28:11–15)*

Between the Galilee pointers of vv. 7, 10 and the Galilee climax of vv. 16–20 comes the final scene of the Gospel in *the city*, Jerusalem. In contrast with the joy, hope and triumph of the risen Jesus and his disciples in Galilee, we see the fear and the sordid deceit of Jesus' priestly opponents in Jerusalem, the city of darkness (see above, on vv. 5–7). Thus the tables are turned, and those who predicted deceit on the part of Jesus' disciples (27:63–64) finish up perpetrating deceit themselves in their futile attempt to thwart his triumph.

On the various arguments against the historicity of Matthew's whole account of the guard, see D. Wenham, *art.cit.*, pp. 22–23, 47–51. A purely fictional story could hardly be expected to have any apologetic value so long after the event that no-one was able to deny it from first-hand knowledge. If the Gospel was written within not much more than a generation of the events (see above, pp. 28–30), such a story about both the Jewish and Roman authorities could hardly be expected to be believed if it were not based on fact. It should be noted that the guards are not presented as witnesses of the resurrection as such (contrast the 'Gospel of Peter'), but as witnesses that the tomb was empty.

Indirect confirmation of the story of the guard has been claimed in the imperial edict against tomb-robbing reputedly found at Nazareth (see Bruce, pp. 284–286). At the least this inscription confirms that the story concocted in v. 13 would have rung true in first-century Palestine: people *did* remove bodies from tombs.

**11.** While the soldiers were ultimately responsible to Pilate, the mission to which they had been assigned was initiated by *the chief priests*, and was of interest to them rather than to Pilate; hence the report back in the first instance to them.

**12–13.** The story suggested by the chief priests was not only discreditable to *the soldiers*, but also dangerous, in that sleeping on guard duty was a serious offence, perhaps punishable by death. To persuade them to spread such a story would need a substantial *sum* (the Greek is literally 'sufficient money' – it would need to be large!). But they may have been the more easily persuaded by the consideration that, even without the story of their sleep, their watch had been a failure. Either way they could expect little mercy from Pilate. The improbability of their all sleeping through a tomb-robbing undisturbed, or of their in that case knowing what had happened while they were asleep, is not likely to have occurred to the priests – such improbability was in any case preferable to the truth!

**14–15.** There was good reason to hope *the governor* would not hear of their failure – it was after all essentially a Jewish concern. But if the cover-up failed, the priests knew their man well enough to expect to be able to *satisfy him* with a bribe.[1] For the subsequent *spread* of *this story*, see above, p. 404.

## (v) Jesus alive and sovereign (28:16–20)

For the relation to 27:57–61, see above, p. 402. It is the striking contrast between these two balancing pericopes which is the measure of the significance of the event of vv. 1–10 around which they are structured. The 'defeat' of Golgotha is transformed into the triumph of Galilee, and on that transformation the church's mission is based 'to the close of the age'. These verses thus

---

[1]See Philo, *Legatio ad Gaium* 302, for Pilate's known venality.

magnificently conclude the final section which began in 27:57; but they also bring the whole Gospel to a dynamic conclusion, which is in fact more a beginning than an end.

Two echoes of the opening chapters serve to round off the framework of the whole Gospel. First, v. 18 presents Jesus as the universal sovereign. In 1:1–17 he was presented as the successor to royal dignity, and 2:1–12 portrayed him as the true 'king of the Jews'. So in due course he entered Jerusalem as her king (21:1–11), but it is this very claim which has brought him to the cross, where it was mockingly displayed (27:37). But now the promise of chs. 1 – 2 is proved true after all, and on a far wider scale than a merely Jewish kingship, in 'the enthronement of the Son of Man' (Davies, p. 197), whose rule is over 'all nations' (v. 19), indeed over both heaven and earth (v. 18). Secondly, and still more wonderfully, 1:23 presented Jesus the baby under the name 'God with us'; now in the final verse Jesus the risen Lord confirms the promise, 'I am with you always.'

Luke, John and Paul (1 Cor. 15:5–7) record other appearances of the risen Jesus. Of these only that of John 21:1–23 is explicitly located in Galilee, and none can certainly be identified with this incident (see further on v. 16), though it is always possible to conjecture that it was recorded in a lost ending of Mark. It is therefore impossible to be sure how it fits into the total picture. Presumably the eleven subsequently returned to Jerusalem before the ascension and the coming of the Spirit at Pentecost (Acts 1 – 2). But in the plan of Matthew's Gospel this scene functions like those events, as Jesus' farewell and commissioning of his disciples for their mission. B. J. Hubbard[1] suggests that the whole scene is modelled on Old Testament stories of the commissioning of God's servants (Abraham, Isaac, Jacob, Moses, Joshua, Gideon, Samuel and the prophets); even if the literary parallels are far from exact, it is certainly true that both the disciples' reactions to Jesus' appearing and the words he speaks recall the awesome experience of those who met with God, and were sent out as his messengers with the assurance of his presence with them.

**16.** After Matthew's emphasis on the fate of Judas (27:3–10) it is

---

[1]*The Matthean Redaction of a Primitive Apostolic Commissioning* (1974).

appropriate that he now describes the 'inner circle' as *the eleven disciples.* Such a specific identification surely renders very unlikely the contention of Stonehouse (pp. 175–181; see above, on v. 7) that a larger group were present, a contention suggested partly by the term 'brethren' in v. 10, and partly by the desire not to identify the 'doubters' of v. 17 with some of the eleven. On the basis of this supposition it has been further suggested that this is the appearance 'to more than five hundred brethren at one time' (1 Cor. 15:6). But if this is so, Matthew was either misinformed or has gone out of his way to disguise the size of the group involved. To accept that only the eleven were present does not, of course, require us to believe that the commission and the promise of vv. 18–20 applied only to them; here, as often, they represent the whole body of Jesus' 'brethren'. For *the mountain,* see on 5:1; here again it is not a specified place, but the general scene of his teaching ministry in Galilee, *to which Jesus had directed them* in 26:32; 28:10. So the wider mission is launched where the original mission began, and the continuity of the disciples' teaching with that of their Master is emphasized. At the same time, as in 5:1–2; 17:1ff., *the mountain* may be intended to remind us of Jesus' role as the new Moses, the giver of new commandments (v. 20), even though what follows will reveal a far higher authority (see Davies, pp. 85–86).

**17.** The mention of Jesus' 'coming' in v. 18 may suggest that at first *they saw him* at a distance, as in John 21:4–7, where it was at first difficult to be sure that it was Jesus. This may partly account for the strangely mixed attitude of the eleven. When they recognized him, it was natural that *they worshipped him,* but the whole experience was so mysterious and overwhelming that *some doubted.* This famous phrase should not be taken as implying that some of the eleven ultimately refused to believe, but that some (like Thomas in Jn. 20:24–28) took longer to accept the reality of the resurrection than others. The verb *distazō* does not denote a settled unbelief, but a state of uncertainty and hesitation (*cf.* 14:31, its only other use in the New Testament). The disciples have often been rebuked for their 'little faith' (*cf.* on 6:30; it is combined with the verb 'to doubt' in 14:31), and it is hardly surprising that such an extraordinary event as the resurrection found them 'in two minds'. 'The same mysterious *chiaroscuro* surrounds the earliest accounts of the reactions of the witnesses: now they fail to recognize the Risen One, now the heavenly brightness blinds them, now they believe that they have seen a ghost. Fear and trembling, anxiety, uncertainty and doubt struggle with joy and worship.'[1] Dunn sees Matthew's mention of this doubt as 'a genuine historical echo' – those who were there would never have forgotten the conflicting emotions and beliefs in that unique experience. (Was their 'hesitation' also increased by the fear that they might not receive a very friendly reception from the one they had recently abandoned and denied?)[2]

**18.** In response to their 'hesitation' Jesus came and spoke to them in reassurance (just as he did in 17:7, the only other place where Matthew uses the verb 'come' of Jesus). His ringing declaration, magnificent enough in itself, is given deeper meaning by the recognition that the words were based on Daniel 7:14, the passage which Jesus has quoted in 26:64 as about to be fulfilled 'from now on'; then it was still future – now it has happened. (See on 26:64 for Jesus' use elsewhere of Dn. 7:13–14.) This 'ingressive aorist' (*has been given*) thus indicates 'that the prophecy that the Son of Man would be enthroned as ruler of the world was fulfilled in the resurrection' (Jeremias, *NTT*, p. 310). Of course Jesus already had *authority* during his earthly ministry (see, *e.g.*, 7:29; 9:6, 8; 11:27; 21:23ff.). But now he has *all* authority, and that word *all* will be repeated insistently in vv. 19 ('all nations') and 20 ('all things', 'always'). In 4:8–9 Satan offered him '*all* the kingdoms of the world and the glory of them; now, by the way of suffering obedience, he has received far more than Satan could offer, all authority *in heaven and on earth.*

**19.** Jesus' universal Lordship now demands a universal mission. The restriction of the disciples' mission to Israel alone in 10:5–6 can now be lifted, for the kingdom of the Son of man as described in Daniel 7:14 requires *disciples of all nations. Ethnē* ('nations') is the regular Greek term for Gentiles, and it has been argued that this command therefore actually excludes the Jews from the scope of the disciples' mission. But to send the disciples to 'the Gentiles' is merely to *extend* the range of their mission, and need not imply a cessation of the mission to Israel which has

[1] Jeremias, *NTT*, p. 303; *cf.* Dunn, pp. 123–125.
[2] For this interpretation, see K. Grayston, *JSNT* 21 (1984), pp. 105–109.

already been commanded, and can now be taken for granted. Moreover, the phrase *panta ta ethnē* ('all nations') has been used previously in 24:9, 14; 25:32 in contexts which probably all include Israel in 'the nations'. And surely there can be no suggestion in Daniel 7:14 of the exclusion of Israel from the dominion of the Son of man, who himself represents Israel.[1] This then is the culmination of the theme we have noted throughout the Gospel, the calling of a people of God far wider than that of the Old Testament, in which membership is based not on race but on a relationship with God through his Messiah (see above, on 3:9; 8:11–12; 12:21; 21:28–32, 41–43; 22:8–10; 24:14, 31; 26:13). The description of the mission in terms of *making disciples* emphasizes this personal allegiance. It is sometimes argued that if Jesus had spoken so clearly, his followers could not have been so hesitant about the admission of Gentile believers as we see them in Acts, but it is worth noting (a) that Luke sees no inconsistency between an equally clear command (Lk. 24:47; Acts 1:8) and the later hesitations, and (b) that in fact the debates in the post-Easter church were not so much over *whether* Gentiles should be admitted as over the *conditions* of their admission (circumcision, keeping the food-laws, *etc.*).

*Baptizing* and 'teaching' (v. 20) are participles dependent on the main verb, *make disciples*; they further specify what is involved in discipleship. *Baptizing* has been mentioned in this Gospel only as the activity of John, though the Gospel of John makes it clear that it was a characteristic also of Jesus' ministry at least in the early days while John was still active (Jn. 3:22–26; 4:1–3). It was against the background of John's practice that it would be understood, as an act of repentance and of identification with the purified and prepared people of God (see on 3:6, 9, 13). But while John's baptism was only a preparatory one (3:11), Jesus now institutes one with a fuller meaning. It is a commitment to (*in the name* is literally '*into* the name', implying entrance into an allegiance) *the Father, the Son and the Holy Spirit* (all three of whom, interestingly, were involved in the event of Jesus' own baptism, 3:16–17). Jesus thus takes his place along with his Father and the Spirit as the object of worship and of the disciple's commitment. The experi-

---

[1] See further, J. P. Meier, *CBQ* 39 (1977), pp. 94–102.

ence of God in these three Persons is the essential basis of discipleship. At the same time the singular noun *name* (not 'names') underlines the unity of the three Persons.

Baptism was in fact performed in New Testament times, as far as our records go, in the name of Jesus, which is surprising if Jesus had laid down an explicit trinitarian formula before his ascension. An explanation for this may be found in the argument that these words, which later came to be used as a liturgical formula, were not originally so intended and used. They were rather 'a description of what baptism accomplished' (*AB*, pp. 362–363). Or it may be that Matthew is summarizing, in the more explicit and formal language of the church in which he wrote, the gist of what Jesus had taught about the God his disciples were to worship, teaching which had clearly associated himself and the Spirit with the Father, even if not in a set formula.[1] It has been argued that these words were not part of the original text of Matthew, since Eusebius regularly in his pre-Nicene works quotes Matthew 28:19 in the shorter form 'Go and make disciples of all nations in my name',[2] but the fact that no extant manuscript of Matthew has this reading suggests that this was rather Eusebius' own abbreviation than a text he found in existing manuscripts.[3]

**20.** Hitherto Jesus alone has been the teacher, and the verb has not been used by Matthew of his disciples' ministry. Now they take over his role of *teaching*, which is the necessary application of his 'authority' (v. 18); see Davies, pp. 198–199. They are to teach not just abstract ideas, but *to observe all that I have commanded you*, the latter verb being from the same root as the noun for 'commandments' in 5:19; 15:3; *etc.* (and *cf.* the same verb in 15:4; 19:7). There is thus a strongly ethical emphasis in this summary of Christian mission and discipleship, as there has been in Jesus' teaching throughout this Gospel. To 'make disciples' is not complete unless it leads them to a life of observing Jesus' commandments.

[1] See my discussion of this possibility in C. Brown (ed.), *History, Criticism and Faith* (1976), pp. 130–131.
[2] So most fully and attractively H. Kosmala, *Annual of the Swedish Theological Institute* 4 (1965), pp. 132–147.
[3] See esp. B. J. Hubbard, *The Matthean Redaction of a Primitive Apostolic Commissioning*, pp. 151–175.

The concluding promise of Jesus' presence echoes both the implication of the name Emmanuel in 1:23 and also the promise to 'two or three gathered in my name' in 18:20. (The latter reference confirms that the promise applies to more than just the eleven, even though only they were present; see on v. 16.) For *the close of the age*, see above, on 24:3. The promise of God's presence often accompanied his call to service in the Old Testament (*e.g.* Ex. 3:12; Jos. 1:5); it is not so much a cosy reassurance as a necessary equipment for mission. That the risen Lord can now make such a promise as God made to his people in the past brings the Gospel's portrait of Jesus ('God with us', 1:23) to a stupendous climax.

P9-BZN-256

3 2487 00076

859317

Chesney, Marion
Deirdre and desire

WITHDRAWN

Newark Public Library
BOOKMOBILE

NEWARK PUBLIC LIBRARY
NEWARK, OHIO 43055

Also available in Large Print
by Marion Chesney:

*Minerva*
*The Taming of Annabelle*

# Marion Chesney

# DEIRDRE AND DESIRE

G.K. HALL &CO.
Boston, Massachusetts
1985

Copyright © 1983 by Marion Chesney.

All rights reserved.

Published by G. K. Hall & Co.
A publishing subsidiary of ITT

Published in Large Print by arrangement
with St. Martin's Press.

G. K. Hall Large Print Book Series.

Set in 16pt Plantin.

*Library of Congress Cataloging in Publication Data*

Chesney, Marion.
    Deirdre and desire.

    (G. K. Hall large print book series)
    1. Large type books.   I. Title.
[PR6053.H4535D4   1985]        823'.914        84–29045
ISBN 0–8161–3824–9 (lg. print)

For my sister, Tilda Grenier,
and her husband, Laurent,
with love

859317

Georgian menu used in this volume of *The Six Sisters* was taken from *Georgian Meals and Menus* by Maggie Black, published by the Kingsmead Press, Rosewell House, Kingsmead Square, Bath, England.

859817

# SPECTATOR AB EXTRA

*Parvenant*

It was but this winter I came up to town,
And already I'm gaining a sort of renown;
Find my way to good houses without much ado,
And beginning to see the nobility too.
  So useful it is to have money, heigh-ho!
  So useful it is to have money.

There's something undoubtedly in a fine air,
To know how to smile and be able to stare.
High breeding is something, but well-bred or not,
In the end the one queston is, what have you got.
  So needful it is to have money, heigh-ho!
  So needful it is to have money.

And the angels in pink and the angels in blue,
In muslins and moirés so lovely and new,
What is it they want, and so wish you to guess,
But if you have money, the answer is Yes.
  So needful, they tell you, is money, heigh-ho!
  So needful it is to have money.
                                Arthur Hugh Clough

# DEIRDRE AND DESIRE

# CHAPTER ONE

It had been a day of heavy rain, but towards sunset the clouds had broken, and an angry, yellow, glaring light bathed the village of Hopeworth and the surrounding sodden fields.

Little choppy golden ripples danced angrily across the village pond. The sun blazed through two huge purple-and-black ragged clouds, and the rising wind sent a shower of wet brown leaves dancing over the cottage roofs.

It was the sort of sunset which presaged a high wind; yellow sunsets always meant a wild night to come.

Squire Radford huddled his thin, old shoulders further into his greatcoat, feeling the heavy material beginning to flap against his spindly legs.

As he hurried in the direction of his cottage *ornée*, he cursed himself for having been stupid enough to accept Sir Edwin Armitage's invitation to take tea at the Hall.

Sir Edwin's haughty wife had been glacially aloof, as usual, and her plain daughters, Josephine and Emily, still

1

unmarried, had giggled and pouted in turns in the most irritating manner.

The squire's thoughts turned from Sir Edwin to Sir Edwin's brother, the Reverend Charles Armitage, vicar of St Charles and St Jude in the parish of Hopeworth. For although the vicar was a close friend of the squire and usually came to call most evenings, Squire Radford found himself hoping for the first time that the ebullient fox-hunting vicar would decide to stag in the comfort of his own home.

It was a sad and lonely feeling to see a dear friend so monstrous changed in character. The vicar had become so puffed up, so swollen in pride, that he seemed another man altogether.

The rot had set in, mused the squire, wincing as the first blast of windy rain tugged at his old fashioned three-cornered hat, with the marriage of the vicar's second eldest daughter, Annabelle.

His eldest, Minerva, had done very well for herself by marrying Lord Sylvester Comfrey, but the vicar had accepted that piece of good fortune with a comfortable sort of gratitude. Then Annabelle had become wed to the Marquess of Brabington and the vicar had accepted that piece of good luck with a

2

comfortable sort of gratitude as well. But after Annabelle's marriage when she had gone off with her husband to the Peninsular Wars, the vicar had found his social standing much elevated by virtue of the aristocracy of his new in-laws. He began to spend as much time in Town as he could out of the fox-hunting Season, returning to the country only to plunge into more wild farming experiments, and more expensive purchases of hounds.

He was now the proud possessor of twenty couple of hounds, a ridiculous quantity for a country parson. Two years had passed since Annabelle's wedding; Lord Sylvester's steward, who had done much to put the Armitage farming land in good heart, was now back managing his master's estates; and once more the vicar was faced with ruin.

He had been faced with ruin before, but never before had Charles Armitage ignored the fact so blatantly.

And he still had four daughters unwed, and two sons at Eton whose future was a weighty matter.

Two whole years had passed since Annabelle wed the Marquess of Brabington. How old were they all now?

The squire pushed open the tall iron gates

leading to his cottage and murmured names and ages over to himself.

'Let me see, the twins, Peregrine and James, will be twelve. Minerva will now be twenty-one! Dear me. How quickly the time flies. Annabelle will therefore be nineteen which will mean Deirdre is just eighteen, Daphne is sixteen, Diana, fifteen, and little Frederica, fourteen.'

The squire's soft-footed Indian servant opened the door and relieved his master of his coat.

'Thank you, Ram,' said the squire. 'I am chilled to the bone. Bring some brandy to the library and if anyone calls—*anyone*—I am not at home.'

Even when the squire felt mellowed by his slippered feet on the hearth, the curtains drawn tightly against the rising storm, and the flames from a blazing coal fire sending golden flames dancing in his brandy glass, he was relieved to be alone.

He had had his cottage *ornée* built some twelve years before to replace the old insanitary Tudor hall which had served his earlier years. He had wanted something simple, and considered his fifteen charming rooms hung with French wallpaper and filled with fine furniture, paintings and china

4

sufficient for his needs. His wife and his daughter had both died a long time ago. The ceiling was low and raftered and the gold lettering of the calfbound books which lined the library wall winked cheerfully in the soft glow from the oil lamps.

As an angry burst of rain struck the windows the squire smiled contentedly and snuggled deeper in his armchair, sipped his brandy, and opened a book.

Then, as the wind slackened slightly, he heard the clip-clop of a horse's hooves coming up his short drive.

The vicar.

He crouched a little further down in his chair, listening guiltily to the sounds of the vicar's arrival, the hammering on the door, the soft murmur of his servant's voice.

Then the closing of the door and no sound other than the howl of the rising wind.

The noise of the wind must have covered the sounds of the rejected vicar's retreat.

Suddenly, Squire Radford got to his feet and walked to the library window nearest his chair and pulled aside the curtains.

He let out a frightened little scream and backed away from the window, his wrinkled old hands to his mouth.

A hideous, squat, fat, distorted face was

5

pressed against the glass.

Then the face retreated a little and resolved itself into that of the Reverend Charles Armitage.

He was mouthing something but the squire could not hear him because of the noise of the storm. Still too shocked to gather his wits together, the squire made flapping movements with his hands to indicate that the vicar should return to the front door.

Then he closed the curtains and sat down in the armchair by the fire, his heart still thudding.

In no time at all, the Reverend Charles Armitage came striding in.

He was a short, round man who normally wore a shovel hat and a pepper-and-salt coat and gaiters. The squire had often thought a Union Jack across his chest would have turned him into the perfect John Bull.

But on this occasion, the vicar presented a very odd figure. His face was painted and roughed and he wore an elaborate cravat and evening clothes, his skin-tight trousers being shoved into hessian boots. As he moved, he unmistakably creaked and snapped.

'Corsets, Charles?' queried the squire faintly.

'Nonsense,' said the vicar, turning even

redder. 'It's my bones creakin'. Being locked out in this demned plaguey weather don't do my old bones a mort o' good. Well, well, well. I'm here, and that's the main thing.'

He sat down by the fire opposite the squire and helped himself to a glass of brandy before removing his dripping hat and putting it down on the hearth where it started to steam.

His light brown hair had been teased and curled and pomaded so that it stood up on his head like a crest, giving him an air of perpetual surprise.

He tossed his glass of brandy off, shuddered, looked at the fire and sighed lugubriously.

The squire said nothing, so the vicar sighed noisily and eyed his friend out of the corners of his twinkling shoe-button eyes.

The squire resigned himself.

'What is the matter, Charles?' he demanded in his high precise voice.

'I have lost my faith,' mourned the vicar. 'Just like that. Just like the thingummy on the road to whatsit.'

'He didn't lose it. He found it,' said the squire crossly.

'Who?'

'St Paul.'

'Oh, him? O' course, it was easy for *him*,'

said the vicar with something like a sneer. 'But does He care if I've lost my faith? Does He send down lights or one small miracle? No. Couldn't even get me some decent hunting weather last year.'

'I do not see, Charles, how you can claim to have lost what you never had,' said the Squire, becoming much flushed 'You are turned exceeding arrogant. Without humility there is no faith.'

'Don't preach,' said the vicar huffily. He poured himself more brandy and sighed again.

The squire looked at him in a mixture of exasperation and compassion.

'You are a great child,' he said gently. 'Faith or lack of faith is not what troubles you. It is money, or the lack of *that*.'

'Aye, that's it,' said the vicar. 'You have it in a nutshell. Two rich sons-in-law and I can't get my hands on them. Brabington's in France and Comfrey had already gone to join him.'

'Indeed! I did not know Minerva and her husband had left the country? I did not expect it. She is soon to present you with a grandson.'

'Another two months,' said the vicar moodily. 'And it'll probably come into the world speaking French.'

'But what took Lord Sylvester to France?'

'I don't know. Went along o' everyone else, I s'pose. At least they're in Paris, and haven't gone to Waterloo to poke around the dead bodies with a stick.'

'My dear Charles!'

There came a silence. The door opened and the servant came in and put two large shovelfuls of coal on the fire.

The vicar watched morosely as grey smoke began to curl up in long trailing wisps. Then little yellow flames sprang through the bank of black coal and green and blue ones danced in the spurts of coal gas.

The clock ticked sonorously in the corner. A great buffet of wind howled round the building.

'There is a solution,' said the vicar at last. 'When I was in London, there was a lot o' talk in the clubs about Lord Harry Desire.'

'The Earl of Carchester's son?'

'Him.'

'And?'

The vicar heaved a gusty sigh. 'Desire's got an uncle who's a nabob, Jeremy Blewett. He says he'll leave all his money to Desire if the man gets married. Blewett's said to be on his deathbed.'

9

'Has Desire no money of his own?'

'Not much. The Carchesters never knew how to keep it. He lives high, does young Desire. He spends more on his tailor than I spend on my pack.'

The squire did some rapid mental calculation.

'Impossible,' he said at last.

'True. He's a great dandy.'

'I do not see how this young man can aid you. How old is he?'

'Late in his twenties. Thirty, say.'

'You have met him?'

'Not I,' shrugged the vicar. 'Heard of him, though.'

'You cannot possibly be thinking of a husband for Deirdre!'

'Why not?' demanded the vicar crossly. 'Had enough trouble with Minerva and Annabelle. Arranged marriage will be just the thing.'

'Deirdre is a highly intelligent lady with a mind of her own.'

The vicar ferreted around in his waistcoat pockets until he found a goosequill and then proceeded to pick his teeth, much to the fastidious squire's irritation. 'Hark 'ee, Jimmy,' he grinned. 'Deirdre's been *told* she's the brainy one o' the family for so long, she's come to believe it herself. But she reads *novels*. So there!'

'I read novels myself,' protested the squire.

'Different for a man,' muttered the vicar. 'Lots o' vices are.'

'I think you are making a great mistake,' said the squire severely. 'I don't know what has come over you this last two years, Charles. You have wasted your money, you have taken to wearing *paint*, and, yes you *are* wearing corsets.'

The vicar flushed and looked mutinous. '*I* haven't changed,' he said, whipping himself up into a fine anger. 'It's you who have changed. Demme, you're worse than the bishop. Always preaching and moralizing and argyfying. I'm off!'

'If our friendship means so little to you that you cannot take a piece of well-meant criticism . . .'

'Pah!' said the vicar, rising, picking up his steaming hat and cramming it on his head.

'Let us not part in anger,' pleaded the squire. 'Join me for supper, I beg you, and let us talk this thing over.'

The vicar marched to the door and then turned.

'"Better a dinner of herbs where love is, than a stalled ox and hatred therewith."

11

Proverbs, Chapter fifteen, verse seventeen.'

'Oh, Charles...' began the squire, but the vicar had already made his exit.

A ride through the night did little to improve the Reverend Charles Armitage's temper. The squire's sorrowful, reproachful face kept rising in front of him as he spurred his horse in the direction of the vicarage. He had felt a new man these past two years. An important man. One of the peerage. By virtue of his daughters' successful marriages, he was invited to all the best houses.

He felt he had regained his youth. And if his corsets pinched and the paint on his face made his skin itch, these were mere pinpricks set against the heady exhilaration of feeling he was one of the bucks and bloods.

He stomped into the tiny, dark hall of the vicarage and was pulled up short by the sight of his daughter, Daphne. She was standing in front of the hall looking-glass, staring at her reflection with a rapt expression on her face.

'Go to your room, miss,' snapped the vicar, 'and stop endlessly preening yourself. And send Deirdre to my study.'

Daphne leaned forward, closer to the glass, and patted one glossy black ringlet into place.

'Yes, Papa,' she said vaguely as she drifted towards the stairs.

'Grumph!' said the vicar. He shoved his head round the door of the vicarage parlour. His wife was lying on a sofa. She raised a brown mask of a face in his direction.

'Gad's 'Oonds!' shrieked the vicar. 'What . . . ?'

'It's mud,' said his wife, moving her lips as little as possible. ''Tis said to be most beneficial.'

'Pah!' snorted the vicar, pulling shut the door and crossing the hall to his study. Mrs Armitage, when not suffering from some imaginary illness or other, was always trying out beauty remedies. He rang the bell for Betty, the housemaid, and demanded a bottle of white brandy and a jug of hot water. The maid went to light the fire but he growled that he would do it himself. As soon as the brandy had arrived, he poured a generous measure into a pewter tankard and added hot water. Then he threw another measure of brandy over the sticks in the grate and struck a lucifer. The fire went up with a satisfying *whoosh*, nearly singeing his eyebrows. He tossed on a log and settled himself behind his cluttered desk.

The door opened and Miss Deirdre Armitage walked in. The vicar looked at her, sighed, and looked quickly away again.

13

Everyone called Deirdre a beauty but her father always thought, uncomfortably, that his daughter reminded him of a fox.

She had thick, shining red hair and green eyes, not the emerald green of Lord Sylvester, but a peculiar jade green like sea-washed glass. They were slightly tilted at the corners. This, together with her short straight nose, high cheekbones and pointed chin gave her an elfin appearance. She had a small, high, firm bosom, a tiny waist, and thin, fragile wrists and ankles. But there always seemed to be some inner joke amusing Deirdre and that was what made the vicar think of a fox. He sometimes thought her sly.

'Well, Papa,' said Deirdre, sitting down opposite him, 'and how was Squire Radford?'

'How did you know I'd been to squire's?'

'Because your coat is in the hall, Papa, and it is wet, and you look guilty and in a bad temper which is the way you always look when you come from Squire Radford.'

'See here, my pert miss, it's time you guarded that tongue o' yours. No man wants a carroty-pated clever shrew for a wife.'

Those green eyes of Deirdre's that gave so little away studied him intently.

'I am to have a Season next year, Papa,' said Deirdre at last. 'Minerva has promised to

14

bring me out. I ... am ... looking ... forward ... to ... it ... very ... much,' she added, slowly and clearly.

'Oh, ah,' said the vicar studying the bottom of his tankard.

'And I shall not put myself through any of the miseries Minerva and Annabelle endured. I shall *know* when I am in love with a gentleman.'

'Oh, *love*. You've been reading novels again. Love has little to do with a good, sensible marriage.'

'On the contrary,' said Deirdre firmly, 'it is everything. As a man of God, Papa, you would naturally never dream of forcing one of your daughters into a loveless marriage contract.'

'Minerva was prepared to,' pointed out the vicar crossly.

'She was fortunate she did not have to do it,' said Deirdre. 'What did you wish to speak to me about?'

The vicar thought rapidly. No need to cross swords with Deirdre until he had seen this Lord Harry Desire. Perhaps nothing would come of it. And he could always wait until one or both his sons-in-law returned from Paris. But he had asked them for money before, and he knew that this time Lord

Sylvester Comfrey might take over the management of the vicarage lands himself as he had threatened to do last time. And Lord Sylvester considered the vicar's private hunt an extravagance.

'I just wanted to tell you I am off to Town in the morning,' he said grumpily. 'So be a good girl and look after your mother and sisters.'

'Oh, Papa,' said Deirdre, her strange eyes shining in the firelight, 'take me with you. *Please.* It is so boring here. Daphne is no fun any longer. All she does now is droop in front of the looking-glass.'

'No. You've your duties. You've got to read to Lady Wentwater. Then you'd best take some cordial to Mrs Briggs what's poorly.'

'What about your sermon?'

'Let Pettifor handle it.' Mr Pettifor was the vicar's overworked curate. 'Time enough for you to be jauntering to London when Minerva gets home.'

When Deirdre reached the privacy of her room, she found her hands were shaking. She knew the vicarage finances were at low ebb. She knew her father probably planned to rescue them by marrying her off to some rich man who would provide a large marriage

16

settlement. Then she smiled to herself and began to relax.

Although she had met many young men when she had visited her two sisters' homes, not one of them had shown more than a passing interest in her. She knew she was always damned as a blue-stocking but that suited her very well. Deirdre was an intense romantic and believed in the marriage of true minds. She was content to wait. And Minerva would not allow Papa to force her into any marriage she found distasteful.

\*     \*     \*

'If she complains to Minerva, then Minerva will put a stop to it,' mused the vicar as he set out for London on the following morning. 'Well, I'll put a spoke in *that* wheel. I'll give a guinea to John-postboy to drop her letters to Paris down the nearest well until I give him leave to do otherwise.' His conscience gave a sudden, vicious stab. But he started to recite the names of his hounds like a litany to comfort himself. Not one would have to be sacrificed if his plans came out right. He had made a few mistakes in breeding, but now he was sure he was on his way to owning the best pack in England. Women were always

17

bleating about love and marriage anyway. It was an attitude. The poor dears were supposed to think that way. Now he, Charles Armitage, had never loved his wife and if he could put up with her plaguey maunderings and moanings for all these years, then so could anyone else, he reasoned, rather incoherently. And women were the lesser breed. Definitely.

Like Lord Chesterfield, he considered women to be 'children of a larger growth', and 'a man of sense only trifles with them, plays with them, humours and flatters them as he does with a sprightly forward child.'

By the time he had reached Town and had made use of his daughter Minerva's town house, he was once more happy within himself.

Barbered and pomaded and laced into a pair of Cumberland corsets under a sky-blue coat of Bath superfine and the latest thing in canary-coloured pantaloons, the vicar creaked and swaggered his way down St James's Street and turned in at the door of White's.

White's Club had changed little since the vicar's salad days, although the entrance had been moved lower down and the old doorway turned into a bow window. The subscription fee had been raised to eleven guineas and the entrance fee from ten to twenty guineas. Beau Brummell passed fashionable judgement on London from his seat in the bow window.

Swift had called White's 'the common rendezvous of infamous sharpers and noble cullies' but White's was, in fact, *the* club. Certainly it was the place to hunt down such an Exquisite as Lord Harry Desire.

The club was remarkably quiet although it was three in the afternoon. It transpired there had been a heavy gambling session the night before and no doubt everyone was still sleeping off the effects. He espied Colonel Brian, and, after some hesitation, approached him.

The elderly colonel had been the paramour of Lady Godolphin, a distant relative of the vicar's wife who had brought out Minerva. Lady Godolphin, that ancient Mrs Malaprop of society, had believed the colonel to be married, when in fact his wife was dead. The colonel had put all that right by asking her to marry him. He had been accepted. For a month afterwards, Lady Godolphin had talked of little else but the preparation of her torso—her word for trousseau—and then, quite suddenly, it had all fizzled out. The gossips would have it that the colonel had jilted her. But no one could find the truth of the matter since both parties refused to discuss the subject.

'I say, Colonel,' said the vicar breezily, 'I haven't seen you this age. You do not seem to be in plump currant.'

For the colonel looked sadly woebegone.

The colonel looked carefully at the painted and groomed vicar for several moments and then his face cleared. 'Charles Armitage!' he exclaimed. 'I would not have known you.'

'Course not,' said the vicar with awful vanity. 'I've growed fashionable.'

'Quite,' said the colonel nervously, taking a step back to escape from the overpowering smell of musk which hovered round Mr Armitage like a great yellow cloud. 'How are your girls? Well, I trust?'

'Minerva and Annabelle are in Paris.'

'The whole of society seems to be in Paris,' sighed the colonel. 'The town is remarkably thin of company. It will be a drab Little Season.'

'I plan to call on Lady Godolphin later,' said the vicar airily. 'Care to accompany me?'

The colonel shook his head sadly, and looked at the floor.

The vicar was longing to ask him the reason for his disaffection with Lady

20

Godolphin, but the thought of his real reason for being in the club made him drop the question he had been about to ask, and demand instead, 'Know Harry Desire?'

'Slightly. I saw him a minute ago.'

'I would like an introduction,' said the vicar. 'I have a private and personal matter I wish to discuss with him.'

'Very well,' said Colonel Brian. 'He is in the coffee room. If you would do me a small favour in return . . .?'

'By all means.'

'When you call on Lady Godolphin, tell her Arthur sends his warmest regards. No. Do not ask me anything.'

'"Arthur sends his warmest regards,"' repeated the vicar impatiently. 'Now, lead me to Desire.'

Lord Harry Desire was sitting barricaded behind a newspaper in the coffee room. He looked up as the colonel stood behind him and cleared his throat. Colonel Brian then introduced the vicar and took his leave.

The vicar sat down opposite Lord Harry and studied him intently.

Lord Harry stared back, his gaze empty, blue and limpid.

He was not quite the fashionable rakish Exquisite the vicar had expected. The first thing that struck the vicar was the man's incredible beauty. Lord Harry had thick, black, glossy hair falling in artistic disarray over a broad white forehead. His blue eyes were clear and innocent like the eyes of a child. The lids were curved, giving him the lazy, sensual look of some classical statues. His mouth was firm, but there was a certain air of lanquid effeminacy about him caused by the girlish purity of his skin and by the slimness of his tall figure.

His clothes were beautifully tailored, reflected the vicar with a pang of envy. His bottle-green coat sat on his shoulders without a wrinkle and his buff-coloured pantaloons looked as if they had been painted on to his legs. His hessian boots shone like black glass. His cravat rose from above his striped waistcoat in intricately sculptured folds.

'You're younger than I thought,' said the vicar abruptly.

'I am remarkably well-preserved for my thirty years,' said Lord Harry earnestly.

'Aye well, just so,' said the vicar.

There was a long silence. Outside, someone was murdering Mozart on a barrel organ.

'Well, well,' said the vicar, rubbing his chubby hands together. 'Well, well, well,'

Lord Harry continued to survey him with a pleasant smiling look.

'You must wonder what it is I want to speak to you about,' said the vicar desperately.

'Oh, no,' said Lord Harry gently. 'I never wonder about anything. It is too fatiguing. And I am sure you will tell me in your own good time.'

The vicar looked at him in irritation. Then he thought instead of the nabob uncle's fortune and leaned forwards and patted Lord Harry's knee in an avuncular manner.

Lord Harry looked at the vicar, looked at the hand on his knee, and looked at the vicar again. His expression did not change, but the vicar's face reddened and he hurriedly withdrew his hand.

'See, it's like this here,' said the Reverend Charles Armitage, beginning to perspire, 'I heard you was in need of getting married so you could inherit your uncle's fortune.'

Lord Harry surveyed him blandly. The vicar felt himself becoming angry. Why didn't the young clod *say* something? This was worse than he had imagined it would be. Better get to the point.

'I have this daughter, see. Deirdre. Eighteen. Beautiful. I ain't got the blunt, you

23

need the wife, what say we strike a bargain?'

A flicker of something glinted in his lordship's blue eyes and then was gone.

'Indeed!' he said politely.

'Well?' said the vicar impatiently. 'What about it?'

'Does she have red hair?' asked Lord Harry, looking vaguely in the direction of the chandelier. 'I can't abide red hair.'

'Dye,' decided the vicar to himself. He thought briefly of God the way one thinks of a nagging, bullying parent, slightly closed his eyes, took a deep breath and said, 'No.'

'And she is in Town?'

'No,' said the vicar. 'But she will be. In four days' time.'

'I met your eldest daughter,' mused Lord Harry. 'Lady Sylvester Comfrey. Very beautiful and very wise. She told me how she despised men who put pride in dress before pride in leading a virtuous life.'

'Oh, Minerva will have her little joke,' said the vicar jovially, privately cursing his eldest for her priggish moralizing.

'Is your daughter—Deirdre—vastly clever?'

The vicar looked at Lord Harry from out of the corner of his little shoe-button eyes and wondered whether Lord Harry wanted a

24

clever wife. Lord Harry looked back with an expression of absolute vacancy on his beautiful face.

'Oh, no,' said the vicar. 'Very womanly. Pretty little thing. Domesticated. Been well-trained. See here,' he went on, improvizing rapidly, 'she will be staying with Lady Godolphin next Monday and we shall behaving a little *musicale*. Perhaps you would like to attend?'

There was a long silence. A bluebottle, brave survivor of summer, buzzed against the glass. A log shifted on the fire and several clocks began to chime the half hour.

'Yes,' said Lord Harry at last. 'I will be there.'

'Good, good, send you a card,' gabbled the vicar, now desperate to escape.

Lord Harry raised one long, slim, white hand as the vicar rose to his feet.

'You are sure your daughter's affections are not otherwise engaged?'

'No,' said the vicar, glad to be able to tell the truth at last. 'Deirdre's never even looked at a man, if you know what I mean.'

'No, I don't,' said Lord Harry pleasantly.

'Well, don't trouble your brain with it,' said the vicar, patting him on the shoulder. 'We look forward to the pleasure of your company on Monday.'

'What an idiot!' muttered the vicar to himself as he left the club. 'Never mind. He's a manageable idiot and Deirdre will be quite happy with a complacent husband.'

He set off at a brisk pace in the direction of Lady Godolphin's house.

He needed all the help he could get!

## CHAPTER TWO

Deirdre Armitage sat reading a novel she did not like to Lady Wentwater whom she did not like either.

The drawing room was dark and musty. Lady Wentwater was white and doughy and musty. As she read, Deirdre wondered about Lady Wentwater's nephew, Guy. No one had seen him in the county since the time it had seemed he was enamoured of Annabelle.

Rumour had it that the vicar had frightened him away. Guy Wentwater had said he was a slave trader, and although he had long quit that ghastly means of earning money, the Armitage family were happy that he chose to stay away.

Then Deirdre's thoughts turned to the

story she was reading. It was called *Ludovic's Revenge* by A Lady of Quality and Deirdre judged it quite the silliest tale she had ever read. Everyone seemed either to turn scarlet or go 'ashen pale'. Men and women fainted with amazing regularity and there wasn't even a decent ghost.

Deirdre took a quick glance at the clock. Then she closed the book firmly.

'It is late, Lady Wentwater,' she said. 'I must return home.'

'Then come tomorrow.'

'Daphne will come tomorrow,' said Deirdre, privately vowing to give her sister's hair a good yank if she did not.

'Oh, *Daphne*. I will need to shroud every looking glass in the house or I won't hear a word out of her,' snorted Lady Wentwater. 'Too taken up with herself, she is.'

'She has reason to be,' said Deirdre, who, though she privately agreed with Lady Wentwater, did not like criticism of any of her sisters. 'She has become even more beautiful than Minerva or Annabelle.'

'Aye, and she knows it. Why, Guy! When did you arrive?'

Deirdre gave a little gasp and leapt to her feet, turning to face the monster slave trader.

Guy Wentwater stood smiling at her,

27

looking so handsome, so normal, and so, yes, *ordinary* that Deirdre lost her fears and was able to drop him a curtsey with an air of composure.

'Permit me to escort you home, Miss ... Deirdre. It is Miss Deirdre, is it not?' smiled Guy.

Deirdre nodded, but added that she was perfectly capable of seeing herself home.

To her annoyance, he walked with her to the door.

'We have not seen you in some time, Mr Wentwater,' said Deirdre, praying that he would leave her at the main door.

'No, I have just returned from Paris. I finally sold out.'

'Sold out? Then you were in the military, sir?'

'Yes,' he sighed, looking grave. 'I know what you and your family think of me, Miss Deirdre. Have you ever considered the disgust I feel for myself? The barbarous trade I briefly engaged in was the senseless folly of a young man. I fought for my country at Waterloo. It was one way to prove to myself that I am not quite so evil.'

'Oh, tell me about Waterloo,' pleaded Deirdre, quite forgetting that she had wished only a moment before to be quit of him.

28

'Everyone says such subjects are not fit for female ears. But it was a wonderful victory.'

He gently took her arm in his and walked with her down the drive. His tale of glory and bravery and courage and death fascinated Deirdre, who hung rapt on his every word.

She could not help admiring his tall, slender figure, the quiet elegance of his dress, and the hard lines about his mouth, 'put there by suffering,' she told herself.

They reached the vicarage all too soon.

He seemed to recollect his surroundings with a start. 'Forgive me,' he said in a low voice, 'if I do not come any further. I do not wish to embarrass your family. In fact, I would be grateful if you would not mention that I am in Hopeworth. It will be *our* secret.'

'Yes,' said Deirdre breathlessly, for he had taken her hand and was holding it in a tight clasp. 'But if I told them how brave you are, how you have made your amends ... well, they would see things differently *now*. As I do.'

'I cannot risk losing a friendship so new and so precious to me,' he said. 'Other people might not have your generosity of spirit.

'I *have* changed, Miss Deirdre. I have put away the shallow affections and affectations of my youth. The friendships I now crave are

29

the friendships of the mind. Do you understand?'

'Oh, yes,' breathed Deirdre.

'Then I shall see you again. Perhaps you would care to walk with me tomorrow afternoon?'

Deirdre hesitated only for a moment. Guy Wentwater was straight out of her private fantasies, a reformed villain, a man of the world, an equal companion, a soul-mate. She felt full of an aching, heady, suffocating exhilaration.

'I will meet you in the churchyard,' she smiled. 'At two.'

He raised her hand to his lips.

'Until tomorrow,' he whispered.

He turned away and strode off down the road. Deirdre watched him for a few moments and then rushed indoors, up to her room, and threw herself face down on the bed, feeling her whole body throb in an aching turmoil of excitement and yearning. All the loneliness and boredom of her days had fled. Had she not known that if she waited there would be one special man? He had been a slave trader, yes. But so long ago. And he had made his amends and paid his debt.

Nothing could spoil her idyll. Papa needed

30

money and Guy Wentwater had money.

Papa would come about. All he wanted was money to breed more and better hounds.

★     ★     ★

The Reverend Charles Armitage sat in the Green Saloon in Lady Godolphin's mansion in Hanover Square and poured out his tale of financial woe and the necessity of arranging a marriage between Deirdre and Lord Harry Desire.

'There, there,' admonished her ladyship when he had finished. 'There's no need to become historical. I can understand the practicality of an arranged marriage. We *all* need money,' she added firmly, in case the reverend had any hopes of asking her for any.

'So you'll do it?' asked the vicar. 'You'll house Deirdre and arrange this *musicale?*'

'Yes, provided you repay me when you can,' pointed out Lady Godolphin. 'You still look worried. What is the matter?'

'It's her hair,' said the vicar gloomily. 'She'll need to dye it. Desire can't abide red-heads.'

'No need to dye,' said Lady Godolphin. 'Wear a wig. I always do.'

She patted her flaxen wig complacently.

31

Like the vicar, she battled the increasing years with a great deal of paint.

Lady Godolphin was in her late fifties, squat, with a bulldog face buried under a layer of blanc and rouge.

'He don't like clever misses either,' went on the vicar.

'Deirdre's a bit of a chatterbox,' said Lady Godolphin. 'Can't understand half what she says. Last time she was here, she was prosing on about bacon and I thought she meant pigs but it turned out she was talking about some Elizabethan philanderer.'

The vicar recollected his message. 'Saw Colonel Brian at White's today,' he remarked casually. 'Sends his warmest regards. Said, "Arthur sends his warmest regards."'

'Oh, he did, did he,' said Lady Godolphin airily. 'Trouble with Arthur is, he's too old for me.'

'Oh,' said the vicar hopefully, waiting for more.

But Lady Godolphin returned to the subject of Deirdre. 'Deirdre always was a bit wild, she and Daphne. Is Daphne still a hoyden?'

'No, she's grown vain. Looks at herself in the glass and does little else.'

'Ah, a narcotic,' said Lady Godolphin,

32

nodding her great head wisely.

'A what?'

'A narcotic. Really, Charles, did they teach you nothing at Oxford? He was one of them Greeks what was so beautiful he wouldn't even have anything to do with echoes and he fell in love with his reflection in a pool, and since he couldn't marry his reflection, he pined away and turned into a narcotic. It's that yellow and white flower.'

'I don't have anything to do with echoes either,' said the vicar in bewilderment.

'Oh, *stoopid*, echoes was not a them but a *her*.'

'It's all heathen talk,' said the vicar righteously. 'And a fat lot o' good it did them Greeks either. Where are they now? Hey? Slavin' for a lot o' Turks.'

'In any case,' said Lady Godolphin firmly, 'you bring Deirdre to me and I'll have her married off in no time. Why, only think what...'

The door opened and Lady Godolphin broke off and simpered girlishly and played with the sticks of her fan.

A young man entered. He was thin and gawky but dressed in the height of fashion, from his frizzed and pomaded hair to his boots with their high heels and fixed spurs.

33

He walked forwards with that peculiarly rolling gait forced on anyone who wears fixed spurs. He wore more scent than the vicar and the vicar's musk met a strong aroma of 'Youth in Springtime'. It was as if two great fog banks of scent had merged, blotting out every other scent in the world.

'My ... er ... friend, Mr Anstey,' said Lady Godolphin, simpering quite horribly.

The vicar left as soon as he could. 'Poor Colonel Brian,' he thought. 'So *that's* the reason.'

The vicar of God told himself that perhaps he ought not to introduce his daughter to such a household. The huntsman dreamed of a pack which would outclass the Quorn, scented the wet, rotten bracken of damp November days when the wind blew from the east, saw his hounds bunched together 'so close you could cover them with a table cloth.' The Huntsman won.

★     ★     ★

The vicar had expected Deirdre to treat the news of her forthcoming visit to London and the glowing description of the superior qualities of one Lord Harry Desire with suspicion and with her usual impertinent questions.

Never had he expected outright rebellion.

'No, Papa,' said Deirdre firmly. 'I wish to remain here.'

'Why?' demanded the vicar, almost pawing the ground.

'Because my duty is to stay home and care for my sisters,' said Deirdre with a saintly expression on her face reminiscent of her sister, Minerva, at her worst.

'Piffle,' said the vicar. 'That's your best gown you got on. It's a fellow. Who've you been fiddling about with as soon as my back is turned?'

'There is no one, Papa,' said Deirdre. How could she explain to this father of hers, who appeared to have harboured not one spiritual thought in the whole of his life, the purity of her friendship with Guy Wentwater? How could she explain the excitement of shared ideas, the tender sweet awakening of love so far above the petty lusts of men?

She thought of the meeting in the churchyard, of his serious grave voice, of the way his blue eyes met hers in a direct and open look.

'It's no use bamming me,' she went on. 'You've got a marriage arranged for me and all because you have squandered good money on a silly pack of dogs.'

'WHAT!' Never had the vicar dreamed of hearing such a piece of blasphemy from one of his own daughters.

They were standing in the vicarage garden, facing each other across a flowerbed, their breath hanging in the frosty air like smoke.

'I'll get my whip,' said the vicar grimly. He turned on his heel and strode into the vicarage.

Deirdre stood frozen to the spot. He would not *dare!*

The vicar emerged brandishing his whip.

Deirdre turned and ran.

After her, hallooing and shouting came her father. Attired in a ridiculously thin muslin gown and thin silk slippers—for Deirdre had been loitering in the garden in the hope that Guy Wentwater would stroll past and see her—she picked up her skirts and fled off down the road with the vicar in hot pursuit.

Deirdre scrambled over a stile beside the road and set off over a ploughed field, feeling like a hunted fox.

The vicar's cries died away behind her, but she was still too shocked at the violence of her father's behaviour to slacken her pace.

Her dress was torn and muddy and her slippers were ruined. Her red hair flew about her face as she stumbled over the frost-hard earth of the fields behind the village, heading for the grounds of the Hall where her uncle, Sir Edwin, lived, knowing instinctively that that would be the last place the vicar would think of looking for her.

She scaled the mossy wall which bordered the grounds, hoping that one of her uncle's gamekeepers would not shoot her in mistake for a poacher.

The woods on either side of her were quiet and dark and still. Deirdre listened hard but could no longer hear any sound of her father's noisy pursuit. She stood still, her heart beating hard. What would happen when she returned to the vicarage, as return she must? There was no Minerva to intercede for her.

She was filled with a sudden, suffocating hatred for her father. Why couldn't he behave like the clergyman he was supposed to be? The vicar of St Ann's in Hopeminster was a quiet, scholarly, aesthetic man, quite unlike her father. When the vicar wasn't reeking of musk he smelled of the stables and seemed to be perpetually covered in dog hair.

The whole vicarage smelled of damp dog, thought Deirdre savagely. Here she was with a whole new love; trembling, innocent and fragile. And there was the vicar, scouring the lanes of Hopeworth for her with his whip in his hands.

'No one understands me except Guy,' whispered Deirdre to the uncaring trees.

In desperation, she sank to her knees and prayed to God for aid. She prayed long and feverishly while a pair of squirrels chattered above her head and a curious rabbit stared at her with unblinking eyes.

And then, all at once, He spoke to her. She could hear a voice in her head telling her exactly what to do.

She must return to the vicarage and apologize to her father and say she would go with him to London. While there, she would make sure this Lord Harry Desire took her in such dislike, he would never want to see her again. Then when she returned in respectable disgrace to Hopeworth, she would seek out Guy and ask him to elope with her.

A great calmness descended on Deirdre. It is quite amazing how the Almighty can occasionally tell people to go ahead and do exactly what they want to do anyway. Only very devout people manage to muddle along as best they can without hearing voices or the whirr of wings.

Feeling exalted and noble, Deirdre brushed down her skirts and made her way back home.

The vicar was already feeling ashamed of his outburst of anger. By the time he had cooled himself off with several glasses of shrub at The Six Jolly Beggermen, he had decided to return home and wait for Deirdre. When she returned, he would simply order her very calmly and quietly to see to the packing of her trunks. His cool dignity would overawe her.

But to his relief—for this calm and dignified picture of himself was beginning to fade by the time he reached the vicarage—Deirdre was waiting to give him a very pretty apology.

The vicar's normal shrewdness deserted him before the pleasure at having got his own way so easily.

Diana and Frederica accepted the news of Deirdre's forthcoming trip to London with all the aplomb of two little girls who were used to their elder sisters jauntering about in the great world. Both still attended the seminary at Hopeminster, the vicar's plans for hiring a governess having never come to anything. Daphne alone seemed shaken out of her narcissistic calm, and started to write out a long shopping list for Deirdre which contained, it appeared, the name of every beauty cosmetic to be had in London.

Mellowed by several glasses of port, the vicar leaned back in his chair after supper and surveyed his family indulgently.

He caught Deirdre looking at him with the sort of blazing green he had seen in the eyes of cornered animals. But as soon as she noticed his suddenly sharpened expression, Deirdre immediately cast her eyes meekly down and presented a demure picture of a dutiful daughter.

Deirdre felt she was seeing her father for the first time. Her acid eye took in the glory of his too-tight coat, his flushed face, the creak of his corsets. Her very biting contempt was armour to her bruised soul. Such a father *deserved* to be deceived. And her mother had never been any help, wrapped up as she was in her various ailments.

All at once, she became aware he was talking about Guy. 'I hear young Wentwater's back,' said the vicar. 'Strange thing about the Wentwaters. Lady Wentwater came to live here nigh on twenty years ago. No one's ever heard of a Lord Wentwater and she don't figure in the peerage. I've asked her time and again about her late husband, but she always goes deaf. But she's a harmless old lady. Pity the same can't be said about her nephew.'

'Hardly, Papa,' said Deirdre sweetly. 'Since no one in their right mind could call Mr Wentwater an old lady.'

The vicar looked at her sharply but she had cast her eyes down again.

'Hey, well,' he said. 'So long as he don't come nosing around here like a fox after the hens. How Bella could have been so stupid as to even look at the man...'

'We all thought him well enough,' pointed out Mrs Armitage languidly, 'until he told us the nature of his trade. You yourself could find no fault with him up until then, Mr Armitage.'

'That's fustian. I...' The vicar broke off and stared at the ceiling in a puzzled way. 'How can it be leakin' in here. Better run upstairs and see if the bedrooms are flooded.'

'It's not the rain,' said Deirdre. 'It's Betty. She's crying,' she added as the maid whipped herself out of the dining room.

'What's she got to cry about?'

'Crying is quite beneficial to the eyes,' said Mrs Armitage, with sudden enthusiasm. 'It exercises the retina.'

'Betty is crying,' said Deirdre, loudly and clearly, 'because she was promised two years ago that she could leave our employ and marry John Summer.' John Summer was the vicarage coachman. He also acted as groom, whipper-in and kennel master.

'Well, she'll just need to wait,' said the vicar testily. 'Can't have servants marrying. Never heard of such a thing. We can't afford another maid at the moment, and we can't afford to pay John Summer enough to set up a household. So there!'

Deirdre thought bitterly of the vast amount of money that had gone to buy new hounds and new hunters and opened her mouth to make an acid retort. But then she remembered her plan and kept silent.

At last the evening meal was over and the girls collected their bed candles from the table in the hall and mounted the stairs to their rooms.

With the departure of Minerva and Annabelle from the family nest, Daphne and Deirdre each had a room to themselves, while Diana and Frederica still shared their old room.

The storm had died down. Deirdre opened the window and leaned out. The chill fresh air smelled of damp, rotting leaves and evergreen.

The figure of a man appeared beyond the high hedge which bordered the vicarage garden, his stock gleaming whitely in the darkness.

'Guy,' murmured Deirdre, her heart beginning to hammer against her ribs.

She threw a cloak over her shoulders and crept out of her room and slowly down the stairs, walking on the edge of each foot so as not to make a sound.

The rumble of her father's voice, and her mother's faint high-pitched replies filtered through the parlour door.

She stood very still in the hall. Betty and cook would still be in the kitchen. The hall door was not yet locked and bolted for the night. She would have to try to get out that way and pray that she did not make a noise or that her father would not choose to look out the parlour window as she made her way down the drive.

The hall door opened with a snap of its hinges like a pistol shot. Deirdre froze, already thinking up excuses. But the voices in the parlour went on, and the clatter of dishes sounded from the kitchen.

She slipped quietly out, forcing herself to take time to close the door slowly and carefully behind her. She made her way down the drive, keeping to the black shadow of the yew trees, for a treacherous moon was bathing everything in a silvery glow.

The iron gate wailed like a banshee, but Deirdre could no longer school herself to wait for possible repercussions. She let it swing behind her with a clang and ran out into the road, looking this way and that.

No one.

She gave a little gasp of disappointment, and then a gasp of fear as an arm came from behind and slid round her waist. She whirled about.

'Guy!'

'I thought you might see me and come looking for me,' he whispered. 'Walk with me a little way. Will they miss you?'

Deirdre shook her head, thinking how handsome he looked in the moonlight with his teeth gleaming white and his eyes glinting in an exciting way.

Her father's remark about a fox after the hens came into her mind, and she said nervously, 'I *hate* this furtive meeting. Oh, how I wish you could call at the vicarage and that papa would be *sensible.*'

'I came because someone told me your father was chasing you with a whip,' he said in a low serious voice. 'I could not sleep. I was worried about you. Believe me, I do not like these clandestine meetings either.'

'Is it not amazing?' said Deirdre softly, 'we should become such friends? It is as if our minds were twins.'

'I think it is because I am tired of simpering, giggling females,' said Guy. 'I admire a woman with a *brain*. Oh, I confess your sister, Annabelle, dazzled me with her beauty, but that was before I learned some sense.'

'Yes,' said Deirdre in tepid agreement. She would have liked Mr Wentwater to say he was dazzled with *her* beauty as well as her brain.

'Oh, Mr Wentwater,' said Deirdre, stopping in the moonlit lane, and clutching hold of both his hands, 'I must tell you. The most dreadful thing has happened.'

The wind sighed over their heads and a shower of damp leaves blew about them.

'Tell me. Why was your father chasing you? If there is anything I can do to help?' said Guy, pressing her hands and holding them to his chest.

'Papa has a marriage *arranged* for me. I am to go to London tomorrow and stay with Lady Godolphin so that some creature called Lord Harry Desire can look me over, check my teeth, and say whether he will have me or nay.'

45

'This is outrageous! Your father already has two rich marriages in the family. What does he need with another?'

Deirdre sighed and the wind over the high hedges on either side of the road seemed to pick up the sigh and send it blowing across the bare autumn fields. 'We are in low funds again,' she said.

'Papa spends a great deal of money on the hunt. This Lord Desire must marry in order to inherit his uncle's fortune, he needs a wife, Papa needs the money, I am to be the sacrifice.'

He released her hands and turned a little away from her so that his face was in the shadows. Deirdre waited, straining to hear him say that he would marry her himself.

'I had hoped,' he said at last, 'that we might come to know each other better . . . that I might establish myself with the county and come to be on calling terms with your family. We have really only just met.'

He gave an awkward laugh. Deirdre shivered and pulled her cloak tightly about her shoulders.

'But,' he brightened. 'There is no guarantee this Lord Harry will want to marry you. Then you may return home and we can all be comfortable again.' He chuckled. 'I am

46

sure you will know precisely just how to give him a disgust of you. An intelligent woman like yourself...'

'Oh, Guy, how our minds do run together,' said Deirdre, forgetting her disappointment in him. 'That is *exactly* what I plan to do.'

'You must return,' he said, tucking her arm in his and leading her back towards the vicarage. 'I do not want your father to get out his pack and hunt me out of the county again.'

'What!' Deirdre stood still, and Guy cursed himself for the temporary slip. She obviously had not heard of his humiliation at the hands of the vicar. She must never know how much he hated her father for that day when he had been hounded, literally, down the summer roads with the vicar's pack in full cry behind him. She must never guess how he had dreamed and plotted revenge. She must never guess that her one attraction for him was that he saw her as an instrument of revenge.

'Papa did *what?*' pursued Deirdre.

He laughed and tugged at her arm so that she had, perforce, to fall into step beside him. 'You misunderstood me. I meant, I *hope* Mr Armitage doesn't hunt me down. A joke, you see.'

47

The parlour lamps were out and the house was in darkness. It would be even more difficult getting back, thought Deirdre. For this time, she did not know where her father was.

But the magic of Guy's presence gave her courage. She glanced up at the firm line of his jaw, the whiteness of his clean linen, his handsome profile, and felt almost unworthy of such an escort. He was worlds removed from her ranting, vulgar father and his petty machinations.

'Goodnight,' he said softly, holding open the gate, and pulling it gently closed behind her.

She turned and faced him through the bars of the tall gate, feeling the cold bite of the iron on her ungloved hands.

'Goodnight,' she echoed softly.

He leaned forwards, and she leaned towards him as well. He kissed her very gently through the bars; a fleeting, chaste kiss.

Deirdre's face blazed with naked love and adoration and Guy watched her intently, feeling a surge of power.

Deirdre floated into the house, not even noticing that the hall door was still unlocked, not even trying to creep quietly up the stairs.

Had her father confronted her at that moment, then Deirdre would have confessed her love, and her idyll with Guy Wentwater would definitely have been over.

But no one met her on the stairs and she reached her bedroom without seeing a soul.

For a long time she sat beside the window, lost in dreams.

Tomorrow, she would go to London. On Monday, she would meet Lord Harry Desire.

And if she played her cards aright, she would be back home very shortly after that, unengaged, and free to pursue her romance with Guy.

After such a failure, her father would surely be glad to marry her off to *anyone*.

## CHAPTER THREE

'If you do not help me, Betty,' said Deirdre Armitage severely, 'I will make sure you slave at the vicarage until the end of your days and die a spinster.'

'If you don't do as vicar says,' sniffed the maid, Betty, 'then you won't be getting married to anyone neither, what with Mr Armitage not having any money and Miss

Minerva and Miss Bella being gone to heathen parts.'

'Lady Sylvester and Lady Peter to you, miss,' said Deirdre tartly. 'Don't be a grouch, Betty,' she went on in a wheedling tone. 'Everything will be all right when Minerva and Bella come back from Paris—Paris isn't heathenish, Betty. Think of the hats!—and I will *make* Papa let you marry your John. But if you aid Papa in forcing me to wear that terrible wig, then I shall do all in my power to encourage him in the idea that we cannot afford to pay John Summer any more money.'

'But I'll get the blame o' it!' wailed Betty.

Deirdre was about to make her curtsey to Lord Harry Desire.

She had told Lady Godolphin that Betty would manage very well as lady's maid. Betty had been told to curl and arrange one of Lady Godolphin's second-best, nutty-brown wigs and to make sure not one offending red curl escaped from beneath it.

The gown which had been chosen for Deirdre by her father and Lady Godolphin was of white muslin embroidered with rosebuds, a dressmaking masterpiece which combined innocence with decadence to a nice degree. The bodice was cunningly boned at the back and fitted at the front to push up Deirdre's breasts into two mounds over the low neckline. The skirt was short enough to show almost the whole of her ankles.

'I know what to do,' said Deirdre. 'I will drop this wig in the basin of water and say it fell off my head when I was washing my face. *I* will take the blame. Come now. I will wear this scandalous dress.'

Betty had not been told of his lordship's aversion to red hair.

So after scowling doubtfully at Deirdre's hair and then at the wig, she suddenly smiled and said she was sure Lady Godolphin had 'been in her altitudes' when she gave the instructions. Anybody could see Miss Deirdre would look much better with her own hair, although it was a pity the rosebuds on her dress were so *pink*, not to mention the broad pink sash which tied under her bosom.

In other circumstances, Deirdre would have been terrified because, in a way, she was to be guest of honour. The *musicale* was simply a piece of stage management. But her aching, tender, delicate love for Guy Wentwater made her feel she could endure anything.

Instead of chiding herself for the speed with which she had fallen in love with a man of doubtful reputation, like many dazzled lovers before, she only prided herself on 'falling in love at first sight'. And like many another love-blinded girl, she was convinced that the rapport of her mind and Guy's was a rare and precious phenomenon.

She stood patiently while Betty dressed her and arranged her hair in an elaborate Grecian style, taught her by Annabelle's lady's maid.

Satisfied that the combination of pink and white muslin with her flaming red hair was sufficiently repellent, Deirdre completed the effect by putting a pink silk stole about her shoulders.

'I look quite dreadful, Betty,' said Deirdre gleefully, as she pirouetted in front of the long glass.

Betty surveyed her young mistress. The maid thought privately that Deirdre had never looked better. The pomade she had added to Deirdre's hair had darkened it to a deeper red, and the pink and white gown showed her excellent bosom and delicate ankles to perfection. The odd combination of pink and white with her red hair and green eyes made Deirdre look oddly and excitingly exotic. Betty decided it would not be wise to praise Miss Deirdre Armitage. Too much vanity had nearly ruined Miss Annabelle and was well on the way to ruining Miss Daphne.

'You'll do,' was all Betty said, and Deirdre went downstairs satisfied that her appearance was quite horrible.

Lord Harry Desire was lounging in quite the latest manner on a sofa in the drawing-room. It was hard to tell from the beautiful blankness of his expression what he was thinking.

At one point, he did put up his glass and stared about the room in a dazed sort of way.

With the exception of the still-not-present Deirdre Armitage and Mr Anstey, Lady Godolphin's simpering cicisbeo, there was no one else present under the age of fifty.

Lady Godolphin had not wanted his lordship's eye, or Deirdre's for that matter, to be attracted by anyone else. Even the soprano who was to star at the *musicale* was fat, florid and fifty and her accompanist turned the pages of the music with a shaking, liver-spotted hand.

Lord Harry recognized old Lady Chester who looked and smelled as if she had been brought out of moth balls for the occasion.

High cracked voices discussed humours and agues and spleen. Lady Godolphin looked the youngest present. She was enjoying herself because all this creaking old age about her made her feel rejuvenated.

But she joined in the conversational illness competition with relish by saying her doctor had told her she had rheumatism but she herself was convinced it was Arthur's Eitis.

She had moved onto a lively dissertation on her Haricot Veins when the door opened and Miss Deirdre Armitage came in.

Lady Godolphin sprang from her chair with amazing alacrity. The vicar uttered a loud oath which caused a shocked murmur of old voices and a fluttering of feathers.

'I'll pretend she's someone else,' thought Lady Godolphin, speeding across the room, 'and get her upstairs and into her wig as soon as possible.'

But right behind Deirdre, Colonel Arthur Brian made his appearance.

Lady Godolphin blushed like a schoolgirl under her paint. She opened and shut her mouth but no sound emerged.

Deirdre smiled benignly on the company, made her curtsey, and walked in the direction of a single chair placed in the farthest corner of the room.

'Hey!' said the vicar, blocking her way. His little shoe-button eyes gleamed as hard as jet but he forced a jovial smile on his face. 'Come along, my girl. There's a handsome gentleman dying to make your acquaintance.'

'Delighted, Papa,' said Deirdre demurely, deliberately sinking in a low obeisance in front of an antediluvian gentleman by the name of Mr Sothers.

'Not him, you buffle-headed jade,' howled her father. There was a stunned silence and the vicar looked around wildly. 'Ha, ha, ha,' he said, baring his teeth in an awful grin. 'We will have our little family jokes. My Deirdre is a naughty puss.' He took his daughter firmly by the upper arm as if he were arresting her, and marched her over to Lord Harry.

Lord Harry Desire uncoiled himself from the depths of the sofa and stood up and made a magnificent bow.

Deirdre studied him from under her lashes with great amusement. This was going to be *much* easier than she had thought. He was a very handsome man, she reflected, but the sheer stupidity of his expression robbed him of any attraction he might otherwise have had.

He stood smiling down at her in a vacant, amiable manner.

'Sit down, sit down!' said the vicar heartily.

He gave his infuriating daughter a mighty

push and she collapsed on to the sofa. Lord Harry sat down gracefully next to her and looked at her with a polite, social expression.

Deirdre played with the sticks of her fan.

'I went to the play the other night,' began Lord Harry amiably. 'Saw Mrs Siddons as Queen Catherine.'

There was a silence.

The vicar, hovering on Deirdre's other side, hissed, 'Well, *stoopid*, ask him how he liked it!'

'How did you like the play, my lord?' asked Deirdre dutifully.

'Very much,' said his lordship after a great deal of serious thought. 'I was wearing my cravat in a new style, entirely my own. Petersham said it looked like a frozen waterfall. But although I confess I was pleased at the compliment, I did not find it very apt. Sculptured snow would have been better, don't you think?'

'No,' said Deirdre. 'I have no interest in fashions whatsoever. My mind would have been on the play.'

A look of almost hellish glee lit up Lord Harry's lovely features but when Deirdre looked up to study the effect of her rudeness, his face was once more a correct and social blank.

'Do you know why you are here?' asked Lord Harry, as the vicar gave a great shrug and moved out of earshot.

'Yes,' said Deirdre. 'I am here to meet you.'

'Do you know *why* it is important you should meet me?'

'I believe my father has marriage in mind,' said Deirdre forthrightly. 'But, of course, as you can see, we should not suit at all.'

'Why, pray?'

Well, the answer to that one was, 'Because you are a stupid lummox and I am not,' but Deirdre felt she had already been rude enough.

She gave a little laugh. 'For a start, you may have noticed I have red hair. My father tells me you can't abide red hair.'

'Did I say that?' exclaimed Lord Harry. 'By Jove, that's right, I did. You see, red hair in a lady has a terrible effect on me. I fall in love with ladies with red hair . . . well, almost on sight.'

'Then it is as well that I am reputed to be something of a Blue Stocking,' said Deirdre quickly. 'For that will surely give you a disgust of me.'

'It certainly would if it were true,' said Lord Harry earnestly. 'But you may be easy

57

on that score, Miss Deirdre, for I do not find you intelligent *at all.*'

Deirdre let out an outraged gasp but the angry retort died on her lips, for the soprano had commenced to sing.

Her name was Madame Vallini. She was possessed of a loud and piercing voice, the delight of the back rows of the gallery who could proudly claim to hear every note.

In a private drawing-room the effect was quite horrendous.

Under Deirdre's fascinated gaze, Lord Harry produced a snuff box from the tails of his morning coat. He flicked it open and took out a small white ball of wax. Then he produced a penknife from another pocket, neatly cut the wax in two, rolled each half in his fingers, and then solemnly popped the resultant wax plugs in each ear. He leaned back at his ease, half closed his eyes, and, it appeared, sent his mind off on a holiday.

'How Guy will laugh when I tell him about this coxcomb,' thought Deirdre with amusement.

Then a great wave of sadness engulfed her. Guy.

Oh, to be back in Hopeworth, walking along the country lanes under the clean, windy country sky, listening to the sound of his voice.

Papa would *not* understand, she realized. How could someone as earthy as her father grasp the spirituality of the meeting and joining of two souls. Guy had talked to her of the army, or the great Battle of Waterloo. He had treated her as an equal.

Two large tears trembled on the edge of Deirdre's long lashes.

Through a hazy blur, she saw with surprise that her indolent companion was holding out a large serviceable pocket handkerchief.

She flushed, but took it, and dabbed at her eyes. He would presume she was affected by the music, thought Deirdre.

She knew that at some period when the singing was over, the vicar and Lady Godolphin would contrive to leave her alone with Lord Harry.

She must try to impress on him the downright unsuitability of this proposed alliance.

Then all at once Deirdre suddenly felt as if Guy were with her in the room, as if he were communicating with her in some way.

She smiled to herself. She knew, in a flash, where he was. He was sitting in the old little-used library in Lady Wentwater's dark mansion. He was leaning his chin on his hand, looking out over the shabby lawns, thinking of her.

All her loneliness and distress fled and she felt loved and comforted and sustained.

★　　★　　★

Not very far away, right at that moment, Guy Wentwater stretched his booted feet in the sawdust of Humbold's Coffee House and smiled at his companion, Silas Dubois.

He was not paying much attention to Mr Dubois. The only reason he was enduring his company was because it had been thrust upon him and Mr Dubois had paid for the wine. Guy's thoughts were firmly focused on the black curls and white bosom of a girl who was strolling up and down the pavement outside.

He was just considering whether to leave abruptly and try his luck with her when a gentleman came up and bowed to the saucy girl and they walked off arm in arm.

Guy sighed regretfully. He would have liked to warm his bed with something like that.

He became aware that Mr Dubois was asking him a question. 'Ever see anything of the Armitage family?' Dubois was asking, his small eyes squinting over the promontory of

60

his large nose.

'No,' said Guy Wentwater. 'The vicar and I had a certain argument once. I am not on calling terms. Not that it matters. A very provincial family.'

'And yet one that has done remarkably well in the marriage mart,' said Mr Dubois slowly.

'So I gather,' yawned Mr Wentwater. 'I hear he is going to marry Miss Deirdre off to Lord Desire.'

'So I hear in the clubs,' said Mr Dubois. 'That must mean the dear vicar is in low funds again.'

'Yes, the reverend has a good number of daughters in the bank, however.'

'Is this Deirdre as fair as Minerva and Annabelle Armitage?'

'Not really,' shrugged Guy. 'Foxy little thing with terribly red hair.'

'I wonder,' mused Mr Dubois, rubbing his one hand with the other. 'Would you say Minerva is particularly fond of this sister, Deirdre?'

'What a fascination the Armitage family does have for you,' sneered Guy. 'Minerva The Good is devoted to the whole pack o' them.'

'And she would be monstrous upset should

anything go wrong?'

Guy looked at Silas Dubois narrowly.

'Oho!' he said. 'Now I begin to remember. Rumour had it that you fought Lord Sylvester in a duel over the fair Minerva and that Lord Sylvester shot the pistol clean out of your hand.'

'A trick, a fluke,' said Mr Dubois. 'He ruined my aim. I was the best shot in England before then.' He nursed his right hand.

'And you want revenge?'

'Why not?'

Guy Wentwater grinned. 'Then perhaps you might be interested in a little proposition which would serve both our ends. I, too, wish revenge on the Armitage family. Lean forwards and listen very carefully, very carefully indeed . . .'

\*        \*        \*

The soprano hit her last high note. There was an arthritic spattering of applause, and then the company began to rise, preparatory to moving to the dining-room.

'What is Arthur doing here?' demanded Lady Godolphin of the vicar.

Mr Armitage threw her a distracted look. 'I

62

talked him into coming,' he said. 'You can't really be interested in that popinjay, Anstey.'

'I don't need to stand here and listen to your muddleactions,' said Lady Godolphin. 'I'll speak to you about it later. What we've got to do at the moment is to get the guests into the dining-room and make sure Deirdre and Desire stay in this one. See?'

'Yes, yes, *yes*,' growled the vicar. 'Better leave it to me. I'll do it tactfully.'

Lady Godolphin looked at him doubtfully, but dutifully waddled off and soon her voice could be heard urging her guests to take a glass of 'Cannery of My-dearer.'

The vicar advanced on Deirdre and Lord Harry, who had risen to their feet.

'If you two are going to make up your minds about anything,' he said, 'you'd better start now.'

And with that, he turned round and shooed the remaining guests in front of him. Lord Harry tried to follow but the vicar stopped that by firmly closing the doors of the drawing-room right in his face, and firmly locking them on the other side.

'Oh, dear,' sighed Lord Harry. 'I am so very hungry.'

'You had better propose to me and be refused and that way we can get the whole silly business over with,' said Deirdre.

He took out his quizzing glass, polished it carefully, raised it to one eye and studied Deirdre carefully from head to foot.

'I *do* apologize,' said Deirdre, becoming flustered. 'I am very embarrassed, you see. I do not want to be married.'

'To me? Or to anyone?'

He had dropped the quizzing glass and his gaze was very level and kind.

'It is not that,' said Deirdre desperately. 'It's just ... oh well, it's just that I would like to become wed to a man of my choice.'

'That's natural,' he said equably. 'Now, I hate being forced to do anything. My nurse used to tell me to eat boiled cabbage because it was good for me and I've detested it ever since. You've been told this marriage is a good thing and so you detest the whole idea. You look on me and you see boiled cabbage.'

'Not quite,' giggled Deirdre nervously. He was standing very close to her. There was a disturbing, almost decadent aura of sensuality about him. She was all too aware of the firmness of his mouth and the breadth of his shoulders.

She wondered idiotically if they were padded. The rest of him was so slim. Except his legs, of course. One could not help noticing his legs since his trousers were so extremely close fitting. Perhaps he wore false calves. But when he moved, one could distinctly observe the hard ripple of muscle under the cloth . . .

Deirdre blushed so violently, she turned almost as red as her hair.

'I have to get married, you know,' sighed Lord Harry. 'Well, I do not really *have* to, but I'm an expensive creature, you see, and uncle has bags and bags of money. Trouble is, I'm too lazy to run about the salons of London courting females. I thought this arrangement of your father's would save me a great deal of unnecessary effort.'

There was a gentle click from the door.

'The vicar has decided we have had time enough.'

'What shall I do?' asked Deirdre. 'I do so want to go home. I *hate* London. There is nothing for me here. If I say to Papa that we shall not suit, he will make me stay in London in the hope that something will eventually come of it.'

'And you would love me more were I able to persuade the vicar to take you away to Hopeworth, say, tomorrow?'

'Oh, I would be most grateful.'

'Then it shall be arranged,' said Lord

Harry comfortably. 'Let us go and join the other guests.'

Deirdre was only too glad to escape from him.

The elderly guests were piling plates high with delicacies from a buffet which had been set up in the dining-room. Lady Godolphin was having a bitter row in the corner with Colonel Brian and seemed unaware that Mr Anstey was paying assiduous court to Lady Chester.

Lord Harry began talking to the soprano. He seemed to have forgotten Deirdre Armitage's very existence. Deirdre saw her father bearing down on her and hurriedly engaged in conversation with the aged Earl of Derham.

Foiled of his prey, the vicar turned his beady gaze on Lord Harry who had just turned away from the *diva*.

While chatting to Lord Derham about the efficacy of vinegar and water to clean the spleen, Deirdre saw Lord Harry put his handsome head slightly on one side as he listened to whatever her father was saying. Then Lord Harry smiled and said a few words. The vicar looked delighted, clapped him on the shoulder and wrung his hand.

'Heavens!' thought Deirdre in dismay.

'That great fool has probably told Papa we are to be married. Nothing else would make Papa look so delighted.'

She hurriedly ended the conversation with the earl and edged cautiously in her father's direction. He saw her coming and beamed on her.

'You're a sensible girl,' he said fondly. 'I always knew you had a shrewd head on your shoulders. When Desire told me this idea of yours that he should travel with us to Hopeworth on the morrow and stay with us until you both get better acquainted, I was fair flummoxed. I didn't expect you to be so sensible about the whole thing and that's a fact.

'"Soul, thou hast much goods laid up for many years; take thine ease, eat, drink, and be merry,"' quoted the vicar gleefully, reaching past Deirdre to grab a plate. 'I was that worrit, I been fair starving myself. But today I shall break my fast.'

Deirdre turned away to hide the blind fury of her face. 'The great fool!' she raged inwardly, cursing Lord Harry.

'But at least I shall be back home, and Guy will only need to see this idiot once to know that he must rescue me.

'Why, this Lord Harry is such a great ox,

such a lumpkin, that he doesn't even realize I *don't* want to become better acquainted!

'Was there *ever* such a fool!'

## CHAPTER FOUR

The vicarage had never seemed so small before. The arrival of Lord Harry seemed to reduce it, although it was a pleasant building with dining-room, drawing-room, parlour and study on the ground floor, six bedrooms on the first and the attics on the top. Deirdre and Daphne once more had to share a room to allow bedroom space for Lord Harry since the dressing-room which had been the boys' bedroom was allocated to him for his personal use. The servants had to double up in the attics to make room for his Swiss.

Then there was the supremely elegant Lord Harry in residence. It was rather like buying a splendid new piece of furniture and noticing that the curtains were faded and the carpet worn.

To Deirdre, he made her home seem shabby and dark and poky.

She had carefully avoided being alone with him. Sir Edwin and his wife, learning of his presence, and, ever-anxious to secure a suitable *parti* for one of their daughters, and hearing that there had, as yet, been no mention of any official engagement to Miss Deirdre Armitage, had asked the whole family to a garden party by way of securing the attendance of Lord Harry. Deirdre had been praying for rain. She did not like her uncle or his cold wife, or their silly, malicious daughters.

But then she overheard her father grumbling to his curate, Mr Pettifor, that Mr Wentwater was to be one of the guests, and, from that moment on, Deirdre could hardly wait for the Saturday of the garden party to arrive.

They had arrived from London on Wednesday morning. Already, it was Friday evening, and so far Deirdre had heard or seen nothing of Guy Wentwater.

She had sat Wednesday and Thursday evening by the window, looking out over the vicarage garden in the hope of seeing him walking in the lane.

She did not know he had been in London at the same time as she, for that vision of him sitting in the library, dreaming of her, was fixed in her mind. Besides, she had prayed to God for guidance, and although He had dealt her an unexpected blow by allowing Lord Harry to come on a visit, she was still sure He meant her to elope with Guy.

The vicarage was in a great bustle with preparations for the garden party. It was difficult to know what to wear. The Almanac promised a fine day. Should one freeze fashionably in muslin? Or be comfortable in wool?

Daphne would, of course, freeze. No sacrifice was too great. Fashion was all.

Had Minerva still been substitute mother, then they would all have had to dress sensibly. But Minerva was married. Minerva was in Paris, and Mrs Armitage had discovered a new and delicate complaint and had as little interest in what her daughters did, or did not do, as she always had evinced.

Deirdre heartily wished the elegant Lord Harry in hell.

He was too much of a favourite with her family for her comfort and they all seemed to see the marriage as good as arranged. In the parlour that evening, after supper, Lord Harry had been playing a noisy game of spillikins with Deirdre and Diana, recklessly gambling away his whole fortune and threatening to go out in the garden and shoot himself, much to Frederica's delight.

'This is worse than Waterloo,' he laughed, tugging Frederica's hair.

'How would *you* know?' asked Deirdre rudely.

There was a shocked silence.

'Deirdre!' said her father. 'I would see you in my study.'

Deirdre folded her lips in a mutinous line. Lord Harry's light husky voice was describing the typhoon which would surely strike the garden party tomorrow and even Daphne was giggling helplessly at the mad descriptions he was drawing.

The whole vicarage seemed too full of Lord Harry Desire, thought Deirdre crossly, as she followed her father across the hall to his study.

She had secretly hoped her family would take a dislike to this indolent, silly lord.

'Shut the door,' snapped her father, breaking into her thoughts. 'What was the meaning of that remark, miss?'

'What remark, Papa?' asked Deirdre sweetly.

'About Lord Harry not knowin' anything about Waterloo?'

'I thought it a just observation, Papa. There are many fine and brave men who fought at Waterloo. He should not dare even to suggest in a joke that he was one of them.'

'And why not? When he most certainly was.'

'You must be . . .'

'See here, my girl, I had it from Lord Brothers that Harry Desire was one of the most courageous officers on the field. Just because the man don't preen and brag, don't mean he ain't brave.'

'I'm sorry, Papa,' said Deirdre meekly, although privately she hated Lord Harry the more for having made her look like a fool.

'I don't know what you've got in that brain-box of yourn,' went on the vicar. 'If there was another fellow in your life, I could understand it. Desire is an amiable chap. He's not too bright, I'll grant you that. He seems nearer Frederica's age than your own half the time. He listened to the belling of my hounds and he said, "The bass is a trifle flat. You should have that animal tuned, don't you think?"

'But intelligence ain't fashionable and never was. He's a gentleman, and your true gentleman is stupid.'

'Would you describe yourself so?' asked Deirdre maliciously.

'Oh, I ain't stupid,' said the vicar seriously, 'but I've got the wit to hide the

72

fact. Now, I've had letters from Minerva and Annabelle. Seems they think your come-out is to be next year. But we can't afford to wait.'

Deirdre clasped her hands and looked at her father with her strange green eyes. 'Papa, if I were to wed a man who had a great deal of money, you would surely not care what type of man he was?'

She looked at her father anxiously, Guy's name trembling on her lips.

'Course I would,' said the vicar stoutly. 'Imagine if our Bella were to have married that Guy Wentwater. He's to be at Edwin's garden party. I told Edwin, I did, "you ain't got any standards". Edwin says Wentwater ain't slave trading and has a mort o' money and he's thinking of him for Josephine or Emily, but I says to him, I'd rather we all starved than let that beast near the vicarage.'

All her new-found hate for her father burned twice as fiercely in Deirdre's bosom.

'I must write to Minerva and tell her of your plans, Papa,' she said.

The vicar looked at her narrowly, then he realized he had remembered to bribe the postboy. 'Very well,' he said with deceptive mildness. 'She's a sensible girl and would approve of my choice. I've been trying to leave you and Lord Harry alone together, but you always seem to make some excuse.

'Now he was brought here, I was told, so that the pair of you should get better acquainted. And you *are* going to get better acquainted, Deirdre Armitage.

'And that's an order!'

'Yes, Papa,' sighed Deirdre.

'It's stupid idea of Edwin's, this here garden party. Whoever heard of a garden party nearly at the end of October? But the grounds of the Hall are pretty enough, and you make sure you and Lord Harry wander off somewhere.'

'Common, disgusting, *vulgar* man,' thought Deirdre, meaning the vicar.

Aloud she said, 'Yes,' now only wanting to escape.

'So go back in there,' said the vicar, 'and let's have no more rudeness from you, miss.'

There was no more rudeness from Deirdre because she did not address one remark to Lord Harry for the rest of the evening. At last, it was time for bed.

Once again, Deirdre sat by the window, watching to see if Guy would walk in the lane, waiting impatiently for Daphne to complete her lengthy bedtime toilet and go to sleep.

Daphne was fortunately too self-absorbed to wonder why her sister spent so much time sitting by the window instead of preparing for bed.

At last Daphne fell asleep, her head full of curl papers gleaming in the darkness.

And then the faint red glow of a cheroot stabbed the darkness of the lane. Deirdre stifled a gasp as she rubbed the pane of the window and peered out. There was the tall figure, there was the familiar gleam of his white stock in the darkness.

She pulled on her cloak and scampered out of the vicarage, too excited even to try to be quiet.

White frost was gleaming on the grass and bushes of the garden. From the kennels, a hound sent up a melancholy howl to the moon. Stars burned in the black night sky.

Deirdre tugged open the gate and darted out into the lane.

At first she thought he had gone, and then she saw that red firefly of the lit end of the cheroot dancing at the turn in the road.

She scampered breathlessly along the lane and turned the corner. Nothing in front of her except the moon shining on the frost-white pebbles of the road.

Beyond the stile to the right, the little,

tantalizing firefly of light danced across the fields.

Frightened to call out in case anyone heard her, Deirdre hitched up her skirt and climbed over the stile and then sped across the frost-hard rutted earth of the field until the tall, dark figure of a man loomed large at the edge of the woods. A cloud had crossed the moon, and she could only make out his silhouette.

'Wait!' she called breathlessly. 'Oh, please wait.'

He threw away the cheroot and turned to face her.

Filled with love and longing, she hurtled towards him and cannoned against his chest.

Strong arms went about her and she sighed and closed her eyes and turned up her face.

The kiss was all she had dreamed it would be, searing, burning, passionate, leaving her shaking and breathless.

He loved her!

When he finally drew back, she gazed adoringly up at him.

The fickle moon swam out from behind a cloud.

The handsome features of Lord Harry Desire looked down at her.

'You!' said Deirdre, putting a hand to her

mouth.

'Who else?' he replied, a note of laughter in his voice.

His arms were still tightly about her. Deirdre struggled to escape. She could not tell him about Guy. For he might tell her father.

'You have a pleasant way of furthering our acquaintance, Miss Deirdre,' said Lord Harry.

'I did not mean ... I was sleep-walking,' said Deirdre desperately. 'And I did not know who ... what I was doing.'

'Are you in the habit of kissing men when you sleep-walk? When we are married, I will need to keep you chained to the bedroom.'

'No. I have never done such a thing before. My lord, you are a gentleman. Pray let us return to the vicarage and say no more on the matter.'

'As you will,' he replied carelessly.

'But I cannot go *anywhere*,' pointed out Deirdre crossly. 'You are holding me so tightly.'

'So I am.' His eyes glinted down at her in the moonlight. 'I am cold, you see, and you are keeping me very warm.'

'Please let me go,' begged Deirdre. She looked wildly about. Mad fears of rape chased through her head. He no longer seemed the silly, indolent lord of the previous days. His masculinity was almost overwhelming and the hard strength of his arms about her made her feel helpless. He had all at once joined that mysterious world of men who told warm jokes, despised women, but undressed them with their eyes. That world of men she now realized she had always feared.

'Of course I will let you go,' he said soothingly. 'You must kiss me again, of course, for I cannot rest quietly tonight knowing I have been kissed by a beautiful young lady who was merely walking in her sleep.'

'No, I will *not* kiss you again!'

'But you see I fear for your health. I feel sure your mother and father should be told of this dangerous malady of yours.'

'No, you must not. They would worry. It happens very rarely. Do not tease me.'

'Then kiss me.'

Deirdre's fears fled before a burst of sheer irritation. Only a very stupid man would keep boring on and on about a kiss when the girl in his arms so obviously wanted to escape.

'Very well,' she said testily. 'One kiss.'

78

She primped up her mouth and screwed her eyes shut. The next moment they flew open in surprise. For he had lifted her off her feet as if she weighed nothing at all. He had one arm behind her shoulders and the other under her knees. The moon sailed behind a cloud again, plunging them into darkness as his mouth descended on her own.

Just before his lips met hers, Deirdre thought savagely, 'Aha, *now* this coxcomb will see the difference . . . now I know he is not Guy.'

His mouth seemed to cling to her own, moving gently against it while she waited listlessly for him to be done.

Then her treacherous body began to shake and ache with all sorts of languorous pains. Her hand stole behind his neck, seemingly of its own volition, and buried itself in his thick curls.

He abruptly released her, swinging her lightly down to her feet, and steadying her with an arm about her shoulders.

She stood very still, looking down at the ground, sick, and shaken and frightened. This rampant lust that had briefly consumed her was terrifying. Love should not be like this. It should be sweet and pure: a delicate communing of minds, a meeting and merging of ideas.

Deirdre felt she had been unfaithful to Guy.

She glanced up at Lord Harry under her lashes. He had taken a flat case out of his pocket and was extricating another cheroot.

'What a beautiful night,' he said happily.

'You . . . you will not tell my parents about . . . about me sleep-walking?' said Deirdre in an odd harsh voice unlike her own.

'No,' he said gently, beginning to walk across the field. 'No, I think not. They might not believe me, you see. Your good father— who sometimes, if you will forgive me, Miss Deirdre, does seem to have evil thoughts for a man of the cloth, might jump to the conclusion that you had mistaken me for someone else.'

Deirdre stumbled and he caught her arm. She looked up at him anxiously and he smiled back, his eyes reflecting nothing more than a rather bovine good humour.

'Which would be very silly of him,' said Deirdre in a low voice.

'Which would be very silly,' agreed Lord Harry, 'since you kissed me back with the same warmth the second time as you did the first.'

'We will not discuss the matter any longer,'

said Deirdre. 'Pray talk of something else. I learn from my father that you fought bravely at Waterloo.'

'I fought, yes.'

'Tell me about it,' demanded Deirdre.

'I don't want to talk about it,' he said lazily. 'I want to talk about your eyes. Do you ever wear jade earrings? I wish we were engaged so that I might buy you a pair.'

'I suppose you consider females too silly to hear stories about war.'

'The only people who want to hear stories about Waterloo are people who either were not there themselves or who have never fought in such a battle. It was not as the others, you know. It was slogging carnage and bloodshed.'

'A battle you obviously think England should not have fought.'

'Now, why would I think that? My French is quite atrocious, you know. I think that's why I had no desire to live under Napoleon. Also, think of their coats! Quite hideous, I assure you.'

'There is one man who has fought bravely at Waterloo and is not ashamed to talk about it,' said Deirdre, her voice tinged with contempt.

'Indeed! Who, pray?'

'You will meet him tomorrow.'

'Ah, I am to be surprised.'

'I think before we reach home, Lord Harry, that I should make it plain we do not suit. Oh, I am grateful to you for telling Papa you were coming on a visit so that I could leave London. But it is time to end this farce.'

'But I am very comfortable,' he said. 'I like your family. I have not had much in the way of family life of late.'

'Do you have brothers and sisters?' she asked curiously, realizing how little she knew of him.

'I have three brothers, all younger than I, and two little sisters.'

'Do you visit your parents very often?'

'As little as possible.'

'I know what it is to detest one's parents,' said Deirdre in a bitter voice, feeling a kinship with him for the first time.

'I did not say I detested them,' he said airily. 'In fact I'm fond of them, but I prefer to live in town.'

He jumped nimbly over the stile and stood on the other side to lift her down.

'I am quite able to get over by myself, sir,' said Deirdre.

But he appeared not to have heard. He

82

held out both arms.

She gingerly put both her hands in his and prepared to jump down.

But he tugged her forwards so that she fell down into his embrace.

Oh, treacherous, disgusting body with its melting lusts and palpitating nerves!

Deirdre wrenched herself free and stalked off down the road in front of him as gingerly as a cat.

He caught up with her. She glanced up at him and started at the look of shrewd, calculating intelligence on his face. But it must have been a trick of the moonlight, for the next second his lovely features looked as bland, stupid and good-humoured as ever.

The vicar met them at the gate. 'Well, now,' he said, rubbing his hands. 'That's what I like to see.'

Deirdre pushed past him and ran into the house.

That night, she cried herself to sleep.

★     ★     ★

The day of the picnic dawned bright and sunny. Deirdre's excitement had affected the other girls who were in a thoroughly strung-up state by the time they were at last ready to

83

leave for the Hall.

Lord Harry had his own carriage and everyone assumed he would drive Deirdre, but Deirdre did not want to appear in his company. She wanted Guy to see her, unescorted, unspoken for, unattached. And so she talked Daphne into taking her place in Lord Harry's dashing phaeton and Daphne was only too ready to oblige.

Deirdre was wearing a jade-green silk gown with a pelisse of the same colour. A charming straw hat *à la bergère* all but hid her red curls. Roman sandals adorned her feet. The frost had melted from the grass and the air still had a sharp nip in it despite the glory of the sun.

She began to wish she had settled for wool. Of what use was a becoming gown if one's nose was red with cold?

All Sir Edwin's tenants had been invited as well as all the notables of the country. Deirdre was surprised to see John Summer driving a farm cart behind the family carriage, piled high with wood and bunting.

The reason for this became all too evident shortly after they had arrived. The vicar, it transpired, felt that garden parties should be in aid of something or other, and what better charity could there be but to raise funds to restore the roof of the church?

A booth was quickly erected, a placard asking for donations propped in front of it, and the beautiful Daphne thrust behind it.

Never had Deirdre seen her younger sister look so enraged.

Sir Edwin and Lady Edwin sailed forwards and neatly cut off Lord Harry and edged him gently towards their giggling daughters, Josephine and Emily.

Josephine and Emily were dressed in identical gowns of violent tartan. They wore enormous poke bonnets from which their giggles echoed as if emerging from the end of a tunnel.

A whole ox was being roasted to one side of the main lawn and members of the peasantry were sulkily dancing around a maypole on the other side, wearing Elizabethan costumes thrust on them by Lady Edwin.

Sir Edwin prided himself on being a good landlord and also prided himself on the fact that not one of his tenants had been known to starve to death. Of course, some of them were quite painfully thin, but, as Sir Edwin liked to point out, that was due to heredity.

Deirdre kept away from the crowds as much as possible. She was watching and waiting for Guy to arrive so that she could tell him of her plight and ask him to elope with her.

Lord Harry appeared to be perfectly happy to entertain Josephine and Emily.

All at once, Deirdre saw Guy with Lady Wentwater on his arm, entering by the south lawn.

But there was a great bustle as Lady Edwin marshalled the guests to the long trestle tables which had been erected down the centre of the front lawn.

Mrs Armitage swam into view. 'You must help me, Deirdre,' she said plaintively. 'All that disgusting smell of roast meat makes me feel quite faint. Be a dear girl and find out where we are to sit.'

'I have found out, ma'am,' said Lord Harry, appearing at their side, a vision in blue cloth morning coat, white waistcoat and biscuit coloured pantaloons. 'Allow me to escort you.'

He held out both arms. Deirdre bit her lip, looking towards Guy who was bowing before Lady Edwin.

He did not look in her direction once.

Deirdre longed to speak to him, to feel the reassuring touch of his hand, to see him smile.

He certainly paled before the glory of Lord

Harry, but that made Guy Wentwater more attractive in her eyes than ever. In truth, Miss Deirdre Armitage was beginning to find Lord Harry Desire somewhat terrifying.

Only see the possessive way he helped her to sickening mounds of that disgusting meat and great horrible mountains of sausages and vegetables.

No, she did not want any game pie, she snapped, close to tears.

Josephine was seated on Lord Harry's other side and determined to make the most of it.

Guy was seated a little way down the table next to Emily. He was laughing and teasing her. Deirdre could not see Emily's face because of the long poke of the girl's bonnet, but the giggles and screams that were emerging from under the straw seemed to show she was well pleased with the attention she was getting.

And so the interminable meal went on, and on, and on.

Clouds covered the sun, the grass under Deirdre's sandalled feet, still wet from melted frost, seeped moisture through the thin soles of her sandals.

She kept squinting down her nose anxiously to see whether it was turning red

87

with the cold, and Lord Harry smiled beautifully upon her and asked her if she were suffering from a fit of indigestion.

At long last, the steward rose to his feet and proposed a toast to the master, and the dutiful peasantry set up a ragged cheer. Many of them were secreting as much food about their person as they could.

Deirdre envied the squire who had his Indian servant standing behind him with armfuls of blankets, and, at a signal from his master, he would unwrap yet another one from the pile on his arm and deftly place it about the squire's thin shoulders.

Daphne was coughing and sneezing. She had arrived at the garden party in a vision of India muslin of the palest pink. Her forced inactivity on duty at the family fund-raising booth had brought her out in a rash of gooseflesh which seemed likely to become permanent, so blue and bumpy it looked. The low neckline of her gown revealed flesh above so blue and mottled, it looked as if she were wearing a blue gauze fichu.

At long last, the company was free to move about and inspect the gardens. Guy took Emily on his arm and headed off in the direction of the rose garden.

'Who is the fellow you said had been at

Waterloo?' she realized Lord Harry was asking her.

'He has just gone towards the rose garden,' said Deirdre, coming to life at last. 'Oh, do let us go there, my lord, and you may share reminiscences.'

'Very well,' he rejoined amiably, tucking her hand in his arm.

The rose garden boasted nothing more than a few frost-blackened, withered blooms but at least it was out of the chilly wind.

Guy was leaning nonchalantly against a sundial, whispering something to Emily, who was giggling and making patterns in the dust with the point of her parasol.

'Mr Wentwater!' cried Deirdre in a shrill voice.

'Oh, tish,' said Emily audibly. 'It's one of the pests from the vicarage.'

Deirdre marched forwards resolutely, almost pulling Lord Harry with her.

'Mr Wentwater,' repeated Deirdre when they had approached. 'Allow me to present Lord Harry Desire. Lord Harry, Mr Wentwater. Miss Emily Armitage, you have already met.'

Guy made his bow. A little silence fell. Lord Harry smiled blandly on the world, holding his curly-brimmed beaver and cane in one hand while the blustery breeze ruffled his glossy black curls. Emily darted a venomous look at Deirdre from the depths of her poke bonnet, like some small and vicious animal staring out of its hole.

'Well,' said Deirdre brightly, 'I felt I simply must bring you two gentlemen together. Lord Harry was at Waterloo as well, Mr Wentwater, and I am dying to hear your shared accounts of that great battle.'

'Good heavens!' cried Guy Wentwater. 'I hear my aunt calling me. She sounds in great distress.'

And he did look most flustered. He made an awkward bow and ran out of the rose garden.

Lord Harry took out his quizzing glass and gazed through it at Guy Wentwater's rapidly retreating figure with interest.

'Marvellous ears that man has,' he murmured. 'Like a demned bat. Now, *I* couldn't hear a thing.'

'We had better go immediately,' said Deirdre. 'Lady Wentwater may be in need of help.'

She ran off in the direction Guy had taken without pausing to see whether the other two had any intention of following her.

But when she returned to the party, she

could see no sign of Guy. The only loud noise was being made by her father and Sir Edwin. Sir Edwin was coldly stating that the introduction of a fund-raising booth to his fête was vulgar in the extreme, and the vicar was hurling biblical quotations at him, like so many stones.

Deirdre searched frantically, running hither and thither until she at last came on the squat figure of Lady Wentwater, sitting under an elm tree with Squire Radford, and sharing his blankets.

'Where is Mr Wentwater?' panted Deirdre, while the squire's kind eyes looked uncomfortably shrewd.

'Blessed if I know,' said Lady Wentwater. 'Why don't you look for him?'

'But I've looked and looked,' said Deirdre, clenching her hands into fists at her sides.

'What's amiss, then?' asked Lady Wentwater curiously. Her little currant eyes turned suddenly sly. 'Why do you *long* to see my nephew?'

'I don't long to see him at all,' said Deirdre, blushing red. 'And he said he heard you calling out in distress.'

'Not I. Keep on looking,' said her ladyship airily.

And Deirdre did.

She not only searched the grounds but the hall as well. But of Guy Wentwater, she saw not the slightest sign.

Her misery was aggravated by the fact that when she left the Hall to enter the grounds again a thin, cold rain was falling.

The tenants were hurriedly leaving, taking as much food with them as they could discreetly carry, and the more illustrious guests were congregating in the drawing-room where tea was to be served. The Armitage family had already left, leaving Lord Harry with instructions to bring Deirdre home, or so Lady Edwin told her in glacial tones.

Deirdre did not want to go home with Lord Harry, did not want to be alone with his suffocating presence.

Using her parasol as an umbrella, she fled down the long drive and let herself out through the tall gates to begin the long, weary walk back to the vicarage.

The rain grew heavier and the village pond had developed smallpox as heavy drops pitted its smooth surface. The burning need to see Guy was like an ache. Suddenly she swung about and headed as fast as she could in the opposite direction, going towards Lady Wentwater's mansion.

She was a sorry mess by the time she reached the old ivy-covered house.

Sending up a fervent prayer that he would be at home, she gave the knocker a resounding bang.

The grim-faced maid evinced no surprise at the wet and bedraggled figure on the step. She led Deirdre into the dark and chilly drawing-room and said she would inform Mr Wentwater of Miss Armitage's call.

Deirdre paced up and down, shivering. Would he never come? If he did not hurry up, Lady Wentwater would be back and all pleas for an elopement impossible.

She had quite given up hope when the door opened and Guy walked in. He strode forwards and took her hands in his.

'What is this?' he exclaimed, standing back to survey her. 'You are soaked to the skin.'

'I *had* to see you,' said Deirdre. 'I am in the most awful trouble.'

'I thought you had decided to accept the marriage to Desire when I saw him return with you,' said Guy.

'But I haven't,' wailed Deirdre. 'It's you I love.'

There, it was out. She had said it. She waited anxiously for him to say he loved her as well, but he dropped her hands and stood very still, staring into the blackness of the empty fireplace.

'What do you want me to do?' he asked at last.

'Elope with me,' whispered Deirdre.

She was now afraid to look at him, terrified of his rejection.

The wind moaned in the trees outside and a spatter of rain hit the windows.

'Why not?' he said with a sudden laugh.

'Oh, Guy!' cried Deirdre thankfully. She waited eagerly for him to take her in his arms, but he only stood a little away from her, looking at her with a sort of brooding, calculating expression she could not understand.

'I have it!' he said at last. 'Meet me tomorrow at the Hopeminster crossroads. I am afraid you will have to walk. Bring very little with you. I will buy you any clothes you need.'

Deirdre wanted to run into his arms, to be held, to have all her worries and doubts soothed away. If only he would say he loved her.

There came the rattle of carriage wheels on the drive outside.

'My aunt!' exclaimed Guy. 'She must not find you here. I'll tell the maid to say nothing. Come with me and I will show you how to leave by the back way.'

He hustled her out of the drawing-room and through the house to where French windows opened from a little-used morning-room into the gardens at the back.

Guy wrenched at the rusty catch and all but pushed her out into the garden.

'Until tomorrow,' he said urgently. 'Meet me at the crossroads at two in the afternoon. Now *go!*'

'Guy,' pleaded Deirdre, hanging on to his arm. 'I do not want to force you to do this. Do you love me?'

'Of course,' he said, with a little laugh. He leaned forwards and kissed her on the lips, then gave her a little shove. 'Be off with you! We can talk tomorrow,' he added, firmly shutting the window on her.

Well, that was that, thought Deirdre, as she scurried through the wet gardens and slipped out by a small gate leading into a narrow lane which skirted the estate.

All the long way home, she was worried and anxious. She had dreamed and fantasized that things would miraculously be splendid and beautiful if he said he loved her and said he would elope with her.

And he had!

But the worry and dread would not go away.

She could only be glad that no one saw her creep into the vicarage. She went up to her room and changed quickly into a comfortable cold wool gown and towelled her hair dry, pinning it back from her face in a severe style.

How on earth was she to pack a couple of bandboxes—for she could not take any more—and escape from the vicarage unseen?

A way suggested itself at supper. Lord Harry was cheerfully planning a visit to Hopeminster the following day. Even Mrs Armitage had roused herself from her customary lethargy to express enthusiasm. The family decided to leave directly after morning service.

'I shall pretend to be sick,' thought Deirdre. 'And when they have all left for Hopeminster, I will make my escape.'

It would take her a full hour to walk to the crossing.

The vicar kept eyeing his daughter throughout supper, noticing the feverish light in her green eyes and the pallor of her face.

His conscience smote him, and finally he listened to its harsh voice. It was a pity

Deirdre showed no signs of forming a *tendre* for Lord Harry. But if the very idea was going to make her ill, then he would need to cancel the whole thing and write to Lord Sylvester and wheedle some money out of him.

The vicar's heart sank at this thought for he stood very much in awe of his elegant son-in-law; his other one, the Marquess of Brabington, could, on occasion, be even more formidable.

Lord Harry seemed in an unusually sombre mood. Knows she doesn't want him, thought the vicar gloomily.

He left the table as soon as he could and fled to the kennels to sit and tell his troubles to his hounds, which sometimes seemed to understand better than any human.

Deirdre was glad to escape to bed. She thought she would not possibly be able to sleep, but she fell asleep as soon as her head touched the pillow, worn out with worry and exhaustion.

The day dawned bright, glittering and cold. Ice had formed in the cans of washing water. While Daphne still slept, Deirdre sat chewing her nails and planning how to pretend to be ill.

But as it turned out, she did not have to

pretend very much. The vicar had gone ahead to the church and the rest of the family and Lord Harry were all assembled in the parlour waiting for her when Deirdre walked in. She opened her mouth to tell her very well-rehearsed lies, closed it, and burst into tears instead, crying and crying as if her heart would break.

Daphne hustled her from the room and led her back upstairs.

'What is it Deirdre?' she asked in her soft voice, forgetting about her own appearance for once.

'I—I'm not well,' hiccupped Deirdre. 'I w-walked h-home in the rain yesterday, and ... and ... I must have caught a chill. My poor head aches so much. All I want is to be left alone. Please go to Hopeminster after the service without me.'

'I know what it's like,' said Daphne, stroking Deirdre's red curls. 'I get blinding headaches sometimes and all I want is to be left in peace. I am really very fond of you, Deirdre. Don't cry. I will not let Papa bully you into coming with us to Hopeminster and I shall tell Mrs Hammer to leave a cold collation for you in the dining-room so you may eat if you feel like it.'

'Thank you,' mumbled Deirdre miserably.

She longed to confide in Daphne, but she knew instinctively that Daphne would go straight to their father.

So Deirdre lay down on top of the bed and turned her face into the pillow.

Daphne picked up a quilt, tucked it around her and with a soft 'goodbye' left the room.

Deirdre fully expected her mother to pay her a visit, for Mrs Armitage could be very firm when it came to family outings although she was remarkably lax in everything else. But Daphne turned out to show a vein of steel that no one had hitherto guessed at, and said decisively that Deirdre must on no account be disturbed.

Daphne had the honour of being escorted to church by Lord Harry. As they walked sedately along the narrow lane behind the rest of the Armitage party, Lord Harry reflected Daphne was a dazzlingly beautiful young girl when she managed to get her mind off her own appearance.

'Tell me,' he said lightly, 'all about Mr Guy Wentwater.'

'Oh, you don't want to know about him,' exclaimed Daphne. 'He is most disreputable, and not a gentleman.'

'And yet he seems to be on calling terms

with your uncle, and Miss Deirdre was furthermore most anxious to introduce me to him.'

'How odd,' said Daphne softly. 'Sir Edwin would invite Mr Wentwater because Mr Wentwater is very rich. But for Deirdre even to go near him!'

'What is so bad about Mr Wentwater?'

'Oh, at one time it seemed as if he would marry Annabelle, but we found out just in time that he was a slave trader. So that was that. He does not trade any more but Papa says once you do that sort of thing, you're apt to go ahead and replace it with something just as nasty.'

'How true,' said Lord Harry. He could almost feel the fair Daphne becoming self-absorbed again. She had paused to glance down at her reflection in a puddle.

'But Miss Deirdre did not seem to hold him in aversion,' he pursued.

'Do you think so?' asked Daphne vaguely. 'Well, maybe she is sorry for him if she found out what Papa did to him.'

'Which was?'

'You mustn't tell anyone, for I am not supposed to know, but I overheard John Summer, our coachman, telling the maid, Betty. They tell each other things because they have an understanding and hope to be married.'

'Yes, yes, and what *was* it that you heard John Summer tell Betty?' asked his lordship with a rare touch of impatience in his voice.

'Only that Papa had taken out his pack and hunted down Mr Wentwater, right in the middle of summer!'

'I cannot see how he could manage to set a pack of fox-hounds on a man.'

Daphne giggled. 'John Summer hid an old fox in the box of Mr Wentwater's carriage. So *that* is what the hounds were chasing although Mr Wentwater was sure it was himself. That was over three years ago and Mr Wentwater has not been seen up until now.'

'How could Miss Deirdre have an opportunity of meeting him then, if he is not allowed to call at the vicarage?'

'Oh, I suppose she might meet him at Lady Wentwater's. Deirdre often reads to her, you see.'

They turned in at the church gate. Daphne realized that in her worry over Deirdre she had quite forgotten to put on her new bonnet and this fact drove all other thoughts from her mind.

Deirdre was packing feverishly, half

unable to believe she was about to take such a drastic step. No longer did the vicarage look shabby and poky; instead it seemed a safe, warm haven filled with happy memories. She longed for Minerva. Somehow, had Minerva still been at the vicarage, Deirdre felt that things would have taken a different turn.

Her heart was beating hard and her fingers were trembling. What would the twins, Perry and James, think of her when they heard the news?

They would be home at Christmas, and she would not be there. She was sure the vicar would not allow her to set foot in the vicarage again.

At least the family and Lord Harry were going to leave the church and go straight to Hopeminster without returning home. She would need to keep away from the main road and make her way the long way round by the back lanes.

She put on a serviceable pair of walking boots and pulled a thick cloak about her shoulders.

She put a poke bonnet on her head, one she had never worn, considering the long poke ugly. But it hid her face, and if the Armitage family should see her, by ill chance, from a distance, they would surely not recognize her.

Finally, she made her way slowly down the stairs, starting at every creak, trying not to bump the two bandboxes against the bannister.

She had reached the bottom step when the door to the kitchen opened and Betty came into the hall.

'What are you doing here?' demanded Deirdre, fighting for composure. 'You were supposed to be at church.'

'I was told by Miss Daphne to wait behind in case you wanted anything,' said Betty, her black eyes snapping with curiosity. 'Where are you going and why have you got them bandboxes?'

'I am taking these things up to the Hall,' said Deirdre. 'Lady Edwin is collecting old clothes for the poor. I feel much better. Don't make a fuss, Betty.'

Deirdre thought of the tear-stained letter she had left on her pincushion. What if Betty saw it too soon and alerted everyone?

'Well, if that's the case, Miss Deirdre, I'd best be fetching my bonnet and come with you,' said Betty cheerfully.

'There is no need for that,' replied Deirdre, forcing herself to be calm, although she felt like screaming at the waste of time. 'A walk in the fresh air is just what I need to clear my head. I shall go back round by the church and join the others.'

Betty hesitated, and then gave a reluctant nod.

Deirdre took great gulps of air as she escaped from the vicarage and hurried off down the lane. Any moment, she expected to hear Betty running after her.

She swung away from the Hopeminster road, keeping to little lanes and footpaths which would lead her to her destination by a circuitous route—and also add several miles to the length of her journey.

★     ★     ★

Lord Harry's phaeton and the vicar's antique travelling carriage had been brought round in front of the church by the servants.

Daphne once again had the honour of being driven by his lordship, torn between worry at the damage the wind would do to her complexion and the thrill of sporting a dash in such a handsome equipage.

But Lord Harry seemed strangely reluctant to set his usual spanking pace and was content to amble along after the vicar's carriage.

Gradually, the woods on either side thinned out. Across the bare fields Lord Harry saw a figure dart behind a tree. He kept glancing in that direction, but only caught a glimpse of a head peering round the trunk.

A frown settled on his forehead. He suddenly urged his team forward so that they passed the vicarage carriage and then, once in front of it, he slowed his team to a halt and waved his arm to signal to the vicarage carriage to stop also. He jumped lightly down and stood, holding his horses, while the vicar ambled up to him.

'I'm afraid you will have to take Miss Daphne. One of my traces is in danger of breaking,' he said. 'I can fix it given some time and I will follow you into Hopeminster.'

Normally, the vicar would have demanded to see the trace and would have offered all sorts of suggestions but Deirdre and his money problems were weighing heavy on his mind. Daphne was only too glad to get into the closed carriage so that she could study her face in her pocket glass and repair the damage done to her hair by the wind.

Promising to see them all at the inn at Hopeminster, Lord Harry waved them all a cheerful goodbye. He stood in the middle of the road until the lumbering carriage had turned a bend and was hidden from view.

Then he led his team back to the crossroads and looked about. Over the fields and far away, a little figure with two bandboxes was climbing over a stile. A gust of wind whipped the figure's hat off and sent it bowling across the fields. Sunlight shone on a flash of red hair.

He looked from the distant figure to the Hopeworth-Hopeminster crossroads and quietly led his team a little away and into a field. He unhitched his horses, setting them free to graze before he left the field, carefully shutting the gate behind him.

There was a stand of alders a short way from the crossroads, set on a mound. He strolled into it. It afforded an excellent view of the crossroads and the surrounding fields.

He leaned his back against the sun-warmed trunk of a tree and studied the little figure, laboriously crossing the fields. The figure grew larger and finally resolved itself into that of a dusty and dishevelled Deirdre Armitage.

She had lost her hat and the wind was whipping her red hair about her face and she kept impatiently setting down the bandboxes and trying to pin it up.

Deirdre finally reached the crossroads and sat wearily down on a milestone.

Gradually the wind died and the sun grew warmer, and Deirdre Armitage waited patiently; hidden in his stand of alder trees, Lord Harry Desire waited patiently as well.

The minutes grew into quarter-hours, half-hours, and then hours. As the sun sank lower on the horizon the little figure on the milestone grew more and more hunched and forlorn.

Lord Harry straightened up and walked back to where his horses were quietly grazing. He hitched his team up to the phaeton again and led them out of the field towards where Deirdre sat patiently on the milestone.

She did not even look up as he approached, but she must have sensed his presence for all she said in a dull voice was, 'Oh, it's you.'

'I had a minor accident to my phaeton,' said Lord Harry cheerfully. 'Are you waiting for anyone? Or can I take you anywhere?'

'No, I'm not waiting for anyone. That is, I'm waiting to see if my father will return from Hopeminster and take me home. I am so very tired, you see.' Tears started to her eyes and she brushed them away with an impatient hand.

'You would have a long wait,' he said gently. 'Your father spoke of taking supper at the Cock and Feathers before returning. Come and I will take you to join them.'

'Only if I can return to the vicarage first,' said Deirdre, thinking of that incriminating letter pinned to the pincushion. 'I am such a mess. I was feeling so much better and decided to walk. I had these clothes, you see, to take to the poor of Hopeminster. But perhaps I should show them to my mother first.'

'Of course,' he said soothingly. 'We will go to the vicarage first, and then we will go to Hopeminster.'

Deirdre was too tired and miserable and humiliated to protest. He drove at a spanking pace, and, in no time at all, she was back home.

Betty looked relieved to see her, and Deirdre dully wondered if the maid had begun to suspect anything. But Betty had obviously not been in her bedroom. Deirdre tore up the letter addressed to her mother, bathed her face, burst into tears, bathed her face again, changed her gown, and found a smart bonnet, and went wearily down the stairs to join Lord Harry.

To her relief, he did not seem inclined to

talk, his horses eating up the miles to Hopeworth and then to Hopeminster at a tremendous pace.

The Armitage family was just sitting down to supper in a private parlour.

Deirdre sent up a prayer that somehow Lord Harry would not mention finding her sitting on the milestone at the crossroads with two bandboxes. *He* was so stupid, he had easily accepted her story. But her father, she was sure, would not believe such a tale. Desperately she wished she had cautioned Lord Harry not to say anything. And what if Betty talked? But that wouldn't be so bad. She could simply add on yet another lie and say she was sure Lady Edwin wanted old clothes. 'But what old clothes have you got that would fill two whole bandboxes?' her mother was sure to ask.

So busy was she in forming lies and excuses, and so subsequently relieved was she when Lord Harry let everyone assume he had collected her from the vicarage that it was some time before the whole weight of depression and humiliation returned.

The vicar saw the look of pain on Deirdre's face and became more than ever resolved to take Lord Harry aside and tell him there was no hope.

He felt quite virtuous at having come at last to this very definite resolve instead of the half-hearted promise he had made to himself the night before. He would tell Jimmy Radford all about it, and impress his old friend with his, the vicar's, nobility of soul.

But every time the vicar looked at Lord Harry's handsome profile, he was reminded of all the couples of hounds he could have bought if the deal had only worked.

The vicar of Chalton St Ann's, six miles on the other side of Hopeworth, was selling his hounds, or about to sell them in order to retrench. Now, they would need to go to some other lucky huntsman.

The vicar heaved a great sigh. God moved in mischievous ways, as Lady Godolphin would put it, his wonders to perform.

Deirdre let out a dry sob which she tried ineffectually to change to a sneeze. The vicar sighed again. The sooner he told her not to worry about the engagement, the better.

'The town's full of Armitages,' said the vicar, realizing he had been sitting silent for some time, and feeling obliged to add his mite of conversation to the company.

'Edwin and those poxy daughters of his were walking past when we arrived. I mentioned earlier we were going so they probably set out to hunt us down.'

'Why?' asked Lord Harry.

The vicar took a pinch of snuff while he debated his reply. The truth, as he knew very well, was that his pesky brother was still trying to capture Lord Harry for one of his daughters. But if Deirdre would not have the Desire fortune—or rather the fortune he would gain when his uncle kicked the bucket—then the vicar was damned if Josephine or Emily were going to get their claws on it. What a repulsive pair of antidotes they were, thought the vicar. And what truly dreadful fashions they always wore. It was amazing their mother did not know how to guide them since she was a bit of a fashion plate herself, if you didn't notice her pale cold eyes and her pursed up mouth and . . .

'Why?' asked Lord Harry again.

'Oh, ah,' said the vicar. 'Er . . . well, because I'm such a fashionable fellow, and Edwin's a bit of an old stick. He likes to imitate me, don't you see.'

'Not quite,' replied Lord Harry in a puzzled way. His gaze was kind and bland but somehow the vicar felt uncomfortable under that childlike stare and tugged at the points of his waistcoat which had ridden up over his middle to expose several bulging

111

inches of shirt.

'Never mind,' said the vicar hurriedly.

Meanwhile, Deirdre had found she was surprisingly hungry. Despite the fact she had had nothing to eat since breakfast, she was quite sure tragedy had robbed her of her appetite. But by the time she had discussed a generous helping of grouse pie, several slices of ham, some smelts and the inevitable potatoes which accompanied every dish, she began to feel as if she might live through the night to come after all. Several glasses of strong wine brought a little spark of hope which gradually grew to a flame.

How could she have been so disloyal in her thoughts of Guy? Of course, something really serious must have prevented him from coming. What if he were ill?

Her colour returned as her fatigue and despair fled.

With the resilience of youth, she shot from hopelessness to the heights of dizzy optimism. Poor Guy. How worried he must be. How his heart must be aching for her.

The ladies were invited to join the gentlemen for port and nuts, the little girls taking theirs with hot water.

Deirdre began to feel sleepy and content. The world had miraculously righted itself.

By the time they were ready to leave, Deirdre accepted the suggestion she should travel home with Lord Desire without demur, although this time the suggestion came from Mrs Armitage, not the vicar.

Deirdre was being helped up into Lord Harry's phaeton by her father when she suddenly stopped short and nearly fell backwards. Two spots of colour burned on her cheeks.

For out of the inn behind them came Sir Edwin, Lady Edwin and their two daughters—and Guy Wentwater. They had obviously just eaten supper as well.

Guy was holding Emily's hand and whispering in her ear and she was giggling and wriggling while her parents looked on with indulgent smiles, and Josephine pouted.

Then Sir Edwin's party saw the vicarage party. The vicar walked forward.

Deirdre took her seat next to Lord Harry and stared straight ahead. Her father said some words to Sir Edwin, Sir Edwin waved a hand to indicate the presence of Guy Wentwater. The little vicar puffed out his chest and raked Mr Wentwater with a beady look from head to foot, then, ignoring his outstretched hand, turned on his heel and walked back to his own carriage.

'Dear me,' murmured Lord Harry. 'The cut direct.'

'Drive on, my lord,' said Deirdre in a harsh voice.

How *could* he, she thought with anguish. What *was* Guy doing, fit and well, and paying court to that awful Emily?

Her thoughts churned and burned all the way to the vicarage. From time to time Lord Harry essayed a few remarks but Deirdre was deaf to everything but the voices clamouring in her own head.

She gave Lord Harry a curt goodnight and escaped to her room.

When Daphne arrived, Deirdre was lying fully dressed on the bed, staring sightlessly up at the canopy.

'We sat and talked downstairs for *hours*,' said Daphne sleepily. 'I wanted to fetch you but Papa told me to leave you alone which is most odd since he has been throwing you at Lord Harry these past few days.'

Deirdre twisted her head and looked at the clock on the mantel. Midnight! And she had arrived home at ten. So absorbed had she been in trying to find a loophole out of her humiliation that she had not noticed the time passing.

'Are you feeling better?' asked Daphne

solicitously.

Deirdre nodded.

'Papa is in a high rage,' went on Daphne, sitting down at the dimity flounced toilet table and picking up a hairbrush. 'He says that Wentwater is a vulgar adventurer and that no man would be attracted to Emily unless he had a mercenary motive.'

'That's rich,' said Deirdre, twisting on to her side. 'When has marriage meant anything to Papa other than a means to get more money for those smelly hounds of his?'

Daphne at last focused on her pretty reflection in the glass. She thought she saw a pimple and leaned forward, holding the candle so close to her face she almost set her dark hair on fire.

Deirdre lay and thought and thought. Daphne eventually appeared on the other side of the bed in her nightgown and begged Deirdre to move so that she could get under the covers.

Rising as jerkily as a martinet, Deirdre moved to her favourite seat by the window and looked out. A small snore from the bed behind her told her Daphne had fallen immediately asleep.

All at once, Deirdre was sure Guy was calling her. She heard his voice inside her brain.

The pain at her heart lessened. This magical communion between their minds was an incredible and beautiful thing. He seemed to be telling her that he had been unable to get away, but had joined Sir Edwin's party to Hopeminster in the hopes of seeing her.

Tired as she was, Deirdre knew all at once she must go to him.

## CHAPTER FIVE

Squire Radford was unable to sleep. A particularly painful twinge of rheumatism stabbed down his left leg. At last, he gave up the battle and climbed out of bed, wrapping himself up in a greatcoat with a blanket over his shoulders.

A breath of air in the garden was just what he needed.

He shuffled out in his slippers across the lawn and stood by the tall hedge, looking through a small gap in it to where the moonlight turned the village pond to a sheet of silver.

It was then his sharp old eyes saw a girl carrying two bandboxes walking quickly along the road on the other side of the pond. He watched until she had disappeared from view, wondering who on earth she could be, abroad at this time of night.

Deirdre half walked, half ran in the direction of Lady Wentwater's.

Over the River Blyne she went, by way of the hump-backed bridge. The river chattered and gurgled underneath, restless and busy like the thoughts in her head.

She now felt disloyal. A gentleman such as Guy Wentwater would not say he loved her or make a firm arrangement to elope with her and just forget about it.

No. Some unforeseen circumstance must have prevented him.

And that is why she was on her road to join him, complete with bandboxes and newly written letter to mother back on the pincushion at home.

Deirdre planned to make her way round to the back of the house and see if Guy had left the window of the morning-room open. She must try to find his bedroom.

How delighted he would be to see her, she told herself firmly. For had not God himself spoken to her, giving her permission to elope with Guy, and was he not yearning for her at this very moment? Every fibre of her being told her it was so.

To her relief, the window had been left unlocked. She gently opened it and crept inside.

Opening the door from the morning-room which led into the hall, she stood very still, listening intently. The sound of laughter and masculine voices was coming from the drawing-room. Then she heard Guy's voice. 'By Jove, it's good to see you fellows. Of course you are welcome to stay. Aunt has bags of room.'

Still clutching the two bandboxes, Deirdre crept across the hall. The drawing-room door was open and a yellow oblong of light sliced across the darkness.

Deirdre looked in.

Guy was lounging at his ease with a bumper of brandy in his hand. Two friends were seated facing him around the fire. They seemed uncouth, they did not seem like gentlemen, but, strangely, Deirdre did not feel alarmed. Their unexpected arrival must have been the reason for Guy abandoning her.

They were so merry and at ease together. They all belonged to that fascinating world of men—a world which Deirdre envied much as she feared.

At times she chafed at being a woman and having to listen to silly women's prattle. She longed to discuss philosophy and world events and politics. Guy had accepted her as an equal. Therefore it followed his friends would do so too.

She took a deep breath and entered the room, still carrying the two bandboxes.

Guy was facing the door. He looked straight at her in dawning surprise and then his blue eyes sparkled with drink and malice.

His friends followed his gaze.

One of them, thickset and burly, with greasy, pomaded locks plastered to his low brow, twisted round.

'The deuce!' he said. 'What's this?'

'A drama from Astley's Amphitheatre,' drawled Guy. 'The Maiden From the Vicarage Leaves Home. Allow me to present Miss Deirdre Armitage.'

Both men arose and made their bows. The thickset one was introduced as Mr Benjamin Rowse and his thin companion as Mr Bill Wilson. Both were obviously well to do.

'There's a story here,' crowed the one called Bill. 'Do tell, Guy. What wickedness have you been up to?'

Guy rose to his feet and walked to where Deirdre stood. He reached forward and for one blissful moment Deirdre's world righted as she thought he was about to take her in his arms. But, instead, he seized her by the upper arm and dragged her towards the mantel.

'Look in the glass, Miss Deirdre,' he laughed. He moved his grip to her shoulders and thrust her face forwards. Deirdre stared at her reflection. Her bonnet was awry, there was a smudge on her nose, and great purple shadows under her eyes.

'Yes, hardly a fashion plate are you?' he jeered.

'Guy!' cried Deirdre, wrenching herself free. 'What has come over you? What happened? I do not understand the cruelty of your manner. You said you loved me. You promised to elope with me.'

Her eyes grew soft and pleading. 'I-I am here, Guy, and I have brought my belongings with me.'

'Oooh, how touching!' said Guy, mincing about the room with one hand on his hip while his friends roared with laughter.

Deirdre's face turned hard and set.

'Good evening, gentlemen,' she said, walking to the door, her back very straight.

'Wait a bit!' called Bill Wilson. 'Guy may be too nice in his taste but Benjie and me ain't above a bit o' fun with a redhead.'

He clipped her round the waist with one beefy arm and thrust his great red face towards her own.

Guy Wentwater smiled lazily and closed the drawing-room door. 'I agree she is not to my taste, my friends,' he said lazily, 'but don't let me stop your sport.'

Appalled, Deirdre tore herself free from Bill's grasp. Benjie rushed to guard the door. Guy sat down in his chair again and picked up his glass and settled back with the air of a connoisseur about to watch a good play.

Now Deirdre looked like the fox of her father's imaginings. Green eyes blazing, she backed away from them towards the fire.

A canterbury filled with old newspapers stood beside the hearth.

She picked one up in one lightning movement, set it alight, and threw the blazing pages full at Guy who jerked back violently in his chair so that he overbalanced and fell on the floor, tearing at the blazing paper which covered his chest.

'Back!' hissed Deirdre as the other two closed in. Why didn't the servants come? Should she scream? No! One thing burned in Deirdre's mind. No one must know she had been here.

Bill and Benjie began to move nearer. Deirdre edged closer to a brass stand on the other side of the fireplace which held a selection of riding whips, polo sticks, umbrellas, and sword sticks.

She seized a sword stick and managed to jerk the blade out of its sheath before Bill found the courage to try to seize her hand.

Slicing the blade through the air in great sweeps, she held them off until she had reached the door.

Then she wrenched it open and ran instinctively to the morning-room. It was as well she did. For the great door at the other end of the hall was barred and bolted for the night and by the time she had unlatched and unlocked everything, they would have been upon her.

She fled down the Hopeminster road which led from Lady Wentwater's estate into the village of Hopeworth. She did not stop running until she had reached the gates of the Hall, determined to rouse the lodge keeper should she hear sounds of pursuit. For Deirdre now felt there was no way her humiliation and stupidity could escape detection.

But no sounds of chase came to her ears. The night was cold and quiet and still.

Deirdre sank down on to a tussock of grass beside the gates of the Hall and buried her face in her hands.

Never again would she believe in God. He had tricked her, she thought illogically, following quite a common line of reasoning— 'He did not help me, therefore I won't believe in Him.'

And as for the marriage of true minds! Piffle! And men? Worse. Some were better mannered and better dressed than others, but *au fond* they were all the same; great, hairy, selfish, hot-handed, slavering satyrs.

Out of the whole pack of them, she hated her father the most. If he had behaved like a true father, then all this would never have happened.

There is nothing more comforting than finding someone else to blame and so Deirdre lashed her rage up against the vicar.

'You do seem to make a habit of sitting around by the roadside,' came a plaintive voice from somewhere above her head.

Deirdre started and looked up. Impeccable and urbane as ever, Lord Harry Desire stood smiling down at her in the moonlight.

Deirdre looked up at him sullenly. 'Have you come to jeer and torment me?' she asked.

'No,' he said amiably, 'only to find you.

Daphne awoke and found your bed empty and raised the alarm. Betty said you had been running around earlier with two bandboxes. The good vicar decided you had run away from home.'

If only, thought Deirdre wildly, she could keep her stupidity over Guy a secret!

'I left a letter,' she said.

'Well, I don't think anyone has found it yet,' he said.

'I must get back and tear it up,' thought Deirdre.

'Thank you,' she said, rising and brushing down her skirts. 'I am ready to go home now. I couldn't sleep. The letter explained all that, you see.'

'The bandboxes!' cried a voice in her head. 'You left the bandboxes!'

'No bandboxes this time?' went on Lord Harry as if reading her thoughts.

Deirdre began to walk down the road with him. She felt very, very tired. She never wanted to see her father again.

There was only one way in which a gently brought up young girl could free herself from home.

Marriage.

'I will marry you,' she said abruptly.

Lord Harry strolled along in silence. Oh,

124

God, thought Deirdre, even this fool does not want me.

Dark figures were scurrying here and there through the village.

'What is the matter?' asked Deirdre.

'You,' smiled Lord Harry. 'Mr Armitage has sounded the alarm.'

He called out to one of the figures. One of the village boys came running up.

Lord Harry fished in his pocket and handed the boy a shilling.

'Go and tell everyone Miss Deirdre has been found,' he said. The boy grabbed the coin and ran off, moving from one figure to the other.

The vicar met them half way down the lane leading to the vicarage.

Even in the moonlight, it was possible to see his face was dark with rage.

Lord Harry put his arm round Deirdre's waist as she braced herself for the tirade to come.

Before the vicar could open his mouth, Lord Harry said quickly, 'Congratulate me, Mr Armitage. Your daughter has done me the great honour to accept my hand in marriage.'

The vicar opened and shut his mouth like a landed cod. Rage was replaced by joy which was promptly replaced by worry.

Did Deirdre want this marriage? Or had she simply broken down under pressure?

'Wonderful,' he said. 'But where on earth did you go in the middle of the night, girl? I have been worried to death.'

Another lie coming up, thought Deirdre wearily.

'I decided to go out for a walk so that I could make up my mind,' she said, not looking at her father. 'Lord Harry found me and I told him of my decision.'

The vicar looked at her narrowly. He did not believe a word of it. Deirdre did not look like a girl who had just been proposed to by an eligible man. She looked . . . numb.

Mrs Armitage had been having one of her famous Spasms, but rallied remarkably on hearing the news. The girls were all delighted, clustering shyly round Lord Harry in their nightgowns and curl papers.

Deirdre accepted hugs and kisses and champagne, wishing all the time she could go to bed.

Somehow, she was sure, the real reason for her journey out into the night would soon be revealed.

She had left those wretched bandboxes. If Guy had not hidden them, Lady Wentwater's servants would find them, and she could not explain that they were clothes meant for the poor when they contained all her best gowns.

Only someone as stupid as Lord Harry would have believed her.

'I'll have a word with you in the morning, Deirdre,' said the vicar, and Deirdre nodded dully.

As she finally went up the stairs to bed, the remembrance of that letter on the pincushion made her teeth begin to chatter. She quickened her steps and burst into her bedroom, her candle held high.

And there was the letter. Just where she had left it.

She snatched it up and tore it into shreds and hurled it into the embers of the fire.

'I didn't read it,' came a soft voice from the doorway. Daphne was standing there, watching.

'Just as well,' said Deirdre, forcing a laugh. 'It was nothing but a series of household notes I meant to give Mama in the morning.'

'I'm glad,' said Daphne, moving into the room. 'When you were missing and after I had sounded the alarm, I saw the letter and I thought you had run away from home. But letters are so final. I thought if they could find you and bring you back, then no harm would have been done.'

'What an imagination you have, Daphne,' said Deirdre with a laugh that ended as a sob. 'Only see how tired I am? I am nearly in tears over nothing at all!'

★    ★    ★

Guy Wentwater tossed and turned, trying to get to sleep. But despite the amount of brandy he had drunk, sleep persisted in eluding him.

His glee over the humiliation of Deirdre Armitage was beginning to turn sour but he would not yet admit to himself that he was heartily afraid of the Reverend Charles Armitage.

There had been his own ignominious hounding out of the county by the vicar. And then there had been that fellow who had tried to break up Annabelle's marriage. He had heard the stories about that. The vicar had whipped him out of the church and the local boys had debagged him and thrown him in the village pond.

Perhaps it would be best to say nothing about it, except perhaps to Silas Dubois, who would enjoy the story. He would leave out the bit about how Deirdre had battled her way free from three grown men. Best tell it that she had left in tears.

Benjie Rowse and Bill Wilson would not remember the name of the girl in the morning. He would make them keep their mouths shut anyway.

But those bandboxes! Burn them. No, that wouldn't do. He would need to wait and see what happened.

If Deirdre didn't talk, then he was safe.

He should have planned some sort of revenge that the vicar would never know about. Even now Mr Armitage could be riding up the road with that dreadful pack of hounds howling before him.

And then the door of his bedroom opened and a tall figure walked in.

'Who's there?' cried Guy, struggling up against the pillows.

'Desire,' said a polite, social voice.

Guy swore under his breath and lit the candle beside the bed.

Lord Harry Desire ambled forward and sat down elegantly on the end of the bed.

'How did you get in?' blustered Guy. 'I locked all the doors and windows.'

'I picked the lock,' said Lord Harry pleasantly.

'Why?'

'To see you, my friend.'

Guy reached out to the bell rope which hung beside the bed. With one graceful, fluid movement, Lord Harry raised his cane and struck Guy across the wrist, a sharp stinging blow.

'Now, now,' said Lord Harry soothingly as Guy cursed and rubbed his wrist. 'We do not want to wake the whole household, now do we?'

'What do you want?' demanded Guy.

'I came to find out about a visit Miss Deirdre Armitage made to this house earlier tonight.'

'That little redhead!' sneered Guy. 'Never saw her.'

Lord Harry's fist flew out and struck Guy full and hard on the mouth.

He yelped with pain and tried to leap from the bed, only to find his shoulders held down by powerful hands.

Lord Harry's face looked as beautiful and pleasant as ever. Guy looked wildly this way and that, searching for another assailant, for this graceful lord who was smiling at him so disarmingly could surely not have dealt him such a ferocious blow.

So Deirdre hadn't talked. And this idiot

was in love with her.

'Very well,' said Guy, leaning back against the pillows and trying to affect a world-weary air. 'I would have told you had I not been trying to protect the poor girl's name. She got it into her head I was going to elope with her because she didn't want to be pressured into marrying *you*.'

He looked quickly and eagerly into Lord Harry's blue eyes for signs of hurt but Lord Harry smiled blandly down on him and begged him to go on.

'She said she loved me and she would be waiting for me at the crossroads at two in the afternoon,' said Guy. 'She came to see me on the day of the garden party. I heard my aunt returning, and fearing for Deirdre's reputation, I just said, "Yes, yes," and pushed her out of the back way, thinking when she heard no more from me that would be an end of it.

'But the silly chit...' Lord Harry's hand moved and Guy quickly changed it to '...I mean, Miss Deirdre arrived in the middle of the night with those wretched bandboxes and started begging and pleading which was most embarrassing because I had two friends with me at the time.'

'Are they still here?'

'Yes, but you don't want to bother with them.'

'We'll see. Go on.'

'Well, that's all there is to it. When Miss Deirdre found out I wasn't going to marry her, she fled out the back way. And that's that.'

There was a silence. Guy eyed the bell rope, wondering if he could reach it. This lord could throw him from one end of the room to the other, and the servants would not come. They had once interrupted one of his noisier revels and he had commanded them never to appear unless called for. And his aunt slept like the dead.

Lord Harry gave a little sigh, and stretched out his legs, and studied the glistening leather of his hessian boots.

Then he raised his eyes to Guy's.

'Now this time,' said Lord Harry in the same easy social tones, 'you will tell me the truth. Begin at the beginning.'

Guy twisted this way and that and fiddled with the bedclothes. 'Let me get up and put on some clothes, and then we can talk,' he pleaded.

'No,' said Lord Harry equably, 'begin at the beginning.'

Guy thought furiously. Obviously this

wretched lord must be madly in love with the girl. Therefore, if he told another story saying he, Guy, had been in love with Deirdre but stopped himself from eloping with her out of the purest motives, *that* might perhaps be accepted.

So he began with much of the truth; the stolen moments in the churchyard and in the lane. Then he proceeded to lie. He said that much as he loved Deirdre, he knew her father would cast the girl off if she married him, and Deirdre would eventually regret the estrangement from her family, and so he had turned her away.

There was another long silence when he finished.

Again Lord Harry sighed.

'Again,' said Lord Harry. 'Start at the beginning and get it right this time.'

'Look here!' blustered Guy. 'You force your way in here and . . .'

He broke off and gazed in horror down the length of a couple of yards of cold steel. Lord Harry had drawn his swordstick and was holding the point of the blade to Guy's throat.

Guy had never felt more terrified in his life. There was something horrible and monstrous about the placidity of the beautiful

133

face looking at him.

'Well, you can't blame me,' he babbled. 'You see, it was all like this...'

Two hours later, Lord Harry Desire, carrying two bandboxes, softly let himself out of Lady Wentwater's mansion. His knuckles were sore and bleeding, but he was sure that neither Benjie Rowse nor Bill Wilson would dare say a word. All three men would be gone from Hopeworth in the morning.

He whistled jauntily as he walked back in the direction of the village.

Squire Radford heard the whistling and swung his stick-like legs over the edge of his bed and felt for his slippers. He walked to the window and looked out.

In the pale grey light of dawn Lord Harry Desire was walking on the other side of the village pond, carrying two bandboxes. His elegant reflection was mirrored in the cold glassy waters of the pond until a bustling duck cut across it and sent little pieces of Lord Harry's reflection shimmering across the surface.

How odd, thought the squire. Some young girl goes out in the middle of the night with two bandboxes, and now here is Lord Harry Desire walking back with them. Perhaps they are different bandboxes. Perhaps it was a

134

wager.

He sighed and turned back to the warmth of his bed. He would dearly have loved to meet this Lord Harry. But for the first time ever no invitation had come from the vicarage, nor had the vicar called.

'Charles must be up to something bad,' mourned the squire. 'I only wish I knew what it was.'

Deirdre awoke in the morning with a pounding headache. The day was all hard and glittery with bright sunlight splintering off the glass bottles on the toilet table.

Betty had already been in and made up the fire and opened the curtains.

Daphne had already awakened and gone downstairs.

Deirdre turned over and buried her face in the pillows as the memory of terrible yesterday flooded over her.

But she could not hide in her room forever. Her father wanted to see her. She twisted round and looked at the clock. Eleven! How could she have slept so deeply and so late with all this trouble awaiting her?

Well, by now the news would be out. Guy and his coarse friends would have made her the laughing stock of the village. Lord Harry would be disgusted because even such a fool as he must have some sort of pride.

As for her father . . .

Deirdre shuddered and climbed from the bed to make a hasty toilet. She was half way down the stairs wearing one of her best ensembles, a round gown of fine cambric under a pelisse of emerald green rep sarsnet with a rich silk cordon with full tassels about her slim waist, when she realised with shock that this very gown was one she had packed and left in the bandboxes.

With faltering steps she made her way back into her room and pulled at the doors of the tall marquetry wardrobe as if she were opening Pandora's box.

Her clothes hung in serried rows, gowns and mantles and cloaks and pelisses. Her shoes were neatly lined up like a regiment underneath. She ran to the clothes press and pulled open the drawers. Her underwear lay in neat folded piles of muslin and cambric, silk and lace.

She sat down on the bed, her heart beating hard. Someone had entered the bedroom while she slept and put away the contents of the bandboxes. And there were the wretched boxes themselves, neatly stacked on the top of the wardrobe!

Betty! Of course, it must have been Betty.

Some servant from Lady Wentwater's had delivered the bandboxes and Betty had put the contents away.

Now, her secret would be out. Well, better to get it over with.

Deirdre walked slowly downstairs and across the hall. Her father poked his head around the study door. 'A word with you, Deirdre,' he called.

This was it!

Deirdre squared her shoulders and walked in.

'Sit down,' said the vicar in a kindly voice.

Deirdre sat down, wondering at his manner.

The vicar sat behind his desk. He fiddled with a snuff box and then he fiddled with the quill of a pen.

At last he looked up. 'Want to marry Desire, do ye?'

'Yes, Papa,' said Deirdre faintly. 'I told you so last night.'

'Well, hey, that's all holiday with me but it's Clarence House to a charlie's shelter, you're only doin' this to please me.'

'When did I ever try to please you, Papa?' said Deirdre, shocked into honesty.

'Never,' said the vicar with a relieved grin. 'Well, that's all right and tight then. Set a

137

date?'

'No, Papa.'

'Well, well, you'll want to wait until the girls get back from furrin parts.'

'Possibly, Papa. I will need to ask Lord Harry.'

'Oh.' The vicar's face fell again before this unusual display of meekness.

He studied her face anxiously. She was upset about something, and, yes, she was frightened too! Why should he feel so guilty? He had not forced her into anything. If only she would look happy.

His face cleared. She hadn't had her breakfast. An empty stomach, in the vicar's opinion, was responsible for most of the humours and sadness in the world.

'Run along then,' he said more cheerfully. 'Have your breakfast and we'll talk later.'

Still Deirdre hesitated, unable to believe her father had heard nothing about Guy Wentwater.

'Betty should have awakened me earlier,' said Deirdre. 'It is my duty to see the girls off to school.'

'They ain't going anywhere today,' said the vicar. 'We were all up and about half the night.'

Deirdre went slowly out into the hall where

138

she nearly collided with Betty, the maid.

'Oh, Miss Deirdre!' said Betty. 'Them bandboxes arrived this morning but you were that tired, I put 'em all away whilst you were asleep. You must have been fair mazed to pack all your best stuff to give to the poor!'

'What?' said Deirdre, blanching. 'Bandboxes? What bandboxes?' she asked, while her thoughts raced this way and that.

'Well, that's what I said to Lord Harry. He was standing right where you are, ever so early, and looking down at these bandboxes. 'What's this?' I asked, and he says they arrived from somewhere because you'd put good clothes in 'em by mistake. So I says they must be from the Hall, 'cos that's where you was takin' 'em.'

'And what did Lord Harry say to that?' asked Deirdre anxiously, remembering she had told him she was taking them to the poor of Hopeminster. So many lies!

'Well, miss, he just looked at me absent-minded like and then he says for me to hang them away and not be rousin' you on account of you being up last night. Ever so thoughtful, he is.'

'Yes,' said Deirdre, walking away to the dining-room. How fortunate Lord Harry was so . . . so *unaware* of things. But if he hadn't been there at those opportune moments, then her father would definitely have found out about Guy Wentwater.

Guy Wentwater.

The dining-room was empty, so Deirdre helped herself to some tea, hardly noticing it was stone cold, and sat down and thought about Guy Wentwater, and the more she thought about him, the more bitter about life and love she became.

He had tricked her, her mind had tricked her with fantasies of spiritual rapport, her God had tricked her, therefore He did not exist, she reminded herself fiercely.

But her love for Guy had been a powerful and heady drug, so suddenly cut off, that a great part of Deirdre's mind longed for reassurance.

If he had walked in the door at that moment and said he had been drunk and apologized humbly for his behaviour, then she would have forgiven him so that she could plunge back into that secure, rosy, exalted world again.

But the memories were dark and filled with humiliation. The malice in his eyes still haunted her.

She absent-mindedly ate two pieces of cold toast.

140

But he *had* been drunk, her mind nagged. Very. And gentlemen were strange when they were in their altitudes. Why, even her own father had become disgracefully drunk after a successful hunt last year and had ridden his horse right into the Hall and up the stairs.

Her brow darkened as she thought of the vicar. It was all his fault, him with his painted face, coarse manners, lack of breeding and awful, awful creaking corsets.

The door opened and Lord Harry Desire sauntered in.

'Ready?' he asked.

'For what?' demanded Deirdre wearily.

'To go driving with me. If you recall, we made the arrangement last night.'

Deirdre could remember no such arrangement but she was too overset to say so. She meekly remarked she would fetch her bonnet and hurried upstairs.

She pulled on the first bonnet that came to hand, which was, fortunately, the one designed to go with her gown. It was of green curled silk and vastly fetching. She remembered it had recently nestled in one of the bandboxes and that she had planned to wear it for Guy. Two large tears hung on her lashes. She brushed them angrily away and went down to join his lordship.

It was only when Deirdre realized they were turning in at the gates of Lady Wentwater's ivy-covered mansion that she burst into speech.

'We cannot call here!' she said desperately. 'We are not expected.'

'But we are,' he said, reining in his team in front of the house.

A groom came running from the stables to take the horses. Lord Harry jumped lightly down and then helped Deirdre to alight.

'I met Lady Wentwater at the garden party,' he said, 'and promised to call. Are you all right? You have gone very white.'

'Yes,' said Deirdre, feeling her knees beginning to tremble. 'Yes, let us go in.'

For she had decided her monumental luck could surely not hold out any longer. Better get it over with.

Lady Wentwater received them in the drawing-room. There were no signs of the fracas of the night before. All was dark and gloomy and quiet. Sunlight filtered through the fluttering ivy leaves which cloaked most of the windows, creating a subterranean effect.

'I'm glad you've called,' wheezed Lady Wentwater, her small currant eyes the only thing alive in the doughy mass of her face.

'It's gone so quiet since Guy left, although I should be glad of that. Why, the noise he and his friends made carousing till all hours! Not that I heard them, I sleep so sound, but my maid told me the servants thought an army had invaded, it got so bad, and at one point she thought she heard a woman's voice, but that can't be the case since there are no lightskirts around here, except Maggie Trumper, who everyone knows is no better than she should be. But Guy had told them all, the servants that is, not to interfere when he was entertaining, but my maid said at one point they heard one of the guests crying blue murder for help and it was as much as they could do to stop themselves from running in to see what the matter was.'

'Mr Wentwater has gone?' asked Deirdre, her lips feeling numb and stiff.

'Yes. Off he went this morning. I'll miss the lad but I wish he'd keep better company. Those friends of his! Such a mess. Faces all beaten up. But they will fight among themselves when they're in their cups.'

'Did he say anything about . . . about me?' asked Deirdre in such a soft voice that Lady Wentwater had to strain to hear her.

'Nary a word,' said Lady Wentwater maliciously. 'But he sent his regards to Miss

Emily up at the Hall.'

She turned and engaged Lord Harry in conversation while Deirdre sat in a daze.

She was free! Free from public humiliation. By a series of strange coincidences, she had escaped. One of Lady Wentwater's servants must have found the bandboxes and sent them to the vicarage without saying a word.

What a miracle!

She sat on in a daze of relief until it was time to go, barely noticing when Lady Wentwater offered her congratulations on their engagement.

When they were driving sedately along the road again, Lord Harry's first words hit her with the effect of a bucket of cold water.

'I would like to be married very soon,' he said.

'Oh,' faltered Deirdre. 'I am afraid I rushed you into things. Perhaps you don't want to marry me at all.'

'Indeed I do,' he laughed. 'So much so that if you were to go back on your word, I would sue you for breach of promise.'

'Nonsense,' said Deirdre, forcing a laugh. 'Only ladies do that. Only a lady is allowed to sue.'

'Then I shall make legal history,' he said

with great good humour.

'We can at least wait until my sisters return from Paris,' said Deirdre.

'Oh, why?'

'I would like them to be there when I am married.'

'Very well,' he said. 'So long as you promise to marry me as soon as they return.'

'Oh, yes,' said Deirdre. Something would arise to save her before then. For had not Minerva said they would not be returning until the following spring?

'In that case, my love,' he said easily, 'I will take myself off to Town today. I have trespassed on your family's good nature long enough.'

He reined in his horses at a quiet bend in the road and kissed her gently and passionlessly. 'You will not break your promise?' he said, his voice unusually serious.

She looked up into his clear blue eyes, childlike, innocent, candid eyes, and realized there was no escape.

'No, I will not break my promise,' she said.

'Remember,' he said lightly as he set his team in motion again, 'should I not be wed when my uncle dies, then I inherit nothing.'

'Where does the money go? I mean who inherits it?' asked Deirdre, although she barely heard the answer since she was still hoping that some miracle would happen so that she need not be kept to her promise.

'Oh, some distant relative. Very unpleasant. Silas Dubois.'

They drove on in silence.

'Hey, what's this?' asked Lord Harry cheerfully. 'Your home is all a-bustle.'

The short driveway was blocked by two magnificent travelling carriages. Liveried servants were bustling here and there.

The door of the vicarage flew open.

Minerva and Annabelle stood on the step, their arms held out in welcome. Deirdre's older sisters had come home.

So she would need to marry Lord Harry Desire.

She *despised* the man. Oh, he was pleasant enough. But she, Deirdre Armitage, who had prided herself on being the most intelligent of the sisters, was to be tied for life to a handsome fool.

Minerva must do something. Minerva had always been able to solve any problem.

But two minutes of her sisters' company shattered her hopes. They were delighted with her choice of husband. They thought

146

Lord Harry was the finest young man on the London scene. Her elegant brothers-in-law, the Marquess of Brabington and Lord Sylvester Comfrey, had also emerged from the vicarage and were thumping Lord Harry on the back and welcoming him to the family.

The vicar stood behind a curtain in the study, watching Deirdre's face.

She looked miserable. She looked trapped.

He cursed himself. Despite his fears, Lord Sylvester had come across with a hefty sum of money and without even one mumble of reproach.

So there had been no need to sacrifice his daughter.

But she had promised to marry the man.

So what was he to do?

## CHAPTER SIX

The Armitage girls were becoming famous for good marriages and short engagements.

In the months preceding her wedding, Deirdre saw much of her two elder sisters and had ample opportunity to unburden herself.

But Annabelle and Minerva had become so fashionable, so *mondaine*, that to confide her infatuation for Guy seemed impossible. The six sisters were all rivals in a way. Annabelle had grown fonder of Minerva than she had ever been, but the old rivalry was still there. Minerva had produced a son, a lusty, adorable baby boy, while Annabelle, as yet, showed no signs of blessing her husband with an heir. And so she envied Minerva and was apt to sympathize with Minerva overmuch about the sad existence of a mother being kept away from the joys of society by a small baby—carefully ignoring Minerva's advantages of having a nanny, a wet-nurse, and a large staff of adoring servants.

Deirdre in her turn had always been jealous of Annabelle's glorious golden beauty. She was also jealous of Minerva's stately manner. But she had always consoled herself with the fact that she, Deirdre, was the *brains* of the Armitage family. How could The Brains confess to such a piece of stupidity. How could she say, 'I fell in love with a villain, and only agreed to marry Lord Harry to get myself out of a humiliating mess?'

Then *not* marrying Lord Harry meant staying at home with Papa, and Deirdre still detested the vicar and considered him the worst of men; vulgar, posturing and bullying.

Deirdre was much in Town, as her two elder sisters threw themselves enthusiastically into the arrangements for the wedding.

But a visit to Lord Harry's family was impending and Deirdre knew she could not put it off any longer. Lord Harry's father, the Earl of Carchester, had estates to the north of London.

Perhaps Lord Harry, sensing her reluctance, had decided that more than an afternoon's visit would be too much for her, or perhaps it was because a longer visit would entail inviting the rest of the Armitages, but it transpired that he and Deirdre would call on the Earl of Carchester and family for tea, and return to London the same day.

Deirdre was dreading the visit. She imagined a whole family of Lord Harrys, stupid, amiable, dressed to perfection.

She had not been alone with him since Hopeworth. He had seemed amazingly content to see her in the company of others, and although there were occasions when he could have contrived to see her alone, he did not make use of them.

Deirdre had rehearsed a whole series of conversations with which to while away the time on the journeys. Silence was too intimate a thing.

She dreaded him making any more of those warm advances. Sometimes, she imagined herself struggling to protect her virtue in some quiet lane, which showed the frantic state of Deirdre's mind that she could even consider such an elegant and languid man as Lord Harry Desire wishing to deflower her under the eyes of two footmen at a damp roadside when he could have her in a warm bed in only a few months time.

So it was with great relief and surprise that Deirdre found out at the last moment that Lady Godolphin was to accompany them.

Deirdre was dressed in a gown of jaconet muslin made with a gored bodice finished with a tucker of fine embroidery. Over it, she wore a cambric pelisse with long sleeves falling over her hands. A bonnet of white sarsnet with raised spots, bound and trimmed with Danish blue satin, ornamented her head.

Lady Godolphin was also dressed in her finest—or what she considered her finest. Because of the youthful years of her lover, Mr Anstey, Lady Godolphin had blossomed out in girlish fashions.

Her muslin gown was a miracle of pink and white gores and tucks and flounces. Her flaxen wig gleamed like the sun above, and rouge burnished her withered cheeks like the autumn russet bloom on fallen crab apples.

It was embarrassing to Deirdre to find out that Lady Godolphin's search for youth did not stop at her appearance. She tittered and giggled and slapped Lord Harry's wrist with her fan and referred to herself and Deirdre as 'we girls'.

Lord Harry smiled vaguely at all Lady Godolphin's sallies and then fell asleep in a corner of the carriage.

They were using his travelling carriage. The day was cold and brisk but Deirdre longed to open one of the windows since Lady Godolphin's perfume was worse than the Reverend Armitage's, being a mixture of musk, lavender water, rose water, Joppa Soap, sweat, garlic, and Something That a Lady Does Not Talk About.

'It's all very romantical,' sighed Lady Godolphin, smiling on the sleeping Lord Harry. 'Such a beautiful young man. Ain't got much in his cock-loft, but then that's all to the good. He has got good legs.'

Deirdre blushed and turned her head away.

'I said, his legs are good,' went on Lady Godolphin cheerfully. 'Can't abide a man

151

with skinny legs. Now, Mr Anstey ain't well-endowed in that direction. Arthur has lovely legs, but he's so old.'

'Do you mean Colonel Brian?' asked Deirdre faintly.

'Yes. Him. I told him I didn't want to be calloused, but that we were obviously not meant for each other. Of course . . . *well!*'

Lady Godolphin's eyes were bulging from her head as she stared out of the carriage window. The horses had slowed down as they negotiated the steep slope of Highgate Hill. Deirdre leaned forwards to see what had caught Lady Godolphin's attention.

Outside a hostelry on a rustic bench in the chilly sunlight sat Mr Anstey and Lady Chester—the octogenarian Lady Chester.

Lady Godolphin leaned back quickly, biting her lips. 'No, I won't go and ask him what he's doing,' she said aloud, although obviously talking to herself. 'It's a chance redervows. He's sorry for the poor old bat, that's all.'

She began to fan herself vigorously, looking the picture of misery.

Deirdre felt dreadfully embarrassed and wished Lord Harry would wake up. A large tear rolled down Lady Godolphin's cheek, turning red as it rolled down through a patch of rouge.

Picking up her parasol, Deirdre stabbed Lord Harry in one of his delicious legs.

'Ouch!' said his lordship, rubbing his leg. His summer-blue gaze came to rest on Lady Godolphin's distressed face.

'You should not become so exercised, ma'am,' he said gently. 'It quite ruins your unique beauty. What is wrong?'

'I am a trifle sick from the motion of the carriage,' said Lady Godolphin, looking woebegone.

He pulled a silver vinaigrette from out of his pocket and handed it to her.

'So I am not the only one who is too cowardly to talk of my folly and humiliation,' thought Deirdre.

She gave Lady Godolphin's hand a squeeze, her own eyes filling with sympathetic tears. Did Guy really hate her so much? Oh, if only by some miracle he would appear again and tell her he had been insane with drink and that he was dying with love for her! Sometimes the weight of shame seemed too much to bear.

She often started from her dreams with the sound of his jeering voice in her ears.

Lord Harry looked hopefully at Lady Godolphin as if waiting for something, but she soon sniffled herself into silence and then nodded off.

Deirdre looked out of the window, hoping he had not noticed her own distress.

To her relief, he went to sleep again.

She fell to wondering about his family. He had said he had three younger brothers and two little sisters. His brothers were called William, Paul and Jonathan. The girls, Amy and Elizabeth. The brothers were not married. That made it all very unnerving. Perhaps they would think Lord Harry had been trapped and would talk him out of marrying her—which would serve her ends but be a very uncomfortable operation all the same.

In her mind's eye, she could see them now, all lined up to meet her; all beautifully dressed, exquisitely mannered, and impenetrably stupid.

At last, the carriage turned into a driveway and began to bowl along a well-kept road through pretty parkland.

The name of the Earl of Carchester's residence was Archer Hall. Deirdre wondered whether Archer was an old family name.

Archer Hall turned out to be a fairly modern edifice, built only about sixty years

154

before when aristocratic families had started moving their saloons and drawing-rooms from the first floor to the ground floor and putting in french windows, the better to enjoy the sylvan beauties of the countryside.

Clouds covered the sun as they swept around under the portico and an icy wind rattled the bare branches of the trees. A mournful, moulting peacock screamed harshly at them before it turned and walked away.

Lord Harry came as neatly and quickly awake as he had fallen asleep. Lady Godolphin rallied bravely as she was helped down from the carriage, although she looked as if she would like to have a good cry.

Some ten minutes later, Deirdre was studying the Carchester family and searching their faces in vain for some resemblance to Lord Harry.

They were all remarkably dark and squat and ugly. The Countess of Carchester, Lord Harry's mother, was a massive, brooding woman with a heavy moustache and a sallow complexion. Her rather wet brown eyes surveyed her eldest son and his fiancée with suspicion. Deirdre was to learn later that the Countess always looked like that.

His father, the earl, was also squat and

sallow, but where his wife was generously endowed with hair in all the wrong places, he had none in the right places, being as bald as a coot.

Lord Harry's three brothers, and two 'little' sisters—they were more or less the same age as Deirdre—were all squat and dark, like so many trolls.

What they lacked in looks, they made up for in exuberance, laughing loudly at family jokes which were unintelligible to the outsider.

They made no effort to engage Deirdre in conversation. The whole afternoon's conversation revolved around when Uncle Jeremy would die and leave his money bags to Harry. Lord Harry's sisters did seem, at one point, to become aware of Deirdre's presence by agreeing it was a shame poor Harry had to marry to get the money.

Deirdre, whose *amour propre* had been pretty much wrecked by Guy Wentwater, was now made to feel a positive dowd by the Carchesters. Without precisely saying so, Lord Harry's family all seemed to consider it a marriage of convenience. They seemed to quite hero worship this one Adonis in their ugly brood and perhaps would not have considered any female good enough for their beautiful brother.

But Deirdre felt herself growing smaller and uglier by the minute, and tried to console herself with a fantasy that a party of simply dashing young men would arrive, and each and every one of them would promptly fall head over heels in love with her.

Time is a strange thing. Sometimes it seems to race along and sometimes it seems to stand still. Deirdre was quite convinced a whole hour had passed and nearly burst into tears when she realized she had only been sitting enduring the company of her future in-laws for ten minutes.

Lady Godolphin was out of sorts. She refused tea and demanded brandy. She insisted on giving Lady Carchester a recipe for a depilatory which used an incredible amount of slaked lime.

Lady Godolphin seemed fascinated by the Countess's moustache and kept returning to the subject. She told a story of how the Earl of Albermarle, ambassador extraordinary to Paris in 1752, had managed to persuade a 'celebrated artist' to cross over to England and pay a professional call on the Duchess of Newcastle, wife of the Secretary of State. This barber successfully shaved her Grace's upper lip. 'The performance lasted but one minute and three seconds.' The Duke was so pleased that he settled four hundred pounds a year on the Frenchman for life.

Then she went on to recommend another depilatory by Marcus Hyams—'a composition for shaving without the use of razor, soap or water.'

Most of this fell on stony ground since Lady Godolphin did not say 'depilatory' but 'debilatory' and confusion was added to confusion when the earl decided she was talking about aids to sexual potency and silenced her by saying it was not a fit subject for the drawing-room.

At last it was time to leave.

Lord Harry took casual but affectionate farewell of his doting and horrible family. Deirdre curtseyed low, hoping they had all taken her in such dislike that they would forbid the marriage.

But, on the other hand, if they did, she would have to return home. Impossible to suggest to Annabelle and Minerva that she come to live with one of them since she could not stand *père* Armitage. Minerva would be shocked to the depths of her Christian soul, and Annabelle would laugh and tell her she was being ridiculous.

Lady Godolphin grumbled on about the

strange and incalculable ways of men to an uncomprehending but sympathetic Lord Harry and Deirdre affected to fall asleep. Soon the act became reality and she dozed off.

★　　★　　★

Meanwhile, Guy Wentwater had almost forgotten about Silas Dubois. He had removed himself and his friends from Hopeworth as quickly as possible. His friends had cursed him roundly for having put them in a position where they were roused from their beds in the middle of the night by Lord Harry Desire who had threatened them into silence in no uncertain manner.

He strolled into Humbold's coffee house in St James's. The announcement of Deirdre's marriage had not surprised him; probably Lord Harry had clubbed her into submitting to the engagement and would drag her off to the altar by the hair.

A shadow fell across him and he looked up into the unlovely features of Silas Dubois.

Mr Dubois had been called a walking lampoon by his critics by virtue of his small, slight figure and very large nose.

He slid into a chair opposite Guy with his usual furtive, crab-like motion and fixed him with his beady eyes.

'I have been looking for you,' said Dubois. 'A fine mull you made of things. Desire is to marry that Armitage chit.'

'The arrangement was to humiliate the Armitages and I achieved just that,' said Guy attempting an air of nonchalance.

'How?' demanded Silas Dubois eagerly.

And so Guy told him a carefully edited account of his promise to elope with Deirdre and his subsequent humiliation of her in front of his friends.

'And what did the good vicar say when he heard of this?' asked Silas drily.

'Well,' said Guy, flushing. 'He did not hear of it from her ... evidently. And I decided it would not be gentlemanly to speak of it. We agreed to humiliate her. I have done so. My part is played.'

'You cowardly fool,' hissed Silas. 'It was to humiliate the whole family. Had you played your part aright, then Desire would never have married the chit.'

'He is not yet married to her,' pointed out Guy huffily.

'Nor must he,' said Silas.

'Eh?'

160

'I have a distant relative, Jeremy Blewett, a nabob. By coincidence, he is Desire's uncle. He will leave his fortune to Desire if he marries. If he does not, the money comes to me. I learned all this from the cagey old fool a bare week ago. Evidently Desire has known of it for some time.'

'Everyone's known about it for some time,' sneered Guy. 'You heard in the clubs that Armitage was planning a marriage between Desire and his daughter. Did you not know the *reason* Desire wanted the marriage?'

Dubois bit his knuckles and stared at Guy over the large promontory of his nose.

'No, I did not know. But you told me you planned to *seduce* the Armitage girl. Not promise to elope with her, tell her you couldn't because she was a dowdy doxy, and then keep the humiliation between yourselves. It seems from your account that she went straight back and told Desire to marry her.'

'No doubt the other way round. Desire's in love with her.'

'Love!' scoffed Silas Dubois.

'"Love is the *fart*
Of every heart;
It pains a man when 'tis kept close;

161

And others doth offend, when 'tis let loose.'''

'Would you say Deirdre Armitage was in love with you?'

'Oh, yes, definitely,' said Guy smugly. 'Mad for me, she was. Not now, of course.'

'Then you must make her so,' said Silas.

Guy stood up. 'Who are you to give me orders, sirrah?' he said coldly.

'I gave you my time before because it amused me to plan a way to revenge myself on the Armitage family. Sooner or later the vicar will learn his precious daughter only became affianced to Desire on the rebound. That is enough.'

'Sit down,' said Silas coldly.

Guy half-turned to leave. 'Sit down, Mr Evans,' said Silas in a soft voice.

Guy whirled about, his face blanching. 'Oh, aye,' chuckled Silas. 'I know the history, you see. Learned it once down Bristol way. That so-called aunt of yours is really your mother. Made a mort o' money running a chain of bawdy houses in Bristol. Biggest abbess in the town. Had you out o' wedlock, brought you up and gave you enough money to start your life and turned you out of the nest. Took herself off to the depths of the country, adopted a fake title, and pleaded genteel poverty although she's as rich as Golden Ball.

'You took to slave trading and made your pile. You sold out because you wanted the rank and life of gentlemen. You play my game and you can keep it and earn money from me besides. You keep on walking and the whole of London and Hopeworth and Berham county will learn by nightfall that you're the bastard son of a brothel keeper.'

'I'll kill you first,' whispered Guy, sitting down again.

'You don't need to,' grinned Silas. 'Just do one little thing for me. Tell this Deirdre Armitage you cast her off because you knew her father would never recognize her again if she married you. Get her to fall in love with you so that Desire will have nothing to do with her. Stop the marriage. Blewett's on his last legs. He's not going to make out a new will until after the wedding. Even if you delay the wedding, that will be enough.'

Guy closed his eyes. He was terrified of Lord Harry punching him in the face again, he was terrified of the vicar and his pack of hellhounds, but now he was even more terrified of Silas Dubois.

'You knew of the will,' he accused Silas, 'when you listened to my plans to seduce

Deirdre Armitage. Well, I did plan to seduce her, but marrying her cousin, Emily, seemed better game. Sir Edwin is very rich and his social standing is high. But you, you wanted me to make her shoddy goods so that Desire would not touch her. You knew about the will.'

'In faith, I did not,' said Silas with a shrug. 'But that is now beside the point. You have a month in which to reanimate the affections of Miss Armitage.'

'But what if I can't!' said Guy, perspiration dotting his brow.

'Then you must do it by other means,' said Silas Dubois, 'or your life in society will come to an end. Oh, it was bad enough you being a slave trader, but then so were a lot of respectable gentlemen and no one thinks the worse of them once their trading days are over. *Now*, you are respectable. See you do all in your power to keep it that way.'

He slid out from behind the table and made his way out of the coffee house, turning every so often to smile over his shoulder at the still, rigid figure of Guy Wentwater.

\*　　\*　　\*

The Reverend Charles Armitage was pacing

the hall of his daughter Minerva's town house, waiting for Deirdre to arrive back.

He was troubled in his conscience. Deirdre had become quieter and quieter and unhappier and unhappier since they had arrived in Town. Neither Minerva nor Annabelle had seemed to notice anything amiss with their younger sister and for a while this had eased the vicar's worries. But all at once he felt he must ascertain whether Deirdre really wanted this marriage or not.

Because he was nervous, he had dressed in his best. His corsets were lashed to suffocating point, his paint was artfully delicate, like the sunset on a watercolour painting, and his white waistcoat had silver stripes.

He heard the rumble of the carriage wheels. Lord Harry did not enter the house with Deirdre but kissed her hand and went back to escort Lady Godolphin home.

The butler held open the door and Deirdre entered, looking weary and dejected.

'Come into the library,' said the vicar.

'Must I, Papa?' said Deirdre listlessly. But she pulled her bonnet from her head, and, dangling it by the ribbons, trailed after him.

The vicar held open the door and ushered her in. He held out his arms and pinned an

165

affectionate, paternal smile on his face.

'My darling, little daughter,' he said, trying to take her in his arms.

Deirdre shrank back with such a look of naked disgust on her face that the vicar stood frozen to the spot. She walked past him and stood with her back to him.

'What is it, Papa?' she asked in a flat little voice.

'Hey, well, don't you see,' blustered the vicar, 'I am worried about you. Seems you are not happy about this here marriage.'

He struck an attitude. 'Well, I tell ye, there's no need for you to worry. I'll cancel the whole wedding. There!' He stood beaming.

Deirdre turned around, her green gaze raking him coldly from head to foot. She had an all-consuming desire to let him know just how much she despised him.

'It does not matter whom I marry, Papa,' she said. 'One man is much like t'other in my opinion. None fortunately disgust me as much as you.'

'What!' screamed the vicar, hardly able to believe his ears.

'Oh, strike me if it makes you feel better,' said Deirdre, still in that horrible, little voice. 'You are a bag of wind, Papa; a selfish,

166

painted, posturing boor. You! A vicar! You would sell your daughters on the slave market if you thought we would fetch a high enough price. I shall marry Lord Harry . . . to escape from you and your repellent presence. How Mama put up with you all these years, I shall never know. You should be happy. Another rich husband tethered in the Armitage stable. Now, if you will excuse me, I must lie down.'

The vicar stood, puffing and panting, his eyes starting from his head, his hand on his heart.

Deirdre walked past him and quietly closed the door of the library behind her.

★    ★    ★

Squire Radford was a very unhappy and lonely man. The long days had passed without gossip or bustle or incident. He had a bad conscience. He had accused his friend, the vicar, of having no faith to lose, and, furthermore, he had insulted his personal appearance.

The sad fact was that life without even a puffed-up posturing vicar was deadly dull. Assailed with nervous boredom for almost the first time in his life and plagued with many of the irritating little pains and stiffnesses of old age, the squire began gloomily to wonder how much longer he could be expected to live. One thing was sure. He must make his peace with his old friend.

But the vicar was in London. The squire had been invited to the wedding, but all of a sudden, he decided he could not wait until then to present his humble apologies to Charles Armitage. He would leave for Town that very afternoon and seek him out.

The gates at the end of his drive creaked loudly on their hinges. He stood up and went to the window.

Muffled up against the cold in a many-caped greatcoat, the Reverend Charles Armitage was riding slowly up the drive.

Excitedly, the squire rang the bell and told his servant the vicar was to be ushered into the library immediately and one of the best bottles of port brought up from the cellar.

Then he scuttled quickly to answer the door himself. The stable boy was leading the vicar's horse away towards the back of the house.

The vicar stood on the doorstep, his shovel hat in his hand. He raised a pair of eyes swimming with tears to the squire's face, and blurted out, 'I need your help, Jimmy. I'm in sore pain.'

'Come in, Charles!' cried the squire, much alarmed.

He tugged his friend's heavy cloak from his shoulders, and with urgent murmurs of comfort and little pushes in the back propelled the vicar into his old seat in front of the fire.

The squire sat down opposite and leaned forward.

'I have missed you, Charles,' he said. 'But I have only myself to blame. I cannot forgive myself for my harsh words to you.'

'Oh, *don't!*' wailed the vicar, completely overset. He knuckled his eyes with his chubby hands and cried and cried. Finally, he took out a huge, red, belcher handkerchief and blew his nose with a sound like the last trump and then mopped his streaming eyes.

'Tsk! Tsk!' said the poor squire, now thoroughly alarmed, despite the comforting glow that was spreading through his old frame. Charles was in trouble and had come to him for advice as he had come so many times before.

'We have had our troubles in the past, Charles,' said the squire earnestly, 'and together we have managed to solve all problems.

'Ah, Ram. Leave the bottle and glasses on the little table and place it between us and then leave us. Now, Charles. Drink a glass of this and tell me your troubles.'

The vicar hiccuped dismally, but nonetheless managed to toss back a full glass of port without pausing for breath. His face lightened and he promptly helped himself to another.

'I'm that ashamed,' he said, his face puckering up like that of a hurt baby. '"Woe, woe unto them that draw iniquity with cords of vanity, and sin as it were with a cart rope." Isaiah, Chapter Four, Verse 18.'

'Dear me!' exclaimed the squire, becoming more alarmed by the minute.

'Yes,' said the vicar, heaving a gusty sigh. 'Vanity. That was my downfall.'

The squire noticed that the vicar's face was free of paint and that his ample figure was no longer confined by a corset.

'Now my own daughter spits in my eye. I have nourished a viper in my bosom!' moaned the vicar, putting out a feeble hand for the bottle of port and helping himself to yet another glass.

'Deirdre?' asked the squire.

'Yes, her,' said the vicar. 'Not my fault. Told me she wanted to marry Desire. *I* didn't force her into it. But she says she's marrying him because all men are the same and I'm the most disgusting of the lot. She ... she called me "a selfish, painted, posturing boor." And, oh, it's true. After she said that I went upstairs and looked at myself in the long glass. The scales were dropped from mine eyes and I saw this awful little painted caper-merchant staring back at me.'

'Now, now,' said the squire soothingly. 'You see the problem is that when you are yourself, Charles, and attired in your usual country good taste, why, you look a very fine figure of a man. With your paint and ... er ... other embellishments, it was like meeting a stranger, and very upsetting it was, too. Only remember how cruel I was to you? It was very harsh and impudent of Deirdre to say such things, but I am sure they were prompted by love ... as my remarks were.'

'Aye, you're right,' said the vicar. 'But Deirdre is dreadfully unhappy about something. She's not the same girl, not by a long chalk.'

'I accused you quite wrongly of lack of faith,' said the squire tentatively. 'Have you thought of placing your daughter in God's hands?'

'Turn my will over to Him? Oh, I find that

mortal hard. I tell 'ee, Jimmy, my prayers are like those coloured soap bubbles. I send 'em up to Heaven, saying, "Here it is, Thy will be done," but afore they can get very high, I say, "Hey, wait a bit. I'll do it my way," and I stick up my finger and pop the bubble before it rises any higher.'

There was a long silence.

A few tiny snowflakes began to spatter against the glass and bounce about the lawn outside. The wind gave a sudden howl in the chimney and great yellow and red flames shot up with a roar, and then died down, leaving a small heaven of red stars burning in the sooty back wall of the fireplace.

'There is a mystery here and I think it concerns Miss Deirdre,' said the squire.

'It was the night you put out the alarm she was missing. I was about to tell you what I knew but by the time I found my coat and boots, a village boy came rushing up to tell me she had been found.' He went on to relate how he had seen a young woman like Deirdre carrying two bandboxes, hurrying along the far side of the pond, and how later, at dawn, he had seen Lord Harry returning with two bandboxes.

The vicar sat up straight, his lips moving soundlessly as he tried to work something out.

'Wentwater,' he said at last, while the squire looked at him with bright eyes. 'By all that's unholy. She tried to go to Wentwater so as to escape the marriage and Desire found out. So why does Desire want to marry her, heh? What do I know of this Lord Harry? Heh? Seemed an amiable enough clod. Where's Wentwater?'

'Gone. He left the morning after Deirdre went missing.'

'Oho! I wonder if I can get anything out of Lady Wentwater. No. Waste of time.' He settled back comfortably in his chair, looking so much like his old self that the squire felt sentimental tears pricking at his eyes.

The wine sank lower in the bottle and the day darkened outside as the vicar sat and thought.

'Deirdre was always a strong-willed girl,' he said. 'She didn't want none of Lord Harry, not a bit of it. Then she suddenly changes her mind, and, while he's at the vicarage, although she's a bit rude with him and off-hand, like, she still has a glow about her. Then when she comes back with him that night, she's gone all hard and cold and bitter. Now she's even more bitter, and demme if I don't think she's frightened of

Lord Harry. See here, Lord Harry found out something about her that night and is making her marry him.'

'Dear me,' said the squire. 'I wonder what it was? You do not think, do you, that there was any ... well ... foul play on the part of Wentwater?'

'No,' said the vicar slowly. 'He was chasing after Emily. But no one saw him near Deirdre. Lord Harry's the problem, mark you. It must be something awful bad for her not to have told Minerva and Annabelle. I asked both of 'em before I left Town but they seemed to find nothing amiss. O' course, Annabelle's so full of all them adventures she had at the wars, and Minerva's so taken up with Julian—my grandchild,' he explained unnecessarily and puffing out his chest, 'that they wouldn't notice anything.

'I'm going back to Town to find out all about it. I'll study them both and think of something to stop the wedding.

'For mark my words, Jimmy, that wedding is not going to take place or my name's not Charles Armitage.'

★    ★    ★

'Minerva!'
'My love?'

Lady Sylvester put down her sewing and smiled on her lord.

Lord Sylvester stretched his elegant legs in front of him and studied the gold tassels of his hessian boots.

'I am a trifle concerned over that sister of yours.'

'Deirdre? But why? She is to be married to a very suitable young man.'

'But I don't think she wants to get married,' said Lord Sylvester, his green eyes meeting those of his wife in an unblinking cat-like stare. 'I think your wretched Papa was groping around to find money while we were absent. Lady Godolphin confessed *he* proposed to Harry Desire.'

Minerva threw back her head. 'My sister shall not be constrained to marry *anyone*. I will talk to Papa.'

'No, my crusading love, there is no need to do that. See that Deirdre and Desire are kept apart as much as possible. If Deirdre seems glad to be kept away from him, then you will have the truth of the matter. It is all very simple. Weddings can always be cancelled, you know.'

★    ★    ★

Annabelle patted her sunny ringlets in front

of the glass and blew a kiss in the direction of her husband. 'Why so solemn?' she laughed.

'Deirdre,' said the Marquess of Brabington, 'is scared to death of marrying Harry Desire.'

'Oh, *Deirdre*,' shrugged Annabelle. 'Fustian! She's always play-acting.'

'But my sweeting, I can assure you . . .'

'You can assure me of a kiss right this minute, Peter, or I shall scream.'

Half an hour later Annabelle murmured lazily, 'What were you saying about Deirdre?'

'What?' said the Marquess of Brabington, running a hand slowly over his wife's hip. 'Oh, nothing. 'Twas nothing at all.'

## CHAPTER SEVEN

Deirdre let herself quietly out of her sister Minerva's town house in St James's Square and took a deep breath.

A light powdering of snow lay on the ground. The day was cold and damp with heavy, lowering clouds above, promising
176

more snow to come.

She had passed a puzzling week. No longer did she have to plot to avoid Lord Harry's company. She had hardly had a chance to see him at all. Minerva took her everywhere, often on the flimsiest of excuses. And then the night before, Lord Sylvester and Minerva had taken her to the opera and Lord Harry was not of the party but two most eligible young men were. When Deirdre had asked the whereabouts of her fiancé, Minerva had replied, with uncharacteristic vagueness, that she had forgotten to invite him.

Then if it was not Minerva who was on hand to keep her out of her fiancé's way, it was her father and Squire Radford. The vicar, looking very much like his normal self, showed a sudden enthusiasm for seeing all the warehouses and shops in London, insisting that she must need extra ribbons and lace for her trousseau. Deirdre found her father's new quiet demeanour more acceptable although she still disliked him, but the squire was, as usual, the complete gentleman, and Deirdre enjoyed his company immensely.

Once, when she was strolling along Bond Street with the squire and her father, Deirdre had seen Lord Harry approaching and had told her father. He and the squire had then behaved most oddly. They had seized her arms and hustled her quickly into the nearest shop.

Then there were the odd conversations. Minerva told of tragic marriages where the couples had been most unsuited; the vicar told her of instances where marriages had been called off at the last moment and the parties concerned had been grateful ever afterwards.

Obviously everyone concerned had gathered she did not really want to marry Lord Harry and was encouraging her with heavy-handed tact to break the engagement.

But if she told Lord Harry the wedding was off, then he would probably be absolutely furious and might even follow through his threat and sue her for breach of promise.

But yet, the prison gates seemed to be opening. Surely Lord Harry would not care to make a cake of himself in the courts by sueing her!

But now that she was kept away from her fiancé, Deirdre became filled with a paradoxical longing to see him, if just for a little.

At times, he had been very pleasant

company indeed. He was not intelligent, but his manners were beautiful. Ladies seemed fascinated by his beauty, and Deirdre was feminine enough to enjoy their jealousy. And she had recently been introduced to a very intelligent member of the House of Lords who was supposed to be famous for his wit. But he had patronized Deirdre quite dreadfully, a thing Lord Harry would never dream of doing.

When she had been escorted by her tall and handsome fiancé, yes, she had to admit it was pleasurable to be looked on with envy. Now, with the Armitage family closing tightly about her again, Deirdre felt as if she were being driven slowly back to the nursery.

Minerva had even volunteered to read to her and kept giving her nasty little glasses of tonic because she 'needed building up'.

Deirdre would gladly have stayed at home at least one evening to play with baby Julian, but she was told that young misses like herself should be gadding about, and not sitting around the house like old, married ladies.

And so the more conspicuous Lord Harry became by his absence, the more Deirdre began to wonder about the strange and tumultuous reaction of her body to his kisses.

Did lust have a place in love?

On that morning she had awoken with a craving to be left alone with her thoughts, and so she had escaped from the house, meaning to walk as far as Green Park. She did not have her maid with her or even a groom, but it was early and all the bucks and bloods who might annoy a solitary female could be guaranteed to be fast asleep for at least another five hours.

A small, slight man with a huge nose stared into her face intently, almost popping his own under the shadow of her bonnet to do so. Deirdre shrank back with a little cry and the man murmured some apology and scurried away.

The hour was nine in the morning. Nothing really came alive in the West End until ten. How still and white and deserted the streets seemed!

There was that strange little man again!

Deirdre was sure she saw him scuttling across the end of the street. She stood still. There was something eerie about it all.

There he was! But it turned out to be the shambling figure of the watch. He touched his hat as he passed. Deirdre half turned towards home. But the broad expanse of Piccadilly lay just ahead. And if she returned,

Minerva would find her and immediately begin making plans for her day.

She bent her head and hurried into Piccadilly. There were a good few people about. Shopkeepers taking down shutters; shopkeepers who served the rich and therefore kept the same hours.

Crossing sweepers were busy with their brooms. A child rolled a large metal hoop this way and that, admiring the patterns it made in the snow. Another ran a stick backwards and forwards across the railings.

Deirdre entered Green Park, only walking a little way in so as not to be too isolated from the road. She brushed the light snow from a bench and sat down and tried to marshal her thoughts.

At last she came to the conclusion that she had treated Lord Harry unfairly. She was the one who had asked him to marry her. It was only fair to the man to tell him of her fears and doubts. In the depths of the country when he had said he would sue her for breach of promise, it seemed believable, since, if he did not marry, he did not inherit his uncle's money.

But in Town, it was all too obvious that a great many ladies would be only too eager to marry Lord Harry if he dropped the handkerchief. And why was she afraid of him? He had been all that was kind and gentlemanly. His family was horrible, but then look at her own father!

Deirdre stood up at last feeling better than she had done for a long time. She *would* talk to Lord Harry. Getting him to understand simple things was often very hard, she thought, but she could try.

She began to walk towards the gates of the Park.

A tall figure was standing right in her path.

Deirdre shied like a frightened horse and put her head down, ready to scuttle round him if he persisted in trying to block her way.

'Deirdre? Is it you?'

Deirdre looked up in amazement into Guy Wentwater's face.

'*You!*' she said in accents of loathing.

She gave him a great push and then hurried past him as fast as she could, the iron ring on the soles of her pattens striking sparks from the pebbles.

He hurried after her, caught her in a strong grasp and twisted her about to face him, his eyes pleading and anxious.

'You must listen to me,' he said intensely.

Guy had been rousted from his bed in his lodging only a short time before by Silas

Dubois and ordered to 'go to it'.

He was frantic. He was tired of his shadowy wandering life and had a mind to settle down as a country gentleman. Marrying Emily Armitage would have made the vicar rage and would have supplied him, Guy, with a respectable wife with a respectable dowry. Now he would need to find some other girl. For when his seduction of Deirdre Armitage became known, he would need to hide out in another part of the country and hope the vicar died of apoplexy. If he could, on the other hand, not seduce her but merely encourage her into some folly that would drive her to cancel the wedding, then there was still hope.

But he must re-engage her affections fast, or Silas would spread the awful secret of his birth all over the place.

'Leave me alone,' said Deirdre savagely, 'or I shall scream for the watch.'

'You must hear me,' said Guy, holding her fast. 'You *will* hear me. I am as much in love with you as I ever was. Yes, I treated you shamefully. But it was for your own good.'

'Indeed?' said Deirdre, standing very still now.

'Yes,' he went on eagerly. 'You must realize I was afraid our marriage would not work. Your family would never speak to you again. I was afraid you would grow tired of being estranged from them. I was frantic when you turned up at my aunt's. I had to be cruel. I felt I had to give you a disgust of me, to drive you away. I was drunk, yes. That I freely admit. But I have not known a night's sleep since then.

'Only look at me and say you forgive me.'

Deirdre kept her head bent.

'You were courting Emily as far as I could see,' she said at last.

'Ah, that was merely to throw sand in everyone's eyes. The minute I heard you were affianced to Desire, I felt ashamed. I felt responsible for you throwing yourself away.'

Deirdre looked up at him at last, her eyes as green and cold as the North Sea. 'I am hardly throwing myself away by becoming affianced to a kind and handsome lord.'

'Of course you are angry with me,' he said in a coaxing voice. 'I deserve more, much more. How can I make you forgive me?'

Deirdre suddenly felt infinitely weary. It had all been too much. All her troubles churned round in her head; her fear of Lord Harry, her hatred of her father, her low self-esteem, all culminating in a great sickening wave of hot self-disgust. She wanted to punish the whole wide world—starting off with herself.

Deirdre took a deep breath. 'By eloping with me,' she said quietly.

Guy's mind raced. Gone were his hopes of Emily's hand in marriage. He need not marry Deirdre, of course. Perhaps he could hide her away somewhere and return her to her family unscathed. Perhaps she would be too ashamed of herself to tell them where she had been. She had obviously told no one of her last try at eloping with him.

But then there was Harry Desire. But he would not want to have anything to do with a girl who jilted him right before the wedding.

'Very well,' said Guy, feeling her penetrating gaze on his face. 'When?'

'Tomorrow,' said Deirdre. 'I mean tonight, but at two in the morning. Wait for me here.'

'You are sure you will be able to escape unnoticed?' asked Guy anxiously.

'Oh, yes,' said Deirdre simply. 'Now, let me go. I must return. It is cold.'

Guy tried to embrace her but she pushed him firmly away. 'Not here,' she said. 'It is too public.'

She broke free from him and hurried off over the snowy ground, moving so quickly that her cloak billowed out about her slight figure.

Guy watched her go, his heart beating hard. He must think where to take her. He must pray she told no one of what she planned to do.

Deirdre walked on, her mind filled with a savage elation. She had no longer any romantic thoughts about Guy Wentwater. She thought him shallow and common. And so, she was bent on marrying him.

We all have a little of the death wish in us ready to rear its ugly head when we fall out of love with ourselves. The depressed commit suicide. But that is not a genteel act. The polite gentleman either commits suicide by regular instalments of hard liquor or by journeying unarmed into the more squalid parts of the city. Young ladies find a rotter to ruin them.

By marrying Guy Wentwater, Deirdre could flagellate herself and make her father thoroughly miserable into the bargain.

Fate seemed determined to aid her in her proposed action, for the vicar had left for a brief visit to Hopeworth on urgent parish business (good hunting weather), leaving Squire Radford behind as a sop to his shaky conscience. The squire had been attacked by

186

an acute attack of rheumatism and was confined to his bedchamber.

Minerva had suddenly become aware that she had spent a great deal of time away from her beloved child while looking after Deirdre and trying to keep her away from Lord Harry. But Lord Harry was keeping himself away, and so Minerva was determined to spend the whole day at home, fussing over her baby to her heart's content.

Lord Harry Desire was paying a visit to his uncle, Mr Jeremy Blewett.

Mr Jeremy Blewett looked very old indeed. He was, in fact, fifty-two, but a life in India under a hot sun combined with a formidable capacity for strong spirits had aged him until he resembled a little dried-up mummy.

He had been talking about death for such a long time that it came as a surprise to everyone to find him still alive. Apart from his eyes which were very bright and twinkling, the rest of him looked dead, and quite often smelled it, since he had a horror of bathing.

'What brings you here . . . as if I need to ask?' cackled Mr Blewett as Lord Harry strolled into his bedchamber. 'Come to see if I've written that will yet? Well, it won't be written till the wedding's over.'

187

'You don't need to worry your pretty little head one way or t'other about my bachelor state,' said Lord Harry amiably. 'I don't need your moneybags.'

''Course you do,' sneered Mr Blewett. 'Carchesters never knew how to keep money.'

'They never knew how to make it either,' responded Lord Harry cheerfully, 'until I came along.'

'Don't tell me you've started working for a living!' exclaimed Mr Blewett.

'No, nothing so horrible. Gambling is my salvation.'

'I should have known. White's and Brooks's have been the sepulchres of many a fortune.'

'Not them. The Stock Exchange. I have a genius for speculation. I am possessor of quite a large fortune, uncle. Wealth has descended on me suddenly. So, you see, you will need to concern yourself with bullying Silas Dubois.'

Mr Blewett looked sulky. 'I never meant to leave him a penny anyway. He doesn't like me and hasn't the grace to hide it.'

'It serves you right for being such a miserable old sinner. Anyway, you don't need to leave me any money, and I don't need to get married.'

'Don't love the girl, eh?'

'I did not say that. I am merely pointing out that due to my exceptional talent for moving around stocks and shares, I am at liberty to marry anyone I please, and when I please. Nonetheless, you can trundle out your bath chair for the wedding and arrive like the bad fairy in time to bring down curses on my nuptials.

'But do, please, put the horrible Silas out of his misery. He's perfectly capable of killing you just to get your money if you tease him too much.'

'That great walking nose! Never! Don't trip over the other relatives on the way out. They gather around me like vultures.'

'And don't you adore it. It's what keeps you alive, dear uncle, all this manipulating and string-pulling.'

Mr Blewett gave a harsh cackle of laughter. 'Perhaps you have the right of it, Harry. But I'll probably leave you the money anyway. You never cared a rap for my bullying and you don't creep around me in that fawning way Dubois has.'

'Oh, I am fond of you in my fashion,' said Lord Harry airily.

'Where are you off to?'

'To see my beloved. A thing I hardly do these days. By the time I meet her at the altar, I shall have quite forgot what she looks like.'

Lord Harry sailed out, and nearly collided with Silas Dubois who was standing outside.

'I wouldn't lurk there, dear boy,' said Lord Harry earnestly. 'The door is so thick, you can't hear a word through it, and you're only likely to get a terrible earache from pressing your ear to the keyhole.'

Lord Harry went off quickly down the stairs before Mr Dubois could think of a reply.

Mr Dubois went into the bedroom.

'Oh, it's you, is it?' snapped Mr Blewett huffily. 'Still waiting for me to die, Silas?'

'Of course not,' said Mr Dubois, his small mouth curving up under the shadow of his nose in what he hoped was an affectionate smile. 'I passed Desire on the stairs. There is a rumour he might not wed after all.'

'Nonsense,' said Mr Blewett, looking slyly out of the corner of his eyes at Mr Dubois. 'Needs to get married.'

'I hear he has been speculating on 'Change to some effect,' said Mr Dubois.

'All a hum,' said Jeremy gleefully. 'The terms of the will still stand. If Desire weds,

190

he gets the money. If he don't, you do.'

Silas grinned. By tomorrow morning, everyone, including this horrible old carcase of a man, would know that Lord Harry's intended bride had eloped with Guy Wentwater.

'What you so happy about all of a sudden?' snapped Mr Blewett.

'Only happy to see you so well and in such good spirits,' replied Silas Dubois, coming forwards and solicitously plumping up Mr Blewett's pillows.

His hands stilled for a moment. How easy it would be, he thought, to jerk out this silk and lace pillow and hold it down on the old man's face!

Silas became aware that Mr Blewett was staring up at him with a sort of unholy glee on his face, almost as if he could read his mind. He quickly finished plumping the pillows, and sidled to the foot of the bed.

Why commit murder? Tomorrow would see a change in the old man's thoughts. And he could not live much longer anyway.

★    ★    ★

Deirdre went into the morning-room to find Minerva busy writing a letter to Mrs

Armitage who had remained behind at Hopeworth with the younger girls.

'Where is His Lordship the baby?' asked Deirdre.

'Asleep,' smiled Minerva. 'Oh, it is so wonderful *not* to have any engagements! I shall lounge for the rest of the day. Oh, dear. Someone has arrived. I shall say we are not at home.'

'Lord Harry Desire,' announced the Comfreys' evil-looking butler.

'Tell his lordship we are not at home,' said Minerva quickly.

'Tell his lordship we *are* at home,' corrected Deirdre crossly. Now that she had set her mind on social ruin and personal degradation Lord Harry held no further fears for her. Besides, all Deirdre's old resentment at Minerva's bossy ways had come rushing to the surface.

'Well, if you *really* want to see him...?' began Minerva. But Deirdre had already left the room. Minerva hesitated, wanting to follow her. Then she relaxed. Sylvester had promised to have things out with Lord Harry some time soon and Deirdre would not have gone rushing to see a man of whom she was afraid.

'Have you come to take me driving?' asked

Deirdre, as she met Lord Harry in the hall.

'No,' he smiled. 'I am come to talk to you, my love, about deep and serious things.'

'Oh,' said Deirdre anxiously. Then she rallied. It did not matter what he said; she would not be seeing him after today. It never crossed Deirdre's mind for a moment that Lord Harry might be hurt in the slightest by being jilted. Such a lummox could only have slow, bovine feelings. He was rather like an aristocratic peasant, she thought, briefly amused at her own wit.

'Well, where shall we go?' he asked, bringing Deirdre to the realization that they were both still standing in the hall.

She led the way into the library.

Lord Harry stood in front of the fireplace, and studied her face with his calm, blue gaze. She was strung up taut like a violin string, he thought. She looked just like someone about to jump off Westminster Bridge . . . or elope with Guy Wentwater.

'Seen anything of that fellow who fought at Waterloo?' he asked. 'Whatshisname. Wentwater?'

'No,' said Deirdre breathlessly. 'Why do you ask?'

'I don't know. Making conversation, don't you see.'

'What are the deep and serious things you want to talk to me about?' asked Deirdre.

'You shouldn't wear brown,' he said severely. 'Don't become you at all. It's a sort of mud colour. Not the thing.'

He put up his quizzing glass and stared at Deirdre's plain round gown with one horribly magnified eye.

'Is *that* one of the serious matters?' asked Deirdre acidly.

'No. Well, yes, it is in a way. Clothes are very important. Now, *I* look rather well in blue. It makes me appear more approachable.'

Deirdre looked at his faultless morning coat, the exquisite ruffles of his shirt, the wide innocence of his eyes, and her lip curled in contempt.

'Ah, but to come to the serious things,' he said. 'I say, can we sit down?'

'Of course.' Deirdre sat down primly on a small sofa in front of the fire and he arranged himself elegantly beside her.

He looked at her anxiously, his black curls tumbling over his forehead. Deirdre noticed for the first time that Lord Harry's lashes were extraordinarily long and thick.

'You see,' he said, 'I don't need to get married. I've made an awful lot of money on

194

'Change.'

'So you don't want to marry me?' asked Deirdre faintly.

'Well . . . to put it bluntly . . . no.'

'Oh.'

'You see, we should not suit. I am afraid I rather misled your father. I was teasing him, don't you see. I said I couldn't abide intelligent women, but I told a lie. I *adore* intelligent women.'

'Are you trying to tell me,' said Deirdre slowly and carefully, 'that *you* don't consider *me* intelligent?'

'You are beautiful and charming,' he said looking at her pleadingly, 'but an intelligent woman has a mind of her own, and you . . . well . . . "*Tu nihil invita dices faciesve Minerva.*"'

'I'm afraid I don't . . .'

'No, of course, I forgot, you probably do not understand Latin.'

'On the contrary,' lied Deirdre, 'I *do* understand Latin . . .'

'I was quoting from Horace . . .'

'So there is no *need* to translate . . .'

'And I said, "You will say nothing, do nothing, unless Minerva pleases."'

'I know very well what you said,' retorted Deirdre, her colour high. 'How *dare* you call

195

*me* unintelligent. How would *you* know? You talk of trivialities the whole time. I *long* for someone to discuss politics with me, for example.'

'Certainly,' he said. 'I would like to hear your views on Parliamentary reform. I think Lord Liverpool and Lord Sidmouth are actually encouraging the radical faction so that an alarmed middle class will support all manner of repressive measures and the Tory supremacy will stand. What do you think?'

'I do not think you would understand my views,' said Deirdre, stalling for time. For she did not have the least idea what he was talking about.

'But an intelligent well-informed mind is capable of communicating his or her ideas. Pray, go on.'

'What is the point!' exclaimed Deirdre, jumping up. 'You don't want to marry me anyway.' And overcome with a sudden realization of her own suicidal folly in rushing headlong into an elopement with a man who would probably abuse her, Deirdre burst into tears, and sat down again next to Lord Harry.

Guy had lounged back that terrible night and let his friends attempt to molest her. God only knew what he would do to her once they were married. Never had Deirdre felt so small or so silly.

A comforting arm stole about her shoulders and a large handkerchief was held out under her nose.

Deirdre took it gratefully and blew her nose and mopped her eyes.

'I thought I would please you,' said Lord Harry's voice at her ear, 'by telling you I didn't need to get married. You see, I could not help noticing you did not seem to favour my company. Also, I sustained a visit from your father before he left for the country. Poor man. He was torn with remorse over having forced you into an engagement you did not want, and the joys of hunting. John Summer, his whipper-in, had written to say the weather was excellent and that there was a wily fox sighted only a few miles from the vicarage. I put him out of his misery by saying I would not marry you. Then right on his heels came Lord Sylvester. *He* said you were frightened of me and he and his wife had done their best to keep you away from me, knowing that if you cared at all for me, you would become upset. But you didn't. Ergo, you don't like me. So I told *him* I wouldn't marry you.'

'Oh,' said Deirdre miserably, wondering why she didn't feel happy.

'I was worried about Mr Armitage. He said you had come to loathe and hate him and it was all his own fault. He was so put about, like a sort of fox-hunting Shylock, running to the window to see if the carriage had arrived and wringing his hands and saying, "Oh, my daughter—oh, the hunt—oh, my daughter—oh, pray God Reynard gives us good chase."

'What misery I have caused you all! So all you need to do is nod your head and I will arrange for an announcement to be sent to the newspapers, terminating our engagement.'

He took both her hands in his.

'I know you wanted to elope with Guy Wentwater,' he said gently.

Deirdre had thought until then that she had tasted the dregs of humiliation, but this last statement proved her wrong.

'How did you know?' she whispered.

'Oh, little things all added up to the one big thing,' he said airily. 'So I went along and collected your bandboxes and had a most interesting talk with Mr Wentwater. After hearing how shockingly he had behaved, I was at least confident that you would never want to set eyes on him again. I thought, you see, that you might come to care for me a little.'

'And Mr Wentwater told you everything

'. . . just like that?' mumbled Deirdre.

'Well, after a certain amount of . . . er . . . pressure. Do not worry. You will not be troubled by him again.'

Deirdre raised shaking hands to her hot face. The very idea of eloping with Guy seemed such a piece of madness now. A madwoman had made that arrangement.

'So,' he went on when she did not speak, 'I told your father I would escort you home to Hopeworth on the morrow, and then all your worries will be over. I know you hate it in Town. Perhaps I shall see you again during the Season.'

'I'm sorry . . . for everything,' whispered Deirdre.

'You are not in any trouble?' he asked. 'Is there nothing you wish to tell me?'

Deirdre thought of her appointment with Guy Wentwater. She shuddered. Over and over again since he had walked into the library, this Lord Harry Desire, the man she had damned a fool, had made *her* appear worse than an idiot. She could not tell him.

Deirdre dismally shook her head.

'Then I think you should tell Mr Radford the glad news of the termination of our engagement,' said Lord Harry. 'He only came to Town because your father begged him for help. I think it would be a great kindness if you could find it in your heart to forgive your father.'

'I must forgive myself first,' whispered Deirdre brokenly. 'I have caused all this distress. Now there are presents to be returned and . . .'

'I am sure your sister, Lady Sylvester, will handle everything admirably. Now, I was to escort you to a ball at Lord and Lady Brothers' tonight. Lady Godolphin is to be of our party. If, however, you do not feel . . .'

'I will go,' said Deirdre wretchedly. She knew all at once, if she stayed at home, then she would fret and worry about Mr Wentwater waiting for her in Green Park, and she would wait in dread in case he called at the house.

'Then I shall call for you this evening. I think perhaps we might be friends, now that you do not need to fear marriage to me.'

'Yes,' said Deirdre in a low voice.

'Good,' he said smiling. 'Perhaps you might choose a bride for me.'

Deirdre looked at the sapphire and garnet ring on her fourth finger and twisted it off and mutely held it out to him. He took it and put it in his waistcoat pocket.

'You are still overset,' said Lord Harry.

'Allow me to tell your sister and brother-in-law and Squire Radford of the termination of our engagement.' He stood up and drew her to her feet.

She looked up into his face. He was looking down at her intently. He raised her hands to his lips and kissed them gently.

'Goodbye, Deirdre. We shall meet again, but as friends.'

He turned and walked from the room, leaving Deirdre shaken and buffeted by a series of emotions: humiliation, shame, and loss.

★　　★　　★

An hour later, Lord Harry entered his lodgings and looked thoughtfully at his Swiss.

'What is today's report, Bruno?' he asked, as he stripped off his driving gloves.

'Ah, milor,' sighed his servant, 'I regret I 'ave sad news. I had Miss Armitage followed as you requested. The man you 'ave watching the 'ouse in St James's Square who was to report if the lady went out alone, 'e come to me and say 'e follow 'er to the Green Park where she meet a man who ... who ... 'ug 'er, like thees,' he added, hugging himself for

201

emphasis.

'Our man keep behind the tree and 'e cannot 'ear everything but 'e 'ear mademoiselle say two in the morning in the Park.'

'Thank you, Bruno. You may call off the watchdog,' said Lord Harry, studying the pleats of his cravat in the glass.

'Milor,' said his servant apologetically, 'our man say mees was preparing, 'e tink, the elopement.'

'Just so. Pay him well.'

'Ver' good.'

Bruno bowed himself out, shaking his head over the peculiar ways of the English quality.


## CHAPTER EIGHT

Minerva was not in the slightest pleased with her sister. She treated Deirdre to a long and severe lecture on the selfishness of allowing the wedding arrangements to proceed as far as they had. Deirdre had *deliberately*, said Minerva, turned poor Papa into some sort of ogre as an excuse for plunging deeper into the whole mess.

Feebly did Deirdre complain that Papa was

not entirely blameless, and that a man who chased his daughter across the countryside with a whip could hardly be described as a loving and sensitive parent, but Minerva would not listen.

Lord Sylvester had had a *most* wretched time of it, talking to Lord Harry. Lord Harry was a perfect gentleman, and, in truth, probably too mature and polished for such a heartless hoyden as Deirdre.

The lecture would have gone on for much longer if Lord Sylvester had not intervened by teasing his wife and saying all her prosing made his head ache.

Deirdre's only ally turned out to be the maid, Betty. Betty had learned that Sir Edwin had offered John Summer a job at the Hall. Had he taken it, then there would have been enough for them to get married. But John had proudly turned it down, saying, 'he would never desert the reverend.'

Men!

'You're not that bad, miss,' said Betty soothingly as she helped Deirdre to prepare for the ball. 'I heard what my lady said. But you are very young for your years and the vicar is a mortal hard man to cross. But all's well that ends well, for now you don't need to marry a man you don't want, and we can all be comfortable again.'

Deirdre sat miserably silent under Betty's ministrations. She had always believed that had she managed to be free of Lord Harry, then her relief and happiness would know no bounds. She never expected to feel as downcast and . . . yes . . . *silly* as this, for all the world like a spoilt child who boasts she does not care for a valuable toy, and yet cries bitterly when it is taken away from her.

Furthermore Lord Harry had *tricked* her. Deirdre now knew he had gone out of his way to appear stupid. Not only that. He had quite deliberately shown her that she was singularly badly informed when it came to politics. Deirdre's idea of discussing politics and world affairs had been a hazy notion of listening to someone's views and promptly expressing those views to the next person she met. She realized she hardly ever read the newspapers.

All she really knew about the Battle of Waterloo was stories passed from one to the other. Guy's story of the battle she now discounted. He had probably never even been there.

Minerva was to blame, for Minerva had always laughed indulgently at Deirdre's opinions and said, 'Oh, little Deirdre is the *brains* of the family,' and what Minerva said other people came to accept and before you knew it, you had been presented with a whole lot of virtues you didn't really possess.

Minerva was apt to tuck people neatly into roles. Annabelle, beautiful and headstrong. Deirdre, intelligent. Daphne, the beauty of the family; modest and stylish. Diana, a wonderful way with animals. Frederica; dainty and funny, a whimsical little thing.

And yet Deirdre had longed for Minerva to interfere and rescue her from marriage to Lord Harry. And Minerva had. Or rather her husband had.

Deirdre's thoughts turned to her father. It seemed he had done his utmost to try to ensure her happiness, even though it meant he would be losing a rich son-in-law. Well, she forgave him, but she still did not think much of him.

And Guy Wentwater? What about Guy who would be waiting patiently in the snow of Green Park at two in the morning?

Let him wait, thought Deirdre savagely.

Yes, she had been mad to make the arrangement. But why should she spend one second worrying about a man who had left her waiting and then had jeered and humiliated her in front of his friends.

And yet, he *had* said he loved her.

How odd that Lord Harry should manage to wring the correct story from Guy, not knowing that Guy had not confessed to his motives of revenge on the Armitages. Lord Harry had mentioned 'pressure' but she could not imagine that entailing any physical violence. He was much too elegant and indolent a creature to resort to that.

During all this hard thought, Deirdre had been standing and sitting and standing again, to allow Betty to dress her and arrange her hair.

'There!' said Betty at last, slamming down the lid of Minerva's jewel box. 'I've never seen you look so pretty. When you cry, Miss Deirdre, it makes your eyes even larger. Me, mine get all puffed up and red.'

Deirdre stood up and shook down her skirts, barely glancing in the looking glass.

She was wearing a slip of grass-green silk covered with a gauze overdress of a lighter green. A necklace of emeralds and dead gold was about her neck. One large gold silk rose had been cunningly embedded in a nest of curls on top of her head, its curling green silk leaves edged with tiny emeralds.

The bodice of her gown was lined and stiffened so that her bosom was pushed up into two swelling mounds. Dainty little grass-green slippers were on her feet and heavy emerald earrings blazed in her ears.

Betty, who considered the colour of Deirdre's hair too violent, had pomaded it so that it was now a rich dark red.

'You look like a fairy queen,' laughed Betty, admiring Deirdre's tilted green eyes and delicate bones. 'I'll fetch your fur-lined cloak for it's mortal cold. It's a good thing you put on them, new drawers.'

Deirdre was wearing the latest in long, skin-tight knitted wool drawers, an underwear fashion much in vogue to counteract the flimsiness of modish outer attire.

The semi-nudity of the last decade's fashions was beginning to go as men once more wanted something to be left to the imagination. But, during the evening, clothes were still almost transparent and some ladies still damped their muslin dresses, causing all sorts of lustful hopes in the masculine bosom.

Men often mistook all those hard and thrusting nipples as signs of hot passion, instead of cold, hard gooseflesh which is what they were.

Deirdre was to be escorted by Lord Sylvester to Lady Godolphin's home in

Hanover Square. Lord Harry would meet her there.

Rather in awe of her tall and handsome brother-in-law, Deirdre sat very stiffly beside him in the carriage on the road to Lady Godolphin's.

'You look enchanting tonight,' said Lord Sylvester, studying the little fairy-like creature that was Deirdre. 'I am glad to see some colour in your cheeks. Lord Harry told me he had sent a notice of the termination of your engagement to the newspapers.'

'Yes,' said Deirdre in a small voice. 'Thank you, Lord Sylvester, for interceding on my behalf.'

'Think nothing of it. I was surprised to observe you seemed to be *afraid* of Lord Harry.'

'Oh, no,' said Deirdre quickly. Then all of a sudden, she became weary of lying. 'Well, as a matter of fact, I was. I do not know quite why,' she added.

'You certainly have nothing to fear from Lord Harry,' said Sylvester gently. 'He is one of the kindest men I know.'

'Yes,' said Deirdre in a suffocated voice.

Deirdre remembered why she was so frightened of Lord Harry. She was frightened of him because of what happened to her body

208

when he touched her. But her silly dream-love with Guy was what had made that physical reaction seen so terrible.

But Lord Sylvester and Minerva were very much in love. There was a radiance about them when they were together. And yet, their love seemed to be of the purest. They never even held hands that Deirdre could see.

Perhaps there was a love which did not involve physical contact, thought Deirdre naively. The fact that her sister and brother-in-law had a son meant nothing to Deirdre since she did not know how babies were conceived.

She knew how the beasts of the fields went about it, but if anyone had ever told her that it was the same performance between humans, well, she simply would not have believed them.

And so Deirdre was sure her emotions when Lord Harry held her had nothing whatsoever to do with love. Lust, yes. Even Papa on his rare appearance in the pulpit pointed out lust was a dangerous and disgraceful thing and one of the worst of the seven deadly sins.

The carriage stopped and Lord Sylvester helped her to alight and saw her safely to the door. He made his apologies for not entering to see Lady Godolphin but explained he was anxious to return to his wife.

Deirdre heaved a sentimental sigh. A little hope came back to her. Perhaps one day, some man would love her as Lord Sylvester loved Minerva; a pure and precious love, free from the hot, heaving, sweating emotions of lust.

Lord Harry had not yet arrived so Deirdre took it upon herself to explain to Lady Godolphin that their engagement was at an end.

'Oh, lor',' said Lady Godolphin. 'Your nipples is off!'

Deirdre glanced down at the bosom of her dress, and then realized Lady Godolphin meant 'nuptials'.

'Didn't he want you?' asked Lady Godolphin sadly.

'We decided we should not suit.'

'Ah, love.' Lady Godolphin sighed gustily. 'I try to forget it but all the poems remind me. Never read poetry, Deirdre. It's too sad. Listen to this one,

"When Love with incontinent wings
Havers around the gates;
And my divine Algae brings
To whimper in the grate;

210

When I lie mangled in her hair,
And frittered in her eye;
The Gods, that want not in the air,
Know no such livery."'

There was a little silence.

'I do not think I have heard that one,' ventured Deirdre cautiously.

'It's by Lovelace,' said Lady Godolphin in surprise. 'You know, the man who wrote the things about, "I could not love thee dear so much, loved I not horrors more."'

'Oh, *that* one,' said Deirdre, realizing that if one sorted out Lady Godolphin's malapropisms, it might take all day, but at least one could understand what she was talking about.

'Will Mr Anstey be joining us this evening?' asked Deirdre, hoping he would not for she had taken him in dislike and thought it disgusting for a woman of Lady Godolphin's great age to have such a young, if unprepossessing, lover.

'No,' sighed Lady Godolphin. 'He has made a fool of me. He has held me up to Reticule. He went off to live with Lady Chester who must be a hundred if she's a day. So now society thinks he was only hanging around my skirts for my money.'

'Is there no one else?' asked Deirdre, hating to see the normally robust and cheerful Lady Godolphin look so woebegone.

'No,' said Lady Godolphin. 'I'm too old.'

'Not you!' Deirdre wanted to scream. It was horrifying hearing Lady Godolphin admit to being old. Although Deirdre had often longed for the reprehensible old sinner to settle down and act her age, there was something appalling in the fact that she was obviously now trying to do just that. Even her gown was subdued, being of brown silk shot with gold. A turban of modest proportions covered her head, and, wonder upon wonders, she was wearing *no paint at all*.

At that moment, Lord Harry was announced.

Apart from casting a look of gloomy lechery at his legs, Lady Godolphin behaved like a sad and respectable dowager.

Lord Harry kissed Deirdre's hand.

Deirdre looked at him with something like awe, seeing him for the first time as many women saw him.

He was wearing a dark blue evening coat with pearl-coloured kerseymere breeches with strings to the knees, white silk stockings and thin pumps.

His only jewel was one enormous diamond pin in his cravat, which might have looked vulgar on another man, but only added to Lord Harry's air of magnificence.

His thick glossy black curls, Grecian profile, clear blue eyes and tall slim figure were enough to seduce the eyes of any lady with a clear brain and normal digestion.

Deirdre held on to her idea of that pure and celestial love as a barrier to all those nasty, gurgling churnings around her insides, and the prickling nervous feeling in the palms of her hands.

'So you are not to be married?' asked Lady Godolphin after they had all been helped to glasses of wine.

'No,' said Lord Harry equably.

'Then you had better return my present,' said Lady Godolphin. 'Cost me a mort of money.'

'Yes, of course,' said Lord Harry and Deirdre in chorus, and then they looked at each other and laughed.

Lady Godolphin's present to them had been an enormous oil painting of a singularly well-endowed Roman matron stabbing herself in a half-hearted way while she rolled her eyes upwards to a stormy sky. She was wearing only a thin wisp of gauze about her massive thighs which seemed to stay up by magical means since she was stabbing herself with one hand and pointing up to heaven with the other. Various hirsute and swarthy Romans rampaged about the background, avenging her, or something-or-other. Lord Sylvester had said it was probably meant to be Lucrece, since Lady Godolphin had proudly presented it as a French picture, called Le Crease.

Lady Godolphin gloomily shook her head at them both, muttering something about the folly of youth, and said it was time to leave.

It was with some surprise that they discovered Lord Harry's high-perch phaeton drawn up outside with his Swiss manservant, Bruno, hovering on the backstrap instead of a groom.

'My dear Desire,' said Lady Godolphin. 'An open carriage! In *this* weather!'

It had not snowed very hard during the day so there was only a thin coating on the ground. Snowflakes were falling through the foggy air; large, light, lace snowflakes drifting slowly down under the flickering lights of the parish lamps.

'We are only going a step,' said Lord Harry cheerfully. 'I have plenty of rugs and hot bricks.'

'But there is barely room for three,' wailed Lady Godolphin.

'What! A sylph like yourself? Come along, Lady Godolphin.'

Grumbling awfully, Lady Godolphin was pushed from the back and pulled at the front until she reached the high perch of the seat. Lord Harry sat on one side of her and Deirdre on the other.

Deirdre gazed about her dreamily, thinking it was wonderful to be perched so high above the London streets, watching the hypnotic dance of the light snowflakes.

She had the beginnings of a sort of excited, suffocating feeling, such as she used to have at Christmas.

Christmas past had been rather disappointing. The boys had come home from Eton and had become very grand, strutting around like Bond Street beaux, and affecting languid airs which sat comically on their cheerful schoolboy faces.

Lord and Lady Brothers' mansion was a blaze of light. Thin strains of music drifted out into the foggy air. After all the worry and self-hate and tension of the past months, Deirdre felt her whole body and mind begin to relax. She would enjoy this one evening. She would imagine she was a respectable young miss with her handsome fiancé and not a disgraceful widgeon who had only such a short time ago been hell-bent on ruining herself.

As they mounted the staircase to the ballroom, Lord Harry slipped her engagement ring into her hand. 'Put it on,' he whispered. 'All the world will know tomorrow we are not to be married but tonight we do not wish to be badgered by questions.'

Deirdre nodded and slipped on the ring.

More than ever before she was conscious of admiring eyes, envious eyes, jealous eyes as the ladies of the ballroom watched her enter on Lord Harry's arm.

Lord Harry danced beautifully. Deirdre found it very hard to pay attention to her steps or listen to her partners when Lord Harry always seemed to be in her direct line of vision, flirting outrageously with one female after another.

She had had the pleasure of performing one country dance with him and was wondering whether he meant to ignore her for the rest of the evening when he came up and led her into the steps of the waltz. The feel of his hand on the small of her back sent fireworks shooting up her spine, the pressure of his other gloved hand in her own made her go numb down one side. He held her the regulation twelve inches away, but she was conscious of every movement of his body. When the dance ended, she promenaded with him as was the custom, but dreading the moment when he would leave her and dance off with someone else.

But he said, 'Let us sit down for a little.'

He led her to a sofa in the corner, behind a bank of hothouse flowers. Deirdre fanned herself languidly because she was once again locked in that dreamy state, and the ballroom was hot. He went to find her a glass of lemonade and immediately she became anxious and worried in case someone would ask her to dance before he returned.

But he was soon back, handing her a glass, and settling himself comfortably beside her on the sofa.

'Here's to liberty,' he said raising his own glass.

'Liberty,' echoed Deirdre, sipping at her lemonade and wishing he had brought her something stronger to ensure that this relaxed dreamy feeling she had in his company did not go away.

'Lady Godolphin is not in plump currant,' he said. 'The horrible Mr Anstey left her for richer, if more withered, pastures.'

'Yes, she is very sad,' agreed Deirdre. 'She was quoting poetry, and getting all the words wrong. Something about love with incontinent wings.'

'Oh, that one,' he grinned. Then he began to quote softly,

'"When Love with unconfined wings
Hovers within my gates;
And my divine Althea brings
To whisper at the grates;
When I lie tangled in her hair,
And fettered to her eye;
The Gods, that wanton in the air,
Know no such liberty."'

'Quite,' said Deirdre huskily, staring into her glass. Then she essayed a laugh. 'I wish I could remember how Lady Godolphin put it, but it was vastly different, I assure you.'

'She should have married Colonel Brian,' said Lord Harry. 'Trouble is, he's always hanging about her, quite obviously dying of love. Now if *he* were to start paying attention to some other female, no doubt she would come about. Which reminds me, I am promised to dance with Lady Coombes, and I think you probably have an anxious partner looking for you.'

'Yes,' said Deirdre reluctantly, wishing they could sit together like this and not have to dance with anyone at all.

A niggling thought entered her mind, a nasty little voice whispering that she had had ample opportunity to enjoy Lord Harry's company these past few months but all she had done was run away from him.

From then on Deirdre danced and danced. Soon it would be two in the morning and soon it would be time for Guy to wait for her in Green Park.

But at one-thirty Lord Harry appeared at her side, yawning, and said he really must go home. Lady Godolphin would not be returning with them since she did not want to 'freeze to death' and had sent for her own carriage.

The night outside was cold and clear. Snow sparkled and shone in broad pools under the street lamps, and, far above the huddled black houses of London a small winter moon rose high in the starry sky.

'It is a beautiful night for a walk, Bruno,' said Lord Harry over his shoulder to his shivering servant on the backstrap. 'I suggest you make the most of it.'

'Ver' good, milo',' said Bruno gloomily.

He climbed down and strode off into the night.

Lord Harry drew on his York tan driving gloves and set his team in motion.

'Come and sit beside me, Deirdre,' he said. 'You will get cold sitting all the way over there.'

Deirdre slid along until she was next to him. He put an arm around her shoulders, holding the reins bunched in one hand, the horses ambling very slowly over the diamonded cobbles of the snow-covered streets.

Deirdre was all too conscious of his hip against her own although they were both bundled up in cloaks and blankets.

His arm tightened about her and she gave a submissive sigh and leaned her head against his shoulder.

After they had been moving along in this dreamlike state for some time, he slowed his team to a halt and looked down at her.

'Keep the ring, Deirdre,' he said softly. 'You need not wear it on your fourth finger.'

She looked up at him, puzzled and bewildered by all the things she felt for him and could not yet analyze.

'And since we are to become friends,' he went on, 'you might at least kiss the lover goodbye.'

Her lips trembled and she put up a timid hand to his cheek.

He took it in his own, and then bent his lips to hers.

This time, because it was all over, she did not feel afraid of him. He would never kiss her again, so there was no harm in kissing him back ... no harm at all.

And so she gave herself gladly, if innocently, up to hot, dizzy, heady passion, totally absorbed in the contours and feel of his mouth, the faint smell of cheroots, wine and cologne from his body, and the feel of his long fingers cradling her face.

They sat on the high-perch phaeton, right outside the gates of Green Park at two in the morning, totally absorbed in each other, oblivious to everything else.

Deirdre did not even know where she was.

Guy Wentwater stood frozen to the spot and stared in mounting savage fury at the two locked lovers, so brightly illuminated by the light of a lamp.

The carriage he had hired for the elopement was waiting out on the street. The driver kept rising up on the box and staring into the darkness of the park as if wondering what on earth this strange Mr Wentwater was doing.

At last, the phaeton moved off.

Guy Wentwater marched out and got into the black stuffiness of the closed carriage, biting his nails and sweating from every pore.

He hated the whole Armitage family more than he had ever hated them before, but this time, he hated Deirdre Armitage much, much more than he had ever hated the vicar. He felt she had deliberately stage-managed the whole thing to humiliate him.

And now Silas Dubois would learn there had been no elopement and Silas would ruin him.

★　　★　　★

Deirdre, Squire Radford, the maid, Betty, and Lord Harry Desire set out for Hopeworth the following day.

They were to break their journey that night at a posting house.

Deirdre was glad to escape from London before curious callers started to arrive, eager for gossip about the broken engagement. Squire Radford was puzzled. Paradoxically, Deirdre and Desire seemed closer than they had ever been before.

The snow had melted and a squally wind

was hurtling grey clouds across the sky.

Weary with thought and confused emotion, Deirdre was glad to be going home. She wondered what Guy Wentwater had thought when she did not appear. Deirdre had been so wrapped up in and by Lord Harry's embrace that she did not even know they had been parked outside the gates of Green Park in full view of Mr Wentwater.

Guy, she thought, would assume she was getting her revenge—which she was, in a way.

'Good hunting weather,' observed Lord Harry. 'I wonder if the vicar has run his fox to earth.'

'I hope he has,' said Squire Radford in his dry precise voice. 'It will take his mind off his troubles. He has had many of late. Besides, he hopes to cut a dash. He took back with him a new coat of hunting pink.'

'Why is it called *pink?*' asked Deirdre idly. 'I assume you mean a scarlet coat.'

'It is named after Mr Pink,' said Lord Harry. 'He was a tailor who was left with a vast amount of red military material when the American war came to an end sooner than expected. So he turned to making hunting coats. Hence pink.'

'Perhaps this fox does not exist,' said the

squire, pulling a bearskin rug more closely about his knees. 'There is a legendary animal which had been plaguing Mr Armitage for some time. It is seen first here and then there, and certainly hounds pick up the scent but they always end up wandering around in baffled circles. Mr Armitage is sure this fox can climb trees.'

Deirdre giggled. 'Papa often sees foxes which don't exist, particularly when he is in his cups.'

There was a reproving silence, and Deirdre felt she had just behaved like a bad child.

'When I get home,' she vowed to herself, 'I will read the newspapers every day and . . . and . . . I will learn Latin, and all sorts of things.' She wondered how long Lord Harry would stay with them this time. She had never really got to know him. She put a hand up to her lips, remembering his kisses. How strange that he was able to be so polite and formal with her now!

She chattered on to him about this and that, but he replied to all her questions and commented on her topics with a lazy smile, like a father indulging a favourite daughter.

Perhaps he will seek me out when we break our journey, thought Deirdre.

But Lord Harry appeared content to spend

most of the evening talking to Squire Radford.

The squire had travelled a great deal, and it transpired Lord Harry had been to many of the countries the squire had visited.

To her disappointment, both men took up the conversation where they had left off at breakfast and continued all the way to Hopeworth.

On the outskirts of Hopeworth they heard the belling of hounds, the winding of the horn, and then streaking across the road behind his pack came the Reverend Charles Armitage with John Summer close behind him. He cleared the hedge beside the road and set off hell-for-leather over a ploughed field.

They had a momentary glimpse of his flushed and excited face and then he was gone.

He did not seem to have seen them.

Squire Radford was deposited at his home, and Lord Harry's carriage swung round the pond, heading for the vicarage.

'How long will you be staying with us?' asked Deirdre.

'I shall not be staying at all,' said Lord Harry, looking surprised. 'I shall return to Town just as soon as I have paid my respects to Mrs Armitage.'

Deirdre's heart plummeted.

But what else could he be expected to do?
She had made it all too clear she did not want
him.

But she hung around anxiously while he
chatted with her mother after their arrival,
tactfully explaining he was the most desolate
of men for he and Deirdre had decided they
would not suit. Then he teased Daphne,
saying she grew more beautiful by the
minute, to which Daphne answered with a
surprised, 'I know.'

Hearing that the little girls were at school,
he decided to take his leave.

Naturally neither Mrs Armitage nor
Daphne dreamed of leaving Lord Harry and
Deirdre alone to say their goodbyes.

Mrs Armitage and Daphne were self-
absorbed in different ways, Mrs Armitage
with her imaginary illnesses and Daphne with
her own beauty, but they had enough
sensitivity to feel it would be monstrous
awkward for poor Deirdre to be left alone to
say goodbye to a man she had decided would
not make a suitable husband.

He bowed very formally before her,
looking more serious than Deirdre had ever
seen him look before.

'I am to have my Season,' said Deirdre. 'I shall see you then, perhaps?'

'I don't know,' he replied. 'Squire Radford has given me a mind to travel. 'Tis a pity, perhaps, we are not to be married. We could have seen all those wonderful places together—Paris, Rome, Naples, Venice...'

He bowed again and entered the carriage. The coachman cracked his whip, Lord Harry raised a white hand in salute, the carriage rumbled down the short drive, out into the lane.

He was gone.

Only dimly did Deirdre hear her mother's anxious questions and lamentations on the end of a most suitable engagement.

★ ★ ★

Lord Harry gazed placidly out at the country fields. He saw the lone figure of a peasant standing by the bend of the road outside Hopeworth, gazing intently across the fields.

Wondering if the vicar had made his kill, Lord Harry signalled to his coachman to stop. He let down the glass and leaned out.

'Watching the hunt?' he called.

The yokel turned slowly and took some time to bring Lord Harry's face into focus.

'No, zur,' he said at last, touching his forelock. 'I bee watching the crops grow. Just watching the crops grow.'

Lord Harry waved his hand and the coach started off again.

'I wonder,' he said to himself, 'whether the crop I have planted will ever come to maturity. Waiting for things, or people, to grow up can be a tedious business.'

## CHAPTER NINE

The vicar of St Charles and St Jude wearily wended his homeward way, slumped over the pommel of his saddle. A string of oaths floated out behind him on the evening air.

'I do believe,' he shouted over his shoulder to his coachman-cum-groom-cum-kennel-master-cum-whipper-in, John Summer, 'that there fox is an invention of the devil. I seen him, with my own two eyes. You saw him too, didn't you John?' he asked pleadingly.

'That I did, master,' said John in a comforting way. 'Saw him with my own eyes. You 'member, the first find was close to Hans Wood and from then onwards, hounds' heads were down and their voices singing well over

228

half the afternoon. Must have run not short of twenty mile.'

'And then what happened?' mourned the vicar. 'Reynard disappears like a puff o' smoke and hounds were running round that great elm in circles. Climbed up it, didn't you? Not a whisker o' Reynard in sight and the scent as cold as last Sunday's dinner.'

'Well, I told you, master,' said John, 'foxes don't climb trees.'

'This poxy one does,' growled the vicar. 'God! I'm mortal stiff. Sharp set, too.'

Wearily, he dismounted outside the vicarage and led his weary horse to the stables.

By the time he had rubbed down his mount and covered it with a blanket, warm from the saddle-room fire, and seen to its feed, the vicar felt every muscle had been wrenched out by some giant hand and put back in all the wrong places.

Groaning heavily, he entered the small dark hall of the vicarage, shouting for Betty to come and pull off his boots.

Betty was stooping over the second boot as the vicar sat on an upright chair in the hall when he had a sort of feeling he was being watched.

He glanced up and saw a huddled figure on

the first landing.

He sent Betty off to bring brandy to the study and waited until the maid had gone into the kitchen and closed the door behind her.

'Come down,' said the vicar, addressing the figure on the landing.

Deirdre rose and came slowly down the stairs. His heart smote him as he saw the telltale marks of tears on her pallid cheeks.

Silently she followed him into the study. 'Don't say a word,' said the vicar, vigorously poking the fire, 'until I get a drop of brandy down me.'

Deirdre slumped in a chair and the vicar sat behind his cluttered desk. Betty came in with the bottle and glass on a tray along with lemons and a jug of hot water.

She glanced curiously at Deirdre.

As soon as she had left, the vicar poured himself a large glass of brandy and tossed it off. He looked narrowly at Deirdre's woebegone face, and poured another glass down him for good measure.

'That's better,' he said, wiping his mouth with the back of his hand. 'Now, what's amiss?'

Deirdre just shook her head dismally.

She wanted to tell someone, but surely anyone was better than this brutish father.

'Well, I'll need to guess,' said the vicar. 'Let's start with Guy Wentwater.'

Deirdre turned as red as she had been pale a moment before.

'Yes,' said the vicar, tilting back his chair and putting his thumbs in his waistcoat, 'him. I think you went and asked that wastrel to elope with you because you didn't want to marry Desire. I think he turned you down that night when you went to Lady Wentwater's carrying them bandboxes. Fortunately for you, her ladyship was in residence or the worst might have happened and you would have ended up with no wedding ring to show for it. Don't you know Wentwater wants revenge?'

Deirdre looked at her father with her mouth open.

The vicar waited to see if she would say anything, and when she did not, he went on, 'And somehow Desire got wind o' it and went up to Wentwater's and brought back them bandboxes. Next thing you says you're going to marry him, but you look so mortal scared o' the man that squire and me decide he's blackmailing you. So we ups to London to try and keep you away from him as much as possible so you might guess we were on your side and tell us the truth. It came as a relief when I finally faced him and he agreed not to marry you. Now would you like to fill in the blanks in my story?'

Deirdre hung her head. She was amazed her father had guessed so much and yet was not ranting and raving.

The need to unburden herself was great, and with a little sigh, she began. She told him the whole story from beginning to end, leaving nothing out, except the last meeting.

'I'll kill him,' said the vicar savagely. 'I'll tell you why he did it.' He related the story of driving Guy out of the county. 'He's weak and vicious,' ended the vicar. 'You look as if you've had punishment enough, but, 'fore George, I cannot but wonder you were so taken in.'

Somehow Deirdre found herself telling him of her love for Guy, of her dreams of the sort of love Minerva had found—'You know, Papa,' she ended earnestly, 'pure and spiritual without any *lust*.'

'Well, they've hardly got a marriage without passion,' said the vicar drily. 'Minerva and Sylvester are too well-bred to paw and ogle in public, but they can hardly keep their hands off each other and it's as well he married her sharpish or I would've been forced to run him up to the altar with my shotgun at his back.'

'Papa!'

'Gad's 'Oonds, daughter! How d'ye think they came to have a child? 'Twas not by reading poetry to each other or by discussing the state of the nation.'

Deirdre stared at him wide-eyed, her eyes very green and sharp—'like that demned fox,' thought the vicar sourly.

He put his elbows on the desk and leaned forwards. 'You don't know what I'm talking about, do you?'

'No, Papa.'

Beads of perspiration began to appear on the vicar's brow. 'Your mother should tell you about these things,' he said crossly, 'but in truth, I don't think she knows. Eight children and she still thinks it's all the fault of the stork. You'd think she was one o' them Greeks, like Leda, to hear her, 'cept that was a swan.

'Did Wentwater kiss you?'

'Yes, Papa.'

'And what did you feel?'

'I felt as a girl in love should feel,' said Deirdre. 'Pure and spiritual and elated.'

'Hey, ho. Desire, did he kiss you?'

'Yes, Papa.'

'And how did you feel?'

'Wanton and lustful,' whispered Deirdre.

'Oh, tut, tut, *tut*,' said the vicar sarcastically.

Deirdre flared up. 'Think of the times you have preached against lust from the pulpit!'

'Aye, but I hadn't a word to say agin passion. Let's get back to Wentwater. You did not see him after the night?'

'I'm afraid I did. He . . . he followed me to Green Park. I went there one morning early to think things out. He must have been watching the house. He said he loved me. He said he had spurned me for my own good. I asked him to elope with me.'

The vicar clutched his hair and gave it a yank. 'Is there any more of this?' he wailed.

'Yes. I was to meet him at two in the morning in Green Park, but I did not.'

'Well, thank God for small mercies. See here Deirdre, you have been playing a dangerous game. Wentwater does not care a fig for you, never has, and never will. He is determined to get revenge, that is all. He wants to marry Emily, if anything. That way, he could anger me, and get himself a wife with a good dowry. But there is something in all this that does not add up. It looks as if Desire put the fear o' God into him, and Wentwater's mortal afraid o' me. So why does he still pursue the matter?'

He sat for a long time, buried in thought. Then he said slowly, 'We never really knew much about these Wentwaters. Lady Wentwater seems to have been missed out of the peerage. Well, we assumed she might have adopted the title and she seems harmless enough. But I wonder where the Wentwaters came from? I am going back to London.' He thought of that pesky fox and a wistful look crossed his face. 'I'll need to smoke out Guy Wentwater and make sure he never comes near Hopeworth again. None of you girls is to go near Lady Wentwater. I'll call on her myself and tell her why.'

He stopped and looked at the drooping picture of misery that was Deirdre Armitage.

'You've made a sad mull o' things,' he said in a kindly voice, 'but it's all over.' He stood up and came round his desk. 'Off to bed with you. It's late and I have not yet had my supper.'

Deirdre stood up and faced him. Large tears began to roll down her cheeks.

The vicar wordlessly held out his arms and she rushed into them.

'There, now,' he said, 'it's all over.'

'But I love him, Papa,' choked Deirdre.

The vicar stiffened. 'Then you will need to

get over it,' he said harshly. 'Wentwater does not set a foot in this house!'

'Oh, not him,' wailed Deirdre, crying harder than ever.

'Who, in Gad's name?'

'Lord Harry.'

The vicar's pudgy hands tightened on her shoulders. He wanted to shake her and shake her until her teeth rattled. Instead he said wearily, 'We'll talk again tomorrow. Now off to bed like a good girl.'

'Oh, Papa,' sobbed Deirdre, 'I love you, too. I have been *such* a fool.'

'You do, do you?' grinned the vicar, suddenly feeling all the troubles of the world slip from his shoulders. 'Well, that's all right. Go and say your prayers.'

He stood beaming until she had left the room. But when Mrs Armitage came in some ten minutes later to ask him whether he was going to eat his supper or not, the vicar of St Charles and St Jude was slowly banging his head rhythmically against the study wall.

Mrs Armitage assumed it was some mysterious masculine hunting ritual—men were so strange, quite like children—and retreated to tell cook and Betty that the master would no doubt be ready to eat in a little while.

Deirdre was glad to have a bedroom all to herself again. She sat by the window, but this time she dreamed of seeing Lord Harry Desire walking in the lane. Why hadn't she realized she loved him before? Why had she hated her father so much? It was as if she had been looking at the world through a distorting glass, and now suddenly she saw things plain for the first time.

How bitter to realize you loved a man, right after you had successfully disengaged yourself from him.

Betty came bustling in, carrying a hot posset. 'Mr Armitage sent me up with this and says you are to go right to bed.'

'Very well, Betty,' said Deirdre. 'Perhaps I have made a mull of things but maybe I shall find a rich husband and then you and John will be able to marry.'

''Tis a pity it wasn't that Lord Harry,' said Betty. 'But he was too handsome. Quite scarey in a way. And don't mind about me, miss, though it's kind of you to bother. Vicar'll make sure I marry John before next harvest is out, never fear.'

'That is wonderful, Betty. But how can you prevail upon Papa to do so?'

'There are ways,' said Betty, grinning. 'Now, I'll put the warming pan between the sheets and you slip into your nightgown.'

At last, when she was tucked up in bed, Deirdre said sleepily, 'Betty, how do I learn Latin?'

'I don't know, miss. Why not ask Mr Pettifor. He has a deal of book learning.'

'Very well, Betty. I do want to learn things.'

'You can read and write, miss, and play the pannyforty. What does a lady need with else?'

'Only, I have found I am really rather stupid, Betty.'

'Oh, not you, miss,' said Betty placidly, as she blew out the candles and lit the rushlight in its pierced canister beside the bed. 'Miss Minerva, I mean Lady Sylvester, always said as how you were the brains of the family.'

'Then she was very much mistaken,' sighed Deirdre.

'Ah, you're young,' smiled Betty, tucking the bedclothes about her, 'and there ain't a body in the whole wide world that don't do stupid things when they're young. You'll feel clever again in the morning.'

And with that, she quietly left the room.

★        ★        ★

A deputation of angry farmers called at the vicarage in the morning to curse the reverend for hunting over their fields while the spring crops were about to sprout. Added to that the day was white with frost, so the vicar had two reasons not to tempt him to take out his hounds.

Instead of flying off to London to scour the clubs and coffee houses for Guy Wentwater, he decided to call on Squire Radford first.

Wentwater had always been on the dubious fringes of society, reflected the vicar. He was the sort of fellow who professed to know everyone, and yet no one knew him. He was unknown in White's or Brooks's or Watier's. He was never to be seen in fashionable saloons or drawing-rooms.

In the county of Berham, he was considered one of the upper set. But he only came on infrequent visits, and Lady Wentwater was considered something of a recluse.

Squire Radford listened eagerly to the ramifications of the story about Deirdre.

'The thing that frightens me,' finished the vicar, 'is that she should go ahead and plan to do the same thing again, that she should ask him to elope with her a second time. Do you think she's addled in her brainbox?'

239

'I think she is very young for her years and that she was very unhappy. Minerva had given her a role to play, the one of highly intelligent girl. And so she played that role and believed in it. Suddenly it was not true and she felt lost and self-disgusted and silly. Sir Thomas Browne said that each man is his own executioner, and I believe that. My poor daughter chose to kill herself by running away with a wastrel. If we do not destroy ourselves, we often find someone else to do it for us. Given a short time to recover, Deirdre will discover she is actually almost as intelligent as Minerva led her to believe herself to be, but very young and sadly uninformed.'

'Aye, but that's not all, Jimmy,' said the vicar eagerly, 'she's in love with him.'

'Dear me!'

'No, not Wentwater. Desire.'

'And when did she discover this? It may be all part and parcel of her temporary madness?'

'Mayhap. Anyway, the silly jade must discover this great fact *after* Lord Harry had broken the engagement and taken his leave. All that money! Jeremy Blewett's said to be richer than Golden Ball. If I was not so worried for my daughter's sanity, I would've given her a beating. Now, there's no hope.'

'I would not say that,' ventured the squire cautiously. 'I could not help observing on the journey to Hopeworth that they are remarkably at ease with each other. The air between them seemed to hold a certain intimacy.'

'Best rush her back to London then.'

'Ah, no. I think Miss Deirdre should be allowed a period of quiet and, if necessary, boredom.'

'But what if Desire goes and gets married to someone else?'

'He told you he had made enough money on 'Change and did not need his uncle's money,' pointed out the squire.

'But some woman's bound to snap him up.'

'They have not succeeded yet and he is surely about thirty years old.'

'But he was at the wars for years and years,' said the vicar. 'No one had a chance to get hold of him.'

'Well, I think we should wait, nonetheless. But to return to Guy Wentwater. It is passing strange that he should even go near Miss Deirdre. I really think we perhaps might return to London, just for a day or two, and call on Lord Harry and ask him to tell us what exactly happened when he went to pick up the bandboxes and whether he threatened Deirdre in any way.'

'She says she asked *him* to marry her.'

'I think it is no use speculating about it until we find out a little more. I've never been much worried about Guy Wentwater, strangely enough, although I fear he is a shiftless and vicious young man. I always thought him too much of a coward.'

'We could maybe start by paying a call on Lady Wentwater,' said the vicar.

Lady Wentwater was at home, as she nearly always was, sitting alone in the dingy, dark drawing-room with its cheap tallow candles, reading a novel.

'My daughters won't be reading to you again,' began the vicar, without preamble, 'on account o' that there nephew o' yours.'

'What's up with him?' asked Lady Wentwater, 'apart from your unusual views on the slave traffic.'

'He's been trying to ruin one of my daughters again,' said the vicar crossly, 'and I may tell you, my lady, that I'm going up to London to hunt him down and make sure he don't put foot in this village again.'

'Guy is always more sinned against than sinning,' said Lady Wentwater, beginning to show rare signs of animation. 'If your girls will throw themselves at him, what else do you expect him to do?'

'Look here, I'll tell you what happened,' said the vicar, 'and if you breathe a word of it, it'll be the worse for your nephew.'

Lady Wentwater listened to the tale of the abortive elopement with her large head on one side, while the ivy leaves rattled against the windows and sent fluttering shadows dancing about the room.

'Just as I thought,' she commented when the vicar had finished. 'More sinned against than sinning. If I have it right, your daughter threw herself at him, begging him to elope with her because you were forcing her into marriage to a man she did not like. He decides not to go through with it. She turns up here. He has been drinking heavily with two friends. He teases her a little to bring her to her senses, and his friends being bosky, try to make sport so she runs away. My poor Guy then fancies himself in love with her and waylays her in London. Again, she begs him to elope with her, but then changes her mind and does not even send him a note to say so. Now, what is so evil and terrible about that? I would not like to be an unescorted female chancing upon you, reverend, when you are

243

in your altitudes.'

The vicar turned red. All at once he remembered when he was much younger, drinking at a wayside inn with two of his friends. A woman had come in and quietly ordered a meal. They had all paid her broad and warm compliments until she had run out of the inn.

It had transpired later that she was a gentlewoman whose maid had fallen sick on the road and whose carriage had then broken down.

The landlord had berated the vicar most roundly and called him an insult to the cloth.

'But I don't think for a minute he's in love with her,' he howled. 'Demme, I swear he's out to get revenge.'

'That's the sort of thing you would do, vicar,' said Lady Wentwater blandly, 'but you must not judge others by yourself. Guy is a sweet and pretty young man who would not harm a fly.'

'Who was your husband, ma'am?' asked the vicar abruptly.

There was a little silence. The asthmatic clock in the corner wheezed preparatory to striking the hour.

'Sir William Wentwater,' she said finally. 'Why do you ask?'

'Never heard o' him,' said the vicar rudely.

'No, why should you? He has been dead for a long time.'

The vicar rolled his eyes in the squire's direction.

The squire coughed gently. 'Perhaps you might furnish us with Mr Wentwater's direction? We are going to London and would like to call on him.'

'I don't know where he's staying,' said Lady Wentwater. 'Try Long's or Limmer's.'

Both men rose to take their leave.

'But if you find him, give him my love,' said Lady Wentwater. Then she picked up her book and appeared to forget their existence.

When both gentlemen had walked a little way down the road, the vicar burst out with, 'I don't like it. Don't like it at all.'

'But the way Lady Wentwater put it, well, it does rather seem as if we are imagining Haymarket villains when they don't exist,' suggested the squire.

'No, no, it stinks,' said the vicar. 'Every time I look at that old bat, I see custom-house goods.'

'Custom-house goods, Charles?'

'Oh, I was talkin' cant,' said the vicar. 'Custom-house goods is the stock and trade of a prostitute, because fairly entered, don't you see.'

'Charles, you shock me.'

'There's something about her,' said the vicar, paying no heed to his friend, 'that calls to mind that Covent Garden abbess, Peggy Jones.' He gave a rich chuckle. 'There was a one. The things that woman could do with a feather duster . . .'

'*Charles!* Enough! Remember your calling. What if one of your parishioners should hear you talk like this?'

'Sorry,' mumbled the vicar. 'Plaguey frost. Do you think it'll be the same tomorrow? Is spring never going to come?'

'If you are longing to go hunting, you had best dream about next season,' said the squire severely. 'I, for one, do not want my spring crops ruined by your hunt.'

'Oh, Gad!' screamed the vicar suddenly. 'Look at that!'

They were passing a thick thorn hedge which bordered part of the Hall's estates. There was a small gap in it. On the other side of the gap sat a fox, studying them with yellow-eyed insolence.

'You see it, too, don't you, Jimmy?' pleaded the vicar.

'Yes,' said the squire, staring at the fox in

amazement. 'I swear that animal knows we cannot reach it because of the thorns.'

'Oh, can't we!' yelled the vicar. He threw himself like a maniac at the gap in the hedge, cursing and shouting as the thorns stabbed his face and hands.

The fox put its head on one side and looked at him curiously.

'I'll get hounds,' gasped the vicar, reeling back defeated. 'I'll *have* that beast, pads and mask and brush.'

'No, no,' said the squire. 'You cannot take hounds out in such a frost. The ground is too hard. It will cut their paws.'

'Then I'll *strangle* that Reynard myself!' howled the vicar, tears of frustration starting to his eyes.

Before the squire could stop him, he was off down the road and in at the gates of the Hall. He doubled back along the other side of the hedge.

The fox studied his approach, and then, with a flick of its brush, it was gone.

The vicar blundered through the woods, shouting and hallooing and cursing fit to wake the dead.

He was nearly shot by one of his brother's gamekeepers, and by the time the squire caught up with him, he seemed fit to die of an apoplexy.

'You see, I can't leave Hopeworth now,' moaned the vicar. 'Not with that gurt beast mocking and sneering at me.'

'Well, we'll see,' said the squire. 'Here's Edwin.'

The vicar's brother, Sir Edwin, made his leisurely way towards them through the trees. He was formally dressed as usual, a contrast to his stocky brother. He raised his quizzing glass and surveyed the mess that was the vicar; bleeding hands, scratched face, dirty clothes.

'Well, Charles,' said Sir Edwin, 'I see you have returned to all your formal glory of dress.' He tittered. 'Quite reassuring to see you looking your old self. May I ask what you are doing cursing and screaming about my property?'

'It's that fox,' babbled the vicar. 'It's in your grounds.'

'Well, I'm sure one of my men will shoot it.'

The vicar reeled with shock. 'Shoot it! You're talking like a coxcomb! Shoot the fox. Did you hear that, Jimmy? The man's insane. *Shoot* a fox!'

'It's my property and I can do what I like, demme,' said Sir Edwin, turning puce. 'I will not have you riding over my grounds and ruining my game, Charles, and if I have to arm men at the gates to keep you out, I will.'

'You are not a Christian. You will go to hell and fry for this wickedness,' howled the vicar, jumping up and down with rage.

'Come along, please,' said the squire, tugging the vicar's sleeve. 'No hunting can be done in such weather anyway. Come along, Charles. Calm yourself.'

The vicar allowed himself to be led away.

Squire Radford accepted an invitation to dinner at the vicarage, although he would have much preferred the comfort of his own home and the vicarage was hardly famous for its cuisine.

The vicar sat like a man who had sustained a severe shock. He mumbled to himself about the wickedness of his brother. He barely touched his food.

'If we are going to London tomorrow,' said the squire at last, 'I must be off home and get an early night's sleep.'

'Oh, ah,' said the vicar dismally. 'Ain't any hope of a thaw, think you, Jimmy?'

The squire shook his head.

'London!' Deirdre's green eyes lit up. 'Oh, Papa, take me with you.'

'Oh, very well,' grumbled the vicar.

'But...' began Squire Radford, and then broke off, feeling it would be bad manners to tell the company at large why Deirdre should not go.

'I really feel this is too much,' said Mrs Armitage crossly. 'Betty must go with her, and now that you do not have the benefit of dear Lord Sylvester's carriage, then you needs must take John as well. Faith, why don't you take cook?'

'Don't be silly,' said her husband rudely. 'The only decent thing about going to London is getting away from her cooking.'

'That is not fair, Mr Armitage,' said Mrs Armitage, turning an alarming colour. 'Mrs Hammer goes very well, very well indeed, on the miserly allowance you give her!'

The vicar looked as if he were about to launch into battle, but Mrs Armitage settled the score by throwing one of her Spasms. Squire Radford crept off and Deirdre went up to her room to dream.

Visions of the old Deirdre running down the lane in search of Guy, meeting him in the churchyard, hating her father, flitted through her brain. It was like looking at the strange antics of another person.

A new Deirdre would go back to London, taking with her her new-found love. She did not know if it would be accepted.

But at least she could try.

★　　★　　★

'You have done very well indeed,' said Silas Dubois.

Guy Wentwater smirked modestly.

'Blewett's money should be coming to me soon,' went on Silas, rubbing his hands. 'He is vastly annoyed that Desire is not to be wed, and furthermore has not had the courtesy to visit him. When I saw the notice in the newspapers that the engagement was broken, I knew it was your work. How on earth did you do it?'

'I told her I loved her,' said Guy, 'and she believed me.'

Both men were sitting in Humbold's coffee house. It had been Guy's first visit to that establishment for some time. He had been hiding out, picturing his reputation in shreds. Only by chance, since he hardly ever read the newspapers, did he learn about the broken engagement. So his reputation was safe, and, not only that, Silas believed him to have been instrumental in the ending of it.

'Well, I certainly must do something to repay you,' smirked Silas.

'I have money enough,' said Guy.

'Oh, I didn't mean money. I feel I owe it to you to give you the news that the dear vicar and that ancient squire from Hopeworth are searching all the clubs and taverns and coffee houses for you. The vicar is crying for your blood. Dear, dear,' chortled Silas, in high good humour, 'you really must have upset the apple cart.'

Guy turned pale. He had carefully kept to places where he would not be likely to come across Lord Harry Desire. But now the hunting vicar was after him, nowhere was safe.

'I must leave,' he said, looking wildly about as if expecting to hear the vicar's halloo and see him charging through St James's with his pack of hell-hounds streaming out in front of him.

He would rusticate somewhere in the country far from Hopeworth. But one day he would return and get his revenge on the whole Armitage family, Deirdre in particular.

A Deirdre trembling with sweet love was one thing; a Deirdre so much in love with another man that she did not even seem to be aware of his presence was another.

He wanted to inflict all sorts of nasty

humiliations on her. If he could only lure her as far as Bristol, there was a bawdy house he knew of where the abbess was skilled in training and breaking down the most God-fearing girl into the tricks of the trade.

A shadow fell across the doorway and Guy started from his seat like a rocketing pheasant. It turned out to be a man he had never seen before, but the shock left him trembling.

He muttered a hurried goodbye to the grinning and malicious Silas and darted out of the coffee house.

Silas ordered another bottle of wine. He had never felt better. He could imagine stiff-necked Minerva wringing her hands over Deirdre's disgrace, for Silas was quite sure Guy had done something awful. And what made the joke so rich was that none of the Armitages knew of his involvement.

★   ★   ★

Perhaps, had Deirdre Armitage been asked, she would have said that Lady Godolphin's dinner party was the most awful thing that had, as yet, happened to her.

Lady Godolphin was giving a dinner and taking the guests to the opera afterwards.

Deirdre had looked forward to it with trembling excitement, for Lord Harry had said he *might* attend but had sent a note to Lady Godolphin, saying if he was not present by six, not to wait for him.

But Deirdre had been so sure he would come. His empty place next to her mocked her dismal eyes.

Although she had not had much time to improve her education, Deirdre had read all the newspapers she could get her hands on and had rehearsed conversation with Lord Harry Desire in which she would dazzle him with her knowledge of contemporary affairs. And she would really like to know what Lord Harry thought of the Prince Regent's latest madness. He had infuriated the Whigs by having it announced in Parliament that he was going to erect a monument in Rome, designed by . . . Casanova? No, that was not right. Canova! That was it. This was to be in memory of the Stuarts. The Whigs were boiling over with rage at this glorification of the Stuarts, a family that might seem glamorous to Highland Tories and Walter Scott but did not inspire any nostalgic affection among English Whigs. Perhaps she would never have a chance to discuss it with him. Perhaps Lord Harry did not want to see her again.

The rest of the party was made up of the vicar and the squire, Lady Chester and Mr Anstey, Colonel Arthur Brian and, of course, Lady Godolphin.

The atmosphere was strained to say the least. The vicar and squire were exhausted from their day's Wentwater hunting. Mr Anstey was more effete, more mincing, and more posturing than Deirdre could remember him being before.

Lady Chester kept sending him killing glances from out of her rheumy old eyes when she was not flashing triumphant ones in Lady Godolphin's direction.

As Lady Godolphin put it, *sotto voce*, 'Asking her was a fox's paw.'

Colonel Brian looked embarrassed and kept drinking rather more wine than was good for him.

Deirdre started at every sound of carriage wheels in the square outside.

Her heart sank as the interminable dinner dragged on and on. Of course he would not come. She had behaved so badly. How could she expect him to come? She had told him they would not suit, she had shown everyone in the world that she was afraid of him. So it was silly to keep jumping at every sound.

In fact, he was probably staying away because he heard she was to be there.

It was only a simple dinner, but the awkward atmosphere and the general lack of appetite made it seem more than it was.

Deirdre tried to keep her mind off the absent Lord Harry, by identifying and counting the dishes, until she had a large ornamental menu printed inside her brain.

## *First Course*

Pigeons Comport
Lambs' Ears, Forc'd
French Pye   Boil'd Turkey
Sheeps' Rumps and Kidneys in Rice
Florendine of Rabbits
Fish Remove   Transparent Soup
Harrico   Pork Griskins
Kidney Beans   Broccoli, etc
Mock Turtle
Bottl'd Peas   Sallad
House Lamb
Larded oysters   Ox Pallets
Beef Olives   Hare Soup
Remove Hanch of Venison
Fricas'd Chickens
Cod's Sounds like little Turkey
Fricando Veal   Small Ham

Sweet Breads à la Royal
Ducks alamode

*Second Course*

Snow balls   Fish pond   Roast Woodcocks
Pistachio Cream   Rocky Island
Pheasant
Crow fish in Savory Jelly
Pickl'd Smelts   Marbl'd Veal
Mince Pies
Stew'd cardoons   Pompadore Cream
Transparent pudding
cover'd with a silver web
Maccaroni   Stew'd Mushrooms
Crocant with Hot pippins
Collar'd Rig   Pott'd Lampreys
Snipes in savory Jelly
Roast'd Hare
Moonshine
Globes of gold web with mottes in them
Pea chick with Asparagus
Floating Island   Burnt Cream

The wines consisted of Lisbon, vintage
Rhenish, champagne, claret (Château
Margaux, Lafite, Pontack), old burgundy,
port and sherry.

257

By the time the tablecloth was removed and the port and sherry, walnuts and sweetmeats stood reflected in the polished wood of the table, everyone was slightly tipsy in a silent and surly way.

'Well, it seems as if Lord Harry is not coming. Waste o' money,' grumbled Lady Godolphin who had been coerced into holding the dinner so that Deirdre could resume her acquaintanceship with Desire. Of course, she had taken the opportunity to renew her own acquaintance with Mr Anstey, fondly picturing that young man spurning Lady Chester and darting to her side.

But Lady Godolphin was clutch-fisted and Lady Chester was not, and so out of sheer pride Lady Godolphin was forced to favour her former beau, Colonel Brian, with her attentions.

Mr Anstey fingered the new ruby pin in his stock and smiled fondly on Lady Chester.

The evening was bad, but worse was to follow. No sooner had they all been set down at the opera than a stern matron descended on their party.

'Oh lor',' muttered the vicar to Deirdre. ''Tis Lady Mason, Lady Chester's daughter.'

'Mama,' said Lady Mason awfully, 'what is this I hear? Is *this* the famous Mr Anstey of whom I have heard so much? Is *this* the ne'er-do-well who preys on elderly ladies for their money? You are the laughing stock of London society.'

''Pon rep,' bleated Mr Anstey, falling back before the venom in Lady Mason's bulging eyes, 'I dote on your Mama.'

'Fustian, you mountebank, you man-milliner, you *counter-jumper!*' hissed Lady Mason. 'Mason!' she called over her shoulder. Her thick-set, brutish husband came ambling up. 'Mason, this is the creature who has been battening on Mama like a leech.'

'Oh, it is, is it?' said Lord Mason with an awful glare and fingering his dress sword.

Mr Anstey looked to his party for help. Mr Armitage and Squire Radford seemed completely absorbed in watching the passing crowd outside the opera. Lady Godolphin was clutching tightly on to Colonel Brian's arm and staring straight ahead.

Lady Chester looked terrified of her daughter.

'I say,' bleated Mr Anstey, 'you mustn't say things like that.'

'What are you going to do about it, hey?' sneered Lord Mason. He stripped off one glove and smacked Mr Anstey across the face with it.

'Name your seconds,' he growled.

'I *won't!*' screeched Mr Anstey, and he turned and fled into the crowd as fast as his spindly legs would carry him.

Lady Chester began to cry but was strong-armed off by her daughter and son-in-law.

The depleted party made their way silently to Lady Godolphin's box.

The opera was Gluck's *Orpheus and Eurydice*. Watching and listening, at first, more for Lord Harry's arrival than anything to do with what was going on on the stage, Deirdre at last became caught up in the story and the music.

And when Orpheus clasped the dead Eurydice in his arms and broke into that famous lament, 'Che faro senza Eurydice' (I have lost my Eurydice), tears poured unchecked down Deirdre's cheeks as the beautiful music rose and fell in the hushed opera house.

And then a hand appeared in front of her nose holding a large pocket handkerchief. She took it gratefully, and, only as the last note of the famous aria died away, did she remember the last time a hand had reached in front of her with a handkerchief. She twisted her head and looked up into the clear blue eyes of Lord Harry Desire who was standing behind her chair.

On stage, Eurydice was restored to life by Amor, and Deirdre was brought back to the present world by the light touch of Lord Harry's hand on her shoulder.

After the opera was finished, Lord Harry made his apologies to Lady Godolphin. 'You didn't miss anything,' said her ladyship, 'except a lot of curst scenes and historicals. That old trout, Lady Chester, was arrested by her daughter, Lady Mason.'

'Mason himself challenges Anstey to a duel and Anstey runs away like the arrant, useless coward he is. My Arthur would never have behaved so cravenishly.' She pressed the Colonel's hand. Colonel Brian glowed with pleasure and murmured, *'Dear* lady,' in a deprecating way.

Lord Harry took his hand from Deirdre's shoulder and she gave a shiver, as if suddenly cold.

When she thought he was not looking, Deirdre glanced up at Lord Harry. He immediately turned and looked full at her. She dropped her eyes and blushed painfully. A terrible blush. She could feel it beginning somewhere around the soles of her feet and coursing in a red tide right to the top of her head.

Inwardly, she cursed the glaring lights of the opera house. Eyes seemed to stare at her curiously from all sides. Through an embarrassed red mist, she dimly saw Lord Harry turn away and say something to Colonel Brian.

At last, they all battled down the stairs in the press of people.

'No one ever wants to sit quietly in their box until everyone else has gone,' thought Deirdre crossly. 'Being tonnish seems to involve a sad degree of crushing.'

Then the press of the crowd thrust her against Lord Harry, who put a protective arm about her, and Deirdre promptly forgot about everything and everyone else.

He would not hold her so if he did not care!

But her heart plummeted as she saw that his *other* arm was around Lady Godolphin's shoulder to protect *her*, Colonel Brian having been thrust back into the crowd.

But she would have an opportunity to talk a little to Lord Harry at Lady Godolphin's—for surely he would come back with them for wine and cakes—and then she might be able to judge if he had any warm feelings towards her.

But no sooner were they all in Lady

Godolphin's carriage and Lord Harry had left in his own than it transpired they were all to go on to a rout at a Mr South's.

There was a little comfort in the fact that Lord Harry was to join them there.

And so after an hour of waiting in a line of other carriages, they alighted at Mr South's mansion and pushed and shoved until they had reached the top of the stairs. Lord Harry was already there, and talking to a dashing matron nearly as tall as himself. She had red hair.

Wedged in a press of bodies with a glass of wine in one hand and a biscuit in the other, Deirdre at last found herself trapped in one of those 'interesting' conversations of which she had dreamed. An intense young man, jammed up against her, subjected her to a strong lecture on the disgraceful state of the economy, the miserable harvests, the sheer ingratitude of the Luddites, and the deviousness and stupidity of the Prime Minister.

In her dreams, she had always replied wittily and intelligently, but she found herself mumbling, 'Indeed,' and 'How true,' while all the while her green eyes kept straying across to where she could see Lord Harry's handsome head.

263

He was looking down at his companion with a lazy, seductive, slightly predatory expression.

'And as for Napoleon,' Deirdre's companion was saying. 'He should have been beheaded on Tower Hill. Do you know he lives like a *king* on St Helena? Do you know . . . ?'

'I don't care,' said Deirdre rudely, 'whether he is surrounded with a harem of dancing girls and eats from gold plates. He is locked away and will never frighten the world again.'

'Good Gad,' said the young man, trying to raise his quizzing glass but finding his arms jammed to his side. 'You are a blue stocking.'

'I am not a blue stocking,' said Deirdre crossly. 'I have said nothing to give anyone that idea.'

'Young ladies,' said the young man firmly, 'should not have views on anything. Their role is to listen to men since their minds are of the inferior variety.'

'They can become bored just like any man. Oh, do excuse me,' said Deirdre, her voice rising on a note of agony as she saw Lord Harry evidently moving off with the redhead. What if he *left* with her? What if he married her?

She elbowed her way frantically through the crowd and came up against him all at once. Of his companion, there was no sign.

'You look as if you are fleeing from wolves,' said Lord Harry. 'I will find us a quiet corner.'

Magically, the crowd parted to let them through and they were soon ensconced in two chairs in a corner, half hidden from the room by a carved screen.

'Someone was talking *at* me,' said Deirdre, 'and I felt suffocated.'

'A rout must be a crush to be a success,' he laughed. 'You are not fashionable, Miss Deirdre, unless you enjoy having sharp elbows rammed in your side, and someone jumping on your feet. Why are you in London? You will become worn to a frazzle with all this junketing back and forth.'

'Papa found out about ... about Mr Wentwater. He means to hunt him down.'

'If anyone can find Mr Wentwater, Mr Armitage can. It is so important? He behaved badly, but you did throw yourself at him, and, I think, you have had your revenge.'

Deirdre grasped her fan very tightly. He could not know of that second elopement. Papa had not time to tell him. Did he know *everything*?

To change the subject she said lightly, 'Are you still of a mind to wave your uncle's fortune goodbye?'

'I don't know,' he said seriously. 'I have to get married sometime, don't I?'

'Why?'

'Among other things, I would like a son.'

'Oh.'

'Would you like to have children?'

Deirdre knit her brows. Children. How *did* one have them? She had studied the women of the village and knew now that the baby was obviously carried inside the belly.

But how did it get *out?* She had some idea that perhaps the navel widened into a sort of door from which the baby would spring fully-clothed like Pallas Athene from the head of Zeus.

It would be all very simple if one could pull babies out of one's head.

Did having them have anything to do with all those warm sensations inside her body when Lord Harry kissed her? Like cheese being churned. Did babies *solidify* inside one after a certain amount of the right kind of kissing? And was that why one was never supposed to let a gentleman do more than press one's hand?

'You have not answered my question,'

pointed out Lord Harry with an amused look at her troubled face.

'Of course I would like to have children,' said Deirdre.

'How many?'

'Do I have a choice?' asked Deirdre naïvely.

'Perhaps. My uncle is anxious for me to have children since no one else in my family shows any signs of becoming wed,' said Lord Harry. 'Of course, Silas may marry someone just to pip me at the post.'

'Silas?'

'Silas Dubois—my rival for uncle's fortune.'

'How very odd,' said Deirdre. 'I know I have heard that name before. I was passing the morning-room when I was staying at Minerva's one time, and she was talking to her husband and I heard her say, "Do you ever hear anything of that dreadful Mr Dubois? I confess I sometimes still have nightmares when I think of him." I did not want to stay and eavesdrop on their conversation, so I heard no more.'

'Indeed!' Lord Harry looked curious. 'Silas has an unforgettable appearance. He is all nose with little beady eyes and he walks like a crab.'

'Why! A man just like that stopped right in front of me one day and looked into my face. Then I thought he was following me and I confess I was afraid.'

'When was this?' he asked sharply.

'Why, it was the morning when...' Deirdre broke off and bit her lip, remembering it was the morning she had met Guy in the park. 'I forget,' she added lamely.

'There would appear to be some connection with your family,' said Lord Harry thoughtfully. 'I shall ask Lady Sylvester.'

Deirdre realized she had not yet tried to impress him with her new-found knowledge, and launched into her speech about the latest iniquities of the Prince Regent.

'Poor Prinny,' said Lord Harry with amusement, although Deirdre had a feeling he was more amused at her lecture than he was at the antics of the Prince Regent.

'But why should he suddenly fall in love with the Stuarts?' demanded Deirdre, narrowing her eyes in what she hoped was a penetrating and intelligent look.

'He is wretched because of his own unpopularity. He is, I think, fascinated by the Stuarts because they have become such a romantic legend, and he would so much like to become a romantic legend himself. And then, the more unpopular he gets, the more determined he seems, in some perverse way, to cultivate more unpopularity.'

At that moment, Lady Godolphin came puffing up to say they were leaving.

Somehow, by the time they had all struggled down the stairs again and were waiting on the step for their carriage to be brought round, Lord Harry had disappeared. Lady Godolphin said he would not be joining them for supper, and Deirdre could not help asking, 'Did he say anything about seeing us again?' to which Lady Godolphin said crossly, 'If you mean you, miss, no he did not and I can't say I blame him.'

Deirdre flushed and hung her head.

But when they were at Lady Godolphin's and Deirdre had retired with Lady Godolphin to her boudoir where they planned to repair their appearance, Deirdre remembered about babies and about her ignorance of how they came to be conceived.

She waited impatiently until the maid had left the room. Lady Godolphin was the very person to ask. There was something so inhibiting about putting delicate questions to Minerva or Annabelle.

As soon as the door had closed behind the

maid, Deirdre took a deep breath and said, 'Lady Godolphin, how does a lady have babies? I mean, how does she *get* them?'

Lady Godolphin looked at Deirdre's red face with indulgent amusement. 'And you a country girl,' she laughed. 'Well, I belong to the old school and go in for plain speaking. I don't believe in gels being kept in ignorants, so I'll tell you direct. Now, sit down and listen.'

Deirdre sat down and leaned forward. Lady Godolphin looked quickly around as if expecting shocked matrons to leap out from behind the curtains.

'See here,' she said hoarsely. 'The man takes out his pinnace and puts it into her virginal and after a bit of fiddley-diddley, a baby is started.'

Deirdre looked blank.

Lady Godolphin groaned.

'I'll try again. The man, see, he takes his Shaftsbury and puts it in her private.'

'Private what?' asked Deirdre.

The maid came back into the room with a warming pan.

'Well, there you are,' said Lady Godolphin. 'I'm glad you asked me. I'm good at explaining delicate matters. In such intimate things, I don't believe anything should be left to the imagination.'

Deirdre was just as baffled as ever.

After she had returned to Minerva's and was lying in bed, still struggling with the problem, Deirdre felt she *had* to know.

Betty would know. Betty, the maid, had been present at the birth of Mrs Armstrong's boy in the village last autumn.

Deirdre decided to go to Betty's room and ask her. It did not seem quite right to ring the bell at this hour of the night—or morning, thought Deirdre with a fretful glance at the clock—but if she, Deirdre, just crept into her room and asked her softly, well, then she would know and then she could sleep.

Carrying a candle in its flat stick, she cautiously and quietly made her silent way to the maid's room, and gently pushed open the door.

She gave a gasp and the candle dropped from her hand, but there was still enough light from the rushlight beside the bed to show Miss Deirdre Armitage the splendid vista of John Summer's bare backside and Betty's startled face peering over his shoulder.

Deirdre picked up the candle and hurried off to her own room.

She fell immediately asleep, because, all at

once, she did not want to think of anything at all.

## CHAPTER TEN

Deirdre was feeling very tired. Her father was making return-to-Hopeworth noises. Her sister Annabelle had scooped her up early in the day—eleven o'clock was early by tonnish standards—and had taken her on a shopping expedition.

Annabelle still had all her old love of new gowns and ribbons and gewgaws. They had spent at least two hours in Harding, Hoswell & Co.'s premises in Schoenberg House in Pall Mall. Unflagging, Annabelle had moved on to Bond Street, very much a masculine preserve with its hotels and apartments, tailors, wig-makers and bookshops, although it had lately become quite *comme il faut* for a lady to shop there. Annabelle had also spent quite a deal of time at Jane Taylor & Son, 'China and Glass Sellers to His Royal Highness ye Prince of Wales' at the Feathers, Pall Mall which sold 'all sorts of China ware, Cutt and Plain Glass,' although she had so far bought nothing at all, and seemed to have endless reserves of energy left to explore Bond Street.

Past the Clarendon Hotel they trudged with Annabelle's maid in stolid attendance. The Clarendon Hotel, famed for its enormously expensive dinners, was run by Monsieur Jacquier, who had been chef to Louis XVIII. It was in the narrow part of the street, known as the Bond Street Straits, and it was there both ladies met Lord Harry Desire, ambling towards them in a leisurely way.

Deirdre had never noticed before her sister's infuriating propensity to flirt with any handsome man she met. Annabelle chattered on breathlessly and Deirdre reflected that she was too forward by half. Of course, Lord Harry was only being polite to pay such complete attention to Annabelle's prattle, but Deirdre could not help wishing her sister's hair was not quite so golden or her eyes quite so blue.

'I am taking my little sister on a tour of the shops,' said Annabelle gaily, and Deirdre could have killed her for that patronizing remark. 'You know how it is, my lord,' went on Annabelle, 'these young things will get up to mischief if one does not keep them truly occupied.'

Lord Harry's calm blue gaze turned on Deirdre.

'And what mischief have you been getting up to, Miss Deirdre?' he said.

'Nothing at all,' mumbled Deirdre, feeling like a gauche schoolgirl.

'Then we shall have to invent some for you,' he said. 'I am going to the Jamesons' masked ball tonight. Would that supply you with mischief enough?'

'I have not been invited,' said Deirdre.

'But *I* have and I can escort you, with your father's permission, of course.'

'You cannot take her without a chaperone,' exclaimed Annabelle, turning from flirtatious matron to stern matron all in a moment.

'Of course not,' said Lord Harry. 'A respectable chaperone will be provided.'

'Oh, in that case,' said Annabelle brightly, 'I can supply my little sister with a domino. It is blue which is not exactly your colour, Deirdre, but 'twill suffice.'

Lord Harry said he would call on Mr Armitage and make all the arrangements, then he made both ladies a magnificent bow, and strolled off.

'What a man!' said Annabelle, watching his well-tailored back retreating down Bond Street. 'Oh, you are such a fool to turn him down, Deirdre!'

'Ooooh! I wish you would stop putting on airs the whole time, Annabelle, and patronizing me in that stupid way. "My little sister," indeed! *And* you were making sheep's eyes at him in front of everyone in Bond Street. I have a good mind to tell Brabington of your behaviour.'

'That's just what a spiteful little cat like you *would* do,' said Annabelle, tossing her curls. 'If you say anything at all to Brabington, I shall pull your disgusting carroty hair out bit by bit.'

'You are very vulgar and common, Annabelle,' said Deirdre haughtily. 'You have learned *no* manners at *all*.'

'And *you* have learned no sense, you widgeon. Imagine letting such a prize as Desire get away. Of course, you are so countrified, such a rustic, you no doubt gave the poor man a disgust of you.'

'If he has such a disgust of me, then why is he taking me to a masked ball?'

'Because it *is* a *masked* ball and he won't have to look at your insipid little face.'

Breathing hard through her nose with rage, Deirdre stamped on Annabelle's toe. Annabelle rammed the ivory tip of her parasol into Deirdre's instep.

Deirdre kicked Annabelle in the shins and Annabelle drew off and punched Deirdre in the midriff.

All this they performed with rigid social smiles pinned on their faces.

Then Annabelle began to giggle, and put an arm around Deirdre's waist. 'I haven't changed, have I?' she laughed. 'Come along and I will get us ices at Gunter's and I will behave myself.'

Deirdre grinned back and they moved off arm in arm down Bond Street. Deirdre wondered whether she should ask Annabelle about babies. But it was well known in the Armitage family that Annabelle desperately wanted a baby and so far nothing had happened. How odd! Perhaps she did not kiss her husband enough.

Deirdre was in such good spirits by the time she returned to Minerva's house in St James's Square that she was able to accept the fact that Lady Godolphin was to be her chaperone without demur. Deirdre was fond of Lady Godolphin, but found her embarrassingly eccentric and often wondered at Lord Harry's very obvious affection for her.

Minerva was delighted that Deirdre should be seeing Lord Harry so soon again. Of course, it had been different when Deirdre had appeared afraid of the man, but now she was not, well, there was no denying that Lord Harry would be a delightful addition to the Armitage family.

Deirdre had seen Betty in the morning before she had left with Annabelle, but had been too embarrassed to ask the maid any questions.

But as Betty was helping her dress for the masked ball Deirdre at last blurted out, 'I'm sorry I went to your room like that, Betty.'

'I'm sorry too, miss,' said Betty, putting the curling tongs on their little spirit stove to heat.

'What were you doing?' asked Deirdre. 'I mean ... I ...' Her voice tailed away.

'Well, miss, seeing as how vicar is never going to let John and me marry, we decided to force his hand. So we were making a baby.'

'Oh.' Deirdre thought furiously. But her thoughts seemed to be dominated by the memory of the nakedness and size of John Summer's bare bottom.

'Oh, so that is how it is done,' she said at last.

'Please don't talk about such things, miss,' said Betty earnestly. 'It is not fitting that a young girl like yourself should know of such matters. I am that ashamed you saw us.'

'I won't tell anyone, Betty,' said Deirdre. 'If one takes off all one's clothes and goes to bed, does that mean one gets a baby?'

'Like as not, miss. Please don't talk about it. What if Lady Sylvester were to hear you?'

'Very well, Betty,' said Deirdre, knitting her brow. One green eye swivelled in the direction of Betty's stomach.

'Is the baby in there now?' she asked. 'I'll not ask you anything else.'

'Maybe it is and maybe it isn't,' said Betty, finally turning brick red. 'Now, be a good girl and say no more.'

'Just like bulls and cows,' said Deirdre at last. *'Ouch!* That hurts. You are burning the back of my neck, Betty.'

'You a vicar's daughter!' exclaimed Betty, tears starting to her eyes. 'I just know you're going to come out with one of them remarks when you oughtn't.'

'No, no, Betty, I promise. But you see it is all very curious.'

'Curiosity kills,' said Betty. 'Now, Lady Peter sent round that domino, and Miss Minerva—I mean, Lady Sylvester says she has a pretty mask. I'll just go and fetch it.'

'It's all right, Betty, I'll go. I feel too restless to sit around.'

Deirdre went along the passageway, the dark blue taffeta skirts of her gown rustling as she walked.

But instead of going directly to Minerva's room, Deirdre sat down at the top of the stairs and propped her chin in her hands. She always sat on landings when she was upset. It seemed a suitably in-between world. Stepping into an actual room seemed to mean she had to take some sort of action.

If she took off all her clothes and went into Lord Harry's bed, she would get a baby and then he would be pleased. Naturally, he would marry her. But perhaps only the lower orders got babies that way. How odd to think of the ton cavorting about like beasts of the fields.

Deirdre gave a little sigh. That must be it. Mrs Armitage was always saying, 'Only very common people do that,' referring to everything from eating peas with your knife to crossing your legs. Therefore, it followed that perhaps one went about having babies in a more genteel way.

Lady Godolphin's lecture had been worse than useless. Her many malapropisms made her quite unintelligible at the best of times.

Then, take the stately Minerva for instance. And her supremely cool and elegant husband. They could *never*... No, it must be something else.

With a little sigh, Deirdre rose and went to Minerva's boudoir, absent-mindedly forgetting to scratch at the door first.

Minerva was locked in her husband's arms. He was only in his breeches and Minerva was clad in the scantiest of petticoats. Her hair was tumbled about her flushed face. Lord Sylvester was kissing her with single-minded passion. Both were completely unaware they were observed.

Deirdre closed the door and stood gasping. She felt as if she had just been slapped in the face.

So it was all the same for everybody!

She went slowly back to her room and mumbled to Betty to fetch the mask 'but not now, later.'

By the time she was to go downstairs and meet Lord Harry Deirdre was in a strung-up, excited state. Her eyes shone green in her pointed face. Her brushed and pomaded hair flamed above her delicately flushed features.

Erotic visions danced through her brain making her go hot and cold by turns.

She fervently hoped Lord Harry would not read her mind as he seemed able to do from time to time.

Grateful for Minerva's blue velvet mask, Deirdre entered the drawing-room to find Lord Harry being entertained by her father and the squire.

The vicar was in high good humour, quite obviously seeing a new fortune about to join the Armitage family.

Lord Harry was wearing a black velvet mask with a black silk domino slung over his shoulders. He no longer looked easy and amiable but quite Satanic. His breeches were moulded to his thighs.

He really had very good legs, thought Deirdre, studying them carefully. Would his bare bottom be as huge and round as John's, or would it. . . ?

Shocked rigid by her thoughts, Deirdre blushed so much that her sympathetic father helped her solicitously to a chair, convinced her garters had fallen down. In the vicar's great experience, that was the only thing that made a girl blush when no one had said a word to embarrass her.

Minerva entered the room on her husband's arm and poor Deirdre blushed again.

Before they were about to leave, Minerva drew Deirdre a little away from the others.

'It seems you do not hold Lord Harry in

dislike,' she whispered.

Deirdre shyly shook her head.

'Then remember to be modest and well-behaved,' said Minerva. 'Gentlemen do not like *fast* young misses, nor do they like girls who encourage liberties.'

'Oh, really,' rejoined Deirdre sarcastically. 'I shall behave just like you.'

'Thank you,' said Minerva simply, failing to notice the sarcasm in her sister's voice. 'I hope I set a good example.'

Lord Harry strolled up to say they were leaving.

'The Jamesons are a rather wild couple,' cautioned Lord Sylvester. 'I believe the company is to be of the most select, but I do not need to tell you, Deirdre, that the most respectable person can behave in the oddest manner when they are in costume.'

'Then there will be nothing in either my dress or Miss Deirdre's to incite us to wild behaviour,' laughed Lord Harry, 'for our only concession to fancy dress is our masks and dominoes.'

It showed the low state of Lady Godolphin's mind that she, too, was wearing ordinary evening dress and carrying a mask on a cane in front of her face, for usually, Lady Godolphin dearly loved fancy dress.

Colonel Brian had not even a mask, and from the way the elderly pair were glaring at each other it looked as if they had been rowing quite ferociously before Lord Harry and Deirdre arrived.

It transpired, however, when they arrived at the Jamesons' in Soho that the rest of the guests were less inhibited. A duke was dressed as an Hungarian Hussar, a knight as a double-man, half-miller, half-chimney sweep. A captain went as a gamester with cards sewn all over his clothes; a countess was an Indian Sultana with one hundred thousand pounds' worth of diamonds on her head-dress; one duchess appeared as a running footman and another as the Witch of Endor.

But there never was a masquerade without its sensation and this time a certain Major Humphries of the Guards provided it. His effort was received with much disapproval. As the *Gentleman's Magazine* later reported: 'A figure of Adam, the unavoidable indelicacy of the dress, flesh-coloured silk with an apron of fig leaves worked in it, fitting the body to the utmost nicety, rendered it the contempt of the whole company.'

Or as one wit described it:

'When we entered this paradise, judge,
my dear madam,
With what pleasure we met
our first ancestor Adam,
Good God! 'twas so awful to see whence we
sprung,
For the dress to his body most prettily
clung.'

But although the company pretended to be shocked the Major's scandalous costume seemed to spice the ball with an air of licence. The guests drank quantities of wine more quickly than usual; they flirted and ogled through the slits of their masks with gay abandon.

One gentleman had arrived dressed as a thatched cottage complete with the insurance company's badge on the front which prompted one noisy party to set it on fire 'since it was covered' and it was fortunately put out with several bottles of champagne before the poor inhabitant of the cottage was incinerated.

Lord Harry twice had to rescue Deirdre from a dancing partner who had become overwarm in his attentions.

'I really should not have brought you,' he

said. 'Now, I have lost Lady Godolphin.'

'No matter,' said Deirdre, delighted to have him by her side again. 'Perhaps, my lord, if it should please you, we could move a little way away from the press of dancers.'

'By all means. There is an empty box over in that corner. If we are very quick, we shall reach it before anyone else decides to take it up.'

The ballroom was formed by a chain of saloons. Round the edge of each saloon boxes had been erected, made of flimsy garlanded lattice work.

Lord Harry helped her into the vacant box and then said he would fetch them some refreshment. The arrangement of the garlands, which were made of silk flowers, afforded a certain shelter from the eyes of the dancers at the ball.

Some couples were making the most of the semi-privacy and were cavorting about in such a manner as to leave Deirdre in little doubt as to how the aristocracy made love.

A young man vaulted into her box and swept her into his arms.

Deirdre let out a scream and tried to push him away but her scream was drowned in all the noise.

His mouth was about to descend on her

own, twist her head as she might, when, suddenly, she was free.

Lord Harry lifted the young man bodily out of the chair next to Deirdre and flung him on to the dance floor.

'And I didn't spill a drop,' he said cheerfully, placing a bottle and two glasses on the little table in front of them.

'It is very strange,' said Deirdre, looking about her, 'that one should receive so many lectures about how to go on in society, and then to have to look at . . . all this.'

'Society is very two-faced,' said Lord Harry. 'I was amazed to find you returning to Town so quickly.'

'Papa would have me go with him.'

'Ah, you must be his favourite daughter.'

His newest marriageable daughter, thought Deirdre. 'He is fond of us all, I think,' she said aloud.

'Do you wish me to volunteer to return with you to Hopeworth on a visit so that you may escape Town? I fear Mr Armitage still views me in the light of a future son-in-law.'

'No, we shall be returning in a few days' time, perhaps.'

She felt uneasy with him. His masked face turned him into a stranger. She was painfully aware of his closeness.

He was looking about him, his eyes glittering through the slits of his mask. 'I think I should take you away from here,' he said. 'Things are liable to get out of hand. Goodness knows what has happened to Lady Godolphin. If I leave you to go in search of her, I may find you being attacked when I return. And if we *both* look for Lady Godolphin, we shall be sadly jostled in the press.

'Then it is not exactly *convenable* to escort you back in a closed carriage without a chaperone, but I feel your family would not like to see you here in such surroundings. So I think escaping with me is the better of two evils.'

'Do let us go,' said Deirdre who did not like to confess the behaviour of the guests shocked her in case she seemed too unsophisticated, and was glad to think she should be alone with him, away from this riot, if only for a short space of time.

As they threaded their way through the saloons Deirdre suddenly saw Lady Godolphin, sitting in a box with Colonel Brian. They seemed to be having a heated argument. Her step faltered.

'What is it?' asked Lord Harry, looking down at her. 'Have you seen Lady

Godolphin?'

'No,' lied Deirdre, turning her head determinedly in the wrong direction.

Once alone with him in the darkness of the carriage, Deirdre found his silence almost unbearable.

All at once, she was afraid she was going to be handed over to Minerva while the night was still young.

And perhaps, after that, she might not see him again.

'It is only eleven o'clock,' she ventured. She gave a little laugh which sounded false in her own ears. 'It is very early to be thinking of going to bed.'

'I agree,' said Lord Harry, 'but since *I* have now become your chaperone, 'twould be best if I took you straight to Lady Sylvester.'

'Where do you live?'

'In lodgings, in Bond Street, near where I met you.'

'Are you comfortable there?'

'Very comfortable.' His voice sounded amused.

'I would like to visit them one day.'

'Gladly.'

'I could visit them *now*.'

'You shock me, Miss Deirdre. You cannot be contemplating visiting my bachelor lodgings at this time of night.'

'No one would know, except your servants. I do not want to go to bed so early.'

'Now, when do you go to bed when you are at home?'

'Hopeworth? About nine o'clock in the winter, later in the summer.'

'Then it is already long past your bedtime.'

'But no one goes to bed here before dawn, no one in the whole world,' said Deirdre, meaning the world bounded by St James's Square and Grosvenor Square.

'Are you not afraid of what might happen to you were you to be alone with me in my lodgings?'

'I am sure you would behave like a gentleman.'

'I might be tempted to kiss you, Deirdre.'

'Well,' faltered Deirdre, 'that would not do at all since we are not to be wed.'

'No. On the other hand, I really should like to marry *someone*, you know, and, as I told you, I am very lazy. The thought of pursuing females and meeting their families exhausts me. I have already met *your* family and you have met mine. What a pity we cannot get married. It would save a great deal of trouble, although this time I don't think anyone would accept the invitation or send us

289

a present. They would say it is all a hum.'

'Yes,' said Deirdre.

The coach stopped outside the Comfreys' residence in St James's Square. The tall house was in darkness. Deirdre peered out. 'I cannot even ask you to accompany me inside,' she said sadly. 'It appears everyone has gone to bed.'

A footman opened the carriage door.

'Close it,' said Lord Harry lazily. 'We are not yet ready to get down.'

The servant closed the door.

'Where were we?' said Lord Harry. 'Ah, we were talking of marriage. Of course, I was quite cast down when your father and Lord Sylvester pointed out you were afraid of me. Now, I ask you, what is there to be afraid of? I am clean, house-trained, have all my own teeth, and am in good coat.'

'It is very hard to explain...'

'Do try. My *amour propre* was quite ruined.'

'I found your attentions ... you treated me to an excess of civility.'

'So I did. Do you still sleep-walk?'

'No.'

'Pity. I like it when you walk in your sleep. Very well, I did kiss you. Was that so very frightening? The last time I did so you did not even struggle.'

'My own feelings frightened me, my lord,' said Deirdre.

'In what way?'

'Oh, I cannot *explain*,' said Deirdre, exasperated. 'Besides,' she added primly, 'I have forgotten.'

'That is easily remedied. Now if I take you in my arms, like this, and kiss you, like this, what do you feel?'

'Breathless and shaken.'

'That sounds unpleasant, perhaps we had better try again...'

Although they were sitting side by side, it was odd how he seemed to manage to get most of her body pressed against his own, how every rushing emotion seemed to be centred in her lips. But if she married him, she would need to lie naked with him in that peculiar way that John was behaving with Betty and she could not.

He felt her body go rigid and quickly released her.

'You *are* frightened of me,' he said gently. 'What is it?'

Overset by all her emotions, Deirdre blurted out a disjointed, rambling, tearful explanation about John and Betty and she could not do *that*, and if *that* was part of marriage then she would die an old maid.

Lord Harry rapped on the roof with his cane. 'Home!' he called up to the coachman.

'Then I will not touch you again,' he said firmly. 'My servants are very discreet so you may examine my lodgings and then I will return you here.'

So that was that, thought Deirdre. How irrational her feelings were! All she now wanted was him to take her in his arms again and kiss away all her fears.

Lord Harry's Swiss made a startled appearance as his master entered the apartment.

'Bruno!' said Lord Harry. 'I know you have been longing for a night off. Now is your opportunity.'

'At nearly midnight, milor'?'

'The perfect time to go roistering,' said Lord Harry firmly.

'Very good, milor',' said Bruno in a hollow voice.

'Well, what do you think of my abode?' asked Lord Harry when his servant had left.

He swung his domino from his shoulders and threw it over a chair. Then he took off his mask.

'Very comfortable,' said Deirdre, looking about her curiously.

'I'll take you on a guided tour,' said Lord Harry. 'This is my living-room.' It was a small cluttered room, full of books and papers which spilled over various seats and tables.

'And this,' he said, leading the way and holding up a candle, 'is my boudoir.'

Clothes seemed to be lying all over the place. A toilet table was crammed with everything except toiletries; magazines, blacking, snuff boxes, a decanter of wine, a card rack, and a pile of letters.

'And beyond that is the bedroom. You have seen it all.'

'All?' said Deirdre in surprise. 'I always thought lords lived in large houses.'

'Not this one. But since I am become rich of late, I plan to find myself a mansion and stretch my legs. Would you care for a glass of wine?'

Deirdre nodded and he grasped the decanter and carried it back into the living-room where he made space for her to sit down by shovelling several books and journals from a chair.

'Your servant does not clean very well,' said Deirdre shyly.

'Bruno's a good sort and can valet me better than any gentleman's gentleman in

London. He loves to clean, but I will not let him disturb my things. Once he has been house-cleaning, I cannot find anything. I am not a domesticated animal.'

He poured Deirdre a glass of wine and helped himself to one.

'Please sit down, my lord,' said Deirdre. 'You make me nervous, looming over me like that. Also, I am doing a very wicked thing. I should not be here with you.'

'It would be very wicked indeed if I took advantage of the situation,' he pointed out. 'And I have no intention of doing so. My servants will not talk, so you may be easy.'

Some devil seemed to prompt Deirdre to move the conversation on to a more intimate footing.

'When I told you about Betty and John,' she said boldly, 'you did not seem shocked.'

'I don't know the parties, except as your servants,' he said. 'Since they are to be married and have found a means to make Mr Armitage marry them, I cannot really say anything much about it. Are they in love?'

'Yes, very much.'

'Then what they were doing was only natural. Other people's lovemaking always looks highly *unnatural*, of course, while one's own does not.'

'But how can *any* lady . . . it is different for servants, surely.'

'Deirdre, talking of such things—I do not know if you are doing it deliberately—is forcibly bringing to my mind the intimacy of our situation. If you go on, I shall be tempted to break my promise.'

'You are right,' said Deirdre, standing up. 'We should go.'

'Aren't you hot with that mask on?'

'Yes, I am a little.' She put up her hands and untied the strings and tucked the velvet mask into her reticule.

'That is better. Masks make most innocent people look wicked. Now you look like a country virgin.'

'Thank you, sir,' said Deirdre, although she was not sure it was a compliment.

'Well . . .' she said, moving from one foot to the other, 'I should return.'

'Of course. Oh, God!' he suddenly screamed. 'Look at that!'

The terror in his voice and face were so real that Deirdre gave a startled shriek and flung herself into his arms, babbling, 'What is it? Oh, is it a *ghost?*'

She hugged him close and buried her face in his chest.

'I am sorry to have alarmed you,' he said

mildly. 'I saw my cravat in the looking glass and it had a *spot* on it.'

'You tricked me,' accused Deirdre, her voice muffled in his waistcoat.

'Not I,' he replied softly. 'Do look up and say you forgive me. You see, I have kept my promise. Your arms are about me, but mine are by my side.'

She looked up and opened her mouth to accuse him again of trickery, but the words died on her lips. His blue eyes were dark in the candlelight, no longer calm and childlike, but blazing down at her with a certain intensity that kept her wide gaze trapped in his.

He stood very still.

She gave a little sigh and stood on tiptoe and kissed him gently on the mouth.

Still, his arms remained at his sides, but his mouth burned and clung, and she kissed him with increasing passion. His mouth slid to the lobes of her ears, then the tip of her nose, then her eyelids, and then ...

'Ow!' yelped Deirdre, her eyes wide with alarm and a hand flying to her neck. 'You *bit* me!'

'Oh, I am so sorry,' he said, drawing back. 'Are you *sure?* I told you Bruno was not allowed to clean. Now only see. It is quite obvious. I have fleas.'

'Sir, this was not a flea bite,' said Deirdre, as cold as she had been hot a moment before. 'I do not understand you. Please take me home.'

'Very well,' he said mildly.

Deirdre kept a very stiff demeanour on the road to St James's Square, her back straight, her face averted from him.

This time, the house in St James's Square was ablaze with lights.

'Confusion,' said Lord Harry, as he helped Deirdre to alight. 'I fear Lady Godolphin has returned and has started an alarm as to your whereabouts. I must think of a good excuse.'

Deirdre and Lord Harry walked into the drawing-room to face a battery of accusing eyes. Ranged up in front of them were Lady Godolphin, Colonel Brian, Minerva and Lord Sylvester, and the vicar and Squire Radford.

'Where have you been?' asked Lord Sylvester.

'We could not find Lady Godolphin,' said Lord Harry easily, 'and I became concerned because the masquerade turned out not to be suitable for a lady of tender years such as Miss Deirdre. In fact, it was not suitable for any *lady*. Lord Sylvester, I assure you, it was like Rome before the Fall. I decided the best thing I could do was to remove Miss Deirdre from the Jamesons' as soon as possible.'

'Forgive me for being a septic,' said Lady Godolphin drily. 'But I do not think you looked very hard.'

'We looked for you at eleven o'clock,' put in Colonel Brian, 'and could not find you anywhere. When we asked at the entrance, we were told you had left a little *before* eleven. Since you did not send the carriage back, I had to escort poor Lady Godolphin here in a hack.'

'We were sitting in the carriage discussing the works of Shakespeare,' said Lord Harry, 'and quite forgot the time. As you can see, Miss Deirdre has come to no harm.'

'Come here, girl,' barked the vicar suddenly, 'And stop lurking in the doorway.'

Deirdre walked forwards, her hand to her throat.

'Is Lord Harry telling the truth?' demanded the vicar.

'Yes, Papa,' said Deirdre.

'Come closer.'

The vicar stared at his daughter's face, and then suddenly his arm shot out and he dragged Deirdre's hand down from her neck.

All eyes fastened on the subsequently exposed purple bruise.

The vicar's eyes were like two black diamonds in his flushed face.

'Where did you come by that?' he asked softly.

'Wh ... what?' Deirdre tried to look innocent and only succeeded in looking miserably guilty.

'You, answer,' snarled the vicar, rounding on Lord Harry.

'No, *I* will answer,' said Deirdre quickly. 'A man jumped into our box at the masquerade when Lord Harry was fetching us refreshments, and ... he tried to kiss me, and in the struggle, I came by this bruise.'

'Such a reason fair pisses my goose,' said the vicar coldly.

'Papa!' shrieked Minerva. 'Such language.'

'Get used to it,' said the vicar. 'There's worse to come, I think. Well, Desire, what's your explanation?'

Lord Harry spread his hands in a deprecating manner, and shot a rueful glance in Deirdre's direction.

'I find it very hard to lie,' he said. 'The truth is, I was holding your daughter in my arms and kissing her and I regret to say I forgot myself.'

'Where did this take place, sirrah? In the carriage?'

Clear as a bell, Lord Harry's voice seemed to ring through the drawing-room.

'In my lodgings, Mr Armitage.'

Green eyes gleaming, Lord Sylvester made a quick move towards Lord Harry. Deirdre threw herself between them.

'It was all my fault,' she gasped. 'I *flirted* with him, quite shamefully. I led him on.'

Lord Harry dropped his hands lightly on her shoulders and pulled her against him.

Then he rested his chin on top of her head and surveyed the outraged company with amused eyes.

Despite all her fright and confusion, Deirdre, nonetheless leaned gratefully back against him, thinking with one little part of her brain that it was the first time she had ever seen Minerva struck speechless.

'So there it is,' said Lord Harry. 'I have sadly compromised your daughter. We will need to be married as soon as possible.'

'That you will,' growled the vicar. 'Come with me, Lord Harry. You have a great deal of talking to do.'

Lord Harry raised Deirdre's hand to his lips and kissed it.

She looked up at him in a dazed and bewildered way. She loved him. He was to marry her, after all. The picture of John and

Betty making love surfaced in her mind and she shuddered. How could she be so in love with the man, and yet so frightened of the idea of her wedding night?

## CHAPTER ELEVEN

Silas Dubois turned a little cloisonné snuff box over in his hands. It had cost a lot of money, and Silas did not like spending money—on anyone other than himself.

He was waiting in a gloomy downstairs saloon in Mr Blewett's residence; waiting to be ushered into the presence.

Mr Blewett had told Silas that he had definitely changed his will in Silas's favour. That was good. But on that last visit, Mr Blewett kept saying eagerly that Silas should inform Lord Harry of this fact.

Cat and mouse games, thought Silas sourly.

The snuff box was an expensive trinket to remind Mr Blewett that his moneybags were to go to the one who appreciated him most.

Silas Dubois had not seen Lord Harry for some time, and had no intention of seeing him now and telling him about the changed will.

For what if Desire should come hot foot to his uncle's bedside and charm the old fool into changing his will again?

A footman entered and told Silas Dubois that Mr Blewett was ready to see him.

'Physician called today?' asked Silas eagerly as he mounted the stairs behind the servant.

'Yes, sir.'

'And what is the verdict?'

'I am sure I do not know, sir,' said the footman haughtily.

Silas glared at his liveried back. Jackanapes! 'You'll be the first to go—and without a reference,' he thought, 'just as soon as I get my hands on Blewett's estate.'

Mr Blewett was propped up against the pillows. He looked as usual. That is, he looked at death's door.

He was clutching a copy of the *Morning Post* and his eyes were bright with malicious humour.

'Well, here's confusion,' he said as Silas sidled up to his bedside. 'You have seen today's newspapers?'

Silas shook his head.

'Desire is to be wed to that Armitage chit after all! I knew he would do what I wanted

302

in the end. I'd no intention of leaving him my money while he was bent on being single. But a wife will settle him down.'

Silas Dubois' fingers curled round the snuff box. 'Do you mean to tell me,' he grated, 'that this engagement of Desire's alters things? You are surely not contemplating changing your will again.'

'Why not?' demanded Mr Blewett pettishly. 'It's my will and my money and I can do what I like with it.'

Silas slid the snuff box into his pocket. He noticed in a detached kind of way that his hands were trembling.

'I would not change your will so soon,' he said forcing a smile. 'The wedding could be off again.'

'Well, I'll confess that's a possibility,' said Mr Blewett cheerfully. 'But I have sent for Desire and expect him directly.'

Silas Dubois thought furiously. He thought of tall and handsome Lord Harry, strolling in and charming this old curmudgeon into changing his will, Lord Harry who was reported to be making money hand over fist on the Stock Exchange.

And then he saw the eager, malicious look on Mr Blewett's face.

'You don't look very comfortable,' said

303

Silas, forcing a smile. 'Allow me to arrange your pillows.'

'Leave them alone,' snapped Mr Blewett. 'I don't like you hovering about me like a demned vulture.' He gave a senile giggle. 'Demme, if you don't look like a vulture with that great nose of yours.'

Well, it was only the matter of a moment to whip the pillow out from under the old man and ram it down on his face.

Silas pressed down with all his strength and tried to think of something else. Who was it who had apologized because he had been an unconscionable time dying? Charles II, that was it.

The frail body on the bed jerked once more and was still.

Silas gently removed the pillow and looked down at the contorted face on the bed.

He composed his features into a suitable expression of mourning and reached for the bell rope.

No. He would go downstairs and make his announcement in soft tones to the butler.

He walked slowly towards the door.

A scrabbling sound behind him made the blood freeze in his veins.

He whipped round and a chamber pot struck him full in the face.

'You don't get rid of me that easily,' cackled Mr Blewett. He tugged the bell rope.

Silas reeled and staggered out of the door. A footman came running up the stairs.

'Murder!' shouted Mr Blewett from the room in an amazingly strong voice. *'Murder!'*

The game was up. Silas took to his heels and fled.

Mr Blewett's house was in Streatham. With hard riding, he, Silas, could reach his lodgings in Brook Street before the Bow Street Runners came to call.

'And no China Street pig is going to haul me off to the cells,' muttered Silas as he spurred his horse.

His one thought was to reach the sanctuary of his lodgings and pack a portmanteau. He had a small fortune in diamonds carefully hoarded away under the floorboards. He had to get out of England as soon as possible.

He hurtled into his lodgings and sent his servant to reserve two seats on the mail coach. 'I have to leave the country,' he gabbled. 'Urgent business. Don't stand there gawking, man. Go to it!'

Once alone, he sank down on a chair and bit his knuckles, his eyes darting this way and that like a cornered rat.

Then all at once, he rose and began to pack

feverishly. He prised up a floorboard in the dark corner of his sitting-room and pulled out a heavy wash leather bag of diamonds and thrust them into a corner of his portmanteau.

He had very little time.

Blewett's servants would have set out after him as soon as they got their wits together.

He heard a quick, light step on the stairs as he fastened the clasp of the portmanteau. His servant had been quick.

The door opened.

'Well, don't stand there like a fool. Take this bag,' snapped Silas.

And then he looked up.

Guy Wentwater stood framed in the doorway, a pistol in his hand.

'So Desire is to be married,' said Guy Wentwater, 'and you are going to blab all over London. You are going to ruin me, heh?'

'No,' screamed Silas. 'Not I. Sit down, dear boy, and put that pistol away.'

'Very well. I'll hear what you have to say.' Guy Wentwater strolled forwards.

'I knew you would see sense,' said Silas mopping his brow. 'A drink. That's what we both need.'

He crossed to the sideboard and seized a decanter of brandy.

Guy took careful aim and shot Silas Dubois through the head, quickly averting his eyes from the subsequent mess. Then he coolly put his smoking pistol away in one of his capacious pockets and made for the door.

All at once, his legs seemed to give way from under him and he collapsed in a heap on the floor. He buried his face in his hands and sobbed bitterly for the wreck of his life and ambitions. He would never become the honoured figure of society he had longed to be. He would be a fugitive, travelling the Continent, living on his wits. He had not even tried to disguise himself and several people must have seen him enter the lodgings.

Damn those Armitages to hell, the whole pack of them.

He finally dried his eyes and crawled to his feet. And then he heard the cries of 'Murder! Murder!' from the street outside. How could anyone know so soon?

Heavy feet sounded on the stairs and two Bow Street Runners backed by Mr Blewett's servants appeared on the landing.

'Mr Dubois?' asked one. Guy waved his hand in the direction of Mr Dubois' body and stood, waiting for his arrest.

'Well, you've saved the law a hanging,'

said one of the officers, straightening up. 'Did he attack you?'

Guy had not the faintest idea what was going on but he began to see a glimmer of hope.

'Yes,' he said. 'I came to call on him and he cursed and flew at me, and I shot him, for I feared he was about to kill me.'

'Don't look so put about, master,' said the Bow Street Runner who stood next to Guy. 'He deserved what he got. Trying to kill an old man. Shameful. Now, if you'll just step along o' us to Bow Street, we'll put all the facts before the magistrate. You'll feel better when you get some fresh air. Come along, now.'

*    *    *

By the time Lord Harry arrived to call on Mr Blewett it was much later that day. Mr Blewett was in a high state of excitement over his own cleverness. The minute he had felt the pillow over his face, he said, he had decided to fake dying, relying on the fact that Dubois would obviously think him weaker than he was.

'And I fooled him!' crowed Mr Blewett.

'And you sent him to the gallows or

308

transportation by playing on his greed,' sighed Lord Harry.

'He's dead. Marvellous thing. Chap called Wentwater shot him. My servants told me,' giggled Mr Blewett.

'What!' Lord Harry was shaken out of his usual urbane calm.

'Yes, seems this young friend called at his lodgings and Silas attacked him, no doubt thinking this Wentwater knew about the attempted murder. So Wentwater shot him.'

Lord Harry sat deep in thought, deaf to Mr Blewett's voice. Minerva had told him of the duel between Dubois and her husband, fought because Dubois and his friends had tried to ruin her. Deirdre had told of the strange man who had looked so closely at her on the day she had gone out walking alone and had then met Guy Wentwater in Green Park. It seemed as if Guy Wentwater and Silas Dubois had been joining forces to attack the Armitage family. That Dubois and Wentwater knew each other came as no surprise to Lord Harry after some more thought. Dubois seemed to have known every weak and shiftless wastrel on the fringes of society.

Lord Harry suddenly decided to call at Bow Street and find an address in London where he could reach Guy Wentwater. That young man had a great deal of explaining to do.

He left Mr Blewett, who was still chortling and chattering over his escape from death, and rode back into London.

But at Bow Street he was informed that Mr Wentwater had announced his intention of leaving the country on business. There had, naturally, been no charges against him. The Runners appeared to think he had acted promptly and bravely.

Lord Harry returned to his own lodgings and told his Swiss to re-hire the watchdog to look after Miss Deirdre Armitage; then he took himself off to see the vicar.

But the vicar was in a bad mood. He said he could not understand any of it, and then glared at Lord Harry and remarked acidly he trusted *he* was not leaving London since his wedding was in two weeks' time and by special licence.

'For you'll have to marry her now,' said the vicar crossly, 'after what you did to her.'

'Yes,' agreed Lord Harry sadly, and Deirdre who was sitting on the other side of the drawing-room looked at him with troubled eyes and wondered if he felt he had been coerced into the marriage.

'Papa,' she said suddenly, '*nothing* happened between myself and Lord Harry.'

'How would *you* know,' said the vicar gloomily. 'Just be guided by your father, and we'll have a respectable matron made of you as soon as possible.'

Deirdre looked pleadingly at Lord Harry but he only smiled blandly back at her.

'Nonetheless, sir,' said Lord Harry, returning to the subject of Guy Wentwater, 'I feel none of your family is safe until we find out exactly where he is. I suggest we get all our servants, that is, mine, the Comfreys', the Brabingtons' and Lady Godolphin's, to search the whole of London.'

'He'll not dare show his face again,' said the vicar.

'On the contrary, I think he will. He is by way of being a sort of hero over the shooting of Dubois.'

'Just think about your marriage,' growled the vicar. 'I am disappointed in you, Desire. Now, I've got the cost of a wedding on my hands, not to mention Mrs Armitage and the girls arriving. Then, there's the boys to fetch from Eton. And the whole world and his wife speculating about the speed of the marriage.'

'It is all very sad,' agreed Lord Harry amiably.

Deirdre studied Lord Harry covertly. All these marriage arrangements were bursting about her head. He had bitten her. Bitten? What other unknown horrors lay waiting for her on the marriage bed. She did not know this man *at all*.

Squire Radford was brought into the discussion, Lord Sylvester arrived, and soon everyone seemed to be speculating about the connection between Guy Wentwater and Silas Dubois.

At last Lord Harry rose to leave. Deirdre stood up as well.

'I would like to have a few words with my fiancé, Papa,' she said, 'in private.'

The vicar scowled awfully. 'I s'pose you're both beyond needin' a chaperone. You may go to the library, but leave the door open, mind!'

Lord Harry held the door open for Deirdre and she walked towards him, aware of the accusing eyes of her father.

'What ails you?' asked Lord Harry, leading her into the library and absent-mindedly closing the door.

'The shame of it all,' said Deirdre breathlessly. 'We did nothing, and yet you allowed everyone to think you had.'

'I knew they would not believe otherwise,'

he said, looking down at her. A red curl had escaped from its moorings and he carefully tucked it back into place on the top of her head. 'Don't you want to marry me?' he asked, noticing the way she flinched from his touch.

'I am afraid, sir,' said Deirdre, hanging her head.

'Of me?'

'You shocked me. You *bit* me.'

'Ah, shameless that I am.'

'It is not a joking matter,' said Deirdre, raising anxious, worried eyes to his. 'It is just that there are a lot of things I do not know about you.'

'It is our wedding night,' he said. '*That* is what troubles you.'

Deirdre hung her head again.

He took her gently in his arms. 'I am a very wicked man,' he said huskily. 'There is something I must tell you . . .'

'Ho!' said the vicar, wrenching open the door and glaring at them with his hands on his hips. 'You'll now wait until you're married, the pair of you. Deirdre! You are coming back with me to Hopeworth and you will return with your mother in a week's time.'

'My dear sir . . .' began Lord Harry, still

313

keeping his arms about Deirdre.

'No, that's final,' said the vicar. 'I'll not rest in my bed o' nights until I see you two *legalized.*'

He stood there glaring until Lord Harry left. Deirdre wondered miserably what wickedness Lord Harry had been about to confess to.

★    ★    ★

Deirdre was to look back on the days before her marriage as a rushed series of comings and goings between Hopeworth and London.

The fact that she did not seem particularly elated about her marriage was, this time, firmly ignored by the Armitage family. She should consider herself lucky she was to be married and not parcelled off to the Continent to live out her shameful days in the obscurity of some genteel spa.

Even Minerva and Annabelle, who should surely have been the ones to be tolerant of pre-marital experiments, privately felt that in their case, it had all been different.

The wedding was to be held in a small church in Islington. Only members of each family were to be present with the exception of a very few close friends.

The newspapers had broadcast the bravery of Guy Wentwater in shooting down Silas Dubois. But a diligent search of London by the staff of the various households had refused to unearth the young man.

The vicar was heartily weary of daughters and marriage. He washed his hands of the whole messy business, he said loudly. The rest could all die old maids for all he cared.

Daphne was secretly disappointed in Deirdre. Deirdre was the last one of them, thought Daphne, that one would ever have thought would allow herself to be rushed into marriage by any man.

She added to Deirdre's uncertainty and distress by treating her like an invalid, talking softly in her presence, and getting cook to make nourishing broths and possets.

Numbly, Deirdre listened to the gossip about the wedding preparations. She was to wear Annabelle's wedding gown which had been refurbished for the occasion and her younger sisters were to wear the bridesmaids gowns they had worn for Annabelle's wedding.

The boy's silk suits were sent to the tailors to be altered to fit their increased size.

A simple wedding breakfast was to be served at an inn near the church.

By the time the whole family set out for London, Deirdre felt crushed. All those tumultuous feelings Lord Harry had caused seemed a vague memory. At times, she was hard put to remember his face. She had feared him and hated him, then she had loved him, and now she was frightened of him again. But this time, no one seemed to care. Her downcast looks were judged to be entirely suitable in a maiden who had fallen from the pinnacle of virginity before her marriage.

Lady Godolphin did not help matters by being eaten up with jealousy because Colonel Brian had finally turned his attentions elsewhere and was reported to be courting a buxom matron, widow of a City merchant, who was only forty years old.

'Men are disgusting,' said Lady Godolphin to Deirdre. 'I should have warned you. When you asked me about having babies, I should not have told you, but how was I to know you would go and lose your virginal? Well, I shall attend your nipples, but if you was expecting Colonel Brian, you will be disappointed. He is flirting with a Cit. Horrible great fat thing. What can he see in her? Oh, follicles!'

And with that Lady Godolphin burst into tears and turned a deaf ear to all Deirdre's

316

pleas of innocence.

Betty was small comfort. The maid shook her head over Deirdre's shame.

'But *you* are not waiting until you get married,' said Deirdre.

'It's different for such as me,' said Betty. 'I had to do it.'

'Well, I did *not!*' howled Deirdre, breaking the sticks of the fan she was holding in her agitation. 'Yes, I went to his lodgings but nothing *happened!*'

'Oh, come, miss, and you with that great bruise on your neck.'

'It just happened. He just ... oh, what's the use,' said Deirdre wretchedly. 'Everyone is creeping about me as if I am going to a funeral, and then there is this havey-cavey wedding, tucked away in the fields of Islington. And now with everyone in the family being so shocked, it has got about London, and *this* was in a print shop in Bond Street.'

She reached over to a small table and held up a coloured cartoon.

Betty looked at it, her eyes wide with horror. In it, Deirdre Armitage in a state of undress was sitting on Lord Harry Desire's knees.

Underneath there was a poem. It read:

317

'The wedding's on, the wedding's off,
Says capricious Miss D.A.
But Desire by name
Desire by fame,
Must needs go have his way

Now whether she desire it,
Or whether she says nay,
Our flighty miss,
Needs wedded bliss,
For Desire has had his way.'

'Oh, *miss*,' said Betty. 'It's a *mercy* he is going to marry you.'

'I cannot understand why he should not make an effort to convince Papa that nothing happened,' said Deirdre fretfully. 'Oh, God. Would that I had never met him!'

'Well, there's nothing you can do about it now,' said Betty, picking up the hairbrush. 'Them gossips will have forgot the whole thing in another few weeks.'

But Deirdre worried and worried. Her father seemed to think that if she saw her fiancé at the wedding rehearsal, then it would be soon enough.

She could not talk openly about it, for the scandal had to be kept from the twins and from Frederica and Diana. Also, it was as if she were to be punished by the parsimony of the wedding arrangements, and she was kept busy, endlessly making and stitching petticoats and handkerchiefs.

The wedding rehearsal was a solemn affair, more like a funeral.

The church was small and dark and smelly. The vicar who was to perform the service was an old University friend of Mr Armitage.

He was one of those muscular Christians who pride themselves on the ease with which they can talk freely on all sorts of delicate subjects, and he teased the young couple jovially about their haste to be married, and was only silenced when Lord Harry Desire roused himself from his reverie and threatened to call the parson out.

'Thank goodness that part's over,' sighed the vicar, after Deirdre had been firmly marched away from Lord Harry and into the family carriage. 'Now we've only got tomorrow to worry about.'

'Yes,' agreed Mrs Armitage. 'It is all very unfortunate. We had two grand weddings already, Mr Armitage, and that is something to be grateful for. Town depresses me these days and I have a monstrous severe pain in my hip. I confess I shall be glad to return to

Hopeworth when this is all over.'

'Why are you getting married in such a poky church?' asked Diana, after a whispered consultation with Frederica.

'Shh!' reproved Mrs Armitage. 'There are things it is better you should not know.'

Suddenly a fit of rebellion assailed Deirdre. She was *not* going to be meekly marched to the altar on the morrow and handed over to Lord Harry Desire. She *must* know what he had been about to confess. What if it were something terrible? There was still a chance to escape. The only way to escape was to ask him.

And, if it were something too terrible, then she would escape this time by facing up to her family.

There was no Guy Wentwater to elope with. What a fool she had been over him. At least she wasn't going to be married to *him*. Deirdre briefly wondered where he was.

★     ★     ★

At that moment, Guy Wentwater was sitting in a hostelry in Bristol waiting for the tide. He signed his name to the foot of the letter he had just written, and then read it over to make sure there were no mistakes in grammar or spelling.

He read: 'My dear Miss Emily, By the time this reaches you, I shall be on the High Seas, bound for the West Indies. I have a certain deal of Business there. As you will have perused in the journals, I am accounted as something of a Hero, by virtue of having struck down one Silas Dubois. They praise me more than I deserve since I was merely protecting my person from a vicious, savage, and armed murderer. He was great and powerful and quite brutal in his madness and I am relieved to have defended myself so ably.

Give my warmest regards to Yr. Family. I hope to return to further our acquaintance. Meanwhile, I remain, Yr. Humble and Devoted Servant, G.W.'

Guy looked at what he had written and frowned. Should he, perhaps, have said something about hoping she would wait for him? Then he laughed. With such a face, Miss Emily would still be unwed by the time he returned.

# CHAPTER TWELVE

Deirdre found herself more worried and agitated than ever as evening arrived. At last she summoned Betty.

'Betty,' said Deirdre, 'I wish you to do something for me. Pray put on your bonnet and cloak and take one of the footmen with you and call on Lord Harry and tell him I must speak to him.'

'Mr Armitage won't like it,' said Betty. 'Nor will Lady Sylvester.'

'Papa is at some coffee house with Squire Radford, Mama, the girls, and the twins have gone to make a brief call on Lady Godolphin, and Minerva and Sylvester are gone to the play. *Please*, Betty. You will be ruining my life if you do not.'

Betty hesitated. In truth, she was sorry for Miss Deirdre. The wedding was to be a poky little affair.

'I'll go, miss,' she said at last. 'But you must get him to say he called round of his own accord.'

'I will, Betty. I promise. Now wait there until I write something.'

Betty waited patiently until Deirdre had

scribbled a letter. 'Tell him to return with you, if possible,' urged Deirdre, 'for Mamma will be coming home soon.'

When Betty had left, Deirdre changed the simple gown she was wearing for one of her best. She went downstairs and sat by the drawing-room window, waiting to see when Lord Harry would arrive.

At last, when she felt she could not bear to wait any longer, a carriage drew up, the door opened and Lord Harry's tall figure alighted on the pavement.

Deirdre flew into the hall and opened the door herself.

'Come in quickly,' she whispered. 'I do not want the servants to know you are here. Come into the library.'

As she led the way, Deirdre noticed Lord Harry was wearing evening dress and had his chapeau bras tucked under his arm.

She realized she would need to say her piece quickly. He was obviously en route for the opera.

Deirdre lit the fire which had been made up and then turned and faced him.

'There is something I must know, my lord . . .' she began.

'How severe you look. And will you not call me Harry?'

'Very well . . . Harry. Please sit down.'

He sat down in an armchair and Deirdre sat on a chair facing him on the other side of the fire and studied him intently.

'Do you love me?' she asked.

'With all my heart,' he answered in his usual light manner.

'I feel . . . I feel you might have tried to make Papa understand that nothing at all happened between us,' said Deirdre miserably, all her worries beginning to come out in a rush. 'And you bit me. And you said you had something to tell me about wickedness, but Papa interrupted us and now I don't know what to expect, and I am to have this poky, little wedding as if I were in disgrace, and no one but family is to attend.

'And I am to wear Annabelle's old wedding gown, and *I am frightened.*'

She looked at him, trembling a little, waiting for him to answer.

He got up and walked to her, and, with one swift movement, gathered her up in his arms. Then he returned to his chair and arranged her comfortably on his knees.

Deirdre was reminded of the cartoon. 'And, oh Harry, they have the most awful drawings of us in the print shop,' she wailed.

'I will begin at the beginning,' he said,

holding her tightly and giving her a little shake, 'and you will listen patiently.'

'Now, I saw you nearly two years ago in the Park with your sister, Annabelle. You were laughing and teasing her and I could not rest until I discovered who you were. I found out you were very young. Your sister had just become married to Brabington. I had to go to the wars but somehow I was determined that when I returned, I would seek you out.

'Shortly after my return your father visited me at White's. You can imagine my amazement. I was being offered marriage to you. I still thought you too young and thought it disgraceful of your father to push you into an unwanted marriage, and so I amused myself by telling him I didn't like girls with red hair and I didn't like clever ones either.

'I wanted you to fall in love with me, but when you really seemed so frightened and miserable and I had ascertained you no longer had any warm feelings towards Wentwater, I decided to agree to a termination of the engagement and then to wait and hope that you would come and miss me.

'Imagine my surprise when I found you back in London so soon! I was persuaded you were not indifferent to me. I was afraid you might run away from me again and so I compromised you—with your help, of course, my love. And you are not to have a poky little wedding. Your father will find I have made other arrangements for the wedding breakfast since I have invited all London society from Brummell to the Prince Regent.

'And the church is to be especially decorated and my army friends will form a guard of honour and society will talk about it for years.'

'Why didn't you tell Papa?'

'I couldn't be bothered,' said Lord Harry lazily. 'I am paying for it, but he would bluster and shout so much before I got a chance to tell him and that does make my head ache.'

Deirdre played shyly with his top waistcoat button. 'You are so generous, and I am sure I love you, only it is a pity,' she said in a low voice, 'that love-making could not be like this ... just being together and being comfortable.'

'Oh, it is, most of the time. I am sorry I bit you. I was simply making my mark, you know, like putting a gold mark on things, except I do not yet have gold teeth. You are naturally afraid of the intimacies of marriage.

It would be strange if you were not. When I said I had been wicked, I simply meant that I had not told you I had been in love with you for a long time.'

'Do we ... do we need to go in for any intimacies right away?' asked Deirdre. 'I mean, could we not become better acquainted first?'

'Of course,' he said, sinking down into the depths of the chair and arranging her head comfortably on his shoulder. 'We could sit many evenings just like this. It would not trouble you if I merely kissed you?'

Deirdre shyly shook her head.

He bent his head and kissed her gently. Deirdre felt the stirrings of passion and decided since he had been so generous, it would only be courteous to kiss him back with some of the enthusiasm she felt.

With equal generosity, Lord Harry replied in kind.

Deirdre finally broke free and sat up on her knees and looked down into his blue eyes.

'I love you Harry,' she said simply.

He mutely held out his arms and she threw herself against his chest with such force that the chair overbalanced and decanted them both on to the library floor.

And then somehow Deirdre could not

seem to stop kissing him, and clothes were becoming an increasing irritation, and when his hand moved down the front of her gown and held one firm breast, it seemed the most natural thing in the world.

Upstairs, Betty waited patiently. The hours passed. The family had long since gone to bed. She had told Lady Sylvester that Deirdre was asleep with the headache and did not want to be disturbed.

She had not taken a footman with her and so she hoped the rest of the servants were not aware of what was going on and that his lordship had had the sense to lock the library door.

At last Betty fell asleep, sitting in a chair beside the fire in Deirdre's bedroom.

She was awakened at five in the morning by Miss Deirdre Armitage creeping into the room.

Betty struggled out of the chair. 'Oh, Miss Deirdre,' she said crossly, 'you do take advantage of a body's kindness. Now into bed this minute or I'll never get you up in time to go to church.'

*     *     *

The wedding was hailed as an outstanding

success. People talked for months about the glory of the choir and the beauty of the flower arrangements, of the reception in striped marquees on Islington Fields and of how the Prince Regent himself had put in an appearance and had danced with Deirdre. The vicar, once he got over his first stunned shock at seeing so many fashionable guests, began to fret and gnaw his nails and worry about the cost of everything and say he always knew Desire was an idiot.

When he was told Lord Harry was paying for everything, Mr Armitage's admiration and gratitude knew no bounds.

'Arranged marriages are just the thing,' he told Squire Radford gleefully. 'If it hadn't been for all my work, this would never have come about.'

'Perhaps,' mused the squire, 'except I have a feeling Desire tricked us and really meant to marry Deirdre all along.'

'Not he! Fine fellow, but ain't got much upstairs.'

'Deirdre is happy at last,' said the squire, watching the new Lady Desire's glowing face. 'You are a lucky man, Charles. Three daughters wed, and all to men they love.'

'Aye, and it was all my doing,' said the vicar, puffing out his chest. 'And His Royal

Highness here as well. Edwin's so jealous, he's near fit to burst.'

The vicar strutted off.

Squire Radford sighed and watched him go. Charles was about to become vain and puffed up again. It was as well Daphne was still young or the vicar would be arranging a marriage for her on the spot, despite his protestations to the contrary.

That young lady was surrounded by a crowd of admirers. She did not do anything to attract them, noticed the squire, but simply stood there, like some beautiful statue.

The squire shook his head. It would not be long before Mr Armitage turned his attention in Daphne's direction.

The vicar was not the man to let a beautiful daughter lie fallow in Hopeworth when he might be adding another illustrious name to the family tree.

Lady Godolphin waddled up, spilling champagne down the front of her gown.

She looked once more her old self, painted and wigged, and dressed in a frivolous white merino gown with broad scarlet stripes.

'My servants had wind o' Wentwater,' she said to the squire. 'Got on a boat bound for the West Indies. We won't be seeing him again. Bad cess to the man. Never could abide him.'

'I did not think you had ever met him,' pointed out the squire.

'Doesn't matter,' sighed Lady Godolphin. 'Heard enough about him. I ain't going to have anything to do with men again, Mr Radford. I am going to remain chased the way a woman's supposed to be. I don't care whether it's Mr Armitage, or Desire, or Comfrey, or Brabington, or that fickle, useless Colonel Brian.'

'Men are all just a load of follicles!'

'Ah, you must not be so bitter,' said the squire in his kindly way. 'Our newly-weds are just leaving. Allow me to escort you, Lady Godolphin. It is not every day an old stick like myself can have the pleasure of escorting such a diamond of the first water.'

'Naughty man!' murmured Lady Godolphin, ogling him quite awfully, and tapping his hand with her fan.

They walked arm in arm to where Deirdre and Lord Harry were getting into the open carriage that was to carry them off to the new town house Lord Harry had bought as one of his many wedding surprises.

Deirdre stood up and tossed her bouquet into the crowd, and then sank down laughing beside Lord Harry.

'Who caught it?' he asked. 'One of your sisters?'

'No. I threw it towards Daphne, and it was caught by a *young man* standing next to her. She held out her hand for it but he was admiring the flowers so much, he didn't even notice. Poor Daphne. It is the first time she has been so ignored.'

'Except by me,' said Lord Harry. 'I only ever saw you.'

'Oh, Harry, how beautiful of you to say so ... Harry! You must not kiss me in an open carriage with everyone looking! Oh, *Harry!*'

The publishers hope that this
Large Print Book has brought
you pleasurable reading.
Each title is designed to make
the text as easy to see as possible.
G. K. Hall Large Print Books are
available from your library and
your local bookstore. Or you can
receive information on upcoming
and current Large Print Books by
mail and order directly from the
publisher. Just send your name
and address to:

G. K. Hall & Co.
70 Lincoln Street
Boston, Mass. 02111

or call, toll-free:

1–800–343–2806